Reading
the Fractures
of Genesis

Reading the Fractures of Genesis

Historical and Literary Approaches

DAVID M. CARR

Westminster John Knox Press
Louisville, Kentucky

Book design by Jennifer K. Cox
Cover design by Vickie Arrowood

First edition

Published by Westminster John Knox Press
Louisville, Kentucky

This book is printed on acid-free paper that meets the American National Standards Institute Z39.48 standard. ∞

PRINTED IN THE UNITED STATES OF AMERICA
96 97 98 99 00 01 02 03 04 05 — 10 9 8 7 6 5 4 3 2 1

Library of Congress Cataloging-in-Publication Data
Carr, David McClain, date.
    Reading the fractures of Genesis : historical and literary
approaches / David M. Carr. — 1st ed.
      p.   cm.
    Includes bibliographical references.
    ISBN 0-664-22071-1 (alk. paper)
    1. Bible. O.T. Genesis—Criticism, Textual. I. Title.
BS1235.2.C34   1996
222'.11066—dc20   95-46693

Contents

Preface

This book attempts to build bridges between methods that are often seen as mutually contradictory: "diachronic" study of a text's formation and "synchronic" study of a text's present form. I was originally brought to this theme by discussions in a consultation and then seminar in the Society of Biblical Literature focused on the "Formation of the Book of Isaiah." The participants in this Isaiah group agreed that there was a need to balance an emphasis from earlier scholarship on divisions in Isaiah with a closer analysis of patterns and images that bind the book as a whole. The issue, however, is What kind of balance? Some in the seminar advocated turning attention almost exclusively to synchronic analysis of the present connections in the book of Isaiah, with minimal or no attention to how the book took shape over time. Others, myself included, argued that the formation of the book of Isaiah has introduced a certain complexity in the final form of the book, a complexity that somehow must be reckoned with in a reading of that form. At the same time, I have become increasingly convinced that precise analysis of the formation of poetic texts in books like Isaiah is often extremely difficult, if not impossible. Without the structure provided by a stream of events, the task of identifying doublets or breaks *within* a given poem is especially subjective. Although we can make certain broad distinctions between groups of texts in Isaiah and recognize some later additions, more precise work is often ruled out by the nature of the evidence.

Exactly this problem in Isaiah studies brought me to Genesis, for the formation process of Genesis is more easily reconstructed than that of Isaiah. First, the narrative form of Genesis allows for the recognition of seams that would not appear in a poetic text. Second, the final stage of the formation of Genesis involved the combination of remarkably large portions of two narrative strands—P and non-P—that fundamentally differed from one another. Their difference also helps in reconstruction of at least this stage of the book's formation process. Third, like Isaiah, Genesis is both a deeply fractured and beautifully shaped text, and it has been the subject of many good diachronic and synchronic studies. Thus, Genesis provides an unusually good opportunity for showing how synchronic study of the present text and diachronic reflection on its process of formation can be interrelated.

I have decided to concentrate in this book on ways the study of a text's past formation contributes to study of its present shape. Nevertheless, it is just as true, if not more so, that careful synchronic study of a text's present form is an essential prelude to methodologically controlled reflection on how that form was produced. Therefore, I began my research process by surveying synchronic studies of Genesis, mapping patterns and tensions in the book. For a variety of reasons I have chosen not to include a separate section reporting the results of this work, but the attentive reader of my text and footnotes will note multiple places where my and other's synchronic work has played a leading role in guiding my perception of the text with which we all must begin.

Overall, I have found myself treading a fine line between overemphasizing the more speculative new frontiers in study of the formation of Genesis and overemphasizing a review of more established results. On the one hand, this book—particularly chapters eight through ten—makes original contributions in the study of the formation of Genesis, whether by offering a new synthesis of older positions or by developing new ones. On the other hand, if this book were devoted exclusively to what is controversial in study of the formation of Genesis, *it would end up focusing on precisely the weakest cases for transmission history in the book.* Yet this book is not just designed for those already familiar with and convinced by earlier transmission-historical studies. Therefore, I devote substantial space in this book to a review of some of the clearer cases of growth in the book of Genesis, such as the distinction between P and non-P. I would urge my more synchronically oriented readers to take special note of the distinctions I make in levels of plausibility in my analysis and concentrate on those cases that are most persuasive to them. I would urge my more diachronically oriented readers to recognize the context within which my review of established arguments is again necessary. Sometimes, as in the case of the distinction between P and non-P, many such arguments remain persuasive. Other times, such as in the case of isolation of J and E sources or dating J, I argue that a review of the classic arguments reveals their weaknesses.

Especially as I now look back on my own book in its present form, I am conscious of how much more could be done. In particular, an ideal work of this kind would comprehensively cover the formation and shape of the Pentateuch as a whole. Unfortunately, the material to be covered in a study of Genesis was already so vast that I could not refer more than cursorily to the broader issues in the study of the rest of the Pentateuch. Nevertheless, Genesis has a certain distinctiveness vis-à-vis the rest of the Torah, and many would agree that transmission-historical issues become—if anything—less clear in the Moses story that follows it. Therefore, this study was focused on Genesis. That was plenty.

I have tried to keep the text free of detailed discussions with secondary literature. At the same time, I have tried at least briefly to reply in the notes to this study to some of the more compelling recent treatments. Because of the immense amount of literature on Genesis, I have confined many of my citations to foundational early works and to works—particularly recent ones—that might not be familiar to the audience I expect for this book. Moreover, I have confined my bibliography only to items that I had occasion to cite in the book. Abbreviations follow the conventions of the Society of Biblical Literature.

All this is to say that I do not pretend to have the final word on either synchronic or diachronic issues in Genesis. No one can. Moreover, this book does not pretend to be a "reading" of Genesis. It involves historically oriented attempts to locate early contexts of texts, but the ultimate focus is on constructing a broader prereading of the book as a fractured, multivoiced whole. Certainly I cover enough ground that there is much here with which one can agree and disagree. Nevertheless, I hope to have demonstrated in this book some of the promise of linking synchronic and diachronic investigations: how synchronic study of interconnections in a text can inform diachronic exploration of its formation, and how diachronic study of the different voices embedded in a text like Genesis can help us hold onto its fractures and, more precisely, identify some of our choices in how we interpret it.

Many people have helped in the gathering of information for this book, discussion of ideas in it, and reading of various chapters of the book as it went through its own formation process. I have already mentioned my indebtedness to the Isaiah seminar, an unusually gifted and collegial group of scholars from whom I have learned very much. Next I would mention the many kinds of tangible and intangible help from the school where I have the privilege to teach, Methodist Theological School in Ohio. I want to mention in particular Datha Myers, the faculty secretary, and Emily Badertscher, whose interlibrary loan wizardry found many a difficult text unbelievably quickly. Also, I thank students of Methodist Theological School in Ohio who participated in several seminars on Genesis over the years, including the most recent Genesis seminar who read and critiqued a penultimate draft of this book. I am especially grateful to Kimberly Barker, James Howell, Julie Peter, Kim Scranton, and Joyce Whippo for their help in assembling an initial bibliography of secondary literature on Genesis and a database of observations in the secondary literature regarding the formation of Genesis. Their work in the summers of 1991 and 1992 was funded by a Methodist Education Fund grant for faculty development, for which I am also grateful. The American Association of Theological Schools and the Alexander von Humboldt Foundation of Germany funded different stages of my work on this book during a professional leave I took in 1993–1994. Later my own school, along with the Humboldt Foundation, funded yet another trip to Europe during the summer of 1995 to finish my work. I am very grateful for this financial assistance without which this book would not have been written.

Finally, I have been unusually blessed with excellent dialogue partners, many more than I can name. I do, however, want to single out several who played a particularly critical role. Carol Newsom was my mentor for the Association of Theological Schools' younger scholar program, and she played a particularly critical role guiding the study, in particular helping me sharpen its methodological focus. While I was in Germany, I benefited immeasurably from the hospitality of and dialogue with some of the best Pentateuch scholars anywhere, my hosts: Erhard Blum, Bernd Janowski, and Rolf Rendtorff. Each gave generously of their time to read and critique portions of this book. Upon my return, John Van Seters and Jeffrey Tigay kindly agreed to read and respond to specific parts of the book. Having listed so many people, often of quite diverging viewpoints, let me make it absolutely clear that no one in this list agrees with all that is here. Nevertheless, much of what is good in this book results from their input and my interaction with them. I am very grateful for their willingness to engage me. In addition, I presented portions of my work and benefited from discussions of it at the Heidelberg Alttestamentliche Sozietät, the 1994 and 1995 International Society of Biblical Literature meetings, the 1994 Annual Society of Biblical Literature meeting, a graduate colloquium at Duke University in the fall of 1994, and the 1995 Congress of the International Society for the Study of Old Testament. Jon Berquist, a specialist in Old Testament himself and my editor at Westminster John Knox Press, deserves much credit for encouraging me and advising me in the final redaction of my work.

In all this, I have not yet mentioned one other person who played a crucial role in helping this book happen: my wife, Sharon. She graciously joined me both at home and away, and her laughter and support helped me keep things in perspective in the midst of this long journey through Genesis. I dedicate this book to her.

Part 1
Introduction

1

The Importance of the Study
of Genesis's Formation

Although biblical scholars have long agreed that the book of Genesis was created out of earlier traditions (both written and oral) through a long process termed here "transmission history,"[1] they intensely disagree right now about how much we can know about that process and how important such knowledge would be, even if it were possible. This book addresses both issues. In it I will argue the following: that our understanding of the present form of Genesis can be substantially deepened through historically informed analysis of its intense multivoiced character. First, I use documented cases of transmission history to contend that ancient texts like Genesis are distinguished from most modern texts in that ancient texts were created over long periods of time by authors with often sharply diverging viewpoints. Then, in the heart of the book, I use criteria and models derived from these documented cases as the starting point for an investigation of the composition of Genesis. Finally, I return to the present book of Genesis, surveying some ways this investigation of the formation of the book can enrich our understanding of its present interpretive potential.

The textual focus of the study, Genesis, is important partly because of the key role this book continues to play in biblical studies and related disciplines. Already in the early 1800s Genesis was the subject of the first attempts to identify sources and editing in a scriptural book.[2] Later, Genesis was the

1. Here the term *transmission history* is used to make clear that this discussion concerns (1) the transmission of written as well as oral materials, and (2) the process of transmission of these materials as well as the traditions themselves. In contrast, the term *tradition history* has often been used exclusively to denote oral transmission history. Toward the end of this study I will also briefly discuss oral traditions in relation to various stages of the development of non-P traditions. Nevertheless, my primary focus will be on the history of written traditions now present in the text of Genesis. For further discussion of the terminological problems here, see R. Knierim, "Criticism of Literary Features, Form, Tradition and Redaction," in *The Hebrew Bible and Its Modern Interpreters* (ed. G. Tucker and D. Knight; Philadelphia: Fortress; Chico, Calif.: Scholars, 1985), 146–48.
2. H. B. Witter, *Jura Israelitarum in Palestinam terram Chananaeam commentatione in Genesi*, 1711 (for exact bibliographical information and comments on this work, see A. Lods, "Un précurseur allemand de Jean Astruc: Henning Bernhard Witter," *ZAW* 43 [1925]: 134–35); J. J. Astruc, *Conjectures sur les mémoires originaux dont il paroît que Moyse s'est servi pour composer le livre de la Genèse* (Paris [though marked as Brussels]: Chez Fricx, 1753). H. J. Kraus, *Geschichte der historisch-kritischen Erforschung des Alten Testaments* (3d ed.; Neukirchen-Vluyn: Neukirchener Verlag, 1982), 95–97.

starting point for subsequent source-critical theories, from Eichhorn to the still prominent "new documentary approach" (JEDP) popularized by Wellhausen.[3] Then, in the first half of the twentieth century, Genesis was a focus of Gunkel's pioneering work on oral forms in the Hebrew Bible,[4] and Noth worked primarily from texts in Genesis in his attempt to trace the preliterary formation of the Pentateuch.[5] Finally, Genesis has been a major locus for the more recent introduction of new methods in biblical studies, including feminist, "new" literary-critical, reader-response, and structuralist approaches to biblical texts.[6]

The aim of this book is to show how historically oriented investigation of Genesis's prehistory can be informed by and inform a broader discussion of the book's present form. Such a synthetic approach to Genesis is important in the midst of the increasing methodological compartmentalization characteristic of contemporary biblical studies. Overall, the newer and older approaches to biblical texts do not often interact with each other in specific ways, but they are all eventually applied to Genesis. This makes Genesis a good test case for looking at how these methods might be brought into relation with each other. Since this methodological linkage is a crucial part of this book, I will digress here for a brief look at some of the ways these methods have interacted up to this point.

Literary and Historical Approaches to the Bible in Historical Perspective

Although some early interpreters of the Bible had already noted certain historical problems in biblical books like Genesis,[7] real investigation of its prehistory first began in a context of increasing consciousness of the importance of the historical dimension in human thought and culture. This point

3. J. E. Eichhorn, *Einleitung ins Alte Testament* (vol. 2; Leipzig: Ben Weidmanns, Erben & Reich, 1781), 294–381; J. Wellhausen, "Die Composition des Hexateuchs und der historischen Bücher des Alten Testaments," *JDT* 21 (1876); 392–450 (reprinted as *Die Composition des Hexateuchs und der historischen Bücher des Alten Testaments* [4th ed.; Berlin: W. de Gruyter, 1963], with citations in this book following the reprint); idem, *Geschichte Israels: Erster Band - Prolegomena zur Geschichte Israels* (Berlin: G. Reimer, 1883); (E.T., *Prolegomena to the History of Ancient Israel* [trans. J. S. Black and A. Menzies; Cleveland/New York: World Publishing, 1957]). Again, for a helpful discussion and overview of the intervening debate on different models for the composition of the Pentateuch, see Kraus, *Geschichte*, 141, 152–60, 178–79, 202–3, 225, 242–69; and C. Houtman, *Der Pentateuch: Die Geschichte seiner Erforschung neben einer Auswertung* (Contributions to Biblical Exegesis and Theology 9; Kampen: Kok Pharos, 1994), 80–114.
4. H. Gunkel, *Genesis* (3d ed.; Göttingen: Vandenhoeck & Ruprecht, 1910).
5. M. Noth, *Überlieferungsgeschichte des Pentateuch* (2d ed.; Darmstadt/Stuttgart: Kohlhammer, 1948); (E.T., *A History of Pentateuchal Traditions* [trans. B. W. Anderson; 1972; reprint, Chico, Calif.: Scholars Press, 1981]).
6. For an overview of literary studies of Genesis up through the late eighties, see M. A. Powell, *The Bible and Modern Literary Criticism: A Critical Assessment and Annotated Bibliography* (Bibliographies and Indexes in Religious Studies 22; New York: Greenwood, 1992), 174–85.
7. Houtman, *Der Pentateuch*, 14–27, 31–48.

is important, for in the current discussion one could sometimes get the mistaken impression that the transmission-historical method was developed exclusively to make sense out of otherwise senseless texts.[8] This was certainly often the case. Nevertheless, as biblical criticism has developed in the modern period, study of the prehistory of texts like Genesis has been built on the following belief: that precise understanding of texts like Genesis requires a determination of the original historical settings of these texts. Insofar as different parts of a text like Genesis were written at different times, one has to place these parts in their respective periods in order to interpret them properly. Failure to do so results in: (1) ignorance of many central elements in a text for which there was no analogy in the reader's culture and (2) anachronistic misinterpretation of elements for which there was an analogy, but a misleading one. Thus, historical-critical scholars have separated a story like the Flood into separate layers not because they had no way of making sense of it as a whole; they have done so because they were convinced that true understanding of the different layers of the flood story was possible only if the layers were located in relation to the original historical setting they addressed.

The best historical-critical scholars have always realized the provisional nature of this project. Nevertheless, they have also believed that progress in it was both possible and desirable. Both suppositions have come under fire in recent years. In particular, many who advocate newer literary methods have argued that exploring the gradual growth of books like Genesis is (1) inherently impossible because of lack of secure data in the text itself and/or (2) hermeneutically uninteresting since the only text really present for interpretation is the final form. For example, in a provocative discussion of these questions, Noble argues that there is an inherent conflict between transmission-historical and literary approaches to the same text. According to his argument, any transmission-historical theory is vulnerable to a competing theory that can posit a plausible present literary function for the doublets, breaks, and the like on which the transmission-historical theory is based. Noble admits that such literary arguments do not prove that a biblical text *did not* have a transmission history. What they show, instead, is that we cannot know much about that history.[9] The transmission-historical indicators are too easily interpreted in another way, and one is faced not with a probable overall theory but with a multitude of equally plausible alternatives.

---

8. See, for example, J. Barton's explanation of the transmission-historical method, *Reading the Old Testament: Method in Biblical Study* (London: Darton, Longman & Todd, 1984), 22–24. In rightly stressing the historical importance of doublets and breaks in the emergence of transmission-historical method, Barton conveys the misleading impression that only such indicators undergird present diachronic studies.
9. P. Noble, "Synchronic and Diachronic Approaches to Biblical Interpretation," *Literature and Theology* 7 (1993): 130–48.

It is not that such advocates of a literary approach necessarily deny the desirability of understanding distinctive aspects of the ancient culture interwoven into biblical texts.[10] Indeed, the classic introductions to literary methods for biblical scholarship typically include comments on how comparative material from cultures neighboring Israel can enable an informed reading of biblical texts.[11] Nevertheless, there is increasing skepticism regarding two items in particular: (1) the precision possible in locating the *specific* original contexts of biblical texts,[12] and (2) previous scholarship's often obsessive search for disjunction in biblical texts so that such texts can be dissected into their component parts. All too often such a search seemed to lead to a stubborn disregard of the compositional art in existing biblical passages. In response, many modern literary critics have urged a focus on the one and only text before us—the biblical text in its present form.[13]

Such study of the present biblical text without primary attention to its history of formation is what is meant here by the term *synchronic*. In contrast, the term *diachronic* designates a transmission-historical investigation of a text's prehistory, its sources, editorial layers, and the like. Each approach has had its characteristic emphases. Historically speaking, diachronic study has tended to stress what might be termed the text's "disunity," that is, the presence in the text of contradictions, narrative breaks, and conceptual crosscurrents.

Only recently have some diachronic studies focused primarily on the shaping of the present form of the text into a whole. Meanwhile, in response to the general emphasis on textual disunity in diachronic studies, most synchronic biblical studies have tended to seek unifying patterns in the given biblical text. Rather than reading for ruptures and other indicators of textual growth, these critics have used modern literary methods to seek cohesion and artistry in the existing form of the biblical text. This form is then often con-

---

10. At this point it is difficult to avoid terminological confusion when referring to the advocates of a literary approach. The problem is that in earlier English language scholarship, the term *literary-critical* applied to the discernment of literary sources and redaction, and the analogous term in German, *Literarkritik,* still refers to this process. For this reason, I will avoid the term *literary criticism* altogether and use the term *literary approach* to designate more recent methods.

11. See, for example, R. Alter, *The Art of Biblical Narrative* (New York: Basic Books, 1981), 13; M. Sternberg, *The Poetics of Biblical Narrative: Ideological Literature and the Drama of Reading* (Indiana Studies in Biblical Literature; Bloomington, Ind.: Indiana University Press, 1985), 12–13.

12. See, for example, R. Alter's critique of Bloom's extremely specific claims for his late tenth-century female Yahwist, in *The World of Biblical Literature* (New York: Basic Books, 1992), 160–69.

13. See, for example, the comments of J. Licht, *Storytelling in the Bible* (Jerusalem: Magnes, 1978), 144–47. As E. Blum has pointed out, this concept of a single "final form" of a biblical text can be problematic in light of the pluralism of textual witnesses to the Jewish canon, each with its own literary and theological integrity. "Gibt es die Endgestalt des Pentateuch?" in *Congress Volume: Leuven, 1989* (ed. J. Emerton; VTSup 43; Leiden: Brill, 1991), 46.

ceived as produced—whatever the text's precise prehistory—through the masterful synthesis of a "final redactor."[14]

Others, still working within a historical-critical framework, have raised questions about so quickly applying literary methods derived from study of modern texts to ancient texts like the Bible. To them the literary treatments in which Noble and others have so much confidence occasionally stretch too far to "harmonize" texts that resist such efforts.[15] By so doing, such treatments go against the grain of the very texts they are purporting to "read closely." For example, Blum argues:

> If one wants to avoid suppressing substantial dimensions of the final form, then one must bear in mind that this form as a whole does not include just *one* meaning level, but more levels next to and in one another. It represents not a flat surface, but a landscape that in its relief at the same time presents its history. To the extent that an interpretation of the transmitted text seeks nearness to the text ("close reading"), it must integrate this relief-structure.[16]

All this does not mean, however, that the final form is a hopelessly confused patchwork. The issue is the extent to which one can explore this final form without explicit attention to the shaping that created that form.

Just such a historical focus on the final shaping of the biblical text has been an interest of various canonical approaches, that is, Child's proposal for a critical focus on the existing (Christian) biblical text as scripture and Sanders's investigation of the interpretive process leading up to (and beyond) the production of canonized biblical texts.[17] Along similar lines, Rendtorff has

14. See, for example, Alter, *The Art of Biblical Narrative*, 20–21, who gives the following quote from Rosenberg ("Meanings, Morals, and Mysteries: Literary Approaches to the Torah," *Response* 9 [1975]: 67–94): "Here the weight of literary interest falls upon the activity of the *final* redactor, whose artistry requires far more careful attention than it has hitherto been accorded." After this citation, Alter argues that "the last clause if anything understates the case, since biblical critics frequently assume, out of some dim preconception about the transmission of texts in 'primitive' cultures, that the redactors were in the grip of a kind of manic tribal compulsion, driven again and again to include units of traditional material that made no connective sense, for reasons they themselves could not have explained." Both Alter's assumptions and those of the scholars he characterizes (indeed at points caricatures) need to be tested before becoming the basis for work with biblical texts.

15. See, for example, the helpful comments of A. F. Campbell and M. A. O'Brien in *Sources of the Pentateuch: Texts, Introductions, Annotations* (Minneapolis: Fortress, 1993), 208–9. On the other hand, compare the subtle literary reflections on complexity in Alter, *The Art of Biblical Narrative*, 19–20, 131–54; and E. Greenstein, "An Equivocal Reading of the Sale of Joseph," in *Literary Interpretations of Biblical Narratives*, (vol. 2; ed. K. R. R. Gros Louis with James S. Ackerman; Nashville: Abingdon, 1982), 114–25.

16. E. Blum, *Studien zur Komposition des Pentateuch* (BZAW 189; Berlin: De Gruyter, 1990), 382.

17. On Childs, see in particular his recent comments on this issue in his *Biblical Theology of the Old and New Testaments: Theological Reflection on the Christian Bible* (London: SCM, 1992), 104–6; in addition to his *Introduction to the Old Testament as Scripture* (Philadelphia: Fortress,

repeatedly called for a theological interpretation of the Hebrew canon in its final form.[18] In each case, the historical aspect of the investigation of the final form is motivated in part by a theological interest in the biblical text as normative. Now the biblical text is not just an object of art to be appreciated—so literary approaches—but a foundational document to be used to regulate a community of faith. This theological interest motivates the attempt of the canonical school of biblical criticism to narrow interpretation.[19] Rather than leaving the text to the whim of divergent synchronic readings, these canonical approaches attempt to specify which readings of the final form count theologically and which do not.[20] Thus, through attention to the final redaction of the Bible or a book in it one might be able to say which reading is a historically appropriate one, even if one can not rule out other nonhistorical readings of the present text. For example, Childs, in his *Introduction to the Old Testament as Scripture*, argues that a theological reading of Genesis as scripture should attend to the "toledot" headings spread throughout the book by a late Priestly redactor (Gen. 2:4a; 5:1; 6:9; etc.).[21] This kind of combined theological and historical interest in canonical approaches has given such approaches much more attention in historically oriented, European scholarship than their literary counterparts.

At the same time, this interest in redactional shaping of the biblical text can lead one to historical difficulties. Indeed, these difficulties also plague literary approaches insofar as they clear historical room for themselves by presupposing that the literary patterns they find are the product of a major final redaction of the text. For, as Friedman and Blum have argued, it is not clear that texts like the Pentateuch were subjected to any kind of systematic final redaction. The idea of a comprehensive final redactor is a diachronic

---

1979); idem, *Exodus* (OTL; London: SCM, 1974). For J.A. Sanders, see in particular his "The Integrity of Biblical Pluralism," in *"Not in Heaven": Coherence and Complexity in Biblical Narrative* (ed. Jason P. Rosenblatt and Joseph C. Sitterson, Jr.; Indiana Studies in Biblical Literature; Bloomington/Indianapolis, Ind.: Indiana University Press, 1991), 154–69; along with his *Torah and Canon* (Philadelphia: Fortress, 1972); idem, *Canon and Community: A Guide to Canonical Criticism* (Philadelphia: Fortress, 1984); idem, *From Sacred Story to Sacred Text: Canon as Paradigm* (Philadelphia: Fortress, 1987).
18. R. Rendtorff, "Between Historical Criticism and Holistic Interpretation: New Trends in Old Testament Exegesis," in *Congress Volume: Jerusalem, 1986* (VTSup 40; Leiden: Brill, 1988), 298–303, and republished in *Canon and Theology* (OBT; Minneapolis: Fortress, 1993), 25–30; idem, "The Paradigm is Changing: Hopes and Fears," *Biblical Interpretation* 1 (1993): 50–53.
19. On the importance of narrowing in theological interpretation of Scripture, see particularly R. Morgan with J. Barton, *Biblical Interpretation* (Oxford Bible Series; New York/Oxford: Oxford University Press, 1988), 11–15.
20. Whereas Childs and Rendtorff lean more toward an exact specification of the meaning of the canonized text, Sanders inclines more toward a hermeneutical narrowing of what constitutes canonical reading of canonized texts.
21. Childs, *Introduction*, 145–50.

hypothesis requiring testing, not an unquestionable postulate.[22] Not only that, but the more one attributes detailed patterns, chiasms, and theological shaping to a final redactor, the more one moves onto diachronically shaky ground. The literary norms used for such analyses are often exclusively modern, and the same could be said for many theological ideas that have been read in relation to the final form of the biblical text.[23] In this context, what we can plausibly argue historically may be much less than what we can see synchronically.[24] This leads to the following methodological paradox: the drive to make (implicit or explicit) historical claims, *however historically directed*, can incline scholars toward ascribing unhistorical certainty to theories regarding the redaction of a particular text. On the one hand, as a historically oriented theologian, I may wish to make certain historical claims. On the other hand, this very wish may lead me to rely excessively on claims about redactional unity in texts that are themselves historically questionable.

Observing that not every text in the Bible has received such a systematic redaction, many have reflected on how this might affect the analysis of a biblical text in its present form. For example, Damrosch argues that a diachronic analysis offers various alternatives to an interpreter. One can choose to interpret an earlier layer over against later ones—so the older approaches—but one can also investigate the self-commenting character of redacted texts and/or read a text through the multiple perspectives offered by its various layers.[25] Fox particularly stresses the intertextual character of redaction history and proposes appropriating Bloom's theory regarding the "anxiety of influence" to elucidate the relationships between various redactional layers.[26] B. Levinson argues for attention to the hermeneutical dimensions of complex biblical texts. In such texts, later additions often contradict the claims of the texts on which they build, even as these additions presuppose the protocanonical

22. R. Friedman, "The Hiding of the Face: An Essay on the Literary Unity of Biblical Narrative," in *Judaic Perspectives on Ancient Israel* (ed. J. Neusner, et al.; Philadelphia: Fortress, 1987), 208–9; E. Blum, *Studien*, 361–80; idem, "Gibt es die Endgestalt des Pentateuch?" 46–57.
23. J. Kugel, "On the Bible and Literary Criticism," *Prooftexts* 1 (1981): 217–36. Childs' *Biblical Theology of the Old and New Testaments* is a good example of how his final form approach has moved toward a conscious interaction between reading of the final form and postbiblical theology.
24. This, of course, is but another version of the problem of "intentional fallacy" raised decades ago by the new literary critics.
25. D. Damrosch, *The Narrative Covenant* (San Francisco: Harper & Row, 1987), 298–326.
26. M. V. Fox, *The Redaction of the Books of Esther: On Reading Composite Texts* (SBLMS 40; Atlanta: Scholars Press, 1991), 151–54. He cites H. Bloom, *The Anxiety of Influence* (New York: Oxford University Press, 1973); idem, *A Map of Misreading* (New York: Oxford University Press, 1975). L. Brisman also attempts to use Bloom's framework for interpreting Genesis, but is hampered by an implausible transmission-historical premise, *The Voice of Jacob: On the Composition of Genesis* (Indiana Studies in Biblical Literature; Bloomington/Indianapolis, Ind.: Indiana University Press, 1990).

status of their precursors by subtly building around them.[27] Along similar lines, I have argued that the Garden of Eden story (Gen. 2:4b–3:24) is the product of exactly such a process of redaction and contradiction. The result of this process is an irresolvably multivalent whole whose interpretive possibilities have been exploited in strikingly different ways by modern interpreters.[28]

Meanwhile, some recent postmodern synchronic approaches to the present biblical text have corrected the earlier emphasis of many biblical literary studies on unity. Rather than seeking overarching patterns in the text, these more recent literary approaches have often stressed the fractured, dialogical, and often irresolvably multivalent character of biblical texts. For example, R. Barthes argued in an influential essay that the story of Jacob wrestling the angel (Gen. 32:23–33; Eng. 32:22–32)[29] is turned in on itself in certain irresolvable ways. The story undoes itself.[30] Miscall argued that the creation narrative and certain portions of the Abraham story work at cross-purposes to each other.[31] Clines and Turner have shown that certain plot announcements in Genesis are never fulfilled.[32] Finally, Bal, Fewell, Gunn, and Pardes have explored ideological contradictions disrupting the dominant

---

27. B. Levinson, "The Right Chorale: From the Poetics to the Hermeneutics of the Hebrew Bible," in *"Not in Heaven"*, 131–53, particularly 150. See also, idem, "The human voice in divine revelation: The problem of authority in Biblical law," in *Innovation in Religious Traditions: Essays in the Interpretation of Religious Change* (Berlin/New York: Mouton de Gruyter, 1992), 35–61. In developing such a focus on hermeneutics, Levinson is quite close to the work of James Sanders mentioned above. In this sense Sanders's hermeneutical interests make his work an important bridge to approaches devoting as much attention to the fractures as to the integrity of the Biblical text.

28. D. M. Carr, "The Politics of Textual Subversion: A Diachronic Perspective on the Garden of Eden Story," *JBL* 112 (1993): 577–95. Note the above survey is not a comprehensive list of explorations of the intersection of synchronic and diachronic approaches. Among the many noteworthy writings on the subject, see in particular J. Barton, *Reading the Old Testament,* especially 8–19; M. Brett, *Biblical Criticism in Crisis?: The Impact of the Canonical Approach on Old Testament Studies* (Cambridge: Cambridge University Press, 1991); and E. Talstra, *Solomon's Prayer: Synchrony and Diachrony in the Composition of 1 Kings 8,14–61* (Contributions to Biblical Exegesis and Theology 3; Kampen: Kok Pharos, 1993).

29. Here and elsewhere I give the alternate versification of the Christian Bible next to that of the Hebrew, labeled "Eng." for my English language readers.

30. R. Barthes, "La lutte avec l'ange: analyse textuelle de Genèse 32.23–33," in *Analyse structurale et Exégèse Biblique; Essais d'interprétation* (Bibliothèque théologique; Neuchâtel: Delachaux et Niestlé, 1971), 27–39. (E.T., "The Struggle with the Angel," in *Image, Music, Text* [trans. Stephen Heath; London: Fontana Collins, 1977], 125–41.) For discussion of how this essay by Barthes already represents a step away from structuralism, see K. Hart, "The Poetics of the Negative," in *Reading the Text: Biblical Criticism and Literary Theory* (ed. Stephen Prickett; Cambridge, Mass.: Basil Blackwell, 1991), 289–303.

31. P. Miscall, *The Workings of Old Testament Narrative* (Semeia Studies; Philadelphia: Fortress; Chico, Calif.: Scholars, 1983); idem, "Jacques Derrida in the Garden of Eden," *USQR* 44 (1990): 1–9.

32. D. J. A. Clines, "What Happens in Genesis," in *What Does Eve Do to Help?* (JSOTSup 94; Sheffield: JSOT, 1990), 49–66; L. Turner, *Announcements of Plot in Genesis* (JSOTSup 96; Sheffield: JSOT Press, 1990).

establishment emphases in the present form of Genesis and other biblical books.[33]

Already this survey suggests a potential convergence between recent postmodern synchronic studies and recent diachronic studies. Just as diachronic studies are focusing more on illuminating the present form of the text, synchronic studies are displaying increasing interest in the very textual disunity that was often the mainstay of transmission history. Indeed, two studies have built on Barthes's essay by integrating diachronic insights into study of a text's present fractured character. Independently of each other, G. Hartman and H. Utzschneider both argued that the process that formed the story of Jacob's wrestling at Penuel introduced fractures into the story that have preoccupied generations of subsequent interpreters. In this way, Hartman and Utzschneider extended Barthes's analysis into both the past and future of the text. On the one hand, they located some of the text's fractures in its formation. On the other hand, they argued that these fractures have influenced the text's subsequent interpretation, provoking generations of interpreters to attempt to pull the text into a unity, determining the identity of Jacob's attacker and who won how.[34] For example, Hartman described his interests as follows:

> What interests me are the fault lines of a text, the evidence of a narrative sedimentation that has not entirely settled, and the tension that results between producing one authoritative account and respecting traditions characterized by a certain heterogeneity.[35]

Thus in Hartman's approach, the "fault lines" become a literary aspect of an irresolvably complex text, not noise to be tuned out.[36] Moreover, both Hartman and Utzschneider's studies are distinguished by their use of an understanding of the text's process of formation to confirm and sharpen a perception of its past and present interpretive potential.

---

33. For examples related to Genesis, see M. Bal, *Lethal Love: Feminist Literary Readings of Biblical Love Stories* (Bloomington, Ind.: Indiana University Press, 1987), 89–130; D. Nolan Fewell and D. M. Gunn, *Gender, Power and Promise: The Subject of the Bible's First Story* (Nashville: Abingdon, 1993), 22–91; and I. Pardes, *Countertraditions in the Bible: A Feminist Approach* (Cambridge, Mass.: Harvard University Press, 1992), 13–78.
34. G. H. Hartman, "The Struggle for the Text," in *Midrash and Literature* (ed. G. H. Hartman and S. Budick; New Haven, Conn./London: Yale University Press, 1986), 11; H. Utzschneider, "Das hermeneutische Problem der Uneindeutigkeit biblischer Texte: dargestellt an Text und Rezeption der Erzählung von Jakob am Jabbok," *EvT* 48 (1988): 182–98 (edited version of a February 1987 lecture).
35. Hartman, "The Struggle for the Text," 11.
36. To be sure, right after the above quote Hartman goes on to add that the text always has a "sometimes laconic, sometimes wordy, but always imperious unity." His following discussion, however, indicates just how complex and unresolved this unity is (pp. 11–17).

The Approach to Be Adopted in This Book:
Focus on the Intratextual Dimension of Genesis

Hartman and Utzschneider enriched study of the text's present form through attention to what might be termed its "*intra*textual dimension." Literary theorists have long spoken of the *inter*textual dimension of a text, where symbol systems from outside the text are transposed into a new, irresolvably multivalent mix within it.[37] At the same time, there has been some discussion in various quarters of "*intra*textual" relationships. For example, G. Lindbeck used the term *intratextual* to refer to the ongoing life of a given text through a particular stream of confessional tradition.[38] Elsewhere, in an essay on the editing of Old English manuscripts that reproduce oral performances, A. Doane also uses the term *intratextual* to refer to the "voices, shifting from performance to performance, within the text."[39] In both cases, these otherwise disparate uses of the term *intratextuality* focus on ways a later text builds itself around an earlier text, claiming to reproduce it. Intratextuality concerns something other than the absorption and clash of various linguistic systems inevitable in any writing. It occurs in a context that values tradition. The resulting text—whether doctrine (Lindbeck) or written record of an oral performance (Doane)—claims the authority of the precursor it incorporates. At the same time, however, this absorption of an earlier text never comes without a transformation. For in each case, whether the development of doctrine, addition of a redactional layer, or textual reproduction of an oral performance, the writer transforms the tradition she or he uses, even as she or he purports to reproduce it.[40]

Insofar as this is true for texts in Genesis, study of their fractured intratextuality can illuminate our understanding of their later interpretation, that is, how they have functioned intertextually.[41] The more wrenching the transformation that occurred in the text's formation, the more complex the result.

---

37. For the classic introduction of the term, see J. Kristeva, *Desire in Language: A Semiotic Approach to Literature and Art* (ed. L. S. Roudiez; trans. T. Gora, et al.; New York: Columbia University Press, 1980), 66; cf. also 36, 86–87.

38. G. A. Lindbeck, *The Nature of Doctrine: Religion and Theology in a Postliberal Age* (Philadelphia: Westminster, 1984), 117 and 136. T. Beal focuses on this use of the term in his "Glossary," in *Reading Between Texts: Intertextuality and the Hebrew Bible* (ed. D. Nolan Fewell; Louisville, Ky.: Westminster John Knox Press, 1992), 23.

39. A. N. Doane, "Oral Texts, Intertexts, and Intratexts: Editing Old English," in *Influence and Intertextuality in Literary History* (ed. J. Clayton and E. Rothstein; Madison, Wis.: University of Wisconsin Press, 1991), 76, cf. 103.

40. For a particularly eloquent exploration of this move in biblical interpretation, see W. D. Edgerton, *The Passion of Interpretation* (Literary Currents in Biblical Interpretation; Louisville, Ky.: Westminster John Knox, 1992), 18–42.

41. Thus I would not as sharply distinguish study of reception of a text from its prehistory and present shape as W. C. Smith. Cf. his "The Study of Religion and the Study of the Bible" in *Rethinking Scripture* (ed. M. Levering; Albany, N.Y.: State University of New York Press, 1989), 18–28, and his later *What is Scripture?: A Comparative Approach* (Minneapolis: Fortress, 1993), particularly his critique of Western Islamic scholarship on 77–91 and his conclusion on 221–23.

One of the particular virtues of Utzschneider's and Hartman's studies of the Jacob story is their demonstration that the intratextual complexity of the story has stimulated variation in the subsequent interpretation of it.[42] Their work suggests that focus on a text's precursor traditions might sharpen our sense of the complexity of its present form.[43] Moreover, study of a text's intratextuality might inform our understanding of how it prompted others to link with it intertextually.

Perhaps this is the most important specific contribution a diachronic approach can make to the investigation of the interpretive potential of the present biblical text: helping a reader *hold on* to the fractures of multiauthored texts like Genesis. As many literary studies over the last decade have shown, synchronic study of the present text can discern numerous potential patterns spanning the text as a whole. Often a diachronic study of the text's prehistory can add little that is unique to this descriptive picture. The patterns are there to see, whether or not one attributes them to this or that redactional stratum. Nevertheless, a diachronic exploration of a text's formation can balance synchronic focus on the whole by tuning the reader's ear to the different voices in the text, voices often impartially harmonized into a broader chorus. Keeping with this chorale image,[44] it is not that the aim here is to separate the biblical chorus into various solo acts. Instead, it is to recognize the often cacophonous character of the biblical work. By attending to these often discordant voices now combined into a complex whole, we can gain a certain critical distance from any one reading of that whole. We can better recognize the element of readerly choice and responsibility in any attempt to master the whole through interpretation.

This book is an attempt to extend such an approach to the book of Genesis as a whole. I will argue for reading Genesis as an intensely intratextual, fractured, and multivoiced text. In contrast to some advocates of the newer literary methods, I maintain that Genesis did undergo a long formation

---

Smith rightly points out the limited character of past, primarily Protestant, scholarly focus on the biblical text and its prehistory. Such an approach often paid little or no attention to the way biblical texts have actually functioned in the communities who cherished and lived from them. Nevertheless, once Smith's point is granted, Hartman's and Utzschneider's approaches suggest a role, though not an exclusive one, for study of a text's prehistory as part of a broader investigation of a text's shape and subsequent interpretation.

42. This formulation consciously crosses concepts that are often kept apart in discussion of intertextuality, "influence," on the one hand, and "intertextuality," on the other. In doing so, I do not mean to imply that the precursor text is the sole determinant of later interpretation. Nevertheless, I do see the fractures of a given text as being a factor in later interpretation.

43. Here is an interesting parallel to how the concept intertextuality has functioned in literary theory. Just as study of intertextuality was — in part — a strategy through which deconstructive literary critics could stress the irreducible multivalency of modern texts, so also study of intratextuality in biblical texts can heighten our awareness of the untamable multivalency in them as well.

44. This image is appropriated from B. Levinson's, "The Right Chorale."

process (its transmission history) *and* that it is possible to explore certain parts of this process. Not all of this process is equally uncertain. In contrast to much historical-critical study of Genesis's transmission history, I maintain that it is not possible to achieve an acceptable level of plausibility on many issues regarding the formation of Genesis. In other words, we must be ever clearer that not all is, or can be, equally certain.[45]

In summary, I am not speaking of transmission history either as a necessary presupposition for further work or as the final arbiter for what counts as a valid interpretation.[46] Instead, I maintain that diachronic analysis has a *contribution* to make in the larger project of interpretation of Genesis. As Frye points out, something like an image of "interpenetration"—or perhaps better, "interrelationship"—of various methods is a more helpful metaphor for interdisciplinary conversation than that of "foundation."[47]

In this study, the primary emphasis will be on distinguishing various textual layers in Genesis from one another, but there will also be some attempt to date these layers and even discuss their function within their probable social contexts. Here too, this is not to maintain that my tentative reflections regarding the social context and function of texts in Genesis exhaust either the original function or subsequent meaning of these texts.[48] Nor is it to maintain that investigation of such social context is required for legitimate study of such texts. Instead, the historical framework functions here as a sort of scaffolding, a different narrative line standing alongside the narrative line

45. To be sure, good transmission historians have long recognized certain limits to their analysis. The point of the following discussion is to sharpen this recognition and nuance it. For example, see the comments on the limits of transmission-historical analysis by W. H. Schmidt, "Elementare Erwägungen zur Quellenscheidung im Pentateuch," in *Congress Volume: Leuven, 1989* (ed. J.A. Emerton; VTSup 43; Leiden: Brill, 1991), 44, who cites a comment along similar lines in Noth, *Pentateuch,* 6; (E.T., 5).

46. When exploring this intersection of diachronic and synchronic approaches, there is a constant danger of trying to recreate the dominance of the historical-critical approach through assertions and/or assumptions of its foundational character. For trenchant critique of this tendency, see D. Gunn, "Narrative Criticism," in *To Each Its Own Meaning: An Introduction to Biblical Criticisms and Their Application* (ed. S. Haynes and S. McKenzie; Louisville, Ky.: Westminster John Knox, 1993), 192–93. Cf. S. Boorer, "The Importance of a Diachronic Approach: The Case of Genesis-Kings," *CBQ* 51 (1989):195–208. She argues that a diachronic analysis can adjudicate between varying synchronic approaches. Such a proposal presupposes that what one is interested in is a historically based synchronic reading, and it sets up a model wherein historical criticism is the context in which other interpretive discourse takes place. This is one option but not the only one.

47. N. Frye, *Spiritus Mundi: Essays on Literature, Myth, and Society* (Bloomington, Ind.: Indiana University Press, 1976), 106. Cf. also Hart's use of Frye in "The Poetics of the Negative," 289–90.

48. On the importance of social context for literary language, see P. N. Medvedev/M. M. Bakhtin, *The Formal Method in Literary Scholarship: A Critical Introduction to Sociological Poetics* (trans. A. J. Wehrle; Baltimore/London: Johns Hopkins University Press, 1978), especially 119–28 and 151–58; and (with an excellent discussion of recent uses of Bakhtin and discussions of the death of the author) S. Stanford Friedman, "Weavings: Intertextuality and the (Re)Birth of the Author," in *Influence and Intertextuality in Literary History,* 146–80.

of Genesis. Locating different voices in Genesis along this alternative narrative line can help us focus on the sometimes subtle distinctions between these voices, rather than blend their perspectives into one. For example, later in the book I will go into some detail on how Priestly texts in Genesis appropriate ancient Priestly concepts to address pressing issues in the late exilic and early postexilic periods. This kind of insight can sharpen our perception of the distinctions between the texture of these Priestly texts and the socioliterary texture of much earlier Jacob and Joseph texts written amidst the emergence of the early Northern monarchy.

The particular character of my approach may be illustrated by the following set of analogies to different approaches to nature. Traditional historical-critical studies have often pursued what might be termed a "strip mining" approach, wherein the fractures in the text are opened up like a seam in the earth, so the early layers of the text can be laid bare for interpretation and extraction of often useful historical information.[49] Newer literary and canonical approaches have often pursued a wilderness preserve approach, wherein the coherence and integrity of the text are carefully protected and admired, or in some postmodern approaches, unmasked and critiqued. I am arguing here for the additional possibility of combining such a primary focus on the present form of the biblical text with a geological approach. In it the contours of the existing biblical landscape, fractures and all, are illuminated by plausible suppositions about how that landscape was produced.[50] Furthermore, I will argue that such a broad exploration of the formation and shape of the biblical landscape can help us better appreciate what various interpreters have seen in that landscape over the years—how the landscape has been not just beautiful, but meaningful.

The Distinctive Character of Texts like Genesis

One important feature of such a geological approach is that it helps keep our attention on the particular textual character and resulting interpretive potential of complex, multiauthored texts like Genesis. To be sure, as deconstructive critics particularly remind us, all texts are somehow fractured. Thus any reader's attempt to overcome the unruly character of a text itself must withstand scrutiny of his or her own interpretive aims and presuppositions.[51] Nevertheless, ancient, multivoiced texts like Genesis have yet another element

---

49. Cf. Alter's depiction of such scholarship as "excavative" in his *Art of Biblical Narrative,* 13–15.
50. This use of the geology analogy for transmission history appears in J. E. Carpenter, *The Composition of the Hexateuch* (London/New York/Bombay: Longmans, Green & Co., 1902), 5. For more recent use of this analogy see Fox, *The Redaction of the Books of Esther,* 149.
51. For a helpful survey of these issues in relation to New Testament texts, see S. D. Moore, *Poststructuralism and the New Testament: Derrida and Foucault at the Foot of the Cross* (Minneapolis: Fortress, 1994), particularly 65–81.

of intratextual complexity that modern readers are not naturally sensitized to acknowledge or perceive. We live in a culture where most texts are written within a fairly short period of historical time by a clearly defined author or group of authors, where the majority of such material is protected by copyright, and where our present literary methods for interpreting narratives like Genesis were developed on modern *fictional* texts with no claim to referential truth and no interest in supporting such a claim through the use of preexisting, time-honored material.[52] This setting can unconsciously shape the way we read texts like Genesis in misleading ways. Thus, for example, even if a modern scholar does not subscribe to the idea that Moses wrote the whole Pentateuch, she or he works in a modern context in which unacknowledged insertion of one's own material into another's work is dishonest. If someone added a chapter to this book and republished it, I would have a ground to sue that person. These preconceptions about texts are present no matter what one's religious beliefs are about the Bible. Moreover, such preconceptions predispose a modern reader to view the ancient process of composition of the Bible as an *anomaly* compared to more familiar, modern processes. A modern context predisposes an interpreter to ignore and/or explain away textual features produced by a long-term textual formation process with which he or she is unfamiliar.

Here it is helpful to review documentary evidence that—whatever their ideas about texts and authors—ancient Near Eastern (including biblical) authors were much more inclined than we are to build on earlier texts, incorporating, combining, and expanding them into a new and complex whole. Such "documentary" or "external" evidence is particularly interesting at this point in our discussion because in these cases we do not have to speculate on the existence of earlier sources in the final form of a text. We have them. Thus, for example, J. Tigay has used separate copies of the Mesopotamian Gilgamesh epic to trace its transmission history over centuries.[53] This epic is particularly important to the discussion at hand because there is documentation of its growth through three quite different stages of composition.

1. *Initial Composition through Linkage of Originally Independent Traditions.* The (Old Babylonian) author of the original Gilgamesh epic appears to have drawn freely on the plots of earlier Sumerian stories in the process of composing a story about Gilgamesh's search for immortality. As Ur-III manuscripts show, these stories once circulated in independent form. Nevertheless, the author of the epic has so thoroughly integrated

---

52. The latter observation comes from Blum, *Studien*, 381.
53. J. Tigay, *The Evolution of the Gilgamesh Epic* (Philadelphia: University of Pennsylvania Press, 1982); and "The Evolution of the Pentateuchal Narratives in the Light of the Evolution of the *Gilgamesh Epic*," in *Empirical Models for Biblical Criticism* (Philadelphia: University of Pennsylvania Press, 1985), 21–52.

these stories and other traditions into his overall theme that it would generally be impossible to say much about their original scope and form if we did not have this earlier attestation of them.

2. *Redirection and Supplementation of the Original Composition.* The Gilgamesh epic continued to evolve over the course of the Middle Babylonian period, and by the end of the period we see a late version that includes—alongside a number of more minor modifications to the tradition—a new wisdom-oriented prologue to the epic and two texts of which we have separate copies: a flood narrative (drawn from Atrahasis or something very close to it) and a translation of an additional Sumerian legend regarding Gilgamesh and his friend Enkidu.[54] Notably, even in this extension of the epic, the revisers continued to build on earlier traditions. In this sense ancient "composition" was "composite" at each stage.

3. *Further Scribal Modification.* Even after this epic had reached relatively stable form, scribes still appear to have introduced minor modifications in the further copying and transmission of the text.[55]

In other cases of documented growth of texts, only one stage in their growth is documented. For example, the Deuteronomistic history itself refers repeatedly to independent source documents upon which it depends,[56] and analysis of it indicates that it was formed out of various traditions regarding Israel's history. Nevertheless, we do not have documentation of the growth of this tradition until slightly different editions of this history are transmitted in the Old Greek and proto-Massoretic traditions, on the one hand, and a still different edition of this history is thoroughly reworked in the books of Chronicles, on the other.[57] So also in other cases, we rarely have direct manuscript access to the traditions used in the initial formation of a given composition (cf. stage 1 of the Gilgamesh epic above), other than in the preservation of parallel and yet

54. Tigay, *The Evolution of the Gilgamesh Epic*, 103–8. Tigay, "Evolution of the Pentateuchal Narratives," 42, points out that although we do have a separate copy of the added legend, we do not have a copy of the end of the Old Babylonian version. Therefore, there is no documentary evidence that the legend in question was only added onto the epic in the Late Babylonian version. Other indicators noted by Tigay, however, lend a very high degree of probability to this hypothesis (*Evolution of the Gilgamesh Epic*, 27, 49; "Evolution of the Pentateuchal Narratives," 42).
55. Tigay, *The Evolution of the Gilgamesh Epic*, 130–39.
56. R. de Vaux, "A propos du second centenaire d'Astruc: Réflexions sur l'état actuel de la critique du Pentateuque," in *The Congress Volume: Copenhagen, 1953* (VTSup 1; Leiden: Brill, 1953), 186. For additional citations and discussion see M. Fishbane, *Biblical Interpretation in Ancient Israel* (Oxford: Clarendon Press, 1988 [original, 1985]), 27.
57. S. McKenzie, *The Chronicler's Use of the Deuteronomistic History* (HSM 33; Atlanta: Scholars Press, 1984). A recent study relating this model to the Pentateuch is W. Johnstone, "Reactivating the Chronicles Analogy in Pentateuchal Studies, with Special Reference to the Sinai Pericope in Exodus," *ZAW* 99 (1987): 16–37.

divergent versions of various individual laws, prophecies, genealogies, and psalms.[58] We only get such documented access to different levels of compositional reworking when we have a given composition. Outside Israel we have divergent editions of texts such as the Sumerian king list, Ashurbanipal inscriptions, and Hammurabi legal proclamations.[59] Now, with the Qumran finds, we are increasingly conscious of how biblical books circulated in different editions even into the second Temple period. For example, recently published "reworked Pentateuch" texts confirm a supposition already suggested by the so-called proto-Samaritan texts: namely, that there was a succession of expansionist, harmonizing editions of the Pentateuch circulating in various circles in Palestine alongside the shorter version of the Pentateuch found in the standard Hebrew version.[60] This kind of evidence has led us to reconsider the testimony of Old Greek translations of biblical books to possible alternative Hebrew editions of those books. Taken together, Qumran and the Greek textual tradition attest to substantial redirection and supplementation of many biblical books such as Jeremiah, Ezekiel, Psalms, Proverbs, Ezra-Nehemiah, and Esther,[61] along with more limited scribal addi-

---

58. For a survey of examples in the Biblical tradition see E. Tov, *Textual Criticism of the Hebrew Bible* (Minneapolis: Fortress, 1992), 12–13, 319. To the best of my knowledge, these texts have not been systematically collected and analyzed. A handy Hebrew synopsis of some texts is provided in A. Bendavid, *Parallels in the Bible* (Jerusalem: Carta, 1972), and Fishbane analyzes some specific cases of ongoing transmission of individual traditions in his *Biblical Interpretation in Ancient Israel*.

59. J. Tigay, "The Stylistic Criterion of Source Criticism in the Light of Ancient Near Eastern and Postbiblical Literature," in *Empirical Models for Biblical Criticism*, 149–73. See references there for earlier literature. Cf. also P. Y. Hoskisson, "Emar as an Empirical Model of the Transmission of Canon," in *The Biblical Canon in Comparative Perspective: Scripture in Context 4* (Ancient Near Eastern Texts and Studies 11; ed. K. Lawson Younger, Jr., et al.; Lewiston, N.Y.: Mellon Press, 1991), 21–32.

60. E. Tov, "The Textual Status of 4Q364–7 (4QPP)," in *The Madrid Qumran Congress, Proceedings of the International Congress on the Dead Sea Scrolls, Madrid, 18–21 March 1991* (ed. J. Trebolle Barrera and L. Vegas Montaner; Studies on the Texts of the Desert of Judah 11; Madrid: Universidad Complutense; Leiden: Brill, 1992), 43–82; E. Tov and S. White, "364–67. 4QReworked Pentateuch[b–e] and 365a. 4QTemple?" in H. Attridge, et al., *Qumran Cave 4*, vol. 8, *Parabiblical Texts, Part I, DJD* 13 (Oxford: Clarendon Press, 1994). The first such expansionist manuscripts found at Qumran were originally termed "proto-Samaritan" because they represent a manuscript tradition that appears to have served as the base for further expansions by the Samaritans. Now, however, with the "reworked Pentateuch" texts, including what seems to be a complete non-Samaritan Torah copy based on the same expansionist base (4Q364), we should probably seek other terminology for this phenomenon. What we have here are various final "editions" of the Pentateuch, including the proto-Massoretic text, various expanded editions found at Qumran and among the Samaritans (related to a similar expansionist base), and the edition used by the Old Greek translators. In light of this phenomenon, variant para-Pentateuchal traditions like Jubilees and the Temple Scroll also appear in a different light. More treatment of this phenomenon, however, must await another context.

61. For an excellent survey of this and other places where the Old Greek presents a different earlier edition of a biblical book, see Tov, *Textual Criticism of the Hebrew Bible*, 313–47. Certain other particularly relevant studies too recent to be cited in Tov's book include: Y. Goldman,

tions.[62] In summary, although we do not always have documentation of transmission history—especially for the initial composition of a text out of originally independent traditions (oral or written)—there is an impressive body of evidence for later stages of textual growth in the ancient Near East. This widely documented growth ranges along a continuum from the substantial redirection and supplementation of an existing composition to more minor scribal modifications.

In addition, there are some other types of growth that are attested under more specific conditions. Tertel has surveyed the abbreviation and patterning of Assyrian royal inscriptions, a streamlining that conformed earlier texts to a certain plot pattern.[63] Van Seters has argued persuasively that the Lagash king list was formed in relation to, but over against the Sumerian king list.[64] Thus, in this case a text builds on the model of an earlier text but fills it with a decisively different content. Finally, there are several examples in the premodern world of conflation: the weaving together of parallel, originally independent documents. Tigay has pointed out how certain early Qumran and Old Greek manuscripts conflate texts from Deuteronomy with their parallels in Exodus and Numbers.[65] Kaufman has studied the often radical process of the conflation of disparate biblical texts in the Temple Scroll.[66] The canonical Christian Gospels of Matthew and Luke stand as another example of conflation, this time of (various editions of) Mark and a Jesus sayings collection. Finally, Moore and Longstaff have studied the conflation of the canonical

---

Prophétie et royauté au retour de l'exil: Les origines littéraires de la forme massorétique du livre de Jérémie (OBO 118; Göttingen: Vandenhoeck & Ruprecht, 1992); Fox, *The Redaction of the Books of Esther;* Z. Talshir, *The Alternative Story: 3 Kingdoms 12:24a–z* (Jerusalem Biblical Studies 6; Jerusalem: Simor, 1993).

In addition, there is J. Sanders' controversial proposal that the divergent psalm scrolls at Qumran reflect the existence of competing editions of the Psalms during the Second Temple period ("Cave 11 Surprises and the Question of Canon," *McCQ* 21 [1968]; 286–95; republished in *The Canon and Masorah of the Hebrew Bible: An Introductory Reader* [ed. Sid Leiman; Library of Biblical Studies; New York: KTAV, 1974], 39–48). For references to the debate regarding this proposal, see J. Barton, *Oracles of God: Perceptions of Ancient Prophecy in Israel After the Exile* (London: Darton, Longman and Todd, 1986), 85–86, 285nn107–11.

62. S. Talmon, "The Textual Study of the Bible—A New Outlook," in *Qumran and the History of the Biblical Text* (ed. F. M. Cross and S. Talmon; Cambridge, Mass./London: Harvard University Press 1976), 328–32; and E. Tov, "Glosses, Interpolations and Other Types of Scribal Additions in the Text of the Hebrew Bible," in *Language, Theology, and the Bible: Essays in Honour of James Barr,* ed. S. Balentine and J. Barton (Oxford: Clarendon Press, 1994), 40–66. In addition, M. Fishbane coordinates such manuscript observations with an exemplary analysis of scribal practice and hermeneutics in his *Biblical Interpretation in Ancient Israel,* 44–88, particularly 82–83.

63. H. J. Tertel, *Text and Transmission: An Empirical Model for the Literary Development of Old Testament Narratives* (BZAW 221; Berlin/New York: De Gruyter, 1994).

64. J. Van Seters, *Prologue to History: The Yahwist as Historian in Genesis* (Louisville, Ky: Westminster John Knox, 1992), 64–66.

65. J. Tigay, "Conflation as a Redaction Technique," 55–57, 61–83.

66. S. Kaufman, "The Temple Scroll and Higher Criticism," *HUCA* 53 (1982): 29–43.

Gospels in Tatian's *Diatessaron*.[67] In most cases, this conflation occurred at a relatively late stage in the transmission of a given tradition, interweaving separate texts that had already achieved some level of authority within the community transmitting them. Conflation was a way to bind these independent, authoritative texts into a single whole.

In Israel and the ancient Near East we see not a single common type of textual modification but a broad variety of types. Some sorts of textual modification, such as the initial building of a composition out of earlier traditions or the substantial reworking of a composition (again based on earlier tradition), are typical of earlier stages in the transmission of tradition. Other sorts, such as more minor scribal modification or the conflation of independent documents, are typical of texts later in their process of transmission. Nevertheless, whatever the type of modification involved, texts in the ancient Near East (including Israel) were often formed in a different way and over a longer period of time than the literary texts on which many of our best modern interpretive methods were developed.[68]

In order to highlight some of the distinctive aspects of the mind-set influencing ancient textual formation, I return to the three aspects of modern textual conceptuality mentioned at the outset of the discussion: singularity of authorship, textual solidity (i.e., modern copyright), and the genre of fiction.

1. *Authorship*. Unlike many modern texts, ancient Israelite historical texts like Genesis were originally circulated anonymously. This means that no kind of authorship rights could impede adaptation or modification. To be sure, already in the postexilic period we see references to the 'Torah of Moses' of which Genesis is a part. Nevertheless, these references seem to be more characterizations of the content of the

---

67. G. F. Moore, "Tatian's *Diatessaron* and the Analysis of the Pentateuch," *JBL* 9 (1890); 201–15 (reprinted in *Empirical Models for Biblical Criticism*, 243–56); T.R.W. Longstaff, *Evidence of Conflation in Mark? A Study in the Synoptic Problem* (SBLDS 28; Missoula, Mont.: Scholars Press, 1977), 10–42; cf. H. Donner, "Der Redaktor: Überlegungen zum vorkritischen Umgang mit der Heiligen Schrift," *Henoch* 2 (1980): 1–30, who compares conflation in the flood story with later gospel harmonies.

68. Already in his introduction to Hexateuchal studies, Carpenter pointed out that this phenomenon of textual growth is hardly confined to the Bible and other ancient Near Eastern documents. He focuses primarily on examples of transmission history from India. *The Composition of the Hexateuch*, 10–12. For comments by specialists on the transmission history of Eastern religious texts see (for Indian religious literature): R. C. Hazra, *Studies in the Purāṇic Records on Hindu Rites and Customs* (1940 ed.; reprint, Delhi: Motilal Banarsidass, 1987); L. Renou, *Vedic India* (trans. P. Spratt; Classical India 3; Calcutta: Susil Gupta, 1957), 3, 9–10, 14–15, 20–21, 25, 42; idem, *Indian Literature* (trans. P. Evans; New York: Walker and Co., 1964), especially 11–13 (on the Mahabharata) and 13–15 (on the Ramayana); T. J. Hopkins, *The Hindu Religious Tradition* (Encino/Belmont, Calif.: Dickenson Pub. Co., 1971), 87–89. For Buddhist religious literature, see: E. Lamotte, "Sur la formation du Mahayana," in *Asiatica: Festschrift Friedrich Weller* (Leipzig: O. Harrassowitz, 1954), 377–96; idem, *Histoire du bouddhisme indien: des origines à l'ère śaka* (Louvain: Institut Orientaliste, 1958), especially 154–210 and 297–319.

Pentateuch—with its focus on the Moses life story and instructions mediated by him to Israel—than expressions of any belief that he was the author of the entire Pentateuch. Explicit attribution of the authorship of the Pentateuch to Moses does not occur until the Hellenistic period (333–64 B.C.E.).[69]

2. *Textual Solidity.* Whereas modern texts are often protected by copyright very early in their formation, ancient texts like Gilgamesh or Genesis often seem to have achieved textual solidity only after they had been in circulation for a long time. This achievement of textual solidity seems connected less with any correlate to modern authorship rights than with these ancient texts' attainment of authoritative status within the communities transmitting them.

3. *The Genre of Fiction (and modern history).* The modern fictional texts on which our literary methods were developed make no claims to exactly report past events, and they are usually the complete creation of their authors. In contrast, ancient historylike texts like Genesis were written to make certain true claims about the past. This means that their authors often did not work at the same level of freedom with their material as a modern writer of fiction does. Indeed, ancient authors did not even have the freedom of modern historians. Whereas a modern historian builds a brand new narrative after having critically evaluated her or his sources, the ancient historian and her or his audience tended to trust much more fully traditions handed down by generations. As a result, they would not just use the traditions, but would reproduce them even as they modified them and/or completely recontextualized them. In summary, rather than creating a fully new text after the manner of a modern novelist or even a modern historian, ancient authors of historylike narratives like Gilgamesh or Genesis would often build their text out of earlier traditions.[70]

Seen within this perspective, Genesis is part of a broader spectrum of originally anonymous, historylike ancient Near Eastern narratives, many of which were formed gradually out of earlier traditions and only achieved textual solidity as they became authoritative in the communities that transmitted them. Within this context, sharp modern contrasts between "author" and "redactor" often miss the point. Ancient Near Eastern authors built on earlier materials yet often intervened in these materials to make them into a

---

69. In a provocative sketch of this process, B. Mack has argued persuasively that this assertion of Mosaic authorship occurred under the direct influence of and in response to Greek concepts of authorship and authority. "Under the Shadow of Moses: Authorship and Authority in Hellenistic Judaism," *SBLSP* 21 (1982): 299–318.

70. On this, see in particular the discussion of tradition and ancient history in H. Cancik, *Mythische und historische Wahrheit* (SBS 48; Stuttgart: Verlag Katholisches Bibelwerk, 1970), especially 20–23, 26–27, 35–39, 61–65, 91–130.

more or less new whole. That is why throughout this discussion and the rest of the book, I often use the term *author* or *author/redactor* to refer to the composer of a biblical text, even when a substantial portion of the composition consists of earlier materials.

Such observations are not new, and they certainly do not suggest that methods developed on modern texts cannot be applied to ancient texts like Genesis. Instead, these reflections indicate that there are aspects of Genesis, such as its distinctive texture produced by its growth over time, that most literary methods developed on modern texts are not immediately equipped to spotlight and interpret. Indeed, I will argue in later chapters that the unusually strong textual crosscurrents and ruptures in a text like Genesis have affected its interpretive potential, that is, how it can elicit readings. As a result of these crosscurrents and ruptures, Genesis is a particularly "open" text, one unusually capable of speaking a variety of messages to interpreters.[71] My supposition of this diachronically based openness is not based on an observation of this doublet or that break in Genesis or on this or that contrast in terminology or perspective. Instead, my overall supposition that Genesis underwent a transmission history is based on the above-described, well-documented phenomenon of gradual growth in ancient Near Eastern and other non-Western, premodern texts.

71. Here I side with Eco, among others, and against a radical reader response approach such as that of Fish, in arguing that some texts are more "open" to interpretations than others, and that one can sometimes define "paths" of interpretation to which they are open. Cf. U. Eco, *The Role of the Reader: Explorations in the Semiotics of Texts* (Bloomington, Ind.: Indiana University Press, 1979); and S. Fish, *Is There a Text in This Class?: The Authority of Interpretive Communities* (Cambridge, Mass./London: Harvard University Press, 1980).

2
Methodology in Reconstruction of Transmission History

This introductory discussion still has not addressed the widespread skepticism in much biblical scholarship about how much we can know about the transmission history of biblical texts. After all, the most significant objection to exploration of transmission history is not that Genesis lacks such a prehistory, but that there is little that we can say about it. To be sure, there are some who argue that a carefully patterned text like Genesis could not have undergone a complex process of transmission history.[1] Such approaches, however, assume a very old and highly dubious contrast between artless redactors and artful authors.[2]

More important are the objections of those who argue plausibly that—whatever Genesis's transmission history—the marks of that history are so obscured in the present form of Genesis that reconstruction of its transmission history is inherently unstable. It replaces the relative certainties of analysis of the present fractured text with unprovable theories about its process of development. Rather than illuminating the fractured character of the final form, such a speculative transmission history would take us away from it.

In particular, in recent years scholars informed by deconstruction have stressed that any text—whether multiauthored or not—is nonunified. It is the reader and his or her interpretive community who attempts to impose a unified reading on a given text. Such readers may, and probably will, claim that the unity they find is *in* the text, but this claim is only a mask for the creative process actually going on. Even the most carefully designed text can not be unified; only the reader's attempted taming of it. Therefore, an attempt to use seams and shifts in a biblical text to discover its textual precursors is based on a fundamentally faulty assumption that one might recover a stage of the text

1. See, for example, I. M. Kikiwada and A. Quinn, *Before Abraham Was* (Nashville: Abingdon, 1985), especially 54–126. Although not a literary critic, a great precursor to such arguments was U. Cassuto. See, for example, his *Commentary on the Book of Genesis*, vol. 2, *From Noah to Abraham. Genesis VI 9–XI 32 with an Appendix: A Fragment of Part III* (trans. I. Abrahams; Jerusalem: Magnes, 1964), 30–33, on the Flood.
2. On this, see the helpful observations by Tigay on the artfulness of the later additions to the Gilgamesh epic, *The Evolution of the Gilgamesh Epic*, 229–31; 237–38; idem, "Evolution of the Pentateuchal Narratives," 46.

that lacked such fractures. When a biblical text is measured against the scholar's own concept of unity and found wanting, this probably says much more about the biblical scholar's concept of unity than about the text's prehistory.[3]

These critiques are extremely important. At the same time, they can be answered. Let us start with the assumption, supported by documented cases of transmission history, that texts like the Bible were often composed over time by different authors. Let us grant that no such text, at any stage of the process, was ever fully unified. Let us further grant that no undocumented stage of the compositional process of a biblical text can ever be fully and reliably reconstructed. The question then is whether there are still certain indicators—or better, combinations of indicators—that might clue us in to the prehistory of biblical texts that have been composed over time.

Our starting point in this chapter will again be documented cases of transmission history. Our goal will not be the creation of a seamless, unified text. Instead, the aim here is to use documented cases of transmission history to see whether in certain cases, parts of a transmission historical process can be reconstructed. Such cases are particularly important in this context because they offer a way out of the usual methodological circle in which transmission-historical approaches often find themselves. Rather than depending on a scholar's own methodological reconstruction for the formulation of the method upon which that reconstruction depends, we are starting with some empirical evidence to see whether certain methods might have helped us unravel the prehistory of the given texts if we lacked such evidence.

An Initial Example

A helpful example of both the possibilities and limits of transmission-historical reconstruction is Tatian's interweaving of the canonical gospels in the *Diatessaron*. Below are reproduced portions of a passage from the Diatessaron given by Longstaff in his analysis of the Gospel sources in the *Diatessaron*'s version of Jesus' reply to the rich young ruler (cf. Matt. 19:23ff.; Mark 10:24ff.; Luke 18:24ff.). The sources are indicated in the following way: Mark is in capitals; Luke is in boldface; Matthew is underlined; and sections where these sources agree are indicated by a combination of these elements:[4]

HOW DIFFICULT IT IS FOR THEM THAT HAVE RICHES TO ENTER INTO THE KINGDOM OF GOD! Verily I say unto you, It is difficult for a rich man to enter into the kingdom of heaven. And again I say unto you, IT IS EASIER FOR A CAMEL TO

3. F. Kermode, *The Genesis of Secrecy: On the Interpretation of Narrative* (Cambridge, Mass.: Harvard University Press, 1979), 49–73 and S. Moore, *Poststructuralism and the New Testament*, 66–81.
4. Longstaff, *Evidence of Conflation in Mark?*, 33–34.

PRESS THROUGH **THE EYE OF A NEEDLE, THAN FOR A RICH MAN TO ENTER INTO THE KINGDOM OF GOD**. . . . VERILY I SAY UNTO YOU, **THERE IS NO MAN THAT LEAVETH** houses, **OR BRETHREN,** OR SISTERS, OR FA-THER, OR MOTHER, or wife, **OR CHILDREN**, or kindred, OR LANDS, for the kingdom of God's sake, OR FOR MY SAKE, AND FOR MY GOSPEL'S SAKE, and that doth not receive twice as many **IN THIS TIME AND IN THE WORLD TO COME** inherit **ETERNAL LIFE.**

At the outset of the quotation, the inclusion of material from two sources (Mark/Luke versus Matthew) is indicated by the duplication of the comment about how difficult it is for a rich man to enter the kingdom of heaven. Coming from the same character (Jesus) at the same point in time, this repetition of the comment is redundant. To be sure, this repetition still serves a compositional function. Within the present literary context, this duplication serves to emphasize how difficult it is for a rich man to enter the kingdom. Nevertheless, the two versions of Jesus' comment about the rich also use slightly different terminology, for example, "kingdom of God" versus "kingdom of heaven." This difference in terminology suggests that the doublet not only serves a literary function in the present text, but is also a mark that it is composed out of two sources at this point. In any case, it is easier to distinguish these two blocks of material in the initial saying about riches and the kingdom than it is to distinguish the different materials in the following comment about the sure reward to all who leave their family, lands, and so forth. Here the list of things that are to be left—brothers (all), father, mother (Mark, Matthew), wife (Luke), children (Mark, Matthew), kindred (close to Luke), lands (Mark, Matthew)—is interwoven in such an intricate way that it would be impossible to form plausible hypotheses about its growth purely on the basis of the *Diatessaron* alone.

Indicators of Transmission History and How to Use Them

Indicators of Seams: Doublets and Breaks

The above discussed example suggests that one can *sometimes* draw certain conclusions about the growth of the passage on the basis of doublets, particularly when one has two fairly complete reports of the same event, made from the same narrative perspective and yet distinguished in minor ways by terminology. This point is important because many recent scholars have correctly argued that transmission-historical analyses are too dependent on observations of doublets without attention to the potential literary function of such repetition.[5] Responding to this trajectory of research, Noble has argued that use of

5. Sternberg, *The Poetics of Biblical Narrative*, 365–440. (See in particular his nuanced comments on 339–40.) See also the earlier work by J. Licht, *Storytelling in the Bible*, 51–95.

indicators like doublets in transmission history is inherently unreliable because any such transmission-historical argument must assert that a repetition is redundant. This assertion in turn makes the transmission-historical argument vulnerable to a synchronic approach, which can argue that such a repetition is not redundant but serves a literary function in its context. Yet in the case of the above-discussed comment about riches, we have a doublet serving a literary function that is nevertheless marked as a transmission-historical indicator by the slight shift in terminology. Moreover, the repetition and distinctions in terminology are not easily explained by a shift in narrative perspective because both comments come from the Jesus character in the same utterance.[6] In this case we know this doublet is a reliable clue to the transmission history of this passage because we have the separate sources that were combined to form this doublet. Nevertheless, in the *Diatessaron* itself there are still indicators that the first portion of the passage was formed from at least two sources.

So, what I am doing here is the following: using a documented case of transmission history to see what kind of rules could be used to reconstruct the transmission history of a given text, even if we did not have its sources and/or earlier versions at hand. I have already suggested that in certain cases doublets from the same narrative perspective can be a clue to transmission history. In addition, one particularly well-documented indicator of transmission history is the doublet that resumes the narrative thread after the insertion of a block of interrupting material, "resumptive repetition" (an English equivalent of the German *Wiederaufnahme*). To be sure, authors can themselves use such resumptive repetition to resume the train of thought after their own digression.[7] Nevertheless, documented cases of transmission history show that resumptive repetition is often a mark of the insertion of new material. I return to Tigay's analysis of the Gilgamesh epic for the first example of this phenomenon. In the Old Babylonian version of this epic, an address by Gilgamesh's companion Enkidu is introduced by a scene in which the elders of Uruk bless Gilgamesh, advise him to rely on his friend Enkidu, and urge Enkidu to bring him back safely. The late (Middle Babylonian) version of this scene inserts four columns of new material between the scene with the elders and Enkidu's speech. In order to resume the train of thought lost in the midst of this insertion, the later version introduces Enkidu's speech with a resumptive repetition: another description of a group (the elders?) urg-

6. This in response to Sternberg and others' observations regarding the potential literary function of repetition from different narrative perspectives and/or narrative times.
7. See examples from the ancient Near East in Fishbane, *Biblical Interpretation in Ancient Israel*, 86n20; and M. Anbar, "La 'reprise'," *VT* 38 (1988): 393–95. Tigay, "Conflation as a Redactional Technique," 74n46 cites some additional examples. Anbar also proposes some biblical examples of this phenomenon on 395–98, as does Z. Talshir, "The Contribution of Diverging traditions preserved in the Septuagint to the Methodology of Biblical Criticism," unpublished paper cited by permission, 7–8. This latter essay is projected to appear in late 1995 in the Proceedings of the International Organization for Septuagint and Cognate Studies.

ing Gilgamesh to rely on Enkidu and charging Enkidu to bring him back safely.[8]

This phenomenon of resumptive repetition occurs frequently in other ancient Near Eastern texts, including the Bible.[9] Take, for example, the example in Chart 2-1 of resumptive repetition observed by Tov in the final redaction of the book of Jeremiah. The resumptive repetition is in boldface and repeats the contents of the first portion of the introduction.[10]

Chart 2-1: Resumptive Repetition in Jeremiah

Jer. 27:19–21 (Old Greek)	Jer. 27:19–21 (Masoretic Text, hereafter MT)
For thus said the LORD	For thus said the LORD of Hosts concerning the columns, the tank, the stands and
concerning the rest of the vessels,	concerning the rest of the vessels which remain in this city,
which the king of Babylon did not take	which Nebuchadnezzar the king of Babylon did not take
when he exiled Jeconiah	when he exiled Jeconiah son of Jehoiakim, king of Judah
from Jerusalem.	from Jerusalem to Babylon, with all the nobles of Judah and Jerusalem
	. . . thus said the LORD of Hosts, the God of Israel, concerning the vessels remaining in the House of the LORD, in the royal palace of Judah and in Jerusalem.

Here, as in many other places in Jeremiah, the resumptive repetition does not mark the insertion of a complete new block of material. Instead, the preceding material appears to have been expanded to the point where the author/redactor felt the need to resume the train of thought interrupted by the expanded material.[11]

---

8. Tigay, *The Evolution of the Gilgamesh Epic*, 73–76; "The Evolution of the Pentateuchal Narratives," 48–49.

9. Fishbane, *Biblical Interpretation in Ancient Israel*, 29n25; 101n41; 162nn49, 50; 196n80; 516n15; Anbar, "La 'reprise'," 386–93; Tigay, "The Evolution of the Pentateuchal Narratives," 49; idem, "Conflation as a Redactional Technique," 74, including n. 46; Z. Talshir, "The Contribution of Diverging traditions preserved in the Septuagint," 3, 8–10. An older, helpful discussion of biblical examples is C. Kuhl, "Die 'Wiederaufnahme'—ein literarisches Prinzip?" *ZAW* 64 (1952): 1–11.

10. Tov, "The Literary History of the Book of Jeremiah," in *Empirical Models for Biblical Study*, 221–22, 235–36.

11. Tov, "The Literary History of the Book of Jeremiah," 235–36.

The particular kind of resumptive repetition we see here, resumption of a divine speech introduction, is particularly typical of redaction of biblical material, and it will appear frequently in Genesis. Another example occurs in the Samaritan Pentateuch's insertion of Deut. 5:28–29; 18:18–22; and 5:30–31 just before the beginning of the covenant code in Exod. 20:22–26. The MT version of this passage proceeds directly from the speech introduction in Exod. 20:22aα—"The LORD said to Moses"—to the early law regarding how to build altars in 20:22aβ–26. The later Samaritan version of this passage inserts the passages from Deuteronomy after the speech introduction in Exod. 20:22aα, but then resumes the train of thought by inserting another speech introduction, "The LORD spoke to Moses," and this then introduces a modified version of the altar command in Exod 20:22aβ–26.[12]

In each of the above cases, the resumptive repetition is an indicator that ancient editors considered what preceded the resumptive repetition to be enough of a digression that they felt the need to resume the train of thought. In other words, when such resumptive repetition occurs, it is a confirmation that the sense of some kind of an interruption in these texts is not just the result of a drive toward unity in a modern scholarly imagination. Whether such an interruption is made up of new material or not is something that must be determined through use of other terminological and ideological indicators, which I will discuss below.

Another clue to transmission history is specifically characteristic of narrative: narrative contradictions and/or breaks in the time continuum of the existing narrative. For example, already in the seventeenth century, Isaac de la Peyrère saw something incongruous in Genesis 20 about Abraham's being so afraid Abimelek would steal Sarah, when we have already heard that she is ninety years old (Gen. 17:17) and advanced in age (Gen. 18:11).[13] Or turning once again to a case of documented growth, Tov argues persuasively that the Old Greek version of 1 Samuel 16—18 preserves a version of the David and Goliath story that lacks the story about Jesse sending David to the battlefield with supplies for his brothers (1 Sam. 17:12–30). This shortened version has only one explanation for David's presence when Goliath issues his challenge: David had previously entered Saul's court as a musician (1 Sam. 16:17–23). In the expanded MT version of the David and Goliath story, however, there are two explanations for David's presence. David entered Saul's court as a musician (1 Sam. 16:17–23), and he was sent with supplies for his brothers (1 Sam. 17:12–30). These conflicting explanations of David's

---

12. Tigay, "Conflation as a Redactional Technique," 69, 74.
13. *Systema Theologicum ex prae-adamitarum hypothesi* (Paris, 1654), book 4, chap. 1, as cited by Carpenter, *The Composition of the Hexateuch,* 39.

trip would be a key to the transmission history of this text even if all we had was the expanded MT version.[14]

Now, once again, a skeptic such as Noble can argue that tensions and breaks such as those noted above only serve as indicators of transmission history when the tension that they produce is "unproductive." Thus, Noble argues that any diachronic explanation of a feature in a given text is vulnerable to a synchronic approach that can explain the present literary function of the given feature. For example, he cites the following example of Prov. 26:4–5 as an example of a contradiction that is productive:[15]

> Do not answer fools according to their folly,
> or you will be a fool yourself.
> Answer fools according to their folly,
> or they will be wise in their own eyes. (NRSV)[16]

This pair of sayings plays on different senses of the expression "according to their folly" to make a clear, easy-to-remember point about the importance of the proper way to respond to fools and their folly. This is a good example of a text with what appears to be a contradiction, but where the contradiction should not be taken as a transmission-historical indicator. Nevertheless, it is striking that Noble draws his prime example of "productive" contradiction from a nonnarrative text. Moreover, in contrast to cases in the Pentateuch where one must often argue at length for the literary productivity of a certain break or contradiction, this nonnarrative example is so obvious that Noble requires a single sentence to comment on it.

To be sure, even in narrative texts one can often make plausible arguments that tensions in them serve some kind of literary function. To presuppose otherwise is to presume that editors were artless. But the point here is that literary treatment of such narrative contradictions and breaks do require more extensive argument than do tensions in texts such as Noble's Proverbs example, and that even with such arguments, the tension or break is often only partially explained. If one is working with a model of textual production where citation and juxtaposition of earlier sources is an anomaly, then such

14. E. Tov, "The Composition of the Samuel 16–18 in the Light of the Septuagint Version," in *Empirical Models for Biblical Criticism*, 98–130. This detailed study persuasively refutes approaches that maintain the MT version is earlier. Cf. the dialogue between Tov and others in D. Barthélemy, et al., *The Story of David and Goliath. Textual and Literary Criticism. Papers of a Joint Research Venture* (OBO 73; Fribourg: Editions Universitaires, 1986). For examples of documented breaks in Esther that might have been otherwise reconstructable, see Fox, *The Redaction of the Books of Esther*, 135–36. Earlier scholars who argued similarly to Tov included first and foremost W. Robertson-Smith, *The Old Testament in the Jewish Church* (London: Adam and Charles Black, 1908), 119–22.
15. Noble, "Synchronic and Diachronic Approaches," 147n17.
16. Unless otherwise indicated, the translations in this book are the author's own.

partial synchronic explanations may suffice. If one recognizes, however, the extent to which ancient Near Eastern texts like Genesis did appropriate and juxtapose earlier sources, then such synchronic arguments are stretched if they are used to argue against the incorporation of earlier text altogether. Although they can help us understand the artfulness of the author/redactor, they do not negate the possibility of investigating the prehistory of the composite text.

Terminological, Ideological, and Structural Indicators

So far I have discussed different types of indicators of seams in ancient Near Eastern narratives: breaks in narrative continuity, contradictions, and doublets—particularly resumptive repetition. As was already suggested in the case of doublets, one element that can be important for the *confirmation* that such indicators are transmission-historically significant is the presence of a distinctive terminological and ideological profile in the material that doubles, interrupts, and/or contradicts other material.[17] As Tigay has observed, the late addition of the Flood section to the Gilgamesh epic is marked by terminological and formulaic shifts from its earlier context, and this is true to a lesser extent for some other documented additions to ancient Near Eastern documents.[18]

The point here is not that narratives all written by one author cannot shift in terminology, emphases, and even apparent ideology within themselves. Rather, the point is that shifts in terminology often correlate with shifts in authorship, and that such shifts can be helpful indicators, *especially when such shifts correlate with indicators of seams* (doublets, breaks, and so forth). Take the following example, where elements of Deuteronomy were combined into an early expansionist (= "proto-Samaritan") edition of the Exodus story of Moses' appointment of judges to help him judge the people (Exodus 18). Tigay has argued persuasively that indicators of seams and shifts in terminology would make possible the identification of the editing of this expansionist version, even if we did not have the earlier version at hand (now reflected in our MT). The primary indicator of a seam in the expansionist version is a set of divergences between Jethro's instructions to Moses and Moses' execution of them.[19] (See Chart 2-2.)

---

17. Cf. Fox, *The Redaction of the Books of Esther*, 134–41.
18. Tigay, *The Evolution of the Gilgamesh Epic*, 232–37; idem, "Evolution of the Pentateuchal Narratives," 42, 45–47; idem, "The Stylistic Criterion of Source Criticism," 154–70.
19. Tigay, "Conflation as a Redactional Technique," 63–68. The following is based on his table on 64–66.

Chart 2-2: Divergences Revealing a Seam

Jethro's Instructions (Exod. 18:17–23)	The Execution (inserted from Deut. 1:9–18)
	Moses asks *the people* to do the choosing, and they agree (inserted from Deut. 1:13).
Moses is to seek out "men from among all the people" (Exod. 18:21).	*Moses* seeks from among the "tribal leaders" (inserted from Deut. 1:15).
Moses is to seek "capable men who fear God, trustworthy men who spurn ill-gotten gain" (Exod. 18:21).	Moses requests and appoints "wise, discerning, and experienced men" (inserted from Deut. 1:13, 15).
Moses is to make them into "chiefs of thousands, hundreds, fifties, and tens" (Exod. 18:21).	Moses makes them into chiefs of "thousands, hundreds, fifties, tens, *and officials*" (inserted from Deut. 1:15).
The people are to "bring" (*bw'*) "major matters" to Moses (Exod. 18:22).	Moses charges the people to "bring near" (*qrb*) matters "too difficult" for them (from Deut. 1:17; cf. Exod. 18:26).

To be sure, these divergences between command and compliance need not just be read as indicators of seams. They could also be interpreted as a subtle narrative comment on Moses' character, as he diverges slightly from the divine command. Nevertheless, the above noted slight divergences between the profile of the Deuteronomy material and its new context provide additional data. Whereas Jethro's instructions in Exodus focus on Moses, the inserted material from Deuteronomy focuses on the people as those who will do the appointing. Jethro speaks of those who are to be appointed in one way ("capable men who fear God . . . "), while the inserted material from Deuteronomy speaks of them in another ("wise, experienced, and discerning men"). And the differences continue as indicated above. Although absolute certainty is never possible in transmission-historical analysis, this correlation of contrast in profile with indicators of seams would be an accurate guide to the documented transmission history of the expansionist version of Exodus 18, even if we did not have an earlier version at hand.

This being said, it is important to emphasize how unreliable such terminological and ideological indicators can be when used alone, that is, not in coordination with indicators of seams such as those discussed above. Insofar as one posits the existence of different layers in a passage *purely* on the basis of certain terminological and ideological contrasts, one must presuppose the significance of these contrasts in order to posit their usefulness in reconstructing separate layers in the passage. Every passage deviates in terminology and theme to some extent. But in order to use a given term or concept as an indicator of transmission history, it must be shown that the deviation in its usage reflects deviation in sources or redactional layers. Unless observations of contrasts in terminology and ideology are coordinated with observations of seams *in the text being analyzed,* the transmission history that results is significantly less plausible than an analysis that uses terminological observations to confirm and coordinate observations of seams in a text. Even if such contrasts corresponded to breaks in another text that has already been analyzed, there is always the possibility that such contrasts are misleading in the text under analysis.

Thus, the best argument from terminology is one that works from the *repeated* correlation of indicators of seams (doublets, and so forth) with certain contrasts in terminology and ideology. For example, in the doublet of Jesus' comment about riches in the *Diatessaron,* we find the deviation between "kingdom of God" and "kingdom of heaven" in the different versions of Jesus' sayings about riches also occurs in many other locations where Matthew is parallel to Mark or Luke. The hypothesis of different sources standing behind the version using the term "kingdom of God" (Mark, Luke) and the version mentioning the "kingdom of heaven" (Matthew) would be more plausible to the extent that one found in the *Diatessaron* other cases of doubled sayings that also had this same divergence in terminology for the kingdom. Lacking other such cases, there is always the chance the author of this passage regarding riches consciously altered the terminology of the two doublets in this particular literary context in order to have a certain effect on his[20] audience. Nevertheless, the more such deviation in terminology is repeatedly correlated with indicators of seams, the more likely it becomes that the given terminology is a clue to the existence of different sources and/or redaction. Such repeated appearance of distinctive terminology confirms the transmission-historical significance of accompanying indicators of seams (doublets, breaks, and so forth). Moreover, such repeated indicators can also help connect disparate parts of a source or redactional layer with each other.

Another element that has often been used in reconstruction of transmission history is what might be termed an "argument from potential continuity." This can work in various ways. One can argue that a passage reads "smoothly" when a certain set of verses are removed. Or one can argue not only that a given passage reads smoothly when certain verses are removed, but also that the removed verses themselves read smoothly as well. Such ar-

---

20. Overall the evidence suggests that the redactor/authors of biblical traditions were male. This apparent gender division of labor in the production of the literature that found its way into the Bible does not measure up to the ideals of modern Western culture. Nevertheless, it was typical of ancient Israelite society. Therefore, male pronouns are used in this book to refer to the probable ancient author/redactors.

guments have been typical in studies that divide the Genesis primeval history into two relatively readable strands, J and P.

A similar type of argument might be termed "argument from potential structure." Here one maintains that a passage has a certain specific structure disturbed at certain points by certain verses. For example, Tigay describes how the Old Babylonian version of the Gilgamesh epic is artfully built around Gilgamesh's search for immortality. This search is embraced by an inclusio structure extending from an initial prologue mentioning the walls of Uruk—"a conventional royal means of securing a form of immortality"—to Gilgamesh's return to those walls after his fruitless search for a way to live forever. This close-knit structure still dominates the late version of the epic but is disturbed in crucial ways by the addition of new materials. The wisdom prologue and the Enkidu appendix both stand outside the elegant inclusio formed by the walls of Uruk, and the inclusion of the flood narrative is not integrally linked to the focus of the epic on the search for immortality.[21] One mark of the secondary character of these materials is their divergence from the immortality-focused structure originating in the Old Babylonian Gilgamesh epic.

Such arguments from potential continuity or potential structure can only play a *retrospective, supporting* role in a careful transmission-historical analysis. In the above example of the Gilgamesh epic, suppositions based on such arguments from potential structure correspond to existing documentary evidence for the formation of the epic. Nevertheless, when used alone, such arguments can be as undependable as arguments depending exclusively on terminological observations. There are probably many ways, for example, to reconstruct the structure of this book (*Reading the Fractures of Genesis*) so that certain sections could be judged secondary because the book reads well without them. This may well mean that this book could have been written better, but it is not necessarily a sign that these sections are secondary insertions. Similarly, one could go through an average business letter written at one sitting, excise a few sentences or a paragraph, and still find that the remainder reads smoothly. This does not prove these paragraphs are late insertions. In summary, although arguments from potential continuity or potential structure can help *confirm* a transmission-historical theory that is first based on other indicators, such arguments are notoriously unreliable when they are not preceded by other considerations.

Conditions Affecting the Reconstructability of Transmission History

One implication of all this is that the reconstructability of the transmission history of a given text is dependent on the extent to which marks of that trans-

---

21. Tigay, *Evolution of the Gilgamesh Epic*, 5–10, 104–5, 138; idem, "Evolution of the Pentateuchal Narratives," 32–35, 41–42.

mission history are left in a text. On the one hand, from the beginning I have emphasized that the premodern redactor/authors of the Bible tended to work more intratextually than modern ones, incorporating and conflating earlier materials where a modern author might well write an entirely new text. On the other hand, these redactor/authors were just that, authors. That means they attempted to form a composition using earlier materials, melding them into a whole that expressed a unified historical-theological truth.[22] Although they were not clearly interested in hiding the traces of their work, neither did they consciously leave clues in their texts of the process through which they grew. In both cases, their interests lay elsewhere.

Often such an author draws so loosely on his sources that they are no longer identifiable. In his study of documented cases of editing of biblical sources in the Temple Scroll, Kaufman terms such an editorial style "paraphrastic conflation" and observes how impossible it would be to work from the Temple Scroll back to its biblical sources, when those sources are drawn on in this way.[23] Likewise, Tigay, in his study of the Gilgamesh epic, persuasively argues that it would be easier to work back from the standard Babylonian version to the general contours of the Old Babylonian one, than it would be to recognize the Sumerian precursors of the Old Babylonian version. There are terminological and other indicators to guide a scholar trying to distinguish Middle Babylonian additions from their Old Babylonian context: stylistic variation, predominant use of different terms for the same thing, and resumptive repetition of material after the insertion of a long block. But when one turns to trying to reconstruct the sources of the Old Babylonian version, the task is almost impossible.[24] Here the author of this version has only loosely drawn on the plots of the Sumerian legends about Gilgamesh. Moreover, he has modified these legends in crucial ways—such as turning Enkidu into Gilgamesh's friend—in order to meld them into a single epic.[25] On this basis Tigay tentatively posits a trend in transmission history from freer use of oral and written traditions in the early stages of transmission history to the less flexible, but more reconstructable, use of such traditions in later stages as the given text gains more authority.[26]

Dealing with a similar set of questions, Noble suggests a helpful distinction between what he terms a "quotation-theoretic" and a "resource-theoretic" mode of composition. In a quotation approach, the editor actually re-

22. Donner, "Der Redaktor," 1–30.
23. S. Kaufman, "The Temple Scroll," 34, 37–38.
24. Tigay, "Evolution of the Pentateuchal Narratives," 44–46.
25. Tigay, *The Evolution of the Gilgamesh Epic*, 29–30, 45–47; idem, "Evolution of the Pentateuchal Narratives," 33–34.
26. Tigay, *Evolution of the Gilgamesh Epic*, 139, 245–46; idem, "Evolution of the Pentateuchal Narratives," 35–46. In the process he cites some suggestive proposals by M. Greenberg, "The Redaction of the Plague Narrative in Exodus," in *Near Eastern Studies in Honor of William Foxwell Albright* (ed. H. Goedicke; Baltimore/London: Johns Hopkins Press, 1971), 245.

produces his sources, while in a resource approach he just draws on certain themes, characters, plots, and so forth.[27] Noble rightly asserts that the former is potentially reconstructable, while the latter is not. For example, Milik and now Davies have argued on the basis of certain parallels that 1 Enoch 6—11 is the written source for the story condensed in Gen. 6:1–4.[28] If this was the case, then this pair of texts, 1 Enoch 6—11 and Gen 6:1–4, would offer yet another example of documented transmission history. Nevertheless, the controversy that has surrounded this proposal indicates the difficulties of establishing exact transmission-historical relationships between texts when they agree on such general terms. To be sure, some of the controversy derives from the inclination of many biblical scholars to presuppose that biblical traditions are earlier than the nonbiblical texts that might be related to them. Nevertheless, even if the author of Gen. 6:1–4 used 1 Enoch 6—11, he used it as a resource. As a result, the relations between these two texts are too tenuous for us to know much definite about their relationship.

Often even when a source is being quoted, it is modified in ways that make reconstruction of it difficult or impossible. For example, above we saw how resumptive repetition in the Samaritan Pentateuch marks the insertion of Deuteronomic material (Deut. 5:28–29; 18:18–22; 5:30–31) just before the Covenant Code altar law in Exod. 20:22–26. As is widely recognized, such Deuteronomic material shares a distinctive terminological and ideological profile, including most prominently the idea that legitimate worship can occur in only one place (Deut. 12:2–14). In contrast, the MT version of the Covenant Code altar law in Exod. 20:22–26 gives instructions for building altars in general, without any presupposition that only one altar is legitimate. If the editor of this passage in the Samaritan Pentateuch had left this altar law unchanged, the preceding insertion of Deuteronomic material might have been distinguished from its context not just by resumptive repetition, but also by the overall Deuteronomic profile of the inserted material and the lack of such a profile in Exod. 20:22–26.[29] But, in fact, the Samaritan Pentateuch

27. Noble, "Synchronic and Diachronic Approaches," 137. The "theoretic" portion of Noble's terminology derives from his interest in different theories of how transmission history might have happened. He is primarily interested in demonstrating that good synchronic analysis will lead a Bible scholar away from postulating a quotation theory for the transmission history of a text and toward postulating a resource theory. This move in turn will then imply that the transmission history of the text is not reconstructable. As indicated in arguments above, I maintain that synchronic analysis does not eliminate the possibility of doing transmission history.

28. J. T. Milik, *The Books of Enoch: Aramaic Fragments of Qumran Cave 4* (Oxford: Clarendon Press, 1976), 30–32; see also P. Davies, "Women, Men, Gods, Sex and Power: The Birth of a Biblical Myth," in *A Feminist Companion to Genesis* (ed. A. Brenner; The Feminist Companion to the Bible 2; Sheffield: Sheffield Academic Press, 1993), 195–99.

29. The term *overall* here is important because the inserted material from Deuteronomy would first have to be recognized as belonging to the overall Deuteronomistic tradition before its profile could be contrasted with Exod. 20:22–26. In and of itself, the inserted material (Deut. 5:28–31; 18:18–22) does not presuppose a centralized cult.

version has a modified version of the Exod. 20:22–26 altar law, one that refers to the building of only one altar (see Chart 2-3).[30]

Chart 2-3: Strategic Modification of a Text
(Modifications are italicized.)

Exod. 20:24 (MT)	Exod. 20:24 (Samaritan Pentateuch)
You need make for me only an	You need make for me only an
altar of earth and sacrifice on it	altar of earth and sacrafice on it
your burnt offerings and your	your burnt offerings and your
sacrifices of	sacrifices of
well-being, your sheep and your oxen;	well-being, your sheep and your oxen;
in every place where I cause	in *the* place where I *have* cause*d*
my name to be remembered	my name to be remembered,
I will come to you and bless you.	*there* I will come to you and bless you.

These strategic modifications have removed a potential indicator that could have been used to reconstruct independently the transmission history of the Samaritan version of this passage, without using the earlier MT version. Such modifications are widespread in documented cases of transmission history. For example, Kaufman cites a number of examples of editing from the Temple Scroll in which the biblical sources are modified to the point that they would be impossible to reconstruct.[31] We must likewise reckon with the possibility of such modifications in Genesis, making reconstruction of parts of its transmission history unreconstructable.

In addition, a glance over the preceding documented examples of transmission history reveals that the editing and combination of quoted sources is often so intricate that the process would be impossible to reconstruct if we did not have separate copies of various editions of the work. Tatian often switches between various gospels for single words or phrases.[32] The reformulations of the Jeremiah passages likewise often feature the seamless inclusion of clarify-

30. Tigay, "Conflation as a Redactional Technique," 73–76. The following is from his table on 73.
31. Kaufman, "The Temple Scroll and Higher Criticism," 34, 39–42. One problem with Kaufman's conclusions is his apparent assumption that the style of editing he finds in the Temple Scroll is typical of the editing books like Genesis went through throughout their development. Although his cautions are well taken, what he has described is a *possible* problem for reconstruction. A broader look at documented cases of transmission history indicates a broader range of redactional styles than are found in the Temple Scroll.
32. See the examples in Moore, "Tatian's *Diatessaron* and the Analysis of the Pentateuch," 203 (reprint, 248–59), and his comments regarding problems in reconstruction on 255 of the reprint. See also Longstaff, *Evidence of Conflation in Mark?*, 10–42, and conclusion in 107–13.

ing words and phrases. And these are but two examples of often unreconstructable, intricate editing of ancient texts.[33] Any transmission-historical method that was sensitive enough to form hunches about these insertions would be so sensitive that it would also read transmission history into passages that had none. Past biblical scholarship has many examples of such hypersensitive attempts to unravel the editorial history of biblical passages. The results of such attempts have been irresolvably diverse and methodologically uncontrolled. In such cases, we must recognize that in the cases where the transmission-historical process was so intricate, we simply can not know much about it.

Thus, much depends on the style of redaction that produced the text with which we must work, or even the style of redaction used by the redactor *in a given portion* of the work under analysis. Studies of documented cases of transmission history have repeatedly demonstrated the extent to which redactional style is variable: small-scale terminological changes are often unsystematic; sources are incompletely incorporated in one case and then relatively completely incorporated in another; and the style of redaction often shifts from one section of a text to another.[34]

In summary, I am arguing for pushing Noble's distinction further. In many respects, a quote type of redaction can be as impossible to reconstruct as a resource type. And there is more. Such problems can be compounded by other factors, such as the lack of clear terminological and/or ideological differences between the various layers of material in a passage. This is not just an issue of a redactor conforming materials to each other. Often the various layers of a text are themselves written in such close temporal and/or cultural proximity to each other and share so much conceptuality that it is difficult to distinguish them from each other. This is one of things that would make Tatian's *Diatessaron* difficult to unravel if we did not have separate copies of his gospel sources. The synoptic gospels are so similar in narrative content and rough ideology that their parallel episodes have been intricately interwoven and they would be particularly difficult to distinguish from one

---

33. Tigay observes that detailed reconstruction of the insertion of Deut. 5:22–30 into the proto-Samaritan version of Exodus 20, would be almost impossible ("Conflation as a Redactional Technique," 73–76). Similarly, Kaufman finds a number of cases of what he terms "fine conflation" in the Temple Scroll, and he points out how difficult they would be to reconstruct from the Temple Scroll alone ("The Temple Scroll and Higher Criticism," 34, 38–39).

34. Longstaff, *Evidence of Conflation in Mark,* 112–13; Fishbane, *Biblical Interpretation in Ancient Israel,* 71, 84; Tigay, "Evolution of the Pentateuchal Narratives," 47; idem, "The Stylistic Criterion of Source Criticism," 162–66, 170–72; Tov, "The Literary History of Jeremiah," 216–17 (see esp. n.22), 228; Talshir, "The Contribution of Diverging traditions preserved in the Septuagint," 14. G. F. Moore, "Tatian's Diatessaron and the Analysis of the Pentateuch," 203 (reprint, 245–46), points out that even Tatian's relatively complete interweaving of the canonical Gospels left out significant sections. On this documented variability in types of redaction, cf. Noble, "Synchronic and Diachronic Approaches," 143. Donner, "Der Redaktor," 1–30, does not reckon significantly enough with the reality of a wide range of different styles of redaction, even in the final formation of Genesis.

another.[35] In contrast, occasionally it would be possible to separate out passages from the gospel of John now in the *Diatessaron*. They are often preserved in blocks because they have no synoptic parallel. Moreover, they are linked with one another and distinguished from the Synoptic Gospel passages by their shared Johannine terminology and theology. To be sure, any isolation of these passages on the basis of the *Diatessaron* alone would be secure only to the extent that such passages were marked as secondary by doublets, contradictions with their context, and other indicators of seams. Nevertheless, once that is granted, it is clear that, relatively speaking, the distinctive profile of the Johannine passages makes them easier to identify than Tatian's Synoptic Gospel sources.[36]

So far I have talked primarily about conditions affecting the reconstructability of a single redactional layer: the style of redaction (quotation or resource, level of intricacy, and extent to which previous material has been modified) and the presence of distinctive profiles in the different layers. The difficulty of transmission-historical reconstruction is further compounded to the extent that a text goes through *successive* stages of revisions. The latest stages of combination and editing may be possible to reconstruct with a comparatively high degree of plausibility. Nevertheless, the traces of earlier stages of the transmission history are often lost in the process of later redaction. Take the example of Tatian's interweaving of the four Gospels into the *Diatessaron*. Whereas it would be impossible enough to reconstruct Matthew, Mark, and Luke from the *Diatessaron* alone, it would be inconceivably difficult to work from the *Diatessaron* back to plausible hypotheses regarding the formation of these gospels themselves, say back to a proto-Mark and a Q sayings source. We see a similar phenomenon in contemporary studies of Genesis. Although there is intense debate right now about the dating and shape of the earlier traditions in Genesis, most studies agree on the existence and overall dating of some kind of Priestly layer in it. The data required for the isolation and analysis of this late stratum in the book still lie close to the surface. This material has not been redacted as often or as radically as earlier materials. Therefore, seams between these various strata remain as clues for a reconstruction of this stage in the transmission history of the book.

All of this should give caution to those who would seek sure answers to every question regarding the transmission history of Genesis. That the book had a transmission history is clear. The shape of the later stages is often relatively clear. But the further back we go into that transmission history and

---

35. W. R. Farmer, "Basic Affirmation with Some Demurrals: A Response to Roland Mushat Frye," *The Relationships Among the Gospels: An Interdisciplinary Dialogue* (ed. W. O. Walker; San Antonio, Tex.: Trinity University Press, 1978), 316–17, in response to R. M. Frye, "The Synoptic Problems and Analogies in Other Literatures," in *The Relationships Among the Gospels,* 283–90.
36. Moore, "Tatian's *Diatessaron* and the Analysis of the Pentateuch," 214 (reprint, 255).

away from the present form of the texts, the more speculative our reflections become. There comes a point where it is important to be explicitly silent.

Such considerations are particularly important because so much of past transmission-historical scholarship regarding Genesis has concentrated on the earliest stages of the transmission history of Genesis. Such stages were the most interesting for the reconstruction of Israel's early history, particularly the history of early Israelite religion. Yet, insofar as earlier scholarship focused on these earliest stages, it attempted an intrinsically difficult, if not impossible transmission-historical task. Although Genesis almost certainly includes some very early material, this material has been so frequently redacted and adapted that it is difficult for us to know much about it. Most would agree that the present form of Genesis is postexilic. Therefore, sources that are centuries older often lie so far behind the present form of the text that we simply cannot know as much about them as about later stages. We can know even less about the nature of oral traditions standing behind and alongside such early written traditions.

Conclusion

This does not mean that we can not even inquire about these earlier stages. What these reflections do mean is that investigation of the transmission history of Genesis must work from the later, easier-to-reconstruct stages to the earlier, more difficult ones.[37] Furthermore, any such analysis must make clear distinctions between the differing levels of plausibility of its transmission-historical conclusions. Indeed, at many points the analysis must make explicit the impossibility of forming defendable transmission-historical hypotheses. To reiterate: Not all is equally certain, or uncertain. This is important to remember, particularly in light of the current debate over the worth of the transmission-historical method in general and the transmission history of Genesis in particular. In another era, Noth was able to begin with a brief justification and overview of the still secure documentary hypothesis, before concentrating the vast bulk of his book on what are really quite speculative reflections regarding the oral prehistory of the Pentateuchal traditions.[38] In contrast, I will dwell on the data for the later written stages of the transmission history of Genesis, giving minimal attention to the undeniable but largely unreconstructable oral counterpart to this transmission of written texts.

---

37. R. Smend, *Die Entstehung des Alten Testaments* (4th ed.; Stuttgart: W. Kohlhammer, 1989), 38–109, moves in this direction, starting with the Priestly layer (including the end redaction) and ending with preliterary materials. See also A. Schart, *Mose und Israel im Konflikt: Eine redaktionsgeschichtliche Studie zu den Wüstenerzählungen* (OBO 98; Göttingen: Vandenhoeck & Ruprecht, 1990), 34–241.
38. M. Noth, *Pentateuch*, 4–44 (E.T., 5–41) and 247–71 (E.T., 228–51) focus on specifically literary problems, while the heart of the book, 45–246 (E.T., 42–227), focuses on oral transmission history (45–215; E.T., 42–197) or combination of traditions that (according to Noth) probably took place largely on an oral level (216–46; E.T., 198–227).

In light of these reflections, the rest of this book is organized as follows. I start my transmission-historical investigation with a series of chapters on the Priestly material of Genesis. This material forms the last major compositional layer in the history of the formation of the book. Then, I proceed to various layers of the remaining non-Priestly material, moving from later layers to earlier ones. By that point it will be increasingly clear how difficult it is to gain methodological control the further back we move into the transmission history of Genesis. Nevertheless, both sections of the diachronic study—one focusing primarily on the P materials and one on the non-P materials—provide significant background for the final step of this study: exploration of how a careful transmission-historical investigation can inform our reading of Genesis in its final form. That will be the focus of the final chapter. In it I review the reconstructed transmission history of Genesis from beginning to end and suggest ways this transmission history might inform an analysis of the book's present interpretive potential.

Part 2

The First Step Backward: Identification of Priestly Material in Genesis

3
Competing
Models for P

The identification of Priestly material, P, in the Pentateuch remains one of the better established results of biblical transmission-historical research. For over a century, opinion has changed little on the identification of certain genealogical and other texts in Genesis as part of a broader compositional layer leading up to more clearly Priestly material in the Moses story. In this section of the book, I take a substantial amount of time reviewing the data leading to this remarkable level of long-standing consensus. Such a review is particularly necessary in light of recent challenges to the viability of the transmission-historical method. Through it, we will see that, with some exceptions, this overall consensus on the scope of P is not just a matter of scholarly inertia. Much of this P material is, in fact, marked off from its surroundings in Genesis both by its distinctive profile and by various seams.

To be sure, some verses are disputed, but the main debate centers not on the scope of the Priestly material but on its nature. From the earliest studies seeking Moses' "sources" onward (Witter, Astruc, Eichhorn), many have thought of the Priestly layer as originally part of a free-standing document. Whenever verses with Priestly characteristics occurred in non-Priestly contexts, such source critics assigned them to a redactor, Rp, who combined the P and non-P source documents. Lately, however, a number of studies have argued that the Priestly material never stood apart from the non-P material surrounding it.[1] Instead, Priestly texts often appear to be modelled on non-P texts, and they often play an important role in relation to their non-P contexts. We will examine examples of this later.

The point right now is that many have read such data as indicating that there never was an absolutely independent P source. Instead, there was just

---

1. F. M. Cross, *Canaanite Myth and Hebrew Epic* (Cambridge: Harvard University Press, 1973), 293–325; J. Van Seters, *Abraham in History and Tradition* (New Haven, Conn.: Yale University Press, 1975), 285; R. Rendtorff, *Das überlieferungsgeschichtliche Problem des Pentateuch* (BZAW 147; Berlin/New York: de Gruyter, 1976), 112–42 (E.T., *The Problem of the Process of Transmission in the Pentateuch* [trans. J. J. Scullion; JSOTSup, 89; Sheffield: JSOT Press, 1990], 136–70); S. Tengström, *Die Toledotformel und die literarische Struktur der priesterlichen Erweiterungsschicht im Pentateuch* (CBOTS 17; Lund: Gleerup, 1981); E. Blum, *Die Komposition der Vätergeschichte* (WMANT 57; Neukirchen-Vluyn: Neukirchener Verlag, 1984), 263–70;

a Priestly redaction much like the Deuteronomistic redaction of Deuteronomy through 2 Kings.[2] Thus we now have two basic models for the Priestly material in Genesis and the rest of the Pentateuch:

A "source" model in which most of the Priestly material is understood to have once existed as a whole separate from its present context

A "redaction" model in which the bulk of the Priestly layer is understood to have been written as an extension of its non-Priestly context and never to have existed apart from it

Each of these models has its counterpart in documented cases of transmission history, and each well explains certain data in Genesis. On the one hand, we do have documented cases of the conflation of independent sources. Moreover, certain doublets and systematic inconsistencies in Genesis suggest that much of the P material was not originally meant to stand alongside the non-P material with which it is now combined. On the other hand, there are also documented cases of redactional extension and redirection of earlier compositions, such as the extension and revision of the Old Babylonian Gilgamesh epic seen in the late version of that epic. And indeed, no one would deny that Genesis has undergone some sort of overall Priestly revision. In light of these models, the transmission-historical issue is the following: whether one can separate from this Priestly revision a Priestly source that once existed *as a whole* apart from its present non-Priestly context.

This ferment in recent discussion of P has prompted many to refine old models, moving from an unquestioned acceptance of the idea of independent sources to some kind of mixed model that can adequately encompass the mix of data before us. Those maintaining a source model for the Priestly material have recognized ways this Priestly material was composed in relation to the non-P material with which it has now been combined.[3] Others, such as Childs and Friedman, have argued for the following mixed position: contin-

420–58; idem, *Studien*, 229–85; R. Rendtorff, "L'histoire biblique des origines (Gen 1—11) dans le contexte de la rédaction 'sacerdotale' du Pentateuque," in *Le Pentateuque en question* (2d ed.; ed. A. de Pury; Le monde de la Bible 19; Genève: Labor et Fides, 1989), 89–91; J. L. Ska, "La place d'Ex 6, 2–8 dans la narration de l'Exode," *ZAW* 94 (1982): 544–46; idem, "Quelques remarques sur Pg et la dernière rédaction du Pentateuque," in *Pentateuque en question*, 102–25; M. Vervenne, "The 'P' Tradition in the Pentateuch: Document and/or Redaction?—The 'Sea Narrative' (Ex 13:17–14:31) as a Test Case," in *Pentateuchal and Deuteronomistic Studies* (ed. C. Brekelmans and J. Lust; BETL 94; Leuven: University Press, 1990), 81–87.
2. For lucid description of how Noth's work on the Deuteronomistic history was a precedent for the P-as-redaction approach, see R. Rendtorff, "Martin Noth and Tradition Criticism," *The History of Israel's Traditions: The Heritage of Martin Noth* (JSOTSup, 182; Sheffield, England: Sheffield Academic Press, 1994), 95, 100.
3. N. Lohfink, "Die Priesterschrift und die Geschichte," *Congress Volume: Göttingen, 1977* (VTSup 29; Leiden: Brill, 1978), 197; R. Smend, *Die Entstehung des Alten Testaments*, 53–54.

uing to posit an originally independent P document but assigning a larger proportion of P materials, such as the toledot structure of Genesis (Gen. 2:4a; 5:1; 6:9; etc.), to a Priestly redactor.[4] Alternatively, Blum has proposed that even the source-redaction opposition is misleading. Instead, he speaks of a P "compositional layer." He argues that under the conditions of the Persian-sponsored gathering of Judean traditions, the Priestly authors were not free to fully replace the earlier non-P material that came to them. Instead they had to put their competing accounts and traditions, sometimes sketched out in some detail, alongside their non-P counterparts.[5]

Much of this debate revolves around a complex interaction between textual data and various models for ancient composition. On at least one point, however, documented cases of transmission history provide some perspective on the recent discussion. In reaction to prominent claims by some scholars that P was almost completely preserved in the Pentateuch,[6] advocates of a redaction approach to P have pointed out major gaps in P, gaps such as the lack of separate P narratives of pre-Flood sin, Jacob's sojourn in Padan-Aram, Joseph's rise to power, or Moses' early life.[7] They ask, How could a P document have lacked such narratives? Nevertheless, all documented cases of conflation suggest that no ancient redactor mindlessly used 100 percent of his source documents. Instead, ancient conflators such as the author of the expansionist Pentateuch, Tatian, or later medieval chroniclers selectively drew on their source materials to form a new whole.[8] In light of such examples, complete or even almost complete preservation of a P source would be the exception rather than the rule for ancient transmission history.[9] If P and

4. Childs, *Introduction*, 147; R. Friedman, *The Exile and Biblical Narrative: The Formation of the Deuteronomistic and Priestly Works* (HSM 22; Chico, Calif.: Scholars, 1981), 76–119.
5. Blum, *Studien*, 229–85. For places where he sees evidence of preliminary sketches for the P rewriting, see Blum, *Studien*, 240–41, 251–52, 305n68.
6. See, for example, the conclusion to Noth's influential discussion of P in his *Pentateuch*, 17: "Generally speaking it can be expected that only the P narrative is preserved completely in its original extent and that therefore the identified P elements connect smoothly with each other."
7. C. Machholz, "Israel und das Land. Vorarbeiten zu einem Vergleich zwischen Priesterschrift und deuteronomistischem Geschichtswerk," (Habil., Heidelberg Universität, 1969), 38–39; Cross, *Canaanite Myth*, 306–7, 317–21; Van Seters, *Abraham*, 285; S. Tengström, *Toledot-formel*, 13, 37–38; Blum, *Vätergeschichte*, 427; 430–31; idem, *Studien*, 231, 240–41 (particularly n.45), 260 (including n.116); Rendtorff, "L'histoire," 89–91.
   To be sure, if one works with a sharply modified Priestly layer, such as the Priestly promise texts as a group, the lack of continuity becomes so conspicuous that it does count against the theory of an originally independent P. See, for example, B. D. Eerdmans, *Alttestamentliche Studien*, vol. 1, *Die Komposition der Genesis* (Giessen: Töpelmann, 1908), 6–33; and Rendtorff, *Problem*, 112–30, (E.T., 136–56). Most of those advocating a redactional/compositional model for P, however, work with a wider-ranging P layer.
8. On the artfulness of this process, see in particular Longstaff, *Evidence of Conflation in Mark?*, 10–113.
9. For this point regarding P, see already W. Eichrodt, *Die Quellen der Genesis von neuem untersucht* (BZAW 31; Giessen: Töpelmann, 1916), 12. Also J. A. Emerton, "The Priestly Writer in Genesis," *JTS* 39 (1988): 385.

non-P materials were conflated with each other, we would expect significant gaps in both.[10] Therefore we need to reflect carefully on how one might determine whether or not an originally separate P source preceded the Priestly redaction of Genesis. On the one hand, the presence of such a source would be suggested by (1) massive numbers of doublets between P and non-P materials;[11] (2) conflicts between an overall pattern in P, such as progression in divine names, and the lack of coordination of such a pattern with intervening non-P material;[12] (3) places where the apparent original impact of the P account, such as the background for Jacob's departure toward Haran/Padan-Aram (Gen. 27:46–28:9), appears to depend on the supposition that the non-P version of the same account (e.g., Gen. 27:1–45) never happened; and (4) the extent to which, despite whatever subtractions that might have happened in conflation, the P material still forms a relatively coherent narrative strand, independently readable apart from the non-P material with which it now stands.[13] On the other hand, factors counting against the existence of such a source would be cases where significant sections of P material are coordinated with and only understandable as part of a narrative including their non-P

---

10. This against Eerdmans (*Studien*, 9–13, 24) and P. Volz ([with W. Rudolph] *Der Elohist als Erzähler. Ein Irrweg der Pentateuchkritik?* [BZAW 63; Giessen: Töpelmann, 1933], 137, 139), who frequently argue against the assignment of a certain verse to P because the given verse is necessary in non-P.

11. Childs, *Introduction*, 147; W. H. Schmidt, "Elementare Erwägungen," 29–30; Lohfink, "Priesterschrift," 200; R. Friedman, *The Exile and Biblical Narrative*, 78–80; E. W. Nicholson, "P as an Originally Independent Source in the Pentateuch," *JBS* 10 (1988): 197; Emerton, "The Priestly Writer in Genesis," 397–98; A. F. Campbell, "The Priestly Text: Redaction or Source?," in *Biblische Theologie und gesellschaftlicher Wandel: Für Norbert Lohfink SJ*. (ed. G. Braulik, W. Groß, and S. McEvenue; Freiburg/Basel/Vienna: Herder, 1993), 42.

12. For similar arguments see Schmidt, "Elementare Erwägungen zur Quellenscheidung im Pentateuch," 30; Friedman, *The Exile and Biblical Narrative*, 77–78, 85; E. Zenger, *Gottes Bogen in den Wolken: Untersuchungen zu Komposition und Theologie der priesterschriftlichen Urgeschichte* (SBS 112; Stuttgart: Katholisches Bibelwerk, 1983), 35–36; F. Kohata, *Jahwist und Priesterschrift in Exodus 3—14* (BZAW 166; Berlin/New York: Walter de Gruyter, 1986), 4; K. Koch, "P-kein Redaktor! Erinnerung an zwei Eckdaten der Quellenscheidung," *VT* 37 (1987):462–66; Lohfink, "Priesterschrift," 200; P. Weimar, "Struktur und Komposition der priesterschriftlichen Geschichtsdarstellung," *BN* 23 (1984): 84n15; Nicholson, "P as an Originally Independent Source," 196–97, 199–200; A. Schart, *Mose und Israel*, 247–48; B. Renaud, "Les genealogies et la structure de l'histoire sacerdotale dans le livre de la Genèse," *RB* 97 (1990): 5–30, especially 29–30; J. Blenkinsopp, *The Pentateuch: An Introduction to the First Five Books of the Bible* (New York: Doubleday, 1992), 77–78.

13. Schmidt, "Elementare Erwägungen zur Quellenscheidung im Pentateuch," 32–33; Kohata, *Jahwist und Priesterschrift in Exodus 3—14*, 3–4; Schart, *Mose und Israel*, 247–48; Emerton, "The Priestly Writer in Genesis," 398; and (with particular emphasis) Campbell, "The Priestly Text: Redaction or Source?," 32–35. One needs to be very careful not to go too far in using this indicator. The more one emphasizes this as primary evidence for a separate P, the more vulnerable one is to observations that the present Priestly compositional layer is not continuous. Therefore, such arguments are more plausible to the extent they maintain that the present Priestly layer has a conspicuously higher degree of continuity than would be typical of a redactional/compositional layer, without claiming the P source has been completely or almost completely preserved.

counterpart. For example, Blum persuasively argues that the irony and particular shape of the P Meribah story at the end of the wilderness period (Num. 20:1–13) are only understandable when the story is seen as standing in the same narrative line as and corresponding to the non-P Meribah story at the outset of the wilderness period (Exod. 17:1–7).[14]

In the end, this discussion can have significant consequences for how one understands the final formation of Genesis and other Pentateuchal books. If one understands P as a reworking of earlier non-P material, then the P material as a whole stands as the most prominent final redaction responsible for the present shape of Genesis. If one understands much of P as having originally existed separately from the non-P material of Genesis, then the last major redaction of Genesis consisted of the compositional interweaving of P and non-P material into a new whole.

My work will proceed in two parts, analysis of P and non-P material in Gen. 1:1–9:17, and then discussion of priestly passages in Gen. 9:18–50:26. In these two chapters, I will argue that the bulk of the P material is dependent on and even designed to correct non-P material. Here I follow the essential thrust of many redactional approaches to P in arguing that P was always dependent on non-P materials for its overall scope and many specific elements. Nevertheless, I will follow source approaches to P in arguing that much of the P material shows signs of not being originally written to stand alongside the non-P material with which it is now combined. Instead, the bulk of Priestly material in Genesis appears to have once been part of an originally freestanding, separate P source. It was a counternarrative apparently designed to *replace* its non-P counterpart.

In summary, I will be arguing for a model of an originally separate, but not independent P source, a source written in constant relation to non-P material (=dependent), but designed to stand separate from and over against it (=originally separate). If this model is accurate, then the final form of Genesis is the product of a remarkable intertextual move. It is the compositional interweaving of an originally separate P source with the non-P material it was originally designed to displace.

---

14. Blum, *Studien*, 271–78. For arguments for other such cross-linkages, see Cross, *Canaanite Myth*, 302–5, 310–17; Tengström, *Toledotformel*, 36–39; Blum, *Vätergeschichte*, 251–52, 269–70, 424; idem, *Studien*, 233–34, 250–55, 263–71; J. L. Ska, "La place d'Ex 6, 2–8," 544–46; idem, "Quelques remarques sur Pg," 98–113; Vervenne, "The 'Sea Narrative,'" 81–87.

4
P from Creation
to Flood (Gen. 1:1–9:17)

Throughout the rest of the discussion, both the selection and order of discussion of texts is determined by where the next clues to the formation of Genesis are to be found. In this case, the first major clues to the identification of Priestly material in Genesis happen to be found at the beginning of the book, in a series of texts extending from the Creation to the Flood (Gen. 1:1–9:17). These texts form the first three-quarters of the first major unit in Genesis, a primeval history that is variously defined as extending from Gen. 1:1 to Gen. 11:9; 11:32, or even 12:3.

This portion of the primeval history is important for our purposes for at least two reasons. First, the texts in it have played a crucial role in defining the overall limits and characteristics of the Priestly layer in Genesis as a whole. In particular, it is here that the link of Priestly genealogical and promise-covenant themes is the clearest.[1] Second, these texts form a major battle-ground for the different models for P. The earliest proponents of a source approach for P started here, and later critics of this approach have returned to these texts in their arguments for an alternative model.

The Flood

The clues to the formation of Genesis are probably the thickest in the flood account and related texts in Gen. 6:1–9:17. Not only is this text dense with doublets and breaks, but it has served a crucial role in past and present discussion of the formation of the Pentateuch. The classic source treatments have long held up the flood account as a prime example of a biblical text that can be explained by positing interwoven P and non-P sources behind it.[2] Already in the middle of the eighteenth century, J. Astruc posited two source strands in Genesis 6—9, and the consensus surrounding his basic approach,

---

1. Just this link in Genesis 1—11 leads Blum (*Vätergeschichte,* 451–2) to concur with previous studies in identifying a broader P layer in Genesis, rather than building on Rendtorff's proposals regarding a more restricted "El-Shaddai" layer, a layer that would have consisted almost exclusively of the P promise texts (*Problem,* 112–30; E.T., 136–56).
2. Gunkel, *Genesis,* 137; O. Eissfeldt, *Einleitung in das Alte Testament* (3d ed.; Tübingen: J. C. B. Mohr, 1964), 240 (E.T., *The Old Testament: An Introduction* [trans. P. Ackroyd; New York/London: Harper and Row, 1965], 181). Smend, *Entstehung des Alten Testaments,* 41–42.

as perfected one hundred years ago by a series of source critics, was not challenged for decades in the mainstream of critical scholarship.[3] Recently, however, many have argued for a bewildering variety of alternative models for the formation of the flood text: that the P layer of the flood account is an expansion of the non-P material (Blum, Van Seters),[4] that the non-P material is an expansion of the P material (Blenkinsopp, Ska),[5] or that much of the non-P material is actually Priestly or post-Priestly (Levin).[6]

It is exactly such lack of consensus that tempts one to despair of the possibility of ever adequately reconstructing the formation of texts like this. One might justifiably ask, If this supposed model of the source approach is now subject to so many alternative theories, then how might one ever hope to reconstruct the formation of less clear texts? Let us take a closer look.

None of the alternative approaches to the flood story adequately accounts for its fundamentally doubled character.[7] To be sure, the doublets of the flood account vary in intensity. At one end of the continuum stand jarring renarrations of the same event, such as a doubled report of the entry of Noah and his family into the ark (Gen. 7:7–9, 13–16a).[8] At the other end are var-

---

3. J. Astruc, *Conjectures*, 49–56, 400–2. Astruc's initial observations were developed by many scholars. The analyses that were most influential in forming the most common contemporary conceptions of source division in the flood narrative include E. Schrader, *Studien zur Kritik und Erklärung der biblischen Urgeschichte* (Zurich: Meyer & Zeller, 1863), 136–55, and K. Budde, *Die biblische Urgeschichte (Gen 1–12,5)* (Giessen: J. Ricker, 1883), 248–89. Even as Schrader and Budde's formulations gained widespread acceptance in a critical scholarship dominated by Christian scholars, Jewish scholars offered important critiques of this approach. See, for example, Cassuto, *Genesis*, vol. 2, 30–33, on the Flood; cf. idem, *La questione della Genesi* (Firenze: F. Le Monnier, 1934), 335–53.
4. Blum, *Studien*, 280–85; Van Seters, *Prologue to History*, 160–64.
5. Blenkinsopp, *The Pentateuch*; J. L. Ska, "El relato del Diluvio: un relato sacerotal y algunos fragmentos redaccionales posteriores," *EstBib* 52 (1994): 37–62. Cf. also B. Gosse, "La tradition yahviste en Gn 6,5–9,17," *Henoch* 15 (1993):139–53, who argues that the non-P flood sections are linked not only with other non-P sections but with the P primeval history material as well.
6. C. Levin, *Der Jahwist* (FRLANT 157; Göttingen: Vandenhoeck & Ruprecht, 1993), 103–17. He assigns some traditionally non-P elements to P (e.g., 7:6–9) or layers that postdate the combination of the P and non-P strands (e.g., 6:5b; 7:1b, 10b, 17a, etc.), and assigns several of the redactional catalogues of animals discussed below (6:7; 7:3a, 23) to his non-P strand.
7. Blum and Levin are partial exceptions to this comment because both posit some kind of interweaving of traditions behind the present flood account.
8. Ska ("El Relato," 42–43) argues on the basis of parallels between Noah's acts in Gen. 7:7–16a* and Abraham's acts in Gen. 17:23–27 that the repetition of entry reports is a stylistic device of P's, stressing the importance of both events and the parallels between Noah and Abraham. There are, however, important contrasts between these texts. The redescription of Abraham's acts in 17:26–27 appears prompted in part by the split dating of his and Ishmael's circumcision in Gen. 17:25–26. In this context, the redescription briefly summarizes the previous acts and asserts that they all occurred on the same day. The redescription of Noah's entry in Gen. 7:13–16a, however, does not follow a complex dating note and serves no such summary purpose. Instead, it is longer than the initial entry (cf. Gen 7:7–9), and diverges from its parallel in Gen. 17:26–27 by reasserting that all was done as God commanded (Gen. 7:16aβ//7:9b; cf. 17:24bβ). Ska has pointed out some interesting parallels here, but they are not compelling reasons to deny that at least 7:7 was once a non-P doublet to 7:13. Of course, it is still possible that the redactor combining the accounts composed Gen. 7:8–9 so that the overall report and dating of Noah's entry in the flood account closely paralleled the notices for Abraham in 17:24–27.

ious nearly parallel elements that could be easily understood as complementary elements of a single narrative (7:17b–18). Nevertheless, the clearer sort of doublets predominate in the flood narrative, particularly at the narrative's beginning (Gen. 6:1–7:16a) and end (Gen. 8:20–9:17). It is at exactly these points that the alternative approaches to the flood account are the weakest, and the approaches that posit two originally independent strands are the strongest.[9]

Indeed, it is the beginning and end of the flood account that provide the clues for interpreting the middle. Not only are the doublets clearest there, but so are the contrasts in profile between parallel texts. If all we had was the middle of the flood account, we could not opt for any of the models being advocated for the flood narrative. Agnosticism on this point would be the best course. With the beginning and end of the flood narrative, however, we have exactly the combination of indicators of seams (doublets) and contrasts in profile (terms, concepts) that can help us disentangle the formation of this text. Together, these indicators help us see that the flood account, however artful, is the result of an author/redactor's careful interweaving of large parts of originally separate sources into a new whole.[10]

Many of the central observations of these doublets and contrasting profiles have been around for a long time, but they have not been presented in the past decades in any kind of detailed form. In light of the recent debate, I

9. Blenkinsopp does not directly address the doubling issue, and Ska ("El Relato," 44–51) focuses many of his central arguments on the soft middle of the flood text (Gen. 7:17–18; 8:2–3, 13–14). Even Van Seters, who assigns part of P's beginning of the flood account to non-P (6:13–16, 22; *Prologue*, 161–3), does not explain how 6:13–16, 22 would have functioned in a non-P context including 7:1–5.

So also, most of Whybray's arguments against the predominence of doublets in the flood account focus on the middle of the narrative. (R. N. Whybray, *The Making of the Pentateuch: A Methodological Study*, 72–91). In the process of arguing against the use of doublets to reconstruct transmission history, he maintains that the flood account does not just have doublets, but in fact several three-, four-, and fivefold repetitions of the same event. The account states four times that God intends to destroy the earth (Gen. 6:5–7, 11–13, 17; 7:4); the waters come on the earth four times (7:6, 10, 11, 12); they abate five times (8:1, 2, 3, 4, 5); the rains come multiple times (Gen 7:6, 10, 11). Interestingly, already in 1753 one of the first source critics, Astruc, argued from similar observations for the positing of a third source, C, in the flood account (*Conjectures*, 19–21).

These arguments spanning two hundred and fifty years indicate just how problematic analysis of the flood account into parallel strands can often be. Nevertheless, a closer look at Whybray's examples indicates that they often group texts that are not in fact parallel. Gen. 8:4 is not parallel to 8:1–3 or 5, and the narrator's description of God's intent to destroy the world in 6:5–7 is not a doublet to God's announcement of this intent to Noah in 7:4. Moreover, Whybray's lists of parallel passages often fail to distinguish processes that are distinguished in both strands. For example, the flood account distinguishes between the arrival of the flood (Gen. 7:10) and the parallel processes that brought it about (7:11//12). So also, it first describes the process leading to the abatement of the waters (8:2a//2b) before narrating the results of that process (8:3a//3b, 5).

10. Blum, *Studien*, 283–84 (including n.210), surveys, extends, and critiques some of the studies that have found careful design in the flood story. See also R. Longacre, "The Discourse Structure of the Flood Narrative," *JAAR* 47 (1979; supplement B): 89–133; and I. Kikawada and A. Quinn, *Before Abraham Was*, 84–106.

will briefly re-present the major indicators of growth in the flood narrative, beginning with a tabular presentation of places in the flood account where the same or a similar event is described more than once. This table collects on one page potentially parallel passages in the flood account, and indicates through numbers and letters the extent to which these parallels are distinguished from each other by distinctive profiles. The column on the right collects passages in the P strand. It is termed "P" because its profile includes a number of terms and concepts characteristic of Priestly texts throughout the Pentateuch. Each small letter—for example *a, b*—indicates that a term or concept particularly characteristic of the P strand occurs in the given passage. The other strand of the flood account is termed, for lack of a better designation, "non-P."[11] Each number—for example, *1, 2*—indicates that a term or concept particularly characteristic of the non-P strand occurs in the passage. Later, in the table following the flood account, a key indicates what terms and concepts are designated by the various letters and numbers. An example of how the table works follows.

6:1–4 (non-P strand)	6:11 (P strand)
1, 2, 3 (4×), 4 and b	a, b (2×), d, e

1 = use of the divine designation YHWH	a = use of the divine designation Elohim
2= use of the term *hā'ădāmâh* for "dry ground"	b = use of the term *'ereṣ* for "dry ground"
b = use of the term *'ereṣ* for "dry ground"	(2×) indicates that feature b occurs twice in 6:11
3 = use of the term *hā'ādām* for "humanity"	
(4×) indicates that feature 3 occurs four times in 6:1–4.	
4 = attributing the Flood to humanity's evil	d = attributing the flood to a more general ruining of the earth
	e = ruining of the earth through violence on it

In summary, Gen. 6:1–4 is distinguished by its focus on YHWH, *hā'ădāmâh* ("dry ground"), *hā'ādām* ("humanity"), and its attribution of the flood to humanity's evil, versus the focus in Gen. 6:11 on Elohim, *'ereṣ* ("land"), and attribution of the Flood to the ruining of the earth. As we look through the rest of the flood account, each of these characteristics occurs again in parallel passages, often contrasting with each other in similar ways. Sometimes, as in the case of the use of the common term *'ereṣ,* a given term occurs in both

---

11. This strand has traditionally been termed *J* for Jahwist. This "Jahwist" is then seen as extending into the ancestral and Moses stories. Later in the book I will argue for an alternative model for the history of this non-P material. For now, before I talk in more detail about this layer, I designate it non-committally as "non-P."

strands but predominates in only one of them. Such a word was hardly the exclusive property of the authors of any one strand. In such cases, the strands are characterized by the predominance but not exclusive use of a given set of terms and concepts.

The Two Accounts

Let us look now (see Chart 4-1) at the potentially parallel passages in the flood account and how various terms and concepts are distributed across it.

Chart 4-1: Doublets and Parallels in the Flood Account[12]
(Parenthetical numbers followed by an × indicate the number of times the term shown in the key is repeated in that context.)

Non-P strand   P strand

Description of problem 6:1–4   Description of problem 6:11
    1, 2, 3 (4×), 4 + b   a, b (2×), d, e
Perception of problem (+ result) 6:5–7 Perception of problem 6:12
Perception of sin 6:5   a, c, d
    1, 3, 4 (2×), 5 + b
(Intent to Destroy 6:6–7)
    1 (2×), 2, 3 (2×), 6, 7, 11 + b, o
Assertion of Noah's contrasting   [Assertion of Noah's unique
    enjoyment of divine favor 6:8   1   righteousness 6:9aβb   a, f]
Divine announcement and instruction   Divine announcement and instruction
    speech 7:1–4   1   speech 6:13–21   a
[Announcement of Flood 7:4]   Announcement of Flood: 6:13,
    2, 6, 13 (2×) + 14   17–18a   b (2×), c (2×), d (2×),
                                                                            e, g (2×), h, i, j

Gather + entry order 7:1–3   Gather + entry order 6:18b–21
    Entry 7:1   Entry 6:18b   k, l
    Gathering and provision 7:2–3a   Gathering and provision 6:19–21
        8, 9, 10, 12 (2×) + n   c, m, n, o, q, r + 2
    Purpose 7:3b   b   (includes Purpose 6:19*, 20*)
Compliance report 7:5   1   Compliance report 6:22   a
[Coming of Flood 7:10]   13   Coming of Flood 7:6   s
[Process of Flood 7:12]   13, 14   Process of Flood 7:11   s, t
Entry report 7:7–9   Entry report 7:13–16a
    Humans 7:7   k, l   Humans 7:13   h, (cf. k), l
    Animals 7:8–9   Animals 7:14–16a
        2, 8, 12, a, m, n, o   a, c (2×), i, m, n, p, q + 12
Waters multiplying and bearing up   Waters multiplying and bearing up
    the ark 7:17b   b   the ark 7:18   b
All life dies 7:22   15   All life dies 7:21   c, h, p, r, u + 3
All life wiped out 7:23aα   All life wiped out 7:23aβ   b
    2, 6, 11 + o

---

12. Note: texts are listed in the order they appear unless the entry for them is in brackets.

Non-P strand		P strand	
End of Flood 8:2b–3a	14	End of Flood 8:1–2a, 3b, 5	
		(Divine initiation 8:1)	a, r, v
Ceasing of cause 8:2b	14	Ceasing of cause 8:2a	t
Result -		Results -	
Receding of waters 8:3a		Receding of waters 8:3b	13
		Uncovering of mountains 8:5	s
Impetus to exit 8:6–12 (Bird Scene)		Earth dry 8:14	
2, 13 (3×) + f (3×)		Dating 8:14a	s
Earth (perceived as) dry 8:13		Drying proper 8:14b	b
Dating 8:13a	s	Impetus to exit 8:15–17(Exit Order)	
Drying proper 8:13b	2, 15	a, b (2×), c, k, l, o, r, u	
Concluding promise scene 8:20–22		Concluding promise scene 9:8–17	
(No more floods)		(No more floods)	
1 (2×), 2, 3 (2×), 4, 5, 7, 8, 9, 10		a (4×), b (6×), d (2×), f, g,	
		[cf. l], o, u (3×), r (5×), j (3×), v (2×)	

Key to the Notations

NOTE: Asterisks in this chart indicate cases where the feature occurs not only in a given strand but in the opposing strand as well. Some features do not span doublets in a given strand but do contrast with an element of the opposing strand. Those cases included purely for contrast with the opposing strand are indicated with brackets.

Features appearing more often in the non-P strand	Features appearing more often in the P Strand
1. "YHWH" (6:3, 5, 6, 7; 7:1, 5; 8:21 [2×])	a. "Elohim" (6:9, 11, 12, 13, 22; 7:9*, 16a; 8:1, 15; 9:8, 12, 16, 17)
2. *hā'ădāmâh* ("earth") prominent either by itself (8:21) or as "surface of the ground" (6:1, 7; 7:4, 23; 8:8, 13) Note also expressions with the root "creep" (rmś/remeś) in 6:20* and 7:8.	b. *'ereṣ* ("earth") prominent (6:4*, 5*, 6*, 11 [2], 12, 13 [2]; 7:17*, 18, 23aβ; 8:7, 9, 11, 14b [cf. *'ădāmâh* in 8:13b], 17 [2]; 9:10, 11, 13, 14, 16, 17
3. *hā'ādām* ("humanity") in 6:1, 2, 3, 4, 5, 6aα, 7; 7:21; 8:21 (2×); 9:6* (3×)	c. "all flesh" (*kol-bāśār*) in 6:12, 13, 17, 19; 7:15, 16, 21; 8:17; 9:11, 15 (2), 16, 17
4. Evil of humanity is cause for flood (6:3, 5a, 5b; 8:21)	d. Combination of "ruin" (Hebrew root *šḥt*) of "earth" (*'ereṣ*; 6:11, 12, 13b; 9:11) or "ruin" of "all flesh" (6:17; 9:15) for sin and punishment of sin
5. Specific focus on "evil"/"inclination" of the "formation" (*yēṣer*) of the [thoughts of the] "heart" of "humanity" in 6:5; 8:21	
6. Destruction is "wiping out" (Hebrew root *mḥh* - N stem) of "humanity" (6:7)/"every living thing" (*yĕqûm*) from "the surface of the earth" (7:4, 23aα)	e. "earth full of violence" (6:11, 13) [Destruction is "wiping out" from "earth" 7:23aβ]

7. Focus on God's inner process (6:6; 8:21)   f.   "generations" (*dōrōt*) in 6:9; 9:12
                                               g.   God's statement of intent is
                                                    introduced with the expression
                                                    hinnî (6:13b, 17; 9:9)
[Use of word *mwt* to refer to death   h.   Use of word "*gwʿ*" to refer to
(7:22)]   death (6:17; 7:21)
                                               i.   Statements regarding breath in
                                                    animals use the phrase "breath of
[Statement regarding breath in animals   life" (*rûaḥ ḥayyîm*) without the
uses the word *nišmat* for "breath" (7:22)]   word "*nišmat*" (6:17; 7:15)
                                               j.   "establishment" of "covenant"
                                                    (6:18; 9:9, 11, 17)
                                                    ["covenant" (9:12, 13)]
[Human group referred to as "you and   k.   Human group referred to as "you,
your house" (7:1)]   your sons, your wife, and your
                                                    sons' wives with you" (6:18b;
                                                    8:16 [cf. 7:7, 13])
                                               l.   Extra preposition "with" (*'et*) in
                                                    6:18; 7:7*, 13; 8:16
8. Focus on clean and unclean animals   m.   One pair of each kind of animal
   (7:2, 8; 8:20)   (6:19–20; 7:9*, 15-16)
9. Provision of/use of animals for food   (Provision of vegetables for food
   and sacrifice through seven clean and   [6:21]; No need for provision for
   one unclean (7:2; 8:20)   sacrifice [see 9:8-17])
   [Gender of animal pairs indicated   n.   Gender of animal pairs indicated
   through the terms "husband" (*'iš*) and   through the terms "male" and
   "his wife" (*'ištô*) 7:2 (2×)]   "female" (*zākār ûněqébâh*) in
                                                    6:19; 7:3*, 9a*, 16
10. Two part categorization of animals   o.   Three-part categorization of living
    (beasts and birds) in 7:2-3; 8:20   things [humans] animals,
                                                    "creeping things" (*rmś, remeś*),
                                                    birds (6:7aβ*, 20; 7:8*, 23aα*;
                                                    8:17); see also three-part
                                                    categorization (birds, domestic
                                                    animals, and wild animals) in 9:10.
11. "From - to" catalog of types of   p.   Four-part categorization of
    animals in 6:7; 7:23 (three-part   living things (wild animals,
    catalogs in a non-P context)   domestic animals, "creeping"/
                                                    "swarming" things and birds) in
                                                    7:14, 21.
                                                    [Two-part categorization of living
                                                    things in ark (wild and domestic
                                                    animals) in 8:1]
12. Reference to animal pairs with the   q.   Catalog "according to their
    phrases of paired numbers—seven by   kinds" 6:20; 7:14
    seven (7:2a), two by two (7:9a, 15*;   r.   Prominence of the word *ḥayyâh*
    also 7:2b in some textual traditions)   for living creatures in 6:19; 7:14,
                                                    21; 8:1, 17; 9:10 (2×), 12,
                                                    15, 16

13. Relative datings given—seven days   s. Absolute datings given by year
    (7:4, 10; 8:10, 12), forty days (7:4,   (7:6) or year, month, and day
    12; 8:6), one hundred fifty days (8:3b*)   (7:11; 8:5, 13a*, 14a)
14. Flood is rain (7:4, 12; 8:2)   t. Flood is opening of portals of
                                                heaven (7:11; 8:2a)
15. Use of the Hebrew root ḥrb to refer   u. Hebrew preposition bĕ introduces
    to dry ground (7:22) or the drying   items that specify the preceding
    process (8:13b)   (7:21; 8:17; 9:10, 15, 16)
                                            v. Emphasis on God "remembering"
                                                (zkr) and then preserving life
                                                (8:1; 9:15, 16)

The foregoing chart does not cover all of the texts in the flood account. Nevertheless, it already indicates the extent to which many items in the flood account are paralleled by other items and distinguished in profile from one another. Even when other texts in the flood story are not considered, there are already several indicators that two originally independent flood accounts have been conflated here.

Doublets

The first such indicator of conflation is the presence of a massive number of doublets. It is difficult to conceive of why an author/redactor would have written such an extensive set of doublets to another narrative. In the case of the flood narrative, these doublets extend across a wide swathe of the first half of the narrative and resume with intensity at its conclusion. This is not a question of whether an author could have put these accounts next to each other. Someone did so. The question is whether narratives such as the doubled divine instruction and execution (6:9–22//7:1–5), the double human entry (7:7//7:13), or the double promise that the Flood will not return (8:20–22//9:8–17) were *first* written in relation to one another, or whether they were originally written separately and only later brought into relation with each other. The nature of many doublets in the flood account suggests that the latter took place. This is confirmed by the next indicator.

Breaks

The second major indicator of conflation here are places where the conceptual systems of the P and non-P passages are broken up by each other. The most prominent and widely recognized example of this phenomenon arises out of a basic difference between the conceptualities of P and non-P. Whereas the non-P strand describes a sacrifice right after the Flood (Gen. 8:20), the P strand assumes that sacrifice did not occur before Sinai. As a result of this difference, there is a contrast between the P strand flood story, which describes only one pair of each kind of animal in the ark (6:13a, 19; cf. 7:15*), and the non-P strand flood story, which provides spare animals to be sacrificed by having six extra pairs of clean animals in the ark for each pair of unclean animals (7:2). This then prepares for the parallel endings of the flood account: P, where no sacrifice occurs (Gen. 9:1–17) and non-P, where sacrifice does (8:20–22).

A less clear example of clashes between the P system and the non-P material is the differing chronologies of the two strands. This clash occurs in two prominent locations. First, the non-P strand dates the onset of the forty days of rain seven days *after* Noah's entry into the ark (7:4–5, 7, 10, 12), while the P strand dates the onset of the flood "on the very day" that Noah enters the ark (7:11, 13). Moreover, the interweaving of these materials has produced a conspicuous seam. The P dating of the onset of the flood "on this very day" in 7:13 originally must have immediately followed the exact dating of Noah's entry on the seventeenth day of the second month of his six hundredth year (7:11). The reference to "this very day," however, now follows the non-P notice that the rains lasted forty days (7:12). To find the day to which 7:13 is referring, one must jump in the present form of the text from 7:13 back to the exact dating in 7:11.[13]

Second, the non-P flood chronology works exclusively with relative dates in seven- and forty-day intervals. In it the flood lasts forty days (Gen. 7:4, 10, 17; 8:6), and the time of drying until Noah's realization that the land was dry lasts a total of fourteen days (8:6, 10, 12). The P Flood chronology is itself multilayered,[14] but it is characterized overall by a predominance of absolute dates determined by Noah's age and an expansion of the duration of the Flood. In P the Flood lasts 150 days (Gen. 7:11 [cf. 7:6], 8:4 and 8:3b [cf. also 7:24]), and the drying and Noah's realization of its conclusion is now stretched over a period of months (8:4b, 5, 13, 14). The redaction responsible for the final form of the text has elegantly meshed these two systems.[15] Indeed, the success of this redactional work is partly reflected by the multiplication of attempts over recent years to construct a consistent system out of these various notices.[16] Nevertheless, as Emerton has shown, these efforts inevitably lead to various improbabilities.[17] The P system does not integrate the non-P system into its framework, nor vice versa.

---

13. H. Hupfeld, *Die Quellen der Genesis und die Art ihrer Zusammensetzung von neuem untersucht* (Berlin: Verlag von Wiegandt und Grieben, 1853), 8–9.
14. S. McEvenue, *The Narrative Style of the Priestly Writer* (AnBib 50; Rome: Biblical Institute Press, 1971), 54–59 surveys the literature up to the writing of his book. Cf. N. P. Lemche, "The Chronology in the Story of the Flood," *JSOT* 18 (1980): 52–62.
15. Donner, "Der Redaktor," 21–22; Blum, *Studien*, 283–84.
16. See, for example, G. J. Wenham, "The Coherence of the flood narrative," *VT* 28 (1978):342–45; and N. M. Sarna, *Genesis* (JPS Torah Commentary; Philadelphia/New York/Jerusalem: Jewish Publication Society, 1989), 376.
17. J. A. Emerton, "An Examination of Some Attempts to Defend the Unity of the Flood Narrative in Genesis: Part One," *VT* 37 (1987): 402–5, 419; idem, "An Examination of Some

Potential Continuity in the Parallel Materials

Another indicator that conflation has taken place in the flood narrative is the remarkable level of potential continuity that we see in both strands of the parallel flood materials. Even considering only the doubled material discussed so far, the two strands in Gen. 6:1–9:17 form remarkably continuous, parallel narratives of the flood. Of course, such a retrospective argument from potential continuity can only confirm a picture arrived at through other means. Nevertheless, it does provide corraborative evidence for a hypothesis of interwoven sources here.

Secondary Linkage of the P and non-P Strands: The Work of Rp

The initial theory of secondary conflation of originally separate strands receives further support from indications that some non-P texts were secondarily modified in order to conform to P models. In the following, I survey three of the most prominent examples.

Gen. 6:7aβ: "from humanity to animals, creeping things, and birds of the air"

This P-strand-like catalog of animals occurs in a non-P context, Gen. 6:7. The catalog of all living things, however, occurs as a specification of God's intent to destroy humanity: "I will blot out from the earth the human beings I have created—from human beings to animals to creeping things to birds." The focus on humanity is typical of the non-P materials, but it clashes here with a more general focus on life more characteristic of the P strand. Indeed, as B. Levinson has pointed out, the catalog of animals at this point moves back from the human starting point to the other classes of animals created on the fifth and sixth days in Genesis 1.[18] Later we will review the data identifying Genesis 1 as part of the P strand seen in the Flood. Genesis 6:7 appears to be an author's attempt to include the animals from this P creation text into a human-focused, non-P text at the outset of the flood account.

Gen. 7:3a: "and also the birds of heaven, seven apiece, male and female"

The description of preservation of birds in 7:3a is awkwardly appended to the preceding divine instruction regarding animals in Gen. 7:2. Moreover, it does not continue the distinction between clean and unclean animals so central to that verse. Here again we appear to have in Gen. 7:3a the work of an author who wanted to secondarily conform a more limited, non-P statement of the need to bring animals into the ark (7:2) to broader P statements about

---

Attempts to Defend the Unity of the Flood Narrative in Genesis: Part Two," *VT* 38 (1988): 11–13.
18. Levinson, "The Right Chorale," 137.

the need to bring in birds as well (Gen. 6:20; 7:14; cf. 1:20–23). Crossover of P terminology into the non-P context—"male and female" (7:3a; cf. 6:19; 7:16) versus the non-P "the man and his mate" (twice in 7:2)—is an additional indicator of the hand of this author, an author accommodating non-P materials into a P-like framework.

Gen. 7:8–9: "from the clean animals . . . as God commanded Noah"

Gen. 7:8–9 is another example of a secondary insertion of P terminology into a non-P context regarding animals. Just after a non-P text has indicated that Noah and his family entered the ark to escape "from" the Flood (7:7), 7:8–9 adds another "from" (Hebrew *min*) and then specifies the animals Noah brought with him and indicates his compliance with "God's" command. Here, as in the secondary addition to 6:7, the *from* at the outset of Gen. 7:7 introduces a catalog of all the animals. In addition, here as in 6:7, we have the apparent expansion of a verse originally focusing on humanity through the addition of a survey of categories of animals created in Gen. 1:20–25. The lack of a conjunction and the close juxtaposition of different uses of the same preposition makes this transition awkward. In this case the expansion combines both P elements ("male and female," one pair entering) and non-P elements ("clean" versus "unclean," "two by two") to make a new whole.[19] In summary, the data suggest that the author of Gen. 7:8–9 had both the non-P and P accounts before him. Working from both, he extended an earlier non-P report of Noah and his family's entry (Gen. 7:7) with a P-like description of how the animals "entered" the ark in accordance with God's instructions (Gen. 7:8–9).

Further Reflections on P, Non-P,
and Rp in the Flood Narrative

Each of the above discussed texts—Gen. 6:7aβ; 7:3a, 8–9—is an example of an author/redactor intervening in a non-P context to conform it to P models. More specifically this author seems to have intervened at the exact point where the break between the P and non-P systems is strongest: in P and non-P's divergent concepts of the importance and role of animals in the flood

---

19. In addition, the idea that one must separately note that animals "came" into the ark is more typical of P than non-P. The non-P materials describe God as merely commanding Noah to "come" with his family in the ark and "take" animals with him. The following note that Noah did all that YHWH commanded, Gen. 7:5, implies that he did take the animals, and Gen. 7:7 completes the report of his execution of the divine commands by describing the entry of Noah and his family into the ark. In contrast, P specifies that the animals of all categories are to "come" along with Noah (Gen. 6:20; see also 6:19). Later the P entry report in Gen. 7:13–16a describes this entry of the animals, noting that this entry was in exact accordance with the divine command (Gen. 7:14–16a). In the present form of the text, Gen. 7:8–9 bridges from the competing divine commands in 6:19–20; 7:2 to 7:13–16a by specifying that what "God" really wanted when asking Noah to bring two of every kind of animal (cf. 6:19–20) was for him to bring the unclean and clean animals in by pairs (Gen 7:9; cf. 7:2).

destruction and rescue. The non-P materials focus primarily on humans, and animals play a role mainly as preparations for Noah's sacrifice in the climax to the non-P account (Gen. 8:20–22; cf. 7:2, 3b). P has no sacrifice and thus no focus on clean or unclean animals, but the P strand does have an intensified focus on the comprehensive destruction and rescue of all of the animals created in Genesis 1 (Gen. 6:19–20; 7:13–16). Later, an author faced with these competing concepts of the role of animals in the Flood intervened in the first three instances in non-P where animals are relevant: Gen. 6:7; 7:2, and 7:7. This overall trend suggests that several other instances of crossover of P terminology into non-P contexts—such as the catalog of animals in 7:23aα (highly similar to 6:7aβ)[20] or the P-like absolute date in 8:13a—are likewise insertions by the same editor.

So far I have focused exclusively on those parts of the flood account that can be divided into doublets or corresponding accounts. Once the two strands of the flood account are identified on this basis, it is possible to assign most of the rest of the flood account to one or the other strand on the basis of terminology and the context of a given passage. For example, the introduction of Noah's sons in Gen. 6:10, instructions for construction of the ark (6:14–16), detailed description of the rising of the waters (7:19–20, 24), exactly dated description of the resting of the ark (8:4), and compliance with the P-strand order to exit the ark (8:18–19) all lack a parallel in the flood narrative. Nevertheless, these texts occur in P-strand contexts and share features with the materials in it.[21] The remaining texts, Gen. 7:16b–17a and 23b, are often assigned to the non-P strand on the basis of isolated non-P characteristics in them. In any case, their treatment does not decisively affect the overall diachronic picture of the flood account one way or the other.

---

20. The catalog of living beings in 7:23aα shares with 6:7aβ a "from - to" construction (feature 11) that is not found in otherwise similar P-strand catalogs. Moreover, 6:7aβ and 7:23aα both focus on the destruction of animals along with humans, much as the other additions discussed above. Together these indicators suggest that 6:7aβ and the catalog of animals in 7:23aα were authored by the same editor. Note that the presence of the latter catalog of animals makes 7:23aα diverge from the (non-P) prediction of this destruction in 7:4.

21. Working with the designations from the above table of the flood account, 7:19–20, 24 has feature *b* and resembles 8:5 (non-P). The date in 8:4 has feature *s*, and its dating of the resting of the ark five months after the onset of the flood (cf. 7:11) conflicts with the non-P strand's dating the *beginning* of the falling of the waters after 150 days (i.e., approximately five months; 8:3b, cf. 7:24; Hupfeld, *Quellen der Genesis*, 16–17 n.). The exit report in 8:18–19 shares features *b, k, l, o,* and *r* with the P strand. Genesis 6:10 occurs in a P-strand context (Gen. 6:9aβb and 11) and is often assigned to the P strand on the basis of its similarities with Genesis 5. That chapter will be discussed later.

As Van Seters points out in his recent analysis of the flood story, 6:14–16 lacks specific P characteristics and is the most prominent gap in the non-P account. On this basis, Van Seters proposes assigning it to non-P, *Prologue to History*, 161–62, an assignment that depends on his overall redactional approach to P. If the above arguments for an overall source approach to the flood account are correct, however, then a gap in P at this point is as problematic as a gap in non-P. In addition, Van Seters argues (163) that 6:13 is a non-P text. Nevertheless, he does not account for how this text would have functioned in a non-P context moving from 6:13–16 to 6:22–7:5.

Such refinements of the analysis of the flood account are inevitably subject to varying degrees of plausibility and agreement. Nevertheless, the data summarized above were clear enough to produce an almost century-long consensus regarding the contours of the two strands in the flood account. Chart 4-2 summarizes the above reflections. Overall, it is quite typical of most such lists since the turn of the century.[22]

Chart 4-2: Overview of the Two Strands and Redaction in Flood Materials

Non-P strand (traditionally labeled "J")	P strand
6:1–7aα, 7b–8	6:9aβ–22
7:1–2, 3b–5, 7	7:6
7:10, 12, [16b], 17, 22	7:11, 13–16a, 18–21
7:23aα* (without the catalog of animals), [23b]	7:23aβ, 24
8:2b–3a, 6–12, 13b, 20–22	8:1–2a, 3b–5, 14–19; 9:1–17

Redactor who combined the strands: Rp

6:7aβ
7:3a, 8–9, 23aα* (just the catalog of animals)
8:13a

The Relation Between the P and Non-P Strands

So far, I have said little about the probable relation between the P and non-P strands. Certainly given the widespread presence of flood narratives across the ancient Near East, one could entertain the possibility that the non-P and P flood stories developed independently. Nevertheless, conspicuous links between the overall design and terminology of the two strands suggest a closer relation between them. First, as the table summarizing doublets indicates, the two strands are extremely similar to each other—matching episode to episode, even subepisode to subepisode, and comment to comment (cf. 6:9 P and 7:1 non-P). Second, the two strands often share rare vocabulary, such as *mabbûl* ("flood") and *tēbâh* ("ark"), or the description of Noah's family as "you, your sons, your wife, and your son's wives with you" (7:7 in non-P; 6:18b; 8:16 in P [cf. also 7:13]).[23] Overall, although each strand has unusually close parallels to flood accounts outside the Bible, they are more similar to each other than to any other.[24]

---

22. Cf. Budde, *Urgeschichte*, 276; Gunkel, *Genesis*, 137–38. The label in Gen. 6:9α will be discussed later in relation to Genesis 1—9 as a whole.
23. McEvenue, *Narrative Style*, 24–27; Van Seters, *Prologue*, 161. Cf. also J. Wellhausen, *Prolegomena*, 309 (E.T., 390) on the parallel of 6:10 (P) with 7:1b (non-P).
24. To some extent, both strands have drawn selectively on earlier flood traditions (manifested most clearly in the Gilgamesh version). As a result, the combination of the two more fully corresponds to the Gilgamesh version than either strand alone. Especially since certain materials

Such specific structural and terminological links between the narratives strongly support the hypothesis that one flood narrative is dependent on the other. Determining the relation of dependence requires attention to different criteria. Two indicators suggest that the P account is dependent on the non-P material.[25] The first such indicator is places where the P strand is more expansive than its non-P counterpart. When the two strands are compared, it becomes evident that the P strand has additions to the basic framework found in the non-P strand, additions such as the expanded description of the rising of the waters (7:19–20, 24), added divine initiation to end the Flood (8:1), new reversal of the Gen. 1:29–30 meat prohibition (9:2–5), and extended transformation of the divine post-flood promise (8:20–22, non-P) into a covenant (9:8–17, P). The extra material in the P account suggests that it is an expansion of a framework found in non-P.

The second indicator that the P flood account is dependent on the non-P flood account is the way the dating system in P appears to imitate the non P system, even though the rationale for the non-P system is no longer maintained in the P account. The non-P strand contains an unusually detailed system of relative dates: for the arrival of the Flood (7:4, 10), duration of the rain (7:4, 12), the end of the rain (8:6), and then the successive sendings of the birds (8:10, 12). In this case, the extra emphasis on the duration of the flood process (7:4, 12) over and above the dating of the initial arrival of waters (7:4, 10) is important because the Flood is caused by the *length* of rain. Such a need for separate dates does not exist in the P strand. Rather than talking of a long rain, it attributes the Flood to a catastrophic opening of the fountains of heaven. Nevertheless, the P strand still has dates corresponding to each date in the non-P strand, including a general date for the arrival of the Flood (7:6) and then a more specific date for the opening of the fountains of heaven (7:11). In addition, the P strand revises the dating system to refer to years (months and days) in Noah's life, and extends the scheme to date Noah's exit from the ark (8:14). Notably, it is at this one point that the redactor who combined the strands apparently saw a need to complete the parallelism between the strands by dating a corresponding event in the non-P strand (8:13a).

The data supporting two documentary strands in the flood account are quite strong.[26] No matter how much study of the final form may illuminate

---

from each strand were excised in the process of conflation, these closer parallels of the present flood story to the Gilgamesh epic do not mean that the present flood story had no transmission history. On the issue of parallels, cf. Emerton, "Examination, part two," 14–15, with Wenham, "The Coherence of the Flood Narrative," 345–47.

25. See in particular McEvenue, *Narrative Style*, 24–27. He presents additional detailed arguments for dependence of the one strand on the other. In several cases, however, his arguments are weakened by his assignment to the non-P strand of materials that are probably part of the redaction that combined the two strands, particularly 7:8–9.

26. Whybray's recent critique of the documentary approach to the flood account and other Pentateuchal material (*The Making of the Pentateuch: A Methodological Study* [JSOTSup 53;

the artfulness of the present redactional composition, the indicators of transmission history remain: a conspicuous number of doublets, along with the multiple and specific similarities in profile that connect their corresponding members with each other. Whatever the weaknesses of a documentary approach elsewhere in the Pentateuch, this text shows that it is possible, at least in this case, to establish documentary strands through attention to just the text at hand. To be sure, we have not yet looked at the implications of such study for analysis of the final form of Genesis. That will only come after a more complete analysis of its transmission history. Instead, I turn at this point to look at P and non-P in the rest of Genesis 1—9. The methodology in what follows will be similar: examination of indicators of seams and then a check for distinctive profiles in the material thus distinguished.

The Creation

I turn next to the creation story of Genesis 1—3. This section is important now mainly because of the close links between blocks of material in it and the flood account that was just analyzed. Through analysis of Genesis 1—3 we will see that the model of textual formation discerned in the flood texts should be extended to cover related texts in the primeval history.

On first glance, the stories here meld more seamlessly than the often jarring doublets of the flood account. Yes, there are a number of parallels between the seven-day creation account in Gen. 1:1–2:3 and the creation and punishment story of Gen. 2:4b–3:24.[27] Chart 4-3 summarizes a number of them, many of which have been observed by recent synchronic studies of the text in its present form.[28]

Sheffield: JSOT Press, 1987]) begins with the weakest criteria for establishing documentary strands, language and style (55–72), before considering the strongest indicators of tradition history, doublets and contradictions of fact (72–91). Later, in his critique of use of "cumulative evidence" to argue for documentary strands (116–117) he again focuses on linguistic and stylistic arguments for the documentary strands. By doing so, he pinpoints a weakness of documentary theory as it has been commonly applied to material outside Genesis 1—9. Nevertheless, Whybray does not adequately account for the above discussed strong cumulative evidence—doublets and contradictions of fact combined with linguistic and stylistic observations—that establishes documentary strands in Genesis 1—9.

27. Gen. 2:4a will be discussed later.

28. See in particular M. Gutiérrez, "'L'homme créé à l'image de Dieu' dans l'ensemble littéraire et canonique Genèse, chapitres 1—11" (Ph.D. diss., University of Strasbourg, 1993), 103–10, 270–82. Cf. W. Shea, "The Unity of the Creation Account," *Origins* 5 (1978): 17–20; J. B. Doukhan, *The Genesis Creation Story: Its Literary Structure* (Berrien Springs, Mich.: Andrews University Press, 1982), 35–80; R. S. Hess, "Genesis 1—2 in its Literary Context," *TynBul* 41 (1990): 151–53; J. F. A. Sawyer, "The image of God, the wisdom of serpents, and the knowledge of good and evil," in *A Walk in the Garden* (ed. P. Morris and D. Sawyer; JSOTSup 136; Sheffield: JSOT, 1992), 64–73. Also cf. Miscall, "Garden of Eden," 1–9, a synchronic study that stresses the differences between Genesis 1 and 2.

Chart 4-3: Correspondences: Genesis 1:26–31 and 2:4b–25

[brackets indicate items in a different order]

Genesis 1:26–31	Genesis 2:4b–25
[(27) And God created humankind in God's image]	(8a) And God *formed* humanity *from the dust of the ground*
[(29–30) Divine gift of every "plant yielding seed *and* every tree with seed in its fruit" (NRSV) as food to humans, while giving every "green plant" to animals]	(8b–15) Planting of garden and placement of the human in it "to work and protect it"
	(16–17) Divine gift of fruit of (all but one of the) trees for food
(26) Divine monologue: "Let us *make* humanity in our image in accordance with our likeness, so that they may rule" fish, birds, animals, etc.	(18) Divine monologue: "It is *not good* that the man should be alone; I will make him a helper corresponding to him"
[(24–25) Divine call for the earth to bring forth animals, followed by divine creation of them]	(19aα) Divine formation of animals out of the earth
	(19aβ–20a) God brings animals to human for human to name (implied domination)
	(20b) Lack of helper *corresponding to* the man
(27) Divine *creation* of humanity, male and female, in God's image	(21–22) Divine creation of woman [result: sexually differentiated humanity]
(28) Divine blessing: fertility and rule	
(31a) Divine pronouncement that all was *very* good	(23) Male's celebration of God's success in creating a truly corresponding helper

---

In this case, however, there is an important difference from the flood account. Whereas the doublets of the flood account were more jarring because they were put right beside each other, in this case the complete parallel accounts of creation have been put one after the other. As a result, the creation and punishment story in Gen. 2:4b–3:24 serves well as an elaboration and specification of Gen. 1:1–2:3. In particular, the description of the creation of and provision for humanity in Gen. 1:26–30 briefly states the idea that God created both genders of humanity in God's image, while Gen. 2:4b–25 describes how God did so.[29]

---

29. Here and elsewhere where the meaning is not compromised, I use the term *God* as a para-pronoun. Nevertheless, in places where such usage would complicate the flow of my discussion, I have adopted the masculine pronoun *he* for God, a usage that reflects the androcentrism of the texts under discussion here, not my theological intentions.

At the same time, however, these parallels are accompanied by some conspicuous divergences in conceptual profile. Gen. 1:1–2:3 depicts an omnipotent God creating a godlike humanity. In contrast, Gen. 2:4b–3:24 depicts a God who can both fail (Gen. 2:19–20) and succeed (Gen. 2:21–23). Humanity is not godlike but is created out of earth and punished for acts leading to humanity's being like God (Gen. 3:1–24). Moreover, the structures and poetics of the creation narratives are distinctively different. Gen. 1:1–2:3 is dominated by a seven-day, regimented scheme, while Gen. 2:4b–3:24 has no such patterns. Most importantly, the creation order is different. In Genesis 1 humans, both male and female, are created after animals, while in Gen. 2:4b–24 the man is created first,[30] then animals, and finally woman as the climax of creation. In summary, not only are the humans and animals created twice in Genesis 1—3, but they are created in different ways. Together this combination of parallel character and contrasting profile point to the different origins of materials in Gen. 1:1–2:3 and 2:4b–3:24, however elegantly they have now been combined.

As briefly indicated above, each of these texts—Gen. 1:1–2:3 and Gen. 2:4b–3:24—show multiple and specific links with a corresponding strand of the flood account. Genesis 2:4b–3:24 provides the wordplay on *'ādām/* *'ădāmâh* ("earthling"/"earth") that is the background for the prominent use of both of these terms throughout the non-P strand of the flood account. In addition, the non-P flood strand implicitly refers to YHWH's "forming" (*yṣr*) humanity in Gen. 2:4b–3:24 when it describes YHWH's perception that humanity's "formation" (*yēṣer*) is only evil (6:5). Now the woman's pain (*'iṣṣābôn*) in childbirth (Gen. 3:16) finds its counterpart in YHWH's pain (root *ʿṣb*, HtD stem) at having created humanity (Gen. 6:6). In these and other ways, Gen. 2:4b–3:24 is the indispensable prelude to the non-P strand of the flood that was isolated above.[31]

So also, Gen. 1:1–2:3 and the P-strand of the flood account are similar to and specifically coordinated with each other. The P strand of the flood account begins with a reversal of the conclusion of creation in Genesis 1. Whereas the creation in Genesis 1 ends with God "seeing" that all God had made was "very good" (Gen. 1:31), now God "sees" that "the earth was corrupt" (Gen. 6:12). In addition, both Gen. 1:1–2:3 and the P strand of the flood account describe a divine wind at the outset of creation/recreation (Gen. 1:2//8:1); both focus on the heavens as a bulwark against the primeval

<hr />

30. Cf. P. Trible, *God and the Rhetoric of Sexuality* (OBT; Philadelphia: Fortress, 1978), 80, 98–99. For critique of her position, see S. Lanser, "Feminist Criticism in the Garden: Inferring Genesis 2—3," *Semeia* 41 (1988): 70–72; Clines, "What Does Eve Do to Help?" in *What Does Eve Do to Help?* 25–41; and the present author's "Politics of Textual Subversion," 585n23.
31. Other, more minor similarities linking Gen. 2:4b–3:24 and the non-P strand of the flood account include: use of *hyh bāʾāreṣ* ("there was in the land") to assert existence/non-existence of something (Gen. 2:5//6:4), focus on the presence and lack of rain (2:5//7:4 [cf.7:12; 8:2b]), and reference to the "breath of YHWH" in humanity (Gen. 2:7//6:3).

ocean (Gen. 1:6–8//7:11; 8:2); both feature similar systematic descriptions of animals with numerous specific parallels in terminology;[32] both describe humans as made in the image of God (Gen. 1:26–27; 9:6); both have a blessing on humans and animals to "be fruitful and multiply" (Gen. 1:28//8:17; 9:1, 7); both specifically state and develop the idea that humans were destined to dominate animals (Gen. 1:26–8; 9:2–3); both have a particular focus on provision of food for animals and humans (Gen. 1:29–30; 6:21; 9:2–3); and God's creation requirement that humans and animals both eat just plants for food (Gen. 1:29–30) is specifically reversed after the flood in the P-strand (Gen. 9:2–3). In summary, Gen. 1:1–2:3 is inextricably connected to the P flood-strand that was isolated above.

These multiple indicators are firm grounds for seeing two parallel strands spanning creation and flood here, 2:4b–3:24 in the non-P strand and 1:1–2:3 in the P strand. If we were merely to extend the model discerned in the flood account, we could suppose that Gen. 1:1–2:3, like the P strand in the Flood, was (1) dependent on its non-P parallel and yet (2) composed to stand separately from it. Nevertheless, this hypothesis requires testing on Genesis 1—3 itself.

To start with, these two stories are complete wholes, neither showing signs of having been composed to supplement the other. Whereas an author/ redactor extending a text in one direction or another can anticipate and soften conceptual clashes with the material he is supplementing, these two creation stories have the range of uncoordinated doublets and conceptual clashes that marks narratives originally composed to stand separate from one another. Genesis 2:4b–3:24 seems to have been harmonized with its P counterpart at only a few minor points, and indeed in much the same way as the non-P flood strand was harmonized. Just as a redactor at certain points in the flood story harmonized non-P lists of animals with P lists using secondary additions (Gen 6:7aβb; 7:3a, 8–9), similar sorts of modifications seem to have occurred in the non-P creation account (Gen 2:19a*, 20a*).[33]

Furthermore, there seems to be some kind of dependence between the two stories. They begin with similar words: "when God first made heaven and earth" (Gen 1:1)//"when YHWH God made earth and heaven" (Gen.

---

32. The descriptions of animals in Gen. 1:25; 6:20; and 7:14 all include the expression "according to their kinds" (*lĕmînâh/lĕmînēhû*). In addition, catalogs in Gen. 1:1–2:3 and the P strand of the flood account include "swarming things" (*šrṣ/šereṣ;* Gen. 1:20–21; 7:21; 8:17; 9:7) and "creeping things" (*rmś/remeś;* Gen. 1:21, 24–26, 28, 30; 6:20; 7:14, 21; 8:17, 19; 9:2, 3). Often the catalogs are three-part, whether covering wild and domesticated animals along with creeping things (Gen. 1:24–25; 7:14, 21) or animals, birds, and creeping things (Gen 1:30; 6:20; 8:17).
33. For treatment of these elements in Genesis 2—3, see P. Weimar, *Untersuchungen zur Redaktionsgeschichte des Pentateuch* (BZAW 146; Berlin/New York: W. de Gruyter, 1977), 118–19; C. Dohmen, *Schöpfung und Tod: Die Entfaltung theologischer und anthropologischer Konzeptionen in Gen 2/3* (SBS 17; Stuttgart: Verlag Katholisches Bibelwerk, 1988), 79–81.

2:4b).[34] They follow a remarkably parallel structure (diagrammed above). And a key part of the P creation narrative (Gen. 1:26–28) links in contrastive ways with the non-P depiction of the problem of divine-human boundaries in Genesis 3.[35] (See chart 4-4.)

Chart 4-4: Contrasts between the P and Non-P Creation Stories

Non-P Narrative	P-Strand Narrative
Human attempts to be "like God" are depicted as problematic (3:5, 22).	Humans are described as created in God's image and likeness (1:26–27).
The immediate result of these human attempts is bodily shame (3:7, 10).	The human likeness to God is repeatedly asserted using terms referring to material likeness (1:26 [twice], 27 [twice]), thus implying that the human body is the very sign of human godlike authority over creation.[36]
The ultimate result of these attempts is a divine curse (3:14–19) and expulsion from the garden (3:22–24).	The sequel to the creation of humans in God's likeness is a divine blessing (1:28).
God's speech to the divine council concludes the narrative with a deliberation leading to separation of the divine and human realms (3:22).	God's speech to the divine council initiates the establishment of a strong link between the divine and human realms: "let us make humanity in our image . . . so that they may rule" (1:26).

---

34. The translation assumed here renders Gen. 1:1 as a temporal clause leading to Gen. 1:2 as the main clause. For arguments supporting this approach to Gen. 1:1–2, see W. Gross, "Syntaktische Erscheinungen am Anfang althebräischer Erzählungen: Hintergrund und Vordergrund," in *The Congress Volume: Vienna, 1980* (VTSup 32; Leiden: E. J. Brill, 1981), 142–45. W. H. Schmidt, *Die Schöpfungsgeschichte der Priesterschrift* (3d ed.; WMANT 17; Neukirchen-Vluyn: Neukirchener Verlag, 1973), 196, proposes that 2:4b was formed in light of 1:1 to serve as a transition from Genesis 1 to Genesis 2—3. Certainly one verse seems to have been formed in light of the other. Nevertheless, Schmidt's hypothesis would not explain why such a transition does not more closely match the text with which it links. Whereas Gen. 1:1 talks of the "creation" of "heaven and earth," Gen. 2:4b speaks of the "making" of "earth and heaven." If 2:4b had been designed to resume 1:1 in a single narrative line, it probably would have been closer in terminology and order. As it is, Gen. 2:4b appears to have been the model for 1:1, and 1:1 in turn was originally meant to stand separate from the verse on which it was modelled, as a distinctively different beginning to a P primeval history.
35. Cf. P. D. Miller, *Genesis 1—11: Studies in Structure and Theme* (JSOTSup 8; Sheffield, England: JSOT, 1978), 21; Gutiérrez, "L'homme," 103–4, 116, 270–74, both of whom focus on the function of the corresponding speeches to the divine council (Gen. 1:26; 3:22) in the final form of the text.
36. The issues surrounding this section of Genesis 1 defy any effort to confine the necessary citations in a single note. The understanding of this verse presupposed here is effectively presented in W. Gross, "Die Gottebenbildlichkeit des Menschen im Kontext der Priesterschrift," *TQ* 161 (1981): 244–64; idem, "Die Gottebenbildlichkeit des Menschen nach Gen 1,26.27 in der Diskussion des letzten Jahrzehnts," in *Lebendige Überlieferung - Prozesse der Annäherung und*

To be sure, it was easier to suppose textual dependence in the flood account where the P and non-P strands were even more closely parallel to each other. Nevertheless, the points of contact are so close and wide-ranging that it is difficult to suppose mere dependence on a common tradition. Notably, the relative lack of exact parallels in this case may have been a factor leading the redactor to put these stories side by side rather than interweaving them as in the flood account. As Moore observed in Tatian's interweaving of the canonical Gospels, Tatian tended to densely interweave parallel Gospel stories, but left nonparallel stories, such as those from John, largely intact.[37]

So far I have not yet discussed which narrative shows signs of being dependent on the other. At this point, the picture is less clear than in the case of the flood narrative. Recent studies have argued the case both ways.[38] One fact, however, strongly suggests that Gen. 1:1–2:3 is dependent on 2:4b–3:24, rather than the other way around. Although the P strand parallels and opposes the non-P creation and crime story as a whole, the non-P story completely ignores major sections of the P-strand creation account (Gen. 1:1–23; 2:1–3). If the non-P strand were dependent on the P strand, it would be difficult to explain why it lacks any discernible relationship—pro or con—to the chronological and other ideological systems dominating Genesis 1. On the other hand, it is easy to see how the more broadly focused P-strand creation account might have appropriated certain elements from the non-P, human-focused account into its overall system. Especially when considered alongside a similar contrast in scope in the flood account, it appears that the P creation account was composed in response to the non-P account, not the other way around.

This suggests the following picture. The formation process of this text started with the writing of the non-P creation account, a depiction of the negative consequences of human movement toward godlikeness (Gen. 2:4b–3:24).[39] Next, the P creation account was written (Gen. 1:1–2:3). This account's description of the creation of humanity contradicts the

---

Auslegung: Festschrift für Hermann-Josef Vogt zum 60. Geburtstag (ed. N. el-Khoury, H. Crouzel, and R. Reinhardt; Beirut: Friedrich-Rückert Verlag; Ostfildern: Schwaben-Verlag, 1992), 130–31; and B. Janowski, "Herrschaft über die Tiere: Gen 1,26–28 und die Semantik von רדה," in *Biblische Theologie und gesellschaftlicher Wandel: Für Norbert Lohfink, S.J.* (ed. G. Braulik, W. Groß, and S. McEvenue; Freiburg/Basel/Vienna: Herder, 1993), 183–98.
37. Moore, "Tatian's *Diatessaron*," 203–5 (reprint, 245–47).
38. For arguments for dependence of the P account on non-P, see P. Humbert, *Études sur le récit du paradis et de la chute dans la Genèse* (Memoires de l'Univ. de Neuchâtel, 14; Neuchâtel: Secrétariat de l'Université, 1940), 198–203; S. Mowinckel, *Erwägungen zur Pentateuch Quellenfrage* (Oslo: Universitetsforlaget, 1964), 27–28; and particularly Gutiérrez, " 'L'homme," 225–44. L. Brisman, *The Voice of Jacob*, 1–8, assumes the opposite (xiv-xvi), and Blenkinsopp, *The Pentateuch*, 64–67, argues for this position.
39. Blenkinsopp, *The Pentateuch*, 64–67, argues against the theory that Gen. 2:4b–3:24 is a tenth-century precursor to the account in Gen. 1:1–2:3. His arguments, however, do not address the issue of relative dating of Gen. 2:4b–3:24 vis-à-vis 1:1–2:3. Instead, he uses a series of

negative claims of its non-P precursor. Only later did the P-strand creation account come to be placed before the non-P narrative it corrected.
Now the non-P narrative (Gen. 2:4b–3:24) is no longer replaced but serves
as a partial renarration of and corrective sequel to the P-strand creation
account.

Genealogies of Adam's Descendants

We turn next to the texts (compared in Chart 4-5) that bridge Creation
and Flood, Genesis 4 and 5. Once again, one does not need criteria derived
from elsewhere to discern that these texts were not composed by the same

---

Chart 4-5: Comparison of Genealogical Sections in Genesis 4 and 5

Chapter 4 (with NRSV English equivalents in parentheses)	Chapter 5 (with NRSV English equivalents in parentheses)
'ādām ("Adam" 4:1–16, 25)	'ādām ("Adam" 5:1–5)
qayin ("Cain" 4:17)	šēt ("Seth" 5:6–8)
ḥănôk ("Enoch" 4:18aα)	'ĕnôš ("Enosh" 5:9–11)
'irād ("Irad" 4:18aβ)	qênān ("Kenan" 5:12–14)
mĕḥûyā'ēl ("Mehujael" 4:18bα)	mahălal'ēl ("Mahalalel" 5:15–17)
mĕtûšā'ēl ("Methushael" 4:18bβ)	yered ("Yared" 5:18–20)
lemek ("Lamech" 4:19–24)	ḥănôk ("Enoch" 5:21–24)
šēt ("Seth" 4:25)	mĕtûšelaḥ ("Methuselah" 5:25–27)
'ĕnôš ("Enosh" 4:26)	lemek ("Lamech" 5:28–31)

---

author. First, as has long been recognized, these two chapters cover a similar
list of names twice, each time in a different sequence. Second, these two chapters diverge significantly in genealogical form. Genesis 4 generally just describes a man's "fathering" of his son (Hebrew G-stem of the verb yld), diverging only slightly from this format at crucial transitions at the end or
beginning of genealogical lines (Gen. 4:1–2, 17–18a, and 25–26).[40] In contrast, chapter 5 carefully follows a more elaborate format now using the H-
stem of the verb yld for "father", rather than the G-stem of yld as in Genesis
4. See, for example, the note regarding Seth's age when he fathered his son
(Gen. 5:6a), the description of his fathering his son (5:6b), the note regard-

---

terminological arguments and arguments from silence (along with a link from Gen. 2:4b–3:24
to his late-dated succession narrative) to argue for a late absolute dating of Gen. 2:4b–3:24.
These arguments could only establish Gen. 2:4b–3:24 as an extension of 1:1–2:3 if Gen. 1:1–2:3
were dated earlier, a thesis Blenkinsopp does not take up.

40. Even at these points, the chapter 4 genealogy has an expanded version of the overall genealogical form (4:1–2, 17, 25). In the latter two of these expanded cases (Gen. 4:17, 25), the
genealogy continues with a passive variation of the same formula (4:18a, 26).

ing the numbers of years Seth lived after fathering his first son (5:7a), the description of his fathering other children (5:7b), and final notices regarding his total age (5:8a) and death (5:8b). In this way Genesis 5 progresses through the above list of names so parallel to that in Genesis 4. Such parallel and yet distinctive coverage of similar sets of names is difficult to explain by viewing one genealogy as an extension or revision of the other. Instead, they appear to be parallel versions.

More particularly, these two genealogies appear to be parallel P and non-P bridges between the parallel P and non-P creation and flood accounts. The Genesis 4 genealogy continues the story from Genesis 3, shares an etiological focus on linking elements of its narrative with the contemporary lives of its audience (see the "Kenites" in Gen 4:11, 15–16, and similar etiological material in Gen. 2:23–24; 3:14–19), and concludes like Genesis 3 and the non-P flood narrative with a short poem (Gen. 4:23–24; see Gen. 3:14–19 and 8:22). More important, the story of Cain and Abel in Genesis 4 almost exactly follows the contours of the story of Adam and Eve in Genesis 3. Both include a divine prohibition/warning (Gen. 2:17; 4:7), misdeed (3:1–6; 4:8), divine interrogations of humans (Gen. 3:8–13; 4:9–10), punishment involving alienation from the ground (3:17–19; 4:11–12), softening of condition (3:21; 4:13–15), and final expulsion of the human eastward (Gen. 3:24; 4:16).[41] The main difference is that the dynamics played out with husband

41. On these parallels, see particularly M. Fishbane, *Text and Texture: Close Readings of Selected Biblical Texts* (New York: Schocken Books, 1979), 26–27; A. J. Hauser, "Linguistic and Thematic Links between Genesis 4:1–16 and Genesis 2—3," *JETS* 23 (1980): 297–305; Gutiérrez, "L'homme," 216–17; and D. Steinmetz, "Vineyard, Farm and Garden: The Drunkenness of Noah in the Context of Primeval History," *JBL* 113 (1994):197–207. These kinds of similarities led earlier scholars, such as Wellhausen (*Composition*, 8–10) to suppose that Gen. 4:3–16 is a late copy of the story in Genesis 3. There is little to indicate, however, that Genesis 4 is from a decisively later stage than Genesis 3, and the two stories balance each other well as a comprehensive view of the breakdown of human relationships: male-female, sibling-sibling. Therefore, this approach has been rightfully rejected by recent scholarship (see C. Westermann, *Genesis 1—11* [BKAT I/1; Neukirchen-Vluyn: Neukirchener Verlag, 1974], 389–90. (Eng. trans., *Genesis 1—11* [trans. J. J. Scullion; Minneapolis: Augsburg, 1984], 285–86.)
That having been said, Genesis 4 itself seems to have undergone its own tradition history. First, there is a good chance that the latter part of the genealogy in Genesis 4 (Gen. 4:25–26) was authored after the first portion (Gen. 4:1–2, 17–24). Scholars differ on whether this took place when the P and non-P strands were linked with each other (example: P. Davies, "Sons of Cain," in *A Word in Season: Essays in Honour of William McKane* [JSOTSup 42; Sheffield: JSOT, 1986], 40–42), or in the midst of the history of the non-P traditions themselves (for example, Gunkel, *Genesis*, 54–55; J. Skinner, *A Critical and Exegetical Commentary on Genesis* [2d ed.; ICC; Edinburgh: T & T Clark, 1930], 99–100; Levin, *Der Jahwist*, 99). Second, much of the genealogical material in Gen. 4:1–24 was probably not an original part of the non-P strand. The primary focus of this material is on locating the origins of various present institutions and groups, with no apparent knowledge of the following flood narrative. These indicators suggest that this genealogy existed before its use as bridge from creation to flood, and was only later adapted for this purpose by the author of the broader non-P strand. Nevertheless, the genealogy seems to have been adapted by the non-P author as a bridge from Creation to Flood. The Cain and Abel story was probably composed as part of this adaptation. In its present form, this story is dependent on and inextricably linked to the genealogical framework in which it is set (Gen. 4:1–2, 17–26).

and wife in Genesis 3 are now being played out with two brothers in Genesis 4. In summary, Genesis 4 has enough specific links with the non-P material in the Flood and particularly Genesis 2—3 to establish securely its role in a non-P strand extending from Creation to Flood.

With the exception of a probable insertion from the non-P strand in 5:29,[42] Genesis 5 corresponds in several ways with the above discussed P creation and flood stories. It would have served well as a genealogical bridge between them. Not only does it use the same divine designation, "God," but it specifically refers to the P creation narrative:

(1) This is the scroll of the descendants[43] of Adam. When God created humanity, in God's image God created them. (2) Male and female God created them, and God blessed them and called them 'humanity' at the time of their creation.

42. This verse follows the naming formula found in the genealogy of Genesis 4, not Genesis 5. Moreover, it uses the divine designation YHWH, rather than the term *Elohim*, which is more common throughout the rest of the chapter (5:1 [twice], 22, 24). Genesis 5:29 is connected to the non-P strand by that divine designation along with specific terminological resemblances with Gen. 3:16–19; 6:5–8; and 8:21–22. For thorough discussion of this verse, see in particular, H. N. Wallace, "The Toledot of Adam," in *Studies in the Pentateuch* (ed. J. A. Emerton; VTSup 41; Leiden: Brill, 1990), 24–29. Part of Gen. 5:28 has also often been seen as part of this insertion, but treatments have varied. For the purposes of this discussion, assignment of this or another part of Gen. 5:28 to the non-P strand is of little import.

43. The Hebrew term translated as "descendants" here, *tôlĕdōt*, is problematic. The noun derives from the root *yld*, "to have a child," and the vast majority of occurrences of the noun *tôlĕdōt* refer to the product of this act: "descendants" or "genealogical series." Because these headings in Genesis consistently introduce sections that focus on the descendants of the figure mentioned, I translate "toledot" as "descendants." For more substantial justification of this translation, see Skinner, *Genesis*, 39–40, and more recently, F. Breukelman's excellent discussion in "Das Buch Genesis als das Buch der תולדות Adams, des Menschen—eine Analyse der Komposition des Buches," in *Störenfriedels Zeddelkasten: Geschenkpapiere zum 60. Geburtstag von Friedrich-Wilhelm Marquardt* (ed. Ute Gniewoss, et al.; Berlin: Alektor, 1991), 75–85.

Primarily on the basis of the headings in Genesis, many have posited a special textually oriented meaning here for the noun, such as "family history." (For references and discussion, see "תולדות" KB 3, 1566). This approach was encouraged particularly by an article by J. Scharbert, "Der Sinn der Toledoth-Formel in der Priesterschrift," in *Wort-Gebot-Glaube: Beiträge zur Theologie des Alten Testaments: W. Eichrodt zum 80. Geburtstag* (ed. J. J. Stamm, et al.; ATANT 59; Zurich: Zwingli Verlag, 1970), 50–52. In this article, Scharbert proposes that with the growth of the text, the word *tôlĕdōt* referred less and less to a specific genealogy and more and more to tribal history, *Stammesgeschichte*.

Although such a translation is possible, it is not the best alternative for the cases under discussion. Other labels like Gen 5:1 generally specify not the text type (e.g., history, prophecy, and so forth) but the major subject matter of the material preceding or following the label. For example, such labels are used elsewhere in the Hexateuch to label an itinerary (Num. 33:1[–2]); outlines of tribal areas (including Josh. 13:28, 32; 14:1; 15:12b, 20; 16:8; 18:20, 28; 19:8; 19:51); lists of officials (Exod. 6:14, 19b, 25b; Num 1:44; 4:37, 41, 45); laws (Exod. 21:1; Deut. 1:1); and various subjects of legal instructions (Num. 4:28, 33). Following these examples, we would expect a label like 5:1; 6:9; 10:1; and so forth to specify the focus of the following text (descendants), not its text type (family history). The above citations and others can be found in H. Holzinger, *Einleitung in den Hexateuch* (Freiburg: J.C.B. Mohr, 1893), 350.

This description of creation then initiates the first step in the Genesis 5 genealogy: Adam/humanity (the Hebrew name *Adam* means "humanity") fathers Seth in his "image and likeness" (Gen. 5:3a; cf. 1:26). The reflections of the P creation account could not be clearer. Moreover, there is no trace in this chapter of any knowledge of the non-P materials in Gen. 2:4b–4:26. Instead, Genesis 5 was probably part of a P creation-to-flood strand that originally stood separate from the non-P material. Within this separate context, the note regarding Creation in Gen. 5:1b–2 would have resumed the theme of human creation after several blocks of intervening material in P: the provision of food for humanity (Gen. 1:29–30); God's approval of God's creation work (Gen. 1:31); and God's observance, blessing, and sanctification of the Sabbath (Gen. 2:1–3). In particular, Gen. 5:1–3 links the overall creation of Adam/humanity *in God's likeness* to Adam's more specific passing on of this image to his descendants, and it links God's blessing humanity with Adam's more specific manifestation of this blessing in having a long line of children.[44]

That having been said, it must also be recognized that the rest of Genesis 5 does not have the same intricate links to the P creation and flood stories. The main reason for this lack of connections is probably that the bulk of Genesis 5 most likely was not written by the author of P. Instead, it was actually a preexisting document that the P author adapted to serve as a bridge from Creation to Flood. There are several indicators of the existence of such a document behind Genesis 5.[45]

First, the heading of Genesis 5 appears to label what was an originally independent document: "This is the scroll of the descendants of Adam." Most places in the Bible we have to speculate on the existence of earlier source doc-

---

44. In the present text of Genesis, Gen. 5:1b–2 functions as a resumptive repetition of material from Gen. 1:26–28 after the interruption of non-P material in Gen. 2:4b–3:24. Working from this observation, H. Holzinger (*Genesis* [KHC; Freiburg: J.C.B. Mohr, 1898], 58–59) and now Blum (*Studien*, 280) and Levin, (*Der Jahwist*, 100) have argued that 5:1b–2 was originally written to resume themes from Gen. 1:26–28 after the long interruption of non-P material in Gen. 2:4b–4:26 (but cf. Wallace, "The Toledot of Adam," 19–21).

Although this matches the present function of the text, this proposal runs into several difficulties. First, Gen. 5:1b–2 would not be a conventional example of such resumptive repetition because it picks up not with the end of the Gen. 1:1–2:3 creation account (2:1–3), nor with the end of the six days of creation (1:31), but with the creation and blessing of humanity (Gen. 1:26–28). Second, the link with the P strand in Genesis 1 is present not only in Gen. 5:1b–2. It is also built tightly into the outset of the genealogical framework in Gen. 5:3a. Such an inextricable element in the genealogy looks more like deep P adaptation of adopted materials (on this see below) than the more sparing work of the Rp editor observed up to this point. Third, 5:1b–2 shows no internal signs whatsoever of links with non-P materials with which Rp would also have been working. Instead, its cross-reference points are exclusively within the P strand. Therefore, the present function of 5:1b–2, though analogous to its initial function as a resumptive repetition after 1:29–2:3, appears to be a later development resulting from its present placement in the combined P/non-P composition.

45. Cross, *Canaanite Myth*, 301; Blum, *Vätergeschichte*, 451–52 (especially n.29).

uments, but in this case we actually seem to have the explicit identification of one.[46]

Second, such an originally independent document in Genesis 5 would have a parallel elsewhere in the ancient Near East. As has long been recognized, the focus in Genesis 5 on the generations before the Flood, its linear focus on the offspring of only one member of each generation, and its ten-generation scope all match the famous Sumerian king list. Thus the bulk of Genesis 5 may have once stood separate as an Israelite parallel to this Sumerian tradition.

Third, the existence of a separate source behind Genesis 5 would help explain the subtle divergences of the P strand from the non-P strand at this point. As we have seen in the creation and flood sections, P appears to have depended to some extent on its non-P counterpart. Moreover, this pattern of P dependence on non-P continues in parallel P and non-P genealogical sections that will be discussed later (cf. Gen. 11:10–16 [P] and 10:24–25 [non-P]). Here, however, the P strand diverges from its non-P counterpart in Genesis 4 in slight ways that are not easily explained as the revisions of the P author. The divergences probably result from the fact that P was dependent here on a "scroll of the descendants of Adam," rather than on Genesis 4.

In sum, there is good evidence for the hypothesis that the bulk of Genesis 5, the "scroll of the descendants of Adam," preexisted the P narrative in which it now stands. The P author used this narrative to bridge the creation and flood stories.[47] At points such as Gen. 5:1b–3a, he adapted this genea-

46. Though others have pointed out that the Hebrew word here, *sēper,* need not label a full "book" (see especially, O. Eissfeldt, "Biblos Geneseōs," now in *Kleine Schriften* [vol. 3; ed. R. Sellheim and F. Maass; Tübingen: J.C.B. Mohr, 1966], 464–65), such a term does generally label some kind of independent document. Eerdmans, *Studien,* 4–5; G. von Rad, *Die Priesterschrift im Hexateuch. Literarisch untersucht und theologisch gewertet* (BWANT 65; Stuttgart-Berlin: W. Kohlhammer, 1934), 35; P. Weimar, "Die Toledot Formel in der priesterschriftlichen Geschichtsdarstellung," *BZ* 18 (1974): 44, 85.

47. Beginning already with Vater, many have supposed that this toledot book continued after Genesis 5 and included texts such as Gen. 11:10–26 (J. S. Vater, *Commentar über den Pentateuch* [vol. 1; Halle: Waisenhaus Buchhandlung, 1802], 48, 172–73). See also Eerdmans, *Studien,* 4–5; Von Rad, *Priesterschrift,* 33–40; Noth, *Pentateuch,* 9–10 (E.T., 10–11); Weimar, "Toledot," 83, 84–87, 92; and Cross, *Canaanite Myth,* 301. This latter genealogy in 11:10–26 is closely linked to Genesis 5 by several features: its similar linear form, similar ending with three sons, and similar genealogical scheme—age notice, birth of first son (using the H-stem of *yld*), additional years, and notice of additional births (again using the H-stem of *yld*). Such similarities were enough to convince Cross, Weimar, and others listed above that both 5:1–32* and 11:10–26 came from the same "toledot book." The Gen. 11:10–32 genealogy, however, diverges significantly from 5:1–32 in lacking death notices and indications of total age. Moreover, it is not obvious how these two genealogies, Genesis 5 and 11:10–26, would have fit together into a coherent document. Instead, those who argue for them once being connected must subtract elements between them, usually the rubric in 11:10. Finally, whereas Gen. 5:1–32 diverges significantly from the non-P strand (thus indicating probable dependence on another source), the 11:10–32 genealogy shows no such distinctiveness vis-à-vis other materials, such as 10:8–19, 21, 25–30. In summary, the evidence suggests that Gen. 11:10–26 was not part of the genealogical book used by P. Instead, the genealogical material used by P was Gen. 5:1a, 3–28, 30–32, and this then was probably used by P as a model for the creation of a largely corresponding genealogy from Shem to Noah (Gen. 11:10–26).

logical book by adding creation themes specific to the P creation story of Gen. 1:1–2:3. Otherwise, however, the source scroll used by P appears to have been left relatively untouched.

The Labels in Genesis 2:4a and 6:9aα

The heading in Gen. 6:9–10 shares the profile of the P-strand genealogical material of Genesis 5*. It is linked to the overall P strand through numerous indicators: the plural reference to "descendants" (6:9; cf. 9:12), full listing of Noah's sons (5:32; cf. 7:13), form of the verb for "father" (H-stem of *yld;* Gen 6:10; cf. Genesis 5), and particular resemblances to parts of Genesis 5 (5:1a, 22, 24), along with shared use of the divine designation "God" rather than the "YHWH" typical of the non-P materials.

Such links suggest that Gen. 6:9–10 is an extension of the structure originally found in the "scroll of the descendants of Adam" used by P. This does not mean that the "scroll of the descendants of Adam" used by P in Genesis 5 also included the flood narrative.[48] Instead, the Priestly author appears to have taken a pattern found in his Genesis 5 "scroll of the descendants of Adam" and extended it to encompass flood narrative materials that were not originally in it. The dating of the flood to the six hundreth year of Noah's life (Gen. 7:6) then represents the P counterpart to the careful notes throughout Genesis 5 of the age of the patriarch when he fathered his heir. Later, after the Flood, we see careful matching of Genesis 5 in the age and death notices for Noah that follow later (Gen. 9:28–29). In this way, the P material regarding Noah is structured by a pattern originating in the Genesis 5 material used by P.

This extension of the structure of Genesis 5 to encompass the flood materials introduced a new construal of their significance. Whereas the flood story adapted by P actually focuses more on Noah than on his sons, Gen. 6:9aα now labels the following section as if it focused on the post-flood generation, his descendants: "These are the descendants of Noah." Almost as if to emphasize the importance of these descendants vis-à-vis the following Noah-focused narrative, the material immediately after the label describes Noah and then *re*introduces Noah's sons:

> (5:32) And when Noah was five hundred years old, Noah became the father of Shem, Ham, and Yaphet.
> (6:9) These are the descendants of Noah. Noah was righteous, blameless in his generation. Noah walked with God.
> (6:10) And Noah became the father of three sons: Shem, Ham, and Yaphet.

---

48. The Genesis 5 material follows a strict genealogical pattern allowing for minor digressions (e.g., 5:22, 24), but nothing anticipating the kind of major narrative focus found in the flood narrative. Therefore, few have supposed that a genealogical book beginning in Genesis 5 originally encompassed the flood narrative. For more discussion of the original contours of this scroll, see n.47 in this chapter.

Although such repetition may look like a doublet, such reintroduction of relevant descendants is typical of more than one genealogical section leading up to Israel (cf. Gen. 11:27//26). In this case the repetition in 6:10 reinforces the introductory focus on descendants (cf. Gen. 6:9), even though the following flood story actually focuses more on Noah himself.[49]

This then represents the first step in a Priestly extension of the Genesis 5 structure to encompass a whole series of narratives leading up to the "descendants" of Israel. The heading regarding the "scroll of the descendants of Adam" in 5:1 probably once introduced just the genealogy of preflood generations that immediately followed it (Genesis 5*). In P, however, this heading now also introduces an entire set of genealogically focused narratives, beginning with the Flood. From this point forward we will continue to see such headings regarding the "descendants" of a given figure (Gen. 6:9; 10:1; 11:10, 27; 25:12, 19; 36:1, 9; 37:2), and the sections regarding them will continue to be structured in a way resembling the pattern in Genesis 5.[50] Within this expanded P context, the heading in 5:1 implies that all the following genealogical material up to the descent into Egypt is part of a scroll of the descendants of Adam. In summary, what was originally an independent genealogy of the generations before the flood (Genesis 5*) was expanded by P into a new genealogical section, one encompassing the Flood and the eventual "fathering" of successive generations culminating in Israel (Gen. 5:1–50:26).

So what about Gen. 2:4a, a genealogical label that *precedes* this expanded P "scroll of the descendants of Adam" (Gen. 5:1)? A number of recent studies have established that this verse serves in the present text to bridge the P creation account of Gen. 1:1–2:3 and the non-P creation materials of Gen. 2:4b–4:26.[51] As such, it introduces Gen. 2:4b–4:26 as concerning the "descendants of heaven and earth." Indeed, there is nothing to suggest that the verse ever served another function. Genesis 2:4a appears to have been written from the beginning to bridge, as well as any text could, two quite different sections of different origins (Gen. 1:1–2:3 and 2:4b–3:24). The author of Gen. 2:4b took the "heaven" and especially the active "earth" of the preceding chapter (Gen. 1:11–12, 24) as the functional equivalent of the "parents" of the first humans, and inserted his label before the following narrative—a narrative that described in detail the making of the first human from a mixture of "ground" and divine breath (Gen. 2:4b–7). In this way the redactional label in Gen. 2:4a moves one step back from the beginning of the

---

49. Tengström, *Toledotformel*, 40–43.
50. The relevant sections will be surveyed in the next chapter.
51. Cf. the overview of past and more recent scholarship in T. Stordalen, "Genesis 2,4—Restudying a *locus classicus*," *ZAW* 104 (1992): 163–65. The redactional understanding of this half-verse has been promoted recently, particularly as an outgrowth of Cross's arguments in *Canaanite Myth*, 302.

Priestly scroll of the descendants of Adam (Genesis 5), and creates room for the inclusion of non-P stories regarding the first humans (Gen. 2:4b–4:26) into the genealogical structure of Genesis. In the process, Gen. 2:4a clashes in subtle ways with the P system it is extending. In particular, Gen. 2:4b diverges from P labels like Gen. 6:9 by describing the "descendants" of things, rather than people. Nevertheless, Gen. 2:4a does its job as well as any genealogical bridge between Gen. 1:1–2:3 and 2:4b–3:24 could.

Some have proposed reading Gen. 2:4a as originally a label for the material that precedes it, Gen. 1:1–2:3. Such an approach, however, requires multiple divergences from the translation of such genealogical labels everywhere else in Genesis.[52] In addition, as Blum has particularly stressed, the label in 2:4a would not fit well into an originally independent P-strand context, between Gen. 2:3 and Gen. 5:1:[53]

> (2:3) And God blessed the seventh day and sanctified it, for on it God rested from all the work which God had done in creation.
> (2:4a) These are the generations of heaven and earth when they were created.
> (5:1) This is the scroll of the generations of Adam. When God created humankind, God made humanity in the likeness of God.

Here we have the immediate juxtaposition of two structural labels without any clear coordination of them with each other.

In summary, there is no good reason to see Gen. 2:4a as a highly divergent label of what precedes it. Instead, the unique relationship of this half-verse to its context is best explained by seeing it as a redactional addition, which—from the beginning—served to bridge two narratives that originally stood separate from one another: Gen. 1:1–2:3 and 2:4b–4:26. It serves a similar coordinating function vis-à-vis these P and non-P narratives that the above-discussed Rp additions (Gen. 2:19b*, 20a*; 6:7aβ; 7:3a, 8–9, 23aα*; 8:13a) served vis-à-vis the P and non-P creation and flood strands.

Concluding Reflections

The main point of the discussion so far has been to demonstrate the strength of arguments that can be made for a source approach to Gen.

---

52. The crucial Hebrew word here is *tôlĕdōt*, as in Gen. 5:1: This is the scroll of the "descendants" (*tôlĕdōt*) of Adam. As many have pointed out, the other *tôlĕdōt* labels of Genesis following Gen. 5:1 all focus on the text following them; all focus the audience's attention on the descendants of a given figure who was important in the preceding narrative; and all name the descendants fathered by a given figure (e.g., Adam in Gen. 5:1; see also 6:9; 10:1; 11:10, 27; 25:12, 19; 36:1, 9; 37:2). Given the pattern established in the ten other examples of otherwise identical labels, one must stretch to read Gen. 2:4a as referring backward to the "origins of heaven and earth" (the traditional translation) rather than looking forward to the "descendants produced by heaven and earth" (the more likely translation). On this problem, see Cross, *Canaanite Myth,* 302; Blum, *Vätergeschichte,* 451–52, and Stordalen, "Genesis 2,4," 170–71.
53. *Studien,* 280; see also Cross, *Canaanite Myth,* 302.

1:1–9:17. First, at each point—Creation, genealogy, and Flood—it has been possible to use indicators internal to each pericope to distinguish strata within them. No criteria derived from other analyses were necessary to distinguish the two strands of the flood account, or Gen. 1:1–2:3 from Gen. 2:4b–3:24, or Genesis 4 from Genesis 5*. Second, once these strata were established in each section, *multiple and specific* terminological and conceptual links could be established between the strata of different sections, links going well beyond mere similarity in divine designation. The P strand of the flood account could be connected to Gen. 1:1–2:3 and Genesis 5*, and the non-P strand of the flood account could be connected to Gen. 2:4b–4:26.

In addition, these two strands, at least for the creation-to-flood section, seem to have been originally separate. In the creation, flood, and intervening genealogy texts we have seen the kind of large number of uncoordinated doublets that is characteristic of conflated sources. Indeed, the number of doublets—with distinct profiles—indicate the existence in Gen. 1:1–9:17 of two remarkably complete narratives extending from Creation to Flood. This completeness of the reconstructed parallel narratives provides a confirming argument for the existence of sources here. Moreover, the completeness of the parallel strands further highlights the extent of the doubling that has occurred.[54] There is, however, one conspicuous place where P lacks much of a parallel to its non-P counterpart. Whereas the non-P materials go into some detail regarding the disobedience and violence of preflood humanity (Gen. 3:1–4:24), P lacks any extensive description of preflood sin. P's brief treatment of this topic occurs at the outset of the flood story:

54. Blum has opposed such an approach, proposing the theory that the P author used various priestly traditions—creation materials in Gen. 1:1–31, the Genesis 5 toledot book, and a pre-priestly flood story—to supplement the non-P narrative (Blum, *Studien*, 279–83). Thus P in Genesis 1—11 is not an overall independent source, but a Priestly reworking of non-P traditions —a reworking that also used various Priestly traditions. According to Blum, these traditions had already received a Priestly stamp from being transmitted in Priestly circles, but the P author further shaped them, placed them in relation to the non-P primeval history, and also modified the non-P materials in certain respects to adapt them to the new supplements. This approach, however, does not account as well as a source approach for at least three features of the Genesis primeval history: (1) the Priestly traditions used by the Priestly redactor form such a complete parallel to their non-P counterparts, and (2) these traditions regarding Creation and Flood do not just have the signs of separate traditions transmitted in Priestly circles, but are thoroughly integrated with each other through an intricate system of cross-references; and (3) this system of cross-references—with the exception of a series of minor and clearly secondary modifications of non-P texts regarding animals—is largely absent from the non-P material this P layer is supposed to have been written to redirect and correct. In other words, Blum's model of compositional extension does not explain as well as a model of interwoven source documents the fact that the Priestly profile of cross-linkages in the primeval history is so confined to specifically Priestly material.

The other main alternative has been sketched by Blenkinsopp. He proposes a return to the older model where the non-P materials were seen as later expansions of the P framework. This approach, however, does not account well for the apparent independence of non-P materials in the creation to flood stories. They too are characterized by conspicuous doublets, interrupted conceptual system, and potential readability, the very indicators that establish the probability of a separate P source.

(6:11) Now the earth was corrupt in God's sight, and the earth was filled with violence.

(6:12) And God saw that the earth was corrupt; for all flesh had corrupted its ways upon the earth.

(6:13) And God said to Noah, "I have determined to make an end of all flesh, for the earth is filled with violence because of them." (NRSV)

Cross, Rendtorff, Blum, and others have argued that these references presuppose the existence of the preceding non-P narratives regarding human sin and violence.[55] Nevertheless, this is not the only way P can be understood. On the contrary, P has its own emphases and its own list of things it does not emphasize. In this case, P appears to have downplayed and rejected the extensive non-P presentation of human sin. For P, the decisive word even in the primeval period is not *disintegration* but *reintegration*. Possibly drawing on non-P materials, P briefly notes in Gen. 6:11 that the earth was corrupted by violence, but this note then serves as the briefest prelude to P's primary emphasis: God's reintegrative power of re-creation and blessing.[56] Assertions that an independent P would have *had* to have an extended account of sin are based on the faulty assumption that P must match the outline and emphases of corresponding non-P material. P is its own text. We can not know what it must or must not have included.[57]

Thus, despite recent challenges, the data in Genesis 1—9 is best explained by the theory that the P layer in Gen. 1:1–9:17, though dependent at points on the non-P material, originally stood separate from it. Indeed, at points such as the creation of humans, P appears to have been designed to refute its non-P precursor. The present creation-to-flood stretch in Genesis is thus the result of a remarkable compositional move, one in which an author/redactor artfully combined large chunks of the P narrative with the non-P narrative it was designed in part to replace. This Rp editor appears to have intervened minimally in the material with which he worked (Gen. 2:4a, 19b*, 20a*; 6:7aβ; 7:3a, 8–9, 23aα*; 8:13a), even as he carefully drew on large blocks of the P and non-P sources to form a new whole. His stunningly creative combination of text and countertext left fractures in the present form of the narrative. So far I have focused on such fractures only as clues to the formation of Genesis. Toward the end of the book I will return to them and see how they make any reading of this remarkable composition itself a creative process.

55. Cross, *Canaanite Myth*, 306–7; Rendtorff, "L'histoire biblique des origines (Gen. 1—11)," 89–91; Blum, *Studien*, 280 with n.193.

56. For other reflections on the P treatment of the human problem in context, see N. Lohfink, "Die Ursünden in der priesterlichen Geschichtserzählung," in *Die Zeit Jesu: Festschrift für Heinrich Schlier,* ed. G. Bornkamm and K. Rahner (Freiburg, Basel, Vienna: Herder, 1970), reprinted in N. Lohfink, *Studien zum Pentateuch* [SBAB 4; Stuttgart: Verlag Katholisches Bibelwerk, 1988], 169–89).

57. Lohfink, "Priesterschrift," 199; Zenger, *Gottes Bogen*, 33; K. Koch, "P–kein Redaktor!," 453–55; Emerton, "The Priestly Writer in Genesis," 392–93; Nicholson, "The P Source," 197–98, 200–1; Campbell, "The Priestly Text: Redaction or Source?" 36.

5

P in the Rest
of Genesis (Gen. 9:18–50:26)

The transmission-historical picture of P in Genesis, however, is still not complete. In the last chapter we saw how a source model for P and non-P made sense for Gen. 1:1–9:17. In this model most of the Priestly material emerges as once having been part of an originally separate narrative. This narrative was written at least partly in response to and over against the non-P strand with which it is now combined.

This is not to assume that this picture extends well into the following material. Indeed, the further one moves into Genesis, the weaker the case for parallel, relatively homogeneous sources becomes. Whereas it is possible to find a clear continuation of the Genesis 1—9 P strand in Genesis 11—50 and following, it is much more difficult to find multiple and specific links between the Genesis 1—9 non-P strand and materials in Genesis 12—50. This led Pfeiffer, for example, to propose a mixed model for P, where P is a source in Genesis 1—11 but a redaction in Genesis 12—50.[1] According to this model, the non-P material now in Genesis 1—11 did not enter Genesis until a later point.[2] To be sure, such a model presupposes that the non-P material in Genesis 1–11 has no early connection to the non-P material that follows it, but as we will see later in this book, this idea has something to be said for it.

For now, however, I will not be investigating the transmission history of the non-P material in Gen. 9:18ff. Instead, in the following section I will focus on the proposed Priestly material in the rest of Genesis. Once again, I will be attempting to determine its scope and the nature of its relation to non-P material. In lieu of the more specific discussion of the non-P material later in the book, I will be working here with an undifferentiated concept of the non-P material. As we will see in that later discussion, most indicators suggest the bulk of the non-P material once existed as a block before it was modified through the addition of the Priestly layer. On this basis I will speak here of "non-Priestly parallels" in Genesis 12—50, "non-Priestly" contexts," and so on.

---

1. R. H. Pfeiffer, "A Non-Israelite Source of the Book of Genesis," *ZAW* 48 (1930): 67.
2. Similarly, Blum in his study of the ancestral stories held open the possibility of such a mixed model. Blum, *Vätergeschichte,* 429 (with n.64) and 452n30. Since then he moved to the previously discussed "composition" model for Genesis 1—11 (*Studien,* 278–85).

As in the last chapter, I will keep moving to points in the text where the next clues to the formation of Genesis are thickest. This method means I will be discussing the Priestly texts as groups, using criteria derived from Genesis 1—9 as my initial guide to Priestly texts elsewhere in Genesis. I will start with those Priestly texts most clearly linked to the Genesis 1—9 Priestly creation and flood narratives: the Priestly set of promise texts in Gen. 17:1–27; 26:34–35; 27:46–28:9; 35:9–15; and 48:3–6. Next comes a group of genealogical texts that extend the (Priestly) Genesis 5 genealogical framework to encompass Israel's ancestors in much the same way Priestly texts in Genesis 1—9 use the Genesis 5 framework to encompass the Priestly flood narrative. With these two text groups as our base, I will then build from them to other groups of texts that are often assigned to P: Priestly age, travel, and settlement notices, along with a few other texts that do not easily fit in one of these categories.

This treatment of texts by groups will mean that I must jump around Genesis a bit. Nevertheless, these groupings will help us better see the links between parallel Priestly texts. By the end of the discussion a remarkably coherent Priestly ancestral strand will have begun to emerge, one binding the Priestly promise texts (Genesis 17 and others) into a broader narrative structured by genealogies and the other above-listed types of notices.

The P Promise Texts

Linkage of the P Promise Texts
to Each Other and P in Genesis 1—9

My starting point in this investigation is the four texts in Genesis 12—50 with the most conspicuous links to the P strand in Gen. 1:1–9:17: Gen. 17:1–27; 26:34–35; 27:(46)-28:9; 35:9–15*; and 48:3–6(7). The links to the P primeval history are particularly evident in Genesis 17, the description of God's covenant of circumcision with Abraham. God's promises to "multiply" and "make [Abraham] fruitful" (Gen. 17:2, 6) link with similar P blessings on animals (Gen. 1:22; 8:17) and especially humanity (Gen. 1:28; 9:1, 7). God's "establishment"[3] of an "eternal covenant"[4] with Abraham and marking it with a "sign" (Gen. 17:4–7, 9–11) closely resembles the P description of God's "establishment" of a covenant with Noah and God's "sign" of the bow in the sky (Gen. 9:1–17). Moreover, there are some more

---

3. The expression *hqym běrît* ("establish a covenant") occurs in Gen. 6:18; 9:9, 11, 17 before appearing again in Gen. 17:7, 19, 21 and further in a P context in Exod 6:4. Cf. also the expression *ntn běrît* ("give a covenant") in Gen. 17:2, already seen in Gen. 9:12 (P) and then later in Num. 25:12 (P). Non-P contexts, e.g., Gen. 15:18, use the expression *krt běrît* (literally, "cut a covenant"). Holzinger, *Einleitung*, 341.
4. Gen. 17:7, 13, 19 already seen in Gen. 9:16 (P). Cf. Holzinger, *Einleitung*, 346, for similar expressions in P and non-P contexts.

minor, specific terminological similarities between elements of the Gen. 1:1–9:17 P strand and Genesis 17.[5]

Chart 5-1: Terminological Similarities Between Genesis 17 and Genesis 1:1–9:17		
"you and your seed after you"	Gen. 17:7–10, 19	Gen. 9:9
"generations"	Gen. 17:7, 9, 12	Gen. 6:9; 9:12
"very very much"	Gen. 17:2, 6, 20	Gen. 7:19
"on this very day"	Gen. 17:23, 26	Gen. 7:13
H-stem of *yld* ("father")	Gen. 17:20	Gen. 5:3–32; 6:10

When considered alone, the predominance of these isolated words and phrases in P contexts could well be ascribed to random language usage. Nevertheless, when combined with the broader similarities between the Genesis 17 Abraham covenant and the P creation (Gen. 1:1–2:3) and covenant (Gen. 9:8–17) texts, this cluster of connections to P in Genesis 1—9 indicates a special link between the P strand there and Genesis 17.

The other three texts listed above then link with the primeval history by way of Genesis 17, relating in various ways to the transmission of the Abrahamic covenant to Jacob. In Gen. 28:1–9 Isaac blesses Jacob with the Genesis 17 blessing and sends him off to Padan-Aram. He begins by wishing "El-Shaddai's" blessing for Abraham on Jacob: "be fruitful and multiply" (28:3a, cf. 1:28; 9:1, 7; 17:1–2, 6). Then, just as God promised to make Abraham into a "father" of a "crowd" of nations (Gen. 17:4b-5), so Isaac wishes that Jacob become an "assembly" of nations (28:3b). Finally, in a blessing framed by references to Abraham, Isaac takes up language from Genesis 17 to pass on the land promise to Jacob.[6] (See Chart 5-2.)

Thus, just before Jacob leaves the land, Isaac passes on from Abraham to Jacob the P formulation of the promise of descendants and land. The specific connections of Isaac's wish for Jacob (Gen. 28:3–4) to the Priestly covenant with Abraham (Genesis 17) are unmistakable.

Later, in Gen. 35:9–15, God fulfills Isaac's wish. God gives Jacob the "blessing of Abraham." First, Jacob arrives from Padan-Aram, mentioned in the previous P narrative of his departure (Gen. 35:9, cf. 28:5–7). "El-Shaddai," seen in Genesis 17 and 28:3–5, introduces himself to Jacob (Gen. 35:11). El-Shaddai then confers on Jacob the Abrahamic fertility blessing (Gen. 35:11;

5. For lists of comparable passages see Holzinger, *Einleitung*, 341–43.
6. In addition to the parallels to Gen. 17:8, Isaac's bestowing of the land promise on Jacob resembles preceding P-strand flood texts in using the particle "with you" as an extra element after listing Jacob and his descendants as recipients of this promise. Such usage was already seen in Priestly lists of those accompanying Noah into the ark (Gen. 6:18; 7:7; 8:16, 18) and later those with him in the covenant (Gen. 9:8). It occurs in numerous other P contexts. For references and discussion see Holzinger, *Einleitung*, 341.

Chart 5-2: Comparison of Blessings on Abraham and Jacob	
Gen. 17:8	Gen. 28:4
And I will give	May he give you the blessing of Abraham
you and your seed after you	to you and your seed with you
	to take possession of
the land of your sojourning	the land of your sojourning
	which God gave Abraham

cf. 17:2b, 6a; 28:3). As Isaac wished, El-Shaddai promises to make Jacob an "assembly of nations" (Gen. 35:11a; cf. 28:3). In addition, God adds the promise that "kings" shall come forth from Jacob's loins (Gen. 35:11b). This promise is an extension to Jacob of a similar promise originally given to Abraham in Genesis 17 (17:6b).

Finally, in Gen. 48:3–7, Jacob refers to God's blessing him in Gen. 35:9–15. The multiple and specific connections to the other P promise texts are summarized in Chart 5-3.

Chart 5-3: Comparison of P Promise Texts				
	17:1–8	28:3–5	35:11–12	48:3–4
"El-Shaddai" as God	1bα	3aα1–2	11aα	3a
Initial reference to a "blessing"		3aα3–4	9	3b
"Be fruitful and multiply" (Gen. 1:28)	2b, 6a	3aβ	11aα	4aα
God will make Jacob into an "assembly of nations"	(4b–5)	3b	11aβ	4aβ
giving of land to the patriarch and his "descendants after [him] as an eternal possession"	8	(4b)	(12)	4b

These multiple and specific links to previous P ancestral texts, along with the specific reference of Gen. 48:3–4 to the P epiphany in 35:9–15, are a secure basis for supposing that at least part of Jacob's speech in 48:3–7 is related in a special way to the Priestly strand seen in the primeval history.

Analysis of the Relation
of the P Promise Texts to Their Contexts

So far, this association of the four promise texts with each other and P material in Genesis 1—9 says nothing about their relation to their existing context, whether as an original part of that context, secondary reworking of it, or parts of an originally separate source. All that has been established so far is the following: that Gen. 17:1–27; 28:1–9; 35:9–15; and 48:3–7 appear to be linked in a special way with each other and the P strand texts of Gen. 1:1–9:17.

At this point let us turn to look at how each text is related to its context. We will see that in three of the four cases—Gen. 17:1–27; 28:1–9 and 35:9–15—there are strong indicators that these promise texts were written in relation to their non-P context but were not meant to be part of it. The ambiguities of the fourth case, Gen. 48:3–7, will be discussed below as well. Overall, this entire set of promise texts appears to have been part of the same originally freestanding Priestly strand that was seen in parts of Genesis 1—9.

Genesis 17:1–27: The Abrahamic Covenant

Several indicators of seams mark Genesis 17 as a later addition to its context. First, in Genesis 17 God begins by introducing himself as "El-Shaddai," in contrast to God's introduction of himself as "YHWH" in Gen. 15:7. Such a deviation in divine name could be read as a simple shift from "YHWH" in Genesis 15 to "El-Shaddai" in Genesis 17ff. Nevertheless, as has been long recognized, Genesis 17 is part of a series of "El-Shaddai" Priestly promise texts (Gen. 28:3; 35:11; 48:3) culminating in Exod. 6:2–3. In Exod. 6:2–3 God refers to the time God was known as "El-Shaddai" (Exod. 6:3) and now introduces himself *for the first time* to Moses as "YHWH." Thus, there is a basic difference between Gen. 15:7 and 17:1. Genesis 15:7 presupposes that God had already introduced himself to Abraham as "YHWH." In contrast, Genesis 17 is part of a layer that claims God was only known to the patriarchs by the name "El-Shaddai." God was not known as "YHWH" until the time of Moses. This divergence hardly means we can then assume all texts with YHWH (or El-Shaddai) belong together. Nevertheless, it does establish a *seam* between the El-Shaddai texts on the one hand, and various YHWH texts, including Gen. 15:7, on the other.[7]

In addition, Genesis 17 doubles promises that are given in the texts before it, yet in a way that shows no consciousness that such texts exist in the preceding literary context. For example, in Genesis 17 God gives Abraham a promise of many descendants (Gen. 17:2b, 4–6) and land (Gen. 17:8), without any reference to God's previous promises to give him the same things (15:4–5, 7–18; cf. also 12:2–3, 7; 13:14–17). Within the present form of the text, this doubling (Genesis 15 and 17) frames the story of Hagar with promises on either side of it. Nevertheless, this concentric relationship between chapters 15 and 17 does not take away the jarring character of the uncoordinated repetition of these themes.

We see a similar doubling in God's announcement of a child in the coming year to Abraham and Sarah in Gen. 17:15–21 and again in 18:10–14. In

---

7. On this, see in particular, Koch, "P–kein Redaktor!," 462–66.

both texts God announces to Abraham that Sarah will bear a child in the coming year (Gen. 17:15–16, 21//18:10a); in both Sarah's old age is mentioned (Gen. 17:17//18:11); and then both have similar inner reactions of surprise and experience divine confirmation of the promise in spite of them—Abraham in Gen. 17:18–21 and Sarah in 18:12–14.[8] In this case, Genesis 18, with its emphasis on the drama surrounding the announcement to Abraham, hardly seems to have been originally written to follow Genesis 17, where God has already announced a child to Abraham. The two announcements probably originally stood separate from one another. Only later were they brought together in a whole that balances Abraham's surprise with Sarah's.

Together these examples of doubling, along with the other above indicators, strongly suggest that Genesis 17 was not originally written to be part of its present context. Given its links to the P strand in Genesis 1—9, Genesis 17 is P. Its context, including Genesis 15 and 18:10–14, is non-P.

In addition, the composition of Genesis 17, like the P creation and flood narratives, appears to have been created in direct dependence on its non-P counterparts in Genesis 15 and 18:10–14. The specific linkages in structure and theme go beyond any kind of generic parallel, to indicate a direct relationship.[9] (See Chart 5-4.)

**Chart 5-4: Parallels between Genesis 17
and Non-P Texts**

	Genesis 17	Non-P Texts
Divine self-introduction to Abraham	Gen. 17:1bα	[Gen. 15:7]
Initial general statement of promise	Gen. 17:1–2	Gen. 15:1
Abraham's reaction	Gen. 17:3a	Gen. 15:2–3
Promise of progeny	Gen. 17:3b–6	Gen. 15:4–5
"Covenant" gift of land to Abraham and the promised descendants	Gen. 17:7–8	Gen. 15:7–18
Promise of child to Sarah in the coming year	Gen. 17:15–16	Gen. 18:10
Laughing response	Gen. 17:17a	Gen. 18:12
	(Abraham)	(Sarah)
Note on Sarah's old age	Gen. 17:17b	[Gen. 18:11]
Divine confirmation of promise	Gen. 17:18–21	Gen. 18:13–14

8. This move from Abraham's reaction to Sarah's has led to the synchronic suggestion that Abraham did not tell Sarah about God's earlier promise that she would bear a child. See, for example, S. Jeansonne, *The Women of Genesis: From Sarah to Potiphar's Wife* (Minneapolis: Fortress, 1990), 24. Nevertheless, this interpretation still does not account for the repetition of the divine promise to Abraham (Gen. 17:15–16, 21; 18:10a) nor the need for a note on Sarah's age in Gen. 18:11, after the comment regarding this in Gen. 17:17.
9. McEvenue, *Narrative Style,* 152–55, particularly 152–53; Van Seters, *Abraham,* 282–85; Blum, *Vätergeschichte,* 423–24.

To be sure, such parallels could be read as indicating a dependent relationship in either direction. Indeed, the late character of Genesis 15 has led some, such as T. Römer, to argue that Genesis 15 is dependent on Genesis 17, rather than the other way around.[10] Nevertheless, at least two indicators suggest that Genesis 17 is dependent on Genesis 15. First, it is far easier to posit that Genesis 17 expanded on the framework in Genesis 15 through the covenant of circumcision than to explain why Genesis 15 would have followed the whole promise sequence of Genesis 17 without more directly anticipating or reflecting its major focus on circumcision. Second, Genesis 17 is not only parallel to the relatively late Genesis 15, but also to the clearly early, non-P birth announcement for Isaac in Gen. 18:10–14. In light of this, Römer opts for the following unlikely progression: first there was the birth announcement in Gen. 18:10–14, then Genesis 17 with its second half based on Gen. 18:10–14, and finally Genesis 15, based *only* on the portion of Genesis 17 that is not dependent on Gen. 18:10–14.[11] On the contrary, the alternative is much more straightforward and likely: Genesis 17 was based on both Genesis 15 and 18:10–14, both of which preceded it. Together these two factors, especially considered in light of the analysis of P in Genesis 1—9, suggest that Genesis 17 was modelled on its non-P counterparts, not vice versa.[12]

Overall, this P promise text, Genesis 17, appears to have been both dependent on and originally separate from its non-P context. A redactor/author would not need to replay completely such promises and announcements. Instead, he could have strategically supplemented and/or modified elements of the narratives with which he was working. Here, however, Genesis 17 is a complete replaying, and sometimes an expansion and/or systematization of non-P materials. The divine self-introduction in Gen. 15:7 is moved to its logical position at the outset of the promise narrative (Gen. 17:1). The covenant theme that was linked to the promise of land in Gen. 15:7–18 is moved to encompass the promise of progeny as well (Gen. 17:2, 4–6, cf.

10. T. Römer, "Genesis 15 und Genesis 17: Beobachtungen und Anfragen zu einem Dogma der 'neueren' und 'neuesten' Pentateuchkritik," in *DBAT* 26 (1989/90): 32–47.
11. "Genesis 15 und Genesis 17," 38n48.
12. Römer, "Genesis 15 und Genesis 17," depends on two major bits of data to suggest the post-Priestly character of Genesis 15: (1) the integral relation of the chapter as a whole to post-Priestly elements in Genesis 14 and 15:13–16 and (2) the focus of Genesis 15 on the Pentateuch as a whole versus the narrower focus of Genesis 17 on issues limited to the Abraham story. The question of dating Genesis 14 and 15:13–16 will be dealt with further in the discussion of the non-P material. With regard to the latter issue, Römer fails to take adequate account of the multiple ways in which Genesis 17 was shaped in order to anticipate the P Sinai material. In addition, the basic principle on which Römer depends is unconvincing. As will be evident by the end of the book, Genesis 15 and 17 were *both* part of compositions extending from the ancestors to Moses. If this is true, a greater or lesser focus by one or the other on the broader scope of the composition would say nothing about relative date. Römer's other more detailed arguments for an anticipation of P material in Genesis 15 are inconclusive (cf. his p. 43). For example, his table of parallels on 39–40 does not indicate direction of dependence.

7–8).[13] The promise of land is now expanded and encompassed in Genesis 17 along with El-Shaddai's broader promise to be Abraham's God (Gen. 17:7b, 8b).[14] Finally, whereas Gen. 18:11 had a brief note about both Abraham and Sarah's old age, Genesis 17 leaves aside the biologically irrelevant factor of Abraham's age and focuses on the main issue that makes God's promise difficult to believe: Sarah's age (Gen. 17:17b).

These are among the clues that suggest Genesis 17 was dependent on its non-P parallels and yet originally stood separate from them. The other main indicator is that the above-discussed divergence in conceptuality between Genesis 17 and its non-P surroundings is never grappled with in either Genesis 17 or its context. Not only does Genesis 15 not anticipate in any way the introduction of God as "El-Shaddai" in Gen. 17, but Genesis 17 does not deal in any way with the earlier self-introduction of "YHWH" in Genesis 15:7. Instead, Genesis 17 is part of a broader layer (cf. Exod. 6:2–3) that works as if events like Genesis 15:7 never happened.

Genesis 26:34–5; 27:46–28:9: The Background of Jacob's Departure

There are a number of indicators of seams that distinguish the promise in Gen. 28:1–9, along with associated texts in Gen. 26:34–35 and 27:46, from the context. First, although Esau marries in Gen. 26:34, he appears to be still unmarried in Gen. 27:1–45, and his mother is still in charge of his clothes (Gen. 27:15).[15] Second, Isaac's passing on Abraham's blessing to Jacob in Gen. 28:3–4 and Esau's observing this in Gen. 28:6 do not fully square with Jacob's already having given Abraham's blessing to Jacob in Gen. 27:27–29 (cf. Gen. 27:29//12:3a), and Esau's anguished perception of the blessing at that time (Gen. 27:34). Third, whereas Rebekah urges Jacob to go to "Laban my brother in *Haran*" (Gen. 27:43b), Jacob ends up sending him to Laban in *Padan-Aram* (Gen. 28:2, 5a). Fourth, Jacob then leaves twice: once to Haran (Gen. 28:10), and once to Padan-Aram (28:7b). Fifth, the present version of Genesis is ambiguous on the importance of proper marriages for Jacob. On the one hand, Rebekah's argument that Jacob needs to go away to get married (Gen. 27:46), coming as it does after her urging Jacob to run for his life (Gen. 27:41–45), seems just a pretext to enlist Jacob's support in sending Jacob away from Esau's wrath (cf. Gen. 27:41–45). On the other hand, the notes regarding Esau's improper marriages (Gen. 26:34–35; 28:8–9) attribute an independent importance to this issue, apart

---

13. Van Seters, *Abraham*, 283.
14. As Blum, *Vätergeschichte*, 423–24, points out, the special P expression "establish [God's] covenant" with Abraham in Gen. 17 (17:7, 19, 21; also 6:18; 9:9, 11, 17; Exod. 6:4) seems to be modeled on a non-P reference to God "establishing" God's oath with Abraham (Gen. 26:3).
15. T. Pola, *Die ursprüngliche Priesterschrift* (WMANT 70; Neukirchen-Vluyn: Neukirchener Verlag, 1995), 44n154. Note, here and elsewhere these citations from Pola were from a set of penultimate proofs of his book and may be off by one or two pages.

from any usefulness it might have for rationalizing Jacob's escape. Indeed, it appears that we have two narratives describing the background for Jacob's trip to Laban, one where marriage is not at all an issue (Gen. 27:1–45), and one where it is the only issue (Gen. 27:46–28:5).[16]

This initial identification of seams between 26:34–35; 26:46–28:9, on the one hand,[17] and 27:1–45, on the other, is confirmed through some arguments from the textual continuity that results when Gen. 27:1–45 is removed from between Gen. 26:34–5 and 27:46–28:9. The notes regarding Esau's marriages to Hittite women and how unhappy these women made Isaac and Rebekah (26:34f.) do not fit particularly well between the story of Isaac in 26:1–33 and the story of Jacob's stealing Isaac's blessing in Gen. 27:1–45. These same notes, however, form a perfect introduction to Rebekah's plea (Gen. 27:46) and Isaac's blessing and sending Jacob to find better wives, along with Esau's angry response (Gen. 28:1–9). Moreover, the story of Jacob's stealing Isaac's blessing and being urged by Rebekah to flee (Gen. 27:1–45) connects seamlessly to Jacob's departure for Haran in Gen. 28:10 and the following protection-focused promise story in Gen. 28:11–22. Thus, Gen. 26:34–35 and 27:46–28:9 are not only defined over against their surroundings by the seams noted above, but they connect well together. Moreover, the texts surrounding them also connect well together. It is this combination of indicators of seams and potential continuity that has led many scholars over the last two centuries to suppose that we have here two parallel descriptions of the transfer of Isaac's blessing and the reasons for Jacob's trip to Laban, Gen. 27:1–45, on the one hand, and Gen. 26:34–35; 27:46–28:9, on the other.[18]

16. For a typical description of this contrast in conceptuality see Gunkel, *Genesis*, 386.
17. In the present form of the text, Gen. 27:46 bridges between Gen. 27:1–45 and 28:1–9. Whether it was originally written for this purpose, or whether it was originally a bridge between 26:34–35 and 28:1ff. is debated. Some have argued that 27:46 was not originally connected to 26:34–35 and 28:1ff. because it terms the wives Jacob must avoid "Hittite women," whereas Jacob's following speech terms them "Canaanite women." Moreover, Rebekah's complaint in 27:46 resembles her complaint in the non-P description of Jacob's and Esau's birth (Gen. 25:22), and her portrayal as a strong character seems to have more in common with the non-P depiction of her in Gen. 27:1–45 than the more exclusively male-focused P materials. Cf. Gunkel, *Genesis*, 315; C. Westermann, *Genesis 12—36* (BKAT, I/2; Neukirchen-Vluyn: Neukirchener Verlag, 1977), 545; (E.T., *Genesis 12—36* [trans. J. J. Scullion; Minneapolis: Augsburg, 1985], 447); Levin, *Der Jahwist*, 215. Nevertheless, the resemblance of the Rebekah character in Gen. 27:46 to her depiction in 27:1–45 could easily be explained by patterns of P dependence on non-P traditions that we already have seen elsewhere in Genesis. Moreover, Rebekah's reference to "Hittite women" links up well with the preceding P reference to Esau's Hittite wives' making life difficult for Isaac and Rebekah (26:35), and there is no reason this theme must be extended into Isaac's response to her request. Thus, although Gen. 27:46 now functions as an elegant link between 27:1–45 and 28:1ff, there is no reason to suppose it did not originally connect 26:34–35 to 28:1–9. For similar assignment of 27:46 to P, see Skinner, *Genesis*, 375, and G. von Rad, *Das erste Buch Mose: Genesis* (ATD 2/4; Göttingen: Vandenhoeck & Ruprecht, 1961), 243, (E.T., *Genesis: A Commentary* [rev. ed.; OTL; Philadelphia: Westminster, 1972], 279).
18. Emerton, "The Priestly Writer in Genesis," 398.

Like the P version of the covenant with Abraham in Genesis 17, the P account of the background to Jacob's departure (Gen. 26:34–5; 27:46–28:9) does not appear to have been written for this context. Instead, this pair of texts offers a radically different picture of Jacob and Esau from that in Gen. 27:1–45, a picture that depends to some extent on the presupposition that the events in Gen. 27:1–45 never happened. Genesis 27:1–45 presents Jacob as gaining the blessing through deceit, and presents Esau as the wronged party. In contrast, Gen. 26:34–35; 27:46–28:9 presents Esau as cheating himself out of the blessing by marrying foreign women who upset his parents (26:34–35), and Isaac as freely turning to Jacob to give him the blessing and send him forth to find a better wife (28:1–5). In the P narrative, Jacob immediately obeys (Gen. 28:7), while Esau in resentment goes to Ishmael and marries Ishmael's daughter, another foreign woman (Gen. 28:6, 8–9).

Here again the P account appears to be based on its non-P parallel and designed to replace it. First, the texts share numerous and specific elements indicating probable dependence of one text on the other: Isaac's passing on to Jacob the blessing of Abraham (Gen. 27:29//28:3–4), Esau's negative reaction to this (Gen. 27:41//28:6–9), Jacob's departure (28:10//28:5), and Rebekah's major involvement in the process (27:5–17//27:46).[19] Second, in this case the direction of dependence is clear. Since the P version offers a much more positive picture of Jacob and lacks many of the folklorist elements of its non-P counterpart, it is much more difficult to argue that the non-P version is a revision of the P version than vice versa.[20] Finally, this P picture of a virtuous Jacob and unworthy Esau seems designed to replace, not supplement, the non-P account of Jacob's unsavory acts. Otherwise, the less positive non-P explanation of Jacob's departure (Gen. 27:1–45) would still stand to make its claims about Jacob to the reader, despite the presence of an alternative, Priestly account (Gen. 26:34–35; 27:46–28:9) encompassing it.[21]

Once it was combined with its non-P counterpart, the P picture of events gained a slightly different spin. Now rather than offering the true explanation for Jacob's departure, Isaac's speech in Gen. 28:1–5 is but one more example of his being manipulated by Rebekah into providing for Jacob. By this point Rebekah has already told Jacob to run for his life (Gen. 27:41–45). Now, however, she uses the "Hittite women" as an excuse to convince Isaac to send Jacob off (Gen. 27:46, cf. 26:35). In summary, the material in Gen. 26:34–28:9 encompasses three different pictures of the background to Jacob's departure: a non-P picture of his stealing of Isaac's blessing and run-

---

19. Even the issue of proper marriage in Gen. 26:34–35; 27:46 (P) relates in certain ways to the non-P context of this text. The P author may well have derived this narrative theme from the non-P account of Abraham's provision of a proper wife for Isaac (Genesis 24). By introducing this theme he anticipates the non-P idea that Jacob got married and had children while he was with Laban (Gen. 29:1–30:24; cf. P in 35:22b–26).

20. On the relation of dependence see especially Blum, *Vätergeschichte*, 264–65.

21. Pola, *Ursprüngliche Priesterschrift*, 44, including n.154.

ning from Esau's wrath (Gen. 27:1–45), a P-sanitized picture of Esau dis-
qualifying himself by improper marriages and Jacob being blessed and sent
to marry properly (Gen. 26:34–35; 27:46–28:9), and a *combined* picture in
which Jacob's being sent to marry properly is but a pretext to get him away
from Esau's wrath (Gen. 27:1–28:9). The distinctiveness of this combined
picture of the background for Jacob's departure from the perspective of both
of its component parts is a major confirming indicator that this section was
formed by joining originally separate sources.

Such a hypothesis of interwoven sources is confirmed by several other
indicators. I have already mentioned the way the P (Gen. 26:34–5; 27:
46–28:9) and non-P sections (Gen. 27:1–45; 28:10–22) both form remarkably continuous narratives sharing similar elements. In addition, Isaac's wish
of El-Shaddai's blessing on Jacob in the P section (Gen. 28:3) appears to have
been written from a perspective that does not acknowledge Isaac's prior blessing of Jacob by YHWH (Gen. 27:29).[22] Finally, this hypothesis of interwoven
sources would help explain why the P narrative in Gen. 28:1–9 does not include central elements of the non-P narrative that precedes it. For example,
since Gen. 27:46–28:9 was probably originally written to stand separate from
rather than after Gen. 27:1–45, it does not continue motifs such as Isaac's inability to recognize Jacob (cf. Gen. 27:1, 18–37).

Multiple indicators point to an oppositional relationship between the P
(Gen. 26:34–5; 27:46–28:9) and non-P (Gen. 27:1–45; 28:10) versions of
Jacob's departure, much like the relationship we saw earlier between the P
(Gen. 1:1–2:3) and non-P (Gen. 2:4b–3:24) versions of creation. In this case,
however, the direction of dependence is even clearer. P in Gen. 26:34–5;
26:46–28:9 provides a corrected version of similar events to those narrated
in Gen. 27:1–45; 28:10. Moreover, this P correction depends for much of
its effect on its standing separate from and replacing its non-P counterpart.
Only later, through a remarkable combination of text (Gen. 27:1–45) and
countertext (Gen. 26:34–5; 27:46–28:9) did the P text come to correct its
non-P counterpart in a new way: by following it, rather than substituting for
it. Now, this new whole offers its audience a different set of interpretive possibilities than either of its component parts would have offered separately.

Genesis 35:9–15: The Bethel Epiphany to Jacob

Like the P Abrahamic covenant and account of Jacob's departure, the P
account of Jacob's epiphany at Bethel (Gen. 35:9–15) is marked off in
multiple ways from its non-P context. In particular, Gen. 35:9–15 duplicates
and even contradicts numerous elements of its previous context.[23] Jacob is
renamed "Israel" in 35:10, although he has already been named "Israel"

22. For discussion of the divine designation issue, see above on Genesis 17.
23. For a survey of these similarities and relevant literature see Ska, "Quelques remarques," 116.

in 32:28–9 (Eng. 32:27–8). The appearance and self-introduction of El-Shaddai in 35:11 presumes that Jacob had not yet met YHWH (cf. Gen. 28:13). Jacob receives the promises of progeny (Gen. 35:11) and land (Gen. 35:12), although he has already had his children (Gen. 29:31–30:24) and has already received the land promise (Gen. 28:13b–14a). Finally and most importantly, the description of Jacob's erecting and naming a pillar at Bethel in Gen. 35:14–15 agrees almost word-for-word with the preceding non-P narrative of him doing the same thing, but the two acts are not linked with each other.[24] Instead, P again contradicts its non-P counterpart. Genesis 28:18–19 describes Jacob's recognition of God's presence at Bethel, "God's house," on his way from home. In contrast, Gen. 35:13 asserts that Bethel was only a place where God appeared in a one-time epiphany to Jacob, and that Jacob named the place "Bethel" only after God had left (Gen. 35:15).[25]

Now, in the present combined Genesis narrative, the oppositions between the Priestly story of Jacob at Bethel and its non-P parallels present certain problems. For example, the earlier non-P narrative claiming that God lives in Bethel (Gen. 28:10–22) is left to make its claims on the text's audience. Yet the P narrative in Gen. 35:9–15 appears to have been designed to replace, rather than supplement, its non-P counterpart. In particular, the P story contradicts the claims of the preceding story that God dwells at Bethel (Gen. 28:18–19) by offering a competing picture of Bethel as a place where God just "spoke to Jacob" (Gen. 35:13 and 14). Within the present text, Bethel appears as *both* the dwelling place of God (Gen. 28:18–19) *and* the place where God talked to Jacob (Gen. 35:13–14). In this way what was a Priestly substitution correcting its non-P counterpart, now simply adds another perspective.[26] In summary, elements in Gen. 35:9–15 indicate not only that it is a later addition to its context, but that it was originally composed to be part

24. Note that libation offerings do not necessarily contradict P's theology since they are not animal offerings and thus are not among the offerings that require a temple (see R. Albertz, *Religionsgeschichte Israels in alttestamentlicher Zeit,* vol. 2, *Vom Exil bis zu den Makkabäern* (ATD-Sup 8/2; Göttingen: Vandenhoeck & Ruprecht, 1992), 385; (E.T., *A History of Israelite Religion in the Old Testament Period,* vol. 2, *From the Exile to the Maccabees* [trans. J. Bowden; OTL; London: SCM, 1994], 377). For arguments that Gen. 35:14 is an inextricable part of this pericope, see particularly W. Groß, "Jakob, der Mann des Segens," *Bib* 49 (1968): 335–37 (esp. n.4); Rendtorff, *Problem,* 119; (E.T. 145); Blum, *Vätergeschichte,* 266–67n22; Ska, "Quelques remarques," 115–16n36. Here much recent scholarship has followed the lead of older analyses up through T. Nöldeke, *Untersuchungen zur Kritik des Alten Testaments* (Kiel: Schivers, 1869), 28; cf. also Eerdmans, *Studien,* 15.

25. Groß, "Jakob, der Mann des Segens," 335–37n4; Blum, *Vätergeschichte,* 267–69. Note that in the present text, particularly as it follows Gen. 28:18–19, God's "going from Jacob" need not represent a definitive departure from Bethel. Instead, it merely signals the end of the appearance to him. It is only in a separate strand that this conclusion of the divine appearance would assume any kind of finality. J. L. Ska, "Quelques remarques," 117–8 argues that "again" in 35:9 refers not just to Genesis 28:10–22 but more immediately to Gen. 35:1, 7. Genesis 35:1 and 7, however, do not describe a preceding epiphany.

26. This text is a key example for Blum of a place where the present form of a Priestly text can only be properly understood if it is seen as having been composed to stand in a composition

of a narrative strand apart from that context. In this Priestly strand, Jacob had not yet been to Bethel or erected a pillar there, God had not yet introduced himself or given promises, and Jacob had not yet been renamed "Israel."

Genesis 48:3–6(7): Jacob's Speech to Joseph

The last P promise text in Genesis is Jacob's adoption speech to Joseph in Gen. 48:3–7. Many have seen in this passage a conflict with the idea in 48:1–2 and 8–22 that Jacob cannot see. Nevertheless, in actuality the seams between 48:3–7 and its context are not clear.[27] Throughout the first scene of the present text (Gen. 48:1–7), Jacob does not realize Joseph's sons are there along with Joseph. This makes narrative sense since Jacob is blind and has not been told they are there. Then in Gen. 48:8 Jacob suddenly notes the presence of the two boys Joseph brought with him, and only here does Joseph tell Jacob who they are (Gen. 48:9). Thus begins the second scene, where Jacob blesses the two sons he has just adopted (Gen. 48:8–22). Overall, the whole chapter describes how Jacob doubled the portion given the favored son of his favored wife (Gen. 48:22, cf. 48:7) by adopting and blessing both of Joseph's sons. The two scenes work well together, and there are no significant indicators of seams to distinguish 48:3–7 from its context.

Thus, in contrast to the other ancestral P texts described so far, we must rely on weaker arguments from potential continuity and profile to distinguish 48:3–7 from its context. Scholars have often pointed out that 48:3–7 disrupts the potential movement from 48:1–2 to 48:8–10. Genesis 48:1–2 describes Joseph's initial entrance with his sons before Jacob, and 48:8–10, the following recognition scene between Jacob and his grandsons. Nevertheless, such arguments from potential continuity are unreliable as a sole basis for isolating a text from its context. The main reason for supposing that 48:3–7 is distinguished from its non-P context is the way the promise in 48:3–4 refers

---

including its non-P parallel (Blum, *Vätergeschichte*, 269–70). He argues that standing alone, the otherwise unique appearance of a Matzebah and the overall etiological focus of Gen. 35:9–15 is strange and serves little purpose. Moreover, Gen. 35:9–15 in its present form seems designed to follow Jacob's trip and thus correspond to the narrative it corrects.

In response to Blum's first point, I argue above that P is writing a narrative that *can* speak to those familiar with the non-P precursor, even as it inverts certain crucial aspects of that narrative. That is the point of including the etiological elements in P. In response to Blum's second point, it is not so evident that Gen. 35:11–15 must have been written to follow Jacob's journey. Gunkel argued plausibly that Gen. 35:11–15 may once have stood much earlier in the P strand, while Gen. 35:9–10 once stood after it, referring to Gen. 35:11–15 through the word "again." In addition, even if Gen. 35:9–15 as a whole always stood near its present location, there are a number of possible reasons the Priestly author would have wanted to transfer this divine promise to the conclusion of his story of Jacob. For example, P may have wanted to imply the blessing transfer as a reward to Jacob for compliance. In summary, neither of Blum's points is decisive, and the mix of the passage's (Gen. 35:9–15) dependence on and doubling of non-P texts is best explained as the P author's tactic for writing a competing Bethel tradition that could stand alone and yet also speak to those in its audience who knew the non-P counterpart.

27. Hupfeld, *Quellen der Genesis*, 35–36.

to several P promise texts, texts that all appear to be secondary to their non-P contexts (Gen. 17:1–27; 28:1–9; 35:9–15). Combined with the disruption of the potential continuity between Gen. 48:2 and 8, these links to other P ancestral texts are a good basis, albeit a weaker one, for the supposition that Gen. 48:3–7 is a later expansion of its surrounding context.

The issue now to be considered is how much of this later expansion is priestly? Jacob's reference to God's revelation to him at Bethel (Gen. 48:3–4) is the only clearly Priestly element, yet it has no point by itself. Instead it is inextricably connected with the next two verses, setting Jacob's adoption of Joseph's sons in the context of Jacob's receiving the promises from El-Shaddai at Bethel (Gen. 48:5–6). Together, Jacob's reference to the Priestly version of the epiphany at Bethel (48:3–4) and his including Joseph's sons through adoption in the promises received there (48:5–6) form an inextricably connected unit. Given the links of Gen. 48:3–4 with the above-discussed Priestly promise texts, Gen. 48:3–6 appears to be a single Priestly unit.

The function of Gen. 48:7 in this context is less clear. Although this note regarding Rachel's death appears to be connected in some way with her son Joseph's prominence in Genesis 48, the note is not necessary as a conclusion to the Priestly section regarding Jacob's adoption of Joseph's sons (48:3–6).[28] Moreover, the note in Gen. 48:7 about Benjamin's birth in Canaan contradicts a Priestly text in 35:22b-26 that lists Benjamin as among the sons born in Padan-Aram.[29] These indicators, along with the fact that 48:7 refers to a non-Priestly text (33:18–20*), have led many plausibly to suppose that 48:7 is an addition to Jacob's speech by a later author who had both Priestly and non-Priestly texts before him.

As we turn to the more clearly Priestly section of Jacob's speech, Gen. 48:3–6, there are not as many indicators as there were for the other Priestly promise texts that this text was originally separate. The main distinguishing indicator is the presence of the divine designation "El-Shaddai" in Gen. 48:3, in contrast to Jacob's constant reference to "God" in his blessings of Joseph's sons (Gen. 48:15, 20–21). Otherwise, the indicators in Gen. 48:3–6 do not point decisively to either this text having originally been separate or having

---

28. Blum, *Vätergeschichte*, 252, argues that this note regarding Rachel's death serves to rationalize Jacob's adoption of Joseph's sons because he can not reproduce anymore through his favored wife. Adoption now represents an important means for him to continue the multiplication promised him at Bethel (cf. 48:3–4). In response, L. Schmidt, *Literarische Studien zur Josephsgeschichte* (BZAW 167; New York, Berlin: de Gruyter, 1986), 254–55, rightly points out that by this point the Priestly multiplication promise to Jacob at Bethel has been fulfilled. Already in Gen. 47:27 P has described Jacob as being "fruitful and multiplying" in Egypt. Moreover, this issue is nowhere explicitly thematized in 48:3–7. Rather than being a further rationale for Jacob's adoption of Joseph's sons, 48:7 is much more loosely connected to the verses that precede it than those verses are to each other. For detailed discussion of possible rationales behind the placement of 48:7, see B. Jacob, *Das erste Buch der Tora. Genesis* (Berlin: Schocken, 1934), 869–73.

29. I will discuss this text below.

been composed for this context. In the present form of Genesis, the Priestly text here appears not as a replacement but as a reconceptualization and intensification of Ephraim's and Manasseh's places in the twelve-tribe system. In P they are not just blessed but fully adopted by Jacob.

On the basis of 48:3–6 alone, one finds no new support for the hypothesis of an originally separate Priestly layer. On the other hand, apart from the loosely connected reference to Rachel's death in 48:7, there is nothing in Gen. 48:3–6 indicating an original connection with the non-P context either.

Review and Conclusion

The four P promise texts in Genesis—Genesis 17; 26:34–35; 27:46–28:9; 28:1–9; 35:9–15; and 48:3–6—build closely on one another and have links through Genesis 17 and the Gen. 1:28 fertility blessing to the P layer in Genesis 1—9. The God of Genesis 1—9 introduces himself to Abraham in Gen. 17:1 as "El-Shaddai," and, parallel to the P covenant with Noah in Gen. 9:8–17, "establishes" a "covenant" with Abraham. This covenant includes the special P versions of the promise of children (including the Gen. 1:28 fertility blessing) and land. Then the other three P texts describe the transfer of these promises to Jacob (Gen. 26:34–35; 27:46–28:9; 35:9–15; 48:3–4), and imply the inclusion of Joseph's children among the offspring who will receive this promise (Gen. 48:5–6). Together these texts reflect a specific theological conceptualization of God's revelation and promise to Israel's ancestors, a description of a period in which YHWH as "El-Shaddai" covenanted with and gave the promise to Abraham and Jacob.

As we have seen, three of these four P promise texts show multiple indicators of having originally stood separate from their non-P contexts. The "El-Shaddai" divine designation in these texts presupposes that the appearances of YHWH to the patriarchs had not happened. Furthermore, the P version of the background to Jacob's departure is only incompletely adapted into its context, so the final form of the text relativizes the original P concern regarding mixed marriages. Similarly, the P version of the epiphany to Jacob at Bethel is only slightly coordinated with the earlier epiphanies by means of the presence at the beginning of the adverb *again* ("God appeared again to Jacob," 35:9), but the coordination stops here. In general, the giving of the promises in the El-Shaddai texts are not coordinated with the previous giving of quite similar promises in non-P texts. With the exception of 48:3–6, the Priestly promise texts parallel and oppose their non-P parallels in a way that suggests some kind of dependence. Yet the lack of coordination suggests that the P texts were not originally composed to be part of the same composition as the non-P texts on which they were based and that they were often designed to correct.

Thus the position being advocated here is similar to a reading like Blum's, one where these Priestly texts are seen as corrections of their non-P counterparts. The one significant difference is the following: in contrast to Blum's work, the analysis here suggests the character of these P texts and the type of correction of non-P tradition they represent indicate they probably once stood separate from the non-P texts they parallel. Blum's compositional approach is an example of how recent redactional approaches to P have illuminated the present function of P texts in their context. Moreover, Blum and others have securely established that the P texts were composed in relation to and often in opposition to their non-P counterparts. Nevertheless, none of this means that these texts were originally written to be part of the same literary context as the texts they correct, and much of the data discussed above works against such a theory. Just how and why these texts came to be placed alongside the texts they were designed to replace is an important question, and one to which I will return at the end of the book after fuller consideration of the non-P texts and their process of growth. Next, however, I turn to consideration of other potentially Priestly texts in Genesis 10—50.

The Genealogical Framework

The other main group of ancestral texts with links to P in Gen. 1:1–9:17 are the texts that are part of the genealogical framework of the patriarchs in Genesis 11—50. As we saw in Genesis 1—9, the Priestly material in Gen. 6:9; 7:6 and eventually 9:28–9 extends to the flood narrative the carefully patterned genealogical pattern found in Genesis 5. Next, the genealogy of Shem in Gen. 11:10–26 extends this Priestly framework, so it now reaches from Adam to Abraham. Despite the minor differences between this genealogy and Genesis 5, the parallels between these texts suggest a special relationship between them. Then, the rest of Genesis is structured by a number of texts that encompass the ancestral stories with a similar genealogical framework. Chart 5-5 summarizes this framework, including some non-P texts that now serve a role in this framework (see the discussion below), and indicating specific divergences from the primeval genealogical pattern with **boldface** type.

Such links to the Priestly "scroll of the descendants of Adam" in Genesis 5 suggest that this overall genealogical framework in Genesis is part of the same Priestly layer seen in Genesis 1—9. To be sure there are significant differences between the way the framework is worked out in the Genesis 5 genealogical scroll and the way it is used to frame the ancestral stories. Most prominently, unlike Genesis 5 and Gen. 11:10–26, these sections in Genesis 11—50 focus not on the firstborn but the second born. Once Abraham is chosen, the promise goes from him to Isaac to Jacob. Also, the Genesis 5 pattern is not present in all the major ancestral sections of Genesis. Since the birth of Jacob's sons is already narrated in the Isaac section (Gen. 29:31–30:24; 35:16–18; cf. 35:22b-26), there is no equivalent to the usual birth narratives in his own descendant section (Gen. 37:2–50:26). Nevertheless, despite such differences, the overall links between the genealogical

Chart 5-5: Genealogical Frameworks in Genesis 5 and 11—50

Frame in Genesis 5 (Example: Adam)	Terah's Descendants	Isaac's Descendants	Jacob's Descendants
Superscription (5:1)	Superscription (11:27aα)	Superscription (25:19a)	Superscription (37:2aα1–3)
Birth and naming of firstborn, including note of age (5:3)	Hagar's bearing of Ishmael to Abraham (16:15a), naming (16:15b)	Rebekah's bearing of Esau and Jacob to Isaac; and naming (25:21–26a)	
	Abraham's age at Ishmael's birth (16:16)	Isaac's age at their birth (25:26b)	
Father's age after birth of first-born (5:4a)	Sarah's bearing of Isaac to Abraham (21:2), naming (21:3), circumcision (21:4), age of Abraham (21:5)	Births of Jacob's first eleven children (29:31–30:24)	
Birth of more sons and daughters (5:4b)		Birth of Benjamin (35:16–18) [**No age notices**] Summary of twelve sons born to Jacob (35:22b–26)	
Concluding notes:	Concluding notes:	Concluding notes:	Concluding notes:
Summary of total years (5:5a)	Summary of years of life (25:7)	Summary of years of life (35:28)	Summary of years of life in Egypt and in all (47:28)
Death (5:5b)	Death **in good old age and gathered to his people** (25:8)	Death **and gathered to his people old and full in years** (35:29a)	Death **and gathered to his people** (49:33b)
	Burial in Machpelah (25:9–10)	**Burial** [in Mamre (Machpelah assumed), 35:29b]	**Extended Mourning and Burial Notice** [in Machpelah] (50:1–14)
			[**Death notice for Joseph (50:26aα), summary of age (50:26aβ), and embalmment notice (50:26b)**]

framework of Genesis 5 and the ancestral texts in Gen. 11—50 are strong, links that suggest both are part of the Priestly strand we are investigating here. That having been said, it must also be acknowledged that this set of

Priestly texts in Genesis 11—50 are often not as distinguished from their non-P contexts as the Priestly promise texts I was just discussing. Only a minority of the Priestly genealogical framework texts in Genesis 11—50 are marked off from their contexts by seams. Here are the main examples:

1. Ishmael is named (Gen. 16:15) by Abraham, not by Hagar (cf. Gen. 16:11).[30]
2. The description of Abraham's burial by Isaac and Ishmael (Gen. 25:7–10) appears to ignore the expulsion of Ishmael in previous non-P material (Gen. 21:8–21).[31]
3. The list of Jacob's sons in Gen. 35:22b–26 is a partial doublet to the earlier narratives of Jacob's fathering children, and has Benjamin born in Padan-Aram (P; cf. Gen. 28:5–7), rather than in Canaan near Bethlehem (cf. non-P Gen. 35:16–18; also 48:7).[32]
4. Jacob's commission of all twelve of his sons to bury him at the cave of Machpelah in Gen. 49:29–33 partially doubles the earlier (non-P) commission of Joseph to bury him in Canaan (Gen. 47:29–31). This commission to his sons to bury him in Canaan (Gen. 49:29–33) appears to have originally stood right before the report of their burying their father in Gen. 50:12–13. The latter text begins with a number of references to their commissioning father—"*his* sons did to *him* just as *he* commanded"—*even though Jacob was not mentioned in the immediately preceding context*.[33] In addition, this preceding context refers exclusively to *Joseph*'s preparations for the burial of his father, thus resulting in a paral-

---

30. As Blum points out (*Vätergeschichte*, 316), even if 16:15 is not from P, it is not original to the preceding narrative. Levin, *Der Jahwist*, 149–50, assigns 16:15 (along with 16:1, 3aαb–4a) to his pre-Yahwistic source, thus accounting for its divergence from 16:11 and its preservation. P, according to Levin, was only used as a supplement and would not have replaced a non-P report here. Such a concept of Rp redaction, however, seems excessively rigid. P has been used at numerous points in Genesis to replace non-P material, particularly for life-cycle events such as birth and death. Particularly given the apparent P character of the following verse (16:16, see discussion below), the simplest theory seems not to see 16:15 as yet another addition (Blum), nor to assign it to a highly hypothetical pre-Yahwistic birth narrative (Levin), but instead to follow classic analyses and assign both 16:15 and 16:16 to P. One element that may have led to the inclusion of this material from P was its connection to the following extensive P account of God's covenant with Abraham. All of 16:15–17:27* was thus inserted as a block into the present non-P context.
31. Cf. Von Rad, *Genesis*, 225; (E.T. 262), who notes a similar problem in 35:29; and Westermann, *Genesis 12—36*, 485–86 (E.T. 397). These narratives can be harmonized through the assumption that Ishmael returned for the burial. The point is that the burial notice in 25:11 ignores the apparently permanent expulsion of Ishmael in Gen. 21:8–21 and lacks any mention of a return.
32. Skinner, *Genesis*, 427; Westermann, *Genesis 12—36*, 677–78 (E.T. 556). See also Blum, *Vätergeschichte*, 446, for parallels with 36:5b and 46:27. To be sure, this list now serves the function of including Benjamin in a comprehensive list, but the narrative shows no signs of presupposing either previous descriptions of these sons' births or the immediately preceding divergent account of the location of Benjamin's birth.
33. C. Westermann, *Genesis 37—50* (BKAT I/3; Neukirchen-Vluyn: Neukirchener Verlag, 1982), 228. (E.T., *Genesis 37–50* [trans. J. J. Scullion; Minneapolis: Augsburg, 1986], 202.)

lel between 47:29–31 and 50:1–11.[34] Here again we seem to have the
narrative continuity of an originally separate Priestly narrative—Gen.
49:29–33; 50:12–13—being broken by being interwoven with its non-
P counterpart.[35]

Aside from these examples, the other genealogical texts are seamlessly integrated with their context. With few exceptions, the superscriptions, births,
dates, death, and burial reports occur just once in Genesis and rarely clash
with their contexts.

This means we must rely exclusively on the Priestly profile to identify many
possible P genealogical texts in Genesis. In this way we can tentatively assign
to some level of P much of the Genesis 5-style genealogical structure in Genesis 11—50, including the bulk of the "descendant" superscriptions (Gen.
11:10aα, 27aα; 25:12, 19a; 36:1, 9; 37:2aα1–3) and related genealogical material (Gen. 11:10aβ–26, 27aβb, 32; 16:15–16; 21:1–5*; 25:7–10, 19b;
35:22b-26, 28–29; 36:1–43*; 47:28b; 49:1a, 29–33; 50:12–13). As emphasized in chapter 2, such an argument primarily from profile is inherently less
reliable than an argument from a combination of indicators of seams and profile. Nevertheless, the Priestly profile in most of these genealogical texts is clear
and well established enough to identify the probable presence of P material.

Yet even in this P genealogical structure, non-P material occurs. Sometimes it is interwoven with P material, and sometimes it is separate from it.
We have already seen this in the case of Jacob's death and burial, but this phenomenon occurs in many other texts, as well. Take the example of the various narratives of the births of Israel's ancestors. The description of the birth
of Jacob's children in Gen. 29:31–30:24; 35:16–18 is purely non-P and
stands quite apart from the P listing of his children in Gen. 35:22b–26. In
contrast, the P dating of Jacob's and Esau's birth (Gen. 25:26b) is connected
to a clearly non-P description of their birth (25:25–26a), one that shows no
P characteristics and is integrated into a non-P context. So here we have P
and non-P elements complementing and connected to each other. So also,
the description of the birth of Isaac in Gen. 21:1–7 seems at least partially interwoven from both P and non-P elements. Its specific formulation, particularly in Gen. 21:3–5, appears Priestly. Nevertheless, elements such as the doubling of the fulfillment notice at the outset (Gen. 21:1a/1b)[36] and the final
hint of different descriptions of Isaac's naming (Gen. 21:3 P; cf. 21:6–7)

---

34. I. Willi-Plein, "Historiographische Aspekte der Josefsgeschichte," *Hennoch* 1 (1979): 309.
35. Notably, the interrupting non-P context refers explicitly to the first (non-P) commission
scene (Gen. 50:5; cf. 47:29–31).
36. Already Eerdmans, *Studien*, 21, disputed whether there is actually a doublet of fulfillment
formulae in 21:1. Nevertheless, as Eichrodt points out (*Quellen der Genesis*, 18), the repeated
comment that Isaac was born "as YHWH said" is an indicator that this verse may stem from two
different hands. Only later were the two fulfillment formulae now found here combined into a
semipoetic, emphatic statement of God's fulfillment of God's promise. That P in this case would

indicate the probable presence of both P and non-P elements here. As a result of the complex mixing of material here, past analyses of this passage have diverged widely without achieving an enduring consensus. The interwoven data defies closure.

The point is that the present Genesis genealogical structure is formed out of a combination of P and non-P material. Another prominent indicator of this is the way the Priestly genealogical headings for the major ancestral sections now introduce predominantly non-P material. The Isaac heading in Gen. 25:19a ("These are the descendants of Isaac") introduces a P-like re-description of Isaac's birth (25:19b), a dated note on his marriage (25:20), and then a block of predominantly non-P material regarding Isaac's descendants (25:21–35:27*). The Jacob heading in Gen. 37:2aα1–3 ("These are the descendants of Jacob") likewise introduces more non-P material than P material in the present text of Genesis. With the possible exception of a Priestly note giving background on Joseph in the rest of 37:2, almost all of the following chapters consist of non-P material regarding Joseph and his brothers. Furthermore, as Blum has pointed out, the P genealogical structure even matches the gaps in the non-P material. Just as the non-P material lacks a separate section regarding Abraham's descendants, Isaac and Ishmael (cf. Gen. 26:1–33 in the Jacob story), so the P genealogical structure lacks a label that would introduce a section focusing on them.[37]

There are two ways to read this data. Many recent studies have argued that the links between the P genealogical structure and non-P material suggest that P was a genealogically focused extension of non-P material. Even Friedman, who argues for a mixed source and redaction model for P materials, attributes the Priestly genealogical structure to his P editor.[38] The other main alternative is to see here a close dependence of P genealogical material on non-P material, even as it—like the Priestly promise texts—may have originally stood separate from the non-P material it now frames. Clearly the P genealogical material matches the outline of the non-P ancestral narratives and is dependent in specific respects on details provided in those narratives. Clearly the P genealogical material is now placed in Genesis so that it elegantly structures the materials on which it is dependent. The question is, Do these connections with non-P materials establish that the Priestly genealogical structure never could have existed separately from the non-P material on which it is based and to which it is now connected?

---

use the divine designation YHWH in narrator speech is not typical of P, but it does not contradict the more central P conceptualization of the progressive revelation of the divine name. All the same, Rendtorff is correct in critiquing those who would use divine designation as a central criteria in 21:3–5 but not here (*Problem,* 126–27; [E.T. 152–53]).

37. Blum, *Vätergeschichte,* 434.

38. Friedman, *Exile and Biblical Narrative,* 77–81. A similar mixed model is proposed by Childs, *Introduction,* 147.

In my judgment, the answer is no. To be sure, there are not as many indicators that the genealogical texts were originally separate as there were for the Priestly texts discussed so far. The above-discussed seams, particularly in the narrative of Jacob's death and burial (Gen. 49:29–33; 50:12–13), are hints in this direction, although they cover only a small portion of the Priestly genealogical structure. But here we must consider the nature of the material. Even if the Priestly genealogical framework originally stood separate from the non-P material on which it was based, it probably still closely matched the earlier non-P material in overall outline and contents. Then when an author/redactor wanted to form a composition out of the P framework and non-P material, he would have been faced with redundant birth narratives, death narratives, and so forth. *Unlike the case of the theologically charged Priestly promise texts,* the redactor would have had little reason to include each redundant detail. After all, can a patriarch die more than once, and what would be the point if he did? So, the author/redactor, in the process of forming a composition out of P and non-P material, included slightly divergent information, liberally combined the P and non-P material (Gen. 21:1–7), and/or simply included one report (Gen. 29:31–30:24; 35:16–18; cf. 35:22b-26). Only a mindless redactor bent on 100 percent inclusion of material, whether relevant or not, would have included complete parallel sets of birth and death notices. Such a compositional move would have left the kind of comprehensive data in the genealogies that would have allowed for the establishment of original independence of the Priestly genealogical framework. Nevertheless, it would have produced a very confusing text.

Such a hypothesis that the P genealogical material was originally independent from non-P texts it now frames does not, of course, mean that P had no knowledge of this non-P material. Once again redactional approaches to P such as Tengström's and Blum's have persuasively argued the contrary. P in Gen. 11:10–16 matches and is probably dependent on the non-P genealogical information in Gen. 10:24–5. Blum argues persuasively that the lack of a separate Abraham genealogical section in P may at least in part reflect the lack of non-P material concerning Isaac.[39] In addition, he observes that P's notices on where Ishmael and his descendants lived seem to draw on non-P material (Gen. 25:11 on 24:62; and 25:18b on 16:12b).[40] Tengström has pointed out that the P inclusion of a father's pronouncement of his sons' destinies in Gen. 49:1 and 28 seems to build on the model of Noah's concluding pronouncement for his sons in (non-P) Gen. 9:25–27.[41] Finally, the Priestly account of Jacob's commissioning his sons to bury him at Machpelah (Gen. 49:29–33) parallels its non-Priestly counterpart (Gen. 47:29–31) in numerous and specific respects.

39. Blum, *Vätergeschichte*, 434.
40. Blum, *Vätergeschichte*, 440.
41. Tengström, *Toledotformel*, 40.

In summary, the Priestly genealogical material is partially dependent on non-P material and yet probably once stood separate from it. As noted above, the nature of the Priestly genealogical material meant that there are fewer of the doublets and breaks that mark an originally separate source. Nevertheless, even here there are some marks of their original independence, particularly in the case of Jacob's burial. Moreover, the status of these Priestly genealogical texts needs to be seen in the context of the strong evidence for original separateness in those P texts that would be more likely to be preserved alongside non-P material: that is, the more theologically charged P creation and flood narratives, along with the Priestly promise texts. Considered in this context, indicators in the Priestly genealogical framework are consistent with the hypothesis of an originally separate P strand.

Excursus: The Priestly Table of Nations in Genesis 10

The above discussion of genealogical materials in Genesis has intentionally omitted one set of texts commonly assigned to P, the framework of Genesis 10: Gen. 10:1a, 2–7, 20, 22–23, 31–2. This framework is composed largely of lists of the sons and grandsons of Noah's sons, starting with a genealogical superscription (10:1a: "These are the descendants of the sons of Noah"), continuing with sections regarding the children of Yaphet (10:2–6), Ham (10:6, 20), and Shem (10:22–23, 31), and then concluding with a summary of the whole in 10:32.

As has long been recognized, these lists and superscriptions contrast in form and content with the material they enclose. The material in 10:8–19 and 24–30 is distinguished from the framework and especially 10:2–6 not only by its narrative form ("Cush fathered Nimrod . . . "), but also by its more explicit focus on linking elements of the genealogy with later civilization. It lists national groups as descendants of Noah (10:16–18), describes territories inhabited by Noah's descendants (10:19, 30), and includes notes on other legends regarding these ancestors (10:8–12, 25). Moreover, this narrative genealogical material diverges from the framework in its treatment of the figures of Havilah (10:29, cf. 10:6) and Sheba (10:28, cf. 10:7),[42] and has Nimrod as a son of Cush (10:8) after the framework material in 10:7 has already listed Cush's grandsons.

These indicators have led most past analyses of Genesis 10 to distinguish between two strands in Genesis 10: (1) a set of narrative genealogical fragments with close resemblances to the above-discussed non-P strand (Gen. 10:8–19, 24–30 along with 10:1b and 21) and (2) a list-focused framework (Gen. 10:1a, 2–7, 20, 22–23, 31–32). In turn, this latter framework is usually assigned to P, partly because P is the other major candidate for material in Genesis 1—11, but also because of the P-like genealogical superscription and conclusion (10:1, 32), along with the overall systematization otherwise characteristic of Priestly material in Genesis.

Be that as it may, Tengström has argued persuasively that this P-like framework in Genesis 10 never existed apart from the material it encloses. The framework presupposes a movement from descendants to nations (Gen. 10:32) but itself only ex-

---

42. Note, Asshur is treated differently in two parts of these materials: 10:11 and 22. This points to transmission-historical complexity already in the non-P materials, probably on the oral level.

ecutes this movement in one section, which lists the descendants of Yaphet. Otherwise, the non-P material carries the burden in Genesis 10 of describing the lands to which the descendants spread (Ham, 10:8–19; Shem, 10:24–30*). Moreover, the framework material in Genesis 10 could never have been part of an originally separate P strand. Without the intervening Tower of Babel story (a non-P text), the verbless material in Gen. 10:31–2 would have produced a jarring doublet to the priestly genealogy of Shem's descendants beginning in Gen. 11:10ff:[43]

> (10:31) These are the descendants of Shem, by their families, their languages, their lands, and their nations.
> (10:32) These are the families of Noah's sons, according to their genealogies, in their nations; and from these the nations spread abroad on the earth after the flood.
> (11:10ff.) These are the descendants of Shem. When Shem was one hundred years old, he became the father of Arpachshad two years after the flood; and Shem lived after the birth of Arpachshad five hundred years, and had other sons and daughters . . .

The verbless material in Genesis 10 resembles Priestly material in important ways, yet never appears to have existed apart from the non-P material in Genesis 10 and 11:1–9. The genealogical framework in Genesis 10 appears to be a Priestly redaction, or more precisely, a Priestly composition built around this portion of the non-P primeval history.

The question then becomes how this relates to evidence regarding the P strand elsewhere in Genesis. Lacking other indicators, the Priestly material in Genesis 10 could be evidence that the Priestly material as a whole is a compositional layer built on and around a preceding non-P composition. Seen in the context of the above analysis, however, Genesis 10 is more likely part of the redaction linking originally Priestly and non-Priestly materials with each other. In the last chapter we saw that the author of the combined P and non-P composition is probably responsible for Gen. 2:4a, a genealogical label that introduces non-P material in Gen. 2:4b–4:26 by extending the Genesis 5 pattern backward. In the case of Genesis 10, the same author, faced with a non-P genealogy of the nations descending from Noah (cf. Gen. 10:8–19, 24–30), probably extended the Genesis 5 framework to encompass fragments of this non-P material. In the process, the redactor wrote one of the few genealogical labels in Genesis that duplicates the starting point of another one (Gen. 10:1; cf. 11:10). This new restructured, P-like survey of Noah's descendants now stands between the end of the Priestly section regarding Noah (Gen. 9:28–29) and the original Priestly sequel to it: the genealogy of Shem's descendants (Gen. 11:10–26). One indicator that this genealogy in Gen. 11:10–26 once stood closer to the end of the Priestly section regarding Noah is the way it begins with a date referring to the Flood (Gen. 11:10b; cf. 9:28; 7:6), a flood now standing fairly distant from this text in the present combined P/non-P narrative.[44]

43. Eerdmans, *Studien*, 4. See also Levin, *Der Jahwist*, 124.
44. Hupfeld, *Quellen der Genesis*, 17. Cf. recently Levin, *Der Jahwist*, 124. In the process, the redactor picked up on the "after the Flood" theme by authoring the P-like genealogical superscription in Gen. 10:1. Nevertheless it serves a new function now. Rather than placing the birth of Noah's sons in a specific chronological system (cf. Gen. 11:10–26), the "after the Flood" notice in 10:1 merely notes that the entire following spread of humanity took place after the Flood. For more arguments for the redactional character of 10:1 and 32, see J.C.F. Tuch, *Kommentar über die Genesis* (Halle: Buchhandlung des Waisenhauses, 1838), 196–97.

Often previous scholars have maintained that P uses the table of nations here to systematically survey the families of humanity who were not included in the promise to Abraham,[45] but this is not yet an issue at this point in P. In P, exclusion from the promise only becomes an issue and is thematized as such from Genesis 17 onward. Indeed, given that P only introduces the promise to Abraham at a late point after his arrival in the land, the idea that P would be compelled to survey those not included in the promise is rather thin. An originally separate P document probably began with two linear genealogical bridges, the Genesis 5 scroll of the descendants of Adam, extending from Adam to Noah, and then an imitation of this form to build a bridge from (1) (the descendant of) the recipient of the first P covenant, Noah, to (2) the one who will receive the other P covenant, Abraham. Then, with the establishment of the covenant with Abraham, P began to introduce genealogies of those excluded from this covenant: Ishmael and Esau.

Relative certainty is no more possible here than in many other cases of transmission history. Nevertheless, the point here is that we need not presuppose that P had a table of nations like the non-P material, and there are some significant indicators that P did not have one. Genesis 10 may be one of the most significant examples in Genesis of the authorial work of the Rp redactor.

Other Texts Commonly Assigned to P

As we turn to consider other texts commonly assigned to P, we are confronted with a continuum extending from clearly Priestly texts that are marked off from their non-P context to texts that have been assigned to P for the weakest of reasons.

An example of the former end of the continuum can be found in Gen. 19:29. This note *re*-reporting God's saving Lot (Gen. 19:29b) stands out from its context as a doublet using different terminology and working from a different conceptuality from the preceding report of the event. Furthermore, this note links up with the P flood strand, particularly by describing God as rescuing Lot because of God's "remembering" a person (cf. Gen. 8:1; also Exod. 2:24; 6:5; also non-P in Exod. 32:13). Although this P note has now been elegantly incorporated into its context as a commentary on the preceding story, it probably originally stood as part of the separate P strand, standing as a brief P reconceptualization of an event already familiar to the audience.

---

45. Eissfeldt, "Biblos Geneseōs," 461–62; Scharbert, "Toledotformel," 45–46; Tengström, *Toledotformel,* 25–27, cf. also 52–53. On this cf. Weimar, "Toledot," 87–92, who argues against this approach on the basis of (1) the predominance of the toledot formula in the blessing-focused primeval history and Jacob sections of P and (2) variations in the formulations of several of the labels that introduce the descendants of those who will not inherit the promise (Gen. 5:1; 10:1; 11:10; 36:9). He interprets all of this latter group of labels on the model of 36:9, as labels introducing subsections that elaborate the blessing focus of the material preceding them. According to Weimar, they are *not* new beginnings representing a narrowing of the promise. These arguments by Weimar rightly stress the essentially positive focus of the Priestly genealogical sidelines on the outpouring of blessing, even on those who did not inherit the promise. Nevertheless, the variations in formulation on which Weimar puts so much weight (cf. 25:12!) do not suffice to negate the way these surveys of the outpouring of blessing on non-heirs in Gen. 25:12–18 and Genesis 36 function to prepare for sections that focus on those who both inherit and transmit the promise.

At the other end of the continuum stand texts like the introduction of Rachel's and Leah's maidservants, Zilpah and Bilhah (Gen. 29:24, 29; 30:4a, 9b). The notes regarding Laban's giving these maids to Jacob (Gen. 29:24, 29) seem secondary to their context.[46] Nevertheless, these verses have no clear connections to P. Assigning these verses to P is the kind of move typical of the weakest sort of source-critical approach. One assumes that the P source had a narrative of Jacob's marriage, and then one automatically assigns elements that are secondary to the non-P narrative of Jacob's marriage to P. In this way one attempts to fill in the gaps in the postulated P source. Nevertheless, the resulting bridge is too weak to hold. One could suppose that Gen. 29:24, 29 and 30:4a, 9b came from P, but there are no solid indicators to help us know this is the case.

In the following material, I turn to look at other postulated P texts in Genesis. As indicated earlier, I will work with these texts in groups to deal systematically with common indicators in them: age notices, travel reports, and settlement notices. Each of these categories of P texts contributes to an intricate, interlocked chronological and geographical system, one that is often disrupted by the intervening non-P material. After considering these specific groups of proposed P texts, I will turn to four other texts that do not completely fit into these categories but contain some Priestly material: the life of Terah (Gen. 11:28–30), the first Hagar story (Genesis 16), the burial of Sarah (Gen. 23:1–20), and the story of Jacob's settlement in Egypt (Gen. 47:5–27).

Age Notices

As noted above, the P genealogical framework includes a regular focus on the age of the given patriarch at the birth of his children and at death. Furthermore, we have seen in the P flood strand a particular interest in dating each stage of the flood story by the years of Noah's life. This kind of special emphasis on chronology in P texts has led many to assign other texts featuring such age notices to P. In three cases, such notices are immediately attached to P genealogical superscriptions. The superscription for Isaac's descendants in Gen. 25:19 is immediately followed by a dating of his marriage to Rebekah (25:20). This note diverges from the preceding non-P notice by identifying her home as Padan-Aram rather than Haran. It is from P. Also, Gen. 47:28a, the notice regarding how long Jacob stayed in Egypt, is immediately connected to the concluding age notice for Jacob in the P genealogical structure (Gen. 47:28b). This verse is securely attributable to P.

Similarly, the Gen. 37:2aα1–3 genealogical superscription, "these are the descendants of Jacob," is immediately followed by an age notice for Joseph, noting that he was seventeen years old when he shepherded the flock with his

46. Blum, *Vätergeschichte*, 104.

brothers and reported on them to his father. This notice is distinguished from what follows by (1) its concept of Joseph as an adult (seventeen years old) versus the following depiction of him as a boy (*yeled*, 37:30), a "son of [Jacob's] old age" (37:3);[47] (2) its implicit limitation of Joseph's conflict with his brothers to a conflict with the sons of Rachel's and Leah's maids;[48] and (3) its explanation of this conflict through reference to his reports on them (cf. Gen. 37:3–11).[49] The awkward comment that Joseph was a "lad" in 37:2 appears to be an insertion of a redactor reconciling the assertion that Joseph was seventeen in 37:2 (P) with the later depictions of him as much younger.[50] We no longer have the P Joseph story that would have followed this notice. Nevertheless, Gen. 37:2 appears to be a brief portion of the story preserved by the Rp redactor at the tail end of a largely Priestly genealogical block extending from 35:22b to 37:2.

The age notice in Gen. 41:46a is not so easily attributable to P. This half-verse notes Joseph's age when he entered Pharaoh's service. It is marked off from its context by resumptive repetition in 46:45b, 46b, and its focus on Joseph's age links it to Gen. 37:2*. Nevertheless, the assignment of the material regarding Joseph in 37:2* to P is itself not certain, and the notice in 41:46a lacks any kind of P context.

Travel Reports

We see a geographical focus in several texts that have already been assigned to P above. The Priestly story of Jacob's departure from Esau describes his departure for Padan-Aram (Gen. 28:5, 7). In addition, the Priestly genealogical structure is linked at two points with travel notices that resemble each other: Gen. 11:31 and 36:6. Genesis 11:31 describes Terah gathering his family and departing for Haran, a description then presupposed in the Priestly death notice in Gen. 11:32. Genesis 36:6 describes Esau gathering his family and possessions gained in Canaan (Gen. 36:6a) and his departure from Canaan for Seir (Gen. 36:6b-8). This latter notice in turn conflicts with non-P texts where Esau has *already* moved to Seir before he comes back to meet Jacob (Gen. 32:4 [Eng. 32:3]; 33:14, 16). Together, these various texts hint at the presence of travel in the P-strand narrative.

The travel notice for Esau is paralleled in turn by several other travel notices scattered throughout Genesis, each of which features a patriarch (or patriarchs) gathering his household before leaving for or from the promised

---

47. Schmidt, *Studien*, 143–44.
48. Skinner, *Genesis*, 443–44. As Redford, points out, the reference to wives by name in 37:2 contrasts with the rest of the Joseph story. D. B. Redford, *A Study of the Biblical Story of Joseph (Genesis 37—50)* (VTSup 20; Leiden: E. J. Brill, 1970), 14.
49. Gunkel, *Genesis*, 492.
50. Schmidt, *Studien*, 143–44.

land. The parallels are indicated in Chart 5-6, with particular terminological similarities boldfaced:[51]

Chart 5-6: Comparison of Travel Reports			
Gen. 36:6–7	Gen. 12:5; 13:6, 11–12*	Gen. 31:17–18 So Jacob **arose**	Gen. 46:5–7 Then Jacob **arose** from Beersheba;
Then Esau **took**	Abram **took**	and he **set**	and the sons of Israel **set**
his wives, his sons, his daughters, and all the members of his household,	his wife Sarah and his brother's son Lot, and	his children and his wives on camels;	their father Jacob, their little ones, and their wives, in the wagons that pharaoh had sent to carry him.
his **livestock** and all his cattle and		and he drove away all his **livestock**,	They also took their **livestock**
all the possessions	all the **possessions**	all the **possessions**	and the **possessions**
that	**that**	that	that
he had acquired	**they had acquired,**	that he had **acquired,** the livestock in his possession	they had **acquired**
	and the persons whom they had gained	that he had **acquired**	
in the land of Canaan;	in Haran;	in Padan-Aram,	in the land of Canaan,
and he went from the land of Canaan[52] away from his brother Jacob.	and they left to go to the land of Canaan.		and they **came** into Egypt,
	They **came** to the land of the Canaan.	to **come** to his father Isaac in the land of Canaan.	

51. As Rendtorff pointed out (*Problem*, 116–17; [E.T., 141–42]), use of words like "possessions" (*rĕkûš*) by themselves are hardly a sufficient basis for assignment of texts to the Priestly layer. Nevertheless, as Blum notes (*Vätergeschichte*, 247–48), it is not just the terminology but the occurrence of the terminology in such similarly worded departure notices that makes the case of a similar layer for 31:17–18 and 46:5ff. persuasive.
52. Here reading with the LXX and Samaritan Pentateuch against the MT.

Gen. 36:6–7	Gen. 12:5 and 13:6	Gen. 31:17–18	Gen. 46:5–7
	(13:6) And the land could not support them **living together;**		
For their possessions were too great for their	for their possessions were so great that they could not		
living together; the land where they were staying could not support them because of their livestock.	live together. (13:11b–12abα) Thus they separated from each other. Abraham settled in the land of Canaan.		Jacob and all his offspring with him, his sons, and his sons' sons with him, his daughters, and his sons' daughters; all his offspring he brought with him into Egypt.
So Esau settled in the hill country of Seir.	And Lot settled in the cities of the plain.		

These parallels, which go beyond the isolated occurrence of this or that vocabulary item, indicate probable common origins for these texts. Furthermore, two out of three of these parallel travel notices are linked to the Priestly strand and secondary to their non-P contexts.

Genesis 12:4b–5; 13:6; and 11b–12abα: Abraham's Travel to and Settlement in Canaan

Genesis 12:4b–5 is marked as Priestly by (1) its resemblance to the Priestly travel notice for Esau (Gen. 36:6–7); (2) the P-like age notice in Gen. 12:4b; and (3) the way this travel by Abraham extends the Priestly account of Terah's trip to Canaan (Gen. 11:31). According to this Priestly account of travel toward Canaan, Terah already set out for Canaan before he died (Gen. 11:31), and Abraham merely completed his trip, knowing all along that he was going to Canaan (Gen. 12:5). In contrast, the intervening non-P material has Abraham depart on the command of God (Gen. 12:1) for an unknown destination—"the land that I will show you." Later, the Priestly and non-Priestly materials duplicate each other by noting that Abraham brought Lot with him toward Canaan (Gen. 12:4a [non-P]//12:5 [P]).[53]

Genesis 12:4b–5 connects directly to two other texts marked off by slighter seams from their context, and together they form a close parallel to the single Priestly travel and settlement report seen in Gen. 36:6–8. Here are the slight seams. Although the description of Abraham's and Lot's riches in Gen. 13:6

53. Hupfeld, *Quellen der Genesis*, 20–21.

fits adequately in its context, the verse's assertion that Abraham and Lot "could not live together" (13:6bβ) prematurely anticipates the more extended description of their conflict and Abraham's proposal for resolving it in 13:7–9. Similarly, the description of Lot's and Abraham's separation (Gen. 13:11b) comes late, since Lot has already departed in Gen. 13:11a. Furthermore, the P-like separation and settlement notice in Gen. 13:11b–12abα disrupts the focus of its surrounding non-P context on decamping and camping (Gen. 12:8–9; 13:3, 11a, 12bβ, 18), with its assertion that Abraham "settled" in Canaan (Gen. 13:12; cf. 13:18), and more specifically interrupts the movement in non-P materials from Lot's decamping in 13:11aβ ("and Lot decamped eastward") and his camping in 13:12bβ ("and moved his tent as far as Sodom").[54]

Genesis 31:17–18: Jacob's Travel to Canaan

The description of Jacob's departure from Padan-Aram in Gen. 31:17–18 links back to the Priestly account of Isaac's sending of Jacob to Padan-Aram and forward to the Priestly description of Jacob's reunion with Isaac in Gen. 35:27. In contrast, in the non-P material Isaac was already near death when Jacob left (Genesis 27), and Jacob's return is presented in the non-P material as just a return to his homeland and brother, without any mention of the possibility of a reunion with his father. Moreover, the departure notice in 31:17–18 is marked off from its more immediate context by its doubling of a following description of Jacob's flight in 31:19ff. The combination of the two descriptions of Jacob's flight produces some crosscurrents in the present text. For example, now Jacob and Rachel are already gone (31:17–18; [P]), before Rachel has a chance to steal Laban's household gods (Gen. 31:19; [non-P]).[55]

Genesis 46:5–7: Jacob's Migration to Egypt

Genesis 46:5–7 is more problematic. The main issue is that the beginning of this P-like travel report connects seamlessly with its non-P context. It balances Jacob's arrival at Beer-Sheba in the non-P material (Gen. 46:1) with his departure from there (Gen. 46:5). As a result, some scholars have wanted to slice off all or part of Gen. 46:5 from P. Nevertheless, there is no indicator supporting such a move,[56] and *all* of Gen. 46:5–7 is parallel to the above-

54. Hupfeld, *Quellen der Genesis*, 22–23. In addition, he notes that Gen. 13:11b–12abα is linked to P by its exclusive focus on the "cities of the plain" (Gen. 13:6, 12; 19:29) in contrast to the non-P focus on either Sodom (with or without Gomorrah: Gen. 13:12bβ–13; 19:1, 4, 24, 28) or the "plain" where it was located (Gen. 13:10; 19:17, 25, 28). For example, Gen. 19:25, a text showing no Priestly characteristics, explicitly mentions the destroyed cities and the "plain" separately.
55. Hupfeld, *Quellen der Genesis*, 32.
56. Genesis 46:5b connects to material regarding wagons in 45:19–21 that is often considered non-P. But there are also good arguments for considering this material as Priestly. See O. Procksch, *Die Genesis* (2d and 3d ed.; Leipzig: A. Dreicherische Verlagsbuchhandlung, 1924), 553; H. Seebass, *Geschichtliche Zeit und theonome Tradition in der Joseph-Erzählung* (Gütersloh: Gütersloher Verlagshaus Gerd Mohn, 1978), 54; Levin, *Der Jahwist*, 300; and particularly Schmidt, *Studien*, 174–77.

discussed Priestly departure notice in Gen. 31:17–18. A case like this brings us up against the limits of the transmission-historical method. Perhaps there is a undetectable divide between P and non-P material in 31:17–18 and 46:5–7. Or perhaps 46:5 as a whole is a P departure notice from Beer-Sheba that fit so elegantly with the preceding epiphany, that it replaced that epiphany's original departure notice.[57] Whatever option or combination of options is chosen, two things are clear. First, it is probably impossible to reach satisfactory certainty on this problem. Second, establishing whether P included Jacob's "arising" (31:17a; 46:5a) and loading (31:17b; 46:5b) is not decisive for consideration of the basic shape and theology of P.

In summary, the P strand seems to have featured a set of remarkably similar travel notices, beginning with Terah's start toward Canaan and ending with Jacob's sons' departure from Canaan for Egypt.[58] These texts then connect both explicitly and implicitly with the above-discussed Priestly promise and genealogical texts. For example, the common geographical referent of this system of travel notices is the land promised to Abraham and then Jacob. Moreover, all of the notices feature a prominent focus on the patriarch's transferring ever increasing numbers of children and livestock, a sign of the accelerating blessing on the heirs of Abraham. Indeed, we move from Terah's

---

57. Another option might be that the P and non-P notices were identical, so the redactor did not have to choose between them. Westermann in particular posits this kind of mix for texts like Gen. 21:1–5, see his *Genesis 12—36*, 405–6; (E.T. 331).

58. In addition to the texts discussed above, there are two other travel texts that have occasionally been assigned to P, Gen. 33:18aβ and 35:6, both of which appear in connection with Jacob's return to Canaan. Some have assigned the phrase "when he came from Padan-Aram" of Gen. 33:18aβ to P because of its reference to Padan-Aram. Cf. for example, A. Dillmann, *Die Genesis* (3d ed.; KEHAT 11; Leipzig: S. Hirzel, 1886), 364; (E.T., *Genesis Critically and Exegetically Expounded*, [vol. 2; trans. W. B. Stevenson; Edinburgh: T. & T. Clark, 1897], 291); Holzinger, *Genesis*, 184; Skinner, *Genesis*, 416; Noth, *Pentateuch* 13, 18; (E.T. 13, 17); and Westermann, *Genesis 12—36*, 643; (E.T. 528). Others, however, have rightly recognized that this phrase is completely dependent on its present context, in contrast to other P travel notices, and is more likely an Rp addition designed to add the P assertion that Jacob sojourned in Padan-Aram to a non-P description of his return (e.g., Wellhausen, *Composition*, 45). Cf. Rendtorff, *Problem*, 118 (E.T., 143) for more recent observations on the problems with assigning this verse to a separate P document.

Parts or all of the other notice, Gen. 35:6, have been assigned by some (e.g., Gunkel, *Genesis*, 387; Holzinger, *Genesis*, 185; Noth, *Pentateuch*, 13, 18; [E.T., 13, 17]; Skinner, *Genesis*, 424; and Westermann, *Genesis 12—36*, 672; [E.T., 551–52]) to P primarily because it names Bethel "Luz" long after Luz has been renamed Bethel in the non-P materials (Gen. 28:19; cf. 35:1). Nevertheless, this verse has no clear P characteristics, and it is immediately followed by a non-P parallel naming tradition for Bethel (Gen. 35:7) for which the preceding reference to Luz in 35:6 prepares. Indeed, the arrival notice in 35:6 is required for all the non-P materials in 35:7–8. In turn, the introduction to the P epiphany in 35:9 does not presuppose 35:6 or 33:18* but instead links seamlessly with the description of Jacob's departure in 31:17–18. Indeed, as a reference to Jacob's travel from Padan-Aram, Gen. 35:9 fits better with 31:17–18 than with any material, such as 33:18aβ or 35:6, that implies he has already arrived in Canaan. Cf. Wellhausen, *Composition*, 47–48; Rendtorff, *Problem*, 119, (E.T., 144); and Levin, *Der Jahwist*, 260.

and Abraham's "taking" modest households to Canaan (Gen. 11:31; 12:5) to the rapid expansion of Abraham's household in the land (Gen. 13:6) and the eventual need for camels (Gen. 31:17–18) and even wagons (Gen. 46:5–7) to transfer all of them. Even Esau, though not an heir of Abraham, experiences this blessing (Gen. 36:6–7).

Settlement Notices

There is one final set of texts to be considered as a group: a set of notices focusing on the settlement of patriarchs and those excluded from the promise. In more than one case, these notices appear to be paired, describing the settlement of the patriarch in the land and the settlement of his counterpart outside the land. For example, after the death of Isaac, Esau is described as moving (because of his many flocks) and "settling" (*yšb*) in Seir (Gen. 36:6–8), while Jacob "settles" in "the land of sojournings of his father, in the land of Canaan" (Gen. 37:1). Similarly, Abraham and Lot must split because of their many flocks (13:6), and Abraham "settles" in the "land of Canaan," while Lot "settles" in the cities of the plain (Gen. 13:12abβ).

This scheme may also be present, albeit without the emphasis on many flocks, with Isaac and Ishmael. After Abraham's death, God blesses Isaac his son, and he "settles" in Beer-la-hai-roi (Gen. 25:11). There is no corresponding notice in the section regarding Ishmael.[59] Nevertheless, we do hear elsewhere of Ishmael's "settlement" outside the land in Gen. 21:21: "he [Ishmael] settled in the wilderness of Paran, and he took a wife for himself from the land of Egypt." The focus on Ishmael's marriages outside Israel links with the later Priestly focus on Esau's similar marriages outside Israel (Gen. 26:34–5; 28:9 and [with different data] 36:2–3), and the focus in particular on his marriage to an Egyptian links with the Priestly focus on the Egyptian origins of Ishmael's mother (Gen. 25:12; also 16:3).[60] Gen. 21:21 is marked off as a secondary addition to its non-P context by (1) its doubling of the preceding notice that Ishmael "settled and grew up in the wilderness" (Gen. 21:20); and (2) its placing of Ishmael in the wilderness of Paran rather than the wilderness of Beer-Sheba (cf. Gen. 21:20 as linked to 21:14).[61] The probable original location of Gen. 21:21 was between the genealogical label in Gen. 25:12 and the list of Ishmael's sons in Gen. 25:13–16. Situated there, it would have corresponded to the same progression found in the nearby Priestly material regarding Jacob (Gen. 25:19–20, 26b): a label regarding the

---

59. The brief comment on the settlement of the Ishmaelites in Gen. 25:18 appears to have been appended to the Priestly genealogical section regarding Ishmael. It contrasts with all of the clearly Priestly settlement notices in focusing on a group rather than an individual (cf. Gen. 13:12; 25:11; 36:6–8; 37:1), and it uses the word *škn* rather than *yšb* for settlement.
60. Hupfeld, *Die Quellen der Genesis*, 30.
61. R. Kilian, *Die vorpriesterlichen Abrahamsüberlieferungen: Literarisch und traditionsgeschichtlich untersucht* (BBB 24; Bonn: Peter Hanstein Verlag, 1966), 235; Westermann, *Genesis 12—36*, 420; (E.T., 343).

descendants of Ishmael/Jacob, a note regarding a marriage, and notices regarding the descendants resulting from the marriage. It may have been moved by the Rp author/redactor from this probable original location to its present location in order to consolidate material regarding Ishmael's settlement in the wilderness.[62]

If this tentative picture is correct, we seem to have in P a closely interlocked system of travel, burial, marriage, and settlement notices dominated by a common Israel- and Canaan-centered perspective. Abraham and Lot travel to Canaan. Lot settles in the cities of the plain, while Abraham settles in the land of Canaan (Gen. 13:12). Abraham fathers Ishmael and Isaac, dies, and is buried by both of them. After his death Ishmael moves to the wilderness of Paran and marries an Egyptian (Gen. 21:21), while Isaac lives in Beer-la-hai-roi (Gen. 25:11) and marries Rebekah (Gen. 25:20). Isaac fathers Jacob and Esau. Esau disturbs his parents by marrying among the Canaanites (Gen. 26:34–5) and then marries among the Ishmaelites (28:8–9; cf. 36:2–3), while Isaac sends Jacob off to find more suitable wives among his kin (Gen. 28:1–2). Later Isaac dies after Jacob's return and is buried by both his sons. After his death another settlement split occurs. Esau settles in Seir; and Jacob, in the land of Canaan. In each case, the death of a patriarch—whether Terah, Abraham, or Isaac—issues in an eventual split in the settlement of his household, with the recipient of the promise settling in the land. The close link between the death and settlement notices may be further reflected by the fact that each time, the burial notice names the sons in the same order in which their settlement notices eventually occur: Isaac-Ishmael in 25:9 (cf. 25:11 and its probable counterpart, Gen. 21:21, originally located after 25:12), and Esau-Jacob in 35:29 (cf. 36:6–9; 37:1).

There may be one more piece of this puzzle. After Jacob dies and is buried by his sons in Canaan (Gen. 49:29–33; 50:12–13 in P), we see yet another settlement notice, this time not for any excluded brother, for there are no excluded brothers at this point, but instead for "Joseph . . . and the house of his father" in Egypt (Gen. 50:22a): "Joseph settled in Egypt, he and the house of his father." This note is immediately followed by an age notice that seems to share the special interest of other P texts in the age of a given patriarch (Gen. 50:22b), a related comment about Joseph's being able to see his grandsons (50:23), and a P-like age and death notice for Joseph in Gen. 50:26a. The special settlement, chronological, and life cycle interests of Gen.

62. This move may have been facilitated by the fact that the preceding non-P notice does not actually specify which wilderness Ishmael grew up in. In any case, 21:21 could now be understood as a sequel to the notice in 21:20, describing where he settled after growing up in the wilderness of Beer-Sheba. Meanwhile, the notice regarding the Ishmaelites in Gen. 25:18 seems to have been added by a redactor linking the thematic interests of non-P, particularly Gen. 16:12, with two elements: (1) the P interest in the geographical area where Esau, another excluded son, settled and (2) geographical information from various sources that puts Havilah near Egypt (Gen. 10:7; though cf. 10:29) and links Ishmael with Shur on the way to Egypt (Gen. 16:7; 20:1).

50:22–23, 26a would otherwise mark these texts by profile as P, and they provide a good link between the burial report in 50:12–13 and the beginning of the P exodus story in Exod. 1:1ff.[63]

In summary, Gen. 50:22–3, 26a seems to be the conclusion to the detailed P system of travel and settlement notices. After Abraham, Isaac, and Jacob have settled and eventually been buried in Canaan, Joseph and his sons settle in Egypt (50:22a). The P story is not finished, but the sojourn in the land of Canaan clearly is (cf. Gen. 17:8; 28:4). After these concluding notices for Joseph (Gen. 50:22b-3, 26a), P begins its Moses story in Exodus 1.

More Texts Often Assigned to P

So far I have covered the texts most critical to perception of fractures and crosscurrents in Genesis. Nevertheless, there are several other texts that do not fit into any of the above groups that are also assigned to P with varying degrees of plausibility. In recent years a number of studies attempted to establish the P connections of the section regarding Terah's life in Gen. 11:28–30.[64] Nevertheless, as Emerton has reminded us, the marriage report in Gen. 11:29 is inextricably connected to the following non-P materials regarding Isaac's marriage (Gen. 22:20–24; 24:1–67).[65] In addition, the location of Haran's death "in the land of his kindred" (Gen. 11:28) appears to provide background for the non-P report of YHWH's later command to Abraham to leave "from your land, your kindred and the house of your father."[66] Furthermore, the assertion of Sarah's barrenness in Gen. 11:30 would have no clear function in the P narrative, but it would serve as a tension heightening element in a non-P narrative that later features a promise that Abraham

---

63. Hupfeld, *Quellen der Genesis*, 36–38; I. Willi-Plein, "Historiographische Aspekte der Josefsgeschichte," *Henoch* 1 (1979): 310. Usually these verses are assigned to the Elohist. The main exceptions are Holzinger and Simpson. Holzinger, *Genesis*, 264, assigns the chronological notice in 22b to another hand, and Simpson builds on Holzinger by tentatively assigning it and the related notice in 50:26aβ to Rp (C. A. Simpson, *The Early Traditions of Israel: A Critical Analysis of the Predeuteronomic Narrative of the Hexateuch* [Oxford: Basil Blackwell, 1948], 157). Nevertheless, Rendtorff (*Problem*, 132n3; [E.T., 158]) rightly notes that these verses are rarely assigned to P despite their chronological focus. In any case, in light of Hupfeld's early analysis, Westermann, *Genesis 37—50*, 235 (E.T., 208), is incorrect in asserting "Zu P aber wird V. 22 von niemandem gerechnet" ("Verse 22, however, is not assigned to P by anyone"). The surrounding material will be discussed in subsequent chapters. It appears to be a mix of an earlier non-P transition to the Moses period (Gen. 50:24–25) and a late addition to the combined P/non-P text (Gen. 50:26b).
64. Van Seters, *Abraham*, 225 (cf. Prologue, 202); Blum, *Vätergeschichte*, 440–41; H. Specht, "Von Gott enttäuscht—Die priesterschriftliche Abrahamgeschichte," *EvTh* 47 (1987): 397–400. In this they were supporting a move back to the mid-nineteenth century position that all of Gen. 11:27–32 should be seen as Priestly. Cf. Hupfeld, *Die Quellen*, 17, and Nöldeke, *Untersuchungen*, 16–17.
65. J. A. Emerton, "The Source Analysis of Genesis XI 27–32," *VT* 42 (1992): 41–42, drawing on the original arguments by Budde, *Urgeschichte*, 414–32.
66. As Budde points out (*Urgeschichte*, 420), the P strand narrator, who described Terah's taking Lot (Gen. 11:31), need not have described the death of Lot's father, Haran, especially to an audience familiar with a Lot character (contra Blum, *Vätergeschichte*, 440).

will be made "a great nation" (Gen. 12:2) whose "seed" will be given the land (Gen. 12:7).[67] In summary, each element of Gen. 11:28–30 anticipates crucial elements of the non-P materials, while P characteristics occur exclusively in Gen. 11:27, 31–32.

Much more plausible is the assignment to the P strand of at least Sarah's giving Hagar to Abraham (Gen. 16:3), as the prelude to the P-strand note regarding the birth of Ishmael (Gen. 16:15–16). There is a conspicuous movement in the present text from the simple reference to Sarah in Gen. 16:2 (non-P) to the *re*identification of her as Abraham's wife in Gen. 16:3 (P), and Sarah's action in Gen. 16:3 does not follow her request of Abraham (Gen. 16:2) as well as the following description of his fulfillment of her request.[68] Furthermore, the dating of Sarah's giving Hagar to Abraham, "ten years after Abraham settled in Canaan" (Gen. 16:3aβ) does not fit its present context, standing as it does long after the earlier-dated notice regarding Abraham's settlement in Canaan (Gen. 12:4–5). Instead, this date is better suited to fit in an exclusively P context that moved directly from Abraham's settlement in Canaan (Gen. 13:12abα; 19:29) to Gen. 16:3: "Sarah, wife of Abraham, took Hagar, the Egyptian, her maidservant after ten years of living in the land of Canaan. . . . " The first half of Gen. 16:1 has also often been assigned to P, but the indicators in this case are far less clear.[69]

The lengthy report of Abraham's purchase of a cave at Machpelah connects directly to material in Priestly burial notices and even features some P-like age notices. At the same time, as Blum has most persuasively argued, this text does not appear to have been an original part of the P strand. Later texts referring to Abraham's purchase of the cave at Machpelah (Gen. 25:9–10; 49:31; 50:13) often appear to expand earlier Priestly burial notices, and the absence of such a reference in the one burial notice without a mention of Machpelah (Gen. 35:29b) suggests that these references to Abraham's purchase of the cave were added onto a Priestly system of burial notices that

---

67. Levin, *Der Jahwist*, 133.
68. Hupfeld, *Quellen der Genesis*, 24. As scholars such as Eerdmans (*Studien*, 12) have stressed, the present text does work, by having the Priestly text in Gen. 16:3 describe Sarah's preparation for Abraham's compliance in Gen. 16:4.
69. This assignment of Gen. 16:1a to P is based on little more than the probably coincidental resemblance between the identification of Sarah as "Abraham's wife" in 16:1a and 3, and the drive to construct a continuous P account. Yet actually this parallel identification of Sarah as "Abraham's wife" is as much a problem for the assignment of 16:1a to P as it is an indicator for it. Including Gen. 16:1a in a P account would mean that P would doubly identify Sarah (Gen. 16:1a, 3). This is not a problem for those for whom repetitive style is an indicator of P, but there is little evidence elsewhere that P repeatedly identifies familiar characters within such a short compass. Moreover, this introduction of Sarah's barrenness is absolutely essential for the non-P narrative, constituting the first part of a two-part introductory exposition to the non-P narrative: Sarah's barrenness (Gen. 16:1a) and the presence of Hagar (Gen. 16:1b). In summary, there is no good data to support assigning Gen. 16:1a to P, and there is good reason to see it as an essential element of the non-P narrative. Volz, *Elohist*, 136; Rendtorff, *Problem*, 124; (E.T., 149–50). For a treatment of Genesis 16 similar to that adopted here, see G. Coats, *Genesis with an Introduction to Narrative Literature* (FOTL 1; Grand Rapids: Eerdmans, 1983), 130–32.

already only irregularly mentioned the cave. On the basis of this pattern and the focus of Genesis 23 on the purchase of the cave, Blum plausibly argues that the layer of material including Genesis 23 is narrowly focused on emphasizing the legitimacy of the purchase of the cave, an interest that then emerged at each point where the Priestly material already mentioned the cave at Machpelah.[70]

Finally, several elements toward the end of the Joseph story appear to have belonged to P. The notice that "they took possession of it and were fruitful and multiplied exceedingly" (47:27b) describes the final fulfillment by Jacob's family of the often-repeated Priestly blessing to Abraham (Gen. 17:2, 6; cf. 28:3; 35:11; 48:4). Yet the plural verb of Gen. 47:27b clashes with the focus on a singular figure in the first half of the verse: "And Israel settled [verb in the singular] in the land of Canaan" (Gen. 47:27a). Rather than providing the continuation of Gen. 47:27a, this Priestly note that "they took possession (*'ḥz*) of it" (Gen. 47:27b) appears originally to have followed on the note in Gen. 47:11 that Joseph gave his family the best part of Egypt as a "possession" (*'ăḥuzzā h//'ḥz*). This "possession" language in turn is a faint link of both Gen. 47:11 and its continuation in 47:27b to Priestly texts that were discussed above (Gen. 17:8; 48:4; also 36:43).[71] We could continue further back in chapter 47 to texts that prepare for this account of Joseph's settling his family in Egypt. Nevertheless, the links between the previous context (Gen. 47:5–6a and 7–10) and P are tenuous, and secure assignment of this material to P, even if it could be done, would not greatly expand our understanding of P's major contributions to the present form of Genesis. So I end here with the Priestly fulfillment in Gen. 47:27b of those Priestly promises with which I began this chapter.

Concluding Overview

Looking back, the data for P in Genesis is varied. Through Gen. 9:17, two strands, a P strand and what I have termed here a non-P strand, are often closely parallel and well preserved. The resulting doublets and contrasting profiles allow for a relatively high degree of plausibility in reconstructing these two strands. Beyond that point I have identified a number of texts in Gen. 9:18–50:26 that are correlated to varying degrees with P texts in Gen. 1:1–9:17 and often appear secondary to their contexts. The P promise texts in Gen. 17; 26:34–35; 27:46–28:9; 35:9–15; and 48:3–6 have close links to

---

70. Blum, *Vätergeschichte,* 441–46. Cf. also Eerdmans, *Studien,* 20–23; R. Smend, *Die Erzählung des Hexateuch auf ihre Quellen untersucht* (Berlin: G. Reimer, 1912), 10–11; Eichrodt, *Quellen der Genesis,* 40–43; Levin, *Der Jahwist,* 193.
71. For discussion of possible theology behind this terminology and survey of the other occurrences of "possession" in P contexts, see L. Ruppert, *Die Josephserzählung der Genesis: Ein Beitrag zur Theologie der Pentateuchquellen* (Studien zum Alten und Neuen Testament 11; Munich: Kösel Verlag, 1965), 148.

each other and the P primeval history texts. Moreover, all except Gen. 48:3–6 show signs of having once existed separately from the non-P context on which they seem to have been modeled. The Priestly ancestral genealogical texts beginning in Gen. 11:10 also occasionally clash with their non-P contexts and have frequent close connections to the P genealogical framework in Genesis 5* and following. And then there are various places where the P strand appears to touch briefly on non-P stories (Gen. 16:3; 19:29; 47:[5–6a, 7–10], 11–27b), and other apparent fragments of P, including P-like age notices (Gen. 25:20; 37:2*; 47:28; 50:22b), travel reports, and settlement notices (Gen. 11:31; 12:4b–5; 13:6, 11b–12abα; 25:11; [21:21]; 31:17–18; 36:6–9; 37:1; 46:5*–7; 50:22a). Although the data for P in these last texts are occasionally thinner because of the smaller amount of material, the same limited scope of material means that the importance of the borderline cases for the reconstruction and study of P is likewise low.[72]

---

72. Emerton, "The Priestly Writer in Genesis," 391.

6

Concluding Reflections on the Priestly Material

Scope, Models, Structure, and Context

Overview of Results

Rp as the Priestly Redactor

P was originally separate from non-P material with which it is now combined, even as it was often modeled on non-P texts and designed to correct them. To be sure, as in all known cases where originally separate documents have been interwoven, not all parts of this postulated separate P document have been preserved. Nevertheless, it appears to have been preserved to a remarkable extent, particularly in the first half of the book. As a result, in much of Genesis we have the kind of conspicuous doubling that often marks conflation. Moreover, the bulk of this posited P document reads remarkably well, much better than a purely compositional/redactional layer, such as the D layer in the Deuteronomistic history, would read if it were separated out.

As we have seen, many of these P texts, though related to non-P traditions in various ways, do not seem to have been originally designed to stand alongside them. The overall P concept of a progression in revelation of divine names (Gen. 17:1; cf. Exod. 6:2–3) is now contradicted in the present text by the intervening non-P material that does not preserve this distinction. Specific P texts—for example, Genesis 17; 27:46–28:9; 35:9–15—are not coordinated with their non-P counterparts and often appear to presuppose that those counterparts do not exist in the same narrative line. Finally, there are a number of cases where once-connected elements of P are now separated from each other by intervening non-P material, cases such as Esau's marriage (Gen. 26:34–5) and Rebekah's plea to Isaac to prevent Isaac from marrying a foreign woman (Gen. 27:46), Joseph's gift of a part of Egypt to his family as a "possession" (Gen. 47:11) and their "taking possession of it" (Gen. 47:27b), or Jacob's commission of his sons to bury him (Gen. 49:29–33) and his sons' execution of this commission (Gen. 50:12–13).

Even the Priestly genealogical framework and above-discussed Priestly fragments show the marks of once having being part of an originally separate source. For example, the above-discussed Priestly chronological framework does not match the non-Priestly materials it now encloses. Now this chronological framework has Sarah 65 years old when she is first seized by Pharaoh (Gen. 12:10–20; cf. 12:4b; 17:17) and 90 the second time (Genesis 20; cf. 17:17; 21:5). Likewise, Ishmael is already 14 when Hagar carries him on her shoulder, puts him under a bush, and does not want to hear his crying (Gen. 21:15–16; cf. 16:16; 21:5). In addition, Joseph is a grown seventeen-year-old when Reuben refers to him as a "boy" (*yeled*, 37:30; cf. 37:2). Someone put some care into this chronological system, but it does not look as if it was originally designed to enclose the non-P narratives it now frames.[1] The same could be said of the system of travel notices in P. We repeatedly see parallel notes regarding the patriarchs' travels in P and non-P, and the P system diverges from the non-P material at crucial points, such as its placement of Jacob's sojourn in Padan-Aram instead of Haran. Similarly, the P settlement notices clash with non-P materials at several points, such as Ishmael's split from Isaac before (non-P) or after (P) Abraham's death. Again and again the P materials, although fragmentary, show signs of originally being a separate source that was only later interwoven with another source into a new whole.

In every documented example of such interweaving outside the Bible, the author of the combined text has composed some material that links the source documents into a new whole. In this respect, Genesis appears to be no exception. At the same time, Genesis is distinguished by the extent to which this author/redactor appears to have worked primarily out of the conceptuality of one of his sources, P. We have seen this author's direct contributions in numerous P-like texts that link P and non-P materials: the Gen. 2:4a genealogical heading, the revision of non-P creation and flood materials to match Priestly models (Gen. 2:19*, 20*; 6:7aβ; 7:3a, 8–9, 23aα*; 8:13a), and the genealogical heading and P-like framework of Genesis 10 (Gen. 10:1a, 2–7, 20, 22–23, 31–32).[2] At a few points, this Rp author/redactor appears to have added to P texts (such as "and he was a youth" in 37:2), but these quite limited modifications merely coordinate P narratives with their non-P counterparts. This leaning toward Priestly conceptuality is the main justification for speaking of this author/redactor as a Priestly redactor, Rp. In the final chapter I will reflect more on the possible background of these Priestly leanings of the redactor who combined P and non-P materials.

Meanwhile, there are some other indicators of redactional work I have not yet reviewed. For example, the Rp redactor is probably responsible for displacing the P reference to the Sodom story in Gen. 19:29 from its original

---

1. These data are the strongest argument against those who would maintain that these chronological notices are secondary additions to the present combined text. It is no easier to explain these problems with a later redactor than it is with an original P author. Cf. Smend, *Erzählung*, 12–13, 99–100; Levin, *Der Jahwist*, 140 (but cf. 150), 271.

2. In addition, in the previous chapter, I identified this redactor's hand in the addition of the P Padan-Aram theme to the non-P notice regarding Jacob's return in Gen. 33:18.

location right after the P description of Lot's settlement in Sodom in Gen. 13:11b-12abα.[3] So also, we have seen another possible example of such displacement in the shifting of an apparent Priestly settlement notice for Ishmael from its probable original location in the section regarding his descendants (after Gen. 25:12) to its present location as part of the non-P story of Ishmael (Gen. 21:21). Such examples of displacement and compensation for it are yet another indicator that P was once a separate document and was not composed from the beginning to stand in the same document as the non-P materials with which it is now combined.

In general, this P author/redactor seems to have almost completely preserved the P primeval history, authored a P-like framework to expand and incorporate the non-P table of nations into the genealogical structure of P (Genesis 10*), and then used blocks of Priestly material clustered around the Priestly concluding death notices and beginning genealogical labels (Gen. 11:10-27; 25:7-20; 35:22b-37:2; cf. 49:29-33; 50:12-13) to frame more detailed non-P accounts of Israel's ancestors. At times, isolated material, such as the probable beginning of the Priestly Joseph story in 37:2, seems to have found its way into the combined narrative by way of its association with one of these larger blocks. In addition, some isolated linking elements of the Priestly composition, such as the above discussed P travel reports, settlement reports, and age notices, have been blended into non-P materials. Nevertheless, where Rp used a full Priestly narrative, such as the P creation text or promise texts, he appears to have strategically inserted it *as a whole* into a non-P context.

Thus, the bulk of Rp's work, at least as far as we can detect it, appears to have consisted of the combination of larger blocks of P and non-P material. Indeed, this block-like character of much of the Rp conflation is one reason it is possible to distinguish P and non-P at all. Already in the methodological discussion with which I started the book, we saw the following principle: the more intricate the interweaving of separate materials, the more impossible it becomes to disentangle the originally separate strands. In general Rp appears to have worked with large blocks. The only place in Genesis where P and non-P narratives are intricately interwoven is in the flood account, particularly in the middle, and this interweaving was probably caused by special factors. Earlier in my discussion of the P genealogical framework, we saw how the Rp redactor consistently avoided preserving parallel P and non-P reports of the patriarchs' deaths. In the case of the Flood, however, Rp has preserved both

---

3. When he did this, he seems to have compensated for the displacement by adding to the end of the original P notice, "when [God] destroyed the cities in which Lot had settled" (19:29bβγ). This temporal notice reproduces part of the context from which 19:29abα has now been displaced. At the same time the notice partially doubles the temporal clause that specifies God remembered and saved Lot "when God destroyed the cities of the plain" (Gen. 19:29aα). The extra temporal notice in 19:29bβγ would not have been necessary when 19:29 came right after 13:11b-12abα. Eerdmans, *Studien*, 11; Levin, *Der Jahwist*, 168.

destruction reports, perhaps because both strands were judged theologically significant.[4] Moreover, he did not put one flood account as a block right after the other. Such a move might have left the impression that the earth died twice. Instead, *particularly in the middle where the destruction takes place*, Rp wove the reports together so skillfully that readers throughout the centuries have been able to read the combined product as the description of a single flood.

The distinctive profile of the P material, along with the remarkable extent to which Rp seems to have preserved competing narratives from P, are additional factors that enable isolation of P material from non-P material.[5] At the same time, however, these distinctive P materials have been carefully combined with their non-P parallels, so many P texts now play a crucial role in the combined P/non-P composition. Thus, for example, the Rp redactor appears to have used the Priestly genealogical labels to structure the overall P/non-P composition, and even to have composed a few extra such labels to encompass non-P materials (Gen. 2:4a; 10:1). So also, Rp placed the P version of the Abraham covenant right after the story of Ishmael's birth, so it now functions in part to clarify that Isaac, not Ishmael, will be the recipient of the covenant.[6] Such powerfully creative fusing of the clearly distinct P and non-P traditions deserves further analysis. We will return to that task at the conclusion of the book, after I have explored the transmission history and character of the non-P material with which Rp worked.

The P Source

For now, let us turn to closer consideration of the reconstructed P document itself. Clearly this reconstructed P source drew on a variety of materials. Foremost among them appears to be some version of the non-P traditions in Genesis. There are striking parallels and oppositions between non-P and P versions of the creation of humanity, the creation-to-flood genealogy, and the Flood; and then between versions of various elements of the ancestral history: the trip to Canaan, the split of Abraham and Lot, the covenant with Abraham and the promise of a child, the destruction of Sodom and Gomorrah, the story of Hagar, the departure of Jacob from his family, the revelation at Bethel, the arrival of Jacob in Egypt, and the burial of Jacob. In addition, P probably drew at various points on other traditions, such as an unreconstructable eight-act creation tradition (Gen. 1:1–31*), a "scroll of

4. Levin, *Der Jahwist*, 345, points out the exceptional character of this report and the Reed Sea narrative.
5. Cf. the case of a text like Tatian's *Diatessaron*, where the texts being combined are enough alike that isolation of them from one another would be almost impossible on the basis of the *Diatessaron* alone. In this case, the differences between P and non-P are pronounced enough that isolation of them from one another is more possible. Here again Farmer's response to Frye is relevant (Farmer, "Basic Affirmation with Some Demurrals," 316–17).
6. Ska, "Quelques remarques sur Pg," 112–13.

the descendants of Adam" (Gen. 5:1–28, 30–32), a genealogy of Esau (Genesis 36*), and a tradition regarding Jacob's stay in Padan-Aram.

In the end, however, the priestly composition is not about appropriating tradition for tradition's sake but about using such traditions as part of a new conceptualization of Israel's prehistory. In order to get a clearer grasp of P material in Genesis, we must take a brief look at the contours of P in the rest of the Torah. The Priestly reconceptualization of Israel's prehistory in Genesis is integrally related to the P account of the formation of Israel and Israel's cult in the Moses story. Furthermore, the P material in the Moses story provides additional data for understanding the theology and sociopolitical context of the P material discussed above.

Excursus: P in the Moses Story

From the outset, the presence of P material in the Moses story is clear. Exodus 1:1–5, 7 begins with a description of the complete fulfillment of the Priestly fertility blessing (Gen. 1:28; 9:1, 7; 17:2b, 6a; 28:3; 35:11; 47:27; 48:4) among the descendants of Jacob. In Exod. 2:24 God "remembers" the covenant with Abraham, Isaac, and Jacob, much like God "remembered" Noah and Abraham in the P material of Genesis (Gen. 8:1; 19:29). In addition, the Sabbath-focused creation account of Gen. 1:1–2:3 links in multiple ways with the Sabbath-focused P tabernacle-building account of Exodus 25—40*,[7] and the P promise texts of Genesis 17—50 are continued in YHWH's speech to Moses in Exod. 6:2–8.

This is not the place for a complete discussion of P in the Moses story. Suffice it to say that the identification of a P layer in the Moses story is relatively undisputed, particularly toward the beginning. For example, the concept of a progression in revelation of the divine name finds its culmination in the call of Moses in Exod. 6:2–8 (cf. Exod. 3:1–4:17), a call that doubles the preceding non-P account of Moses' call in Exod. 3:1–4:17.[8] The portions of the following plague narrative that are usually assigned to P (Exod. 7:8–13 [introduction], 19–20a, 21b–22 [plague 1]; 8:1–3 [Eng. 5–7], 11 end [plague 2; Eng. 8:15], 12–15 [plague 3;

---

7. A. Klostermann, *Der Pentateuch: Beiträge zu seinem Verständnis und seiner Entstehungsgeschichte* (Leipzig: A. Dreicherische Verlagsbuchhandlung, 1907), 44; Jacob, *Genesis*, 67; M. Buber, "Der Mensch von heute und die jüdische Bibel," in *Die Schrift und ihre Verdeutschung* (Berlin: Schocken, 1936), 39–41. For newer literature and observations, see particularly Blum, *Studien*, 306–12; B. Janowski, "Tempel und Schöpfung: Schöpfungstheologische Aspekte der priesterschriftlichen Heiligtumskonzeption," *Jahrbuch für Biblische Theologie* 5 (1990; reprinted in *Gottes Gegenwart in Israel: Beiträge zur Theologie des Alten Testaments* [Neukirchen-Vluyn: Neukirchener Verlag, 1993], 214–46, especially 223–24, 236–40); and J. Blenkinsopp, *The Pentateuch*, 60–63, 217–19.

8. Ska, "Quelques remarques sur Pg," 98, argues that 6:2–8 can not be a call narrative because it lacks an actual sending of Moses and the standard objection to the call. Such arguments rightfully point out that Exod. 6:2–8 is not as close to the prophetic call scheme as Exod. 3:1–4:17. Nevertheless, Moses is sent at the heart of the speech (Exod. 6:6), and the deviations from the form appear to arise out of particular priestly theology. Ska among others has done much to illuminate the function of Exod. 6:2–8 within its present context. Nevertheless, the passage also could have served in an independent priestly document as the introduction of Moses, albeit an introduction presupposing the audience's familiarity with Moses as a figure in Israel's history.

Eng. 8:16–19]; 9:8–12 [plague 6]) show a clear structure and theology, bearing the marks of material that once existed separately.[9] Then, the P version of the Reed Sea crossing is an almost complete, parallel, alternatively conceptualized account of an event also reported in the non-P material with which it is now interwoven (Exodus 14),[10] and the P Sinai account appears deliberately to exclude an account of a Sinai covenant. Instead it presents the Sinai events as an outgrowth of the covenant with Abraham (Genesis 17).[11] To be sure, there is a good deal of debate about layers in P. In particular, there is lack of consensus on the extent to which substantial blocks of the Priestly Sinai legislation and P-like narratives at the end of Numbers were parts of the earliest P document.[12] Nevertheless, even here there are some striking similarities in dynamics with the situation in Genesis. P in Genesis is most clearly present as an originally separate source in the primeval history and less clearly preserved at the end in the Joseph story. So also, P in the Moses story is most clearly present in the oppression, call, plague, and Reed Sea episodes at the outset, and increasingly disputed as one moves into Leviticus and Numbers.

To be sure, as we look at P in the Moses story, there are the kinds of gaps we see in every documented example of conflated sources. Nevertheless, one must once again be careful not to presuppose that certain things would be in P because

9. Blum, *Studien*, 250. On 250–52, however, Blum goes on to argue that this material is but a pre-Priestly source used by the P author. Following Noth, he has already argued for the assignment of additional material to P (9:22–23aα, 35; 10:12–13aα, 14aα, 20–23, 27; pp. 245–50). Building on this analysis, he argues that this additional Priestly material is dependent on the non-P/Kd material not only for content but for structural function. Moreover, P material regarding the Passover in Exodus 12 appears to presuppose a narrative regarding the killing of the first-born that is now found only in non-P (Exod. 11:1–8; 12:29–32; cf. also 11:9–10). As Blum points out, Rp as usually conceived of (particularly by Noth) would not have eliminated such a crucial block of P material. Such conceptions, however, have proven faulty, particularly with regard to the idea that an Rp who was conflating would have mechanistically preserved all of his source material. Therefore, this gap, though striking, would not be a decisive argument for an original link between the Priestly compositional layer and non-P material. The rest of Blum's argument depends largely on his defense of Noth's particular assignment of additional material to P. These arguments deserve closer analysis but fall outside the range of this study.

More recently, J. Van Seters has likewise argued that certain gaps in the P plague account indicate it must have been composed from the outset to supplement the non-P material (*The Life of Moses* [Louisville, Ky.: Westminster John Knox Press, 1994], 103–12). His biggest argument is that certain details of the P introduction to the plagues in Exod. 7:1–7 occur only in the non-P plague accounts, such as the prediction that Moses and Aaron will speak to pharaoh. Nevertheless, P handles this through an execution formula at the outset: "Moses and Aaron did so; they did just as the LORD commanded them. Moses was eighty years old and Aaron eighty-three when they spoke to pharaoh" (Exod. 7:6–7, NRSV). There is no gap in P at this point. It just narrates things less fully than its non-P counterpart.

10. Cf. Vervenne, "The 'P' Tradition in the Pentateuch," 81–87, who relies heavily on Zenger's and Weimar's complex analysis of the material (on the latter, cf. Blum, *Studien*, 259). Blum, *Studien*, 260 (with n. 116) points out that here, as elsewhere, P does not represent a completely continuous, readable strand. Nevertheless, he recognizes enough continuity here (along with a gap in the Priestly material at Exod 14:15a) to posit alongside the non-Priestly Reed Sea episode a pre-Priestly source used by the Priestly author (260–61).

11. W. Zimmerli, "Sinaibund und Abrahambund: Ein Beitrag zum Verständnis der Priesterschrift," *TZ* 16 (1960): 268–80; E. Nicholson, "P as an Originally Independent Source," 199–200; Blum, *Studien*, 293–94 (cf. n. 26 on 294–95 regarding Zimmerli).

12. For comprehensive collection of all possible arguments against assignment of this material (along with everything else after Exodus) to Pg, see Pola, *Ursprüngliche Priesterschrift*, 49–145.

they occur in non-P texts. For example, as a result of the non-P analogy, we would expect P to have an account of Moses' birth and marriage (cf. Exod. 2:1–22), but P moves smoothly from God's "remembering" the Israelites in Exod. 2:25 to God's call of Moses in Exod. 6:2. Perhaps Rp has eliminated the P account of Moses' early life in favor of the non-P material. Yet it is also possible the smoothness of the potential continuity between Exod. 2:25 and 6:2 reflects the absence of a corresponding P account. It is impossible to know. In either case, the gap at this point is not a decisive argument against the hypothesis that much P material in the Moses story was once part of an originally separate source.

Looking at the contours of P in the Moses story, the prominence of the Sinai account is striking. No other event in the preserved material from P receives so much attention. To be sure, this could simply reflect a particular interest of Rp in the Sinai material. Nevertheless, a number of the P-source texts isolated in Genesis lead up to this event: the sabbath-focused Genesis 1 creation account, the P account of the building of the ark (which anticipates the tabernacle account), P covenants with Noah and Abraham, and so forth.

Finally, as we turn to look at what follows Sinai in P, the relative paucity of material is striking. Even if one follows the traditional assignment of material toward the end of Numbers to P, there is not much of it. Much of Israel dies in a plague following their lack of belief in God's gift of the land (Numbers 13—14*). Some kind of material regarding leadership and challenges to it may have followed (Numbers 16—18), and the (traditionally reconstructed) story concludes with Moses himself being excluded from the land on account of his lack of faith (Numbers 20). The potentially Priestly material then ends with accounts of the deaths of Aaron (Num. 20:22b–29) and Moses (Deut. 34:1*, 7–9).[13] Although P may have included some material regarding the settlement of the land, establishment of the existence of this material and identification of its contours is quite uncertain.

The Nature of the Reconstructed P Document

Text: Structure and Genre

As we look at the parts of the posited P document that appear to be preserved in the Pentateuch, there are two major breaks in the material. The first is between the cosmology in Gen. 1:1–2:3 and the genealogically focused material introduced by the superscription in Gen. 5:1, "This is the book of the descendants of Adam." As we saw previously, this superscription does not just introduce the genealogical material in Gen. 5:1–32*. Instead, it now labels the entire range of P genealogically focused material, from 5:1 to the death and burial of Jacob in Gen. 49:29–33; 50:12–13. At this point, however, the pattern of relating the naming of the patriarch, his fathering, and his

---

13. For critiques of assignment of these texts to P, cf. L. Perlitt, "Priesterschrift im Deuteronomium?" *ZAWSup* 100 (1988): 65–88. (This article focuses on Deut. 34:1*, 7–9. It is reprinted in *Deuteronomium-Studien* [FAT 8; Tübingen: J.C.B. Mohr, 1994], 123–43.) Cf. also P. Stoellger, "Deuteronomium 34 ohne Priesterschrift," *ZAW* 105 (1993): 26–50, especially 27–30, 36–46; and Pola, *Ursprüngliche Priesterschrift*, 93–95, 99–104. On this problem, cf. L. Schmidt, *Studien zur Priesterschrift* (BZAW 214; Berlin/New York: W. de Gruyter, 1993), 241–51.

death introduced in Genesis 5 ends,[14] and Exod. 1:1, a P text, begins a history of Israel's formation that extends to Deut. 34:9. The section that it begins (Exod. 1:1–5, 7) reviews the one aspect of the preceding narrative essential for what follows: the bringing of the sons of Jacob to Egypt and the fertility of their descendants.[15] This review introduces the formation of these descendants into God's people with the tabernacle cult at their center (Exodus 1—Deuteronomy 34*).[16] From here on the history is dominated not by the production of children and choosing of heirs, nor by the death of patriarchs and transmission of the blessing, nor by the making of covenants and response to them, but instead by the movement of Israel from Egypt into Canaan. As Weimar and Zenger have observed, Sinai is the orientation point for this journey. The major sections of the Moses story are defined not by the lifetimes of progenitors, but by the itinerary for their movement to and from Sinai.[17] Moreover, following Knierim, the overall scope of this formative history is defined by a lifetime, although not the lifetime of a progenitor but of a leader, Moses.[18] This final major section of P extends from a prologue to Moses' work in Exod. 1:1–7, 13–14; 2:23–25, to an account of his call and pivotal leadership in Exod. 6:2–Num. 27:23*, to its probable conclusion with Moses' death and burial in Deut. 34:1, 7–9.[19]

14. The presence of a P "descendants" heading in Num. 3:1 only highlights the shift that has occurred by this point. The heading introduces an isolated list of Aaron's descendants and in no way defines a broader macrostructural unit in the way the P genealogical headings in Genesis do.
15. For summary of the arguments that Exod. 1:6 belongs not to P but to non-P, see particularly W. H. Schmidt, *Exodus* (BKAT 2; Neukirchen-Vluyn: Neukirchener Verlag, 1974), 10.
16. Weimar, "Struktur," 98–99, and Zenger, *Gottes Bogen*, 38–39, have argued that Exod. 1:1–7 is the conclusion to the first half of P, not the beginning of a new section (see also Hupfeld, *Quellen der Genesis*, 37–38). This thesis has two major difficulties. First, the P material in Exod. 1:13–14 develops and is inextricably linked to the comment in Exod. 1:7. Exodus 1:13–14 is hardly the beginning of Israel's national history as Weimar and Zenger would have it. Second and more important, Exod. 1:1–7* shows signs of being just such a beginning. The superscription in Exod. 1:1, although it just introduces 1:2–4, marks a structural break. Furthermore, even the links of Exod. 1:1–7 with what precedes already indicate that this break coincides with a significant shift in focus in the Priestly writing, from the ancestors of Israel to the people descending from them. The material in Exod. 1:1–7 does not so much report the completion of the various narrative threads of P in Genesis, as *review* the completion of those threads, particularly the bringing of Jacob's sons into Egypt (Gen. 46:5–7) and the fulfillment of the fertility blessing (Gen. 47:27b). Now the P narrative of Genesis is not being pulled forward but is presupposed to prepare for the following national history. To be sure, the "filling" of the land of Egypt does represent a particular parallel to the "filling of the earth" of Gen. 1:28; 9:1, (7). Nevertheless, the particular focus of this formulation on Egypt indicates that Exod. 1:7 is not a fulfillment of the creation blessing. Instead, it is an echoing of that blessing *in the process of pointing forward* to God's formation of the nation through the exodus from Egypt. The issue is not just connections between units but the structural function of the connections. In the case of Exod. 1:1–7, material from the preceding Priestly material is presupposed and selectively reviewed and developed *in order to introduce* the following national history of Israel.
17. Weimar, "Struktur," 98–105; Zenger, *Gottes Bogen*, 138–40.
18. R. Knierim, "The Composition of the Pentateuch," *Society of Biblical Literature 1985 Seminar Papers* (ed. K. H. Richards; Atlanta: Scholars Press, 1985), 394–96.
19. For arguments that this material was not part of P, see the literature cited in n. 13 in this chapter.

Between these three major sections are two transitional texts that link the major sections, even as they mark the seams between them. Genesis 5:1b–2 introduces the scroll of the descendants of Adam by briefly reviewing God's creation of Adam in the divine image. In this way the genealogy steps back to make the transition from cosmology to genealogy. More particularly, the note clearly shows that "Adam" is no longer "humanity in general" but the first progenitor of the human race. Similarly, Exod. 1:1–5, 7 introduces the following national history of Israel by redescribing Israel's multiplication in Egypt (cf. Gen. 47:27). Yet this is now but the prologue to the description of their oppression in Egypt (Exod. 1:13–14; 2:23) and God's response, calling Moses (Exod. 2:24–25; 6:2–8). Just as the review in Gen. 5:1b–2 accomplished the shift from humanity in general to a single progenitor of the human race, so also the redescription of Israel's multiplying and filling the land of Israel in Exod. 1:1–5, 7 helps accomplish the shift from a genealogically focused family history giving an account of Israel's ancestors (Gen. 5:1–50:26*) to a national history culminating in the founding of the cult at Sinai (Exod. 1:13–Deut. 34:9*).

As we look more closely at the genealogical subsection in P, the most fundamental division in it is between (1) the internationally focused genealogical sections culminating in the covenant with Noah (Genesis 5—9*) and (2) the Israel-focused genealogical sections developing God's covenant with Abraham (Genesis 11—50*).[20] The former has a cosmic setting, while the latter is distinguished by its narrower focus on Israel's sojourn in Canaan, a sojourn beginning with Abraham's move to Canaan (Gen. 12:4b–5; 13:6, 11b–12abα), continuing with the burial of the fathers in Canaan and the splitting of the sons into two groups—the heirs who stay in Canaan and the nonheirs who do not, and concluding with Jacob's move to Egypt and his and Joseph's death there. This land schema dominating the P travel and settlement notices throughout Gen. 11:31–50:26* is one among many indicators of the importance of the land in the covenant featured in this Israel-focused series of genealogical sections. For example, the Priestly system of burial and settlement notices makes clear that it is the heirs of the promise, and they alone, who are buried in the land. Insofar as Israel shared the belief (attested elsewhere) that a family has a special claim to the land in which its ancestors' bones lie, this description of the burial of multiple generations of ancestors in the land is at the same time a claim of the Israelites' right to possess it.[21]

Within this context, the genealogy of Shem's descendants in 11:10–26 provides a bridge from the internationally focused section to the Israel-focused ancestral accounts. Genesis 11:10–26 is closer to what follows in its

---

20. Albertz, *Religionsgeschichte*, vol. 2, 531–32; (E.T., 489–91).
21. I am indebted to Brian B. Schmidt (University of Michigan, Ann Arbor) for the oral communication that legal documents from Emar indicate a concern about this issue and that some Japanese and Chinese texts reflect a presupposition that a family owns a given plot when three or four generations of their ancestors are buried in it.

narrow focus on the ancestors of Abraham. At the same time, it forges a link with what precedes by specifically linking Abraham with the descendants after the Flood. In Gen. 11:10–26 we are led from the broader circle of international history culminating in God's covenant with Noah and the postflood humanity descending from him, to the narrower circle of family history leading to God's formation of the nation of Israel. Notably, both these histories of P are in turn enclosed by the yet broader cosmic circle presented in the cosmology of Gen. 1:1–2:3, where the overall creation framework for all that follows is presented.[22] Thus in P we have the cosmic creation as the setting for the Noah covenant, which in turn is the setting for God's covenant with Israel. Genesis 11:10–26 links these covenant-centered Flood and Israel-focused sections of P with each other.

These major units in P are of different genre. The first distinctive unit in P is the cosmology in Gen. 1:1–2:3, distinguished from what follows by the heading to the genealogical book in Gen. 5:1. The following genealogically focused bridge from creation to nation in Gen. 5:1–50:26* is probably best characterized as an "expanded genealogy." It is expanded in two senses: (1) it combines both linear genealogy and a horizontal listing of descendants of a given progenitor; and (2) it goes beyond the brief notes or stories that are often part of shorter genealogies (cf., for example, Gen. 5:1b–3, 22, 24)[23] to enclose in the genealogical framework more extended narratives: the flood story, ancestral travel and settlement reports, and the giving and transmission of the Abrahamic covenant. Notably this expanded genealogy is distinguished from the material in Exodus and following by both its intensive life-cycle focus and its overall focus on the "sojourn" (and burial) of Abraham, Isaac, and Jacob in Canaan. Moreover, its genealogical form of organization takes precedence over a linear progression. According to chronological notices (Gen. 21:5; 25:7), Abraham was 140 years old at the outset of the section regarding Isaac's descendants (Gen. 25:20), and Isaac must still have been alive throughout much of the section on Jacob's descendants (Gen. 25:20; 35:28; 47:9), even though he is not mentioned. In each case, the swerve from a straight chronological progression, both by excluding certain genealogical lines and by resolutely focusing on certain father-son pairs, indicates the importance of this overall genealogical structure.

The following national history in Exodus is more difficult to characterize generically. For the purposes of this study I will characterize it in terms of its scope, the lifework of Moses, and I will term it a "lifework story." Form-

22. Albertz, *Religionsgeschichte,* vol. 2, 532–35; (E.T., 491–93).
23. See also the expansions of the genealogy in 1 Chronicles 1—8: 1:10b (Nimrod); 2:3b (Er); 7 (Achar), 22b (Jair); 4:9–10 (Jabez), 38–43 (leaders in clans); 5:1–2 (Reuben), 6 (Beera of Reuben), 8–10 (Bela of Reuben), 18–22 (battle of Reubenites, Gadites, and Manasseh), 25–26 (rebellion of Manasseh), 36b (Johanan; Eng. 6:9); 7:21b–23 (Beriah's background). These extend from brief notes identifying a given figure (e.g., 1 Chr. 1:10; 2:3b, 7b; 5:36b [Eng. 6:10]) to more extended stories connected to them (4:9–10; 5:18–22; 7:21–23). Although this genealogy is significantly later than P, it is culturally close enough to be a useful comparison.

critical work by Baltzer and Knierim, among others, has established the existence in the ancient Near East of a career-focused genre, one distinguished
from the more individualistic and psychologically focused modern genre of
biography by its interest in the function of a given individual vis-à-vis a given
community.[24] The term *lifework story* reflects the scope of the P unit extending from Exodus to Deuteronomy *and* its focus on Moses' function vis-à-vis
Israel, rather than on his personality per se.

Building on these insights, I offer the following tentative structure of P:

Outline of P Genesis Materials

I. Cosmology: Sabbath-focused creation starting point   *Gen. 1:1–2:3*
II. Expanded genealogy: Covenant-focused prologue to
national formation   *Gen. 5:1–50:26**
  A. International context: Noachic covenant and blessing   *5:1–9:28**
    1. Adam's descendants: Prologue to the Flood   *5:1–28, 30–32*
    2. Noah's descendants: Establishment of the
Noachic covenant   *6:9–9:28**
  B. Genealogy of Shem's descendants: Intracovenant bridge   *11:10–26*
  C. Israel Center: Abrahamic covenant and blessing   *11:27–50:26**
    1. Terah's descendants: Establishment of the
Abrahamic covenant   *11:27–25:11**
      a) Superscription   *11:27aα*
      b) Body   *11:27aβ–25:11**
        (1) Life of Terah: Birth of sons and initiation
of trip toward Canaan   *11:27aβb, 31–32*
        (2) Life of Abraham: Initiation of sojourn
and covenant   *12:4b–25:11**
          (a) Background leading up to the covenant
12:4b–19:29abα; 16:3,15–16
          (b) Establishment of the covenant   *17:1–27*
          (c) First consequence of the covenant:
Birth of Isaac   *21:1–5**
      c) Conclusion: End of life of Abraham, transfer
of blessing   *(23:1–20 addition) 25:7–11*[25]
    2. Next generation pair   *25:12–35:29**
      a) Ishmael's descendants: Fertility of the
excluded offspring   *25:12–18[+21:21]*
      b) Isaac's descendants: Fertility and
transmission of blessing   *25:19–35:29**

24. Knierim, "The Composition of the Pentateuch," 406–15, building in particular on the
work of K. Baltzer, *Die Biographie der Propheten* (Neukirchen-Vluyn: Neukirchener Verlag,
1975), 19–197.
25. The concluding notices for the life of Abraham in Gen. 25:7–11 serve double duty as the
conclusion to the section concerning him (and thus parallel to 11:32) and as a conclusion to
the section on Terah's descendants as a whole.

(1) Superscription   *25:19a*
(2) Body   *25:19b–35:29**
   (a) Birth: Jacob and Esau   *25:19b . . . 26b*
   (b) Travel narrative (to and from
      Padan-Aram)   *26:34–35:27**
      (i) Departure for Padan-Aram   *26:34–35; 27:46–28:9*
      (ii) Return from Padan-Aram   *31:17–35:27**
         (*a*) Trip to Canaan   *31:17–18*
         (*b*) Bethel epiphany upon return   *35:9–15*
         (*c*) Final approach/conclusion   *35:22b–27*
   (3) Conclusion: End of life of Isaac   *35:28–29*
3. Final generation pair   *36:1–50:26**
  a) Esau's descendants: Fertility of the excluded
    offspring   *36:1–37:1*
  b) Jacob's descendants: Fulfillment of Abrahamic
    version of the fertility blessing in Egypt   *37:2–50:26**
    (1) Superscription   *37:2aα1–3*
    (2) Body   *37:2aα*–47:27**
      (a) Exposition [leading to unpreserved
         P story of Joseph]   *37:2**
      (b) Migration   *46:5–47:27**
    (3) Concluding Notes:
      (a) End of Life of Jacob: Burial in Canaan   *47:28–50:13**
      (b) End of Life of Joseph   *50:22–23, 26a*
III. Life work story: Formation of cult-centered Israel
    through Moses   *Exodus-Deuteronomy**

Intertext: The Relation of P to Non-P Materials

This look at the structure clarifies certain aspects of the relation of P to non-P materials (see Chart 6-1). Three characteristics stand out. First, P in Genesis is remarkably parallel to non-P in its overall outline. It begins with Creation, a preflood genealogy, Flood, and postflood covenant and genealogy. Then it continues with similar accents at each major stage of the ancestral story, a promise-focused Abraham story, travel-focused Jacob story, and migration-focused Joseph story. Despite significant differences, the similarity in overall contours of the P and non-P materials is striking.

Second, whereas P in the primeval history is expanded in comparison with its non-P parallels, P's ancestral history seems to be less extensive than non-P's. To be sure, such suppositions are particularly dangerous given the tendency of redactors to selectively preserve material from their sources. Nevertheless, the relative readability of much of the P material, particularly in the first half of Genesis, suggests that Rp preserved a larger than average amount of both sources. Moreover, at precisely these points the remarkably preserved material from P appears to be much less extensive in the Abraham section than in the primeval history section. Whereas the primeval history P narra-

Chart 6-1: Corresponding Units in P and Non-P Materials

P	Non-P
Creation (1:1–2:3)	Creation of life (2:4b–3:24)
Genealogical scroll (5:1–28*, 30–32)	Seven-generation bridge (4:1–26*, 5:29)
Flood history (6:9–22; 7:6, 11, 13–16a, 18–21, 23aβ, 24; 8:1–2a, 3b–5, 14–19; 9:1–17)	Flood history (6:1–7aα, 7b–8; 7:1–2, 3b–5, 7, 10, 12, [16b–]17, 22, 23aα*, [b]; 8:2b–3a, 6–12, 13b, 20–22)
	Postflood genealogy (10:1b, 8–19, 21, 24–30)
Genealogical bridge (11:10–26)	[*No corresponding material in Non-P*]
Terah's/Abraham's journey to Canaan (11:27–32; 12:4b–5)	Call and journey of Abraham (12:1–4a, 6–8)
Split with Lot (13:6, 11b–12abα)	Split with Lot and confirmation of promise (13:1–5, 7–11a, 12bβ–18)
Birth of Ishmael (16:3, 15–16)	Birth of Ishmael (16:1–2, 4–14 . . .)
Covenant with Abraham (17:1–27)	[Covenant with Abraham (15:1–21)]
Sodom and Gomorrah note (19:29)	[Sodom and Gomorrah story (19:1–28)]
Birth of Isaac (21:3–5+)	Birth of Isaac (21:1a . . . 6–7)
Death and burial of Abraham (25:7–10)	[*No corresponding material in Non-P*]
Transfer of blessing (25:11)	[Demonstration of transfer of blessing (Genesis 26)]
Ishmael's genealogy (25:12–17)	[*No corresponding material in Non-P*]
[Settlement and marriage of Ishmael (21:21)]	Life of Ishmael (21:20)
Isaac's marriage and children (25:19–20, 26b)	[cf. Genesis 24]
Jacob's departure for Padan-Aram (26:34–35; 27:46–28:9)	Jacob's stealing of blessing and departure (27:1–45)
Departure from Haran (31:17–18)	Jacob's departure and Rachel's stealing of gods (31:19–20)
Bethel epiphany(ies) (35:9–15)	Bethel epiphany (28:10–22) and Penuel renaming (32:29 [Eng. 32:28])
Full list of Jacob's children (35:22b–26)	[cf. Birth narratives (29:31–30:24; 35:16–20)]
Return (35:27)	[*No corresponding material in Non-P*]
Death and burial (35:28–29)	[*No corresponding material in Non-P*]
Esau genealogy (Genesis 36*)	[*No corresponding material in Non-P*]
[Settlement and marriage of Esau (36:2–8)]	[cf. Gen 32:4 (Eng. 32:3), 33:16]
Jacob's settling (37:1)	[*No corresponding material in Non-P*]

Introduction of Joseph and conflict (37:2)	Introduction of conflict (37:3–11)
Jacob's departure for Egypt (46:5–7 [8–27])	Epiphany and departure (46:1–4, 28a)
[?Presentation to pharaoh (cf. LXX, 47:5–6a, 7–10)]	Presentation to pharaoh (46:28–34; 47:1–4, 6b)
Settlement (47:11)	Settlement (47:27a)
Jacob's enjoyment of blessing (47:27b)	Jacob's enjoyment of privilege (47:12–26)
Adoption of Manasseh and Ephraim (48:3–6)	Blessing of Ephraim, Manasseh (48:1–2, 8–22)
[*No equivalent*]	Blessing of twelve sons (49:1b–27)
Burial commission and death (47:28; 49:1a, 29–33)	Burial commission (47:29–31)
Execution of burial commission (50:12–13)	Execution of burial commission (50:1–11 . . .)
End of life of Joseph (50:22–23, 26a)	End of life of Joseph (Exod. 1:6)

tives are comparable in length to their non-P counterparts, the P Abraham narrative appears to have been much shorter. This P Abraham story only briefly touches on the Hagar (16:3, 15–16; cf. 16:1–2, 4–14) and Sodom and Gomorrah stories (19:29; cf. 19:1–28). Moreover, it appears to have lacked a number of other elements present in the Genesis non-P traditions, such as the first wife-sister story (Gen. 12:10–20), the expulsion of Ishmael (Gen. 21:8–20), and the near sacrifice of Isaac (Gen. 22:1–19).[26]

Rp has preserved enough of P for us to conclude that its emphases were different from those in the non-P materials. Overall, P appears to have drawn selectively on Israel's ancestral traditions in the process of presenting a covenant-focused expanded genealogy, rather than a complete Priestly review of all non-P stories.

The third major aspect of P's intertextuality to be discussed is already implicit in the first two: P represents a major reconceptualization of non-P traditions. The connections between P and its non-P precursors have been evident all along. The P creation story (Gen. 1:1–2:3) is in part a radical recontextualization and correction of the non-P creation and punishment story in Gen. 2:4b–3:24. The P flood story adds a new covenant focus to a flood tradition otherwise quite parallel to non-P. The P account of Abraham has him receive the promise only after he has arrived in the land (Genesis 17).

26. Other non-P traditions for which there is no counterpart in P include: the rescue of Lot from the Eastern kings (Gen. 14:1–24); covenant with Abimelek (Gen. 21:22–34), and genealogy of Nahor's descendants (Gen. 22:20–24).

Moreover, the entire covenant account has been systematized and revised in comparison with its non-P parallels in Gen. 12:1–3; 15:1–21; and 18:10–14. P completely revises the picture of Jacob's departure from his family. Now rather than fleeing from Esau's wrath, Jacob is leaving on his father's orders to find more proper wives than those married by Esau. The P version of the Bethel epiphany no longer implicitly describes Jacob's founding a temple (cf. Gen. 28:22). Instead it reinterprets this event as a one-time drink offering at the location where God spoke to Jacob (Gen. 35:14). These are but some examples of an overall trend in P not just to draw selectively on certain non-P traditions but to reconceptualize them as well.

Just as important, however, is the way the P document revises the broader outlines of the non-P pre-Moses history. The non-P pre-Moses story described a history of human's striving and divine frustration with that striving, on the one hand (non-P Genesis 2—11*), and a history of promise on the other (non-P Genesis 11—50*). In contrast, P presents the whole as a working out of the divine blessing given at the outset of creation. Now the P covenants with Noah and Abraham stand as indestructible divine structures for insuring the continuance and working out of the created order and blessing, despite the corruption of the world and chaos of humanity. Creation is unreservedly good (Gen. 1:31), and God's response to corruption (Gen. 6:11–12) and unbelief (Exod. 6:9; 14:10–12; 16:2–3, 20; Num. 13:32–14:10) is consistently decisive. Although humans may rebel, there is no counterpart in P to the non-P accounts of persistent and deep-rooted rebellion. Whether in the Flood, the spy episode, or elsewhere, God simply destroys the evildoers, while preserving the created and covenantal structures God has introduced. Overall, the world of P is one in which God is unmistakably sovereign, as is clear from the immediate execution of God's commands in creation to the immediate and complete execution of God's commands by Noah, Abraham, and Moses. In P, order triumphs.

One textual reflection of this is the orderly character of the reconstructed P document itself. Creation days and ancestral sections are clearly marked with labels. Each genealogical unit marches through a similar framework, from superscription ("these are the descendants of"), through birth, to death and burial. The various circles of cosmic, international, and ancestral history preceding Moses are neatly put one inside the other. As we will see when we turn to the non-P traditions, this P order contrasts with the relative lack of such order in the traditions it uses. Not only does P describe an overall orderly cosmos, but P does so in a more orderly way than its precursor texts.

To borrow Harold Bloom's term, P appears to be a "strong misreading" of its non-P precursors.[27] This concept of misreading highlights the respon-

---

27. Cf. particularly Bloom, *Anxiety of Influence*. As noted previously, Bloom's approach has been previously applied to biblical texts by Fox, *Redaction of the Books of Esther*, 151–54, and Brisman, *Voice of Jacob*.

sive character of P. As we have seen, P is neither a simple repetition of Israel's pre-P traditions, nor does P stand completely independent of them. Instead, P makes its points by strategically drawing on, but twisting or excising parts of, its precursor traditions. The above-discussed relations between the contents of P and its non-P precursors establish the interpretive linkage between the two. This, however, only heightens P's departure from traditions on which it builds. Moreover, if the above arguments are correct, the earliest P materials were not meant to stand alongside their non-P precursors as a derivative interpretation of them. Instead, cases like the creation narrative and Jacob stories suggest that the earliest P narrative was intended to displace the non-P accounts.

Pre-text:
The Sociohistorical Context of P

Although P does not itself make clear its sociopolitical locus, such a wide-ranging reformulation of Israel's traditions does not happen in a vacuum. Instead, it is a creative response to the challenges of a particular time, coming from authors working within a particular context. Analyzing this context goes against the grain of their work, since they are arguing for the timeless, unconditional truth of their representation of Israel's prehistory. Nevertheless, focus on the sociohistorical context of P need not reduce P to its context. At best, such sociohistorical analysis helps us reconstruct some of the questions to which P was the answer, and understand better the sociopolitical circumstances in which the answer provided by P would prove particularly compelling to certain groups.

Social Locus

Specification

The identity of the group behind P is clear and already implicit in the name given to this material: Priestly. Although the priestly character of the material in Genesis is only implicit, the predominance of technical priestly material in the Priestly version of the Moses story makes such an identification likely. Only priests would have been so interested in and competent to describe in such detail construction of the tabernacle (Exodus 25—28; cf. Exodus 30:30–31, 35–40), ordaining of the priests (Exodus 29; Leviticus 8—9), or clan organization and census of the Levitic house (Num. 3:11–4:49). Moreover, there is much additional material reflecting the concerns of priests in various P layers of the rest of the Moses story, such as specific instructions for various sacrifices (Leviticus 1—7), distinctions of pure and impure foods (Leviticus 11), specification of the length of impurity of a woman after giving birth (Leviticus 12), and purity of people with bodily secretions or diseases (Leviticus 13—15; cf. Num 5:1–4).

More exact identification of the priestly group is less certain. The prominence of Aaron vis-à-vis the Levites in the Priestly material suggests that Aaronides were probably responsible for all or part of the Priestly layer. In addition, there are connections between the Priestly material and material in Ezekiel 40—48, such as the similar positions on self-administration of the temple cult and distinction of priests and Levites. Such similarities suggest some kind of broad connection between the Aaronide group and the priestly group behind Ezekiel 40—48. Nevertheless, there are also some important differences between Ezekiel and the Priestly material. For example, Ezekiel 40—48 focuses on the Zadokites; and P, on the Aaronides.[28] Beyond these general reflections, it is difficult to be more specific about the exact author(s) of the Priestly material.

The Cultic Background to Space and Time in P

Despite our inability to specify the exact author(s) of the Priestly material, the overall priestly attribution does key us into the cultural matrix out of which P was written. This Priestly matrix was a factor not only in the creation of cultic laws outside Genesis but also in the shaping of the perspective, emphases, and presuppositions of the P presentation from Genesis 1 onward. For the Priestly material betrays the marks of a specific set of beliefs present in city cultures across the ancient Near East. Stated quite briefly, the temple cult stands in this matrix as a community's discourse with nature, holding community and nature together through language and rite.[29] The cult is a divinely given way for a specific community to grapple with random forces outside humans' control by drawing on the power of divine order established in Creation. A given cult is consistently localized in a particular social structure in a particular land. The result of a properly maintained cult is the outpouring of blessing on the land, preservation of order, and the prevention of divine attack or neglect. We can see this in the fertility imagery that characterized temples in the ancient Near East, including the Jerusalem temple. Within this context temples are understood to be built on the mountain of creation as a bulwark against chaos, linked with the primal springs watering the world, decorated with signs of fertility such as trees and lotus blooms and with signs of vitality such as bulls, and lit with lamps representing the life-giving power of God.[30] When the temple is properly maintained, the creative power of God is manifest in the land around it: the land and people are fertile, the king lives long, and disasters—famine, defeat in war, overturning

---

28. Albertz, *Religionsgeschichte*, vol. 2, 519, especially n. 104; (E.T., 481–82; 629, n. 104).
29. Janowski, "Tempel und Schöpfung," 38–46 (reprint in *Gottes Gegenwart;* 215–23).
30. O. Keel, *Die Welt der altorientalischen Bildsymbolik und das Alte Testament am Beispiel der Psalmen* (Darmstadt: Wissenschaftliche Buchgesellschaft, 1972), 99–155; E.T., *The Symbolism of the Biblical World: Ancient Near Eastern Iconography and the Book of Psalms* (trans. T. J. Hallett; New York: Seabury, 1978), 112–76.

of established political structures, and so forth—are averted. Overall, ancient Near Eastern temples served as divine beachheads of created blessing and order.

Working out of this matrix, the Priestly writing is dominated by the narrative span extending from Creation to cult. This span is then filled in with conceptual struts drawn from the above-outlined Priestly theology: order, blessing, fertility, light. Thus, just as the Jerusalem cult included a significant creation component, so also the first section of the Priestly document is a majestic, programmatic creation story (Gen. 1:1–2:3). Moreover, just as blessing and fertility stood at the heart of the temple cult, so also blessing and fertility stand at the head of the Priestly creation. The next major unit in P, the Noah story, is profoundly shaped by its placement on the Priestly creation-to-cult axis. Its description of watery uncreation and recreation echoes the primal establishment of order over watery disorder in Genesis 1, while its description of Noah's divinely directed construction of the ark anticipates the later description of Moses' divinely directed construction of the tabernacle.[31] The next major station on the creation-to-cult theological axis is the creation of the cult itself. Within the Priestly document this is presented—largely in response to non-P materials—as a gradual process, moving from an ancestral prologue to the itinerary-organized Moses story. The first, ancestral portion of this movement is characterized within this scheme first by its relative brevity. God covenants with Abraham and creates Israel and other peoples through an outpouring of the creation blessing on Abraham and his heirs (Genesis 12—50*). Then, with both the Noachic and Abrahamic covenants in place, the Priestly Moses story describes the transformation of Jacob's descendants into a cult-centered community with the tabernacle in their midst, and their procession—with structures intact despite drastic shifts in the personnel—to the land promised to Abraham.

This creation-centered cultic background to P helps clarify the restructuring of space and time in P, as compared with non-P. P's critical time is that leading up to the constitution of the people with the cult at their center. P's space consists of concentric circles moving outward from God's presence in the tabernacle. Whereas the non-P traditions either ignore or disparage the world outside Israel, the P tradition more closely links cosmos and ethnos, humanity and Israel, earth and "the land." Thus, for example, Israel's fertility is but a specific and intense instance of God's blessing on humanity in general. Israel's possession of the land echoes God's broader creation intent for humans to fill the earth and subdue it. Furthermore, P diverges from its non-

---

31. J. Blenkinsopp, "The Structure of P," *CBQ* 38 (1976): 277–78, 283–86; Zenger, *Gottes Bogen*, 174–75; S. Niditch, *Chaos to Cosmos: Studies in Biblical Patterns of Creation* (Scholars Press Studies in the Humanities 6; Chico, Calif.: Scholars Press, 1985), 22–24; S. W. Holloway, "What Ship Goes There: The Flood Narratives in the Gilgamesh Epic and Genesis Considered in Light of Ancient Near Eastern Temple Ideology," *ZAW* 103 (1991): 328–55.

P precursors by describing God as covenanting not just with Israel's progenitor, Abraham, but with Noah, the progenitor of postflood humanity as well (Gen. 9:8–17). Indeed, P's post-Sinai human world is defined as much by spatial nearness to God's tabernacle as by the genealogical background of the given person.[32]

Time as defined by the limited scope of P is divided between (1) God's institution and development of the created order up through the constitution of Israel as a cultic community and (2) all time afterward. In this sense P lends a primeval tinge to all of Israel's formative history.[33] Yet there are also important differences between P's primeval history of Israel and its counterparts in cultural founding myths of the ancient Near East. Instead of having the cult and other aspects of human culture established at creation or in a time span extending from Creation to Flood, the Priestly writing describes the cult and other human potentialities as being established over a stretch of cosmic history extending up through Moses. Moreover, these potentialities are not the simple outgrowth of the original creative impulse, but instead are outgrowths of God's indestructible, covenantal responses to human history. By the time Moses dies, the basic possibilities of human life, from the Noachic law to the indwelling of God's glory in the midst of Israel, are already in place. At or by this point, the Priestly writing comes to an end. Israel can hope for no more and no less than actualization of the potentialities already established at the dawn of its history.[34]

Overall, there is a consistent two-level character to P. P depicts the world outside Israel as the faint prototype for Israel's world, and the time up to Moses as the normative context for its audience's time. In other words, Israel's present and potential reality is implicitly depicted in P as throbbing with the rhythms established in the broader cosmos and in a formative time long before it. In contrast, the non-P materials depict the world outside Israel more ambivalently, and the non-P primeval history functions primarily as a negative backdrop to the story of Israel's special blessing. P, however, includes the world outside Israel as the context of God's foundational blessing and the overarching (Noachic) covenant. Then, working from the outside in, P reenvisions Israel in its cosmic context.

---

32. F. Crüsemann, *Die Tora. Theologie und Sozialgeschichte des alttestamentlichen Gesetzes* (Munich: Kaiser, 1992), 359–60.

33. Zenger, *Gottes Bogen*, 170–75; Lohfink, "Priesterschrift," 202–15; P. Weimar, "Sinai und Schöpfung. Komposition und Theologie der priesterschriftlichen Sinaigeschichte," *RB* 95 (1988): 383–85. Compare, however, the qualifications of Blum, *Studien*, 330–32 (including n. 159), and Janowski, "Tempel und Schöpfung," 65–67 (reprint in *Gottes Gegenwart*, 242–44), regarding the tendency of the previous discussion toward a characterization of P as non-historical. What is argued here is not that the Priestly material retreats from history, but that it reformulates history with a primeval accent.

34. For provocative comments on the mixing of ongoing ritual "time" with historical focus, see Damrosch, *The Narrative Covenant*, 282–84.

Historical Locus

So far I have discussed only how the overall parameters of P have been shaped by the cultic understanding that informs it. Yet we can say more once we gain a clearer picture of the historical context to which P was addressed. For this reason I turn here to a discussion of (1) the dating of P and then (2) the way a more exact dating can illuminate P's presentation in Genesis and following.

Dating P

Since Wellhausen, discussions of dating P have been heavily infused from both sides by a broader debate regarding the legitimacy of Judaism and Christianity. This issue must be raised at the outset because it provides important background for the discussion and the various interests driving it. The context for the modern discussion was set into motion by the synthesis of the "newer" documentary hypothesis by Wellhausen. In this synthesis P was dated well into the postexilic period and associated with the late books of Chronicles and Ezra-Nehemiah. Much of this position was carefully argued. To dismiss Wellhausen's position as a mere reflex of his own—or his time's— romanticism, Hegelianism, or anti-Judaism is to ignore the power of many of his observations, a power that transcends the limitations of his and his contemporaries' perspectives. Nevertheless, it must be recognized at the same time that part of what made Wellhausen's position so compelling among Christian scholars was its claim that the earliest core of the Hebrew Bible tradition was not cultic or legal, indeed not "Jewish." In this way Wellhausen's formulation provided a seemingly scientific tool for Christians to claim legitimacy vis-à-vis their older sibling, Judaism, to claim greater antiquity for their non-Torah-observing worship of the God of Israel.

In this context, a number of Jewish scholars have marshalled evidence to argue that numerous parts of P not only predate the postexilic period to which Wellhausen dated P, but predate the exile and even the late preexilic Deuteronomic law.[35] In this way the Torah law so central to Judaism once again finds its place alongside the earliest biblical traditions. Once again, this position has been carefully argued, and it would be a mistake to dismiss the

---

35. Y. Kaufmann, *The Religion of Israel: From Its Beginnings to the Babylonian Exile* [Heb.], vol. 1 (7th ed.; Jerusalem: Bialik Institute and Dvir, 1967), 113–42; (E.T., trans. and abridge., M. Greenberg [New York: Schocken Books, 1960], 175–200); Y. Grintz, " 'Do Not Eat the Blood': Reconsiderations upon Setting and Date of the Priestly Code [Heb]," in *Studies in Early Biblical Ethnology and History* (Tel Aviv: Hakibbutz Hameuchad Publishing House, 1969), 201–21; M. Haran, "Behind the Scenes of History: Determining the Date of the Priestly Source," *JBL* 100 (1981): 327–30; Friedman, *Exile and Biblical Narrative*, 47–76; H. Hurvitz, "The Evidence of Language in Dating the Priestly Code," *RB* 81 (1974): 25–55; idem, *A Linguistic Study of the Relationship between the Priestly Source and the Book of Ezekiel* (CARB 20; Paris: J. Gabalda et Cie, 1982); Z. Zevit, "Converging Lines of Evidence Bearing on the Date of P," *ZAW* 94 (1982): 481–511. Also, for arguments that Deuteronomistic texts are dependent on P, see W. L. Moran, "The Literary Connection between Lv. 11,13–19 and Dt. 14,12–18," *CBQ* 28 (1966): 271–77; M. Weinfeld, *Deuteronomy and the Deuteronomic School* (Oxford:

full range of challenges to Wellhausen as a mere reflex of their frequently Jewish sociocultural context. Data have been brought forward and they deepen the complexity of the transmission-historical picture.

In response to this debate, several reflections are in order. First, although Wellhausen was well aware his various sources drew on earlier traditions, our consciousness of the importance of this process has been augmented since Wellhausen's time. Particularly following Gunkel's work, the significance of presource traditions is recognized on both sides of the debate. On the one hand, advocates of a late dating of P recognize that it contains earlier elements. For example, Kaiser in his most recent introduction to the Old Testament cites the example of the Keteph Hinnom bracelet, a preexilic copy of the Aaronide blessing found in Num. 6:24–26, as an example of early material finding its way into a late stratum of P.[36] On the other hand, some of those inclined toward an early dating of P legislation, such as Knohl and Milgrom, advocate a multilayered approach, where preexilic Priestly legal corpora are seen to have undergone a redaction from the perspective of the holiness code, including addition of narrative material, extending to the exilic and even postexilic periods.[37] To be sure, these various approaches are by no means identical to each other. Nevertheless, they make clear that a dating of the overall framework of P, whether early or late, is not decisive for the date of its elements. In other words, the Wellhausen link between dating of P and historical placement of the law in it has been loosened, if not broken.

Clarendon Press, 1972), 180–82; J. Milgrom, "Profane Slaughter and a Formulaic Key to the Composition of Deuteronomy," *HUCA* 47 (1976): 9–13; S. Japhet, "The Laws of Manumission of Slaves and the Question of the Relationship Between the Collection of Laws in the Pentateuch," in *Studies in Bible and the Ancient Near East: Presented to S. E. Loewenstamm on his Seventieth Birthday* (Jerusalem: E. Rubenstein's Publishing House, 1978), 231–49; (cf. on this essay, S. Kaufman, "Deuteronomy 15 and Recent Research on the Dating of P," in *Das Deuteronomium: Entstehung, Gestalt, und Botschaft* [ed. N. Lohfink; Leuven: University Press, 1985], 273–76); I. L. Seeligmann, "Loans, Security, and Interest in Biblical Law and in Its World-View," *Studies in the Bible and the Ancient Near East*, 202–4.

36. O. Kaiser, *Grundriss der Einleitung in die kanonischen und deuteronkanonischen Schriften des Alten Testaments* (Gütersloh: Gerd Mohn, 1992), 60.

37. See particularly I. Knohl, *The Sanctuary of Silence: The Priestly Torah and the Holiness School* (Minneapolis: Fortress, 1995) and Milgrom, *Leviticus 1—16*, 3–35. To be sure, Knohl briefly assigns the bulk of material in Genesis to his earlier "Priestly Torah" because "we find no linguistic features of HS [holiness school]." Genesis 17:7–8 is the primary exception, but here he runs into difficulty, because the promise in these verses is so central to other Genesis Priestly texts. Since he has already assigned the bulk of Genesis to the Priestly Torah, he concludes, without indicators to support him, that his holiness school editor intervened in a limited way in Gen. 17:7–8, while adding other smaller portions of P material elsewhere in Genesis (e.g., Genesis 23; 36). Presupposing his model, one could just as easily conclude that his holiness-school author/editor composed Genesis. Criteria derived from his detailed analysis of legal corpora may not be adequate for analysis of the decisively different sort of material in Genesis. This approach, however, would mean a significant revision of his concept of the relation between the ideology of the Priestly and holiness schools (cf. 124–98).

This is perhaps particularly true for the priestly instructional corpora making up a substantial portion of the Priestly compositional layer in the Pentateuch. Wellhausen argued on the basis of a romantic concept of religion that early Israelite religion was spontaneous and unstructured, while detailed Priestly regulations and institutions were late, postexilic creations. That approach has now been shown to be fundamentally mistaken.[38] Moreover, particularly as we enter the Sinai section, we encounter various Priestly instructional traditions transmitted in some form within the temple cult long before they were incorporated into this narrative context. Thus, we must distinguish in this case between the publication of professional traditions as part of P and their earlier background.[39] Israel long had priestly/cultic traditions. For the purposes of this analysis of Genesis the crucial question is, When was P *as a whole* written?

Because of the potential distinction between the age of P and the age of its cultic contents, dating the language or legal content of P's individual elements is not necessarily helpful when dating the overall writing. Although such arguments have the appearance of a certain scientific objectivity, they can at best date individual elements of P. Even then, studies of P's language suffer from several additional problems: the presupposition of a unilinear linguistic development, a thin set of language samples from which to construct statistically significant linguistic comparisons, the phenomenon of an overall archaizing tendency in P that extends to its language, failure to distinguish between different levels of material in P, and the lack of distinction between various layers in the material with which P is compared, particularly Ezekiel.[40]

---

38. See in particular M. Weinfeld's survey, "Social and Cultic Institutions in the Priestly Source Against Their Ancient Near Eastern Background," in *Proceedings of the Eighth World Congress of Jewish Studies, Jerusalem, August 16–21, 1981* (Jerusalem: World Union of Jewish Studies, 1983), 95–138. Weinfeld's arguments, however, do not establish an early dating of the Priestly source as a whole either. They merely establish that the Priestly source can not be dated late on the basis of the institutions and practices described in it.

39. Precursors of this basic model for P traditions include: A. Dillmann, *Die Bücher Numeri, Deuteronomium und Josua* (2d ed.; Leipzig: S. Hirzel, 1886), 666–67; M. Weinfeld, "Towards the Concept of Law in Israel and Elsewhere," *Beit Miqra* 8 (1964): 61–63; M. Haran, *Temples and Temple Service in Ancient Israel* (Oxford: Clarendon Press, 1978), 10–12, 143–44; idem, "The Law Code of Ezekiel XL–XLVIII and its Relation to the Priestly School," *HUCA* 50 (1979): 62–71; idem, "Behind the Scenes of History," 327–30; see also J. Begrich, "Die priesterliche Torah," *Werden und Wesen des Alten Testaments* (ed. P. Volz, F. Stummer, and J. Hempel; BZAW 66; Berlin: de Gruyter, 1936), 86–87.

40. See Lohfink, "Priesterschrift," 201n33; B. Levine, "Late Language in the Priestly Source: Some Literary and Historical Observations," in *Proceedings of the Eighth World Congress of Jewish Studies* (vol. 5; Jerusalem: World Union of Jewish Studies, 1983), 69–94; Blum, *Vätergeschichte*, 453–54n35; Y. Hoffman, "The Lexicography of the P Document and the Problem Concerning its Dating," in *Studies in Judaica* (Te'uda 4; Tel-Aviv: Tel-Aviv University, 1986), 13–22 (Heb.); Pola, *Ursprüngliche Priesterschrift*, 35–38. The importance of the distinction of various levels of material in P for linguistic analysis is demonstrated in R. Polzin's book, *Late Biblical Hebrew: Toward an Historical Typology of Biblical Hebrew Prose* (HSM, 12; Missoula, Mont.: Scholars Press, 1976), particularly 85–122.

This leaves us with no escape from the more difficult task of exploring the context within which P's overall character and theology make the most sense. Here comparison of broader aspects of the reconstructed P source as a whole with datable biblical literature points toward dating P no earlier than the late exilic period. First of all, Wellhausen's central argument still holds. Whereas the late preexilic Deuteronomic law must assert the need for cultic centralization, the regulations of the Priestly writing have all been built around this assumption. For example, there is no animal sacrifice in P before Sinai. Second, whereas the Deuteronomic law is presupposed in exilic works such as the Deuteronomistic history, P is not clearly reflected by non-Pentateuchal texts until the late works of Chronicles and Ezra-Nehemiah.[41] Third, the overall dating system in P, where months are numbered, appears to enter the biblical tradition in the Babylonian period, that is the late preexilic and exilic periods.[42] Fourth, P appears dependent on the non-P traditions in Genesis. To be sure, many of these traditions may be early. Nevertheless, P's dependence on Genesis 15, a text that appears to be a semi-Deuteronomistic addition to the Abraham tradition, points to a date no earlier than the late exile.[43] In light of such evidence, an exilic or postexilic date for the bulk of P makes the most sense, despite the probable presence in P of often ancient legal materials.

As we turn to attempt a more specific dating, we are faced once again with the slippery task of dating a tradition that has grown over time. Thus Wellhausen, among others, was able to draw on certain elements of P to argue that P was the constitution of a postexilic, Jewish theocracy. Nevertheless, already in the tabernacle material, one can discern an important distinction in P. This material appears to shift from a more utopian picture of a movable cult in God's first speech to Moses (Exod. 25:1–29:45) to the addition of various other elements to this vision, which more closely anticipates the cult of the Second Temple period (Exod. 30:1–31:18).[44] This suggests that one

---

41. The classic argument along these lines is Wellhausen, *Prolegomena,* 175–307; (E.T., 171–294).
42. E. Auerbach, "Die babylonische Datierung im Pentateuch," *VT* 2 (1952): 334–41; cf. Y. Kaufmann, "Der Kalender und das Alter des Priesterkodex," *VT* 4 (1954): 307–13. Kaufmann rightly points out that establishing a late date for the priestly dating system would still not make the laws late (308–9), but his other arguments (309–13) do not successfully account for the appearance of a semi-Babylonian month-numbering system precisely in texts like Jeremiah and the Deuteronomistic history, which are datable, at the earliest, in the Babylonian period of Israel's history.
43. For more detailed discussion of P innovations vis-à-vis the non-P tradition, see in particular Pola, *Ursprüngliche Priesterschrift,* 331–34.
44. Cf. for example, the introduction of elements of a functioning cult such as the half-shekel tax (Exod. 30:11–16) and the bronze altar (Exod. 30:17–21). The distinctively different origins of these materials is highlighted not only by their separate speech introductions, but also by the break in organization represented by the elements in Exod. 30:1–31:18. Exodus 25:1–29:45 moves methodically from inside to outside the sanctuary and then to the court (25:1–27:19) before moving to the priestly vestments (Exod. 28:1–40), consecration (29:1–37), offerings

should distinguish in P between (1) an earlier, more utopian Priestly retelling of Israel's formation and (2) the (probably gradual) later postexilic Priestly modification/concretization of this retelling in the context of the reestablishment of Israel's cult.[45] The early retelling was a Priestly construal of Israel's prehistory working out of the matrix of temple ideology. The later additions transformed this utopian construal into an increasingly concrete temple etiology articulating the legitimacy of the Second Temple cult and priesthood. In summary, the social function of the P material shifted from the grounding of hope to the legitimating of structure.

Past scholarship has demonstrated that distinction of these two levels is extremely difficult.[46] Nevertheless, it is significant that the tabernacle section is probably the first major part of P that was effected by this postexilic redirection of P. For it is with the Sinai section that P begins to treat matters most relevant to the Second Temple cult: the constitution of Israel as a cultic community surrounding the tabernacle. Here most of all we must distinguish between the origins of P traditions and their inclusion in the broader P framework. Insofar as the establishment of the Second Temple cult involved the reintroduction of often ancient Priestly customs, the modification of P to anticipate the Second Temple could have involved the *late* addition of *early* Priestly traditions. Particularly in this material we must distinguish between the age of the component parts of P and the time when these components were published as part of the broader P document.

In any case, the text stretching from Genesis to Exodus 19 was probably relatively untouched by these developments, since this section presents Israel before the introduction of its sanctuary. Instead, the text's scope and emphases are dominated by the concerns of diaspora life. Not only does P in Genesis focus on Israelite characters in "the land of [their] sojourning," but the practices in the P narrative up through Exodus 19 are all customs that assumed particular importance in the exile: circumcision (Genesis 17), Passover (now

---

(29:38–42), and final rationale (29:43–45). In contrast, the additional speeches in Exod. 30:1–31:18, standing as they do after the careful organization of Exod. 25:1–29:45, add elements that have their place at various points throughout what precedes. This problem appears to have been perceived already by the tradents of the text. In the later execution report that was added to the tabernacle account, they reorganized the older and later elements so all fit together in the broader scheme.

45. Zenger, *Gottes Bogen*, 48–49; Crüsemann, *Die Tora*, 330–32; Pola, *Ursprüngliche Priesterschrift*, 33–34, and for an early recognition of this basic move, see already, P. Wurster, "Zur Charakteristik und Geschichte des Priestercodex und Heiligkeitsgesetzes," *ZAW* 4 (1884): 132–33.

46. Rendtorff, *Problem*, 83–84; (E.T., 104–6); Blum, *Studien*, 223. The problem here lies in the history that has produced our evidence. The postexilic period is characterized by successive waves of exiles returning to Judah and an effort culminating in Nehemiah and Ezra to reorganize life in postexilic Judah in accordance with the insights and revisions stemming from the exile. This means that there is a substantial continuity between exile and the importation of exile perspectives into postexilic Judah. This continuity can make it difficult to assign texts to one period or the other.

a clan festival that can be celebrated outside Jerusalem; Exodus 12*), and Sabbath (Exodus 16 [cf. Gen. 2:1–3]).[47] In addition, the P narratives up to Sinai reflect a more broadly documented move in Israel toward nonstate social and leadership structures.[48] They articulate a genealogical (as opposed to state) definition of Israel; encourage endogamous marriage as a patriarchal custom (Gen. 26:34–35; 27:46–28:9) and ultimately as part of a broader trend toward ethnic boundary reinforcement; and even develop a nonland-centered utopia featuring a movable tabernacle, a kinglike priest, a community defined in nonland-focused terms as a "congregation," and a cult-centered camp.[49]

Finally, although P's earliest form does not seem to presuppose the Second Temple,[50] crucial elements of the P narrative already unite traditions of the late exilic period: (1) the late Ezekiel tradition's "glory" theology, "I am YHWH" credo, and utopian vision with (2) exilic Isaiah's focus on the importance of return and his picture of a creator God powerful enough to bring the Israelites out of a foreign land and reveal himself to non-Israelites in the process.[51] Indeed, P's focus on land in the Israelite covenant (cf. especially Exod. 6:2–8) and argument against those who lack enough belief to return to the land (Num. 13:32; 14:36–37; cf. Ezek 36:13–14) suggest a stance al-

47. R. Kilian, "Die Hoffnung auf Heimkehr in der Priesterschrift," *Bibel und Leben* 7 (1966): 39–41; W. Wood, "The Congregation of Yahweh: A Study of the Theology and Purpose of the Priestly Document," (Ph.D. diss.: Princeton, 1974), 167–79. The case of the Noachide law is more complex. See Crüsemann, *Die Tora*, 339–40. Circumcision is particularly significant here because it became a significant marker only during life among the Babylonians, who did not circumcise males.

48. Albertz, *Religionsgeschichte*, vol. 2, 378–82; (E.T., 371–75).

49. K. Elliger, "Sinn und Ursprung der priesterlichen Geschichtserzählung," *ZThK* 49 (1952): 142–43; M. L. Henry, *Jahwist und Priesterschrift: Zwei Glaubenszeugnisse des Alten Testaments* (Arbeiten zur Theologie 3; Stuttgart: Calwer Verlag, 1960), 29–30; Wood, "Congregation of Yahweh," 29–30; N. Gottwald, *The Hebrew Bible: A Socio-Literary Introduction* (Philadelphia: Fortress, 1985), 480. For further arguments regarding P as an attempt systematically to decouple Israel's legal traditions from land possession, see Crüsemann, *Die Tora*, 330, 335–36, 343, 350–60. On the importance of boundary maintenance for displaced groups, see D. Smith, *Religion of the Landless: The Social Context of the Babylonian Exile* (Bloomington, Ind.: Meyer-Stone Books, 1989), 56–63.

50. See the discussion of the tabernacle text above and Friedman, *Exile and Biblical Narrative*, 47–61 (who builds on initial arguments along similar lines by Kaufmann).

51. On this mix see in particular Smend, *Entstehung*, 57. This theory is simpler than one that posits Ezekiel and/or exilic Isaiah drawing on different halves of the P tradition. Moreover, it allows for a close link between P and the possibility of return. Nevertheless, as A. Kapelrud particularly persuasively argued, the links between the P narrative and Second Isaiah are so close that the latter may be dependent on the former. A. S. Kapelrud, "The Date of the Priestly Code (P)," *ASTI* 3 (1964): 58–64; cf. also A. Eitz, "Studien zum Verhältnis von Priesterschrift und Deuterojesaja," (Ph.D. diss., Heidelberg, 1970) and M. Weinfeld, "God the Creator in Gen. I and in the Prophecy of Second Isaiah," *Tarbiz* 37 (1967–68): 105–32 (Heb.). The latter argues that Isaiah is later. He depends heavily in his argument, however, on the presupposition that elements shared with other cultures of the ancient Near East must be earlier, while critiques of such themes must be later. Although this may be the case, it is not necessarily so. It is just as likely that the Priestly authors drew on a fund of ideological resources shared with their counterparts in other ancient Near Eastern cultures when presenting a picture that contradicted elements of exilic Isaiah's prophecy. Direction of dependence must be determined on other grounds.

ready oriented toward the opportunity for return and an argument against those failing to take advantage of it.[52]

To be sure, such arguments are notoriously difficult to control, particularly when they focus on certain themes and emphases in the given document. Nevertheless, the main issue here is not whether P was preexilic or not. The case for an exilic/postexilic dating for P was already made above. Instead, the issue at this point is the extent to which the P material in Genesis is part of the early layer of P that preceded the building of the second temple. In this case, both external and thematic indicators converge to support this idea. Whatever the dating of P material in much of the Moses story, the P narrative in Genesis was probably composed some time in the late exile or early postexilic period.

P's Response to Its Historical Context

If this dating is correct, then P represents an important reconceptualization of Israel's traditions in response to the struggles and hope of diaspora life. As Smith's survey of studies of refugees suggests, displacement of a group almost inevitably is a major shock to the cultural traditions the group maintained in its homeland. Such a group, especially if it is able to stay together in its new home, adapts its culture to adapt to the decisively different circumstances.[53] Standing as a separate and often radical reconceptualization of Israel's non-P traditions, P appears to have been part of this broader movement in Israel.

Building on the logic and parameters of their own tradition, the Priestly authors were able to provide an orderly reconstrual of Israel's story. This construal in turn was compelling to a broader community living in a context where nonstate structures, cultural boundaries, and order in general were appealing. The resulting story is half narrative and half vision. Later apocalypses, also often authored by displaced priests, would present eschatological visions in which history up to that present time was presented as if it were being predicted, and then the author's utopia was presented as the decisive final step to this history.[54] Likewise P begins with a narrative reflection of the experience the audience already knows, a description of Israel's pre-Sinai history

---

52. Elliger, "Sinn und Ursprung der priesterlichen Geschichtserzählung," 135–42; R. Kilian, "Hoffnung auf Heimkehr," 41–45; Lohfink, "Priesterschrift," 194–95, 211–12; Schart, *Mose und Israel*, 247.

53. Smith, *Religion of the Landless*, 49–90.

54. On this, see in particular H. Stegemann, "Die Bedeutung der Qumranfunde für die Erforschung der Apokalyptik," in *Apocalypticism in the Mediterranean World and the Near East: Proceedings of the International Colloquium on Apocalypticism, Uppsala, August 12–17, 1979* (ed. D. Hellholm; Tübingen: J.C.B. Mohr, 1983), 496–526, especially 507 with citations of earlier literature. Cf. also J. Smith's suggestive, "Wisdom and Apocalyptic," in *Map is Not Territory: Studies in the History of Religions* (Studies in Judaism in Late Antiquity; Leiden: Brill, 1978), 67–87, where he argues that "Apocalypticism is Wisdom lacking a royal court and patron" (86). The "Wisdom" of which he speaks is scribal, and often linked to the institution of the royal cult.

featuring diaspora practices familiar to the audience, before presenting as the decisive final step in this history the P author's utopia, the constitution of Israel as cultic community and procession into the land.

Thus the early P was a sort of legal *vaticinum ex eventu*. Only now P is not displacing into the past a prediction of present and future events (so apocalypses), but instead retrojecting legislation shaping the present and future cultic community of Israel. Of course, there are important differences. The visions of the apocalypses are placed in the distant past, while the encoded history in them reaches into the audience's present. In contrast, P itself does not thematize its time of narration, and the history it describes is all confined to the distant past. This makes a significant difference in how elements such as the wilderness tabernacle are developed. Nevertheless, both apocalypses and P work out of the above-discussed, Priestly, two-layered concept of primeval and present time.

P builds a bridge between these two layers of time by using the themes of eternity and memory. God "establishes" "eternal" covenants with Noah and Abraham, and then "remembers" them at crucial junctures. On the other side, Israel is "reminded" of its paradigmatic history (as conceived by P) by elements such as circumcision (an "eternal covenant") and Passover ("an eternal decree").[55] In other words, the etiological dimension of the pre-Sinai P narrative reinterprets the diaspora culture of the audience—circumcision, Sabbath, Passover—as a testimony to P's representation of Israel's history. This history has certain eternal structures now present in the life of the audience that they must "remember." In this oblique way, the P text itself reminds its audience of these structures and in the process thematizes the importance of its project. The world has certain created and covenantal structures. God has always remembered. Now Israel, standing at the brink of possible return to the land and reestablishment of its cult, must remember as well.

---

55. R. W. Klein, *Israel in Exile* (Philadelphia: Fortress, 1979), 134–36.

Part 3
Probing Further Back: Transformations of Meaning in the Non-P Material

7

Competing Models for the Development of the Non-P Materials

As we turn to the non-Priestly materials of Genesis, the transmission-historical picture begins to blur. The indicators of transmission history are not so clear as those used to isolate Priestly from non-Priestly material. Moreover, the non-P material is not cross-linked in the same way as the P materials. The emphasis has shifted from the whole of the narrative to its parts. The major covenant and genealogical texts of P were integrally linked with each other in a Creation to tabernacle stretch. In contrast, the non-P texts often focus on a narrower narrative segment. Despite significant links across narratives, much of the narrative interest has shifted to more limited plots, whether the garden of Eden or Abraham and Abimelek stories or the lengthier Jacob-Esau and Joseph narratives. This is but our first, very rough indicator that the non-P material has undergone a different sort of formation than the P material in Genesis.

Even the background of the non-P material is less clear. The P material shows clear signs of emerging out of a priestly institutional background in the exile or early postexilic period. In contrast, the non-P material is not so easily located. Indeed, the most crucial non-P texts have been dated from the tenth century to the postexilic period shortly before P. Thus, with the non-P material we encounter a concrete example of a principle stated more abstractly above: The farther one moves back in transmission history, the more difficult and tentative the reconstructive task becomes.

The Development of the Classic Source Approach to the Non-P Materials

This difficulty in analysis of non-P materials is reflected in the greater degree of debate surrounding the basic models for reconstructing the transmission history of non-P materials. We can already see this in the earliest development of models for the transmission history of the Pentateuch. When Witter, Astruc, and Eichhorn first isolated P and non-P materials in Genesis, their primary criterion was the variation of divine designations (Yahweh, Elohim) in Genesis 1—11. The model that arose out of a focus on this variation was a vertical one, one that posited the presence of parallel, now interwoven

Pentateuchal sources, both of which narrated a similar storyline. Neverthe-less, as Astruc already realized, this model did not completely account for the complexity of the material. Therefore, he posited the existence of a third block of fragmentary material alongside his two sources. In addition, he con-cluded that the two strands he presented were in fact only parallel collections of sources, preserved by Moses in separate columns but mixed up by later copyists.[1] Others, A. Geddes and J. Vater, went further. They posited what might be termed a horizontal model for the transmission history of the Pen-tateuch. According to this model, the Pentateuch as a whole was formed by connecting discrete compositions (or fragments of compositions) not origi-nally meant to stand alongside each other. The line ran not *through* the Pen-tateuch but *between* its stories.[2] (See Chart 7-1.) Still others (De Wette, Ewald, Bleek, Tuch) combined these approaches, continuing to posit a Priestly source but arguing that the non-Priestly materials, at least as they stand now, are fragments from various sources used to supplement the con-tinuous Priestly writing. Thus the Priestly source was recognized as a con-tinuous vertical presence through the Pentateuch, while a greater role was al-lowed in a horizontal model for accounting for non-Priestly materials.[3]

Ultimately, however, the model that triumphed was the extension of the vertical, interwoven-source model.[4] First Ilgen (1798) and then, with a greater following, Hupfeld (1854), argued that the bulk of the Pentateuch was created out of not two, but three parallel, now interwoven sources: the

---

1. Astruc, *Conjectures*, 483–90. Here he is working on analogy with Origin's *Hexapala*.

2. I was not able to locate Geddes' own discussions of these issues. In any case, we will not find discussion of the formation of the Pentateuch in his sometimes-cited *Critical Remarks on the Holy Scriptures, corresponding with a new translation of the Bible*, vol. 1, *Containing Remarks on the Pentateuch* (London: Davis, Wilks and Taylor, 1800) or in his proposal for a new translation and replies to various responses to this proposal. An overall discussion of his theories with cita-tions of fuller treatments can be found in Houtman, *Pentateuch*, 80–82. For Vater, see his *Commentar über den Pentateuch*.

3. H. G. A. Ewald, "[review of J. J. Stähelin, *Kritische Untersuchungen über die Genesis*]," *The-ologische Studien und Kritiken* 4 (1831): 602–5; F. Bleek, *Insunt de libri Geneseos origine atque indole historica observationes quaedam contra Bohlenium* (Bonn: Typis Caroli Georgii, 1836), 6–30; Tuch, *Genesis*, xxxii, lxv–lxxxv; W. M. L. de Wette, *Lehrbuch der historisch-kritischen Ein-leitung in die kanonischen und apokryphischen Bücher des Alten Testaments* (6th ed.; Berlin: G. Reimer, 1845), 195–216. (This position also seen in the fifth, 1840, edition). On this stage of research, see Houtman, *Pentateuch*, 91–95, and references there.

4. In actuality this sometimes involved the division of non-Priestly material into not two but three non-P sources: the Elohist and two Yahwists. Cf. Smend, *Erzählung des Hexateuch*, especially 16–30; O. Eissfeldt, *Hexateuch-Synopse* (Darmstadt: Wissenschaftliche Buchgesellschaft, 1962), 6–30 (on Genesis); idem, *Einleitung* 253–64, (E.T., 191–99); Pfeiffer, "A Non-Israelite Source," 66–73; idem, *Introduction to the Old Testament* (2d ed.; New York: A. and C. Black, 1948), 158–67; C. A. Simpson, *The Early Traditions of Israel* (Oxford: Basil Blackwell, 1948); G. Fohrer, *Einleitung in das Alte Testament* (10th ed.; Heidelberg: Quelle & Meyer, 1965), 173–79; (E.T.; *Introduction to the Old Testament* [trans. D. Green; Nashville: Abingdon, 1968], 159–65). Since the basic data upon which these proposals depend is better explained through the assumption of oral prehistory to the written materials, the hypothesis of parallel "Yahwistic" doc-uments has not been pursued in the last few decades. Therefore, the following discussion will fo-cus exclusively on the often-made distinction between parallel Yahwistic and Elohistic documents.

Priestly source, *a newly identified non-Priestly Elohistic source,* and the Yahwistic source.[5] Once again, variation in divine designation was a crucial criterion. Its importance can be seen in the fact that Hupfeld felt compelled to define his new non-Priestly source not over against the Yahwist, but over against the other "Elohist," the Priestly source. Starting in the Jacob story he tried to show that Genesis 25—35 contained Elohistic traditions that were non-Priestly (Gen. 28:10–22; 31; 35:1–7). Only after establishing this beachhead for his Elohistic source in the Jacob story did he argue that one can also see the same source in the Joseph story. Then, after analyzing the latter half of Genesis, he identified the same non-Priestly Elohistic strand in the Abraham story (Genesis 20—22*), although in this case "with much less probability" than he claimed for his analysis of the other materials.[6] On the basis of his overall analysis he concluded that for two main reasons this Elohistic material must be the remnants of a source parallel to the Yahwist: (1) the Elohistic material extends across the whole of Genesis from Abraham onward, and (2) despite its gaps, Elohistic back-references such as Gen. 35:1–7 and 48:20–21 indicate that the Elohistic source once contained material that has now been omitted by the redactor who combined the sources.[7]

Chart 7-1: Competing Early Models for the Formation of Non-P Materials

Vertical—Example of the traditional source model

Concept of Overall Non-P text	jjjjjjjjjjjjeeeR^{je}jjjjeeejjjjejeR^{je}jjjeejejjjjjeeeeeee

Reconstructed sources	Yahwist source	jjjjjjjjjjjjj... jjjj...jjjj.j. jjj..j.jjjjj.....
	Elohist source	..........eee ....eee....e.e ...ee.e.....eeeeee

Key: Periods indicate material that is posited in the source but does not exist in our text. R^{je} symbolizes the posited author/redactor who combined the sources

Horizontal—Example of a fragment model positing originally independent Jacob and Joseph stories

Concept of Overall Non-P text	JaJaJaJaJaR^{jj}JaJa	JoJoJoJoR^{jj}JoJo
Reconstructed sources	JaJaJaJaJaJaJa	JoJoJoJoJoJo
	Jacob story	Joseph story

Key: R^{jj} symbolizes the posited author/redactor who combined the stories

---

Ilgen's and Hupfeld's isolation of a non-Priestly Elohistic source was as much a matter of redefining and narrowing the Priestly layer as it was of carving an Elohistic source out of non-Priestly materials. Indeed, Hupfeld's analysis of P was so successful that by the end of the century, Wellhausen

---

5. Hupfeld, *Quellen der Genesis;* cf. K. D. Ilgen, *Die Urkunden des Jerusalemischen Tempelarchivs in ihrer Urgestalt . . . : Theil I: Die Urkunden des ersten Buchs von Moses* (Halle: Hemmerde und Schwetschke, 1798).
6. Hupfeld, *Quellen der Genesis,* 48.
7. Hupfeld, *Quellen der Genesis,* 194.

largely presupposed Hupfeld's isolation of P. In his *Composition des Hexateuchs* he devoted most of his labor to distinguishing E and J from each other in the non-P materials. Moreover, from Wellhausen onward, the beginning point was not the Jacob narrative but the Abraham narrative. The task had shifted from distinguishing a non-Priestly Elohistic tradition from the later Priestly strand (Hupfeld), to distinguishing Elohistic traditions from their Yahwistic counterparts (Wellhausen).[8] The Abraham narrative, with its cluster of Elohistic traditions regarding Abraham in Genesis 20—22, provided a better locus for the latter sort of argument. Once Wellhausen had made the case for an Elohistic source there, he moved backward to identify traces of the Elohistic source in Genesis 15, and then forward to isolate certain key Elohistic passages (Gen. 28:10–22*; 37:2b-11), before searching for the continuation of this Elohistic source in the surrounding material.[9]

In this way, Wellhausen exemplified a typical type of argument already present in Hupfeld's analysis of the Jacob narrative. Analyses of E tend to seek certain textual beachheads, such as Genesis 20—22; 28:10–22*; and 37:3–11, 21–30, and then work outward from them to find the missing Elohistic context of these passages. This does not just involve locating passages using the divine name "Elohim." Instead, such early Elohistic passages are identified through an ever-expanding range of vocabulary and thematic indicators developed first from the Elohistic beachhead texts, and then from subsequent texts linked with them. Subsequent analysis then tends to proceed in two steps: (1) presuppose that E "must" be in a given section, and (2) use the fund of terminological indicators drawn from other texts to identify Elohistic fragments in the material that can be shaken loose from the Yahwistic context. Alternatively, in some cases, like the Joseph narrative, the process moves in the reverse direction: presuppose that J must have had sections corresponding to the E source; then use terminological indicators from other Yahwistic texts to isolate fragments of the Yahwistic source; and finally pry verses and half-verses loose from an Elohistic context.

The result is both similar to and different from a basic vertical distinction between P and non-P sources. On the one hand, this isolation of (non-Priestly) Elohistic and Yahwistic materials involves the resolute application of the same conflation model to non-Priestly materials that was first developed in the distinction of Priestly and non-Priestly materials in Genesis 1—11. Moreover, the initial criterion that was so important to the earliest source critics, variation in divine designations, is the same. On the other hand, there are a number of significant differences.

8. For example, Wellhausen, *Composition*, 15–16, devotes only a few sentences to the chronological problems with assigning Genesis 20—22 to P before arguing at more length for isolating 20—22 from J.
9. Wellhausen, *Composition*, 30–48 (on Jacob) and 53–60 (on Joseph).

1. *Size of Blocks:* Whereas the previously discussed posited P and non-P materials occur in big blocks and interweaving of them is the exception (the Flood, Reed Sea), we can only reconstruct parallel J and E sources by isolating fragments of each, fragments now intricately interwoven into the context of the other source. Therefore, analysis of J and E involves a new level of slicing texts into sources, texts that often do not provide grounds for doing so.

2. *Type of Criteria Used to Identify Sources:* Whereas distinction of P materials from non-P materials can draw on numerous explicit cross-references (Creation-Flood, successive covenants, toledot superscriptions) and extensively parallel phraseology, J and E materials are often distinguished by little more than their supposed diverging preferences for certain common words and genres. Yet such an approach is inherently problematic. Mere similarity in the use of common words, genres, and narrative themes can be explained by all sorts of models: that the materials belong to the same compositional level, that one text was composed in light of the other, or that both texts developed parallel to each other because they were written in environment with similar linguistic and narrative possibilities. Therefore, the use of common language and thematic stock has proven a foundation of sand beneath the source-critical house. As a result, the structure has thus shown a striking tendency to shift. This leads to the next point.

3. *Level of Attainable Consensus:* The level of consensus attained in isolation of the sources is lower. Whereas scholars have been able to achieve relative unanimity on isolation of P and non-P materials, the divisions between J and E have remained irresolvably fluid.

The Rise of Alternatives to the Classic Source Approach

In light of these differences, it is no wonder that the number of advocates of a source approach to non-P materials has significantly decreased in recent years. Instead, a combined redaction and tradition-historical model is now increasingly used to describe the written transmission history of the non-P material. On the one hand, most agree that the earliest origins of the Pentateuch are to be found in various discrete, shorter oral and/or written *traditions.* Thus, most posit a basic set of horizontal divisions *behind* the non-P material. We can see the faint traces of various originally independent traditions in the often discrete subplots and confined character groupings of the non-P material: Creation, Flood, Abraham and Lot, Hagar and Ishmael, Jacob and Esau, Jacob and Laban, Isaac, Joseph, Judah and Tamar, and so forth. On the other hand, these elements are now connected into a continuous narrative. Thus scholars posit a vertical layer or layers of *redactional* or, sometimes, *compositional* appropriation of these traditions by the author(s) responsible for producing the non-P material as we now see it.

This mixed tradition/composition model matches well the evidence we have for the production of literature elsewhere in the ancient world. Take the example of the Gilgamesh epic. The Old Babylonian version of this epic appears to have been created through a fluid borrowing from the plots of several earlier, independent Sumerian traditions regarding Gilgamesh.[10] This resembles the apparent fluid appropriation of Abraham and Jacob traditions that many posit for the earliest stage of the composition of these ancestral traditions. Later, this Old Babylonian version was extended and redirected, particularly in the Middle Babylonian period.[11] So also, many posit successive layers of compositional extension and redirection of the Genesis non-P materials. Indeed, as we saw at the outset of the book, there are numerous other documented examples of such extension and redirection. We have fewer empirical examples of borrowing of earlier traditions only because such borrowing is more difficult to document and the traditions used were often more fluid.

In any case, from Gunkel onward this transmission-historical model of tradition and composition history has often been used to describe the prehistory and subsequent development of the J and E sources. The difference is that in recent years this model has increasingly been used *exclusively* to describe the transmission history of non-P materials. The older source critics argued for two parallel acts of compositional appropriation of tradition, J and E, that were later combined with each other. Now, however, one can account for many of the most important features in the non-P material by positing that it has undergone a single compositional process, extending from the earliest compositional appropriation of tradition to later modifications and extensions of this early compositional work.[12] The combination of traditions and successive layers of composition accounts for many of the most important indicators once used by critics searching for J and E. When this model is considered, Hupfeld's main arguments for an independent E source fall by the wayside. Indeed, the most extensive attempt to trace Elohistic cross-references to missing material, Kessler's 1972 Heidelberg dissertation, ended up arguing *against* the existence of E. Instead, he decided that the cross-references in the Pentateuch are better explained by a theory of successive redactions of originally independent traditions.[13] Such a combined model allows us to avoid the questionable terminological arguments and arbitrary slicing into strands that characterized the attempt to find parallel sources in the non-P materials.

10. Tigay, *The Evolution of the Gilgamesh Epic,* 23–54.
11. Tigay, *The Evolution of the Gilgamesh Epic,* 55–109.
12. For an early advocate of this model see A. Jepsen, "Zur Überlieferungsgeschichte der Vätergestalten," *Wissenschaftliche Zeitschrift der Karl-Marx-Universität Leipzig, gesellschafts- und sprachwissenschaftliche Reihe* 3 (1953/4): 265–81, particularly 278–81.
13. R. Kessler, "Die Querverweise im Pentateuch. Überlieferungsgeschichtliche Untersuchung der expliziten Querverbindungen innerhalb des vorpriesterlichen Pentateuchs" (Ph.D. diss., Heidelberg, 1972).

In light of this background, the main issue for transmission-historical work on the non-P materials of Genesis is less isolation of parallel sources. Instead, the central transmission-historical task appears to be exploration of the ways the various traditional building blocks of Genesis have been linked together into the non-P material as we have it. The question facing us at this point is the following: To what extent was there a broader history to this linkage of materials, and how much of this history can we reconstruct? Some, such as Schmid and Van Seters, focus primarily on the description and placement of the final non-P composition.[14] Others, such as Rendtorff, Crüsemann, Blum, and Levin, are more optimistic about our ability to reconstruct earlier stages in the compositional process. They isolate both successive layers of composition and various core compositions that preceded the non-P narrative: an originally independent primeval history, Abraham history, and Jacob history, alongside the long-hypothesized Joseph novella.[15]

Overview of the Model to Be Developed in the Following

In the following chapters on the non-P materials, I will once again work backward, this time through the following stages.

1. *A Layer of Late Scribal Revision of Earlier Non-P Materials.* As we will see, this retouching apparently partakes of a more widespread tendency in exilic and postexilic Israelite discourse to draw on Deuteronomistic themes and emphases in the process of articulating various viewpoints. The closest correlate to this retouching is the limited scribal revision seen in the late development of many textual traditions, such as that for the book of Jeremiah.

2. *The Earliest Genesis: A Composition Spanning the Primeval History and All Three Patriarchs.* Once we lift the identifiable late revisions from the text and move further back, we come to an intricate web of compositional connections spanning the major primeval and ancestral parts of Genesis: the primeval curses and subsequent promises, the working out of the Abrahamic blessing in the ancestral history, the theme of "calling on the name of YHWH," the analogous travel commands and itineraries of the three major patriarchs, and so forth. To

---

14. H. H. Schmid, *Der sogenannte Jahwist: Beobachtungen und Fragen zur Pentateuchforschung* (Zurich: Theologischer Verlag, 1976); Van Seters, *Prologue to History,* but there are places where Van Seters does propose possible earlier stages. Cf. *Prologue to History,* 246–48 (affirming his work in the second half of *Abraham*), 277–78 (on 29:31–30:24), and 317 (accepting the basic contours of Redford's work on the Joseph story).
15. Rendtorff, *Problem,* 29–173, (E.T., 43–206); F. Crüsemann, "Die Eigenständigkeit der Urgeschichte: Ein Beitrag zur Diskussion um den 'Jahwisten'," *Die Botschaft und die Boten: Festschrift für H. W. Wolff* (ed. J. Jeremias and L. Perlitt; Neukirchen: Neukirchener Verlag, 1981), 9–29; Blum, *Vätergeschichte;* idem, *Studien;* Levin, *Der Jahwist.*

be sure, some such terminological and thematic parallels could be the result of parallel development of traditions regarding various ancient figures. Nevertheless, this web of connections is specific, cohesive, and sequential. Taken as a whole, the connections suggest that this promise-centered compositional stage in Genesis always included a primeval history and traditions regarding all three patriarchs.

3. *Precursor Compositions Apparently Used in the Earliest Genesis Composition: A Non-P Primeval History and Jacob-Joseph Story.* Upon further analysis, many of these broader cross-Genesis connections show signs of having been introduced at a late stage of some of the stories in which they occur. This is particularly true of broader cross-Genesis connections located in the non-P primeval history and Jacob-Joseph sections. For example, in the Jacob-Joseph story, the promise-centered, cross-Genesis connections seem to have been added to their present contexts. Once such secondary linkages with broader Genesis are removed, the Jacob-Joseph section shows signs of having existed on its own, prior to its inclusion in Genesis. Furthermore, this composition shows signs of having undergone yet earlier growth, a process extending back to separate Jacob and Joseph compositions.

As is already evident from this anticipatory survey, my study partakes of the recent trend toward replacement of the source model for non-P materials with a mixed tradition and composition model. Where traditional documentary approaches posit two successive stages of conflation (J/E and JE/P), I argue instead that the non-P materials developed in a way more analogous to the Gilgamesh epic, Deuteronomistic history, and other non-conflated compositions. This process moved from (1) initial linkage of independent traditions into broader composition to (2) more limited redirection and extension of that composition. Only after this process had taken place and this non-P Genesis had achieved some authority of its own did the Priestly authors countertell the story of Israel's early history.

In summary, we must be careful about too quickly extending conflation models from the later transmission history of Genesis, P and non-P, to Genesis's earlier transmission history. Indeed, throughout the rest of the book, I will maintain that exactly such an extension of the source-conflation model to the non-P materials was a fundamental misstep in research on the Pentateuch. It produced many of the most notoriously weak arguments in the history of transmission-historical research. Moreover, our documented cases of such conflation suggest that such interweaving of separate documents tends to be done at a later stage in the growth of tradition rather than during earlier ones. In light of such considerations I will be proposing a fundamentally different model for the formation of the non-P material. Rather than positing an early Southern Yahwistic source and later Northern Elohistic source, I posit a growth from preexilic Northern Jacob and Joseph compositions to later Southern extension of those materials into a promise-centered proto-Genesis. The case for this model, however, will only emerge gradually as we move backward through the formation of the non-P materials. Let us turn to that task now.

8
Reinforcing the Promise

The Late Revision of the Non-P Materials

I start the trip back through the transmission history of the non-P materials with texts that appear to have been part of a process of late retouching and revision of the non-P material in Genesis.[1] As we saw earlier, many ancient textual traditions were revised and retouched in the process of their transmission. The Jeremiah tradition underwent various layers of revision between the version of the book reflected by the Old Greek tradition and that represented by the Massoretic tradition. The expansionist Pentateuch manuscripts found at Qumran seem to reflect a similar process of ongoing revision of books like Genesis, one that continued in the production of the "Reworked Pentateuch" manuscripts of cave four on the one hand and the Samaritan Pentateuch on the other. So also, the multiple versions of the books of Kings indicate the many ways the basic form of a text can change in the process of its being used and reproduced.

Genesis, including its non-P tradition, would be an exception if had not undergone such a process. The problem is that such minor revisions are often unreconstructable. As one compares the later Jeremiah tradition with the earlier one, or the later versions of Esther with earlier ones, it is often clear that the revisions of a term here or a sentence there would have been undetectable if we did not have manuscript evidence for such shifts.[2] That having been said, even in these later versions there are occasional obvious additions that could probably be identified even in the absence of a copy of the earlier version. These more obvious additions stand as marks in the later versions of a broader process that preceded them. They are the tip of the iceberg.

In this chapter, I will look for such marked revisions in the non-P portions of the book of Genesis. In doing so, I will have to presuppose many of the findings of the next chapter. In that chapter I argue that Genesis owes its basic form to a promise-centered network of compositional connections that span it. Through texts like the initial command and promises to Abraham in

---

1. The term "retouching" is used to refer to smaller-scale revisions, whereas "revision" is a more encompassing term including larger-scale changes, like the addition of Genesis 14—15 and related texts.
2. Tov, "The Literary History of Jeremiah," 217–35.

Gen. 12:1–3, 7, the story of his almost-sacrifice of Isaac in Genesis 22, the texts focusing on Isaac in Gen. 26:1–33, and subsequent promise texts like the promise to Jacob at Bethel in Gen. 28:13–15, the author of this first non-P "Genesis" bound various traditions together into an inextricably connected whole. When we see additions *to these connecting texts uniting the first Genesis,* we have evidence for a secondary revision of this overall non-P tradition.

Isolation of Late Revisions of the Non-P Material in Genesis

The Link of the Promise to Abraham's Obedience: Genesis 22:15–18; 26:3bβ–5

Perhaps the best place to start is with two texts that are at the same time (1) composed in relation to and integrally linked with the above-mentioned, earlier Genesis compositional context and (2) marked secondary additions to that context. In Gen. 22:15–18 YHWH calls "a second time" from heaven to specify not only that Abraham did pass the test (Gen. 22:11–12) and will receive his son back (Gen. 22:13–14), but that God will also "swear" to do yet other things for him: bless him, multiply his seed/offspring, allow that offspring to take possession of the land, and make it so other nations bless themselves by Abraham's descendants. Later, after YHWH has commanded Isaac to stay in Gerar and has promised to be with him, bless him, and give him land (Gen. 26:2–3abα), YHWH promises to "establish the oath" that YHWH swore to Abraham (Gen. 26:3bβ; cf. 22:15). The text that follows is closely parallel to that in Gen. 22:17–18 in the wording and order of the promises and in the conclusion of the promise series with a similarly formulated reference to Abraham's obedience.[3] (See Chart 8-1.)

These texts are integrally related to each other. The main difference is that Gen. 22:15–18 shares its context's focus on Abraham's offspring (cf. Gen. 22:1–14, 19), while Gen. 26:3bβ–5 adds a new focus on "these lands" in a literary context where offspring are no longer such an issue (cf. Gen. 25:21–26).[4]

One other shared characteristic is that both these texts, however related they are to their contexts, appear to be additions to those contexts. The oath promise in Gen. 22:15–18 represents a parallel, second divine recognition of Abraham's obedience long after God has already recognized his passing the "test." The original reward for this passing the test was the return to Abraham of his son (Gen. 22:13), indeed his heir around whom much of the pre-

---

3. R. Kilian, *Die vorpriesterlichen Abrahamsüberlieferungen,* 205–6; Kessler, "Querverweise," 88–89; Blum, *Vätergeschichte,* 363–64.
4. Blum, *Vätergeschichte,* 363. Note, in addition, Gen. 26:3bβ–5 does not start with a promise of blessing (cf. Gen. 22:17a). This is probably because this promise is already part of the earlier context of this addition (Gen. 26:3).

Chart 8-1: Initial Promises to Abraham and to Isaac	
Gen. 22:17–18 (To Abraham)	Gen. 26:4–5 (To Isaac)
I will certainly bless you and	
I will certainly multiply	I will multiply
your offspring	your offspring
like the stars of heaven	like the stars of heaven
and like the sand on the seashore	
	And I will give your offspring
	all these lands
And by your seed	And by your seed
all the nations of the earth	all the nations of the earth
shall bless themselves	shall bless themselves
Because (*ʾēqeb ʿăšer*)	Because (*ʾēqeb ʿăšer*)
you [Abraham]	Abraham
obeyed my voice	obeyed my voice
	and kept my charge, my commandments,
	my decrees, and my instructions.

ceding narrative has revolved. With the provision of an alternative sacrifice, the narrative tension surrounding this son of promise is resolved. Abraham celebrates God's provision of the sacrifice by naming the mountain "God will see [to it]," after his initial statement of faith that God would "see to" the sacrifice (Gen. 22:8; cf. also 22:5b). The second divine speech in Gen. 22:15–18 names an additional reward for Abraham's obedience and thus interrupts the probable original movement of the narrative from Abraham's naming of Moriah (Gen. 22:14) to his departure from there (Gen. 22:19). Moreover, this speech adds a condition to promises of blessing and descendants, promises Abraham has already received. God had already promised him these things, but Gen. 22:15–18 now asserts that God now will provide these things for one reason: *because* Abraham did not withhold his only son (Gen. 22:16–17).[5]

Genesis 26:3bβ–5, the oath-focused section of YHWH's first promise to Isaac, likewise appears to be an expansion of the command and promise in Gen. 26:2–3abα. As we will see in the next chapter, the entire command and

5. Wellhausen, *Composition,* 18; A. Dillmann, *Genesis,* 285–86 (E.T., 140–41); Gunkel, *Genesis,* 239–40; Westermann, *Genesis 12—36,* 445, (E.T., 363); Blum, *Vätergeschichte,* 320. For early isolation of this section, actually 22:14–18, see already J. W. Colenso, *The Pentateuch and Book of Joshua Critically Examined,* Part 5, *Critical Analysis of Genesis* (London: Longmans, Green & Co., 1865), 95–97.

promise in Gen. 26:2–3abα is closely paralleled in several connecting texts in Genesis (Gen. 12:1–3; 31:3, 13; 46:1–4) and appears to be part of Genesis's earliest overall compositional layer. These parallels stop, however, with the oath-focused section in Gen. 26:3bβ–5. Already its secondary character is suggested by the way it doubles the land promise in the preceding material (Gen. 26:4; cf. 26:3bα). Moreover, it adds to preceding promises the same conditional element that we saw in Gen. 22:15–18. In these preceding promises, YHWH had already promised to bless Isaac and give his seed "these lands" (Gen. 26:3abα). Now, however, in Gen. 26:3bβ–5, YHWH promises to do so *as an outgrowth* of Abraham's obedience at Moriah and YHWH's resulting oath to him (Gen. 22:15–18).[6]

One more confirming argument is that both Gen. 22:15–18 and Gen. 26:3bβ–5 diverge from surrounding texts in Genesis in the way they formulate the promise of blessing (see Chart 8-2).

Chart 8-2: Blessing Promise Formulations

Gen. 12:3	all clans of the earth [*hā 'ǎdāmāh*]	shall bless themselves *or* shall be blessed [N-stem of *brk*]	by you through you
Gen. 18:18	all nations of the world [*hā 'āreṣ*]	shall bless themselves *or* shall be blessed [N-stem of *brk*]	by him through him
Gen. 22:18	all nations of the world [*hā 'āreṣ*]	shall bless themselves [Htd-stem of *brk*]	by your seed
Gen. 26:4	all nations of the world [*hā 'āreṣ*]	shall bless themselves [Htd-stem of *brk*]	by your seed
Gen. 28:14	all clans of the earth [*hā 'ǎdāmāh*]	shall bless themselves *or* shall be blessed [N-stem of *brk*]	by you through you

---

Genesis 12:3 and 28:14 perfectly match each other and are part of the above-mentioned compositional layer spanning Genesis. Genesis 18:18 is a secondary addition to be discussed below. The versions of the blessing promise in Gen. 22:18 and 26:4 both build on part of Gen. 18:18, the shift to "all the nations of the world," but they diverge in at least two ways from the earlier texts before and after them. First, they share a special focus on the nations blessing themselves by the *seed* of Abraham and Isaac. All the other texts

---

6. Here I follow the delimitation of the addition from Noth, *Überlieferungsgeschichte des Pentateuch*, 30; (E.T., 29); cf. Colenso, *Genesis*, 117–18; Dillmann, *Die Genesis*, 317–18; (E.T., vol. 2, 201–3); Gunkel, *Genesis*, 300; Kessler, "Querverweise," 105; Blum, *Vätergeschichte*, 362–63. These treatments, however, tend to depend more exclusively on terminology than the arguments given above do. For critique of such terminologically oriented approaches, see Van Seters, *Prologue to History*, 269.

focus on how the clans/nations will bless themselves by the patriarch himself. Second and more important, both 22:18 and 26:4 now use a new form of the verb for "bless," one that makes it absolutely clear that the nations will not *be blessed through* Abraham, but will *bless themselves by* him.[7]

Alone, such a deviation in promise formulation would not be significant, but considered alongside the above-discussed indicators of seams, this shift becomes one part of a broader picture. Overall, Gen. 22:15–18 and 26:3bβ–5 are marked as secondary additions to their context by multiple converging factors: (1) *doubling:* the doubling of the divine response to Abraham's obedience in Gen. 28:15–18 (cf. 22:12) and the doubling and recontextualization of the land promise in Gen. 26:4 (cf. 26:3bα); (2) *slighter indicators of seams:* the interruption in its context by Gen. 22:15–18, and the expansion beyond the command/promise form by Gen. 26:3bβ–5 (cf. Gen. 26:2–3abα//12:1–3; 31:3, 13; 46:1–4); and (3) *divergence in profile:* the deviation of both Gen. 22:15–18 and 26:3bβ–5 from other formulations of the divine blessing by/of other nations. Furthermore, both the command/promise in Gen. 26:2–3abα and the story of Abraham and Isaac at Moriah (Gen. 22:1–14, 19) are part of the earliest compositional layer spanning Genesis. Thus Gen. 22:15–18 and 26:3bβ–5 are additions to that layer. They are part of an extension and redirection of an earlier form of Genesis as a whole.

So much for arguments for the secondary character of these texts. What is more important for our purposes is a brief look at how these texts link with and redirect the material they extend. First, especially if one expects obedience to produce a reward greater than the return of Abraham's heir, then the added promise in Gen. 22:15–18 provides this extra reward. Indeed, there is a striking precedent for this pattern elsewhere. As Van Seters points out, the Deuteronomistic history states that Judah and Jerusalem remained in the hands of David's ancestors "for the sake of David, my servant, who kept my commandments and my statutes" (1 Kings 11:34). So also now, with the addition of 22:15–18 and 26:3bβ–5, the Abraham and Isaac stories describe how Abraham's descendants, starting with Isaac, would receive the promise of blessing, descendants, and land "because Abraham listened to [God's] voice, and kept [God's] charge, commandments, decrees and instructions."[8]

---

7. Regarding this pair of shifts, see H. H. Schmid, *Der sogenannte Jahwist,* 132–33; Rendtorff, *Problem,* 43 (E.T., 59–60). The probable original meaning of the earlier blessing formulation in Gen. 12:3/28:14 will be discussed in more detail in the following chapter. Van Seters, *Prologue to History,* 220, rightfully argues against excessive dependence on such formulaic shifts for identification of layers and relative dating. He does not, however, consider these shifts in the context of other indicators for the secondary character of Gen. 28:15–18 and 26:3bβ–5 (see *Prologue,* 262–64 and 269). It is exactly this *correlation* of indicators that is important in the argument here.

8. For Van Seters (*Abraham,* 239; idem., *Prologue to History,* 262–64) this testing and reward pattern is strong evidence that the testing story in Gen. 22:1–19 always had the promise in Gen. 22:15–18. Nevertheless, the indicators of seams and profile that were discussed above suggest that Gen. 22:15–18, however well-fitted to its context, was secondarily added to it. Moreover, the earliest form of the story probably did focus exclusively on the restoration of the heir

Second, standing in a strategic position between God's earlier promise of blessing to Abraham (Gen. 12:3) and God's promise of the same to Jacob (Gen. 28:14), these texts artfully redirect their broader context. Through the above discussed shift in formulation, the additions in Gen. 22:18 and 26:4 specify that God was promising in Gen. 12:3 and 28:14 that all nations would *bless themselves by* Abraham's heir, Isaac, and his children. Furthermore, Gen. 22:18 and 26:5 stress that this promise was transmitted to Isaac *because of Abraham's obedience*. In summary, these new additions relating especially to Isaac (Gen. 22:15–18; 26:3bβ–5) attribute the transmission of the promise from Abraham (Gen. 12:3) to Jacob (Gen. 28:14) *by way of Isaac* to one thing: Abraham's obedience, particularly at Moriah.[9]

This sharp focus on the centrality of obedience is one of several elements in this pair of texts that link them with late trends in Israelite literature, trends often linked to varying extents with the theology and language of specifically Deuteronomistic literature (e.g., the Deuteronomistic history, present edition of Jeremiah, and related texts). This literature is characterized by many elements, including (1) an emphasis on the importance of obedience by the people to YHWH's Torah in Deuteronomy; (2) opposition to foreigners and their influence on Israel—especially to Canaanites, the paradigmatic pre-Israelite inhabitants of the Promised Land; and (3) use of certain patterned language to express these and other themes.[10]

Recent scholarship has shown a tendency to find such "Deuteronomistic" influences behind every stone and tree in biblical literature, and such efforts have been rightly criticized. Nevertheless, we do see quite divergent late Israelite texts appropriate various aspects of the Deuteronomistic tradition, from the Chronistic revision of the Deuteronomistic history and the

---

to Abraham. As will be discussed more in the next chapter (see also Van Seters, *Abraham,* 238–39; idem, *Prologue to History,* 265), Genesis 22 stands parallel to and yet over against the preceding story in Gen. 21:8–20, a story where Abraham is forced by God, against his objections, to permanently give up a son. In this context, the restoration of the son to Abraham in Gen. 22:13 completes the narrative circle begun in Genesis 21. Note that the parallels between these chapters end with the verbal links between Gen. 21:17, 19 and 22:11–13 (on these see Blum, *Vätergeschichte,* 314).

Now Van Seters argues that the inclusion of the promise in Gen. 21:13 and 18 prove that its parallel in Gen. 22:15–18 is an original part of the story. Such an approach misses the point of the special focus of the promise in Genesis 21: to stress that Ishmael, though now expelled from the household of Abraham, is nevertheless still included in the promise of blessing to his descendants. Isaac's role as heir of the promise is already clear from preceding texts, including Gen. 21:12. This promise certainly *could* have been reiterated in a story like that in Genesis 22, but the indicators discussed above suggest that in the earliest written form of the story the focus was exclusively on the restoration to Abraham of his son, already the clear heir of the promise. Only later did an author, very likely with the test-reward schema in mind, see Abraham's fulfillment of the test as an apt compositional opportunity to stress the link of obedience with fulfillment of the promise. Van Seters' observations pertain to the artfulness of that author's work.

9. Rendtorff, *Problem,* 59–60, (E.T., 77–78).

10. See Weinfeld, *Deuteronomy and the Deuteronomic School,* 320–65.

Deuteronomistic revisions of the book of Jeremiah, to certain texts in the post-exilic sections of Isaiah that build on selected Deuteronomistic themes in the process of opposing some central developments of Deuteronomistic theology in the postexilic period.[11] In the present day a Southern politician, whether liberal or conservative, will often use the conservative, evangelical language of the Bible belt to articulate her or his beliefs. So also it appears that the themes and language of Deuteronomistic religiosity pervaded much Israelite religious discourse in the exile and beyond.[12]

As we turn to Gen. 22:15–18 and 26:3bβ–5, this pair of texts exemplifies certain so-called Deuteronomistic themes, while opposing others. In this sense they belong to a broader stream of Israelite literature that is probably best termed semi-Deuteronomistic. Their emphasis on the importance of Abraham's obedience links them to broader trends in post-Deuteronomistic Israel on the centrality of obedience. At the same time, however, these texts are distinguished in important respects from properly Deuteronomistic literature. For example, as Van Seters has particularly stressed, properly Deuteronomistic texts focus not on the patriarchal promise but instead on the absolute necessity for Israel to obey the Deuteronomistic Torah in order to enter and stay in the land. This pair of texts in Gen. 22:15–18 and 26:3bβ5 diverge from this central part of the Deuteronomistic tradition by grounding Israel's claim to the land not in Israel's *own* obedience to Deuteronomistic law, but in YHWH's prior oath commitment to Abraham.[13] Thus the language of the Deuteronomistic tradition is being used against itself in this pair of strategic semi-Deuteronomistic additions to Genesis.

So also, the antiforeign elements of the Deuteronomistic tradition may be reflected in the reformulation of the blessing so that it is clear that other nations are not *being blessed* through Isaac and his children, but will *bless themselves* by them. Even so, the differences from properly Deuteronomistic tradition must again be acknowledged. There is no exact analogy in Deuteronomistic literature to the nations blessing themselves by Israel.[14] This theme in Gen. 22:15–18 and 26:3bβ–5 is prompted in large part by the author/reviser's creative interaction with material regarding this blessing in Genesis.

---

11. O. H. Steck, *Israel und das gewaltsame Geschick der Propheten: Untersuchungen zur Überlieferung des deuteronomistischen Geschichtsbildes im Alten Testament, Spätjudentum und Urchristentum* (WMANT 23; Neukirchen-Vluyn: Neukirchener Verlag, 1967), 60–218; idem, "Strömungen theologischer Tradition im Alten Israel," in *Zu Tradition und Theologie im Alten Testament* (ed. O. H. Steck; Biblische-Theologische Studien 2; Neukirchen-Vluyn: Neukirchener Verlag, 1978), 48–54.
12. Rendtorff, "Paradigm," 48–49. See also the comments of Lohfink on undifferentiated Deuteronomistic influence and the lack of a specific Deuteronomistic movement in this period, "Gab es eine deuteronomistische Bewegung?" in *Jeremia und die "deuteronomistische Bewegung"* (BBB 98; Weinheim: Beltz Athenäum Verlag, 1995), 313–82, especially 370–73.
13. Van Seters, *Abraham*, 273; idem, *The Life of Moses*, 467.
14. Probably the closest analogy would be a passage in Deuteronomy where "the peoples" look to Israel's law and wonder at the wisdom of the people (Deut. 4:6–8).

Finally, there are some reflections of Deuteronomistic language in Gen. 22:15–18 and 26:3bβ–5.

> The promise to "multiply [Isaac's] descendants" (Deut. 7:13; 13:18; Josh. 24:3; cf. Isa. 51:2) "like the stars in the heaven" (Gen. 22:17; 26:3bβ; cf. Deut. 1:10; 10:22; 28:62) or the "sand at the sea" (1 Kings 4:20; Jer. 33:22)[15]
>
> The final reference in both texts to Abraham's "listening to [YHWH's] voice" (22:18b; 26:5a) and "keeping" YHWH's "charge, commands, decrees, and instructions" (Gen. 26:5b)[16]
>
> YHWH's promise to "establish the oath which [YHWH] swore to Abraham, [Isaac's] father" (Gen. 26:3bβ; cf. Gen. 22:16 and Jer. 11:5)[17]

Not all the language in these texts is Deuteronomistic. Moreover, as we have seen, even the expressions that are Deuteronomistic occur in the context of a non-Deuteronomistic emphasis on Abraham's foundational obedience and God's resulting promise. Nevertheless, the occurrence of these expressions in conjunction with the above-described semi-Deuteronomistic themes suggests that Gen. 22:15–18 and 26:3bβ–5 were authored in a late Israelite environment where such specific Deuteronomistic language had become part of the culture's more general literary repertoire.

In sum, this pair of texts is certainly not the work of a strictly "Deuteronomistic" editor, one who simply conformed non-P texts in Genesis to Deuteronomistic models. Instead, they are the work of an author/reviser who creatively revised and extended the non-P Genesis tradition, while working in a context where Deuteronomistic themes and language are "in the air." Let us look now to see whether other traces of such revision can be found in Genesis.

Predicting Future Obedience of Abraham's Heirs: Genesis 18:19

Genesis 18:17–19 has two explanations for YHWH's speaking to Abraham about his plans for Sodom and Gomorrah: (1) Abraham will be powerful nation and object of blessing (Gen. 18:17–18), and (2) God "takes a special interest in him" (*yĕda'ttîv*)[18] in order that "he may charge his sons and his house after him to keep the way of YHWH" so that "YHWH will bring about for Abraham what he has promised him." Later in this chapter I will discuss the first rationale in Gen. 18:17–18. For now, however, it is important to recognize how Gen. 18:19 offers an alternative explanation to that given in Gen. 18:

---

15. Schmid, *Sogenannte Jahwist,* 131.
16. Holzinger, *Einleitung,* 290; Gunkel, *Genesis,* 300; Blum, *Vätergeschichte,* 363.
17. W. Thiel, *Die deuteronomistische Redaktion von Jeremia 1—25* (WMANT 41; Neukirchen-Vluyn: Neukirchener Verlag, 1973), 143–44.
18. On translation of this form see KB 3, 374.

17–18. Furthermore, one crucial aspect of the profile of Gen. 18:19 is shared with the secondary additions discussed above: the intense focus on obedience. Whereas Gen. 18:17–18 already justifies YHWH's speech through reference to the promise, Gen. 18:19 additionally mentions YHWH's interest in making sure Abraham will teach his children to "keep the way of YHWH," *and this then is the precondition* for YHWH fulfilling his promises to Abraham and his descendants (Gen. 18:19b). This addition of obedience as a precondition to already-given promises was one of the above-discussed markers of the secondary character of Gen. 22:15–18 and 26:3bβ–5. In summary, Gen. 18:19 is marked as a probable addition to its context by at least two indicators: (1) the partial doubling of Gen. 18:17–18 in Gen. 18:19, and (2) the *particular* focus in this verse on Abraham's obedience as a precondition for fulfillment of already-given promises, an element of profile that links Gen. 18:19 with additions to the Abraham and Isaac stories in Gen. 22:15–18 and 26:3bβ–5.[19]

This verse shows other signs of being part of a revision of non-P material like that seen in Gen. 22:15–18 and 26:3bβ–5. Not only does Gen. 18:19 share the emphasis on the importance of Abraham's obedience; not only does it likewise appear to ground previously given promises in obedience; but in addition, the language of Gen. 18:19 draws on the Deuteronomistic tradition. In particular, it describes Abraham as fulfilling the programmatic Deuteronomistic stipulation to teach children righteousness (cf. Deut. 6:1–3, 20–25).[20] At the same time Gen. 18:19, like the above-discussed texts, deviates from the Deuteronomistic tradition. It grounds YHWH's relationship with Israel in an ancestral righteousness that long predates the all-important Deuteronomistic law. As a result the "justice and righteousness" Abraham will teach his children (Gen. 18:19a) is distinguished from the "decrees and commandments" the Deuteronomistic tradition envisions later Israelites teaching their children (Gen. 6:1–3, 20–25).[21]

---

19. Another possible indicator, albeit much weaker, is the particular concentration of Deuteronomistic themes in Gen. 18:19 (more on this below). Arguments for Gen. 18:17–19 as a whole as "Deuteronomistic" have tended to find most of their evidence in Gen. 18:19. Cf., for example, Colenso, *Genesis,* 73–74, and Blum, *Vätergeschichte,* 400, both of whom assign both 18:18 and 19 to a Deuteronomistic reviser but find substantially more evidence for this in 18:19.

Others have argued that Gen. 18:19 is marked as secondary because God refers to Godself in the third person here. See, e.g., Kilian, *Die vorpriesterlichen Abrahamsüberlieferungen,* 106; L. Schmidt, *'De Deo,' Studien zur Literarkritik und Theologie des Buches Jona, des Gesprächs zwischen Abraham und Jahwe in Gen. 18, 22ff. und von Hi 1* (BZAW 143; Berlin/New York: De Gruyter, 1976), 134–36 (see for references to earlier studies). Nevertheless, as Blum points out (*Vätergeschichte,* 401), this does not explain why a redactor, one who himself probably began in the first person, was able to bear such a contradiction, and an author of the speech as a whole was not. Moreover, the range of biblical examples shows that divine speech was often used as a broad medium for communication about God, so that one can not just automatically assume that third-person speech about God in a divine speech is a reliable indicator of the secondary character of the text in question.

20. See in particular Blum, *Vätergeschichte,* 400, and references. In contrast, no such noticably Deuteronomistic terminology appears in this verse's preceding context, Gen. 18:17–18.

21. Schmidt, *De Deo,* 136; Van Seters, *Abraham,* 273–74; idem, *The Life of Moses,* 467.

Overall, Gen. 18:19 serves as a strategic modification not just of its immediate context but of the ancestral history as a whole. The text implies that Isaac and Jacob were able to pass on the promise because their obedience was like Abraham's, although we do not have texts that specifically assert this. By asserting that Abraham would pass on his obedience, Gen. 18:19 makes other semi-"Deuteronomistic" additions to the Abraham and Isaac materials (Gen. 22:15–18; 26:3bβ–5) function for the ancestral history as a whole. Not only will Abraham's obedience ground YHWH's gift of the promise to Isaac and his children (Gen. 22:15–18; 26:3bβ–5), but his teaching of obedience will ensure the ongoing transmission of the promise to his grandchildren and great-grandchildren.

The Beginning of the Fall of Canaan: Retouching the Aftermath of the Flood

So far I have surveyed identifiable semi-"Deuteronomistic" revisions in the ancestral section of Genesis, revisions that have often been discussed in previous studies. Indeed, most discussion of semi-"Deuteronomistic" material in Genesis has focused on the ancestral material. Perhaps this is because Israel-focused, semi-"Deuteronomistic" revisers, working as they did with a theology heavily influenced by the Israel-focused theology of the Deuteronomistic tradition, were preoccupied with the story of Israel itself, and thus left more material in the ancestral section than in the cosmic history that preceded it. Nevertheless, there is some evidence that the primeval history was at least partly revised out of a similar semi-"Deuteronomistic" perspective. In particular, these revisers appear to have modified the primeval history at precisely the two points where that history touches the one nation outside Israel of central importance for Deuteronomistic theology: the Canaanites. These revisions in turn prepare for later semi-"Deuteronomistic" revisions in the ancestral history.

One such revision occurs in the non-P survey of the nations who followed the flood, Gen. 10:8–19, 24–30. In large part this survey, like the non-P genealogy in Genesis 4, covers the fabled progenitors of various peoples and how they "fathered" various other peoples: Cush fathers Nimrod, Canaan fathers Sidon and Heth, Arpachshad fathers Shelah, and so forth. In Gen. 10:16, however, just after this material has described Canaan's fathering Sidon and Heth, the text shifts from individual progenitors of nations to the national groups themselves:

> (Gen. 10:15) Canaan became the father of Sidon, his firstborn, and Heth, (Gen. 10:16–18a) and the Jebusites, the Amorites, the Girgashites, the Hivites, the Arkites, the Sinites, the Arvadites, the Zemarites, and the Hamathites. (NRSV)

This is the only place in Genesis 10 where whole national groups are listed, and the gentilic used in 10:16–18a (Jebusites, Amorites) distinguishes this list from the set of names in Gen. 10:15. Moreover, the particular form of this list closely resembles widespread Deuteronomistic lists of the nations *who are to be displaced by Israel in its conquest of the land.* Both the nations listed and the form in which they are listed in Gen. 10:16–18a are similar to those of these Deuteronomistic lists, with the exception that Gen. 10:16–18a expands its Deuteronomistic precursors through the addition of more peoples.[22] This striking deviation of Gen. 10:16–18a from the other non-P material in Genesis 10, combined with its close resemblance to distinctive Deuteronomistic lists of displaced nations, suggests that Gen. 10:16–18a is a semi-"Deuteronomistic" extension of its context. In this case it is an expansion of an earlier mention of Canaan in the Genesis 10 table of nations. It reflects the special interest of much post-Deuteronomistic Israelite literature in the Canaanites as those whom Israel conquered and as the paradigmatic example of the foreign nation with whom Israel must not mix.

A similar special interest in Canaanites is also present in the story of Noah's sons (Gen. 9:20–27). Interpreters have long puzzled at the fact that Ham was the one who viewed his father's nakedness, but it was his son Canaan who was cursed. In the past, most historical-critical scholars have "solved" this problem by eliminating "Ham, the father of" from Gen. 9:22, so that Canaan is the one who sees his father's nakedness.[23] Nevertheless, as Westermann points out, there is no other evidence for a tradition that Noah's sons were Shem, Japhet, and Canaan. Moreover, aside from some peripheral mentions of Canaan around the margins of the story about Ham (Gen. 9:18b, and "father of Canaan" in 9:22), the majority of references to him in this story (five out of seven) are in the curse on him (Gen. 9:25–27). As a result of this evidence, Westermann proposes that the curse on Canaan has been appended by the Yahwist to a story of Ham's outrage.[24] The original story in 9:20–24 shows every sign of having focused on Ham, and the original curse probably described some kind of enslavement of Ham to his "brothers" (cf. Gen. 9:25).

Given the evidence elsewhere for semi-"Deuteronomistic" additions to Genesis, I argue that the focus on Canaan in the present Gen. 9:25–27 curse derives from the late author/retouchers who produced texts like Gen. 22:15–18;

---

22. On these lists cf. W. Richter, *Die Bearbeitungen des 'Retterbuches' in der deuteronomistichen Epoche* (BBB 21; Bonn: P. Hanstein, 1964), 40–43. Richter treats Gen. 10:16 and 15:19–21 as "pre-Deuteronomistic." Nevertheless, the expansion of this list vis-à-vis its Deuteronomistic parallels leaves little doubt that it is later. There is little evidence here of the "more detailed knowledge" Richter presupposes in order to maintain that longer lists like Gen 10:16 and 15:19–21 predated the Deuteronomistic lists of the Deuteronomistic history. Indeed, if those Deuteronomistic lists postdated Gen. 10:16 and 15:19–21 as Richter supposes, then they could have drawn on the information in these two Genesis texts. On the contrary, the Deuteronomistic lists predate those in Gen. 10:16 and 15:19–21. Such lists tend to expand over time, not contract.

23. For the most influential examples, cf. Wellhausen, *Composition*, 13, and Budde, *Urgeschichte*, 300–2. This revised version of the beginning of Gen. 9:22 would read, "and . . . Canaan saw the nakedness of his father."

24. Westermann, *Genesis 1—11*, 646–68; (E.T., 483–84).

26:3bβ–5 and the above-discussed list of Canaanite nations in Gen. 10:16–18a. In particular, the anti-Canaan focus of Gen. 9:25–27 links with Gen. 10:16–18a. Noah curses Canaan (Gen. 9:25–27), and then the to-be-displaced nations coming from him are specified in the addition in Gen. 10:16–18a. Together these texts reflect a special interest in Canaan typical of much late, semi-"Deuteronomistic" literature. In this case, the probable retouching of the Noah story (Gen. 9:18–27) and extension of the nations list (Gen. 10:16–18a) anticipate later texts that will describe Israel's conquest of the Canaanites in the process of taking the Promised Land from them. In other words, these semi-"Deuteronomistic" revisions of non-P material in Genesis 9—10 describe the primeval origins of the future subjugation of Canaan.

Genesis 14—15: The Initial and Future Subjugation of Canaan under Abraham and His Descendants

I turn last to a pair of texts that have long been recognized as distinct from their context: Genesis 14 and 15. Genesis 14 reintroduces Abraham as "the Hebrew" (Gen. 14:13), although he has been featured in the previous two chapters. Moreover, the story of conquest and rescue in Genesis 14 does not integrally link with or continue the major themes of the early compositional material that precedes it, Genesis 12—13. For these and other reasons, most scholars have rightly seen Genesis 14 as originating in large part from an independent source and have given the chapter widely varied datings.[25] Genesis 15 takes the promise that occurred in the preceding early compositional material (Gen. 12:1–3; 13:14–17) and builds a whole promise scene around it, culminating in the designation of YHWH's land promise as a "covenant" with Abraham. This perspective finds its closest analogy in the later semi-"Deuteronomistic" oath that appears in Gen. 22:15–18 and 26:3bβ–5, but is otherwise not reflected in the central promise texts of the earlier compositional layer.[26] For this and other reasons, it appears Genesis 15 is not an original continuation of the material in Genesis 12—13.[27] Instead, it breathes a life of its own, as a strategic reconceptualization of the promise of children and land to Abraham, and of Abraham's response to it.

In recent years a handful of literary studies of Genesis have pointed out another dimension of Genesis 14—15 that had escaped the notice of historical-

---

25. For the original arguments for the independence of the chapter and a late dating, see Gunkel, *Genesis,* 288–90, but cf. Sarna, *Genesis,* 102, for a survey of some ways the chapter does link with the broader assumptions of its context. For a survey of previous studies, see W. Schatz, *Genesis 14: Eine Untersuchung* (Bern: H. Lang; Frankfurt am Main: P. Lang, 1972), 13–61; and J. A. Emerton, "Some False Clues in the Study of Genesis XIV," *VT* 21 (1971): 24–46; idem, "The Riddle of Genesis XIV," *VT* 21 (1971): 403–39; idem, "Some Problems in Genesis xiv," in *Studies in the Pentateuch* (VTSup 41; Leiden/New York; Brill, 1990), 73–102.
26. Gen. 50:24 will be discussed below.
27. See already, Colenso, *Genesis,* 56–62. For a review and discussion of more recent scholarship, see Blum, *Vätergeschichte,* 367–83.

critical scholars working on these texts: the way these two chapters work together to continue themes already seen in Gen. 9:18–27 and 10:16–18a. The
studies of Cassuto, Sykes, and Steinmetz are particularly important in this respect.[28] Building on Cassuto's work, Steinmetz observes that Genesis 14 links
in multiple ways to the present form of Gen. 9:20–27. There Noah proclaims
a curse on Canaan, saying that he will be "enslaved" to his brothers (Gen.
9:25–27), while Shem will be blessed. This curse is then reflected in the first
half of Genesis 14, where the five Canaanite kings are "enslaved" by certain
descendants of Shem, Yaphet, and Ham (Gen. 14:1–4; cf. 10:19), and are
defeated when they attempt to rebel (Gen. 14:5–12). At this point Abraham
conquers the conquerors. This act hints at his supremacy over the others who
descended from Noah and at his appropriation of the blessing on Shem that
was given by Noah.[29]

Next, Genesis 15 implicitly links with the conquest narrative of Genesis 14
through the royal war oracle at its very beginning: "Do not be afraid, Abram.
I am a shield for you, your reward/booty will be very great."[30] The "shield"
(*māgēn*) mentioned here resembles the "delivering" (*miggēn*) of Abraham
that Melchizedeq just mentioned in his blessing of Abraham (Gen. 14:20);
the promise of reward in 15:1 takes the place of the booty Abraham had rejected in 14:22–3; and the overall promise in Gen. 15:1 stands as a reassur-
ance to Abraham after his encounter with the eastern kings in Genesis 14.[31]
Moreover, as Sykes has particularly emphasized, the continuation of Genesis
15 includes a later prediction of the Israelites' sojourn in Egypt that goes out
of its way to use terms that echo Genesis 14. Just as Abraham conquered the
conquerors at "Dan" (which means "judgment"), and came forth from that
encounter with "riches" (*rĕkûš*), so also YHWH proclaims that he will "judge"
(*dān*) the Egyptians, and Israel will leave Egypt with "riches" (*rĕkûš*;
15:14).[32] Genesis 15 then concludes with a Deuteronomistic list of the Ca-

28. Cassuto, *Genesis,* vol. 2, *From Noah to Abraham,* 168–70; D. K. Sykes, "Patterns in Genesis," (Ph.D. diss., Yeshiva University, 1985), 66–70; D. Steinmetz, *From Father to Son: Kinship,
Conflict and Continuity in Genesis* (Literary Currents in Biblical Interpretation; Louisville, Ky.:
Westminster John Knox, 1991), 146–47.
29. Steinmetz, *From Father to Son,* 146–47.
30. For analogies to this oracle in ancient Near Eastern literature, see O. Kaiser, "Traditionsgeschichtliche Untersuchung von Genesis 15," *ZAW* 70 (1958): 111–15. (See this article also
for discussion of this translation of *śĕkārkā* as "your booty.") Van Seters, *Abraham,* 254–55;
Westermann, *Genesis 12—26,* 258–59 (E.T., 218–19).
31. Blum, *Vätergeschichte,* 464n5.
32. See J. Halevy, *Recherches Bibliques,* vol. 1, *L'histoire des origines d'après la Genèse* (Paris: E.
Leroux, 1895), 334–35, 390; A. Caquot, "L'alliance avec Abraham (Genèse 15)," *Semitica* 12
(1962): 63–65; Sykes, "Patterns in Genesis," 68–70; N. Lohfink, *Die Landverheißung als Eid*
(SBS 28; Stuttgart: Verlag Katholisches Bibelwerk, 1967), 84–88; and Sarna, *Genesis,* 112, for
other links between Genesis 14 and 15. Note that I am interpreting the term *rĕkûš* ("possessions") here not as a post-Priestly use of a term unique to the Priestly material, but as a prominent theme in a particular layer of non-Priestly material, a theme that then gets radically reinterpreted in the Priestly material as a thoroughgoing component of Israel's special blessing.

naanite nations to be displaced (Gen. 15:19–21), a list that resembles the primeval history list of nations to be displaced in Gen. 10:16–18a.[33]

Thus, Genesis 14—15 *as a whole* presents the story of Abraham's conquest in Genesis 14 not only as a fulfillment of Noah's proclamations on Canaan and Shem, but also as an anticipation of the final fulfillment of these proclamations through Israel's exodus and conquest. In the process this section of the Abraham story extends and resonates with both the above-discussed semi-"Deuteronomistic" elements of the primeval history: Gen. 9:25–27 and 10:16–18a.[34] In addition, Genesis 15 has long been recognized as itself reflecting late Deuteronomistic themes and language. In particular, the focus throughout the chapter on the Deuteronomistic theme of "inheritance" (Gen. 15:3, 4, 7–8), the Exodus-like description of God as the one who "brought [Abraham] out of Ur to give [him] this land" (Gen. 15:7), and the concluding focus of the chapter on the making of a covenant (Gen. 15:18) mark this text as being formed in a period when Deuteronomistic terminology and conceptuality had become widely influential.[35] Like Gen. 22:15–18 and 26:3bβ–5, Genesis 15 is distinguished from properly Deuteronomistic material by its grounding the land promise in YHWH's promise to Abraham, rather than in the people's later obedience to the Deuteronomistic Torah. Nevertheless, even at points like this where Genesis 15 opposes the Deuteronomistic tradition, it has a special oppositional relation to it.

That having been said, an important qualification is in order. Both the bulk of Genesis 14 and crucial parts of Genesis 15 appear to have predated their use in this part of the Abraham story. I have already mentioned some of the indicators that Genesis 14, or more likely, some earlier form of it, predated its insertion in an ongoing story of Abraham. In addition, there are faint signs that Genesis 15 may have been built out of some kind of ritual description (cf. Gen. 15:9–11, 17) and another precursor tradition regarding YHWH's promise to Abraham (cf. Gen. 15:1–6*).[36] In any case, these traditions have

33. Again cf. Richter, *Bearbeitungen*, 42.
34. For other possible semi-Deuteronomistic elements in Genesis 14, see M. C. Astour, "Political and cosmic symbolism in Genesis 14 and in its Babylonian sources," in *Biblical Motifs: Origins and Transformations* (ed. A. Altmann; Cambridge, Mass.: Harvard University Press, 1966), 65–112, especially 68–73; Van Seters, *Abraham*, 303–4.
35. For more detailed observations, see in particular M. Anbar, "Genesis 15: A Conflation of Two Deuteronomic Narratives," *JBL* 101 (1982): 39–55; and Blum, *Vätergeschichte*, 367–72.
36. For example, whereas it is already night in Gen. 15:5, night appears to arrive for the first time in Gen. 15:17. Other marks of probable earlier traditions include Abraham's parallel objections in 15:2 and 3 and the striking interruption of the ritual in 15:9–11, 17 by the speech in 15:12–16. (For a survey of other indicators, cf. J. Ha, *Genesis 15: A Theological Compendium of Pentateuchal History* [BZAW 181; Berlin/New York: Walter de Gruyter, 1989], 27–29 [with a survey of solutions on 30–38]). In the past such indicators have been exploited by those seeking parallel non-P sources in the Abraham story. Nevertheless, these indicators point not to a vertical model of parallel Yahwistic and Elohistic strands (Elohim does not occur here), but to a model in which the composition has been built out of successive traditions with no marked

been so thoroughly reworked that they are now unreconstructable. The important point for our purposes is the following: whatever earlier traditions were used, there is no sign that they were earlier parts of Genesis. Instead, traditions like Genesis 14 or the traditions behind Gen. 15:9–11, 17 were separate building blocks used by later revisers of Genesis in the process of redirecting the Abraham story to fulfill the primeval history and anticipate the exodus and conquest.[37]

In summary, although portions of Genesis 14—15 probably predated their use in this part of Genesis, the block as a whole resonates with other late additions to Genesis and has a similar special relation to Deuteronomistic themes and language. Set in the midst of earlier compositional material of Genesis—Genesis 12—13 and 16:1–2, 4–14—this pair of chapters adds a new focus on linking Abraham with both the primeval history and the exodus-conquest story. It presents Abraham's departure from his homeland and his conquest of non-Israelites (Genesis 14) as a fulfillment of the curse on Canaan and an anticipation of Israel's exodus from Egypt and conquest of Canaan. Furthermore, it puts God's covenant with Abraham in the center of the Abraham narrative. From this point forward, Abraham begins having children who will bear the promise (Genesis 16ff.).

Much later, in a related text at the very end of non-P Genesis, Joseph announces to his brothers that God will fulfill his "oath" to bring them out of Egypt (Gen. 50:24; cf. Gen. 15:14; also 22:15; 26:3bβ). Moreover, he makes them "swear" to bring his bones back with them when YHWH does so (Gen.

---

connection to material regarding Abraham outside Genesis 15. Moreover, the above-sketched model better matches the data than the hypothesis that 15:1–6 is a Deuteronomistic expansion of a pre-Deuteronomistic story following it. Such a model would not explain the indicators of growth in 15:1–6 and 7–18, where the former text prematurely anticipates the arrival of night and the divine approval of Abraham. Instead, these fractures, combined with the closely parallel structure of the two units, are best explained as the result of overall compositional shaping of originally independent traditions.

37. This treatment contrasts with those that posit a late postexilic dating of Genesis 14. Cf. Gunkel, *Genesis*, 288–90; R. de Vaux, *Histoire ancienne d'Israël: Des origines à l'installation en Canaan* (EB; Paris: J. Gabalda et Cie, 1971), 211–2 (E.T., *The Early History of Israel* [trans. D. Smith; Philadelphia: Westminster, 1978], 219–20); Van Seters, *Abraham*, 305–8. There are basically two arguments for such a dating late in the postexilic period: (1) the purported mixture of Priestly language into a non-Priestly text (e.g., "riches" 11, 12, 16, 21; "children of the household" 14; "living beings" 21), thus making Genesis 14 a post-P (and Rp) text; and (2) the affinities of this narrative of Abraham's victory over the eastern kings with postexilic Jewish legends such as those regarding Esther, Daniel, and Judith. Regarding the first indicator: the occurrence of these terms in both Genesis 14 and the Priestly layer could just be parallel language usage, and if there is a relation of dependence, P could as easily be dependent on the language of Genesis 14—15 as the other way around. Regarding the parallels to Judith and other postexilic legends: the focus of such late legends on the often crafty victory of lone Israelites over world powers does suggest that Genesis 14 in its present form dates from a time when Judah was dispersed, humiliated, and without an army. These considerations, however, do not decisively establish a late postexilic date for Genesis 14. Instead, they suggest a dating any time from the exile onward. For arguments for a broader diaspora background for such stories, see D. Smith, *Religion of the Landless*, 162–64.

Chart 8-3: Parallels in Joseph's Final Speech

Gen. 50:24	Gen. 50:25
I am about to die,	And Joseph made the sons of Israel swear,
but God will surely come to you	"When God so surely comes to you,
and bring you up	you must bring up
out of this land	my bones from here."
to the land that he swore to Abraham, Isaac, and Jacob.	

50:25). As Lohfink has pointed out (see Chart 8-3), these two acts are integrally intertwined.[38]

In this way, Joseph takes God's solemn commitment to Israel as a model for the solemn commitment he wants from his brothers. Both parts of this final section in non-P Genesis appear to be part of the layer of revision of the non-P material we have been discussing. The first half of Joseph's speech points backward to YHWH's covenant promise to bring the Israelites out of Egypt (Gen. 15:14–21) and to YHWH's oath to Abraham (Gen. 22:15–18; 26:3bβ–5), all texts that appear to be secondary extensions of the non-P material. The second half of Joseph's speech points forward to a series of texts extending into the Deuteronomistic history, from taking Joseph's bones out of Egypt (Exod. 13:19) to burying them in Shechem (Josh. 24:32; cf. Gen. 33:19).[39] Neither Gen. 50:24 nor Gen. 50:25 makes as much sense alone as it does with the other, and both are tightly linked with a layer of extended non-P materials, reaching in this case to the Deuteronomistic history itself.[40]

Further Signs of Revision
of the Non-P Jacob-Joseph Story

So far I have focused primarily on secondary additions to the primeval history and Abraham sections. Nevertheless, already in Gen. 50:24–25 we saw

38. N. Lohfink, *Landverheißung als Eid*, 23n43.
39. Kessler, "Querverweise," 88–89, 175–77; Rendtorff, *Problem*, 75–79, 163–64 (E.T., 95–97, 195–96); Blum, *Vätergeschichte*, 255–56.
40. The description of Joseph's embalmment appended to the probable P death notice in 50:26a is probably the work of Rp. This addition completes the P death notice in 50:26a, using the model of embalmment already found in the non-P material of 50:2 and the model of burial in the other P death notices for Abraham (25:9–10), Isaac (35:29b), and Jacob (50:12–13). The probable distinction in layers between 50:26b and texts related to it is evident in the fact that the later notices regarding Joseph's eventual burial in Canaan (Exod. 13:19; Josh. 24:32) focus exclusively on the "bones" mentioned by Joseph in 50:25 and not on the "ark" mentioned in 50:26b. In summary, the author of 50:26b is not the author of Gen. 50:24–25; Exod. 13:19; and Josh. 24:32. On this cf. Blum, *Studien*, 363–65 (altering his position from *Vätergeschichte*, 256), who assigns his entire "Joshua 24 Redaction" to the very latest stage of the development

a text in the Joseph story that presupposes and builds on several of these secondary additions. In addition, there are a couple other texts in the Jacob-Joseph story that likewise appear to be secondary additions to their non-P contexts. For example, a number of scholars have pointed out that Jacob's vow to make YHWH his God (Gen. 28:21b) does not exactly fit with his earlier condition that "Elohim" be with him and protect and provide for him on his way (Gen. 28:20–21a). As Blum observes, the emphasis on the identity of the deity is quite central in Gen. 28:21b, and one would have expected this deity to appear earlier in Jacob's description of what the deity must do for him. For example, the text might have read "if YHWH is with me and protects me on this way . . . , I will make *him* my God."[41] As it is, Jacob's specification of what "God" must do in Gen. 28:20–21a does not seem to have been written to anticipate Jacob's promise to make "YHWH" his God in Gen. 28:21b. Such indicators suggest that Gen. 28:21b is a later addition to a saying that originally moved from Jacob's condition (Gen. 28:20–21a) to Jacob's vow to make the pillar he had laid on into a "temple of God" and to tithe to "God" in return for "God" being with him on his way from home to Haran (Gen. 28:22). The later addition (Gen. 28:21b) had Jacob commit to making YHWH his God in anticipation of later Deuteronomistic descriptions, particularly in Joshua 24, of Israel making YHWH their God.[42]

The final text to be discussed, Gen. 32:10–13 (Eng. 32:9–12), comes as Jacob anticipates his final encounter with Esau. As many exegetes have pointed out, this prayer interrupts the movement from his division of the

---

of the Pentateuch. Blum does not appear to distinguish between 50:26b and the other additions anticipating Josh. 24:32.

41. Blum, *Vätergeschichte*, 91. This is a refinement of earlier proposals that merely pointed to the variation in divine designation here (cf. Dillmann, *Genesis*, 331 (E.T., vol. 2, 229); Wellhausen, *Composition*, 31; Gunkel, *Genesis*, 321; Skinner, *Genesis*, 379n; E. Otto, "Jakob in Bethel," *ZAW* 88 (1976): 169–70. Van Seters does not accurately represent Blum's proposal in his presentation of Blum's position in *Prologue*, 293.

42. Blum, *Vätergeschichte*, 89–92. Van Seters's objections in *Prologue*, 293, do not suffice to refute Blum's position. First, Van Seters argues that Gen. 28:20 can not mean just any god, but must mean instead a specific deity, YHWH. Yet Blum does not argue that 28:20 means just any god. Instead, "Elohim" in Gen. 28:10–22* and elsewhere in the Jacob story often functions as a designation for the specific God whom Jacob meets at Bethel and who protected him on the way. Second, Van Seters argues that the identity of YHWH as the "God" mentioned in Gen. 28:20–21a is already clear in Gen. 28:16a, a text Blum assigns to the early Bethel story. But, Van Seters himself has already pointed out the weaknesses of Blum's assignment of that verse to an early Bethel story (*Prologue*, 291), and I have agreed with him in the previous chapter. Third, Van Seters points out that the presence of Gen. 28:21b means Jacob promises three things in return for God's doing three things. This observation, however, only establishes the original link of 28:21b to its context if it can be proven that a vow almost always has a match in the number of conditions and promises, an unlikely thesis. Van Seters is more likely pointing to the artistry of the reviser than to the artistry of an original author of Gen. 28:20–22 as a whole. Fourth and finally, Van Seters notes that Gen. 28:21b, along with the establishment of the stone in 28:22, nicely anticipates the scene in Joshua where the people declare YHWH to be their God and Joshua sets up a stone to witness to that. This is true and is part of Blum's argument that Gen. 28:21b is built on Deuteronomistic models (*Vätergeschichte*, 92).

camp (Gen. 32:8–9; Eng. 32:7–8) to his sending the divided camp to Esau as a gift to him (Gen. 32:14–22; Eng. 32:13–21), and the piety and intensity of its theological focus contrasts with the emphasis on Jacob's trickery in the surrounding context.[43] Moreover, as Blum has argued, the wording and movement of the prayer—humility, petition, and reference to divine promises —resembles certain Deuteronomistic royal prayers quite closely (e.g., 2 Sam. 7:18–29; 1 Kings 3:6–9). Finally, the otherwise unexplainable reference to "this Jordan" in 32:11 (Eng. 32:10) corresponds to similarly theoretical references to "this Jordan" throughout the Deuteronomistic conquest narrative. In the Deuteronomistic conquest narrative, the term "this Jordan" serves as a technical expression describing the crucial eastern boundary of the land (Deut. 3:27; 31:2; Josh. 1:2, 11).[44] Now in Gen. 32:11 (Eng. 32:10), Jacob, like Moses, is depicted as on the threshold of the land. He is on the edge of "this Jordan" theologically, although the context of Gen. 32:10–13 (Eng. 32:9–12) places him at the Jabbok. Once again, we have the convergence of Deuteronomistic elements with indicators of seams: evidence for the presence of semi-Deuteronomistic retouching at this point.

Concluding Reflections

Identifying the Limits of the Late Revision
of Non-P Material in Genesis

So far I have focused on a group of texts that are marked by *both* indicators of seams and profile as part of a layer of revision of the non-P material in Genesis. Indicators of seams mark off each of the above texts from the first overall compositional layer in Genesis. Moreover, despite the fact that they contradict central tenants of properly Deuteronomistic texts, these additions to the non-P material of Genesis share an overall linkage to some late Israelite semi-Deuteronomistic themes and language. Finally, several of these texts link with each other: Gen. 22:15–18 and 26:3bβ–5 with 18:19, and the Canaan-focused retouching in the primeval history (Gen. 10:16–18a and the anti-Canaan redirection of 9:18–27) with Genesis 14—15. This does not mean that all these texts were part of the very same compositional layer. It does suggest, however, that certain of these additions were either added at the same time or carefully coordinated with earlier ones.

43. Gunkel, *Genesis,* 356–57; Skinner, *Genesis,* 406; H. J. Boecker, *1 Moses 25.19–37.1* (ZBK 1,3; Zurich: Theologischer Verlag, 1992), 97.
44. Blum, *Vätergeschichte,* 155–58. Deuteronomy 4:22 has "this Jordan" only in some Greek and Syriac manuscript traditions. On Gen. 32:10–13 (Eng. 32:9–12), cf. Van Seters, *Prologue to History,* 295–96. He points out ways Gen. 32:10–13 has been composed in light of its context. Blum does not dispute this and makes a number of observations along these lines himself. Van Seters does not account for the way this prayer interrupts and introduces new, specifically Deuteronomistic elements into its surrounding context, nor does he deal with Blum's observations regarding the "Jordan" reference in 32:11 (Eng. 32:10).

The further we go in identification of such secondary additions to non-P material, the more we need to rely exclusively on the slippery criterion of profile, particularly "Deuteronomistic" profile. Already in my discussion above I moved from texts where the indicators of seams were clearer (e.g., Gen. 22:15–18; 26:3bβ–5) to texts where such indicators were comparatively weak (e.g., Genesis 14—15). Following the lead of previous studies, I could go yet further. For example, Blum has argued primarily on the basis of Deuteronomistic profile that texts such as Gen. 16:10; 28:15; 35:1–5; and Genesis 24 as a whole are likewise part of a Deuteronomistic compositional layer. Indeed, in cases such as Gen. 28:15aβb and 35:2bα, linkages with Deuteronomistic elements and texts are especially striking.[45] Nevertheless, such arguments from profile are inherently unstable.[46] Part or all of these texts may well have been components of a much larger layer of semi-Deuteronomistic revision of non-P Genesis. As emphasized above, we probably can see only the tip of the iceberg here. The problem is that we can not know much more about this layer. The indicators are not there for further analysis.

One major problem with heavy reliance on "Deuteronomistic" profile to identify late additions to Genesis is the way such a method depends on the presupposition that the preceding Genesis material, as a whole, is non- or pre-Deuteronomistic. In the next chapter I will argue that the earliest overall Genesis composition dates from sometime in the period from the fall of the Northern Kingdom to the middle of the exile (722–560). If this range is correct, then there is a chance that the proto-Genesis composition was written after Josiah's reform and could have been influenced by it. To be sure, this composition does not have the same special link to Deuteronomistic elements we saw in the above-discussed additions to non-P Genesis material. Nevertheless, the presence of such Deuteronomistic elements in the first Genesis composition would not be surprising, nor would such elements be decisive evidence for the secondary character of the texts in which they occur.

As we look at the overall character of this revision of non-P material, one more note is in order: some of this revision may have actually lacked any identifiable relation to later semi-Deuteronomistic strands in Israelite culture. The

---

45. See in particular Blum's arguments in *Vätergeschichte,* 158–61 (on Gen. 28:15; cf. S. McEvenue, "A Return to Sources in Genesis 28,10–22?" *ZAW* 106 [1994]: 379), and 43–61 (on Gen. 35:1–5; see also H. J. Boecker, *1 Moses 25.12–37.1,* 123). I am inclined to identify smaller amounts of this material as secondary than Blum does. The clearest parallels to Deuteronomistic material occur exclusively in Gen. 28:15aβb and 35:2bα (along with "foreign gods" in 35:4a).
46. For Blum's assignment of other texts to his D compositional layer, see *Vätergeschichte* 121 (on 31:3), 257 (on 48:20–21; see also Kessler, "Querverweise," 177), 365 (on 26:24; cf. Van Seters's persuasive critique in *Prologue to History,* 269–70); 383–87 (on Genesis 24 as a whole). Each of these proposals has a measure of plausibility. Nevertheless, these assignments depend heavily on arguments from profile, and indeed on an interlocking set of terminological arguments based on other semi-Deuteronomistic texts in Genesis, a dependence that weakens their overall claim to probability.

best example of this is the addition of Abraham's and YHWH's dialogue (Gen. 18:22b–33), along with its anticipation (Gen. 18:17–18), to an earlier context moving from Mamre (Gen. 18:1–16) to Sodom and Gomorrah (Gen. 18:20–22a, 33; 19:1–28). As we will see in the next chapter, this earlier context, particularly the speech in Gen. 18:20–21, shows multiple signs of being part of the earliest compositional layer spanning Genesis. In contrast, Gen. 18:17–18, though carefully formed in light of this context, is marked as secondary to it by (1) its doubling of the speech introduction to Gen. 18:20 (cf. Gen. 18:17); (2) the way its description of YHWH's intent to inform Abraham of what he will do (Gen. 18:17) prematurely anticipates YHWH's later speech where YHWH is still deciding what to do (Gen. 18:20–21); and (3) the way it breaks from the indication in the surrounding material that Abraham was visited by *three* messengers, by having YHWH stay while the messengers go on (18:22; cf. 18:33–19:1).[47] So also, the dialogue Gen. 18:17–18 anticipates, Gen. 18:22b–33, interrupts the probable original movement between YHWH's decision to investigate (Gen. 18:20–21), and the narrative's presentation of YHWH's/his messengers' execution of that intent (Gen. 19:1ff.).[48]

The themes of this secondary layer in Gen. 18:17–18 and 22b–33 and the elegance of its connections to its context deserve a separate discussion for which there is not space here. The two points relevant for our discussion are the following: (1) these texts show no clear connection to specifically Deuteronomistic themes and language,[49] and yet (2) they address a problem of collective destruction and individual righteousness first documented in a broad spectrum of exilic texts.[50] Thus, Gen. 18:17–18 and 22b–33 appear to be part of an *ongoing,* complex process of revision of non-P material in Genesis, one often but not necessarily always characterized by nearness to late Israelite semi-"Deuteronomistic" language and theology. In this case, the material in Gen. 18:17–18 is built upon further by the more Deuterono-

---

47. Coats, *Genesis,* 140. See also *Gen.Rab.* 49:7, which goes so far as to posit a scribal emendation in 18:22 because of the way it shifts from the standpoint at the outset of the chapter.

48. Wellhausen, *Composition,* 26; Gunkel, *Genesis,* 202–3; Schmidt, *De Deo,* 133–36 (see especially 136, where Schmidt establishes the link between 18:17–18 and 22b–33). Cf. Van Seters, *Abraham,* 213–14; idem, *Prologue to History,* 259–60; and Westermann, *Genesis 12–36,* 350; (E.T., 287–88). The latter scholars point to how the present form of the text makes sense, but they do not establish that 18:17–19 and 22b–33 always must have been integral parts of the text. Indicators surveyed above suggest otherwise.

49. Blum, *Vätergeschichte,* 400–1, argues for the Deuteronomistic character of Gen. 18:18 on the basis of its use of the expression "all the nations of the earth" in anticipation of Gen. 22:18 and 26:4, and on the basis of its use of the term "great and mighty nation" (*gôy gādôl vě'āṣûm*) to describe the great nation Abraham will become (cf. on the latter, see also Schmid, *Sogenannte Jahwist,* 131). On the contrary, Gen. 22:18 and 26:4 are modeled in part on Gen. 18:18, the formulation of the blessing they follow. Moreover, one occurrence in Deuteronomy of one expression, "great and mighty nation," (Deut. 26:5; cf. also Num. 14:12) is not sufficient grounds for assigning Gen. 18:18 to a particularly Deuteronomistic or semi-Deuteronomistic layer.

50. Schmidt, *De Deo,* 139–64; Blum, *Vätergeschichte,* 402–5.

mistically colored addition in Gen. 18:19, on the one hand, and by the blessing formulations found in Gen. 22:15–18 and 26:3bβ–5, on the other.

The Characteristics and Background of the Later Additions to Non-P Material in Genesis

Even when we look at only the more noticable examples of late additions
to non-P Genesis, certain patterns emerge. I briefly note a few of them here.

1. *Intratextuality in the Additions:* The author(s) of this material worked
   intensely *intra*textually. For example, Gen. 22:15–18 links integrally
   with the narrative in which it occurs. Especially if this text is read through
   late eyes influenced by the Deuteronomistic tradition, one expects Abraham to get a reward once he has passed the "test" (Gen. 22:1; cf.
   22:12).[51] For the author of the addition in 22:15–18, this story in Gen.
   22:1–14, 19 was a compositional opportunity to deepen the connection
   between the promise on the one hand and obedience on the other. So
   he authored a promise that picked up the wording of the previous divine
   recognition of Abraham's obedience (Gen. 22:16b, cf. 12b), composed
   a promise reward that in turn corresponds with the outset of the Abraham narrative (Gen. 22:17–18; cf. 12:2–3), and inserted the whole just
   after the etiology where Abraham names Moriah (Gen. 22:14).

   Similarly, the insertion in Gen. 18:19 allowed these late author/re-
   touchers to assert that obedience was important not just for Abraham but
   was also passed on by him to Isaac and Jacob. Through the addition of
   just one dependent clause, the authors could reconceptualize the relationship of the three patriarchs without having to intervene in the texts
   concerning them. As a result of this addition, we know that Abraham will
   pass his love of YHWH's commandments down to Isaac, Jacob, and Jacob's sons, and that YHWH will therefore fulfill YHWH's promises to Abraham. Toward the very end of Genesis, Joseph is able to refer to God's
   "oath" to all three patriarchs (Gen. 50:24), despite the lack of explicit intervening texts describing the transfer of this oath to them.

2. *Direct speech:* Notably, all the additions discussed above occur in direct
   speech. Even in the composition of Genesis 15, the most obvious
   Deuteronomistic elements all occur in direct speech while the action elements in 15:9–11, 17 appear to have been drawn from a preexisting tradition. This does not mean the late author/redactors could not write
   action elements. Instead, it seems as if they used the particularly dis-
   course-intensive means of represented speech to strategically recast the
   narrative, rather than to rewrite it completely. As Hardmeier observes in
   his survey of text-linguistic studies of narrative, direct speech often is the

---

51. Cf. Van Seters, *Abraham,* 239; idem, *Prologue to History,* 262–64.

most direct way to engage a reader, and it often serves strategic roles in propelling a reader in one direction or another.[52]

In this case, direct speech is a particularly apt medium through which later retouchers could have maximum effect with minimum intervention. With the exception of Genesis 15, all of the above-discussed semi-"Deuteronomistic" elements are quite limited in scope, often involving the modification of a given context through the addition of a phrase, sentence, or small set of clauses. Documented cases of transmission history suggest that such limited modification is often typical of the late revision of a given textual tradition. Nevertheless, partly because these limited elements are direct speech, they exert an influence on the narrative that is disproportionate to their size.

3. *Interlocking Themes:* Although the above-discussed texts do not all seem to have been written at one time, they do share some themes and foci. The series centering on Abraham focuses on establishing the obedience-promise connection (Gen. 15; 18:19; 22:15–18; 26:3bβ–5), or more specifically, a belief-promise connection (Gen. 15:1–6; 22:15–18). In addition, several texts share a special emphasis on the land. This emerges not only in the special emphasis of several additions on the land's pre-Israelite inhabitants (Gen. 9:18b, 22aα3–4, 25–27*; 10:16–18a; 15: 19–21), but also in the strengthening of the land promise into a covenant (Gen. 15:7–18) and/or oath (Gen. 26:3bβ–5; cf. also 24:7 and 50:24).

It is difficult to go much beyond the above description of the character of the handful of texts that can be more securely isolated as part of the late revision of non-P material in Genesis. In particular, they do not provide many indicators that would help us more exactly date them or place them in a particular social and institutional context. Yes, later additions like Genesis 15 appear to be presupposed by P texts like Genesis 17. Yes, these additions appear to build on an earlier promise-centered proto-Pentateuch that I will argue in the next chapter is late preexilic or exilic. Such considerations of relative dating would then lead us to place these additions to the non-P material between (1) the earliest composition of non-P Genesis in the late preexilic or early exilic periods and (2) the early postexilic Priestly counterwriting of that tradition; that is, sometime in the exile and/or early postexile.

This time also happens to be a period when the Deuteronomistic history was being retouched and indeed occasionally retouched to include more references to elements of Israel's preland history, such as the patriarchs. Nelson

---

52. C. Hardmeier, *Prophetie im Streit vor dem Untergang Judas: Erzählkommunkative Studien zur Entstehungssituation der Jesaja- und Jeremiaerzählungen in II Reg 18—20 und Jer 37—40* (BZAW 187; Berlin/New York: de Gruyter, 1990), 56–57.

in particular has observed an extra interest in Israel's preland history in exilic additions to the Deuteronomistic history.[53]

Given the presence of semi-Deuteronomistic revisions of both the Pentateuch and the Deuteronomistic history, and given the common interest of both sets of revisions in Israel's preland history, it is likely the revisions of non-P Genesis were part of a broader process of revision of the entire primary history, from Creation to exile. In other words, this entire stretch of non-P history from creation to exile appears to have been subjected to a similar set of gradual additions, often influenced by semi-Deuteronomistic ideology and language. Not all these additions were done at the same time, and they were not necessarily part of a comprehensive revision of that history.[54] Nevertheless, such changes were probably done in a similar intellectual climate. Moreover, some additions to Genesis may have been done with an explicit view toward the continuation of the story in Joshua and other parts of the broader primary history. Certainly Joseph's final will in Gen. 50:24–5 looks forward to a series of texts in Exodus and the Deuteronomistic history (Exod 13:19; Josh. 24:32). So also, the anticipation of the conquest of Canaan in the additions to the primeval history (Gen. 9:20–27*; 10:16–18a) and Abraham section (Genesis 14—15) may be intended to anticipate in turn the report in Joshua of the Israelites' conquest of Canaan.

As we turn to social location, it is impossible to be as specific as with the Priestly materials. Weinfeld persuasively argues for a scribal context for the earliest Deuteronomic tradition.[55] Nevertheless, we are almost certainly not dealing here with a direct outgrowth of the original Deuteronomic tradition. Instead, these revisions of non-P Genesis material appear to be part of a broader adaptation of both the non-P proto-Pentateuch and an early version of the Deuteronomistic history. The great diversity of semi-Deuteronomistic elements found in various Hebrew Bible texts suggests that they were not the

---

53. R. D. Nelson, *The Double Redaction of the Deuteronomistic History* (JSOTSup, 18; Sheffield: Univ. of Sheffield, 1981), 45–46, 52–53, 96–98.

54. H. C. Schmitt has proposed a similar hypothesis of a "late Deuteronomistic" redaction of the primary history. On this, see most recently his stimulating lecture at the 1995 IOSOT Congress in Leuven, "Das spätdeuteronomistische Geschichtswerk Gen 1—II Reg 25 und seine theologische Intention," to be published by E. J. Brill in a Vetus Testamentum Supplements volume. The proposal being made here is distinct from his in two ways: (1) I see no clear evidence that this gradual process of revisions was a cohesive, comprehensive "redaction" designed to restructure the composition as a whole; and (2) *at least for Genesis,* I see no decisive evidence that this revision process was post-Priestly. For example, the use of the term *br'* ("create") in Gen. 6:7 or of *rěkûš* ("riches") in 15:14 shows that non-P material has certain terms in common with Priestly material, but hardly demonstrates that the non-P material must be drawing on the Priestly material. The relation of dependence could be reversed (as is probably the case with *rěkûš*), or the common language may just result from parallel use of limited Hebrew vocabulary (as is probably the case with *br'*). Such terminological arguments have been used too rigidly in transmission-historical studies, without sufficient awareness of the extent to which vocabulary use in Hebrew can not be easily slotted into neat transmission-historical boxes.

55. Weinfeld, *Deuteronomy and the Deuteronomic School,* 158–78.

possession of a single group. As a result, any overly precise attempt to delineate the authors of this material is doomed to fail. As Blum points out in a discussion of the origins of Deuteronomistically influenced literature in general, "hardly more is left than the silhouette of non-Priestly (= 'non-Zadokite') circles, who had the necessary intellectual and 'professional' prerequisites at their disposal and knowledge of/access to such diverse traditional materials, as are incorporated in DtrG, KD and Jer. (!)."[56]

Unfortunately we do not know much about non-priestly leadership groups in the exilic and postexilic periods when this revision of Genesis most likely occurred. Indeed, traditional pictures of postexilic Israel in the introductions are often marked by an almost exclusive emphasis on the priestly character of the Judean community. Nevertheless, recent research has highlighted the importance of specific lay groups and lay leaders alongside the priests. In several sources we see the appearance of a lay council of elders in the exile, whether the "elders of the exile" (Jer. 29:1), the "elders of Judah" (Ezek. 8:1; cf. 8:11–12), or the "elders of Israel" (Ezek. 14:1; 20:1). Later in the postexilic period we see a similar council of "elders of Judah" mentioned in the Aramaic source materials of Ezra (Ezra 5:5, 9; 6:7–8, 14), a group who should probably be identified with the "nobles [of Judah]" mentioned in an letter from the Jewish colony at Elephantine to leaders in Jerusalem (AP 30, lines 18–19)[57] and the "nobles" often associated with the work of Nehemiah in his memoir (Neh. 2:16; 4:8, 13 [Eng. 4:14, 19]; 5:7; 6:17; 13:17). This council of lay nobles/elders of Judah stood alongside the priestly college as one of the two major leadership groups under the Persian governmental administration of postexilic Judah.[58] This group, along with Nehemiah, was an important lay leadership component in late Judah.

Just as the priestly college or a subgroup in it probably transmitted and developed the Priestly material, so also the lay council of the elders/nobles of Judah probably transmitted and developed the non-P proto-Pentateuch. The biggest difference in the two cases is the following. When we seek to identify the social location of the Priestly material, we can compare texts in Genesis to our knowledge of priestly conceptuality through both Israelite and extra-Israelite sources. In contrast, when we seek to identify the social location of

56. Blum, *Studien*, 342.
57. A. Cowley, *Aramaic Papyri of the Fifth Century B.C.* (Oxford: Clarendon Press, 1923), 112 (translation on 114).
58. On this picture of lay groups, see J. Jeremias, *Jerusalem zur Zeit Jesu: Eine kulturgeschichtliche Untersuchung zur neutestamentlichen Zeitgeschichte* (3d ed; Göttingen: Vandenhoeck & Ruprecht, 1962), 252–53; H. G. Kippenberg, *Religion und Klassenbildung im antiken Judäa: Eine religionssoziologische Studie zum Verhältnis von Tradition und gesellschaftlicher Entwicklung* (Göttingen: Vandenhoeck & Ruprecht, 1978), 69, 83–84; and Albertz, *Religionsgeschichte*, 472–73; (E.T., vol. 2, 446–47); cf. E. Meyer, *Die Entstehung des Judentums: Eine historische Untersuchung* (Halle: Max Niemeyer, 1896), 132–35. As Albertz in particular points out (474; E.T., 447), these groups in postexilic Judah all have ancient antecedents.

the tradents of non-Priestly material, we have very little comparative material for the conceptuality of the lay leaders of exilic and postexilic Judah. Nevertheless, Nehemiah may provide some clues to the broader orientation of such lay leaders. During his work as governor he appears to have conflicted with priestly groups in his promotion of certain characteristically Deuteronomistic themes such as antipathy toward intermarriage with non-Israelites (Neh. 13:4–9, 23–29) and securing of the rights of Levites (Neh. 13:10–14; cf. 12:44–47). Indeed, Nehemiah's description of his discouraging intermarriage echoes 1 Kings 11:1–2, a negative description of Solomon's marriages to foreign women and itself among the late layer of exilic additions to the primary history under discussion here.[59] This supports the initial suspicion that returnee lay leaders like Nehemiah were probably those responsible for transmitting the primary history and adding further semi-Deuteronomistic elements to it.[60] More specifically, the kind of distancing from foreigners evident in Nehemiah's conflict with the priests over intermarriage correlates with the frequent anti-Canaanite elements of the above-discussed revisions of non-P Genesis.

All this is not to say anything specific about what subgroups of lay leaders may have been specifically responsible for the transmission and development of the non-P Genesis materials or when this process took place. Nevertheless, especially given the common impression that Judah was a priestly theocracy during the postexilic period, it is important to draw attention to this parallel, non-priestly institutional locus of political and textual authority. The significance of such reflections can be put another way: in exilic and postexilic Judah, there was what might be termed "social space" for the ongoing transmission and development of a non-priestly presentation of formative history.

Further discussion of the shape and significance of the additions to the non-P material in Genesis will need to wait until we have gone further back into the shape and transmission history of the book. So let us continue moving backward, turning now to the compositional core of non-P material in Genesis that precedes the above-discussed late layer of compositional redirection and retouching.

59. Fishbane, *Biblical Interpretation,* 123–26.
60. For other, necessarily more speculative attempts to connect the social praxis of non-P legislation and postexilic groups, see F. Crüsemann, "Israel in der Perserzeit: Eine Skizze in Auseinandersetzung mit Max Weber," in W. Schluchter, ed., *Max Webers Sicht des antiken Christentums: Interpretation und Kritik* (Frankfurt am Main: Suhrkamp, 1985), 213–17; idem, *Die Tora,* 381–82, 394–98. See also Albertz, *Religionsgeschichte,* 509–12, (E.T., 475–6); Blum, *Studien,* 342–44.

9
Constructing
the Promise

The Proto-Genesis Composition

Whatever one might say about the presence or absence of retouching in the non-P material of Genesis, the basic non-P substratum of Genesis is a carefully composed whole. To be sure, the limited subplots and generic elements of the non-P stories manifest their often separate origins. Nevertheless, this material is now bound together by a complex web of narrative connections. Furthermore, as we will see, these connections are so specific and intricate that it is impossible to separate them into Yahwistic and Elohistic strands or detectable redactional layers. Instead, we have reached the level of the "proto-Genesis composition." This term, "proto-Genesis," designates the earliest stage at which the primeval history and material regarding all three ancestral figures was linked into a single narrative. Indeed, some indicators in this proto-Genesis material would suggest that we might be dealing here with a "proto-Pentateuch." That question, however, can be revisited only after a survey of connections linking the major sections of Genesis with each other and, potentially, the Moses story.

The task of this chapter is to survey and then analyze these linkages across the major sections of Genesis, looking for clues to the formation of the first proto-Genesis. By "linkages" I mean specific *and* sequential connections between texts that link them into a broader narrative framework. For example, several similar divine travel commands and accompanying promises—Gen. 12:1–3; 26:2–3bα; 31:3, 13; 46:3–4—link Abraham, Isaac, and Jacob.[1]

As indicated in Chart 9-1, the departure commands for Abraham and Jacob to leave Mesopotamia are particularly parallel (Gen. 12:1; 31:13b, cf. 31:3). Furthermore, the narrative following these commands describes their trips as parallel. Both trips include stops at Shechem and Bethel and even Hebron (13:18; cf. 37:14), and both Abraham and Jacob are described as descending into Egypt after their arrival in Canaan because of a famine in the land (Gen. 12:10–20; 45:28–46:5*, 28–29). Meanwhile, Isaac is explicitly

---

1. The previous mention was in the last chapter's discussion of Gen. 26:3bβ–5 as an extension of the travel command and promise discussed below (Gen. 26:2–3bα). The chart here has been adapted from Blum, *Vätergeschichte*, 300. For further discussion of these parallels, see Westermann, *Genesis 12—36*, 169; (E.T., 169), and above all, Blum, *Vätergeschichte*, 297–301.

Chart 9-1: Travel Commands and Promises

Gen. 12:1–2	Gen. 26:2–3	Gen. 31:13b (cf. 31:3)	Gen. 46:3b–4
Go from your country and your kindred and your father's house	Do not go down to Egypt;	Leave this land and return to the land of your kindred.	Do not be afraid to go down to Egypt,
to the land that I will show you.	settle in the land that I shall show you.		
	(3) Reside in this land as a resident alien,		
(2) I will make of you			for I will make you
a great nation,			a great nation there.
	and I will be		(4) I myself will go down
	with you,		with you to Egypt,
and I will bless you	and will bless you;		
and make your name great, so that you will be a blessing.			
	for to you and to your descendants I will give all these lands . . .		and I will also bring you up again.

portrayed as the exception. Although Abraham himself came from Haran and although Jacob will later go there, Abraham goes to great lengths to avoid sending Isaac out of the land. Instead he sends a servant his place (Gen. 24:2–9). Later, Isaac is explicitly told *not* to go to Egypt (Gen. 26:2) when he encounters a famine like that Abraham experienced (Gen. 26:1). This means that when Jacob receives the similar and yet quite different travel command to go to Egypt (Gen. 46:3b), he is being told to imitate Abraham and not Isaac, descending into Egypt without fear.

Such specific coordination of various figures in Genesis is important because such terminological connections and sequential relationships between texts reflect a level of the composition that interrelate Abraham, Isaac, and Jacob. To be sure, there are important indications that many traditions regarding Abraham, Isaac, and Jacob have their own separate prehistories. Nevertheless, given the specific and sequential relation between the above texts, it is highly unlikely that *these texts* were composed completely independently of each other. Instead, their parallel wording and sequential coordination are indicators that these travel commands reflect a compositional level that includes all three figures.

To be sure, there are many possible compositional models that could explain such connections. One might suppose that all of these texts were written by the same author. Alternatively, it is possible that one author modeled one or more of the travel commands on an earlier such command regarding only one patriarch. For example, an author could have added the command regarding Isaac (Gen. 26:2–3bα) in order to contrast him with the parallel travel commands to Abraham and Jacob, or one might argue that the final travel command for Jacob (Gen. 46:3–4) is later than the previous ones for Abraham, Isaac, and Jacob (Gen. 12:1–3; 26:2–3bα; 31:3, 13). Whatever the model chosen, the point here is that such specific and sequential connections between texts can be an *initial* key to deciphering the transmission history of Genesis. Through study of such connections, we can go beyond speculation about the dating and background of specific traditions in Genesis and investigate the emphases and probable context of the shaping of the whole. More reflection on the exact model for these connections, however, must await a survey of other such specific and sequential connections in the non-P material of Genesis.

Survey of Trans-Genesis Compositional Connections

My survey of these connections begins with a section of non-P material surrounding the first of the above-discussed travel commands, Gen. 11:28–30; 12:1–8. As we will see, this text is distinguished by an unusual density of specific linkages to texts both before and after it. In particular, promise material such as Gen. 12:1–3 and 7 appears to have played a strategic role in the early linkage of disparate non-P Pentateuchal materials into a single narrative.[2] Whatever one thinks about the early and largely unreconstructable history of independent traditions behind the non-P narrative, the promises in it appear to span the present whole.

For this reason, I start my survey of linkages with the promises in Gen. 12:1–3 and 7. After looking at the promises themselves, I will examine how certain non-P texts regarding Abraham develop this promise theme and at the same time coordinate him and his heirs with the periods before (primeval

2. Rendtorff, *Problem,* particularly 40–79; (E.T., 55–100). Cf. also D. J. A. Clines, *The Theme of the Pentateuch* (JSOTSup, 10; Sheffield: JSOT, 1982) for an early synchronic study that argued persuasively for the centrality of this theme in the final form of the Pentateuch.

history) and after (Moses story) them. Next, I will move outward from Gen. 12:1–4a, 6–7, looking at the way Gen. 11:28–30 and 12:8 likewise feature specific themes that coordinate various sections of the non-P material with each other. By the end of the survey I will have outlined a detailed, multiply intersecting system of compositional connections spanning the non-P material. As we will see, this system is particularly evident in Gen. 11:28–30; 12:1–4a, 6–8, but it also appears throughout much broader stretches of the non-P material and links its sections into a single narrative line.

The Travel Command of Genesis 12:1
and the Land Promise

The importance of the promise as a linking factor can already be seen through an examination of the narrative development of the first travel command: "Go from your land, your kindred, and your father's house to the land which I will show you" (Gen. 12:1). At this point, any idea of a land promise is merely implicit.[3] YHWH commands Abraham to leave his own land for "a land that God will show him." Nevertheless, when Abraham complies with this command (Gen. 12:4a, 6), God initially certifies his compliance through promise of this land in an epiphany at Shechem, saying "to your seed I will give this land" (Gen. 12:7aβγ). Later, upon Abraham's split from Lot, God finally "shows" him this land, a land now promised to him and his descendants.

Chart 9-2: Correspondence of the Promise
to Show Abraham the Land and Its Fulfillment

Gen. 12:1, 7	Gen. 13:14–15
(1) Go . . . to the land I will show you.	(14) . . . Raise your eyes now, and look from the place where you are, northward and southward and eastward and westward;
(7) To your seed I will give this land.	(15) For all the land that you see I will give to you and to your offspring forever.

Significantly, it is only at this point that Abraham finally stops moving (cf. Gen. 12:4a, 6, 8–10; 13:1, 3) and "settles" in the land, at Hebron (Gen. 13:18; cf. also 13:12).[4] This chain of texts with specific, sequential connections to each other links a span of non-P material into a single narrative line. The line ex-

---

3. Kilian, *Die vorpriesterlichen Abrahamsüberlieferungen*, 1.
4. M. Köckert, *Vätergott und Väterverheißungen: Eine Auseinandersetzung mit Albrecht Alt und seinen Erben* (FRLANT 142; Göttingen: Vandenhoeck & Ruprecht, 1988), 250–54; see also D.J.A. Clines, "What Happens in Genesis," in *What Does Eve Do to Help?*, 56. Köckert's observation led Blum to a simplification of his transmission-historical model for the formation of the Abraham materials; see his *Studien*, p. 214, n35.

tends from (1) the command to go to a land that God will show Abraham (Gen. 12:1–3), to (2) Abraham's departure for and arrival in the land (Gen. 12:4a, 6–8), (3) his split from Lot (Gen. 13:2–13*), and (4) God's final showing of the land to Abraham and his settlement there (Gen. 13:14–18).

The specific, sequential linkage does not stop there. Just as Abraham received the confirmation of God's promise to him after his split from Lot, so also Jacob receives a similar confirmation of the promise *after he has separated from Esau*.[5]

Chart 9-3: Correspondence of the Promises to Abraham and Jacob

Gen. 13:14–16	Gen. 28:13b–14
(14) . . . Raise your eyes now, and look from the place where you are, northward and southward and eastward and westward;	(13b) I am YHWH, the God of Abraham your father and the God of Isaac;
(15) For all the land that you see I will give to you and to your offspring forever.	the land on which you lie I will give to you and to your offspring
(16) I will make your offspring like the dust of the earth; so that if one can count the dust of the earth, your offspring can also be counted.	(14) And your offspring shall be like the dust of the earth,
(17) Rise, walk through the length and breadth of the land,	and you shall spread abroad to the west and to the east and to the north and to the south; . . .
for I will give it to you.	

---

5. Gunkel, *Genesis,* 319; Rendtorff, *Problem,* 54; (E.T., 71–72); and especially Blum, *Vätergeschichte,* 290–91 (with critique of Rendtorff's focus on formulation in n.5 on 290). Cf. Westermann, *Genesis 12—36,* 554; (E.T., 455); and especially L. Schmidt, "Väterverheißungen und Pentateuchfrage," *ZAW* 104 (1992): 2–9, who argue that 13:14–17 is later than its parallel in 28:13–15. First, Schmidt points out the lack of counterparts in Gen. 28:13–15 to the theme of the uncountability of Abraham's progeny (Gen. 13:16b; cf. 28:14) and the idea that God is giving the land to his progeny "forever" (Gen. 13:15b). This suggests to him that the version in 13:14–17 must be an expansion of the model found in 28:13–15. Second, Schmidt argues that the language of "the land on which you lie" and then of "spreading" Jacob's seed in Gen. 28:13–15 preserves a link between the promise of land and the promise of offspring that is lost in the secondary adaptation of this promise in 13:14–17. Whereas Gen. 28:13–14 talks of spreading Jacob's seed across the promised land on which he lies (cf. Isa. 54:3), 13:14–16 merely has Abraham touring the promised land and receiving successive but unconnected promises of land and offspring. These arguments build on two quite questionable premises: (1) later tradents were necessarily less artful than their predecessors, and more importantly (2) agreement must be total for texts to belong to the same compositional level. Certainly the contexts and characters of Gen. 13:14–17 and 28:13–15 are different, and a storyteller would not necessarily want to repeat exactly the same formulation in any case.

In both cases, God first promises land (to the patriarch and his offspring), then multiplication of offspring (like the dust of the earth), and finally the spreading of this offspring across the promised land. Moreover, both promises stand as confirmations of a previous divine promise of land. Genesis 13:14–17 stands as a final confirmation of Abraham's compliance with God's command in Gen. 12:1 and explication of the land promise. Genesis 28:13–14 comes after Isaac has himself received a version of this land promise (Gen. 26:2) and then has accidentally blessed Jacob (Gen. 27:27b-29). Within this context, the promise in 28:13–14 confirms that both the blessing and the associated land promise have in fact been passed on to Jacob.[6] Overall, the explicit link to Abraham at the outset of Gen. 28:13, the verbal linkages, and overall similar placement of the two divine speeches all suggest that either Gen. 28:13–15 or Gen. 12:1–3 was composed in light of the other, or that both are part of the same compositional level. Decision on which model best fits the evidence must await a later analysis of the linkages as a whole.

For now I will just note the way these promises of land are linked in multiple ways with the above-discussed travel command network. First, explicit land promises often occur in connection with the travel commands. The land promises in Gen. 12:7 and 13:14–15 follow on and develop a promise sequence beginning with the travel command in 12:1, and the (non-)travel command in Gen. 26:2 likewise leads to a promise of "these lands" to Isaac in 26:3bα. Second, the land promise is implicitly part of the background to the travel command network. Everything in the travel command system centers on travel to *the Promised Land* and the proper time for descent from that land into Egypt. Thus, for example, the land promise is implicitly part of the background of the travel command in 46:4, one that includes an assurance that although Jacob is leaving the [promised] land, God will descend with him into Egypt and bring him back out again. Such linkage of the land promise theme with the travel command theme is but our first indication that both elements are part of a broader system of compositional linkages spanning the non-P material.

Perhaps this link of the travel command to the promise of the land explains why it does not occur in the primeval history. There is no promised land there. Instead, there is just the garden from which the first humans were expelled at the outset. Notably, the primeval history is characterized by *east-*

---

6. At the same time, there are differences in the two promises that correspond to their different settings. Aside from the initial reference to the "land on which you are lying" (Gen. 28:13bα), we do not have an equivalent in Gen. 28:13–14 to YHWH's showing the land to Jacob (Gen. 13:14; cf. 12:1). Instead, YHWH's speech in Gen. 28:13 begins by focusing on the chain of promise transmission that has led to this point: "I am YHWH, the God of Abraham your father and the God of Isaac." Thus, even the deviation from Gen. 13:14–17 at this point provides further evidence that Jacob is being coordinated with Abraham in Gen. 28:13–15.

ward movement away from the garden. This begins with the expulsion of Adam and Eve in Gen. 3:23–24a (note the guards east of Eden in 3:24b), and continues with the movement of Cain eastward into Nod in 4:16, and then the movement of Yoktan, a nonheir of Shem, eastward (Gen. 10:30).[7] Next, already at Babel, the people begin moving westward (Gen. 11:2). This then provides the broad Mesopotamian starting point for Abraham's westward movement into Canaan (Gen. 11:28; 12:4a, 6), and implicitly back in the direction of the Garden of Eden. To be sure, the texts never make an explicit connection between the garden on the one hand and the Promised Land on the other (cf. Gen. 13:10 for Sodom). Nevertheless, these directional correspondences in the Genesis travel reports set up an implicit network of associations between the two.

The Promises in Genesis 12:2–3

Let us turn back to Gen. 12:2–3 to examine the promises YHWH gives Abraham there, promises that have already begun to emerge in my discussion of Gen. 12:7; 13:14–17; and 28:13–15. Indeed, formulated in prefix form just after God's travel command in Gen. 12:1, these promises are integrally linked with that command as the promised reward for obedience.[8]

> (12:1aβb—Command) Go . . . to the land which I will show you.
> (12:2–3—Promised Reward) And I will make you into a great nation, and bless you, and make your name great, so that you will be a blessing.[9] And I will bless those who bless you, but those who treat you lightly I will curse. And all the clans of the earth shall bless themselves by you.[10]

Thus, when Abraham complies with God's travel command in Gen. 12:1 (Gen. 12:4a, 6–7; cf. 13:14–17), he puts in force several divine promises: that he will be made "a great nation," "be blessed," and have a "great name"/be famous.

These promises are in turn confirmed and developed in the following narrative concerning him and then transferred to his descendants. For example, once Abraham has arrived in the land (Gen. 12:6), YHWH promises the land *to his descendants,* the very descendants who had been promised in Gen. 12:2 (Gen. 12:7). In this way broader themes converge. Abraham's departure and

---

7. Steinmetz, *From Father to Son,* 145.

8. T. Vriezen, "Bemerkungen zu Genesis 12:1-7," in *Symbolae Biblicae et Mesopotamicae: Francisco Mario Theodoro de Liagre Böhl Dedicatae* (ed. M. Beek, et al.; Leiden: E. J. Brill, 1973), 386; also T. Mann, *The Book of the Torah: The Narrative Integrity of the Pentateuch* (Atlanta: John Knox, 1988), 29 and 166n44; J. Rosenberg, *King and Kin: Political Allegory in the Hebrew Bible* (Indiana Studies in Biblical Literature; Bloomington, Ind.: Indiana University Press, 1986), 74; Van Seters, *Prologue to History,* 272n32.

9. Vriezen, "Bemerkungen," 386–87.

10. The translation of the latter portion of this verse presupposes the discussion below.

arrival in Canaan (Gen. 12:1, 4a, 6) is part of the travel-command network; the promise of the land (Gen. 12:7) is likewise part of the travel-command series of texts; and both themes intersect in 12:7: the promise of *land* to *descendants*.

Thus, we once again have the tight intersection of different compositional connections. This kind of intersection shows that we are not dealing here with separate compositional layers, one coordinating the travel of the patriarchs, another promising them the land, and yet another promising them descendants. Instead, all of these themes are part of an intense web of multiply intersecting compositional linkages, linkages connecting disparate ancestral texts. This will become yet clearer as we further investigate the narrative development of each of these promises of blessing and protection, starting with the promise of descendants.

"I will make you a great nation"

God promises to make Abraham a "great nation" (Gen. 12:2), make his offspring numerous (Gen. 13:16), and give his offspring the land (Gen. 12:7; 13:15). This theme of descendants in turn stands in a tensive relationship with the note regarding Sarah's barrenness in Gen. 11:30. Especially once the non-P material of Gen. 11:30; 12:1–3 is read continuously without the (later) Priestly material standing in the middle, the strength of this tension is clear. Just after we hear that Sarah is barren (Gen. 11:30), YHWH promises Abraham that he will make him a "great nation" (Gen. 12:2) and give his "offspring" the land (Gen. 12:7).[11]

Much of the narrative following this verse focuses on Abraham's and Sarah's lack of offspring in the face of God's promises to him. For example, in Genesis 16*, Abraham and Sarah engender Ishmael in an attempt to produce the promised offspring (Gen. 16:1–2, 4–14). This theme is then further developed in (1) God's following promise of a child to them (Gen. 18:10–14); (2) the narrative describing the birth of the promised child (Gen. 21:1–2, 6–7* non-P material); (3) a reference to God's gift of the promised child in the story about finding a wife for Isaac (Gen. 24:36); and (4) the description of the birth of yet additional children to Abraham (Gen. 25:1–4). All these texts develop in a single narrative line the above-described tension between a barren Sarah (Gen. 11:30) and the series of promises concerning descendants (Gen. 12:1, 7; 13:15).

Even once the narrative tension surrounding the promise of descendants diminishes with the birth of Isaac (cf., however, Genesis 22), the rest of the narrative still describes the fulfillment and transfer of the promise of descendants. Not only does Abraham have more children (Gen. 25:1–4), but the promise of many descendants is extended to his heirs and fulfilled with them

11. W. Zimmerli, *1. Moses 12–25: Abraham*, 18; Levin, *Der Jahwist*, 133.

as well. First, God promises protection, blessing, and many offspring to Isaac in Gen. 26:24, all "on account of Abraham, [God's] servant."[12] Then, in Gen. 28:13–14, a text already discussed above in connection with the land promise, YHWH promises to make Jacob's descendants "like the dust of the earth" (Gen. 28:14; cf. Gen. 13:16). Later, in the travel-command speech just before Jacob descends into Egypt, God promises to make him into a "great nation" and bring him out of there (Gen. 46:3–4; cf. 12:2). The last reflections of this promise in non-P material occur outside Genesis. In the non-P Moses story pharaoh states that the Israelites have become "more numerous and mightier than we are" (Exod. 1:9), and then the Israelites later decamp from Rameses with 600,000 warriors (Exod. 12:37).[13]

Overall, particularly in Genesis, we see how the promise of descendants is integrally interlinked with the above-discussed travel command texts (Gen. 12:1; 46:3) and promises of land (Gen. 13:14–17; 28:13–14). This makes sense given the way the promise of descendants has been linked with other promises from the very outset (Gen. 12:1–2, 7). These themes have been interlocked with each other from the beginning, and they are further interlocked with each other in their development.

"I will bless you"

The second promise to "bless" Abraham is fulfilled within Genesis. Just as Job was blessed with "fourteen thousand sheep, six thousand camels, a thousand yoke of oxen, and a thousand donkeys" along with "seven sons and three daughters" (Job 42:12–13) so the Genesis narrative repeatedly stresses that Abraham and his descendants are not only blessed with children but also with numerous flocks and other riches. A series of riches lists occurs in connection with the wife-sister story immediately after God's promise to bless him (Gen. 12:16; 13:2, 5; cf. 19:12; 25:5). Riches are referred to again in the second wife-sister story about Abraham (Gen. 20:14), and then this blessing through flocks is referred to in the story about finding a wife for Isaac (24:35; cf. 24:1). Then with Isaac we once again see the giving of the blessing promise (Gen. 26:3), the wife-sister story about life among strangers (Gen. 26:6–11), and a following description of God's blessing of Isaac (Gen. 26:12–14). Jacob is blessed by Isaac (Gen. 27:27b-29), and then is blessed like Isaac with offspring, and numerous flocks, while living abroad with Laban (Gen. 30:43;

---

12. Blum, *Vätergeschichte*, 365, argues primarily on terminological grounds that this verse is a secondary addition to its context (cf. also Gunkel, *Genesis*, 303). Nevertheless, as Skinner (*Genesis*, 366n) and Van Seters (*Prologue*, 269–70) have observed, there are no clear grounds for seeing a addition here. Blum also links the emphasis in the verse on Abraham with the secondary additions in Gen. 22:15–18 and 26:3bβ–5. Nevertheless, this verse lacks an explicit reference to the *obedience* of Abraham so stressed in the other texts, and one could just as easily argue that 22:15–18 and 26:3bβ–5 are later explications of what it meant for God to make promises to Isaac "on account of Abraham" (Gen. 26:24).
13. Levin, *Der Jahwist*, 45–46, 313, 324.

cf. 32:6 [Eng. 32:5]). Immediately upon being taken to Egypt, Joseph is made successful by God in both Potiphar's house and the prison into which he is thrown (Gen. 39:2, 5, 21), before he rises to a level of power second only to pharaoh's own might (Gen. 41:39–40). Finally, the Israelites as a group enjoy blessing in Egypt, not only multiplying themselves but following Abraham's first example by leaving Egypt "very heavy" with livestock (Exod. 12:37–38; cf. Gen. 13:2). As Levin has pointed out, this theme is developed with similar terminology in the riches lists, and in each case the patriarch receives the blessing in the context of life in a foreign culture. Indeed, each patriarch always receives this blessing of riches in connection with the successful negotiation of marriage issues within the foreign culture (Gen. 12:10–13:1; 26:6–14; 29:1–30:43; 39:1–23; cf. 24:1–67).[14]

"I will make your name great, so that you will be a blessing, . . . all clans of the earth shall bless themselves by you"

As others have observed, the closest biblical parallel to this set of promises occurs in Ps. 72:17, a royal psalm. This text is particularly interesting because of the way it combines the theme of the king's "great name" (cf. 2 Sam. 7:9; 1 Kings 1:47) and that of his special blessing (cf. 2 Sam. 7:29; Ps. 21:4, 7 [Eng. 21:3, 6]). The psalmist prays first that the king's "name" be eternal—that his fame endure—and then that all nations bless themselves by the king and pronounce him happy. And this is but one biblical example of a more widespread phenomenon of ancient Near Eastern belief in and prayers for special blessing that will bring fame for the king.[15] The hope is that his blessing will so distinguish the king from his contemporaries that they will look to him as a paradigm of blessing. The paradigmatic character of this blessing likewise appears in another Genesis text, Gen. 48:20, where Jacob prays that Ephraim and Manasseh become paradigms of blessing for Israel: "by you Israel will invoke blessings, saying 'God make you like Ephraim and Manasseh.'" Although this text does not concern a king, the same idea of paradigmatic blessing is being applied here to tribal groups, indeed groups viewed as dominant among their peers. Now, Gen. 12:2–3 is speaking of the blessing that will bring fame not to a king nor to a dominant group, but instead to a sojourner in a foreign land. As in Ps. 72:17, the text focuses first on Abraham's future "name," his fame (Gen. 12:2aβ), before climaxing with the promise that his blessing will be so pronounced that others will look to him as a paradigm of blessing (Gen. 12:3b; cf. 72:17b). Living among foreigners, prone to be seen as cursed, he will instead enjoy blessing famed far and wide (cf. Zech. 8:13).

---

14. Levin, *Der Jahwist*, 36–46 and passim.
15. For thorough discussion of this issue including the ancient Near Eastern parallels, see in particular Schmid, *Der sogenannte Jahwist*, 133–36; Van Seters, *Abraham*, 274–76; Blum, *Vätergeschichte*, 349–59; Köckert, *Vätergott*, 276–97; and Van Seters, *Prologue to History*, 252–55.

This understanding of Gen. 12:3b is confirmed by the focus of the following narrative on the recognition by foreigners of Abraham and his heirs' famed blessing. After this promise is given (Gen. 12:3), Abimelek of Gerar asks for a treaty with Abraham because God is with him (Gen. 21:22), and Laban recognizes Abraham's servant as the "blessed of YHWH" (Gen. 24:31). Later, God promises to "be with" Isaac, and Abimelek likewise recognizes that "YHWH is with [Isaac]" and asks for a treaty with Isaac like the one he made with Abraham (Gen. 26:28; cf. 21:22 and 27). After Isaac passes on the blessing to Jacob (Gen. 27:27–29), Jacob receives the same promise of famous blessing from YHWH (Gen. 28:14), and Laban later sees that God has blessed him because of Jacob (Gen. 30:27; cf. 30:29–30). The promise continues to work for Jacob's descendants. Potiphar turns all he owns over to Joseph because God was with him (39:3–5), as does Joseph's jailer (Gen. 39:21–23). Finally Pharaoh (Exod. 1:9), Jethro (Exod. 18:10–12), and Balaam (Num. 24:1; cf. 22:12) perceive that God is with the Israelites as a whole. In every case, from Abraham to his Israelite descendants, foreigners recognize them as specially blessed by YHWH.[16] Indeed, in the case of Jacob and Joseph, the blessing is so strong that others are blessed on their account (Gen. 30:27, 29–30; 39:5). The patriarchs are, as promised in 12:2, a "blessing."[17]

I am suggesting in this survey that the fame being promised to Abraham, the "great name," is intricately connected to the broader theme of blessing. Not only does this promise of a "great name" occur in the midst of the promises of the blessing of descendants and overflowing fertility (Gen. 12:2), but the subsequent narratives describe Abraham and his heirs as being famous for one thing: their blessing. In this way, this *one* theme of the ancestral narratives contrasts with *two* elements that were separate in the preceding primeval history: (1) the repeated appearance of curse there (Gen. 3:14–15, 17–19; 4:11; 9:25–27*; cf. 8:21), and (2) the repeated occurrence of various themes surrounding the theme of the "name." Previous primeval figures and the land beneath them were cursed. Now Abraham and his descendants will be blessed. Previously the people of Babel tried to make a "name" for themselves (Gen. 11:4), a name like that the preflood "men of the name" once had (Gen. 6:4). Now, God's blessing of Abraham, the heir of Shem ("name"), will make him and his descendants famous (Gen. 12:2).[18] Abraham's special blessed status will make him shine like a beacon in the midst of

16. H. W. Wolff, "Das Kerygma des Jahwisten," *EvT* 24 (1964): 90–93 (reprinted in *Gesammelte Studien zum Alten Testament* [TB 22; Munich: Kaiser, 1964], 364–67; trans. W. Benware, "The Kerygma of the Yahwist," *Int* 20 [1966]: 149–51 and again in *The Vitality of Old Testament Traditions* [ed. W. Brueggemann and H. W. Wolff; Atlanta: John Knox, 1975], 58–61); and more recently, Levin, *Der Jahwist*, 36–46.
17. L. Schmidt, "Israel ein Segen für die Völker?" *Theologia viatorum* 12 (1975): 138–39.
18. A. K. Jenkins, "A Great Name: Genesis 12:2 and the Editing of the Pentateuch," *JSOT* 10 (1978): 41–57.

the primeval world that has been fractured by human rebellion. Using language otherwise used for promises to a king, God promises that others will bless themselves by Abraham's example (Gen. 12:3b).

"I will bless those who bless you, but those who treat you lightly I will curse"

Schottroff and many following him have observed that the promise of protection in Gen. 12:3a is stronger than biblical and ancient Near Eastern parallels. The formula usually reads: "those who bless you will be blessed, but those who curse you will be cursed" (Gen. 27:29; Num. 24:9), but Gen. 12:3 replaces the term *curse* with the term "treat lightly" (*qll*): "I will bless those who bless you, but *those who treat you lightly* I will curse" (Gen. 12:3a).[19] Notably, the narrative never describes anyone being blessed because they blessed Abraham. Instead, the narrative stress seems to lie on the modified portion of the standard curse/bless formula.[20] This modified promise in turn connects with the preceding promise to make Abraham's name great (Gen. 12:2aγ), a promise otherwise only present in promises to kings to make them famous.[21] In Gen. 12:2aγ, 3a God is promising to make Abraham famous and curse those who have contempt for his royal greatness.

Indeed, as befits the royal parallels to the promises earlier in Gen. 12:2 and later in Gen. 12:3b, this promise of protection in Gen. 12:3a appears to apply not just to Abraham's person, but also to what might be loosely termed his *realm,* that is his clan. The promise is fulfilled vis-à-vis members of Abraham's clan on at least three occasions: when pharaoh unknowingly takes Abraham's wife during his time in Egypt (Gen. 12:10–20); when the eastern kings take Abraham's relative, Lot, hostage (Genesis 14); and when the Sodomites attack Lot (Gen. 19:1–25). In each case, foreigners who treat Abraham and/or those belonging to him lightly are defeated.

In this way the narrative describes God's protection of Abraham and his clan as they live precariously amidst foreigners more powerful than they are. This theme then develops in multiple ways in the following narrative. God transfers the protection promise in different form to Isaac and Jacob (Gen. 26:3, 24; 28:15; 31:3; 46:4), and this promise is then fulfilled in multiple encounters of both patriarchs with foreigners. Isaac successfully negotiates with Abimelek (26:6–11, 17–33), and Jacob is likewise successful with Laban (31:25–32:1 [Eng. 31:55]; cf. 31:24), Esau (Gen. 33:1–17), the Shechemites (Genesis 34), and Pharaoh (Genesis 46*).

With the above discussion in mind, the promise-centered connections often drawn between the non-P primeval and ancestral sections look different.

---

19. W. Schottroff, *Der altisraelitische Fluchspruch* (WMANT 30; Neukirchen-Vluyn: Neukirchener Verlag, 1969), 29–30; Schmidt, "Segen?" 137–38; Levin, *Der Jahwist,* 134–35.
20. Levin, *Der Jahwist,* 134–35.
21. Westermann, *Genesis 12—36,* 173; (E.T., 150).

Many theologically oriented, Christian analyses of this non-P material have proposed that the promise of blessing to Abraham in Gen. 12:3b is God's antidote to the curse so prominent in Genesis 1—9.[22] According to this understanding, Gen. 12:3b is God's promise to mediate blessing to the world through Abraham in place of the curse that has dominated it so far. The transfer of blessing to Laban and Potiphar are then taken as prime examples of the mediation of blessing to the world through Abraham.[23] Nevertheless, if Gen. 12:3b was a promise to mediate blessing to the whole world through Abraham, then the transfer of blessing to Laban and Potiphar would be a pitiful fulfillment of this promise.

Above I have advocated a different understanding of Gen. 12:3b and the texts preceding it. If Gen. 12:2–3 in fact speaks of the fame and paradigmatic character of Abraham and his descendants' blessing, then the following narrative describes the fulfillment of this promise. Occurring in a non-P narrative world colored in the somber tones of primeval curses, the exceptional blessing of Abraham and his descendants shines all the brighter. Foreigners still standing largely outside the blessed circle are all the more conscious of the contrast, seek the blessing, and occasionally touch it. Indeed, here we see an apparent pattern of depicting the patriarchs in contrast to the prepromise history that has already appeared elsewhere. Just as Sarah's barrenness provides a backdrop highlighting the promise to make Abraham a great nation, just as the failure of humans at Babel to make a name for themselves highlights God's promise to make Abraham's name great, so also the curse prominent in the primeval history provides a backdrop for the exceptional blessing of Abraham and his descendants.

This contrastive relationship between the non-P and primeval histories means the connections between these two portions of Genesis can not be as direct as those between the ancestral sections themselves. The ancestral sections develop the *ongoing* theme of the promise and as a result repeat specific terminology and narrative patterns. Therefore, it is comparatively easy to see how the Abraham, Jacob, and Joseph sections of the non-P material are all connected by the promise theme. This same theme, however, contrasts with the preceding primeval section. This contrast between the primeval and

---

22. Procksch, *Genesis*, 96–97; G. Von Rad, "Das formgeschichtliche Problem des Hexateuch," in *Gesammelte Studien zum Alten Testament* (TB 8; Munich: Kaiser, 1961), 71–75 (E.T., "The Form-Critical Problem of the Hexateuch," in *The Problem of the Hexateuch and Other Essays* [trans. T. Dicken; New York: McGraw Hill, 1966], 64–67); idem, *Theologie des Alten Testaments*, vol. 1, *Die Theologie der geschichtlichen Überlieferungen Israels* (4th ed.; Munich: Kaiser, 1962), 174–78 (E.T., *Old Testament Theology*, vol. 1, *The Theology of Israel's Historical Traditions* [trans. D. M. G. Stalker; New York: Harper & Row, 1962], 161–65); Wolff, "Kerygma," 86–88 (in *Gesammelte Studien*, 359–61; E.T. in *Int* 145–46, and *Vitality*, 53–55); O. H. Steck, "Genesis 12,1–3 und die Urgeschichte des Jahwisten," in *Probleme biblischer Theologie: Festschrift für G. von Rad* (ed. H. W. Wolff; Munich: Kaiser, 1971), 531–54.
23. Wolff, "Kerygma," 90–92 (in *Gesammelte Studien*, 364–66; E.T. in *Int*, 150–51, and in *Vitality*, 58–60).

ancestral sections on this point makes the connections between them more difficult to pin down.

Nevertheless, there are some such connections. The most prominent ones appear at the point where the destructive forces seen in the primeval history break into the ancestral history: the story of the destruction of Sodom and Gomorrah, Gen. 19:1–28.[24] Already we have a hint of a connection to the primeval history in two elements preceding Genesis 19:

1. the comparison of Sodom to the "garden of YHWH" (Gen. 13:10; cf. Genesis 2—3) and description of the "sin" and "evil" of the Sodomites (13:13; cf. Gen. 4:7; 6:5; 8:21)
2. the similarity between God's decision to "descend" and "see" what is going on in Sodom (18:20–21), and the previous description of God's "descent" to see what was going on in Babel (11:5; cf. also the divine self-reflection in 3:22; 6:3, 5–7; 11:6–7)

Then, in Genesis 19 and the flood story we have more similar elements:

1. a story of some kind of sexual misdeed (19:4–11; cf. Gen. 6:1–4)
2. the introduction of a figure who is uniquely righteous in his context and "finds favor" with YHWH (19:1–11, 19; cf. 6:5–8)
3. an announcement to this righteous one of the destruction of the rest of humanity/the community, and the command for him to prepare himself and his family to escape (19:12–3; cf. 7:1–4)
4. subsequent compliance with the command (19:14; cf. 7:5)
5. actual escape of the figure along with his wife and children (19:15–23; cf. 7:7) before the "rain" of destruction on the rest of the community (19:24–5; cf. 7:10, 12)

Of course, there are important differences. Most importantly, although the Lot figure, like Noah, "finds favor" in the eyes of YHWH (Gen. 19:19; cf. 6:8), both the context and substance of the narrative make clear that Lot is rescued *because of his connection to Abraham*. God has already rescued Sarah from the clutches of pharaoh, when the Egyptians unknowingly treated her and Abraham with contempt (cf. Gen. 12:2), and God now rescues Lot when the Sodomites do the same. Although Lot distinguishes himself from the evil Sodomites by his hospitality, he is qualified only as a possible recipient of protection by his association with Abraham. Even the rescue narrative implicitly contrasts his hesitant cooperation with the divine messengers, with Noah's and Abraham's immediate compliance with God's commands.[25]

24. I am indebted to the following works for the survey of these parallels: W. M. Clark, "The Flood and the Structure of the Pre-patriarchal History," *ZAW* 83 (1971): 194–95; G. J. Wenham, "Method in Pentateuchal Source Criticism," *VT* 41 (1991): 108–9; Levin, *Der Jahwist*, 48, 134–35, 143, 159–63.
25. For comparison of Genesis 18 and 19, see *Gen.Rab.* 50:4; R. C. Culley, *Studies in the Structure of Hebrew Narrative* (Philadelphia: Fortress; Missoula, Mont.: Scholars Press, 1976),

Finally, Lot's solidarity with fallen Noachide humanity is depicted through specific links to the story of the aftermath of the Flood:[26]

1. Just as Noah got drunk, and exposed his nakedness to his sons (Gen. 9:20–21), so now Lot is made drunk by his daughters so they can have sex with him (19:32–33, 35).

2. Noah founds postflood humanity in the broader context of God's earlier command to "preserve seed on the earth" (Gen. 7:3). So also Lot's daughters mistakenly decide there is no one left on the earth to impregnate them (Gen. 19:31; cf. similar terminology in 2:5; 6:4, 6). They then likewise act to "preserve seed," this time that of their father (Gen. 19:32, 34).

3. Noah's story ends with a curse on one of his grandsons (Gen. 9:25–27), while Lot's ends with offspring tainted by incest (Gen. 19:36–38).[27]

This then represents a final contrast with Abraham. Abraham gave hospitality, and this culminated in a specific promise of a son through Sarah (Gen. 18:10–14). Lot gave hospitality, and this likewise culminated in offspring, but offspring produced by incest (Gen. 19:30–38). Such contrasts make clear that whatever Lot gets, it is by virtue of his connection to Abraham.

To be sure, some of these parallels between the flood and Sodom stories could be explained through a combination of (1) use of common Hebrew terminology in both narratives and (2) the parallel development in both narratives of widespread ancient Near Eastern motifs regarding collective destruction.[28] Nevertheless, the intense cluster of specific linkages extending across both the rescue/destruction and aftermath accounts suggests that these stories have some kind of more direct compositional relationship with each other. Moreover, these resonances between Sodom and various aspects of the primeval history play an important coordinating role in the overall non-P narrative. It is as if the specialness of the promise to Abraham is highlighted here by the depiction of his nephew Lot's continued life in the primeval

---

54–55; Kilian, *Die vorpriesterlichen Abrahamsüberlieferungen,* 150–51; T. Rudin-O'Brasky, *The Patriarchs in Hebron and Sodom (Gen. 18—19): A Study of the Structure and Composition of a Biblical Story* (Heb.) (Jerusalem: Simor, 1982), 140–41; Blum, *Vätergeschichte,* 280–81; Rosenberg, *King and Kin,* 77; G. J. Wenham, *Genesis 16—50* (WBC 2; Dallas: Word Books, 1994), 43–44.

26. The parallels here are drawn primarily from R. Alter, "Sodom as Nexus: The Web of Design in Biblical Narrative," in *The Book and the Text: The Bible and Literary Theory* (ed. R. M. Schwartz; Oxford: Basil Blackwell, 1990), 153–54.

27. Steinberg, *Kinship and Marriage in Genesis,* 72 (especially n.81) suggests we need not presuppose incest is viewed negatively here. Instead, it might just be an example of the lengths to which one may need to go to perpetuate a family. Such a reading, however, misses the fact that the text is first and foremost interested in the perpetuation at all costs of a specific family line, that extending from Abraham to Israel. Lot functions consistently throughout as a negative contrast to Abraham, and the grouping of incest and drunkenness at the close of Genesis 19 make it absolutely clear that his fathering children through incest with his own daughters is not being presented neutrally.

28. For a survey related to these texts, see Westermann, *Genesis 1—11,* 536–46; (E.T., 399–406); and idem, *Genesis 12—36,* 363–64; (E.T., 297–99).

world depicted in the non-P material of Genesis 1—11*. The chaos-and-establishment-of-order pattern seen in similar stories in the ancient Near East is developed here in a very specific way. Through parallel stories standing in sequence, the non-P composition points to the ongoing presence of chaos outside Israel and God's particular protection of those under Abraham's semiroyal care.

This pattern continues in the one other location where these motifs cluster in the non-P narrative, the exodus from Egypt. To be sure, there are important differences between the story of the Israelites' exodus from Egypt and Lot's exit from Gomorrah. Nevertheless, the parallels are striking.[29]

Chart 9-4: Stories of Water, Destruction, and Rescue

	Flood (Gen. 6—9)	Babel (Gen. 11:1–9)	Sodom (Gen. 18:16–19:38)	Exodus (Exodus 3—4, 14)
God sees/hears that evil "big"	6:5		18:20	cf. 3:7 (see *'ny*)
Problem is "evil"	6:5		13:13; 19:7, 9	
God hears "cry" (cf. 4:10)			18:20–21; 19:13	3:7; 14:10
God descends		11:5, 7	18:21	3:8
God tells righteous	7:1–4		18:20–21	3:1–4:17
God provides escape instructions	7:1–4		19:12–13	3:16–4:17 (14:13–14)
Righteous are saved	7:7 (cf. 7:1)		19:15–23	3:8; 14
Destruction by water	7:4, 12;		19:24 ("rain" of fire)	14:21–27

In this way the Sodom story not only draws on certain primeval history themes to depict the destruction of an immoral community outside the promise, but these same themes help the Sodom story anticipate the ultimate rescue by God of the people of promise from Egypt.

The exodus is anticipated in specific ways by yet another story in the non-P Abraham cycle, that regarding Abraham's sojourn in Egypt in Gen. 12:10–13:1. The links between this story and the Exodus begin already in

---

29. Levin, *Der Jahwist*, 326, 341. In addition, as W. H. Schmidt points out, God threatens Pharaoh in Exod. 10:28 with the same death penalty with which the primeval humans were threatened at the outset of time (Gen. 2:17). W. H. Schmidt, "Ein Theologe in solomonischer Zeit? Plädoyer für den Jahwisten," *BZ* 25 (1981): 85; (E.T., "A Theologian of the Solomonic Era? A Plea for the Yahwist," in *Studies in the Period of David and Solomon and Other Essays* [ed. T. Ishida; Tokyo: Yamakawa-Shuppansha, 1982], 59). Once again, the proto-Pentateuch composition appropriates certain motifs from the non-P primeval history to depict the situation of humanity outside the promise.

12:10. Just as the exodus is preceded by Jacob's descent into Egypt because of a famine (Genesis 42—47*), so also this story is preceded by Abraham's descent into Egypt because of a famine (Gen. 12:10). Later the exodus story will describe how the pharaoh will call for each male Israelite child to be killed while each daughter is to be "allowed to live" (Exod. 1:16). In eerie anticipation of that event, Abraham is afraid in Gen. 12:12 that the pharaoh will see Sarah's beauty, kill him, and "let her live."[30] Later, pharaoh "takes" Sarah because of her beauty, thus echoing the incident in the primeval history where the divine beings "took" the daughters of humanity because they were beautiful (Gen. 6:1–4).[31] Once again, God intervenes, this time to exact revenge on those who "treat Abraham lightly" by seizing his wife (cf. Gen. 12:3). Furthermore, God does this in a way that anticipates the final fulfillment of this promise in the exodus. As in the exodus story, God "strikes" pharaoh with plagues (Gen. 12:17; cf. Exod. 11:1); as in the exodus story pharaoh "lets" the chosen go (Gen. 12:20; cf. Exod. 5ff.); and as in the exodus story, Abraham leaves with riches (Gen. 12:16, 20; 13:2; cf. Exod. 12:35–38).[32] Indeed, in both cases the Egyptians incur judgment against their will, first by unknowingly taking Abraham's wife (Gen. 12:18–19), and then by having their "hearts hardened" by God after each plague (Exod. 4:21; 7:3; then Exod. 7:8–14:8).[33] Overall, Gen. 12:10–20 serves as the first demonstration of a trans-moral distinction in humanity that has been introduced by the promise in Gen. 12:1–3, 7 and will culminate in the story of the exodus. Whatever the variables in the Israelite response to the promise and whatever the variables with non-Israelites, Abraham will be blessed, and any non-Israelite who treats lightly Abraham or those who are his will be cursed.

We have already seen how Lot was rescued from destruction like that of primeval times as a result of his connection to Abraham. The last link of the promise with the exodus to be considered here concerns another member of Abraham's household, Hagar. Once again, as in Gen. 12:10–13:1, Abraham and Sarah are not relying on God to fulfill the promise, this time attempting

30. Sykes, "Patterns in Genesis," 107–11.
31. Westermann, *Genesis 1—11*, 495–96; (E.T., 366–67).
32. *Gen.Rab.* 40:6; Jacob, *Genesis*, 355–56; (E.T., 90); U. Cassuto, *Genesis*, vol. 2, 334–37; Fishbane, *Biblical Interpretation*, 375–76; Miscall, *The Workings of Old Testament Narrative*, 42–44; Westermann, *Genesis 12—36*, 193; (E.T., 166); Blum, *Vätergeschichte*, 309–11; Ha, *Genesis 15*, 199–200.
33. To be sure, particularly in the case of the Exodus, Egypt is portrayed as oppressive and deserving of punishment. Nevertheless, the extended punishment, even after initial willingness to let Israel go, is the parallel being argued here. Cf. Miscall, *Workings of Old Testament Narrative*, 42, who argues that Gen. 12:10–20 contrasts with other texts in portraying the Egyptians as "good guys." I am arguing here that Gen. 12:10–20 actually shares with the later exodus story an emphasis on the trans-moral element of God's choice of the Israelites. Although the Egyptians are "bad" in both stories, both narratives simultaneously emphasize that the Egyptians' badness or goodness does not matter in comparison with God's choice of Israel and intent to demonstrate his might to protect it.

to produce the offspring promised in Gen. 12:2; 13:16. Moreover, just as in the case of Gen. 12:10–20, the result of their efforts is not ideal. It produces discord in the camp, and eventually Hagar flees into the wilderness (Gen. 16:6bβ), where she is told by God to return (Gen. 16:9), and then does so. There is, however, at least one important difference between Gen. 12:10–20 and the story of Hagar in Genesis 16. Genesis 12:10–20 anticipated the exodus by describing Abraham's proto-exodus from Egypt. In contrast, the Hagar story describes a *non-Israelite's,* indeed an Egyptian's, exodus experience. Like the Israelites, Hagar is "oppressed"; like the Israelites at Sinai, Hagar meets God in the wilderness (Gen. 16:7–12) and even names God (Gen. 16:13; cf. Exod. 3:13–14); but unlike them she is fleeing toward Egypt, not away from it (Gen. 16:6bβ–7).[34] To be sure, the son's fate does not sound particularly good (Gen. 16:12), and Hagar, unlike Israel, is eventually forced to return and submit to the oppression from which she fled (Gen. 16:9; cf. Gen. 21:8–20). Nevertheless, her membership in Abraham's household puts her in the sphere of promise. God interacts directly with her in a way similar to the way he interacts with Abraham and his heirs, and God extends to her son the promise of offspring given to Abraham (Gen. 16:10). Thus this story is not only linked to the promise of descendants (on this see above), but also to the above-discussed network of non-P promise/destruction stories, especially Gen. 12:10–13:1 on the one hand and the non-P Exodus story on the other.

Material Surrounding the Initial Promises: Genesis 11:28–30 and 12:8bβ

So far I have focused on the promises to Abraham in Gen. 12:1–4a, 6–7 and the fulfillment of them in the following ancestral narratives. These promises in Gen. 12:1–7* are preceded and followed by two other texts that are part of this cross-Genesis compositional network: Gen. 11:28–30 and 12:8bβ. For example, "calling on YHWH's name" in Gen. 12:8bβ is a quite specific expression for worship, one that contrasts with other descriptions in Genesis of characters offering sacrifices (Gen. 8:20; 22:13; 31:54; 46:1) or anointing pillars (e.g., Gen. 28:18). The expression occurs at crucial points across the non-P material, starting with the establishment of the preflood line leading to Israel (Gen. 4:26), continuing in the stories of Israel's ancestors (Gen. 12:8; 13:4; 21:33; 26:25), and culminating at Sinai (Exod. 34:5). The distribution of this expression suggests that it marks crucial points in the narrative spanning from the initial calling on YHWH's name to Sinai.

Genesis 11:28–30 likewise manifests certain specific themes that work themselves out in the following narratives. I have already mentioned the way

---

34. P. Trible, *Texts of Terror: Literary-Feminist Readings of Biblical Narratives* (OBT; Philadelphia: Fortress, 1984), 14–17; Sykes, "Patterns in Genesis," 66–67; Rosenberg, *King and Kin,* 88.

the juxtaposition of Sarah's barrenness in Gen. 11:30 with the promise in Gen. 12:1–3, 7 sets up a tension that dominates much of the rest of the non-P Abraham narrative. So also, the note regarding Haran's death in the "land of his kindred" in Gen. 11:28 prepares for God's later command to Abraham to leave his "land, kindred, and father's house" (Gen. 12:1). Finally, Gen. 11:29, the note regarding Abraham and Nahor's marriages sets up a genealogical structure that spans both the Abraham and Jacob sections of the non-P narrative. As Steinberg has particularly emphasized, the following transmission of the promise then occurs exclusively through these intermarriages within Terah's clan, between the lines of Abraham, on the one hand, and Nahor, on the other. Thus, the Jacob and Abraham sections are specifically linked not only by the Abraham-Isaac-Jacob genealogical sequence but also by a Nahor-Betuel-Laban sequence. Both Isaac (Gen. 22:20–23; 24:1–67) and Jacob (Gen. 29:1–30) marry descendants of Nahor.[35] This emphasis on intermarriage within the clan is an important link between genealogy and promise, particularly the promise of the land. As Steinberg points out, such emphasis on linear transmission of heirship through a limited family line is typical of cultures where inheritance of limited land resources is a major issue.[36] By emphasizing that the promise was transmitted through such interclan marriage, Genesis stresses the legitimacy of that process.[37]

Analysis of the Connections

I have surveyed an extensive system of specific and sequential connections spanning the non-P Pentateuchal material. The system links the genealogies of Israel and the Nahor sideline, provides similar divine travel commands at

35. N. Steinberg, "Alliance or Descent? The Function of Marriage in Genesis," *JSOT* 51 (1991): 51–53; idem, *Kinship and Marriage in Genesis: A Household Economics Perspective* (Minneapolis: Fortress, 1993), 12–14. Steinberg tentatively suggests ("Alliance or Descent?" 52–53; *Kinship and Marriage*, 14) that Abraham's excuse to Abimelek that Sarah is his half sister (Gen. 20:12) implies that even Sarah comes from Terah's household. This is an interesting observation, particularly given the patrilineal tendencies of the broader narrative. Nevertheless, as Steinberg herself acknowledges ("Alliance or Descent?" 53), Abraham's interest in defending himself here decreases the believability of this comment (cf. Miscall, *The Workings of Old Testament Narrative*, 14–15). Given the context in which it occurs, Abraham's claim about Sarah is on a decisively different narrative level from the narrator's statements about the parentage of Rebekah (Gen. 11:29; 22:20–23), Rachel, and Leah (29:16).
36. Steinberg, "Alliance or Descent?" 49–53; *Kinship and Marriage*, 26–34.
37. As Levin stresses (*Der Jahwist*, 139–40), the relationship between the Abraham mainline and the Nahor sideline is set up with texts that in turn resemble the conclusion of the description of first genealogical sideline in Genesis, that extending from Cain to Lamech (Gen. 4:19//11:29; 4:22//20:20–22). Both marriage reports move from an initial description of taking two wives to naming both, and both birth reports use similar language to describe the birth of an additional son. Such similarities set up a potential resonance (1) between Lamech's marriages and Abraham's and Nahor's and (2) between Lamech's descendants on the one hand and Nahor's on the other. Nevertheless, this is probably one of the weaker potential connections in Genesis, and it may just result from the use of common language to describe both marriages and births.

the outset of each patriarch's travels, parallels Abraham's and Jacob's journeys and contrasts Isaac's lack of descent into Egypt with Abraham's and Jacob's trip there, coordinates the promise across all the sections, details the development of people "calling on YHWH's" name from Enosh to Sinai, and
describes similar patterns of primeval-like divine destruction of groups on the
one hand and rescue of the oppressed on the other. Throughout I have
stressed the way these various linkages crisscross each other. This is not just
a case of separate themes, which might be distinguished from one another as
separate compositional layers, each occurring in a distinct set of texts. Rather,
the travel commands, land promise, descendant theme, blessing and protection theme, calling on YHWH's name, and so forth, all occur across the full
stretch of texts and are constantly intertwined with each other. Although
these themes do not all occur in every text, the different combinations of
themes form an intricate web of connections. Any attempt to separate one
strand destroys the whole.

As we have seen, each verse of the transition in Gen. 11:28–30; 12:1–4a,
6–8 is part of this broader system of interconnections. Indeed this is the one
text in which all of the above-discussed themes occur. Nevertheless, as we
have seen, many other primeval and ancestral traditions are linked in various
ways to this network. For example, Isaac's sojourn in Gerar, whatever its prehistory, is now linked to this broader system by the travel command and
promise in Gen. 26:2–3bα. So also, Jacob's epiphany at Bethel, whatever its
background, is now integrally linked into the broader non-P narrative by the
promise in Gen. 28:13–15. So far, I have explicitly left open the question of
how these different texts were linked. In the following sections, I will argue
for a particular transmission-historical model that can best account for the
sort of connections we see here.

"Elohistic" Traditions
and the Non-P Compositional Network

Having surveyed this system, my first point is that it seamlessly spans "Yahwistic" and "Elohistic" traditions alike. In the next chapter I will discuss the
Jacob and Joseph sections. Now, however, I will focus on the usual starting
point (since Wellhausen) for source analyses of the non-P material: the Abraham section. Such source analyses typically assign Gen. 11:28–30; 12:1–4a,
6–8 and most subsequent texts regarding Abraham to the "Yahwist," and the
bulk of Genesis 20—22 (aside from parts of Gen. 21:1–2, 6–7*) to an "Elohist" or redactor responsible for combining the Yahwist and Elohist (Rje).
Nevertheless, *all* these traditions—"Yahwistic" and "Elohistic" alike—develop the above-discussed themes spanning the non-P materials of Genesis.
For example, Abraham does not just receive the promised blessing of riches
in the first wife-sister story (Gen. 12:16; cf. 13:2, 5; all "J") but also in the
second (Gen. 20:14). Moreover, as promised in Gen. 12:2–3, this blessing

does not go unnoticed. Just as Isaac's (Gen. 26:28), Jacob's (Gen. 30:27–30), and Joseph's (Gen. 39:2–5, 21–3; 41:39–40) blessings were recognized by foreigners, so also Abraham's blessing "in all" (Gen. 24:1b, 35) is recognized by Abimelek in a supposedly separate, Elohistic text (Gen. 21:22; cf. 26:28). A "Yahwistic" source lacking this text would have a promise of famed blessing to Abraham (Gen. 12:2–3) but no foreign recognition of such blessing. Instead, reception of the promised *famed* blessing would be limited to his descendants (Gen. 30:27–30; 39:2–5, 21–23; 41:39–40; also Exod. 1:9).[38]

In addition, the supposedly separate "Elohistic" stories of Genesis 20—22 often presuppose the existence, in the same storyline, of preceding "Yahwistic" stories in Genesis 13–19*. For example, as Van Seters has pointed out, the wife-sister story in Genesis 20 presupposes that the preceding story in Gen. 12:10–20 stands in the same storyline. Otherwise the audience does not know why Abraham immediately presents Sarah as his sister (Gen. 20:2).[39] Furthermore, in this story Abraham justifies his behavior toward Abimelek by referring to the time when God "made [him] wander from the house of [his] father" (Gen. 20:13). This reference has no existing "Elohistic" referent but instead refers to Abraham's initial request that Sarah say she was his sister (Gen. 12:11–13) after YHWH had called him to leave "the house of [his] father" (Gen. 12:1).[40] So also, Genesis 22 is tightly linked to the overall non-P Abraham narrative. There are close parallels between God's travel command in 22:2 and the command in 12:1 (both in parallel formulation [*lek-lĕkā*] and unknown destination, the "land/place I will show you"); between Abraham's giving up his family of origin in 12:1 and his family of the future in 22:2; between his silent and immediate execution of the command in both cases; and between the emphasis in 22 on God's "seeing" to the sacrifice (Gen. 22:8, 14) and similar emphases on God's "seeing" throughout other,

38. Cf. Levin, *Der Jahwist*, 174–75, who isolates Gen. 21:22 from this series that he otherwise describes so well. Rather than seeing this as an outgrowth of the same compositional layer seen in Gen. 12:1–3, he assigns this text to a series of Elohistic additions to the Abraham narrative.
39. Van Seters, *Abraham*, 171; Westermann, *Genesis 12—36*, 391–92; (E.T., 320–21). Westermann has citations and arguments against earlier treatments of this gap.
40. Van Seters, *Abraham*, 171–72. To be sure, there are some differences. First, Abraham uses the divine designation "Elohim" at this point, yet this does not affect the intelligibility of the interreference. After all, the audience would not expect Abimelek to know YHWH, and so Abraham's reference at this point to a more generic God is natural. Second, Abraham's report of his request in Gen. 20:13 is slightly different from the narrator's description of this request in Gen. 12:11–13. Nevertheless, at least some of these differences can be explained as reflexes of a presentation of Abraham adjusting his story to fit the circumstances. Merely reporting his request to Sarah in Egypt would not serve to explain his behavior in Gerar. Instead, the narrator has him report a new version of his request, one where he wants her to say that she is his sister in every place they enter.
For more discussion of links between Genesis 20 and 12:10–20, see Smend, *Erzählung*, 38–39; Volz, *Elohist*, 34–36; Westermann, *Genesis 12—36*, 399—400; (E.T., 326–27); Blum, *Vätergeschichte*, 406–7; and (for synchronic discussion of tensions and connections here) Miscall, *The Workings of Old Testament Narrative*, 14–15.

above-discussed, linking parts of the non-P composition (Gen. 6:5; 16:11–12, 13; 18:21; Exod. 3:7; cf. also 29:31–33).[41] These links of Genesis 22 to the broader non-P composition are especially significant because this chapter is so closely linked to the Ishmael story in Gen. 21:8–20, as well: both concern divine calls to Abraham to put a child in a life-threatening situation; in both cases he gets up early and preparing to execute the command (Gen. 21:14//22:3); and in both cases the child is delivered when "an angel of God/YHWH" "calls from heaven" and gives a command (Gen. 21:17; 22:11–12) and Hagar/Abraham "sees" a way out of the life-threatening dilemma (Gen. 21:19//22:13).[42] Genesis 21 serves as a prelude to Genesis 22, showing how Abraham was forced by God to expel the nonheir from his clan before being asked to sacrifice his heir as well, *but* then had that son returned to him.[43] These narrative connections confirm the picture already suggested by the above-discussed thematic connections between "Yahwistic" and "Elohistic" sections of the Abraham story: that Gen. 20:1–18; 21:8–20; and 22:1–14, 19 together all build on the compositional layer beginning in Gen. 12:1–8.

Finally, as many since Cassuto have previously observed, the "Yahwistic" and "Elohistic" portions of the Abraham story are structurally coordinated with each other:[44]

A Prologue: including genealogical material on Abraham and Nahor marriages (Gen. 11:28–30)

B Initial call to leave family of origin and promise (Gen. 12:1–3)

C First wife-sister story (Gen. 12:10–13:1)

D Initial split with Lot (Gen. 13:2–18)*

E Hagar-Ishmael proto-exodus story (Gen. 16:1–2, 4–14)

D' Split hospitality/progeny episodes, Lot vs. Abraham (Genesis 18—19*)

C' Second wife-sister story (Genesis 20)

41. Cassuto, *Genesis,* vol. 2, 296; Volz, *Elohist,* 46; Rendtorff, *Problem,* 50; (E.T., 66–67); Westermann, *Genesis 12—36,* 436–37; (E.T., 357); P. Trible, "Genesis 22: the Sacrifice of Sarah," in *Not In Heaven,* 172–73; and (on the motif of "seeing") Levin, *Der Jahwist,* 104–5, 147.
42. J. Magonet, "Die Söhne Abrahams," *Bibel und Leben* 14 (1973): 206–10; Blum, *Vätergeschichte,* 314; P. Trible, "Genesis 22," 187–88; Van Seters, *Abraham,* 238–39; and idem, *Prologue to History,* 265; S. E. McEvenue, "The Elohist at Work," *ZAW* 96 (1984): 317–18.
43. Blum, *Vätergeschichte,* 314.
44. Cassuto, *Genesis,* vol. 2, 294–96; Coats, *Genesis,* 28, 97–98; Kikiwada and Quinn, *Before Abraham Was,* 96; Rosenberg, "Is there a story of Abraham?" 73–98; Rendsburg, *The Redaction of Genesis,* 28–29; among others. Such proposals agree in placing the call of Abraham in 12:1–8 in correspondence with his (almost) sacrifice of Isaac in 22:1–19, the two wife-sister stories in correspondence with each other (12:10–20 and 20:1–18), and the story of Abraham's rescue of Lot in Genesis 14 in correspondence with the rescue of Lot on Abraham's account in Gen. 18:16–19:38. Their major divergence lies in whether Genesis 16 is considered the center of the Abraham story (Coats, Rosenberg), or Genesis 17 or a part of it is put at the heart of the pattern (Cassuto, Kikiwada, and Rendsburg).

B' Final test: call to leave family of future (Gen. 22:1–14, 19; cf. also leaving Ishmael in 21:8–20)

A' Epilogue: including genealogical material regarding Nahor's line (Gen. 22:20–24), the story of securing a wife for Isaac from that line (Gen. 24:1–67*), and a list of Abraham's additional children by yet another line (Gen. 25:1–4)

Thus, the above-discussed parallels and cross-references between the Genesis 20 wife-sister story and the preceding one (Gen. 20:13; cf. also 20:14), and between Genesis 22 and Gen. 12:1–3, occur in an overall context where large swathes of the second half of the Abraham story—whether "Yahwistic" (e.g., Gen. 18:1–19:28, 30–38 and 22:20–24; 24:1–67*) or "Elohistic" (e.g., Genesis 20; 21:1–2*, 6–7*; 22:1–14, 19)—are coordinated in a concentric structure with their counterparts in the first half.[45]

The weakness of the case for separate Elohistic and Yahwistic sources is highlighted by the intricate links of Genesis 26, a purportedly "Yahwistic" text, to the *entire* Abraham story, "Yahwistic" and "Elohistic" traditions alike. The main similarities are listed below.

1. An introduction to the Isaac narrative (Gen. 26:1) links the famine Isaac experienced at the outset of his adult life with the famine Abraham experienced at the outset of his (Gen. 12:10).
2. A divine travel command and promise to Isaac (Gen. 26:2–3bα) links in multiple and specific ways with the above-discussed parallels in the Abraham and Jacob stories (J: Gen. 12:1–3; 31:3; E: Gen. 22:2; 31:13; 46:3–4).[46]
3. Just as Abraham's travel command and compliance was followed by a wife-sister story, so is Isaac's (26:6–11). Moreover, this wife-sister story presupposes and builds on both Gen. 12:10–13:1 and 20:1–18 (J: Gen. 12:10–13:1; E: Gen. 20:1–18).[47]
4. The story of blessing for Isaac (Gen. 26:12–14) shows the transferral of the blessing originally promised to Abraham in Gen. 12:2–3 and given to him in Gen. 12:16 ("J") and 20:14 ("E").

---

45. Cf. McEvenue, "The Elohist at Work," 329–30, who notes that the Elohistic material of Genesis 20—22 "complements" the preceding Yahwistic material, but nevertheless maintains separate authorship on the basis of various stylistic parallels between the three main stories in 20—22. Certainly there are differences here, but whether they link 20—22 over against the non-P material in 12—19 as a block remains to be seen. McEvenue is much stronger in arguing for his conclusion that there is a singularity of authorship in 20—22, than in establishing disunity of authorship with 12—19. Many of the differences he notes are the products of (1) his particular exegesis of the significance of 20—22 and (2) the differing traditions that lie behind the entire non-P account of Abraham.

46. The parallels in travel notices have already been discussed above. On the links between 22:2 and 26:2, see Rendtorff, *Problem*, 50; (E.T., 66–67).

47. Van Seters, *Abraham*, 177–81.

5. Abimelek's recognition of this blessing (Gen. 26:28) resembles his earlier recognition of such blessing with Abraham (Gen. 21:22; "E"). In addition, it anticipates the above-discussed blessing recognition by other
   foreigners: Laban, Potiphar, Joseph's jailer and pharaoh.
6. The note regarding Abraham's digging wells (Gen. 26:15) creates room
   in the Isaac narrative for the story of Isaac's digging and naming the well
   at Beer-Sheba (Gen. 26:26–33) after the "Elohistic" story of Abraham's
   doing the same (Gen. 21:25–33).[48]

Previous source-oriented studies have tended to take the bulk of Genesis 26
as "Yahwistic" and then assigned some connections with E texts to the Rje
redactor. There are not, however, any clear grounds for distinguishing the
"Yahwistic" linkages, on the one hand, from the "Elohistic," on the other.
Instead, the non-P "Yahwistic" Isaac narrative in Gen. 26:1–33* *as a whole*
seems to have been formed in correspondence with the Abraham narrative *as
a whole*, "Yahwistic" and "Elohistic" elements included. This correspondence
then helps Genesis present Isaac as a figure who is in many ways like Abraham and specifically able to pass Abraham's blessing to Jacob. Later, in Genesis 27, Isaac will bless Jacob. By describing Isaac in terms quite parallel to
Abraham, Gen. 26:1–33 indicates that Isaac's blessing of Jacob in Genesis 27
is actually a transferal of Abraham's blessing to Jacob.

The thematic, narrative and structural connections between "Yahwistic"
and "Elohistic" sections of the Abraham story and the reflection of the entire
Abraham story in the supposedly "Yahwistic" Genesis 26 suggest that the
bulk of the non-P Abraham story is one written fabric, although almost certainly formed of disparate traditions. Its mix of complexity and overall design
resemble the artistry of a quilt formed out of patches of various kinds of cloth.
The patches give a quilt its complex quality. At the same time they have been
cut and coordinated into an overall design that brings them together in a single whole. So also, the non-P Abraham story appears to have been created
out of various tradition patches, all of which have been integrally linked in a
concentric whole centered on the themes introduced at the outset in Gen.
11:28–30; 12:1–4a, 6–8. Traditional source analyses have recognized this but
have argued that we have essentially two different groups of patches, as if the
Abraham quilt were formed of two earlier quilts, say a "Yahwistic" wedding
ring quilt and an Elohistic heart quilt.

Any evaluation of the significance of divine designation, "God" versus
"YHWH," in the non-P Abraham story must be seen in the context of the
above survey of how "Yahwistic" and "Elohistic" portions of the Abraham
story are integrally connected with each other. Yes, it is true that certain of

---

48. Wellhausen, *Composition*, 21; Gunkel, *Genesis*, 302; Blum, *Vätergeschichte*, 301–2. (The last
responds to the different treatment by Rendtorff, *Problem*, 32–34; [E.T., 47].)

these Abraham traditions appear to favor a given divine designation, whether YHWH or Elohim, much as there are predominantly "Yahwistic" or "Elohistic" versions of various psalms in the Psalter (Pss. 53//14; 70//40:13–17 [Hebrew 40:14–18]; 108//57:7–11 [Hebrew 57:8–12]; 60:5–12 [Hebrew 60:7–14]).[49] Yes, it is true that these predominantly Yahwistic and Elohistic traditions regarding Abraham are roughly grouped together (Genesis 12—19* and 24*, versus 20—22) and even sometimes parallel each other (e.g., Genesis 20//12:10–13:1; Gen. 21:8–20//16:1–2, 4–14). Nevertheless, the present forms of these stories presuppose each other, even as there are indicators of separate origins not just for "Yahwistic" and "Elohistic" traditions, but also among Yahwistic traditions themselves and among Elohistic traditions themselves. For example, source critics have often pointed to the parallels between the "Yahwistic" Hagar story in Gen. 16:1–2, 4–14 and the "Elohistic" version in Gen. 21:8–20.[50] Nevertheless, this Yahwistic Hagar story in Gen. 16:1–2, 4–14 also appears to have been originally separate from its context in the "Yahwistic" Lot-Abraham complex of Genesis 13, 18—19, and the "Elohistic" Hagar-Ishmael story (Gen. 21:8–20) appears to have been inserted into an Elohistic story of Abraham in Gerar that moved from the wife-sister story featuring Abimelek in Genesis 20 to the subsequent treaty between Abraham and Abimelek in Gen. 21:22–34. All of these traditions—the "Yahwistic" Abraham-Lot cycle, the "Elohistic" story of Abraham in Gerar, and the "Yahwistic" and "Elohistic" Hagar traditions—appear to have originated separate of one another. Moreover, all these traditions are so carefully linked to one another in the non-P material that it is impossible to reconstruct a form of "Elohistic" Genesis 20—22 that did not build on the "Yahwistic" Genesis 12—19*.

In light of this, we would need strong data, data we do not have, to argue that the "Yahwistic" traditions were linked in one composition and the Elohistic traditions linked in another composition before both groups of traditions were then radically adapted to form our present non-P Abraham composition. Perhaps these "Yahwistic" and "Elohistic" traditions circulated orally in different tradition circles and thus came to the author of the non-P Abraham story in two groups of some sort. Alternatively, this author himself may have seen some wisdom in sorting out the traditions into an overall "Yahwistic" beginning and "Elohistic" conclusion. In neither case, however, is there sufficient evidence to suggest any separate, parallel "Yahwistic" and "Elohistic" Abraham stories were written prior to the non-P Abraham story. Lacking the kind of evidence used to establish parallel P and non-P sources

49. G. Fohrer, *Einleitung*, 318–19 (E.T., 293–94).
50. See especially H. Seebass, "Que reste-t-il du yahwiste et de l'élohiste?" in *Le Pentateque en Question*, 199–214. The other classic parallel was the wife-sister stories. Cf. in particular Noth, *Pentateuch*, 21–23 (E.T., 22–24).

in Genesis, the application of that source model to the non-P Abraham material adds a hypothesis for which there is no need. Yes, we have largely unreconstructable separate traditions standing behind the Abraham story. Yes, we have a whole formed out of those traditions. The data in the Abraham story does not require one to posit an additional source stage here. Ockham's razor eliminates it.

In conclusion, there is no good evidence for a special distinction between "Yahwistic" traditions *as a whole*, on the one hand, and "Elohistic" traditions *as a whole*, on the other. Instead, the non-P Abraham story appears to be woven out of a variety of disparate traditions, Yahwistic and Elohistic alike, and predominance of divine designation is only one potential criterion helping us to distinguish these traditions from one another.[51] The delimited plots and shifting casts of characters help one identify the faint outlines of a number of these largely unreconstructable oral and/or written precursors: an Abraham-Lot cycle behind Genesis 13 and 18—19, a wife-sister story behind Gen. 12:10–13:1, a pair of Hagar traditions behind Gen. 16:1–14* and 21:8–20, and an Abraham-in-Gerar tradition behind Gen. 20:1–18; 21:22–34 parallel to the traditions regarding Isaac in Gerar (cf. Genesis 26).[52] Nevertheless, these traditions have been so thoroughly integrated into the broader sweep of the non-P composition that it is impossible to say anything much about their earlier shape. At least in the Abraham story, the compositional connections spanning these stories are often too dense to separate the traditions from the compositional context in which they now occur.[53]

---

51. As Blum and others have pointed out, divine designation is already a quite slippery criterion because the divine designations YHWH and Elohim are not equivalent (Blum, *Vätergeschichte*, 471–77, with an overview of earlier literature). Instead, each is used in certain contexts. At the same time, in certain contexts such as the flood story, variation in divine designation appears to correspond to distinctions between various layers of material. This means that such variation may be a criterion, but also that each divine designation must be considered in context and in coordination with other indicators of profile and breaks.

52. Van Seters (*Abraham*, 184–87) argues persuasively for a distinction between an original core of tradition in Gen. 21:22–34 and a later layer in that text that has affinities with 26:26–32. Others have argued that many of the above-discussed supplements were actually the original continuation of the wife-sister story in Genesis 20, moving from the initiation of the covenant in 21:22–24, to the gift of livestock and covenant in 21:27, to a conclusion in 21:31 or 34 (Gunkel, *Genesis*, 233; cf. Blum, *Vätergeschichte*, 411–12). Nevertheless, the gift of livestock is hardly a "covenant." This association only entered the story when the author of the non-P material modified an early "well of seven" gift story in Gen. 21:22–34* into a "covenant" similar to that with Jacob through the addition of texts like Gen. 21:22–24, 27, and 31b–33. Moreover, Van Seters's model of the secondary assimilation of parallel narratives is the most plausible explanation for the agreement of (1) doubled material in Gen. 21:22–34 (Gen. 21:22–24//25; 21:27a//28–30; 21:27b, 31b–32a//21:30–31a) with (2) elements of the broader non-P composition, particularly 26:26–33 (Gen. 21:22–24//26:28–29; 21:27a//12:16 and other such riches lists; 21:27b, 31b-32a//26:28, 30, 33).

53. The weaknesses of Levin's detailed attempt to do just this demonstrate the difficulty of the task. Cf. his *Der Jahwist*, passim. Although some of his arguments are plausible, he must often build on very slippery preconceptions about the probable early foci of narratives and their original continuity.

An Alternative to the Source Model
for the Formation of the Non-P Proto-Genesis

The question to be addressed at this point is what transmission-historical model can best account for the above-surveyed linkages spanning the non-P material. I have already suggested that a model of parallel sources is not warranted by the evidence, at least in the Abraham story. Nevertheless, at least two major options remain: (1) that not just the Abraham story but the entire non-P composition was created by one author (or group of authors) out of various largely unreconstructable precursor traditions, or (2) that the author of the non-P composition worked from larger precursor compositions, in addition to gathering and reformulating traditions concerning figures like Abraham. Taking up the quilt image introduced earlier: the question is whether the broader non-P composition is one quilt created out of various patches, or whether there might have been an earlier primeval history quilt and/or a Jacob-Joseph quilt (each with its own prehistory) that the author of the non-P composition used in the process of making the broader non-P proto-Genesis quilt.

Here I will make the case for a version of the latter option: that the author of the above-surveyed non-P composition (1) built on and modified earlier primeval history and Jacob-Joseph compositions and (2) linked them with sections regarding Abraham (Genesis 12—25*) and Isaac (Genesis 26*) that were woven out of earlier traditions concerning both figures. This argument has two parts. In the first, I maintain that the author of the Abraham and Isaac sections was responsible for many of the broader non-P connections surveyed above. This portion of the argument will be brief because it has been prepared for by the above discussion of these connections. The second portion is longer. In it I argue that this author was *not* responsible for the bulk of the primeval history and Jacob-Joseph sections. Instead, he built around these units and/or modified them so they fit a broader scheme most evident in the Abraham story.

The Author of the Non-P Abraham Story = the Author of the Broader Non-P Connections

The above survey has already been structured to show how the author of the Abraham story and the author of the broader non-P story are one and the same. In it I indicated how one text absolutely essential to the Abraham story, Gen. 11:28–30; 12:1–8*, is also absolutely central in the web of connections spanning the non-P material. This text introduces the problem of descendants that dominates much of the Abraham story, the promises of protection and blessing that are partially realized in it (e.g., Gen. 12:10–13:1; 19:1–28), and the two genealogical lines—Abraham's and Nahor's (Gen. 11:29)—that are featured in the final search for a proper wife for Isaac (Genesis 24*). This is not just a question of secondary links of the Abraham stories to the broader themes of the non-P composition. Instead, the very substance of the Abraham stories is so infused with the promise and other foci of Gen. 11:28–30; 12:1–4a, 6–8 that we can not reliably isolate any form of the Abraham story that preexisted these themes. Consider the major units of the non-P Abraham story (aside from later revisions): the protection and blessing of Abraham during his sojourn in Egypt (Gen. 12:10–13:1); his split with Lot and confirmation of promise (Gen. 13:2–18*); the echoes of the promise in the story of a member of Abraham's household, Hagar (Gen. 16:1–2, 4–14); the paired hospitality scenes for Abraham and Lot (Gen. 18:1–15; cf. Gen. 19:1–38*); the description of God's protection of the designated matriarch (Genesis 20); and the outlining of the later destinies of the heir and nonheirs of the promise (Gen. 21:1–25:6*). All these stories, particularly linked as they now are into a continuous narrative sequence, specifically develop themes of travel, promise, and transmission of the promise that were first introduced in Gen. 11:28–30; 12:1–8*. Moreover, all of Gen. 11:28–30; 12:1–8 is so saturated with these themes that it is impossible to isolate any form of it that might have preexisted the broader Abraham composition.[54] From the implicit placement of Abraham with his family in the "land of [his] kindred" in Gen. 11:28 to the final "calling on YHWH's name" (Gen. 12:8), the clustering of connecting themes in Gen. 11:28–30; 12:1–4a, 6–8 is intense. These integral links of all the non-P material in Gen. 11:28–30; 12:1–8* to such substantial elements of each pericope in (non-P) Gen. 12:10–25:6 lead to the following conclusion: the author of Gen. 11:28–30; 12:1–8* put together the Abraham story in its present form.

The Author of the Non-P Connections ≠ the Author of the Jacob-Joseph and Primeval History Materials

As we have seen, the themes introduced in Gen. 11:28–30; 12:1–8 are not confined to the boundaries of the Abraham story. Instead, they continue into the Jacob and Joseph materials while linking as well to certain stories in the primeval history. There is, however, an important difference. The Abraham traditions appear to have been so thoroughly organized around the themes of Gen. 11:28–30; 12:1–8 that any earlier, non-promise-centered form of the Abraham story is indiscernible. In contrast, both the Jacob-Joseph story and the primeval history appear to have been organized around other emphases. Moreover, especially in the Jacob-Joseph story, the themes of Gen. 11:28–30; 12:1–8 appear to have been secondarily added to their contexts. In the next

---

54. Some, such as Kilian (*Vorpriesterlichen Abrahamüberlieferungen*, 1–15) and Van Seters (*Abraham*, 223), have argued that the promises in Gen. 12:2–3 and/or 7 have been secondarily inserted into an Abraham story originally beginning with just his itinerary to Canaan. Nevertheless, a closer look at non-P material in Genesis indicates that this passage *as a whole* is a crucial binding element in the overall non-P compositional system. For other arguments for the unity of this section see Köckert, *Vätergott*, 255–62, and Levin, *Der Jahwist*, 136–37.

chapter I will survey the apparent themes and major emphases of the primeval history and Jacob-Joseph stories. For now, I will concentrate on the main texts in the broader non-P Genesis narrative where the themes of Gen. 11:28–30; 12:1–8 are developed, starting with the clearer case of the Jacob-Joseph story.

Genesis 26:1–33

The Isaac story of Genesis 26* serves in the broader non-P composition to link the story of Jacob's stealing Isaac's blessing (Gen. 27:1–40) with the Abrahamic blessing first given in Gen. 12:2–3. The close links of Genesis 26 with Gen. 12:1–3 and the Abraham story as a whole have already been explored in depth. What is significant for our purposes here is that this story interrupts the movement from Jacob's initially buying the birthright (Gen. 25:27–34) to his stealing the blessing (Genesis 27). Moreover, the focus of this chapter on Isaac's blessedness apart from any offspring or conflict between them distinguishes it from its context. The children just born in Gen. 25:21–26 are absent. Such indicators have long led scholars to recognize a shift in the tradition behind Genesis 26. My point here is that these indicators of divergent origins for Genesis 26 converge with the above-discussed links of Genesis 26 to the Abraham story. Together, they suggest that the Jacob story was modified through the introduction of the Isaac traditions in Gen. 26:1–33. This chapter was composed through the modification of earlier Isaac traditions *from the promise-centered perspective* first seen in Gen. 11:28–30; 12:1–4a, 6–8 and the rest of the Abraham story. By thus presenting Isaac in promise-centered terms that recall Abraham, Isaac's blessing of Jacob in Gen. 27:27–29 becomes an unwitting transmission of the Abrahamic promise. Although Isaac did not mean to bless Jacob, YHWH "blesses the one [Isaac] has blessed" (cf. Gen. 12:3a).

Genesis 28:13–16*

The subsequent divine confirmation of the gift of the promise to Jacob after his split from Esau (Gen. 28:13–15) has already been mentioned above as a parallel to YHWH's confirmation of the promise to Abraham after his split from Lot (Gen. 13:14–17). The relevant point here is that this promise similar to the one made to Abraham appears to be a secondary insertion into a carefully constructed cult etiology. As a result of the insertion, the appearance of YHWH in Gen. 28:13–15 now competes with an earlier theme in which Bethel was distinguished as the locus of a stairway *for angels of God* (Gen. 28:12; cf. also Gen. 28:17).

In addition, the author of some subsequent texts in the Jacob narrative does not appear to know of the promise material in Gen. 28:13–15. The later reference to Bethel in Jacob's speech to Rachel and Leah (Gen. 31:13) mentions only Jacob's oath there (Gen. 28:20–22) and demonstrates no knowledge of the divine appearance and promise to him there.[55] Later in the Jacob narrative, God (*'ĕlohîm*) tells Jacob to make an altar to the God (*'ēl*) who appeared to him there (Gen. 35:1), and Jacob tells his family of his intent to build an altar to the God (*'ēl*) who appeared to him there and "answered" him in the day of his trouble (Gen. 35:3). Although this pair of texts can now be read in relation to Gen. 28:13–15, they do not necessarily presuppose it. Genesis 28:13–15 emphatically identified the god who was speaking as YHWH, and the promises given there were not an "answer" to a request by Jacob. Instead, they precede his oath (Gen. 28:13–15 . . . 20–22). In contrast, Gen. 35:1 and 3 stress two things: (1) the link of the divine messengers Jacob saw (cf. Gen. 28:12) with the singular God (*'ēl*) found in the place name Bethel[56] and (2) the idea that this divinity after whom Jacob named Beth*el* (Gen. 28:17–19) has, in fact, protected Jacob as he had asked, thus "answering" his call in 28:20–22. We have a contrast here. On the one hand, we have a prepromise form of the Jacob narrative that features and refers to an appearance by divine beings/God ("Elohim"/"El") to him at Beth*el* (Gen. 31:13; 35:1; cf. Gen. 28:12, 17–19) and his oath there (Gen. 31:13; 35:3; Gen. 28:20–22). On the other hand, we have the apparent addition of a promise speech from YHWH (Gen. 28:13–15), a speech that introduces the themes so integral to the preceding Abraham and Isaac narratives.

Furthermore, the contrasts do not stop here. As many source critics have observed, Jacob's response to Gen. 28:12–15 also has two parts: (1) Gen. 28:16, an initial wake-up scene that mentions the very "YHWH" who made the promises in Gen. 28:13–15; and (2) Gen. 28:17, Jacob's exclamation over the "gods/God" and "gate of heaven" featured in Gen. 28:12. The

55. Blum, *Vätergeschichte*, 8, 118–19. Cf. Van Seters, *Prologue to History*, 295, who asserts that 31:13 refers to 28:10–22. Actually 31:13 refers exclusively to the "God" to whom Jacob made his oath. Van Seters argues on other grounds (*Prologue to History*, 293–94) that the oath in Gen. 28:20–22 *must* have had the promises before it: "to suppose that the author would include a vow just because Jacob had seen a vision of angels hardly seems credible" (294). Only in this way can he read the reference to the oath in Gen. 31:13 as a reference to the whole of Gen. 28:10–22. Van Seters does not, however, back up his claim that the oath must be preceded by the promise. On the contrary, Gunkel, *Genesis*, 316–17, argued that the oath trying to bind God into protecting Jacob (Gen. 28:20–22) stands in some tension with God's having already promised to do just that (Gen. 28:15). Certainly Jacob never refers to God's promise in Gen. 28:20–22 with an expression such as "as you have said." Now, contra Gunkel, it must be maintained that there are a variety of ways to make sense of the relationship between 28:13–15 and 28:20–22 (Volz, *Elohist*, 76–77; Blum, *Vätergeschichte*, 22). Therefore, it would be mistaken to put too much weight on Gunkel's argument. Nevertheless, it does point out the weaknesses of Van Seters' assertion that the idea of an oath without a preceding promise "hardly seems credible."

56. To be sure, there is still a tension here between an earlier tradition regarding the presence of divine beings at Bethel (Gen. 28:12, 17) and a broader context that identifies these beings with a single deity (Gen. 28:20–22; 31:13; 35:1, 3). As will be discussed in the next chapter, the layer of material seen in Gen. 28:20–22; 31:13; 35:1, 3 is probably distinct from the earlier Bethel tradition that has been adapted (Gen. 28:10–12, 17–19*).

doubling of Jacob's surprised response in Gen. 28:16 (cf. 28:17) and the link of 28:16 to the secondary promise material in Gen. 28:13–15 (cf. 28:12) suggest that both 28:13–15 and 28:16 were not originally part of the Bethel story in which they now appear.[57]

The problem comes in deciding how to interpret this data. Advocates of a documentary approach to the material took these data as indicators of two parallel documents. The "Elohist" had a Bethel story consisting solely of the vision of angels, complete with later references to this vision (Gen. 31:13 and 35:1, 3). The "Yahwist" had the promise in 28:13–15, one much resembling that in Gen. 12:2–3.[58] Nevertheless, there is no evidence for such a complete,

---

57. Cf. Blum, *Vätergeschichte*, 11, 14. He argues energetically that 28:16 as well as the beginning of 28:13 were parts of the prepromise form of the Bethel epiphany. Nevertheless there are several reasons to suppose that whatever links are here, are the result of careful redaction rather than organic connection. First, the main arguments for the secondary character of Gen. 28:16 have already been given above. Note particularly the parallel surprised recognition by Jacob of the presence of divinity at Bethel in 28:16 and 17 (see G. Fleischer, "Jakob träumt. Eine Auseinandersetzung mit Erhard Blums methodischem Ansatz am Beispiel von Gen. 28,10–22," *BN* 76 [1995]: 86–87). Second, as McEvenue argues, the force of Blum's artistic argument weakens at precisely the point where he tries to link Gen. 28:12–13aα into a chiasm with 28:16–17 ("A Return to Sources?" 378–81). Third, as Van Seters points out (*Prologue to History*, 291), Blum's proposal that the original vision extended only up to YHWH's standing on the stairway ends up with an unprecedented example of a God who appears and says nothing (so also L. Schmidt, in a paper, "El und die Landverheißung in Bet-El," which he kindly shared with me in prepublication form). In light of this, it is much easier to see a seam between the angels of Gen. 28:12 and YHWH in 28:13ff, than between YHWH in 28:13aα and YHWH's speech. Blum's observations on the ways 28:13aα and 16 fit into the concentric structure of Gen. 28:10–19 confirm the artfulness of the author who developed this expansion of the Bethel story. Nevertheless, they are not decisive reasons for assigning these texts to the earlier Bethel epiphany.

Be that as it may, in so far as McEvenue's critique of Blum's identification of layers in this text purports to be a critique of Blum's overall theory (and along with it Rendtorff's), it represents a serious misconstrual of the role of this analysis of Gen. 28:10–22 in Blum's work as a whole. McEvenue is right that Blum's analysis of Gen. 28:10–22 receives disproportionate emphasis in his study and is problematic in some important respects. Nevertheless, McEvenue's claim to have put in question Blum's two large volumes of work on the entire Pentateuch by picking at Blum's analysis of one thirteen-verse text is absurd. As McEvenue himself notes (388n25), Blum's specific divisions are not essential to his following analysis. What is far more important for broader scholarship is (1) Blum's replacement of the new documentary hypothesis E with prepromise Jacob and Joseph narratives and (2) his isolation of the core of Gen. 28:13–15 (along with other texts) as part of a broader promise-centered compositional layer that focused on Abraham. McEvenue misses this fact and misconstrues Blum's analysis of Gen. 28:10–22 as the key to everything else Blum does.

Fleischer's analysis is more focused on methodology and so theoretically might have broader implications for Blum's theory. Nevertheless, a closer look reveals that his points do not touch Blum's broader argument. Fleischer criticizes Blum's arguments for division of 28:13–15 into two levels (85), a theory inessential to Blum's overall approach and given up by Blum himself (*Studien*, 214n35). Most of the rest of Fleischer's critique relates to Blum's assigning the beginning of Gen. 28:13 and all of 28:16 to his early Bethel story (85–90), neither of which are decisive for Blum's further analysis. Again, just picking at the first chapter of Blum's first book is not enough to refute his basic model for the non-P material.

58. For overviews, see A. de Pury, *Promesse divine et légende cultuelle dans le cycle de Jacob: Genèse 28 et les traditions patriarcales* (EB; Paris: J. Gabalda et Cie, 1975), 32–35, and K. Berge, *Die Zeit des Jahwisten. Ein Beitrag zur Datierung jahwistischer Vätertexte* (BZAW 186; Berlin/New York: W. de Gruyter, 1990), 147–50.

parallel "Yahwistic" Bethel story in Gen. 28:10–22. Genesis 28:13–15 and part or all of Gen. 28:16 do appear to have been inserted as promise-centered redirections of an earlier story in Gen. 28:10–12, 17–22.[59] Yet attempts to isolate a Yahwistic introduction or conclusion to this story are forced.[60] Moreover, far from being a fragment of an independent narrative, 28:13–16 is linked in multiple ways with its existing context: (1) at the outset, by having YHWH stand over Jacob to give the promise (Gen. 28:13aα); (2) in the middle, by having the promise include the theme of protection so central throughout the broader Jacob narrative (Gen. 28:20–22; 31:25–33:20); and (3) at the end, by having Jacob pick up terminology from the introduction of the narrative ("this place" in Gen. 28:16//"the place" in 28:11 [twice] and "that place" in 28:11).[61] The promise-focused material in 28:13–16 appears to be an insertion composed in light of the context into which it has been inserted.

The Fulfillment of the Abrahamic Promise in Jacob's and Joseph's Lives

Not only are the texts transferring the Abraham promise to Jacob secondary, but so are *some* of the more specific descriptions of the fulfillment of this promise in Jacob's and Joseph's lives. For example, the proto-Genesis author would not have needed to add an emphasis on blessing to the Jacob

---

59. See Schmid, *Der sogenannte Jahwist,* 120; H. C. Schmitt, *Die nichtpriesterliche Josephs-geschichte: Ein Beitrag zur neuesten Pentateuchkritik* (BZAW 154; Berlin/New York: de Gruyter, 1980), 104–7. The initial awakening notice at the outset of Gen. 28:16 may have preexisted the insertion of Gen. 28:13–15 and the rest of 28:16. The textual data does not allow a decision either way.

60. Procksch, *Genesis,* 171; Noth, *Pentateuch* 30; (E.T., 29); de Pury, *Promesse divine,* 36, 349; and Berge, *Zeit des Jahwisten,* 150–54, argue that Gen. 28:10–11aα was the introduction to a self-contained Yahwistic narrative featuring Gen. 28:13–16. According to them, the notice that Jacob spent the night (Gen. 28:11aα) could not have been followed in the original text by a description of him subsequently "lying down" (Gen. 28:11aβb). In response (to Berge), Van Seters (*Prologue,* 290) argues that Ruth 3:13 is an example of an initial command to "spend the night" followed by a specification of the command, "lie down until morning." In an unpublished paper, "El und die Landverheißung in Bet-El" (n.11), L. Schmidt counters that the command to lie down in Ruth 3:13b is actually a resumptive repetition of the initial command to spend the night after Boaz's description of what might happen the next day (Ruth 3:13a). The fact that "lie down" in Ruth 3:13b could resume "spend the night" at the outset of the verse proves to Schmidt that these two expressions are doublets of one another in 28:11. Be that as it may, the ending of Berge and Schmidt's Elohistic narrative, Gen. 28:17–18, relates both to the "place" featured in Gen. 28:11aα and the "stone" in 28:11aβ. Whatever resumption is present in Gen. 28:11aα ("he spent the night") and 11b ("he lay down there") serves a similar function to that in Ruth 3:13, resuming the narrative thread after the narrator's own brief digression to introduce a crucial element, in this case a stone (Gen. 28:11aβ).

The assignment of Gen. 28:19a to J has always been based on the weakest of grounds, as Blum, *Vätergeschichte,* 23n62, shows. Berge (*Zeit des Jahwisten,* 160–61) excludes this verse from his self-contained Yahwistic narrative.

61. Blum, *Vätergeschichte,* 9–17; Boecker, *1. Moses 25.19–37.1,* 57.

tradition he used. The prepromise Jacob story began with a focus on the father's blessing, continued with a focus on Jacob's blessing of children and flocks during his sojourn in Haran, and mentioned blessing yet again in the story of his wrestling with God at the Jabbok (Gen. 32:27, 30; Eng. 32:26, 29). Within this context, the account of Laban's recognition of Jacob's overflowing blessing (Gen. 30:27–30) need not be an addition by the proto-Genesis author but could just as well be yet another element of the Jacob story that the proto-Genesis author presupposed and on which he even modeled other texts.[62]

In contrast, the core of the Joseph story is not so clearly focused on blessing. Instead, the blessing-focused texts within it are often marked as secondary by indicators of seams. I start with two sets of texts at the outset of the Joseph story, Gen. 39:2–3, 5–6aα and 39:21–23, which are distinguished from their context as the only places in the Joseph story outside of Gen. 46:1–4 (cf. 12:1–3, etc.) where God intervenes directly. In the case of Genesis 39, an early narrative focusing more exclusively on the favor Joseph found in Potiphar's house (Gen. 39:1, 4, 6aβb), has been supplemented by theologically oriented interpretive material that: (1) asserts that God was with Joseph (Gen. 39:2), (2) bases Potiphar's transfer of authority to Joseph on this blessing (Gen. 39:3), and (3) describes God's blessing of Potiphar on account of Joseph (Gen. 39:5–6aα). Indeed, the secondary character of Gen. 39:5–6aα is marked not only by its explicitly theological profile but also by an indicator of a seam, the resumptive repetition of the description of Potiphar's delegation of all to Joseph (4bβ//6aα).[63] Similarly, Gen. 39:21–23 is not only marked by its distinctively theological profile but also by a slight clash between its picture of Joseph's rise to prominence and the later depiction of him in Genesis 40 as a prison slave.[64] This description of Joseph's enjoyment of divine favor culminates in yet another text marked as secondary to its con-

62. Cf. Z. Weisman, "The Interrelationship between J and E in Jacob's Narrative," ZAW 104 (1992): 183–84, and Levin, Der Jahwist, 40–41, 232–33. The latter identifies 30:27, 29–30 as secondary to the surrounding narrative primarily on the basis of the double speech introduction in 30:27//28 and resumptive repetition of Laban's request for Jacob's wage in 30:28//31. Yet the doubled speech introduction could just be functioning to mark the structural division between Laban's specification of the background of his request (Gen. 30:27) and his request for Jacob to specify his wages (Gen. 30:28). Furthermore, as Gunkel points out (Genesis, 326), the doubled request for Jacob's wage in 30:28, 31, could be understood as a representation of standard bargaining banter. Laban keeps asking Jacob to name his price. I am indebted to a personal communication from E. Blum for the reflections in this note and text above.
63. Wellhausen, Composition, 54; Levin, Der Jahwist, 36–40, 274–76; cf. Holzinger, Genesis, 231; N. Kebekus, Die Joseferzählung: Literarkritische und redaktionsgeschichtliche Untersuchungen zu Genesis 37—50 (Internationale Hochschulschriften; Münster/New York: Waxmann, 1989), 35. Kebekus and Levin also assign 39:4a to this compositional layer, but their arguments are too dependent on the use of the common expression "find favor" in this half-verse. It is possible that 39:4a was part of the insertion, but this is not as clear as in the case of the other materials here.
64. Levin, Der Jahwist, 36–40, 274–76, building on classic source analyses.

text, Gen. 41:39–40. Just as in the cases of Gen. 39:2–3, 5, and 21–23, Joseph is placed in authority over everything belonging to his master, once again this placement is justified by God's being with him, and once again the text is marked as secondary, doubling the speech introduction (complete with both speaker and addressee) and content of a preceding speech (Gen. 41:38), as well as a later report of pharaoh's transfer of power to Joseph (Gen. 41:44).[65] In all three of these cases we see the hand of an author binding Joseph's success to God, more specifically binding Joseph's rise to the Abrahamic blessing, which is established as a theme already in Gen. 12:1–8*.

The author of the broader non-P narrative appears to have intervened in a similar way toward the end of the Joseph narrative in Genesis 48. First, Jacob's blessing of Joseph in 48:15–16 has long been recognized as secondary, interrupting a context moving from the reversal of Jacob's hands in 48:14 to Joseph's reaction to this reversal in 48:17.[66] Furthermore, this secondary addition is integrally linked to the broader promise theme of Genesis. Indeed, the addition explicitly extends the entire sequence of promises that began with Abraham: "May the God before whom my fathers Abraham and Isaac walked . . . bless the boys . . . and let my name and the name of my fathers, Abraham and Isaac, be perpetuated through them, and let them grow numerous in the midst of the land" (Gen. 48:15–16). Once again, we have the apparent modification of an earlier, prepromise text (Gen. 48:1–2, 8–14, 17ff.) by the insertion of material linked with the promise-focused themes of Gen. 11:28–30; 12:1–8 and the rest of the Abraham narrative (Gen. 48:15–16).

So also the final promise and gift to Joseph in 48:21–2 appears to be secondary and is linked to the promise themes of the Abraham and Isaac narratives. This speech appears to be appended to what precedes. Whereas the rest of the chapter has Jacob exclusively addressing Joseph and his sons, Gen. 48:21–22 shifts to second person plural language and focuses now on the return of all of the Israelites to the land of their fathers.[67] The rest of the chapter is focused on the relative priority of Manasseh and Ephraim, and it concludes with the climactic reversal of their birth order in Gen. 48:17–20a, and the comment, "And he set Ephraim before Manasseh" (Gen. 48:20b). The speech in Gen. 48:21–22 does not link specifically with these themes and comes after this climax in the chapter.[68] Genesis 48:21–22, however, does have an important function vis-à-vis the broader, promise-centered Genesis

---

65. Gunkel, *Genesis,* 433, Holzinger, *Genesis,* 234; Von Rad, *Genesis,* 372; Kebekus, *Joseferzählung,* 69–70; cf. Westermann, *Genesis 37–50,* 97 (E.T., 94).
66. Noth, *Pentateuch,* 38 (including n.136; E.T., 36); Kessler, "Querverweise," 170; H. Donner, *Die literarische Gestalt der alttestamentlichen Josephsgeschichte* (Heidelberg: Carl Winter Universitätsverlag, 1976), 32–34; Rudolph, *Elohist,* 171–72; Westermann, *Genesis 37—50,* 212; (E.T., 188–89); Blum, *Vätergeschichte,* 253; Kebekus, *Joseferzählung,* 200–1.
67. Blum, *Vätergeschichte,* 257, points out that this is the only place in the chapter where Jacob speaks in the second person plural of the Israelites and their return. In the rest of the chapter he speaks exclusively to Joseph, and he speaks only about him and his sons.
68. Gunkel, *Genesis,* 474; Kessler, "Querverweise," 171–72.

narrative. With the addition of this blessing, Jacob now looks to his grandchildren for the fulfillment of God's promise to bring him out of Egypt
(48:21; cf. 46:3) and gives them a specific portion of the land promised to
Abraham (Gen. 48:22; cf. 12:7; etc.).[69] In this way, 48:15–16 and 21–22
bind Joseph, a major figure throughout Genesis 37—47, into the promise
themes introduced at the outset of the ancestral section.

The Case of the Travel Commands

I have already discussed how the travel command and promise in Gen.
12:1–3 is an integral part of the introductory section in the Abraham story.
In addition, the travel command and promise for Isaac in Gen. 26:2–3bα is
part of the same compositional layer. As we look at the remaining three travel
commands, Gen. 31:3, 13, and 46:3–4, we see that two of these travel commands, Gen. 31:3 and 46:3–4, appear to be secondary additions to their
contexts. In contrast, Gen. 31:13 appears to have preceded the promise-
centered network of which it is now a part. First, however, let us look at Gen.
31:3 and 46:3–4.

As we have seen, the travel command and promise to Jacob in Gen. 46:3–4
is integrally linked to a broader system of such commands and promises beginning in Gen. 12:1. What is important for our purposes now is that God's
command for Jacob to go to Egypt in 46:3 comes after Jacob has already decided to go there in 45:28. Moreover, we have clash in profile coinciding with
this ripple in the explanation of Jacob's trip. On the one hand, we have the
broader Joseph narrative in which, aside from the above-discussed texts,
there are no divine encounters and only human perceptions and decisions like
that seen in Gen. 45:28. On the other hand, in 46:2–4 we have a limited text
describing God's retrospective sanction of Jacob's decision, a sanction that
sets the command given to Jacob parallel to the travel command given to
Abraham (Gen. 12:1–3), and both, then, stand over against the command
given to Isaac (Gen. 26:2–3bα). Many elements—the initial divine encounter
(46:2; cf. Gen. 22:1, 7; 31:11; Exod. 3:4), the mention of Isaac, and the emphasis on promise—distinguish 46:2–4 from the broader Joseph story that
lacks these elements.[70] Moreover, all of these elements link 46:2–4 in turn

---

69. The tradition of Jacob conquering Shechem with the sword in 48:22 is probably an older
element appropriated by the author responsible for these connections, much as this same author
used older Abraham and Isaac traditions to compose the Abraham and Genesis 26 Isaac sections.
As in those cases, the older tradition in 48:22 is taken up into a broader promise focus, this time
by Jacob's initial speech in 48:21. Gunkel, *Genesis*, 474–75; De Vaux, *Histoire*, 584–85; (E.T.,
637–38); Von Rad, *Genesis*, 414.
70. Rudolph, *Elohist*, 149, 165; H. Eising, *Formgeschichtliche Untersuchung zur Jakobserzählung der Genesis* (Emsdetten, 1940), 336; Jepsen, "Vätergestalten," 141, n2; Von Rad, *Genesis*,
396–97; Redford, *Joseph*, 19; Donner, *Josephsgeschichte*, 29; Willi-Plein, "Josefsgeschichte,"
306–7; W. L. Humphreys, *Joseph and His Family: A Literary Study* (Studies on Personalities of
the Old Testament; Columbia, S.C.: Univ. of South Carolina, 1988), 196–97.

with the above-described broader system of compositional connections spanning the non-P material. Genesis 46:2–4 appears to be part of a broader layer of additions coordinating Jacob and Joseph with the promise focus introduced in the Abraham story.[71]

We see a similar pattern in Gen. 31:3. In this case, Jacob's decision to leave is already justified by his perception of the enmity of Laban and his sons toward him (Gen. 31:1–2). In response, Jacob speaks to Laban's daughters (Gen. 31:4–13) and secures agreement from this portion of Laban's family that he is in the right (Gen. 31:14–16). The direct narrative report of YHWH's command to leave in Gen. 31:3 interrupts the movement from 31:2 to 31:4 and adds a reliable narrator's report of the divine sanction for his decision.[72] This narrator's report diverges in significant ways from Jacob's own report of this command in Gen. 31:13. Not only is 31:3 worded differently, but it depicts him as receiving the command at a different time. Whereas in his speech to Leah and Rachel he implies that he heard the command while in the fields multiplying Laban's flocks (Gen. 31:12–13), 31:3 places his reception of the command long after this, when Laban and his sons realized what he has done.[73] To be sure, such divergences can serve various narrative functions in presenting Jacob as a character. Nevertheless, they probably signify more than that in this case. These divergences between 31:3 and 13 also correspond with the above-described, more broadly evident phenomenon in which texts that are part of the broader non-P system clash in various ways with their contexts in the Jacob-Joseph story. In this case, the direct narrative report of the divine command and the double emphasis on the idea that Canaan is Jacob's homeland link Gen. 31:3 into a broader system of such narrative reports of travel commands, starting with Gen. 12:1.

The travel command in Gen. 31:13, however, shows no signs of being secondary to its immediate context. Instead, this text appears to be an integral part of the broader rationale Jacob offers Rachel and Leah for leaving their kindred, Laban and his sons (Gen. 31:1–2, 13–16): "Now rise, leave this land and return to the land of your kindred" (Gen. 31:13b). This call to "leave this land" and "return to the land of your kindred" in turn links to a broader emphasis in the Jacob narrative on the separation of Rachel and Leah from their family. This begins with Jacob's perception of hostility from Laban (Gen. 31:1–2), continues with Jacob's focus on Laban's misdeeds (Gen. 31:4–8), and concludes with Rachel's and Leah's statement of dissolution from their family (Gen. 31:14–16), Rachel's stealing her father's household gods (Gen. 31:19), and the final treaty sealing, among other things, Jacob's

---

71. Blum, *Vätergeschichte*, 246–49, 297–301. These observations pertain exclusively to 46:2–4. Whether 46:1 is part of the same secondary layer is not clear on the basis of them.
72. Rendtorff, *Problem*, 58, (E.T., 75); Blum, *Vätergeschichte*, 121, 153–54; Levin, *Der Jahwist*, 237.
73. Blum, *Vätergeschichte*, 121, 152.

right to take the daughters and grandchildren with him (31:43ff.). Thus, Jacob's report of a divine command to return to his "land of kindred" in 31:13 has a particular reference *to the family dynamics of the immediately surrounding narrative.*[74]

As discussed above, the broader system of narrative travel commands in Gen. 12:1–3; 26:2–3bα; 31:3, and 46:2–4 closely resembles Jacob's report of such a command in Gen. 31:13. Nevertheless, these parallel commands feature a distinctive emphasis on the promise, an emphasis not found in Gen. 31:13. When Abraham is told in Gen. 12:1 to "go from [his] land, kindred and house of [his] father," he is leaving the land of kindred *for the land of promise* (Gen. 12:7; 13:15). Gen. 31:13, on the other hand, appears to presuppose a form of the Bethel epiphany that did not yet include the insertion of the land promise (Gen. 28:13–16*). Instead, it refers exclusively to Jacob's anointing the pillar and his vow at the end of that narrative: "I am the God who is at Bethel, where you anointed a pillar and to whom you made a vow there" (31:13a).[75] To be sure, this verse now plays an important role in the broader promise-centered composition by certifying that the land of promise has become the land of kindred. Nevertheless, its form and more immediate connections to its context suggest that it once served a different function in a prepromise form of the Jacob narrative.

I am suggesting a distinction between the original referents of 31:13 and its use in the broader proto-Genesis composition.[76] On the one hand, we have an apparent prepromise form of the travel command theme in Gen. 31:13, one integrally related to the clan dynamics of the surrounding Jacob narrative: Jacob's versus Laban's. This verse was part of the prepromise Jacob materials modified from the perspective seen most clearly in the Abraham and Isaac narratives. On the other hand, this report of a travel command in 31:13 is now embedded in a broader, promise-centered context composed by the author of the Abraham and Isaac narratives, a context in which divine travel commands are integrally linked to the theme of promise. This author knew of the command reported in Gen. 31:13. Moreover, similarities between this command and the others (12:1; 26:2; 31:3; 46:3–4) suggest that he even modeled the later promise-centered commands on Gen. 31:13. In summary, the report of a travel command in 31:13 appears to have preexisted the broader, promise-centered system of narrator comments (12:1–3; 26:2–3bα; 31:3; 46:3–4).

---

74. For these and other links between 31:13 and its context, along with discussion of the relevant previous treatments, see Eising, *Jakobserzählung*, 203–7; J. P. Fokkelman, *Narrative Art in Genesis. Specimens of Stylistic and Structural Analysis* (SSN 17; Assen: Gorcum, 1975), 151–62; and especially Blum, *Vätergeschichte*, 119–26.
75. For translation of this passage see Blum, *Vätergeschichte*, 186–90, and see the same work, 298, on the lack of an explicit reference to the promise in this passage.
76. This model is from Blum, *Vätergeschichte*, 299–301.

Intermediate Reflections

Several overall trends emerge from this analysis. First, the Abraham and Isaac (Gen. 26:1–33) narratives appear to have been composed from the perspective of the broader themes of the proto-Genesis composition, from Gen. 11:28–30; 12:1–4a, 6–8 onward. Second, many of the texts describing a specific development of these promise themes in the Jacob and Joseph stories are distinguished as secondary additions to their contexts by multiple indicators. Third, in certain cases, central texts of the Abraham and Isaac narratives (e.g., Gen. 12:1; 26:2) and even insertions in the Jacob and Joseph materials (e.g., Gen. 31:3; 46:3–4) appear to have been modeled on portions of the prepromise Jacob and Joseph stories (Gen. 31:13). In this way, the author of the broader proto-Genesis composition coordinated his picture of Abraham and Isaac with that of Jacob.

Other indicators confirm this picture. For example, in the present broader proto-Genesis composition, Jacob's stops on his way home from Haran resemble Abraham's stops at Shechem (Gen. 12:6–7; cf. 33:18–35:4) and between Ai and Bethel (Gen. 12:8; cf. 35:5–8) during his trip to Canaan. Nevertheless, there is an important difference. The Jacob narrative is built around various local traditions regarding Shechem and Bethel. In contrast, the materials regarding Abraham (Gen. 12:4–8*) appear to function largely to put Abraham on a track similar to Jacob's. Indeed, the Abraham material appears to be modeled on the older traditions regarding Jacob. In this way, the travel narrative regarding Abraham (Gen. 12:4a, 6–8), along with the other connecting materials in Gen. 11:28–30; 12:1–3, coordinates Abraham's activities with those of Jacob in the following story. Now, Jacob follows in Abraham's footsteps when he stops at Shechem and Bethel on his way home from Haran to Hebron.[77]

This model in turn would explain several other elements in the Abraham narrative. For example, the specific linkage of genealogical information in Gen. 11:28–29 with the Isaac and Nahor clan dynamics described in the Jacob narrative (Gen. 27:43; 29:10, 12–14) probably resulted from modeling Gen. 11:28–29 on information in the following Jacob material. So also, the overall composition of the Abraham narrative in light of the Jacob-Joseph materials would explain the predominance of comparatively later elements—anachronistic place names and peoples, later family arrangements, and so forth—in the Abraham section.[78] Nevertheless, all this is but confirmation of a model based on the evidence outlined above: the thorough building of the

---

77. Gunkel, *Genesis,* 165; Cassuto, *Genesis,* vol. 2, 307; Noth, *Pentateuch,* 217; (E.T., 221); de Pury, *Promesse divine,* 59–60; Blum, *Vätergeschichte,* 336.
78. Z. Weisman, "Diverse Historical and Social Reflections in the Shaping of Patriarchal History [Heb.]," *Zion* 50 (1985): 2–6.

Abraham and Isaac narratives (Gen. 26:1–33) around themes only secondarily inserted in the Jacob-Joseph materials.

The Primeval History

As we turn back to the primeval history, the situation appears more analogous to that in the Jacob and Joseph stories than to that in the Abraham
and Isaac sections. To be sure, the connections between the non-P primeval
and ancestral sections are strong. Within the non-P composition, the non-P
primeval history serves as an excellent backdrop to the story of blessing for
Abraham and his descendants. Abraham's famed blessing contrasts with (1)
the curse frequently featured in the primeval history as a whole and (2) the
failed attempt to achieve fame described in the Tower of Babel story. Once
this promise, among others, is given to Abraham, humanity is divided between those belonging to him, and everyone else. Abraham's clan now en-
joys special blessing and protection, while those who threaten it—Egypt
(Gen. 12:10–13:1), Sodom (Gen. 19:1–28), Egypt (Exodus 1—15*)—re-
enact patterns already seen in the primeval history and eventually experience
primeval-like divine destruction. Most of these observations are not new to
this study. They have long been used in arguments that the author of the
proto-Genesis narrative, the Yahwist, wrote not only the Gen. 12:1–8*
promise text but also large swathes of the non-P primeval history.

A closer study of the central themes and structure of the primeval history,
however, suggest it was not originally written to serve as a negative backdrop
to the shining picture of promise beginning in the Abraham story. The details of this study will not be presented until the next chapter, but its results
will be anticipated here because of their relevance to this discussion. Overall,
the non-P primeval history appears to be an intricately designed reflection on
both positive and negative aspects of the present human condition. In close
dialogue with the Mesopotamian Atrahasis tradition, this primeval history describes the gradual creation of civilized humanity through an interaction between YHWH and YHWH's initial creation, and this interaction centers in large
part on the establishment of a secure divine-human boundary. The result of
this interaction is a sociocosmic structure that is by no means uniformly bad.
When we venture into the non-P ancestral history, however, the focus on divine-human boundaries has disappeared, and only the most somber of the
primeval history themes are revisited. The multisided reflection on humanity
as a whole is over, along with the intricate structural system that developed
it. In its place is a *particular* usage of certain primeval history themes in the
context of a new story of promise. Whereas both positive and negative aspects
of general human existence are explored in the non-P primeval history, only
its negative elements are emphasized in what follows, particularly in the
Sodom and Gomorrah story.

These indicators suggest a contrast between the primeval history and its use in the broader proto-Genesis composition.[79] On the one hand, we have a non-P primeval story moving from Creation to Flood and its aftermath. The scope and theme of this story correspond in particular to the Mesopotamian Athrahasis epic, but it incorporates numerous other themes from the cultures surrounding Israel, as well. On the other hand, we have a broader proto-Genesis story that lacks any such connections. Instead, the proto-Genesis compositional level features an entirely different set of traditions, ancestral traditions used to depict the *special* blessing enjoyed by Abraham and his heirs. Moreover, the emphasis on the specialness of Abraham's blessing is heightened through the description of (1) foreigners' complete dependence on Abraham and his heirs for blessing and (2) their suffering of a curse that seems almost primeval when they threaten his household. The result is a more uniformly negative picture of the broader human condition than that seen in the primeval history. The proto-Genesis author who composed the non-P Abraham section probably did not develop the non-P primeval history. Instead, he built around it and *selectively* used its themes in the process of telling a story of Israel's special promise.

That having been said, there are some parts of the early non-P primeval history that may have been added in the process of its incorporation into the broader Genesis story. For example, Gen. 4:26b is the first occurrence of the theme of "calling on YHWH's name," a theme much more prominent in the Abraham and Isaac stories (Gen. 12:8; 13:4; 21:33; 26:25; cf. Exod. 34:5). This theme's distribution in the very sections where the proto-Genesis author seems to have been most active suggests it was important to him. One might suppose that he developed the theme from the notice in 4:26b, but there also indicators that 4:26b may have been added secondarily to its context. It is only loosely connected to the genealogy of Seth (4:25–26a), and the following primeval history narrative does not develop the theme of calling on YHWH's name.[80] Such indicators suggest that this theme of calling on YHWH's name was inserted at its appropriate point by the proto-Genesis author. As a result of this insertion, Abraham's and Isaac's characteristic form of worship is anticipated by humanity's calling on YHWH's name, a calling that begins the founding of the genealogical line that will eventually lead to Israel's ancestors.

Be that as it may, aside from examples like Gen. 4:26b, there is not much evidence of the proto-Genesis author's hand in the non-P primeval history, certainly not as much as there was in the Jacob-Joseph story. As we will see in the next chapter, the substance of the pre-Pentateuchal primeval history

79. Here I build from the basic insight of Crüsemann, "Die Eigenständigkeit der Urgeschichte," although developing this contrast in a somewhat different way, based on an analysis of the emphases in both the proto-Genesis and non-P primeval history material.
80. Eerdmans, *Studien*, 81; Levin, *Der Jahwist*, 95.

revolves as a whole around its own issues. The proto-Genesis author merely used it as a prologue and backdrop for his own story of Israel's reception and enjoyment of the promise. Once this promise is given, however, he intervened more extensively in the stories of Abraham's descendants, showing how they too received and enjoyed the benefits of the promise. Thus, the proto-Genesis author may have intervened less in the non-P primeval history because he was far more interested in Israel and its destiny.

Excursus: The Moses Story

I have consistently referred up to this point to "proto-Genesis" in order to leave open the question of the relation of this compositional level to material in the Moses story. So far we have seen numerous connections between this proto-Genesis material and elements of the Moses story. The connections are not limited to the parallels between elements of the exodus story and portions of the Abraham account (Gen. 12:10–13:1; 16:1–2, 4–14; 19:1–28). In addition, the exodus story represents the specific, sequential culmination of themes introduced in the Abraham story. The promise of many descendants and blessing to Abraham, Isaac, and Jacob reaches its final fulfillment in Israel's exodus as a great and rich people from Egypt (Exod. 12:37–38). The recognition of Israel's special blessing by Jethro (Exod. 18:10–12) and the Moabites (Num. 22:3) continues the previous theme of recognition of this blessing by Laban, Potiphar, Joseph's jailer, and pharaoh. Finally, the "calling on YHWH's name" that happens in Genesis (Gen. 4:26; 12:8; 13:4; 21:33; 26:25) culminates in Moses' "calling on the name of YHWH" (Exod. 34:5).[81]

What does this mean? Given the specificity of many of these connections and the fact that they link a narrative that ends in Egypt (non-P Genesis) with a narrative that begins there (the non-P Moses story), the above-discussed, promise-centered proto-Genesis composition probably extended in some form into the Moses story. Some have argued on various grounds that Genesis was a self-contained unit before being connected to the following Moses story. Wagner, following on some earlier observations, stresses the unique character of the traditions in Genesis.[82] Nevertheless, this does not yet point to the independence of the overall composition in which these traditions are incorporated into a broader whole. Blum argues that the promises in the ancestral section do not require a textual fulfillment in the Moses story but only presuppose the audience's knowledge of the broader outlines of Israel's history.[83] Nevertheless, the number and specificity of connections between the ancestral section and the Moses section that follows on it strongly sug-

81. Levin, *Der Jahwist*, 95–96, 134, 143, 326, 334, 359, 363.
82. A. Bentzen, *Introduction to the Old Testament* (vol. 2; 4th ed.; Copenhagen: Gad, 1958), 20–21; Y. Kaufmann, *The Religion of Israel*, 206–7; and especially N. E. Wagner, "Pentateuchal Criticism: No Clear Future," *Canadian Journal of Theology* 13 (1967): 229; idem, "Abraham and David?" in *Studies on the Ancient Palestinian World Presented to F. V. Winnett* (ed. J. W. Wevers and D. B. Redford; Toronto Semitic Texts and Studies 2; Toronto/Buffalo: University of Toronto Press, 1972), 124–25.
83. Blum, *Vätergeschichte*, 360–61.

gest that, in fact, this proto-Genesis story *did* continue in some form into the Moses story, required or not.[84]

The exact delimitation of proto-Pentateuchal material in the Moses story is an intrinsically difficult, often impossible task.[85] It will not be attempted here. Indeed, the lack of clarity of the data in the Moses story suggests that analysis of it would not contribute significantly to clarity of the picture of Genesis. On the one hand, the links of the non-P Genesis material to what follows are so strong it is difficult to suppose this proto-Genesis did not extend in some form into the Moses story. On the other hand, the exact shape of this extension, if any, is quite difficult to specify.

The Background of the Composition of the First Genesis

As a result of the above analysis, the model being advocated here for the composition of non-P can be further specified. The basic proto-Genesis non-P composition appears to have been a mix of (1) appropriation and minor adaptation of preexisting compositions (primeval history and Jacob story) and (2) new formation of major sections through liberal use of other ancestral traditions (non-P Abraham section and Genesis 26*). To the best of my knowledge, there are no exact analogies of an extension on this scale in documented cases of transmission history. The closest example would be the Middle and Late Babylonian extension and modification of the Old Babylonian Gilgamesh epic through the addition of prologue material, the flood narrative, and so forth. In this way an earlier epic was both modified and extended. Furthermore, just as the new Abraham section appears to have been built around earlier traditions, so also the new material in the late Gilgamesh epic seems to have been built around earlier materials.[86] Thus the late development of the Gilgamesh epic provides a precedent not only for the addition of substantial amounts of new material but also for the significant use of earlier traditions in the process of creating that material.[87]

---

84. Blum's later work, *Studien*, 9–218, has stressed the links between the non-P Moses story, the Deuteronomistic tradition, and later additions to the non-P Genesis (e.g., Genesis 15; 22:15–18; etc.). This then stands over against the lack of such connections in his pre-Deuteronomistic ancestral story (his Vg2; cf. *Vätergeschichte*, 339–59). If one, however, dates the bulk of the non-P material to a point after the earliest Deuteronomistic history, then one can allow for a significant reflection of that material in a proto-Pentateuch, especially at the Moses story, where the non-P proto-Pentateuch would have overlapped with the numerous Moses-focused texts in the Deuteronomistic history.

85. See in particular Blum's cautions on this point in his *Studien*, 213–17.

86. Tigay, *The Evolution of the Gilgamesh Epic*, 140–77.

87. That being said, there is an additional analogy between the type of use of traditions in the new material in Genesis and an earlier stage in the creation of the Gilgamesh epic, the composition of the Old Babylonian version. Just as the author of the Old Babylonian Gilgamesh epic drew on the plot and characters of various early Gilgamesh traditions, so also the author of the non-P Abraham story seems to have drawn freely on various Abraham traditions. Furthermore, just as the author of the Gilgamesh epic wove his traditions into a narrative arch beginning and ending with Gilgamesh at his city wall, so also the author of the non-P Abraham story wove his Abraham traditions into an overall compositional arch beginning and ending with the formation of the family of promise. On the artful design of the Gilgamesh epic, see in particular Tigay, *The Evolution of the Gilgamesh Epic*, 3–10.

A later analogy to the proto-Genesis composition would be the formation of the canonical Gospels. If one follows the overall two-document approach to the transmission history of the canonical Gospels, then Matthew and Luke both represent substantial extensions and modifications of slightly variant editions of Mark. Furthermore, just as the proto-Genesis author drew heavily on Abraham and Isaac traditions to extend the Jacob-Joseph materials back to the primeval history, so also the authors of Luke and Matthew probably drew heavily on a sayings source (Q), among other materials, in the process of supplementing the Markan story of Jesus. To be sure, this compositional move is far distant in time from that being posited here for the proto-Genesis composition. Nevertheless, it does occur in the same Jewish stream of tradition, and this model is a better candidate for ancient modes of composition than many models we modern authors would tend unconsciously to assume.

One final analogy to the above-argued model for the formation of proto-Genesis would be the formation of the Deuteronomistic history. The Deuteronomists appear to have appropriated and modified substantial blocks of fixed tradition (succession narrative, Elijah cycle) into a new whole through the strategic addition of crucial bridging material. For example, the above analysis suggests that the non-P proto-Genesis composition was formed through the author's composition of an Abraham section that linked the non-P primeval history with the Jacob-Joseph story. So also, on a much smaller scale, the authors of the Deuteronomistic history appear to have bridged from the succession narrative to what follows by adding a heavily edited version of the story of Solomon at Gibeon (1 Kings 3:1–15).[88] To be sure, the compositional process being posited for the Deuteronomistic history is reconstructed, not documented (cf. Gilgamesh). Nevertheless, this widely accepted picture of the composition of the Deuteronomistic history closely resembles the linking and modification of disparate documents in the formation of proto-Genesis being posited here. Moreover, this would be an Israelite analogy to the model being proposed here for Genesis.

Analysis of the context and ideology of the Deuteronomistic history usually includes a special focus on specifically Deuteronomistic material. So also, in this analysis of the context and ideology of proto-Genesis, I have focused in particular on the new Abraham and Isaac sections in proto-Genesis, and on the related modifications of the older Jacob-Joseph and primeval history compositions. This specifically proto-Genesis material is

---

88. The basic contours of this position are not new. For a particular picture of the development of 1 Kings 3:1–15, citation of earlier treatments, and discussion of the role of this text in its context, see my *From D to Q: A Study of Early Jewish Interpretations of Solomon's Dream at Gibeon* (SBLMS 44; Atlanta: Scholars, 1991), 7–30, 57–62, 75, and (for more detail on the transmission history of the text) idem, "Royal Ideology and the Technology of Faith: A Comparative Midrash Study of 1 Kings 3:2–15," (Ph.D. diss., Claremont Graduate School, 1988), 80–139.

found primarily in the non-P sections regarding Abraham and Isaac (Gen. 26:1–33*), along with promise-centered material added at points to the Jacob-Joseph story (Gen. 28:13–16*; 31:3; 39:2–3, 5–6aα, 21–23; 48:15–16, 21–22; cf. also 4:26b). The question I wish to answer here is, What can we say about the probable sociohistorical context and ideology of this material?

Socio-Historical Context

Usually the promise material so central to this proto-Genesis composition, particularly Gen. 12:1–4a, 6–8, is assigned to a tenth-century "Yahwist." Nevertheless, scholarship over the last century proves just how difficult it is to find firm handles to date this proto-Genesis composition. Any analysis that puts undue stress on a particular setting of this promise-focused compositional layer risks building a house on a very sandy foundation. Therefore, rather than stressing a particular dating of the proto-Genesis layer at this point, I will survey some of the variables that consistently come into play in any such discussion. My starting point is a consideration of the major types of arguments often used to date the Yahwist to the tenth century. As we will see, many of these arguments do not pertain to what is under discussion here as the proto-Genesis layer but instead relate to traditions used by the layer. Moreover, many of these arguments themselves are problematic. In either case, this discussion of problems dating the Yahwist will serve as a cautionary prologue to my own reflections on dating the proto-Genesis materials that bind the non-P Genesis materials together.

Critique of the Criteria Often Used to Establish a Tenth-Century Dating for the First Promise Materials

Arguments for a tenth-century dating of the Yahwist depend on several major types of criteria, each of which has its problems. First and perhaps most prominent are the links scholars draw between Yahwistic material and developments they see in the tenth century. Particularly influential have been arguments linking the formation of the proto-Pentateuch to the profound shifts involved in formation of the state under David[89] or the emergence of a purported enlightenment under Solomon.[90] The problem is that many such arguments are based on a picture of the tenth century that is no longer plausible. Neither the archaeological evidence nor sociologically informed analysis of the textual material confirms any picture of a Solomonic empire or

89. H. Seebass, "Zur geistigen Welt des sog. Jahwisten," *BN* 4 (1977): 40–43, 46; cf. P. Ellis, *The Yahwist: The Bible's First Theologian* (London/Dublin/Melbourne: G. Chapman, 1969), 42.
90. Von Rad, "Problem," 62–68, *Gesammelte Studien*, 75–81; (E.T., 68–73); Wolff, "Kerygma," 77, *Gesammelte Studien*, 349; (E.T., *Int*, 135; *Vitality*, 44); Schmidt, "Ein Theologe in solomonischer Zeit?" 94; (E.T., 66); R. B. Coote and D. R. Ord, *The Bible's First History* (Philadelphia: Fortress, 1989), 5.

rest. "I'll take care of it, Adam. But I won't be able to if I'm worried about you."

The moment the words were said, Adam relaxed and stopped struggling. "He . . . he said he wanted you to call . . . call off your men. He . . ." said Miss Sarah is his ticket out."

Ira stood back and Jeb took his place. "I'll stay with him." Ira lifted his pistol and out of habit checked it before slipping it back in his holster.

"What are you going to do?" Cole asked quietly. "You're not thinking of facing him down, are you?"

"I'm going to go find the bastard and kill him." Ira met his brother's serious gaze. "I want you to get your rifle, then find Harris and tell him what's going on. I want you both to spread the word that I'm gunning for Josh. I don't need any innocent folks getting caught in the crossfire. After that, get on the roof over at the bathhouse and don't let me out of your sight until he shows."

Sarah shivered as she glanced down the deserted street. Josh had said something about meeting up with his father, but they'd been holed up at the livery for over an hour and Silas never showed. A cold wind picked up dirt and bits of debris, swirling them along the boardwalk.

She had no idea that Cole was on the roof of the bathhouse, nor could she know that Deputy Harris was in the alley between the bakery and the butcher shop on the same side of the street, three doors down. The only thing she was painfully aware of was that the man holding her at gunpoint was deranged.

During the hour she'd been his prisoner, he had talked in circles, telling her how all his life he'd hated Ira, and that he was just as good and just as fast and no matter what Jonah said, he could outdraw the famous marshal. Then he started

"You might want to stop by the telegraph office and send word to Mayor James," Ira suggested.

Cole leaned on the table after the deputy left. "It's hard to believe so many were in on it." Cole toyed with the handle on his beer mug then looked over at Ira. "Whatever happened to Sheriff Finch?"

"Sarah said he's dead."

"Is that all she told you?" Jeb asked, scratching the whiskers on his chin.

"Yes, but I can tell from your expression that there's more to it."

"That's puttin' it mildly." Jeb told them the whole story, and then took a drink. When he finished his beer, he dragged the back of his hand across his mouth. "I swear she's one hell of a little lady to have the guts to do what she did."

Ira was about to respond when Mrs. Baca's grandson burst through the doors. "Marshal Farrell, come quick."

Mrs. Baca intercepted Ira the moment he walked into the boarding house. "I'm so sorry. I did not hear anyone come in until it was too late."

A tight fist closed around Ira's chest as he set her aside so he could climb the stairs. Cole and Jeb were already inside Adam's room when Ira walked through the door.

"He took her! He took her!" Adam said desperately. Cole rushed over to hold him down when Adam tried to get up. There was fresh blood on his bandage and smeared on the floor where it looked like he'd dragged himself to the door.

Ira came to Adam's side. "Easy now. We're here. Just tell me who took Sarah." Ira didn't need to hear his name. He already knew, but nevertheless the moment Adam said the name "Joshua Pruitt," Ira's stomach lurched with dread. He calmly pressed his younger brother down and told him to

an enlightenment to go with it. Many of the architectural structures that used to be assigned to the tenth century have now been more accurately placed in other periods, and the picture of Solomon's kingdom in many biblical texts looks more like an idealized picture of the past than an accurate portrayal of the tenth century. Overall, careful analysis of both the texts and the archaeological evidence suggests that we only have a proto-state structure under David and Solomon, one that might better be termed a "chiefdom" than a full-fledged "monarchy."[91] Moreover, Jamieson-Drake's thorough analysis of material culture associated with writing indicates that we do not see in the tenth century any significant concentration of population, acceleration of building, or proliferation of luxury objects that would point to a state apparatus requiring extensive written communication.[92] It is difficult to know just how many peoples Judah actually did subject in this time[93] or whether it achieved "nationhood" in its own terms (cf. Gen. 12:2).[94] What is clear is that postulating of an expansive empire or massive literary production in this time is no longer as likely a hypothesis as it once appeared to be. Instead, this picture of a glorious united kingdom seems to have more to do with later Judah's glorification of its foundational past and hopes for the future than with historical reality.

Another major type of data is texts outside Genesis that appear to presuppose the proto-Genesis material. For example, several texts in the Deuteronomistic history refer to God's oath promise of the land to "fathers" (Deut. 1:35; 6:18, etc.) and/or to Abraham, Isaac, and Jacob (e.g., Deut. 1:8; 6:10).[95] These references are particularly significant because they may represent a later development from the non-oath forms of the promise found in

---

91. J. W. Flanagan, *David's Social Drama: A Hologram of Israel's Early Iron Age* (The Social World of Biblical Antiquity Series 7; Sheffield: Almond, 1988), 119–318.

92. D. W. Jamieson-Drake, *Scribes and Schools in Monarchic Judah: A Socio-Archeological Approach* (JSOTSup, 109; Social World of Biblical Antiquity Series, 9; Sheffield: Almond, 1991).

93. Some have argued that the mix of nations present in the non-P ancestral stories—Philstia, Amon, Moab, Edom, Aram—suggests a dating in the tenth century because these nations are said to have been subjugated by David. See, for example, Schmidt, "Ein Theologe in solomonischer Zeit?" 94; (E.T., 65); and Coote and Ord, *The Bible's First History*, 6. Nevertheless, domination is only predicted over Edom in the non-P Genesis materials (Gen. 27:29; cf. 25:23), while such domination rhetoric is conspicuously lacking in the description of interaction with the Philistines and the ancestors of Aram, Amon, and Moab. These other nations are merely neighbors of ancient Israel, and thus are featured in various descriptions of the interactions of Israel's ancestors with their most closely related counterparts among the ancestors of neighboring nations.

94. This relates to the argument, prominent in recent years, that God's promise that Abraham will be a great "nation" in Gen. 12:2 needs to be understood as a prediction of the full-fledged nation that emerges under David and Solomon. See L. Schmidt, "Überlegungen zum Jahwisten," *EvTh* 37 (1977): 237–38; Berge, *Zeit des Jahwisten*, 51–76. In actuality, this promise could be understood as an anticipation of the nation at any point in the preexilic period, or as a hoped-for restoration of nationhood in the midst of the exile.

95. For a complete list and discussion, see S. Boorer, *The Promise of the Land as Oath: A Key to the Formation of the Pentateuch* (BZAW 205; Berlin/New York: W. de Gruyter, 1992), 37–38.

crucial proto-Genesis texts like Gen. 12:7; 13:14–15; and 28:13.[96] Never-theless, two problems have been raised vis-à-vis these texts. First, Van Seters and Römer have argued that these mentions of "Abraham, Isaac, and Jacob" are all later additions to a Deuteronomistic history that previously only knew of a promise to the "fathers" of the exodus generation.[97] Nevertheless, at least in some cases, this interpretation is difficult to maintain.[98] The second and more significant issue is that this indicator only suggests a relative dating of proto-Genesis material vis-à-vis Deuteronomistic history texts whose dates are themselves disputed. Almost no one would date the core of the overall Deuteronomistic history earlier than the seventh century, and most would date its various redactions across the sixth century. Therefore, even if one grants that the promise layer of Genesis predates these mentions of a promise to the fathers, this would only mean that the proto-Genesis material was no later than the early seventh century. In other words, at the very most, men-tions of a land oath in the Deuteronomistic history suggest a date of the proto-Genesis material in the early seventh century or earlier, and even this is not secure.

Another non-Pentateuchal text that has been used to argue for an early date of the Yahwistic material is Hosea 12:5–7 [Eng. 12:4–6]:

> He strove with the angel and prevailed
>   He wept and sought his favor.
> He met him at Bethel,
>   and there he spoke with him.
> YHWH, God of hosts,
>   YHWH is his name!
> But as for you, return to your God
>   hold fast to love and justice,
>   and wait continually for your God. (NRSV, alt.)

Especially when this text is read in connection with Gen. 28:10–22, it is not hard to read the second half of verse 5 (Eng. 12:4), "and there he spoke with him," as referring to God's promises to Jacob in Gen. 28:13–15. Neverthe-less, this text is fragile evidence on which to base dating the proto-Genesis ma-terial in the early preexilic period. First, the text may not be referring to God's

96. J. A. Emerton, "The Origin of the Promises to the Patriarchs in the Older Sources of the Book of Genesis," *VT* 32 (1982): 29–31; L. Schmidt, "Väterverheissungen und Pentateuch-frage," *ZAW* 104 (1992): 20–26. Cf. also the thorough study by Boorer, *The Promise of the Land as Oath,* who focuses on land oath texts outside Genesis, but whose reflections are relevant for the question being dealt with here.
97. J. Van Seters, "Confessional Reformulation in the Exilic Period," *VT* 22 (1972): 448–59; T. Römer, *Israels Väter: Untersuchungen zur Väterthematik im Deuteronomium und in der deuteronomistischen Tradition* (OBO 99; Freiburg and Göttingen: Vandenhoeck & Ruprecht, 1990).
98. Cf. N. Lohfink, *Die Väter Israels im Deuteronomium mit einer Stellungnahme von Thomas Römer* (OBO 111; Göttingen: Vandenhoeck & Ruprecht, 1991).

"You still have some of that whiskey I brought to the ranch?" Lily asked.

"I-I do," Jeb stammered. "In fact, before I leave town, Miss Lily, I'll come by for a few more bottles."

Lily laughed. "We'll see that you do. I reckon with a few bottles it'll be another five years." Lily bent down and placed a kiss on the old man's cheek. "Those bottles are on me, Jebson, but don't take so long to come back for more."

As soon as she walked away, Ira and Cole teased their uncle until the beers arrived. Ira took a long drink, then turned his attention to his deputy. "Tell me what you found."

Deputy Harris leaned back in his chair. "No more bodies. We arrested Earl Watts. He was very cooperative. He gave us several other names. As soon as you're up to taking over, I'll head up to the Rocking R Ranch and arrest the owner. Earl said his name is James Roland."

"What else?" Ira pushed his hat off his forehead, taking another sip of his beer.

"The other two prisoners were just where you said they'd be. We're using the doctor's office as a jail. I've a man guarding them. We also found a short bald man coming out the back door at the bank. He tried to run for it when he saw us, but he was carrying quite a large sum of money with him." Harris grinned. "I guess it slowed him down some."

"That'll be Silas Pruitt," Ira confirmed. "Did he say anything about Josh, his son?"

"Oh, he had plenty to say, but nothing about any kin." Harris paused to take a long drink of beer. "A couple of men came up and volunteered to help. Since I'm not sure who to trust, I've got them watching the streets. They're supposed to report anything suspicious."

Deputy Harris finished his beer, then pushed away from the table. "Well, I've got to go check on a few things."

The Price of Pride

"No," Sarah pleaded. "Please, don't hurt him. I'll go with you, but please, don't hurt him."

"Ain't that sweet," Josh turned his gun on her and cocked it. "Get up," he ordered, grabbing Sarah's sleeve and yanking her to her feet. She inwardly winced at the flicker of insanity in his gaze as he turned his attention back to Adam. "You'd best find your brother and tell him to call off his deputies and let me and my pa ride out of here if he ever wants to see his woman again."

Ira sat at a table with Cole, his uncle and Deputy Harris.

"Four beers," he ordered as he stretched his injured leg out a little to ease his discomfort.

"Beers are on the house," Lily stated as she walked up and put one hand on Ira's shoulder. She'd dusted a little powder over the bruises on her cheek, and a little on the dark circles under her green eyes. "Gotta say, it sure is good to see you boys alive after all the fireworks last night. Where's Adam?"

"Back at the hotel recovering," Ira replied. "He took one in the leg."

Lily went to the bar and motioned to Sam. A few minutes later she returned with a bottle of imported rum. "Here, you give this to him." She winked at Ira. "Tell him it's for the pain."

"Hell, you never brought me anything like this," Ira complained.

"Had I done that," Lily replied with a sultry smile, "your lady would have scratched my eyes out." Lily turned to Jeb.

"Well, Jebson Farrell. You're looking fit as a fiddle. I'm thinking it's been about five years since you've put a foot in the Crystal Slipper."

Ira grinned as his uncle turned red.

315

speech to Jacob. Instead, it may be describing *Jacob* speaking to God at Bethel when he made his oath: "He [Jacob] met God at Bethel, and there he [Jacob] spoke with him [YHWH]." This would serve well as an introduction to the following admonition for later Israel to return to God (Hos. 12:7; Eng. 12:6). Certainly the overall focus of the Hosea passage is not on God's behavior toward Jacob but on Jacob's behavior toward God. Second, even if 12:5 (Eng. 12:4) is a description of a divine speech to Jacob at Bethel, the text says nothing about the contents of the speech. It is possible the story of Jacob at Bethel did include an earlier promise of protection for him, a promise of protection on his way out that would have corresponded to the promises of protection he receives later when he starts back (Gen. 31:3, 13). If it did include such a promise, there is no way to know much about it. In any case, we must be careful here not to harmonize unthinkingly the traditions in Hosea 12 and those in Genesis.[99] This text is not an adequate basis for an early dating of the proto-Genesis promise material.

The next major type of criterion used to argue for a tenth-century Yahwist is an argument from silence in the proto-Genesis material on certain themes some scholars say would have stood in it if it were post-tenth century. For example, many assert that a history written after the split of David and Solomon's united kingdom would have had to include some reflection of this fact, such as animosity between Judah and his brothers, distinction in the composition between Southern and Northern cult places, or something in the composition corresponding to the borders between North and South.[100] So also, many miss the presence of certain features characteristic of eighth century prophecy, such as the focus in Hosea and Jeremiah on the problem of foreign gods, prophetic focus on the fall of the North, or the overarching problem of Assyria and its domination of the area.[101] The problem with such

99. For discussion and citations of earlier literature on Hos. 12:5 (Eng. 12:4), cf. Blum, *Vätergeschichte*, 161–63; D. Daniels, *Hosea and Salvation History: The Early Traditions of Israel in the Prophecy of Hosea* (BZAW 191; Berlin/New York: W. de Gruyter, 1990), 33–39, 51; and W. Whitt, "The Jacob Traditions and Their Relation to Genesis." *ZAW* 103 (1991): 35–38.

100. Ellis, *The Yahwist*, 41–42; Coote and Ord, *The Bible's First History*, 5–6; cf W. Zwickel, "Der Altarbau Abrahams zwischen Bethel und Ai (Gen. 12f)," *BZ* 36 (1992): 207–19. Zwickel argues that the non-P material in Genesis 12—13 actually originates from the time shortly after the divison of the kingdoms, when the boundary between North and South was between Bethel and Ai, and when Shechem and Hebron were still living symbols of North and South. The core of his argument, however, depends on (1) a tenuous link between Josh. 16:1b–3 and Abraham's reception of the promise between Bethel and Ai, (2) dating Josh. 16:1b–3 to the early ninth century, and (3) a series of arguments in which Zwickel argues that places *featured in later texts*— Ai, Shechem, Hebron—would actually have passed out of living memory of all but Jews living in the ninth century. Although Zwickel's construction of a possible context for the non-P narratives in Genesis 12—13 is vivid and plausible as far as it goes, it requires testing against other data for the rest of the proto-Genesis material. In my judgment, other factors, particularly the dating of the Jacob-Joseph material the proto-Genesis composition built upon and around, suggest a later date than Zwickel's reflections would allow.

101. Schmidt, "Ein Theologe in solomonischer Zeit?" 96; (E.T., 68); Coote and Ord, *The Bible's First History*, 6; E. W. Nicholson, "The Pentateuch in Recent Research: A Time for Caution," *The Congress Volume: Leuven, 1989* (VTSup 43; Leiden: E. J. Brill, 1991), 18–19.

arguments is that they depend so heavily on a scholar's expectations of what would have had to stand in a ninth century or later proto-Pentateuch. This is particularly problematic when so many of these expectations seem to have been shaped by the particular emphases of specific bodies of materials, and indeed, in the case of prophetic texts, materials of different genres and foci from those in Genesis. As we look at the myriad ways a composition might deal (or not deal) with historical events, it is highly dangerous to presuppose that any composition, irrespective of genre, dating after a certain event would have had to directly reflect that event. For example, the books of Samuel and Kings focus on the division of North and South partly because they are discussing events leading up to and beyond that event, but it is more difficult to find such a reflection of the division of the kingdoms in Deuteronomy through Judges. A proto-Pentateuch lacking such reflection might just be ignoring it or presenting an idealized picture of a unified Israel before the division of the kingdoms following Solomon's reign. We cannot know.

This takes us to another set of indicators of dating used to establish a tenth-century date for the Yahwist, indicators of dating that relate to a specific text or group of texts not necessarily part of the broader proto-Genesis layer under discussion here. For example, many would see the stories regarding Jacob and Esau in Gen. 25:27–34 and 27:1–45 as aimed at legitimating David's subjection of Edom in the tenth century.[102] These texts, however, appear to be part not of the proto-Genesis material but instead of the very earliest material used by it. The proto-Genesis material builds around and resonates with the specific promises of domination in Gen. 25:27–34 and 27:1–45, but there is also a clear distinction between the sort of promise to be found in these Jacob-Esau materials and the broader promises of blessing and land that are the consistent focus of proto-Genesis texts both before (Gen. 12:1–3; 13:14–17) and after (Gen. 26:2–3bα; 28:13–15; 46:2–4) the Jacob-Esau stories. These Jacob-Esau materials may well date back to the tenth century, but they can not be used to date the proto-Genesis materials because they are not a demonstrable part of the overall proto-Genesis compositional layer.[103] The same could be said for the argument that the Yahwist should be dated to the tenth century because of parallels between it and the succession narrative.[104] Not only is a tenth century date for the succession narrative not assured, but the clearest parallels to the succession nar-

102. Von Rad, *Genesis*, 243; (E.T., 279); O. Eissfeldt, *Die Genesis der Genesis: Vom Werdegang des ersten Buches der Bibel* (2d ed.; Tübingen: J. C. B. Mohr, 1981), 27; Wolff, "Kerygma," 77–78, *Gesammelte Studien*, 349; (E.T., *Int*, 135; *Vitality*, 44–45); Schmidt, "Ein Theologe in solomonischer Zeit?" 94; (E.T., 65); Nicholson, "A Time for Caution," 17–18.
103. This same problem attends attempts to date the proto-Genesis materials on the basis of other isolated texts, such as Num. 24:17–19. On this text, cf. Henry, *Jahwist und Priesterschrift*, 15; Schmidt, "Ein Theologe in solomonischer Zeit?" 94; (E.T., 65); Ellis, *The Yahwist*, 41.
104. Ellis, *The Yahwist*, 41; Schmidt, "Ein Theologe in solomonischer Zeit?" 93–94, 101–2; (E.T., 65); Coote and Ord, *The Bible's First History*, 6; cf. also Jacob, *Genesis*, 1048–49.

rative all occur in a demarcated layer of secondary texts in the Jacob-Joseph story (Gen. 30:21; 34:1–31; 35:21–22a; 37:36–38:30; 49:1b–28) that lack a specific connection to the proto-Genesis materials.[105] Even here, this Judah-focused layer in the Jacob-Joseph story appears to presuppose the succession narrative in some form. It is not necessarily contemporary with it.[106] In sum, dating proto-Genesis must focus on texts such as Gen. 12:1–4a, 6–8; 13:14–17; 28:13–15, etc., which are clear parts of its compositional layer.

Finally, the classic argument used by Wellhausen to date his overall non-P layer, his JE, to the pre-Deuteronomic period was the lack of a reflection in non-P materials of the cultic centralization under Josiah.[107] This argument, however, is not decisive in dating the proto-Genesis materials under discussion here. First, Wellhausen's argument depends particularly on the mention of sacrifice in non-P texts such as Gen. 8:20; Gen. 22:13; or 31:54. Nevertheless, a closer look at compositional connections spanning Genesis indicates the proto-Genesis materials that carefully bind together the non-P materials speak of "calling on the name of YHWH" (Gen. 4:26; 12:8; 13:4; 21:33; 26:25; cf. Exod. 34:5), a practice easily compatible with worship outside Jerusalem even when sacrifice was centralized there. Only 46:1 mentions a sacrifice by Jacob to the God of his father Isaac, and this verse may have predated the proto-Genesis material that now follows it (46:2–4). Second, even if 46:1 was a part of the specifically proto-Genesis compositional layer, it is not decisive for dating that layer before Josiah's reform. Composers could respond to such events in a variety of ways, and even with 46:1, the specifically proto-Genesis materials would still focus predominantly on a form of worship outside Jerusalem, "calling on the name of YHWH," that is not explicitly sacrificial.

This covers the most important types of argument often used to locate a Yahwistic proto-Pentateuch in the tenth century.[108] As we have seen, some

---

105. This limited text basis is also a problem in arguments for a tenth-century dating that rely on the prominence of Judah and demotion of Reuben in this series of texts. On this, see H. P. Müller, *Ursprünge und Strukturen alttestamentlicher Eschatologie* (BZAW 109; Berlin: Töpelmann, 1967), 52; Ellis, *The Yahwist*, 41; Coote and Ord, *The Bible's First History*, 6.

106. As Wagner points out, the dating of the Yahwist to the tenth century on the basis of parallels to the succession narrative depends on the thesis that the succession narrative postdated the Genesis materials and was based on them. This thesis is severely weakened by the lack of any mention of Abraham in the succession narrative. Wagner, "Abraham and David?" 117–40.

107. On this see Müller, *Ursprünge und Strukturen alttestamentlicher Eschatologie*, 52; Coote and Ord, *The Bible's First History*, 6; Schmidt, "Ein Theologe in solomonischer Zeit?" 96; (E.T., 68).

108. Other arguments tend to work with a basic presupposition of a tenth-century date and elaborate on it by reading certain themes in non-P Genesis as responses to purported issues in tenth-century Israel. For example, R. Clement's reading of the non-P Abraham traditions in relation to David (*Abraham and David* [Studies in Biblical Theology, 2d series, 5; London: SCM, 1967], 47–60) would illuminate these materials if they could be dated on other grounds to the tenth century, but the basis for this dating is nowhere near as secure now as it was when Clements wrote his book. Cf. Wagner, "Abraham and David?" 131–35.

of the arguments, such as those based on belief in a large Israel in the tenth century or those based on the silence of the non-P materials on certain subjects, are based on faulty assumptions and are not usable for dating proto-Genesis materials. Other arguments, such as some of those relating to specific texts in the Jacob-Esau story or the pro-Judah layer in the Jacob-Joseph story (Genesis 38; 49:1b–28; and related texts) relate to texts that lack a specific link to the proto-Genesis materials. Such arguments may pertain to dating the traditions used in the proto-Genesis composition but are less reliable for dating the compositional layer itself. Finally, there are no references to proto-Pentateuchal material outside the Pentateuch that can be used to establish a tenth century dating. Hosea 12:5–7 (Eng. 12:4–6) does not unambiguously refer to the promise in Gen. 28:13–15, and the dating of the Deuteronomistic land oath texts is uncertain. If one takes the various oath promises of land in the Deuteronomistic history as early parts of that history, then they would establish a date for the proto-Genesis materials sometime before the mid-sixth century. Such texts can not be used to place the proto-Pentateuch in the tenth century.[109]

Reflections on a Range of Contexts for the Proto-Genesis Materials

If we did not have such a strong, recent scholarly tradition of dating these materials in the tenth century, the dating debate for the earliest proto-Genesis materials would probably vary in a significantly later dating range. What I wish to do here is consider the scope of such a dating range and the variables that might influence us to go toward one end or the other of that range. This discussion will highlight one major aspect of the rhetorical orientation of proto-Genesis materials: that rather than legitimating an existing Solomonic kingdom, these materials are intensely oriented toward bolstering an audience's faith in a non-existent or threatened *future* of nationhood, blessing, land possession, and protection.

As we will see in the next chapter, there are texts in Genesis that seem oriented toward predicting and legitimating the particulars of existing political arrangements. Nevertheless, these texts are found in the prepromise layers of the Jacob and Joseph materials, and they anticipate elements in the Northern Kingdom of Israel. Both the prepromise Jacob story and the prepromise Joseph story appear to have been designed to anticipate and legitimate an emergent Northern Kingdom, and they have been bound by materials, primarily found in Genesis 48, that further anticipate the domination of Ephraim over Manasseh, among the Northern tribes of Joseph. Furthermore,

---

109. Note that, although the above discussion has focused on proto-Genesis materials including some texts regarding Abraham that are traditionally assigned to the Elohist, these texts have not played a role in moving these materials to a later date.

these Northern-oriented Jacob-Joseph materials have been revised by a series of closely connected pro-Judah additions—Gen. 30:21; 34:1–31; 35:21–22a; 37:36–38:30; 49:1b–28—additions that revise this Jacob-Joseph story, moving from anticipation of Ephraim's domination over the other tribes of the North to anticipation of Judah's ultimate domination of all tribes, a domination that will never end: "the scepter will not turn away from Judah" (Gen. 49:10). All these Jacob-Joseph materials anticipate specific power structures, whether in the North or South. In addition, even the latest layer of this material, the pro-Judah materials with the promise of eternal domination for Judah, does not seem to presuppose the exile.

If these conclusions from the next chapter are secure, then the proto-Genesis materials that build around this multi-layered Jacob-Joseph story must date from a time after the division of the North and South. Indeed this layer dates from a time after a Northern-oriented Jacob-Joseph composition would have been adopted and revised from a Southern perspective. As I will argue in more detail in the next chapter, such a Judean adoption and revision of Northern Israelite materials most likely occurred in the period following the destruction of the Northern Kingdom by the Assyrians in 722. This establishes the probable *terminus post quem* (earliest possible date) for the proto-Genesis materials.

The *terminus ad quem* (latest possible date) for these materials belongs somewhere in the exilic period. If we take the above-discussed land oath texts in the Deuteronomistic history as early parts of that history, then we can not date proto-Genesis any later than the early exile, and we can only do this if the early layer of the Deuteronomistic history dates to the middle of the exilic period. Even if we do not consider such Deuteronomistic land oath texts, the proto-Genesis composition would still probably date no later than the end of the exile because a modified form of this composition appears to be presupposed by the Priestly layer, and there are good reasons for dating the earliest overall Priestly layer in the early postexilic period.

The combination of these considerations suggests a date for the proto-Genesis composition sometime in a range extending from the fall of the Northern Kingdom in 722 to sometime in the exile around 560, the approximate date of the last event found in the present Deuteronomistic history. Dating within this range depends on how different sorts of indicators are weighted. On the one hand, if the Deuteronomistic land oath texts are dated to the time of Josiah's reform, then we must work with a narrower dating range extending from 722 to around 626. On the other hand, it is only toward the late end of this dating range, during the exile, that we first see the central elements of the above-discussed proto-Genesis composition enter datable texts: Abraham, Isaac, and the promise. To be sure, this is largely an argument from silence. Nevertheless, it is an argument from *relative* silence. Genesis Jacob traditions appear to be reflected in eighth-century Hosea (Hos.

12:3–5, 13; [Eng. 12:2–4, 12]; cf. Gen. 25:26; 27:43; 28:10–22*; 30:15–30; 32:23–33 [Eng. 32:22–32]),[110] Jacob/Israel's name appears repeatedly as an epithet for Israel, and Joseph's name appears as an epithet for the Northern group of tribes (2 Sam. 19:21 [Eng. 19:20]; 1 Kings 11:28; Amos 5:6).[111] In contrast, Isaac is only mentioned in passing in two potentially late oracles attributed to Amos (Amos 7:9, 16), along with some Deuteronomistic texts, Chronistic texts, a psalm that seems to presuppose the final form of the Pentateuch (Ps. 105:9), and a late Jeremiah passage (Jer 33:26).[112] So also, aside from mention of Abraham in an undatable enthronement psalm (Ps. 47:10; Eng. 47:9), all other non-Pentateuchal references to him occur in the Deuteronomistic and Chronistic histories or in prophetic material whose exilic or postexilic date is securely established (Isa. 29:22; 41:8; 51:2; 63:16; Ezek. 33:24; Micah 7:20).[113] Furthermore, whereas almost all of the (late) references featuring Abraham and Isaac occur in some connection with the promise theme so central to the proto-Genesis composition, there is no such unambiguous reference to the promise in the datable references to Jacob.[114] We do not see clearly datable, unambiguous references to the promise until Ezekiel's angry refutation of such ideas in Ezek. 33:23–29 and exilic "Isaiah's" promotion of them (Isaiah 40—55). This pattern in prophetic texts outside the Pentateuch suggests an external benchmark for developments within Genesis.

To be sure, we can not presuppose a text is only to be dated to the time when its major themes appear in other datable texts.[115] The proto-Genesis author must have worked with earlier Abraham and Isaac traditions, and

---

110. A pair of recent publications have cautioned against too quickly assuming that Hosea knew Genesis or that the non-P Jacob traditions preceded Hosea's prophecy. At the very least Hosea probably had access to a mix of oral traditions regarding Jacob, along with whatever written traditions he had access to. Whitt and, to a lesser extent, Daniels argue further that Hosea may have depended exclusively at points on oral traditions not otherwise attested in written materials available to us, traditions whose variant forms appear refracted through the material in Genesis. See Daniels, *Hosea and Salvation History*, 43–46, 51, and Whitt, "The Jacob Traditions," 18–43. In either case a number of traditions regarding Jacob that are close to those we see in Genesis appear to have been in some kind of circulation in preexilic Northern Israel. In the next chapter I will argue for a closer relationship than this, but that point is not essential for the purposes of the present argument.

111. On Joseph see Blum, *Vätergeschichte*, 183, 242–43n46, and 490n71.

112. The latter passage appears to postdate the Hebrew edition of Jeremiah translated in the Old Greek.

113. The citations come from B. Diebner, " 'Isaak' und 'Abraham' in der alttestamentlichen Literatur außerhalb Gen. 12—50. Eine Sammlung literaturgeschichtlicher Beobachtungen nebst einigen überlieferungsgeschichtlichen Spekulationen," *DBAT* 7 (1974): 38–50. See also the more detailed discussion of these and more difficult-to-date texts in H. Vorländer, *Die Entstehungszeit des jehowistischen Geschichtswerkes* (Europäische Hochschulschriften, Theology Series 109; Frankfurt am Main/Bern/Las Vegas: Peter Lang, 1978), 50–68.

114. Hosea 12:5 (Eng. 12:4) does not refer unambiguously to the promise. For discussion, see above, pp. 222–23.

115. Blum offers some nuanced reflections along these lines (*Studien*, 218n44) despite his agreement with the thesis this evidence would support.

Chart 9-5: External Attestation to Genesis Traditions	
Internal Analysis of Genesis	External Attestation of Traditions
Prepromise Jacob and Joseph traditions	Preexilic attestation of Jacob and Joseph without clear reference to the promise
Later extension of Jacob-Joseph composition through addition of Abraham and Isaac sections, along with an overall promise focus	Exilic attestation of Abraham and Isaac, almost always in connection with a clear promise focus

there could well be a gap between the publication of these traditions in the proto-Genesis composition and the increasing reference to these traditions in other genres like prophecy. Nevertheless, the sudden prominence of Abraham, Isaac, and the promise theme during the exile suggest, at the very least, that the exile was the time when the material covered in the proto-Genesis composition reached wider circulation. Furthermore, dating the proto-Genesis composition during the exile would help explain the particular focus of the composition on God's provision of riches, protection, offspring, and fame to landless patriarchs living among foreigners and attempting to negotiate tricky diaspora issues such as proper marriage.[116]

Clearly, consensus on this subject is not possible. What is important for our purposes is the suggestion that this material is more prospective than retrospective. The history of Judah from 722 to the exile is not a time of glory to be anticipated by the promises to the patriarchs, but a time of progressive disintegration of the Judean state structure and of intensifying hope among its officials for restoration of past glory. Within this context, the Judean audience could identify themselves with the Judean figures, Abraham and Isaac. More importantly, once they had climbed into the Genesis story world in this way, they could identify their future with Abraham's and Isaac's future. The proto-Genesis composition encouraged them to believe in a promise that was not yet executed but would, against all outward appearances, be fulfilled.

Ideology, Dating, and Social Setting

We can deepen our sense of how the proto-Genesis composition works by briefly considering the way it draws on (1) royal ideology and (2) traditions of personal piety to construct hope for its audience in late preexilic or exilic Israel.

Let us turn first to royal ideology. Another argument that has sometimes been used for a tenth-century dating of the proto-Genesis material is its

116. For additional reflections linking the promise and other themes in the proto-Genesis material to the exile, see Schmid, *Sogennante Jahwist*, 143–66; Blum, *Vätergeschichte*, 293–96, 349–59 (with expansive citations of earlier literature); and Levin, *Der Jahwist*, 415–17, 418–19, 426–28.

multiple linkages to Judean royal ideology. Within Israel and other ancient Near Eastern societies, the king was regarded as specially blessed, and we have several texts that (1) describe divine promises to give the king a "great name" (cf. 2 Sam. 7:9; 1 Kings 1:47; Ps. 72:17), (2) envision the overflowing of blessing on the king and through him to others (cf. 2 Sam. 7:29; Ps. 21:4 [Eng. 21:3]), and/or (3) call for others to bless themselves by him (Ps. 72:17).[117] Furthermore, just as royal texts speak of the god's special protection and empowerment of the king for world rule (e.g., 2 Sam. 7:9–11; Pss. 2:8–12; 21:2–14 [Eng. 21:1–13]; 89:23–24 [Eng. 89:22–23]; 110:1–3, 5–6), so also God's promise to curse those who treat Abraham lightly extends not only to his person but to his "realm" in the form of his clan and household. In this way Abraham is depicted as enjoying a semiroyal promise, and as anticipating the establishment of a full-fledged Israelite "nation."

At the same time, there is one crucial difference between the proto-Genesis promises and its royal parallels: in the proto-Genesis composition these themes are applied not to a king but to an ancestor of Israel. Royal ideological texts tend to celebrate actual kings or the founders of a dynasty. In contrast, our other datable examples of transfer of royal themes to nonroyal characters are from the exile and postexilic period.[118]

Thus, the application of royal promises of blessing, protection, and nationhood to Abraham speaks for a dating of the proto-Genesis promise to a time when the actual kingship has become a problematic referent for these themes.[119] This supposition is supported by the way the ancestor narratives, particularly those regarding Abraham, stress *God's steadfast commitment to the promise in the face of human lack of reliance on it.* Far from being a royal-ideological celebration of a present reality, this proto-Genesis composition about a landless ancestor appears to have been written to bolster a shaken faith in Israel's continuing national destiny. Where its audience might be tempted to laugh like Sarah at the promise of a son (Gen. 18:12), the narrative assures them through the divine voice that God can do all things (Gen. 18:13–15). It is exilic and postexilic texts that speak of doubt about whether Israel will (again) be a nation (Jer. 33:23–26) and lament how Israel has become a "curse" among the nations (Zech. 8:13aα). In response to such doubts the proto-Genesis promise narrative assures its audience that God promised their ancestor Abraham he would be a great nation and a "blessing" (Gen. 12:2; cf. Zech. 8:13aβb), so that he would be a paradigm of blessing to the clans of the earth (Gen. 12:3b). Combined with the preland setting reminiscent of the exile that is chosen by the proto-Genesis author,

117. Steck, "Gen. 12,1–3," 551–52, and n.70; Schmid, *Sogenannte-Jahwist* 133–38; Köckert, *Vätergott*, 276–94; Van Seters, *Abraham*, 274–75; idem, *Prologue to History*, 252–55.
118. Schmid, *Sogenannte Jahwist*, 132–36; Van Seters, *Abraham*, 275–77; and Köckert, *Vätergott*, 296–97.
119. Schmid, *Sogenannte Jahwist*, 130–31, 135–38, 143–44; Van Seters, *Abraham*, 271–78.

the focus on the *future* in this promise framework was ideally suited for articulating a hope to people who had lost their king along with his "mighty nation," "great name," and blessing.

As Daniel Smith points out, one frequent aspect of community building in the midst of social chaos is the tendency for displaced groups to discard and adapt elements of their previous state ideology in the process of emphasizing nonstate community and conceptual frameworks that are better suited to structuring life in their new nonstate setting.[120] Just such social disintegration is the most probable background for the use of Israelite personal piety in the proto-Genesis composition to construct communal hope. Such piety tended to focus on a deity's unconditional and unshakeable commitment to an individual, a commitment that manifested itself in divine provision for individual needs: children, fertile crops, and protection. Just such concerns dominate the proto-Genesis composition. It focuses on God's unshakeable commitment to several generations of a given family, describes the fulfillment of that commitment in God's protection and blessing of the ancestors, and uses the image of God's provision of a son to Abraham and Sarah as a metaphor to stress the surety of God's fulfillment of the promise God made to the people as a whole. When we look elsewhere for examples of such appropriation of personal piety for corporate use, the parallels begin with the late preexilic use of such personal piety in Deuteronomy and intensify in the exilic and postexilic periods. This was the major time when personal piety entered the communal realm of Israel.[121]

As we turn to try to specify the author responsible for this remarkable ideological move in Genesis, the first thing that emerges is that this author was Judean. This supposition of Judean origins is confirmed by at least two indicators: (1) all the above-discussed, datable references to Abraham and Isaac come from Judean sources; and (2) with the exception of Gen. 12:1–8 (modeled on Jacob), all of the localized Abraham traditions are placed in Southern loci: Hebron (Genesis 18), the Dead Sea (Genesis 19), the way to Shur (Gen. 16:1–14*), and Gerar and Beer-Sheba (Gen. 20:1–18; 21:8–26, 28–31a, 34; and 26:1b, 6–11, 17, 19–23, 25aβ–33).[122]

In addition, this Judean was probably part of the Judean intellectual elite. This is suggested by the fact that we are speaking here of the composition of an extensive written work. Only a few in the ancient world had either the knowledge or other resources to do this.

Finally, this Judean is was probably part of the non-priestly governmental

---

120. *Religion of the Landless*, 74–80.
121. H. Vorländer, *Mein Gott. Die Vorstellungen vom persönlichen Gott im Alten Orient und im Alten Testament* (AOAT 23; Kevelaer: Butzon & Bercker; Neukirchen-Vluyn: Neukirchener Verlag, 1975), 293–98; R. Albertz, *Persönliche Frömmigkeit und offizielle Religion. Religionsinterner Pluralismus in Israel und Babylon* (CTM A9; Stuttgart: Calwer Verlag, 1978), 178–98; idem, *Religionsgeschichte*, 377, 413–27; (E.T., 370, 400–11).
122. Blum, *Vätergeschichte*, 290.

elite. Not only does the specifically proto-Genesis material lack any uniquely Priestly characteristics, but its saturation with semiroyal themes speaks for this possibility. Indeed, especially insofar as royal ideology represented a specific form of personal piety, all of the resources drawn on in this reconceptualization of Israel's preland history would have been an immediate part of the ideological repertoire of an ex-royal official.[123] At this point, however, we are beginning to venture into the realm of plausibility rather than probability. I stop here.

Concluding Reflections

The proto-Genesis composition, if not some form of proto-Pentateuch, was written sometime in the late preexilic or (more likely) early exilic periods by a present or former member of the Judean governmental elite. This (ex-) court official appropriated the non-P primeval history and Jacob-Joseph story, along with various largely oral traditions regarding the Judean figures Isaac and particularly Abraham, to reground Israel's hope for restoration and return in Israel's preland history. The personal piety framework already featured in his sources (Jacob-Joseph) was combined with elements of royal ideology to depict a protoroyal Abraham who travels from Mesopotamia back to Canaan. Then this promise theme was used to bind the Isaac and Jacob-Joseph stories as well. The result was hardly a sum of its various parts. Instead, it was a radically new, future-focused vision for a disspirited people, a depiction of God's unbelievable and yet absolutely reliable promise to bless, protect, and return God's people to Canaan, leading them in the footsteps of their ancestors Abraham and Jacob. Let us turn now to look more closely at the precursor traditions the proto-Genesis author built around to construct this remarkable picture of hope: the non-P primeval history and the pre-promise Jacob-Joseph story.

---

123. Vorländer, *Mein Gott*, 36–44, 231–40; Albertz, *Persönliche Frömmigkeit*, 150–52.

10

The Earliest Reconstructible Precursors to Genesis

The Preexilic Primeval History and the Jacob-Joseph Materials

As we move to consideration of the primeval Jacob and Joseph sections, we reach a yet greater level of methodological uncertainty. Here we now stand at least three layers back from the final form of the book, behind (1) the final formation of the book through incorporation of the Priestly counter-writing of non-P material, (2) the revision of the non-P material through the addition of texts like Gen. 22:15–18 or Genesis 14—15, and (3) the initial shaping of that non-P material by the author of proto-Genesis. This proto-Genesis author intervened extensively enough in the material he appropriated that reconstruction of it is much more difficult. P was more easily isolated because of its distinct profile and parallel character (as a separate document). Profile also helped identify at least parts of the retouching of non-P material. In contrast, the proto-Genesis author appears to have been the first to gather the various traditions behind Genesis and unite them in a fundamentally new whole. The question to be explored here is, To what extent are the precursors of this proto-Genesis composition reconstructible?

The answer to this question is already implicit in the preceding chapter: only to a limited extent. In the case of the Abraham and the (Genesis 26) Isaac stories, we can not do much more to reconstruct the traditions used by this author. To be sure, these sections were almost certainly created out of earlier, largely oral traditions. Nevertheless, they have been so interlinked with their broader context that we can do little more than posit that they existed, and—especially in the case of parallel traditions—speculate about their general outline and form.[1] Many of these traditions themselves

---

1. Cf. Levin, *Der Jahwist*, on the one hand, and Van Seters, *Abraham* (154–312) and *Prologue to History*, on the other. The former shows the methodological difficulties that attend an attempt to be overprecise when identifying the precursor traditions of the Jahwist. The latter goes too far in the other direction by maintaining on the basis of the present interdependence of the sub-plots and parallels in proto-Genesis that most stories in it never had an oral background. Many of Van Seters's observations are helpful and were used in the last chapter. Nevertheless, it is striking that in every case of parallel tradition, he finds the first parallel to be the earliest one, with the next one in the narrative dependent on the first, and so on. This is clearest in the wife-sister stories, where he argues that Gen. 12:10–13:1 can stand alone, Genesis 20 presupposes 12:10–13:1, and Gen. 26:6–11 presupposes both. So also with the present form of the Hagar-Ishmael stories. Van Seters takes Gen. 21:8–20 to be later than the layer found in Genesis 16*. In the process of his analysis he makes a number of observations that suggest these stories have

were probably fluid enough, being mostly oral, that their boundaries are no longer visible. Moreover, the proto-Genesis author so freely adapted them, whatever their initial form, that his contributions are not distinguishable from the material upon which he built. We no longer have any methodologically controlled access to these Abraham and Isaac traditions; we have access only to their textual reappropriation. At this point the proto-Genesis composition is truly analogous to the free adaptation of tradition in the Old Babylonian Gilgamesh epic.

In the case of the primeval Jacob and Joseph sections, however, the clear linkages with the broader proto-Genesis composition are more limited in scope and more clearly identifiable as secondary to their contexts. Here we seem to have fixed traditions and often limited adaptation of them. To be sure, even here, the proto-Genesis author has intervened deeply in the material. Nevertheless, these interventions are usually identifiable from seams and profile as secondary to their contexts. The vast bulk of the primeval Jacob and Joseph stories is not linked tightly to the overall proto-Genesis compositional framework. Instead, each section is governed by its own network of cross-linkages and thematic foci. In the following, I will investigate these linkages and foci further, examining the prehistory of the proto-Genesis composition.

The Primeval History

Most previous scholarship has seen the author/redactor of the non-P primeval history and the author/redactor of the first layer of the non-P ancestral story as one and the same: the "Yahwist." This understanding was largely based on a reading of Gen. 12:1–3 as inextricably connected with the themes of the primeval history. According to this reading, Gen. 12:1–3 is not just a contrast to the picture presented there but instead presents YHWH's solution to the problems laid out in the primeval history. This reading reached the point that Gen. 12:1–3 was interpreted as a primeval history text, describing Abraham as the new humanity through whom blessing would flow

---

been shaped in relation to one another. His chronological theories, however, ignore the fact that an author putting parallel traditions at different points in a narrative would almost certainly adapt the traditions that come late in the narrative more than the ones put earlier. For example, the proto-Genesis author who put Genesis 20 into its present form could presuppose that the audience was already familiar with the story in Gen. 12:10–13:1 and build on it. So also, he could adapt the tradition in Gen. 26:6–11, presupposing knowledge of the preceding versions of the story, Gen. 12:10–13:1 and 20:1–18. In summary, Van Seters's observations have helped establish that these stories *in their present form* are not independent of one another. Moreover, he has provided a helpful corrective to attempts to claim a great oral antiquity behind the Abraham stories of Genesis. Nevertheless, the general oral culture of Israel and the limited contours and character of the ancestral traditions suggest that this oral background was still there. Indeed, in some cases, the general outlines of these traditions can be seen, even in the midst of their appropriation in the present textual form.

to the world.[2] In this way the ancestors of Israel have significance for humanity as a whole, and Abraham became a prototype of the new Adam.

The links to specifically Christian interpretive tradition and concerns are unmistakable in this approach but will not be discussed further here. What is important for our purposes is the following: neither the language of Gen. 12:1–3 nor the development of its themes *in the following non-P narrative* support such an interpretation. Genesis 12:1–3 does not introduce a solution to problems in the non-P primeval history. Instead, it builds on this history by contrasting (1) God's gift of blessing and a great name to Abraham with (2) the curse of broader humanity and their failed attempt to get a name for themselves. In this way, this promise text introduces a specific set of themes developed throughout the proto-Genesis layer of Genesis 12— 50* and indeed onward in the Moses story: foreigners' recognition of Abraham's famed blessing and God's special protection of Abraham and his heirs.

Initial Survey of the Whole

As already suggested in the preceding chapter, this understanding of the non-P ancestral tradition reopens the question of the nature of the relationship between non-P primeval and ancestral texts. There I focused primarily on the one-sided negative picture of the non-Israelite world in the non-P ancestral story. Here I will explore in more detail the more multisided picture of the world outside Israel in the non-P primeval materials.

The starting point for such an analysis is the system of cross-references spanning the non-P primeval history.[3] In Gen. 5:29 Lamech asserts in naming Noah that Noah will bring rest from the "toil" given by YHWH in the garden (Gen. 3:17). This comment is then partially born out in the later description of Noah as the first wine maker (Gen. 9:20). In Gen. 6:5–7 YHWH looks back on the preceding history of sin and rebellion in Gen. 3:1–6:4. He refers with regret to having "made" (*yāṣar*) humans as narrated in Genesis 2, because the "inclination" (*yēṣer*) of the thoughts of their hearts is evil. Later, after YHWH has purged the bulk of humanity (*hā'ādām*) from the ground from which they were made (*hā'ădāmāh*), God returns to the terminology of 6:5–7. Now he states his intention to preserve humanity despite their evil "inclination" (*yēṣer*, Gen. 8:21). These and other linking passages (e.g., Gen. 9:18–19; 10:25) function exclusively within the primeval history to draw together the primeval stories into a broader theological concept, one focusing on the emergence of a stable natural, agricultural, and corporate order through the interaction between God and humans.

---

2. See especially the influential position of Von Rad, *Theologie*, 174–78; (E.T., 161–65); cf. Steck, "Gen. 12,1–3," 531–54.
3. Kessler, "Querverweise," 45–58.

In addition to these cross-references, there are a number of subtle ways in which the non-P primeval pre- and postflood stories correspond to each other. Indeed, many of these patterns did only emerge into sharp focus through the synchronic studies by Sasson, Cohn, Rendsburg, Jensen, Gutiérrez, and Steinmetz. The correspondence of creation of humanity from the ground and the removal of humanity from the ground in the Flood was already clear from the above-discussed cross-references. Now, however, it is more clear how the *contents* of the surrounding parts of the non-P primeval story correspond to each other. Overall, both sections begin with a primeval ancestor (Adam, Noah) and then move through the following sequence of scenes: from scenes regarding the first generation (Adam and Eve in Gen. 2:4b–3:24, Noah in 6:5–8:22*), to scenes regarding the children (Cain and Abel in 4:1–16, Noah's sons in 9:18–27), to genealogical information (Gen. 4:17–26; 5:29; 10*), to a final shorter story concerning the human community as a whole (Gen. 6:1–4; 11:1–9).[4]

The similarities between these stories make clear the continuity in human nature before (Gen. 6:5) and after (Gen. 8:21) the Flood, while differences between them indicate the shift that occurred there. For example, there are a number of correspondences between the story of the sequel to the Flood in Gen. 9:20–27 and the initial story of humans' first sin in Genesis 2—3. Both stories portray the father of humanity as the primeval farmer (Gen. 2:7; 9:20). Indeed, in both cases this ancestor is defined by his relation to the ground: Adam is made from the " *'ădāmāh*" ("ground") to work it (Gen. 2:7–8, 15), and Noah is a "man of the *'ădāmāh*" (Gen. 9:20) who will bring relief from God's curse of this "ground" (Gen. 5:29; cf. 3:17–19). Both stories deal with the products of their gardens, whether fruit in the Garden of Eden (Gen. 2:17; 3:2–6), or wine, in the case of Noah (Gen. 9:20–21). And finally, in both cases consuming this product leads to trouble: eyes are opened (Gen. 3:7; 9:22), nakedness is seen (Gen. 3:7; 9:22), and a curse is soon given (Gen. 3:14–19; 9:25–27).[5] All the while there are crucial differences in the replay

---

4. R. L. Cohn, "Narrative Structure and Canonical Perspective in Genesis." *JSOT* 25 (1983): 5. Here Cohn develops a pattern initially pointed out in J. M. Sasson, "The 'Tower of Babel' as a Clue to the Redactional Structuring of the Primeval History (Gen. 1–11:9)," in *The Bible World: Essays in Honor of Cyrus H. Gordon* (ed. G. Rendsburg; New York: KTAV and the Institute of Hebrew Culture and Education of New York University, 1980), 211–19. Cf. also S. Niditch, *Chaos to Cosmos*, 11–69, particularly 59–67. Although she puts the most fundamental division of the primeval history at 6:1 (rather than 6:9 as below), she observes a pattern of correspondences similar to that diagrammed and discussed below: the move to "reality" in Genesis 1—3 and 6:5–9:19 (pp. 13–24), the "shake-up of family structure" in Gen. 4:1–16 and 9:20–27 (pp. 45–55), the genealogical "further definition" in Gen. 4:17–5:32 and 9:28–10:32 (pp. 55–56), and the corresponding moves from ideal order to reality beginning in Genesis 3, and continuing in 6:1–4 and 11:1–9 (pp. 25–43).

5. K. R. R. Gros Louis, "Genesis 3—11," in *Literary Interpretations of Biblical Narratives* (vol. 2, ed. K. R. R. Gros Louis with James S. Ackerman; Nashville: Abingdon, 1982), 47–48; H. J. L. Jensen, "Über den Ursprung der Kultur und der Völker: Eine transformationskritische Analyse von Komplementarität und Verlauf in der jahwistischen Urgeschichte," *SJOT* 2 (1987): 39–40; Gutiérrez, "L'homme," 188, 218–21.

of this pattern in Genesis 9. In Genesis 2—3 *God* planted the garden, cursed Cain, and expelled him from the ground. Now in Gen. 9:20–27, however, a human (Noah) plants the vineyard, curses his grandson, and metaphorically expels him from Shem's tent (cf. 9:27).[6] A crucial shift in the divine-human relationship has occurred in the postflood world, a shift involving the displacement to humans of dynamics that were formally divine. I will look more at this shift in a moment.

For now let us turn to the close parallels between the postflood stories and the postcreation stories. The story of Noah's sons (Gen. 9:18–27) is parallel not only to the Garden of Eden story (Genesis 3) but also to the story of Adam's sons in Gen. 4:1–16. Both Gen. 4:1–16 and 9:18–27 begin with an explicit description of the sons as the first children of Adam and Noah respectively (4:1–2; 9:18); both focus on farming the "ground" (*hā'ǎdāmāh*) shortly afterward (4:3; 9:20); both describe division between brothers and a misdeed by one of them (4:4–8; 9:21–23); both narrate God/Noah's recognition of what happened (4:9–10; 9:24); and both conclude with a curse on one of the brothers (4:11–12; 9:25–26). At the same time, there is a contrast between *God's* cursing in Genesis 4, and Noah's in Genesis 9.[7] As in the case of the comparison of Genesis 3 and 9:18–27, the prominence of humanity in Gen. 9:18–27 contrasts with the prominence of the divine character in Genesis 4.[8]

These stories in Gen. 4:1–16 and 9:18–27 have similar aftermaths. Both are followed first by a genealogically focused section in the non-P material. Genesis 4:17–24 focuses more on the founding of city culture, while the non-P material of Genesis 10* focuses more on national groups.[9]

Finally, both primeval story sequences culminate with stories that stress an issue already implicit at the beginning: the vulnerability of the divine-human boundary. This issue emerges with clarity at the end of the Garden of Eden story. There YHWH decides to expel the humans out of fear that by eating of the tree of immortality they may become even more like God than they already have (Gen. 3:22–24; cf. 3:5). The issue next reappears at a strategic point, at the culmination of the preflood story sequence when this boundary is threatened from the divine side of the divine-human boundary: divine beings have children by human wives (Gen. 6:1–4).[10] Indeed, the stories have similar beginnings. Just as the garden crime began when the woman imitated God by looking at a part of creation and seeing that it was "good" (Gen. 3:6),

6. Gros Louis, "Genesis 3—11," 48; Davies, "Sons of Cain," 38–39; Jensen, "Über den Ursprung der Kultur und der Völker," 39–40; Steinmetz, *From Father to Son*, 144; and especially eadem., "Vineyard, Farm and Garden," 197–207.
7. G. A. Rendsburg, *The Redaction of Genesis* (Winona Lake, Ind.: Eisenbrauns, 1986), 14; Gutiérrez, "L'homme," 222.
8. For nuanced reflections along these lines, see in particular Steinmetz, "Vineyard, Farm and Garden," 197–207.
9. Jensen, "Über den Ursprung der Kultur und der Völker," 38.
10. Gutiérrez, "L'homme," 194–97.

so also this last step in preflood chaos begins when the sons of God "look" at women and see that they are "good" (Gen. 6:2). Both acts result in a blurring of the divine-human boundary and a divine response limiting human life.[11] In Genesis 3 God prevents human immortality by setting a geographic boundary between Eden and the land to the east of it (Gen. 3:24). In Gen. 6:1–4 God sets a temporal boundary by limiting the length of human life. This latter move thus completes the limitation begun in Genesis 3.[12]

The next time this issue of boundaries appears is at the conclusion of the primeval history in Gen. 11:1–9. Humans have returned by the time of Babel (Gen. 11:1–9) to the condition they were in just before the Flood (Gen. 6:1–4). Whereas the former sequence ended with the "men of the name" produced by the divine beings taking human women "for themselves" (Gen. 6:4), the postflood sequence now features humanity seeking to make a "name for themselves" by building a tower to heaven (Gen. 11:4). In both cases we see God deliberating, whether deciding that God's "spirit" can not abide forever in human flesh (Gen. 6:3; cf. 2:7) or proposing to the divine council that the God-given human power is getting out of hand with the Tower of Babel (Gen. 11:6–7).[13] The latter text is particularly significant because it concludes the second of the two primeval history narrative sequences. Moreover, it is the first time after Gen. 3:22 that God uses the first person plural to talk to the divine council.

> The LORD said, "Look, one people and one language for all. This is but the beginning of their actions, and nothing that they decide to do will be too much for them. Come, let *us* go down there and confuse their language so that each will not understand his neighbor's language."

This speech, with its strong echoes of Gen. 3:22, is the culmination of the primeval history.[14] God supplements the horizontal and temporal boundaries of Gen. 3:24 and 6:3 with a decisive defense: a vertical boundary between heaven and earth.[15]

---

11. Sykes, "Patterns in Genesis," 46–47.
12. H. J. L. Jensen, "Über den Ursprung der Kultur und der Völker," 42.
13. Miller, *Genesis 1—11*, 22–26; Sasson, "The Tower of Babel," 219; J. G. Williams, "Symphony No 1: The Genesis - An Analysis of the First Two Movements," *JRelS* 9 (1982): 26–29; Rendsburg, *The Redaction of Genesis*, 20; C. Uehlinger, *Weltreich und 'eine Rede': Eine neue Deutung der sogenannten Turmbauerzählung (Gen. 11,1–9)* (OBO 101; Göttingen: Vandenhoeck & Ruprecht, 1990), 569–70; Jensen, "Über den Ursprung der Kultur und der Völker," 42; Gutiérrez, "L'homme," 194–96. Uehlinger adds that both 6:1–4 and 11:1–9 feature the use of the H-stem of *ḥll* ("begin") and similar terminology for human and divine beings: *běnôt hā'ādām* ("daughters of humanity") versus *běnê-hā'ělohîm* ("sons of god"/"divine beings") in 6:2 and *běnê hā'ādām* ("sons of humanity") in 11:5. He also raises persuasive criticisms of some of Rendsberg's parallels (569n274).
14. Miller, *Genesis 1—11*, 20–25; Gutiérrez, "L'homme," 196–97.
15. Jensen, "Über den Ursprung der Kultur und der Völker," 38–39, 42.

As we look back at the general human history before this point, a clear trend emerges: there is a link between a threat to the divine-human boundary, on the one hand, and the multiplication and development of humanity, on the other. Other things may vary, but this linkage remains the same. The preflood sequence is characterized by escalating human strife and divine curse (Gen. 3:8–19; 4:3–16, 23–24). The postflood sequence is dominated by a focus on the separation and division of the postflood human family (Gen. 9:18–19; 10:1–11:9*). In each case, however, the stories concerning humanity's emerging from a single progenitor—Adam, Noah—end in the same place: a threat to the divine-human boundary and God's work to reinforce it.

Standing between and closely linked to this pair of parallel primeval storylines stands the non-P flood story as the turning point in God's response to humanity. This story describes the introduction of God's self-imposed limit when responding to human rebellion. First the story refers to the escalating rebellion in Genesis 3—4 (Gen. 6:5–7), and later it describes God's coming to terms with the rebellious nature that caused the Flood (8:20–22).[16] God's self-imposed limit then allows a permanent place for human engagement in agriculture and for building civilization. The stories coming after the Flood demonstrate the functioning and development of this basic state of affairs. Each story parallels earlier ones but decisively shifts away from divine engagement. Postflood human behavior appears relatively unchanged, but the nature of its consequences has shifted. Whatever the parallels to preflood affairs, human misbehavior after the Flood now occurs without the previous divine attempts at prevention. Moreover, there is no divine curse or threat of death penalty, only human curse and divine frustration of human aims.[17]

As a result, there is an important difference between the sequel to Gen. 11:1–9 and its parallel in Gen. 6:1–4. Whereas Gen. 6:1–4 is followed by a world-destroying flood, Gen. 11:1–9 is not. Instead of ending with watery chaos, the primeval narrative concludes with this picture of civilized humanity, a picture complete with agriculture (Genesis 3) and vitriculture (Gen. 9:18–27), cities (Gen. 4:17–24; cf. 10:9–12; 11:9) and national groups (Genesis 10*), limited life (Gen. 6:1–4) and reach (Gen. 11:1–9), along with many other elements of civilization (striving toward knowledge, clothes, crafts, and so forth). (See Chart 10-1; adapted and translated from H. J. Jensen):[18]

16. E. Zenger, "Beobachtungen zu Komposition und Theologie der jahwistischen Urgeschichte," in *Dynamik im Wort: Lehre von der Bibel, Leben aus der Bibel* (ed. E. Zenger and J. Gnilka; Stuttgart: Verlag Katholisches Bibelwerk, 1983), 49.
17. Zenger, "Urgeschichte," 45–46.
18. "Über den Ursprung der Kultur und der Völker," 41.

Chart 10-1: Patterns in the Non-P Primeval History

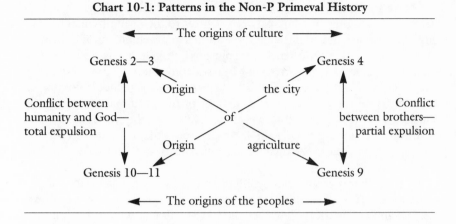

All of this balanced whole now stands under the umbrella of YHWH's post-flood promise.

As Batto has argued, the whole of this primeval history is an intricately nu-anced picture of the gradual creation of humanity, from the first individual to the multilanguage peoples scattering from Babel. This picture moves from an initially incomplete creation to the reality of the text's audience, from a human mixed of clay and divine breath to mortal peoples spread over earth, from an unclear relationship between God and humans to a situation where God has come to terms with their rebellion and created human culture in the process.[19] The intense etiological elements of this subtle picture invite its au-dience to interpret their present agriculturally focused city life as the out-growth of this process. Their cities, professions, languages, and so forth, are transformed by the non-P primeval history into testimonies to the truth of a narrative in which God carefully created humanity. According to this story, their present condition evolved out of God's interactions with an often un-ruly creation.

Analysis of the Original Scope
and Background of the Non-P Primeval History

Comparison and Contrast with the Proto-Genesis Composition

As already suggested, none of this subtlety in depicting the general human condition continues past Genesis 11, nor does the terminology used to de-velop it, the cross-linkages used to knit it, or the structural parallels used to frame it. Instead, only select parts of the non-P primeval history appear to have been drawn on in the broader proto-Genesis composition to character-

19. B. F. Batto, *Slaying the Dragon: Mythmaking in the Biblical Tradition* (Louisville, Ky.: West-minster John Knox, 1992), 50–68.

ize the world outside Israel. In the process, the proto-Genesis material renders a narrative world where foreigners engage in primeval-like crimes against Israel, and God strikes them with the same kind of destructive power seen "in the beginning." Not only does such a picture contrast strongly with the structural movement in postflood portions of the non-P primeval history *away* from such divine destruction, but this echo of primeval themes in the non-P sections of Genesis 12—50 fails to develop the crucial theme of divine mercy and provision for broader humanity that is a part of the primeval history. Overall, the non-P material in Genesis 12—50 builds selectively on that in Genesis 2—11, but Genesis 2—11 does not refer to what follows.[20]

Christians—who identify with the Gentile, pre-Israelite narrative world of Genesis 1—11—have tended see Genesis 1—11 as the problem to which Genesis 12 is the answer. Nevertheless, a closer look suggests that the non-P primeval history was not a statement of any problem. Instead, the non-P primeval history is an articulation of the belief that the audience's present reality is a divine response to problems present at the dawn of creation.

There are a number of subtle differences between the perspective of the non-P primeval history and that of the non-P ancestral history that follows it. The primeval history focuses not on any specifically Israelite issues but on the overall status of humanity in relation to God. The crucial problem in this primeval history does not foreshadow any later foreign threat to Israel but describes human rebellion and the emergence of threats to the divine-human boundary. The featured characters in the non-P primeval history are not on the move, like the Israelites of the preland history. Instead, they are the founders of settled, agriculturally focused city culture.[21] Finally, the non-P primeval history does not in any way appear to articulate hope for threatened or displaced people. Instead, it offers a more general, highly etiological exploration of the human condition. In sum, the creation-to-tower, non-P primeval history reads as a complete whole, with its own foci, cross-references, and structure, each of which is distinct from those of the broader proto-Genesis composition into which it has been incorporated. It shows every sign of having once stood free of the proto-Genesis ancestral material that now follows and builds on it.

The Non-P Primeval History and the Atrahasis Epic

As has long been recognized, the scope and themes of this non-P primeval history have particularly close parallels in a freestanding primeval history from

---

20. Köckert, *Vätergott*, 264–65.
21. On these and other differences see in particular, Crüsemann, "Genesis 12,1–3," 18–29. Cf. also L. Ruppert, "'Machen wir uns einen Namen . . .' (Gen. 11,4). Zur Anthropologie der vorpriesterschriftlichen Urgeschichte," in *Der Weg zum Menschen: Zur philosophischen und theologischen Anthropologie: Für Alfons Deissler* (ed. R. Mosis and L. Ruppert; Freiburg/Basel/Vienna: Herder, 1989), 40–41.

Mesopotamia: the Old Babylonian Atrahasis epic. Especially since the new re-construction of this epic in the late 1960s an increasing number of scholars have recognized the close parallels between it and the non-P primeval history. Both the Genesis primeval history and Atrahasis epic are set in Mesopotamia; both extend from Creation to Flood; and the two share a number of specific parallels, as well.[22]

Chart 10-2: The Atrahasis Epic and Non-P Primeval History

Atrahasis Epic (OB = Old Babylonian; LA = Late Version)	Non-P Primeval History
The igigi (lower) gods are the first farmers (OB I.1–38)	YHWH plants the first garden (Gen. 2:8)
The primordial humans are created as substitute laborers for the igigi gods (OB I.189–242)[23]	The first human is created to work and till the garden (Gen. 2:7–8a, 15)
humans formed from a mix of clay and a rebel god's blood (OB I.203–39)	humans formed from a mix of clay and YHWH's breath (Gen. 2:7)
implicit immortality (cf. OB III vi.45–48)	the chance for immortality (Gen. 2:9b; 3:22, 24)
Beginning of sexuality and marriage (OB I.271–76; cf. I.300–305)[24]	Beginning of sexuality and marriage (Gen. 2:24)
The divine midwife, the goddess Mami, is renamed "Mistress-of-All-the-Gods" in celebration of her role in creating humans (OB I.246–47)	The first woman is called "Life" because she is "the mother of all living" (Gen. 3:20)
Continual multiplication of the	The humans multiply from the first pair

---

22. This table is based in large part on Batto, *Slaying the Dragon*, 51–52, and the translation of the Old Babylonian and Late Assyrian versions of the Atrahasis epic by B. R. Foster, *Before the Muses: An Anthology of Akkadian Literature*, vol. 1, *Archaic, Classical, Mature* (Bethesda, Md.: CDL Press, 1993), 159–83 (Old Babylonian) and 186–98 (Late Assyrian). Some other discussions of links include A. R. Millard, "A New Babylonian 'Genesis' Story," *TynB* 18 (1967): 3–18 (reprinted in *"I Studied Inscriptions from before the Flood": Ancient Near Eastern, Literary, and Linguistic Approaches to Genesis 1—11* [ed. R. S. Hess and D. T. Tsumura; Winona Lake, Ind.: Eisenbrauns, 1994], 114–28); W. von Soden, "Der Mensch bescheidet sich nicht: Überlegungen zu Schöpfungserzählungen in Babylonien und Israel," in *Symbolae Biblicae et Mesopotamicae*, 355–57; R. Oden, Jr., "Divine Aspirations in Atrahasis and in Genesis 1—11," *ZAW* 93 (1981): 210–15; idem, *The Bible without Theology: The Theological Tradition and Alternatives to It* (San Francisco: Harper & Row, 1987), 98–105; and T. Frymer-Kensky, "The Atrahasis Epic and Its Significance for Our Understanding of Genesis 1—9," *BA* 40 (1977): 147–55. (The articles by Oden and Frymer-Kensky both work with the combined P/non-P primeval history. The book by Oden focuses on Gen. 3:21, a non-P text.)
23. Cf. also the Old Babylonian fragment CT 44 20, translated in Foster, *Before the Muses*, vol. 1, 164–65.
24. Batto, *Slaying the Dragon*, 205. For English translation of this section, see Foster, *Before the Muses*, vol. 1, 167.

primordial humans (OB I.352–53; II i.1–2; LA I iv.1–2, 38–39)

(Genesis 2—3) to their children (Gen. 4:1–16) to the generations following them (Gen. 4:17–26; 6:1–4)

Successive outbreaks of rebellious noise and cries from the primordial humans that disturb the gods (OB I.334–39; II i.3–8; LA I iv.3–8, 40–41)[25]

The first humans disobey the first commandment (Gen. 3:1–6; cf. 2:17), their first son murders their second (Gen. 4:3–16), and the daughters of subsequent generations become the objects of desire for the "sons of gods" (6:1–4)

The gods respond with successive strategies to reduce human population through plague (LA I iv.9–16; cf. OB I.360, 371), drought/famine (OB II i.9–21; LA I iv.42–v.26), allowing the land to become salty (OB II iv.1–18; cf. LA vi.1–15).

YHWH responds with successive expulsions of the humans eastward from the garden (Gen. 2:24; 4:10–16).

YHWH's final preflood act is setting a limit of 120 years on human life (Gen. 6:3).

Flood and rescue of Atrahasis (OB III.i.1–v.51; LA II.iii[?].1–23)

Flood and rescue of Noah (Gen. 6:5–8:22) (with close parallels to Atrahasis)

When the gods smell the sacrifice of Atrahasis, Nintu criticizes Anu's decree of a flood (OB III.iv.40–45)

YHWH smells Noah's sacrifice and swears not to disrupt the natural cycle again (Gen. 8:20–22)

The gods come to terms with the multiplication that had troubled them before by creating sterile women and women set aside to be priestesses (OB III.vi.41–vii.7)

YHWH comes to terms with humanity's "evil inclination" (Gen. 8:21)

Postflood structure: provisions for natural death of primordial humans (OB III.vi.45–48) establishment of sterile women, death in childbirth, and taboo priestesses (OB III.vii.1–7)

Postflood structure: hierarchy of Noah's three sons (Gen. 9:18–27*) separation into nations and languages (Gen. 10:1–11:9*)

---

25. The cause of the flood in the Atrahasis myth is highly disputed. For interpretations of the problem as rebellion and/or overreaching by the primordial humans, see W. von Soden, "Schöpfungserzählungen," 350–55; G. Pettinato, "Die Bestrafung des Menschengeschlechts durch die Sintflut," Or 37 (1968): 171–200; Oden, "Atrahasis," 204–10; B. Batto, "The Sleeping God: An Ancient Near Eastern Motif of Divine Sovereignty," Bib 68 (1987): 159–64; idem, Slaying the Dragon, 30, 196. For interpretations that stress the problem was overpopulation, see A. D. Kilmer, "The Mesopotamian Concept of Overpopulation and Its Solution as Reflected in Mythology," Or 41 (1972): 160–75; W. L. Moran, "Atrahasis: The Babylonian Story of the Flood," Bib 52 (1971): 54–57; Frymer-Kensky, "The Atrahasis Epic," 149–50; Van Seters, Prologue to History, 52–54.

In addition to these parallels, Batto has pointed out that both these histories deal with a similar overall theme: the move from an initial incomplete, problematic creation to gradual clarification of human status in relation to God and animals.[26]

The differences in the substance of the Atrahasis epic and the non-P primeval history are also clear. Most fundamentally, the Israelite version features none of the interaction between gods so prominent in Atrahasis. Instead the entire plot line is organized around the interactions between just YHWH and humans.[27] Moreover, the overall aim of humanity is conceived differently. Atrahasis depicts a humanity destined to serve the gods through service in the Mesopotamian temple state. The gods bestow this destiny on humans to fulfill the gods' own needs. In contrast, the non-P primeval history has a more ambivalent view of work. Humans are both destined (Gen. 2:7–8, 15) and cursed (Gen. 3:16–19; 4:17–24) to the settled life of farming and reproducing (Gen. 3:16–19; 9:18–27).[28] This structure of human life emerges out of divine actions characterized in the end by resolute firmness in preserving the divine-human boundary combined with mercy in otherwise tolerating the humans. This latter theme then is developed in a series of stories after the Flood (Gen. 9:18–11:9*) that end up going beyond the outlines of the Atrahasis epic. As argued above, this postflood extension of the primeval myth replays central themes of the earlier preflood stories but without the same level of divine involvement.[29]

In the past, such parallels have generally been taken as evidence that the author of the proto-Genesis material drew on Mesopotamian traditions like Atrahasis to compose his primeval history, but I propose that the relation may be closer than that. Above I surveyed signs that the non-P primeval history once existed separately from the broader Genesis story in which it is now located. This suggests that the earliest non-P primeval history may once have had a *similar scope* to that of the Atrahasis epic. Just as the Atrahasis epic moves from creation to flood and its aftermath, so also the non-P primeval history moves from creation to flood and aftermath. As noted above, the main difference is that the aftermath in Genesis is extended to completely parallel the preflood sequence of stories (9:18–27//3:1–4:24; 11:1–9//6:1–4). Thus we have a mixture of similarity and difference. The non-P primeval his-

---

26. Batto, *Slaying the Dragon*, 50–69.

27. For parallels to this in Neo-Assyrian and Neo-Babylonian literature, see Van Seters, *Prologue to History*, 123.

28. R. Albertz, "Die Kulturarbeit im Atramḥasīs-Epos im Vergleich zur biblischen Urgeschichte," in *Werden und Wirkung des Alten Testaments: Festschrift für C. Westermann* (ed. R. Albertz, et al.; Göttingen: Vandenhoeck & Ruprecht; Neukirchen-Vluyn: Neukirchener Verlag, 1980): 55–56.

29. This against Clark, "The Flood," 209–11, and Batto, *Slaying the Dragon*, 69–70, who argue that these stories are just added to the outline by the Yahwist to bridge to Abraham. A genealogy would suffice for this function.

tory in Genesis appears to be an originally independent Israelite creation-to-flood text that revisits many of the themes and foci of its Mesopotamian counterpart, albeit in a distinctly different way.

Seen in this light, the non-P primeval history might be described as an originally independent Israelite "Atrahasis." It retraces the creation-to-flood scope of the Atrahasis epic yet fills it with decisively new content. As such it is a counterwriting of its Mesopotamian counterpart. Just as the Lagash king list offers a fundamentally reconceptualized counterversion to the Sumerian king list,[30] so also the Israelite non-P primeval story was hardly a repetition of Atrahasis. Instead, it used the overall outline and motifs of Atrahasis along with other traditions to offer a competing conceptualization of the divine-human relationship and the human condition. Indeed, at the conclusion of the non-P primeval history, in the Tower of Babel story, one can detect an implicit anti-Mesopotamian polemic in this reconceptualization.[31]

To be sure, the non-P primeval story draws on other Mesopotamian themes as well. In the Garden of Eden story, the deity lies in order to preserve the divine-human boundary, much as in the Adapa epic (*Adapa* is the equivalent to Hebrew *Adam*).[32] In addition, in Eden a snake plays a crucial role in denying humans the chance at immortality, as in the flood section of the Gilgamesh epic.[33] The humans grow into full adulthood through acquisition of wisdom, clothing, and sexuality, much like Enkidu of the Gilgamesh epic and other primeval figures.[34] In addition, the lack of focus on divine rivalry in Genesis 2—3, the freshwater spring (Gen. 2:6), and the combining of creation of humans with creation of plants and animals in Genesis 2—3 are paralleled by Neo-Assyrian and Neo-Babylonian creation traditions, particularly the prologue to a Neo-Babylonian temple purification incantation that describes Marduk's creation of the world.[35] Finally, there are numerous and specific parallels between Mesopotamian flood traditions and the non-P flood story.[36] In all these respects and more, the non-P primeval history draws on a rich fund of motifs from Mesopotamia and possibly the Mediterranean culture as well,[37] even as each motif receives a decisive new twist in its new con-

---

30. For discussion of this tradition in relation to Genesis see Van Seters, *Prologue to History*, 65–67.
31. Ruppert, "Machen wir uns einen Namen," 28–41, discusses the anti-Babylonian coloring of 11:1–9 in the context of the primeval history as a whole. On this, see in particular the thorough argumentation in Uehlinger, *Turmbauerzählung*, 406–546.
32. On lying in Genesis 2—3, see Carr, "Politics of Textual Subversion," 590.
33. Batto, *Slaying the Dragon*, 57–58.
34. Batto, *Slaying the Dragon*, 53–57.
35. Van Seters, *Prologue to History*, 123–24. Van Seters also argues that there is a verbal parallel between the goddess Aruru's creation of the seed of humankind with him (line 21) and Eve's statement that "I have created a man together with YHWH" (Gen. 4:1b).
36. Van Seters, *Prologue to History*, 165–69 (though note that his parallel of types of construction on 165 depends on his implausible assignment of Gen. 6:14–16 to J); Batto, *Slaying the Dragon*, 67–69.

text. Nevertheless, the overall framework and problematic of the non-P Genesis story is particularly similar to that found in the Atrahasis story. This Mesopotamian epic seems to have been a special intertextual precursor to the non-P primeval history, a precursor that the author of the non-P primeval history strove to build on and overcome.

Sociohistorical Placement
of the Non-P Primeval History

Most have dated the non-P primeval material to the tenth century, but there are no clear indicators within it of such origins. Indeed, its very primeval character, purporting to explain timeless structures of human existence, makes it inherently difficult to date. Some might be tempted to place it in the Babylonian exile, especially given its multiple links with Mesopotamian traditions. Nevertheless, Mesopotamian cultural links are documented throughout the history of Israel. Moreover, there is nothing in the history that can be specifically linked to life in the exile. Considerations of relative dating suggest an earlier date. If the above dating of the broader proto-Genesis composition to sometime in the exile or earlier is correct, it is likely the primeval history was composed sometime in the preexilic period. A more exact date is difficult to determine and not particularly important for our interpretation of it.

In any case, a tenth-century date certainly should not be taken for granted. The non-P primeval history is the product of a highly sophisticated scribal culture, and as Jamieson-Drake persuasively argues, the infrastructural correlates of a writing culture do not really emerge in Judah until the late preexilic period.[38] Especially in Jerusalem we see in this period a population concentration, acceleration of building, and proliferation of luxury objects that would point to a state apparatus requiring extensive written communication.[39]

The non-P primeval history, like its Atrahasis model, was probably written within such a state apparatus, more specifically by scribes working within the preexilic temple cult. Of course, the history does not involve the

---

37. Van Seters, *Prologue to History,* 125, 145–46, 155–58, 177.

38. In addition, certain internal thematic indicators, such as the law-wisdom debate behind Genesis 3 (see Carr, "Politics of Textual Subversion," 588–91) or elements of the tower of Babel story (Uehlinger, *Weltreich und eine Rede*) point to a late preexilic dating. Furthermore, Mesopotamian influence is best documented in preexilic Judah during the late preexilic period, when Syrian and Mesopotamian links (often by way of Syria) were strongest. See H. Spieckermann, *Juda unter Assur in der Sargonidenzeit* (FRLANT 129; Göttingen: Vandenhoeck & Ruprecht, 1982), 226–381; R. Albertz, *Religionsgeschichte Israels,* vol. 1, *Von den Anfängen bis zum Ende der Königszeit* (ATDSup 8/1; Göttingen: Vandenhoeck & Ruprecht, 1992), 291–304; (E.T., *A History of Israelite Religion in the Old Testament Period,* vol. 1, *From the Beginnings to the End of the Monarchy* [OTL; Louisville, Ky.: Westminster John Knox Press, 1994], 186–95); O. Keel and C. Uehlinger, *Göttinen, Götter und Gottessymbole: neue Erkenntnisse zur Religionsgeschichte Kanaans und Israels aufgrund bislang unerschlossener ikonographischer Quellen* (2d ed.; Questionones Disputatae 134; Freiburg/Basel/Vienna: Herder, 1993), 322–401.

39. Jamieson-Drake, *Scribes and Schools in Monarchic Judah,* 74–80, 105, 133–34, 147–49.

democratization of priestly concepts and the publication of professional priestly instructions as seen in the later Priestly response to the exile (P). Nevertheless, the temple was the context within which the Atrahasis epic was probably developed, as were most other documents with cosmological interests as pointed as the Genesis non-P primeval history. Moreover, there are faint echoes of a probable temple context in the non-P primeval history. These echoes are particularly prominent in the Garden of Eden story with its divine garden (Gen. 2:8–9, 15), world-watering spring and rivers (2:10–14), mention of the Jerusalem Pishon as the first among these rivers (2:11), tree of life (2:9; 3:22, 24), and cherubim and fire at the garden's eastern gate (3:24).[40] Furthermore, such echoes continue in the focus of the Cain-Abel narrative on divine acceptance/rejection of a pair of sacrifices, and in various foci of the flood narrative: the central focus in the flood narrative on the disruption of natural rhythms, the careful provision of enough "clean" animals for a later sacrifice, and then the sequence of sacrifice and restoration of seasons (Gen. 8:20–22).[41] All these themes, along with the more general cosmological focus of the non-P primeval history, suggest that it was composed in a priestly context.

If this is so, then the early primeval history was a preexilic priestly counterwriting of a Mesopotamian precursor, much like the later Priestly document was a priestly counterwriting of its "non-P" precursor. This not to say that there was necessarily any continuity between the groups who produced these two documents. Nevertheless, the parallel relations with precursors may point to a concentration of this sort of countertextuality among priestly groups. Be that as it may, this picture suggests that the term "non-P" might be misleading when discussing the strand of Genesis 1—11 that is not part of the broader Priestly document. For if we can say anything about the background of this non-P primeval history, it is that this history features priestly imagery and foci. Most probably it was a preexilic Priestly document, one that itself was later counterwritten by priestly authors in the Diaspora.

---

40. For particular treatment of temple links in Genesis 2—3, see H. Gese, "Der bewachte Lebensbaum und die Heroen: zwei mythologische Ergänzungen zur Urgeschichte der Quelle J" in *Wort und Geschichte: Festschrift für Karl Elliger zum 70. Geburtstag* (ed. H. Gese, H. P. Rüger; AOAT, 18; Neukirchen-Vluyn: Neukirchener Verlag, 1973), 82 (reprinted in *Vom Sinai zum Zion: Alttestamentliche Beiträge zur biblischen Theologie* [Beiträge zur evangelischen Theologie, 64; Munich: Kaiser, 1974], 106–7); and M. Görg, "'Wo lag das Paradies?' Einige Beobachtungen zu einer alten Frage," *BN* 2 (1977): 30–32.

41. Also a major temple-focused theme in Atrahasis. On the link of these themes to the temple, see the discussion of temple imagery in Keel, *Bildsymbolik*, 118–26, 131–33, 144–46, 164–69; (E.T., 135–44, 149, 163–65, 186–89). On these parallels throughout Genesis 1—11, see G. J. Wenham, "Sanctuary Symbolism in the Garden of Eden Story" in *Proceedings of the Ninth World Congress of Jewish Studies, Jerusalem, August 4–12, 1985* (vol. 1; Jerusalem: World Union of Jewish Studies, 1986), 19–25; reprinted in *"I Studied Inscriptions from before the Flood,"* 399–404.

Moving Further Back?

The history of scholarship regarding the prehistory of the non-P primeval history is a sea full of wrecked theories.[42] On the one hand, the traditions display clear signs of having once existed separately of one another and of having undergone redaction. For example, the elements of the primeval history that focus most on the divine-human boundary—Gen. 3:22, 24 (cf. 2:9b); 6:1–4; and 11:1–9—are linked together and appear secondary to their context to varying degrees.[43] On the other hand, any step toward further reconstruction of the prehistory of the primeval materials must (1) disassemble the above-discussed primeval composition, including its striking mirroring of both the rebellion and divine-human boundary issues so often seen in the Atrahasis epic,[44] and (2) step so far from the final form of Genesis that the probability of repeatable results diminishes radically. So I stop at this point, four steps removed from the final form, having reconstructed an originally independent, preexilic Israelite "Atrahasis" standing behind four later layers of Genesis 1—11: proto-Genesis, retouching of that proto-Genesis, a Priestly counterwriting of the non-P composition, and Rp.

The Jacob-Joseph Story

The other major complex of tradition that appears to have preceded the proto-Genesis composition is an earlier form of the Jacob-Joseph story. As we will see, the bulk of this material originates from two precursor compositions: an independent Jacob story on the one hand, and an independent Joseph story on the other. Only a few texts secondarily added to these two stories in-

42. Houtman, *Der Pentateuch,* 141–48, surveys some prominent examples of theories, from Budde to Fohrer, that attempted to distinguish two Yahwistic sources, usually starting in the primeval history. To his survey can be added S. Mowinckel, *The Two Sources of the Pre-Deuteronomistic Primeval History in Genesis 1—11* (Oslo: J. Dybwad, 1937).

43. The expulsion of the humans from the garden in 3:24 doubles the expulsion in 3:23, and it is closely connected with 3:22 by the focus in both verses on God's interest in preventing the humans from gaining godlike immortality after having already gained godlike knowledge. The story of the sons of God in Gen. 6:1–4 has often struck interpreters as an odd prologue to the flood story. Whereas YHWH in 6:5–8 focuses on the evil of humanity, the heart of 6:1–4 in fact focuses on the behavior of divine beings. The story of the tower of Babel (11:1–9) contrasts with the preceding non-P table of nations in presuming that humanity is united, rather than already spread into different land and languages. The concern for divine-human boundaries and the divine self-reflection is shared with both 3:22, 24, and 6:1–4*. (On these texts, cf. H. Gese, "Der bewachte Lebensbaum und die Heroen," 77–85; reprint, 99–112). For a provocative and plausible proposal of a still earlier, genealogically focused primeval history, see Levin, *Der Jahwist,* 86–87, 96–99, 119–20, 123–24.

44. As indicated above (see n. 25), scholars are not agreed on whether the Atrahasis epic means to attribute the divine destructive actions in Atrahasis to overpopulation or some kind of rebellion. Be that as it may, the very debate over this issue suggests the present form of Atrahasis can be read either way. As we turn to later appropriation of themes from Atrahasis, such as in the non-P primeval history, the issue is not the original intention of Atrahasis but its interpretive potential. In this case, the non-P primeval history seems to have actualized both aspects of the demonstrated interpretive potential of its main precursor text.

extricably link the two, and these additions are mostly located in the Joseph story. Moving backward as usual, I will discuss these later texts first. Only then will I move to discussion of the Jacob and Joseph stories respectively.

The Judah Additions
in Genesis 38; 49:1b–28 and Related Texts

I begin with two secondary texts that function within their Joseph-focused context to present *Judah*'s future destiny to rule. Genesis 38 interrupts the movement from Genesis 37 to 39 and diverges from the Joseph story in its focus on Judah *apart from his brothers* and in its implicit presupposition that settlement in the land has already begun.[45] Genesis 49:2–27 contrasts with its context in its archaic language and imagery and is only loosely linked to that context by framing elements in 49:1b and 28.[46] Together, Genesis 38 and 49:1b-28 redirect the surrounding Joseph story. Whereas the context develops a narrative world where Joseph's *present* dominance is divinely destined, these insertions at the beginning (Genesis 38) and end (Gen. 49:1b–28) of the Joseph story implicitly relativize this picture by predicting Judah's *future* dominance over his brothers, including Joseph. The claims of the surrounding narrative for Joseph are left in place, but they are overcome by being relegated to a narrative past: Joseph was dominant, but in the future *Judah* will be the one who ends up on top (Gen. 49:8, 10).

Genesis 38 follows the outset of the Joseph story (Genesis 37) by implicitly anticipating Judah's future dominance: he will father the Davidic dynasty. Much of the drama of the chapter revolves around the fact that David's future line is at stake.[47] This becomes particularly clear when the story concludes with a birth report anticipating the future dominance of the Davidic dynasty. It does so by describing how the purported ancestor of David's clan was actually the firstborn, although he came out second (Gen. 38:27–30). In addition, the story is full of encoded references to the story of David. It is set near the cave where David fled from Saul and built his army (Gen. 38:1 "Adullamite"; cf. 1 Sam. 22:1; 2 Sam. 23:13). Tamar as "Bat Shua" ("the daughter of Shua") can be linked to Solomon's mother, "Bat Sheba."[48]

---

45. See for example, Gunkel, *Genesis,* 410.
46. Cf. Rudolph, *Elohist,* 172; L. Schmidt, *Literarische Studien,* 128; Van Seters, *Prologue to History,* 322–23; Levin, *Der Jahwist,* 311–12, who argue that the distinctive character of Genesis 49 and the present framing of this text by probable P material (Gen. 49:1a, 29) indicate that 49:1b–28 only entered Genesis with P material or later. Here I follow scholars from Wellhausen, *Composition,* 60, to Blum, *Vätergeschichte,* 260–61 (cf. also Gunkel, *Genesis,* 395, 478; Skinner, *Genesis,* 509, 512), who see this material, however distinctive, as originally a secondary addition to the non-P material. Only later did Rp skillfully include it at the outset of the P version of Jacob's charge to his sons.
47. Blum, *Vätergeschichte,* 226.
48. As Blum, *Vätergeschichte,* 227 notes, this wordplay may not have worked in ancient Hebrew.

Finally and most importantly, the Genesis 38 Tamar story has numerous parallels and contrasts to the Tamar story in 2 Samuel 13.[49]

The tribal blessings in Genesis 49, particularly the first three (Gen. 49:3–12), are the ones that concentrate on Judah's future destiny to rule. The first two tribal blessings exactly follow the order of Gen. 29:31–35 and disqualify Jacob's first three sons from the right of the firstborn because of various misdeeds (Gen. 49:3–7). Then the blessing for Judah not only anticipates his future empire (49:10) but predicts Judah's sovereignty over his brothers (49:8). Indeed, it predicts this sovereignty by using the same term "lie prostrate" (*hštḥvh*), which is used elsewhere to describe the brothers' "lying prostrate" *before Joseph* (42:6; cf. 44:14; 50:18). Thus, the first portion of Genesis 49 disqualifies Jacob's older sons from the right of the firstborn and presents Judah as the future dominant figure, even using terminology for obeisance that was previously applied to Joseph. Its interest in establishing firstborn rights links it with the similar interest manifest at the end of Genesis 38.

A further look indicates that while the present form of both Genesis 38 and 49:1b–28 are dependent on their context, the core traditions behind both texts seem to have been originally independent of the Joseph story. Scholars have long plausibly hypothesized that much of Genesis 38 was once part of a group of traditions describing the direct settlement of the patriarchs in the land.[50] Nevertheless, whatever the prehistory of Genesis 38, it is now closely linked to its context by both loose (37:32–33//38:25–26) and close (37:36//39:1) resumptive repetition of the end of Genesis 37.[51] Moreover, through its overall structural parallels to the Joseph story, it describes Judah in terms quite close to those describing Joseph.[52] Similarly, the substance of Gen. 49:1b–28 seems to have been an old or archaizing set of tribal blessings that have no direct connection to the preceding traditions. Yet the first three sayings, Gen. 49:3–12, are distinguished from the rest by their close connections to aspects of the Ja-

---

49. Y. Zakowitch, *'For Three and for Four'* [Heb.], (vol. 1; Jerusalem: Makor, 1979), 74–75; Blum, *Vätergeschichte*, 227; F. van Dijk-Hemmes, "Tamar and the Limits of Patriarchy: Between Rape and Seduction," in *Anti-Covenant: Counter-Reading Women's Lives in the Hebrew Bible* (JSOTSup, 81; Sheffield: Almond, 1989), 137–55. For more links between Genesis 38 and the story of David and Judah, see Sarna, *Genesis*, 264.

50. Noth, *Pentateuch*, 162–63, 252–53; (E.T., 148, 233); Von Rad, *Genesis* 312; (E.T., 356–57).

51. *b.Soṭa* 10b; *Gen. Rab.* 84:19; 85:11; *Num. Rab.* 13:14 (along with later parallels). For other links of Genesis 38 with its context, see Sarna, *Genesis*, 263–64. On the probable compositional background of Gen. 38:25–26, see W. Dietrich, *Die Josephserzählung als Novelle und Geschichtsschreibung. Zugleich ein Beitrag zur Pentateuchfrage* (BThSt 14; Neukirchen-Vluyn: Neukirchener Verlag, 1989), 51n144 (building on but reversing Blum, *Vätergeschichte*, 245).

52. G. W. Coats, "Redactional Unity in Genesis 37–50," *JBL* 93 (1974): 17; J. Ackerman, "Joseph, Judah, and Jacob," in *Literary Interpretations of Biblical Narratives* (vol. 2; ed. K. R. R. Gros Louis with James S. Ackerman; Nashville: Abingdon, 1982), 98–113; Steinmetz, *From Father to Son*, 45–57; and Noble, "Synchronic and Diachronic Approaches," 137–40.

cob and Joseph stories. Whereas the last eight blessings diverge from the birth order in Gen. 29:31–30:24, the first three blessings closely follow that birth order. In addition, there are major contrasts in the forms and content of the sayings themselves. The last eight blessings focus exclusively on the destiny of each brother, show no interest in issues of guilt or innocence of the brothers, and refer in no way to preceding narratives. In contrast, the first three blessings lead up to the prediction of Judah's future dominance, which will be reminiscent of Joseph's (49:8; cf. 42:6; 44:14; 50:18; also 37:7, 9). They do so by referring to previous misdeeds of Judah's older brothers, misdeeds that implicitly disqualify them from any privilege of the firstborn (49:3–4, cf. 35:21–22a; 49:5–7, cf. 34:1–31).[53] This contrast between the Judah-focused sayings in 49:3–12 linked to the broader Jacob-Joseph story and the following sayings, which lack such elements, suggests that Genesis 49 was modified by an author who had the Jacob and Joseph narratives in view and wanted to represent Judah's relation to his brothers in light of those narratives.[54]

Finally, there are three texts in the Jacob story that appear secondary to their contexts and serve to illustrate the misdeeds referred to in the first two

53. Westermann, *Genesis 12—36*, 253; (E.T., 223). In addition, Westermann points out that the sayings regarding Reuben, Levi, and Simeon are distinguished by a reversal of the typical prophetic judgment oracle, so that now the announcement of their destiny (//prophetic pronouncement of sentence) precedes a reference to their misdeeds (//prophetic accusation). This then prepares for a protoroyal coronation oracle in 49:10–12 (cf. Pss. 2; 110; and Isa. 9:1–6 [Eng. 9:2–7]).

With regard to the "privilege of the first born," the recent work of F. Greenspahn, *When Brothers Dwell Together: The Preeminence of Younger Siblings in the Hebrew Bible* (New York/ Oxford: Oxford University Press, 1994) must be mentioned. He rightly argues against an excessively rigid concept of the right of the firstborn, where the firstborn—along models of later English aristocracy (37–38)—"inevitably" (82) inherits *all* of the father's wealth and blessing. In the process, however, he goes too far in arguing that there was no "default" assumption that the firstborn did not receive some kind of preferential treatment in the inheritance process (9–83). This takes him to rather forced interpretations of texts like Gen. 35:22 and 49:3–4, where it is absolutely clear that some kind of firstborn privilege is lost through a character's actions (122–23). To be sure, as Greenspahn points out, the patriarch had freedom to designate another privileged heir. Nevertheless, only the presence of some kind of assumption of preferential treatment of the firstborn makes sense of Greenspahn's later arguments that the preeminence of younger siblings represents a literary device to stress the divine role in choosing them (85–109) or to focus on a character (112–40).

54. Thus this position does not imply that 49:3–12 was all composed by this author. Indeed, a portion of Judah's blessing, Gen. 49:9, conforms particularly well to the third-person, metaphor-explication pattern found elsewhere in the last eight blessings (cf. 49:14, 21, 22, 27) and may be an early core to the section concerning him. In addition, there may well have been earlier antecedents to the blessings on Reuben, Simeon, and/or Levi as well. The point here is that a Judah-focused author has intervened almost exclusively in this portion of the tribal blessings in 49:3–27.

Notably, the author/adaptor of these blessings was probably also responsible for inserting the blessings to their present context. The framework that links the blessings to their context begins with an emphasis on the future crucial to compositional replacement of Joseph's dominance with Judah's (Gen. 49:1b). Moreover, the framework concludes with an emphasis on the suitability of the blessings (49:28) that particularly closely matches the emphasis on the worthiness/unworthiness of the recipients in the first three blessings.

blessings of Gen. 49:3–7. Reuben's misdeed is described in Gen. 35:21–22a, a text that diverges from its context by (1) naming Jacob "Israel", (2) focusing on a place with Southern associations,[55] and (3) lacking a naming or cult-founding etiology for the place (cf. 33:18–20; 35:6–8, 16–20). Simeon's and Levi's misdeed is described, with slight deviations from Gen. 49:5–7, in the story of Dinah, Gen. 34:1–31.[56] As in the case of Gen. 35:21–22a, this chapter appears to be secondary to its context. It disturbs the movement from Jacob's settlement in Shechem through the purchase of land (Gen. 33:18–20) to God's express command to uproot and leave Shechem (Gen. 35:1). Moreover, the chapter contrasts with its broader Jacob-story context by describing Jacob's children as already old enough to lay waste a local town (Gen. 34:25–29), rather than as young children (Gen. 31:41; cf. 29:31–30:24) who were vulnerable targets in the preceding encounter with Esau (Gen. 33:1–8).[57] Finally, Genesis 34 is prepared for by an addition to the Jacob-story birth narratives. The birth notice for Dinah, Gen. 30:21, lacks an etiology for Dinah's name, and Dinah is not numbered among the children born to Jacob (Gen. 32:23 [Eng. 32:22]).[58] The secondary character of this anticipation of Genesis 34 in Gen. 30:21 adds support to the theory that the placement of Genesis 34 in the non-P material postdates the birth narratives and the broader Jacob story of which they are a part.[59]

  Together, the insertions in Gen. 30:21; 34:1–31; and 35:21–22a suggest that the Judah-focused material in Genesis 38 and 49:1b–28 is part of a broader compositional level spanning the Jacob-Joseph story. The author of this level prepared for Judah's ascendancy in the Jacob story by inserting

55. See Blum, *Vätergeschichte,* 209.

56. This text has been the subject of numerous and highly divergent analyses, from Wellhausen's isolation of parallel Simeon/Levi and all-Israel narratives (*Composition,* 45–46) to B. Edele's forthcoming study in *Vetus Testamentum* ("A Diachronic Analysis of Genesis 34," cited in Van Seters, *Prologue to History,* 306, and summarized on 278), which argues for the secondary character of the Levi and Simeon material. The latter picture is able to stay closer to the text by not having to find completely parallel narratives. Notably, such a compositional model would then agree with the above picture of Genesis 38 and 49. In each case, an earlier independent tradition has been modified to serve its function in the Judean redirection of the Jacob-Joseph story. Nevertheless, this is not the context to explore the complex and to some extent irresolvable transmission-historical problems of Genesis 34.

57. Westermann, *Genesis 12—36,* 654; (E.T., 537); cf. Astruc, *Conjectures,* 442–46.

58. Dillmann, *Genesis,* 339; (E.T., vol. 2, 244); Gunkel, *Genesis,* 336; Kessler, "Querverweise," 135–36; Blum, *Vätergeschichte,* 110. To be sure, Genesis 34 does not seem to have been written in light of 30:21. For Dinah, like her brothers, would have been rather young for the narrative to take place. Instead, Genesis 34 appears to have had its own prehistory before being inserted into its present context (cf. above, n.56 in this chapter), probably by an author who prepared for the insertion by adding Gen. 30:21 to anticipate Genesis 34. In this, the complex mix of links to the narrative context and original independence from it would make Genesis 34 resemble the above-discussed cases of Genesis 38 and 49:1b–28.

59. Genesis 30:21 provides only supporting evidence because it could also have been added by a later reviser who noted Dinah's absence from the birth notices in Gen. 29:31–30:24.

traditions regarding Judah's older brothers (Gen. 30:21; 34:1–31; 35:21–22a). He anticipated the Davidic dynasty in the Tamar story near the beginning of the Joseph story (Gen. 38:1–30). Finally, near the conclusion of the Joseph story, he modified and added the tribal blessings of Genesis 49, so that these adapted blessings now balance the claims for Joseph and his sons in the surrounding narrative and anticipate Judah's future hegemony (Gen. 49:1b–28; see especially 49:1b, 3–12*, 28).

Genesis 48

Genesis 48* (Gen. 48:1–2, 8–14, 17–20)[60] is the next step backward. It too appears to be a compositional addition building on both the Jacob and Joseph narratives. On the one hand, it shares a focus on Joseph with the surrounding Joseph narrative. Indeed, Genesis 48 could not exist outside its context in the Joseph narrative, focusing as it does on Joseph's sons born in Egypt (cf. Gen. 41:50–52) and referring as it does to Jacob's previous expectation not to see Joseph again (Gen. 48:11; cf. 37:32–35; 42:36; 45:25–28; 46:30).[61] On the other hand, the narrative itself is formed in close relation to the Jacob story. Joseph's reference to "the sons that God gave [him]" in 48:9 echoes Jacob's description of his children in Gen. 33:5.[62] More importantly, the whole of Genesis 48* concludes the Jacob-Joseph complex with a picture much like the earlier story of Jacob and Esau with which the complex began. Both the beginning (Genesis 27) and end (Genesis 48*) of the Jacob-Joseph story feature a deathbed blessing scene in which the patriarch aims to express his preference for one descendant over the other. In both cases, the patriarch is nearly blind. Both times the younger is placed over the older, Jacob over Esau in Genesis 27, and Ephraim over Manasseh in Genesis 48:8–20. Finally, as Blum has pointed out, the beginning of the Jacob-Esau narrative and end of Genesis 48 both feature remarkably similar predictions of the dominance of the younger over the older.[63] (See Chart 10-3.)

In summary, Genesis 48* appears to have functioned in an early form of the Jacob-Joseph complex to conclude it with an ordering of Joseph's sons, Ephraim and Manasseh, that is similar to the ordering of Jacob and Esau in Genesis 25:21–34; 27:1–40.

To be sure, there are also important differences between Genesis 48* and its parallels earlier in the Jacob story. These too can be important keys to its composition and setting. In Genesis 27 the nearly blind Isaac is deceived into

---

60. Above, I have already discussed elements of P (Gen. 48:3–6), Rp (48:7), and proto-Genesis (48:15–16, 21–22) in the chapter. This discussion focuses exclusively on the rest of Genesis 48 and indicates this through use of the asterisk in citations.
61. Blum, *Vätergeschichte*, 253.
62. Kessler, "Querverweise," 168–69.
63. Blum, *Vätergeschichte*, 253n63.

Chart 10-3: Predictions of the Dominance of Esau and Manasseh

Gen. 25:23	Gen 48:19
Two nations are in your womb, and two peoples born of you shall be divided. The one shall be stronger than the other, the older shall serve the younger.	He [Manasseh] also shall become a people, and he also shall be great. Nevertheless, his younger brother shall be greater than he, and his offspring shall become a multitude of nations.

giving the younger Jacob the blessing. In contrast, in Genesis 48 the nearly blind Jacob firmly chooses to place Ephraim over Manasseh, even over against Joseph's attempt to point Jacob's error out to him (48:18). The former story still partakes deeply of trickster motifs, while Genesis 48 is a more straightforward legitimation of one group over the other. The honored patriarch of established structures is now the center of legitimation, not the subversive, trickster son. As a result, the elements of blindness and reversal so central to Genesis 27 are no longer linked with one another to develop a deception theme. Instead, these motifs serve mainly to establish the connection between Jacob's placement of Ephraim over Manasseh, on the one hand, and the earlier description of Jacob's placement over Esau, on the other.[64]

Just as in the case of the Judah additions in Genesis 38 and 49:1b–28, so also the blessing material in Genesis 48* is characterized by specifically political interests. Yet the characters and respective groups connected with them are decisively different. In this case, purported ancestors of Northern groups, Ephraim and Manasseh, are the focus, rather than a Southern figure, Judah. Ephraim and Menasseh both bask in the glow of Joseph's reunion with Jacob (Gen. 48:11). Furthermore, both receive a special blessing from him: "By you Israel will invoke blessings, saying, 'God make you like Ephraim and Manasseh.'"(Gen. 48:20a). This blessing places Ephraim and Manasseh over the rest of Israel, and it does so using a formula of blessing typical of royal liturgy for the king.[65] Furthermore, Genesis 48* argues more specifically for the precedence of Ephraim over Manasseh. This precedence is presented as Jacob's express choice, made even over against the attempt by Joseph to reverse the order (Gen. 48:13–14, 17–18). Jacob's justification of this choice reaches into the audience's present experience by stating that Ephraim will become a greater people than Manasseh (48:19). The climactic concluding blessing places Ephraim's name before Manasseh's (Gen. 48:20a), and

64. Blum, *Vätergeschichte*, 253.
65. Cf. Ps. 72:17. Steck, "Gen. 12,1–3," 552n70; Schmid, *Sogenannte Jahwist*, 133–34; Van Seters, *Prologue to History*, 253–55; Köckert, *Vätergott*, 276–83; Blum, *Vätergeschichte*, 353.

then—just in case the audience might have missed the interest in community placement earlier—Genesis 48* concludes with the narrative comment, "So [Jacob] put Ephraim over Manasseh" (Gen. 48:20b). By this point the precedence of Ephraim over Manasseh and the implicit dominance of both over the rest of Israel is clear.[66]

This overall argument both builds on and yet is secondary to the surrounding Joseph story.[67] First, Genesis 48* is introduced with a standard redactional formula, "after these things" (Gen. 48:1aα).[68] Second, Genesis 48* (along with Gen. 49:1b–28) interrupts the movement in non-P materials from (1) Jacob's dying descent toward his bed after getting Joseph to swear to bury him (Gen. 47:31) to (2) Joseph's execution of his oath after Jacob's death (Gen. 50:1–11 . . . 14). Genesis 48 breaks into this context by introducing Joseph's sons (Gen. 48:1aβ–2a), revivifying Jacob to offer a blessing on them (Gen. 48:2b), and adding them to the previous narrative of Jacob's and Joseph's reunion (48:11; cf. Gen. 45:27–28; 46:30).[69] Third, Genesis 48* is distinguished from the surrounding Joseph story by its compositional relation to the preceding Jacob narrative. This is not just an issue of shared

---

66. Blum, *Vätergeschichte*, 254.

67. Here I am working with Gen. 48:1–2, 8–14, 17–20 as a unit. Source analyses have traditionally built on a previous identification of J and E in the surrounding story and found J and E here as well. The primary indicators of seams have been the following: (1) Joseph's double presentation of his sons in 48:10b and 13, (2) the reference to Jacob's blindness in 48:10 and his exclamation over seeing Joseph's sons in 48:11, and (3) the above-discussed interruption represented by the blessing in 48:15–16. Cf. Seebass, *Geschichtliche Zeit*, 67–68; Schmitt, *Die nichtpriesterliche Josephsgeschichte*, 68; Schmidt, *Literarische Studien*, 256–57. Building from such indicators, scholars since Dillmann (*Genesis*, 440–41; [E.T., 434]) have used arguments from profile and potential continuity to distinguish a Yahwistic version focusing on Joseph from an Elohistic version focusing on Ephraim and Manasseh. As L. Schmidt points out, however, such arguments have reconstructed an Elohistic strand that deviates from the rest of the Elohistic Joseph story by using "Israel" as the designation for Joseph's father (*Literarische Studien*, 257–58). Schmidt himself proposes a yet more complex picture of J with various expansions he himself recognizes as comparatively uncertain (*Literarische Studien* 257–71).

Contra Schmidt, there are no clear indicators of growth in Genesis 48 once one has isolated 48:2–6(7), 15–16, and 21–22 as secondary additions. Joseph presents his sons once for the initial greeting and extension of the reunion (Gen. 48:1–2, 8–11) and then again for the announced blessing (48:12–14, 17–20). Jacob's "seeing" Joseph's sons does not contradict the statement that his eyes were weak with age (Gen. 48:10). This comment serves as background for the later interaction where Joseph thinks his father has mistakenly confused the oldest with the youngest (Gen. 48:17–19). Nevertheless, it does not imply such a total blindness that he could not "see," i.e., meet, his son and grandsons (see Rudolph, *Elohist,* 170–71). Furthermore, the indicators discussed above suggest that 48* as a whole is a later addition to its context. It does not form an extension of any strand in the surrounding Joseph story. On this, see in particular, Blum, *Vätergeschichte*, 250–54, 259.

68. This quite general formula has often been mistakenly used as an indicator of the Elohist. Cf. Wellhausen, *Composition*, 59; Holzinger, *Einleitung*, 190; and (for critique of this move) Gunkel, *Genesis*, 243, and Westermann, *Genesis 12—36*, 435; (E.T., 356).

69. For critique of interpretations of this as a deathbed ritual on the basis of 1 Kings 1:47, see Blum, *Vätergeschichte*, 250n37; cf. Schmidt, *Literarische Studien*, 256. Note the original non-P death notice has been omitted, as in other similar cases, replaced by a Priestly death notice from the Priestly genealogical framework (49:33).

characters and information. Such elements could be shared by independent narratives. Instead, Genesis 48 develops certain patterns first seen at the outset of the Jacob story, so that the non-P Jacob-Joseph complex is now begun (Gen. 27:1–45) and ended (Genesis 48*) with similar deathbed blessing scenes. This kind of inclusio is characteristic of narratives composed to stand in the same narrative sequence. As we will see, the bulk of the pre-promise Jacob and Joseph narratives do not show such clear signs of having been written to stand next to each other. Genesis 48, however, links the two.[70]

Before we move on, however, I will note another text that seems to be a part of the same compositional layer as Genesis 48*: the paired birth notices for Ephraim and Manasseh in Gen. 41:50–52. These notices introduce the sons of Joseph who will be the focus of Genesis 48* and share numerous other characteristics with that chapter. Like Genesis 48*, the notices focus on the original ordering of Joseph's sons. Like Genesis 48*, the notices appear to be composed in relation to the Jacob materials, reproducing the birth and etiology pattern seen in Gen. 29:31–30:24 and 35:16–18. Finally, like Genesis 48*, the birth notices appear to be secondary to their context in the Joseph story. Although they build on their surrounding context by mentioning Joseph's wife Asenath (Gen. 41:50, cf. 41:45), they do not develop the themes central to the surrounding story of Joseph's rise to power and provision for Egypt, and they interrupt the specific movement from Joseph's storage of grain (41:46–49) to the beginning of the famine for which it was stored (41:53–57).[71] Like Genesis 48* for which they prepare, these birth notices in 41:50–52 seem to be composed in relation to and yet later than the Joseph-story context in which they occur.

The Jacob Story

Initial Survey and Analysis of the Composition

Although we now stand four steps removed from the final form of the Jacob narrative, the material to be discussed at this point is remarkably similar to the canonical Jacob narrative before us. In previous chapters I have isolated marginal chunks of the narrative as later additions by the Rp editor (Gen. 25:19–20; 26:34–35; 27:46–28:9; 31:17–18; 33:18aβ; 35:9–15, 22b–29), semi-Deuteronomistic retouching (Gen. 26:3bβ–5; 28:21b; and 32:10–13 [Eng. 32:9–12]), compositional adaptations of the story to fit in a broader promise-centered narrative (Gen. 26:1–33*; 28:13–16*; 31:3), and additions by a Judean editor anticipating the Davidic dynasty (Gen. 30:21; 34:1–31; 35:21–22a). The vast bulk of the narrative remains, a narrative ex-

70. Blum, *Vätergeschichte*, 253–54.
71. Donner, *Literarische Gestalt*, 27–28; Rudolph, *Elohist*, 159; Kebekus, *Joseferzählung*, 79–80.

tending from the birth and initial encounters between Jacob and Esau (Gen. 25:21–34; 27:1–45), through the Bethel story (Gen. 28:10–12, 17–22*) and Jacob-Laban encounters (Gen. 29:1–32:1* [Eng. 31:55]), to Jacob's return to Canaan (Gen. 32:2–9 [Eng. 32:1–8], 32:14–33:20 [Eng. 32:13–33:20]; 35:1–8, 16–20). Already this narrative has the concentric form so often noted in synchronic studies of the final form of the Jacob story:[72]

A   Initial encounter between Jacob and Esau (Gen. 25:21–34; 27:1–45)

B   Jacob's divine encounter on the way out of Canaan (Gen. 28:10–22*)

C   Jacob's initial acquisition of wives from Laban at the outset of his sojourn in Haran (Gen. 29:1–30)

D   Fertility: the birth of Jacob's children (Gen. 29:31–30:24)

D' Fertility: the multiplication of Jacob's flocks (Gen. 30:25–43)

C' Jacob's extrication of his wives from Laban's clan at the conclusion of his sojourn (Gen. 31:1–32:1* [Eng. 31:55])

B' Jacob's divine encounter on the way back in to Canaan (Gen. 32:23–33 [Eng. 32:22–32])

A' Final encounter between Jacob and Esau (Gen. 33:1–33:1–17)

Later additions to this structure have either augmented various components in it (e.g., P in Gen. 26:34–35; 27:46–28:9) or added blocks of material toward its margins (e.g., proto-Genesis material in 26:1–33; early Judean material in 34:1–31; and P in 35:9–15). Nevertheless, the basic contours of the Jacob narrative appear to have preceded the work of these later revisers.

As we turn to this overall prepromise Jacob narrative, the first and most important thing to note is its relative independence from everything that precedes and follows it. Once the above-discussed materials are excerpted, the Jacob story shows signs of once having existed independently.[73] Its plot and structure form a cohesive, self-contained whole. Although Abraham is mentioned peripherally in Jacob's references to the "God of his father" (31:42, 53),[74] there is nothing integral to the Jacob materials under discussion that

---

72. M. Fishbane, "Composition and Structure in the Jacob Cycles (Gen. 25:19–35:22)," *JJS* 26 (1975): 15–38 (cf. also his *Text and Texture*, 40–58); Fokkelman, *Narrative Art in Genesis*, 86–241; J. Gammie, "Theological Interpretation by Way of Literary and Tradition Analysis: Genesis 25—36," in *Encounter with the Text: Form and History in the Hebrew Bible* (ed. M. J. Buss; Philadelphia: Fortress; Missoula, Mont.: Scholars, 1979), 121–22; Coats, *Genesis*, 177–80; Mann, *The Book of the Torah*, 52; Wenham, *Genesis 16—50*, 169–70.

73. Blum, *Vätergeschichte*, 7–151, especially 149–51.

74. As others have noted, these mentions of Abraham may be elaborations of original references just to the "god of my/your father." In Gen. 31:42, "the God of my father" (singular) now stands in apposition to a twofold specification of that God, "the God of Abraham and the Fear

requires the presence of the Abraham *narrative* before them. Moreover, although there are a number of characters in common with the following Joseph narrative, there is nothing in the prepromise Jacob narrative that requires continuation in the Joseph narrative. Indeed, as we will see in a later discussion, the Joseph narrative diverges in some important respects from the Jacob narrative, even as it appears to presuppose that its audience is familiar with some form of the Jacob story.

As Kessler and Blum in particular have highlighted, this self-contained Jacob narrative is bound together by a network of explicit textual cross-references and anticipations.

1. The final scene of Genesis 27, where Jacob is sent by Rebekah to her brother Laban because of Esau's plans to kill Jacob (Gen. 27:41–45), looks forward to Jacob's sojourn in Haran and links it to the conflict with Esau.

2. Jacob's vow at Bethel to tithe in return for protection on his way looks forward to his journey to Haran (Gen. 28:20–22; 29:1) in light of the preceding Jacob-Esau narratives where his life was in danger (Gen. 25:21–34; 27:1–45). It builds on the references to "angels of God" and the "house of God" in the preceding narrative (28:12, 17, 19), but focuses specifically on "God's" protective power for him on his journey.[75]

3. The story of the birth of Jacob's first eleven children, Gen. 29:31–30:24, anticipates the later narratives regarding his reunion with Esau (Gen. 32:23 [Eng. 32:22]; 33:1–14) and the description of Benjamin's birth (Gen. 35:16–20; cf. 30:24).

4. The extended speech of Jacob to his wives Rachel and Leah (Gen. 31:4–13) and their reply (Gen. 31:14–16) starts the transition from the Jacob-Laban materials back to the Jacob-Esau theme. Once again, as in the Bethel oath, the narrative now refers to a singular divine "Elohim," who protects Jacob. Notably, Jacob's speech to his wives refers to his oath at Bethel but not to any divine appearance there. This cross-

---

of Isaac." In Gen. 31:53a, the specification "the God of Abraham and the God of Nahor" is different from the "Fear of Isaac" by whom Jacob swears in Gen. 31:53b. Moreover, this description of "the God of Abraham and the God of Nahor" stands strikingly distant from "their God" ("your God" in early Greek manuscripts) at the end of the clause. This suggests that 31:42 may have originally read, "may the gods of your father judge between us, and Jacob swore by the fear of Isaac." Only later was it adapted to refer to the parallel lines of Abraham and Nahor introduced at the outset of the ancestral section (Gen. 11:28–29).

Especially given the presence of other texts in the Jacob-Joseph story that link Jacob and Joseph to Abraham and the promise theme, and especially given the fact that the parallels to these texts in Gen. 31:5 and 29 have a reference exclusively to "the god of your (singular) father," it is likely that the mentions of Abraham and Isaac in Gen. 31:42 and Abraham and Nahor in 31:53a are secondary. Nevertheless, the argument above does not depend on this point.

75. The reference to "YHWH" in Gen. 28:21b was identified as a secondary addition to non-P in chapter 8 of this book.

reference appears to predate the insertion of the (proto-Genesis) YHWH divine speech in Gen. 28:13–15.

5. The narrative describing Jacob's and Laban's encounter in Gilead continues the linkages to the broader Jacob narrative. First, it links with the Bethel story by describing how "the god of [Jacob's] father" appeared to Laban in a dream (Gen. 31:24) and protected Jacob from Laban, as Jacob had asked (31:29b; cf. Gen. 28:20–21). Second, Jacob's speech to Laban at this point (Gen. 31:36–42) reaffirms this protection theme and reiterates the construal of Jacob's sojourn in Haran that was first heard in his speech to Rachel and Leah (Gen. 31:4–13). Finally, this treaty is sealed through Jacob's oath by the "fear of Isaac" (Gen. 31:53b), a mention of the father standing at the outset of the narrative concerning him.

6. Genesis 32:4–33 [Eng. 32:3–32] then bridges from the Jacob-Laban encounters to a Jacob-Esau section. This section begins and ends with accounts like the earlier Bethel story (Gen. 32:3, 23–33 [Eng. 32:2, 22–32]//28:10–22*), and these accounts enclose a description of Jacob's preparing to encounter his potentially murderous brother (cf. Gen. 27:41–45) by giving him family and flocks gained in Haran (Gen. 32:4–9, 14–22 [Eng. 32:3–8, 13–21]; cf. 29:31–30:43).[76]

7. The description of Jacob and Esau's encounter in Gen. 33:1–17 is saturated with references to the previous Jacob narrative. It describes the gift of flocks and family gained in Haran (cf. Gen. 29:31–30:43) offered to the brother cheated of birthright and father's blessing (cf. Gen. 25:21–34; 27:1–45). At the same time there is an often-noted swerve at this point: whereas Esau was predicted to serve Jacob (Gen. 25:23; cf. 27:29), it is Jacob who is obeisant to Esau here (Gen. 33:3).[77] Whatever domination Jacob will enjoy is thus projected outside the narrative framework, indeed implicitly into the present of the audience. At this point the network of the Jacob story focuses not on Jacob's dominance of Esau as predicted in the oracle. Instead, it describes Jacob's successful escape from the threat of death at Esau's hands. This escape theme is yet another continuation of the protection theme already seen in Gen. 28:20–22.

8. Jacob's constructing and naming an altar at Shechem in Gen. 33:18–20 links directly with his oath in 28:20. Just as he looked forward at that time to God's bringing him home "in peace," so now this text describes

---

76. This double explanation of the Mahanaim place-name is a key place where source critics found elements of J and E in the Jacob narrative. Yet as Van Seters has persuasively argued (*Prologue to History*, 96, 181–250, 212), such double etiologies are quite characteristic of ancient narratives formed out of earlier materials. Especially since there is no evidence of ongoing, parallel sources elsewhere in the Jacob narrative, it makes sense to interpret this doubling as the result of this normal combination of traditions, rather than positing a rather abnormal process of source combination.

77. Turner, *Announcements of Plot in Genesis*, 119–24; Clines, "What Happens in Genesis," 59–60. See also *Gen. Rab.* 94:5.

how Jacob came to Shechem "in peace" after his encounter with Esau.[78] Moreover, his naming the altar he built there "God [El] is the god of Israel" links with the preceding account of his own renaming as "Israel" (Gen. 32:23–33 [Eng. 32:22–32]). After having been brought by God in peace to Shechem (33:18), Jacob recognizes God's power through this sentence name (33:19). This recognition, just as with the renaming of Jacob in Gen. 32:23–33 [Eng. 32:22–32], shows again how the narrative works on two levels. On the one level stands the intricate narrative of personal dynamics surrounding Jacob and his family. On the other, the narrative anticipates the later national connection of the people of Israel to the God of Jacob.

9. Genesis 35:1–7 links with the initial Bethel story, the theft of the household gods in Genesis 31, and the general theme of protection seen throughout the previous Jacob story. After being commanded to return to the place where God appeared to him at Bethel (Gen. 35:1, cf. 28:10–22*), Jacob passes the command along and buries the household gods along with jewelry at Shechem (Gen. 35:2–4) and travels to Bethel (Gen. 35:6). Then, in a narrative closely paralleling the previous account of building the altar at Shechem, Jacob anticipates the later establishment of the Northern Kingdom sanctuary at Bethel by building an altar there and naming the place after God's appearance to him (Gen. 35:7).

10. Finally, as Blum has pointed out, the death, burial, and place naming for Deborah in 35:8 and Rachel in 35:19–20 closely resemble each other.[79] (See Chart 10-4.)

Chart 10-4: The Death, Burial, and Place Naming for Deborah and Rachel

Gen. 35:8	Gen. 35:19–20
And Deborah, Rebekah's nurse,	And Rachel
died,	died,

and she was buried
    under an oak below Bethel.
	and she was buried
	    on the way to Ephrath (that is
	    Bethlehem)

So it was called "Oak of Weeping."	and Jacob set up a pillar at her grave; it
	    is the pillar of Rachel's tomb, which
	    is there to this day.

---

78. *Gen. Rab.* 79:2, 3; Rashi, ad loc.; Dillmann, *Genesis,* 364; (E. T., vol. 2, 291–92); Gunkel, *Genesis,* 368; Procksch, *Genesis,* 540, 542; Fokkelman, *Narrative Art,* 229–30; Sarna, *Genesis,* 232. Blum's objections (*Vätergeschichte,* 206) to connecting these two expressions are not persuasive. The use of *šālēm* ("in peace") here is rare but easily understandable. Moreover, contra Blum, it occurs at a place exactly appropriate to mark the fulfillment of the condition in 28:21, indicating Jacob's survival of his encounter with Esau immediately after that encounter has occurred.

79. Blum, *Vätergeschichte,* 204–5.

Together, these notices take Jacob's travels up to the very border with Judah. Between these two notices, Benjamin (Gen. 35:16–18), the son looked for in the initial set of birth notices in Gen. 29:31–30:24, is born. His birth appears originally to have been placed in a Benjaminite border region, on "the way to Ephratah" (cf. 1 Sam. 10:2), and only later attached to Judah through the gloss "it is Bethlehem."[80] In sum, the birth and death notices of Gen. 35:8 and 16–20 bind up the loose ends of the Jacob narrative and end the story at the border between the Northern and Southern Kingdoms.

As in the case of the primeval history and the broader proto-Genesis composition as well, these explicit cross-references are important keys to the viewpoint and setting of the author of the Jacob composition. Through them we can move beyond a focus on the traditions used by this author to suppositions about the one who drew these traditions into the present narrative whole.

Indeed, in some important respects the profile of many of these cross-reference texts is distinct from that of the traditions they connect. Further analysis of these distinctions can sharpen our sense of the perspective and background of the author of the Jacob story. Take Jacob's speech in Gen. 31:4–13, for example. This speech diverges from the material preceding it in its presentation of at least two crucial items. First, whereas Laban only specifies Jacob's wages three times in the preceding narrative (Gen. 29:15–17, 27; 30:27–34), Jacob says in Gen. 31:4–13 that Laban has changed his wages ten times (31:7). Second, whereas the preceding narrative describes Jacob gaining his flocks through trickery (Gen. 30:37–43), in this speech in Gen. 31:4–13 Jacob asserts that he gained them through divine intervention (31:11–12). In both cases, Jacob comes off better in his speech than in the narrative that precedes it. Given this, these divergent descriptions of single incidents in the present narrative are easily read as further characterizations of Jacob that contrast Jacob's own speech with that of the narrator.[81] Nevertheless, as Blum points out, such a reading would put in question not only Jacob's exoneration of himself in Gen. 31:4–13 but also theological elements of the speech, such as the otherwise unreported divine command to return in Gen. 31:13. Yet these and other elements of the speech are essential parts of the presentation of Jacob and of God in the broader prepromise Jacob narrative. However one makes sense of the present form of the text, there is an apparent ancient gap between the narrator's report of events in Genesis 29—30 and the narrator's theological-moral re-presentation of those events through Jacob's mouth in Gen. 31:4–13.

---

80. Blum, *Vätergeschichte*, 207–8.
81. Eerdmans, *Studien*, 55–56; Westermann, *Genesis 12—36*, 599; (E.T., 491); cf. Volz, *Elohist*, 95–96; Fokkelman, *Narrative Art in Genesis*, 157–59.

The classic source analyses of this gap identified J as the main source in Gen. 30:25–43 (analyses of Genesis 29 differed), while E was the source of the presentation in Gen. 31:4–13.[82] Nevertheless, such studies could not find any clear signs of the specific E narrative to which 31:4–13 refers. Instead, they had to satisfy themselves with prying loose various pieces of Gen. 29:1–30 and 30:25–43 from their contexts, and then identifying them on the basis of fragile linguistic grounds as fragments of the missing E source that "must" have been there. In the past few decades, however, an increasing number of scholars have recognized the futility of such an approach and have argued instead that Gen. 31:4–13 was designed from the beginning as a moralizing, theocentric re-presentation of the preceding events. Its prologue was not a non-existent E source but Genesis 29—30 itself.[83] By inserting this speech, the author of Gen. 31:4–13 could elegantly redirect crucial parts of the Jacob story, without having to intervene massively in the often convoluted traditions before him (especially Gen. 30:25–43).[84]

In summary, there is a strong crosscurrent to be observed in the pre-promise Jacob narrative here. On the one hand, we have trickster traditions that unself-consciously present Jacob as deceiving his father-in-law and Rachel as stealing her father's gods. On the other hand, the expansion in 31:4–13 (along with the reply in 31:14–16) strategically modifies the overall narrative. It uses the medium of a dialogue between Jacob and his wives to exonerate Jacob from any charge of wronging Laban, and to clarify and theologize the preceding convoluted account of Jacob's acquisition of flocks from Laban. Now, through the addition of this material, Laban's sons in 31:1 are balanced by Laban's daughters (31:14–16). Now, Rachel's theft of the household gods is not only a continuation of the deception theme (cf. Genesis 27, 29—30) and background for the treaty (31:33–37) but an outgrowth of hers and Leah's expression of solidarity with Jacob's cause (31:14–16). Now, Laban's insistence that his daughters, grandchildren, and flocks are his (31:43) does not go unanswered but instead is refuted first by Jacob (31:5–13) and then by his own family (31:14–16).[85]

Thus, Gen. 31:4–16 is not just a linking of diverse traditions with each other but provides a moral reconstrual of them. It is a partial taming of an unruly, trickster character into one who can better fit in an orderly moral universe. Genesis 31:4–16 and related texts, even if formulated in light of their context, represent an important theological reconceptualization of surrounding traditions. Through them the author of the Jacob materials was able to re-present Jacob as having the moral high ground. Furthermore, he

82. Hupfeld, *Quellen der Genesis,* 42–43; Wellhausen, *Composition,* 38–39; Dillmann, *Genesis,* 333, 343–44; (E.T., vol. 2, 232, 252–53); Gunkel, *Genesis,* 336–37.
83. Kessler, "Querverweise," 119–25; Blum, *Vätergeschichte,* 123, 127.
84. Blum, *Vätergeschichte,* 123n21.
85. Kessler, "Querverweise," 119–25; Blum, *Vätergeschichte,* 123–26.

was able to do so exclusively through the medium of a large block of direct speech, without extensive modification of the preceding, often complex descriptions of Jacob's and Laban's interactions.

So also, other cross-reference texts, particularly in Genesis 25—31, are distinct from and appear to be secondary to their contexts.

1. Jacob's oath in Gen. 28:20–22 appears to be an addition to an earlier epiphany report designed to legitimate the sanctuary at Bethel. The earlier epiphany story followed a careful concentric structure focusing on Jacob's discovery of the Bethel "gate of heaven" and his erecting a pillar there (cf. 28:11//18; 28:12//16*–17), and concluded with the naming of Bethel (28:19).[86] Jacob's oath in 28:20–21a, 22 falls outside this concentric structure, after its conclusion. Moreover, the oath shifts from the relentlessly local focus of the preceding epiphany report. Now, with the presence of the oath, the overall Bethel story is a theological link between the Jacob-Esau and Jacob-Laban stories. Whereas the early, originally independent epiphany report focused exclusively on legitimating the Bethel sanctuary, the author of Gen. 28:20–22 made that tradition into a description of Jacob's encounter with God upon exiting the land. This encounter then balances the later narrative of Jacob's encounter with God upon reentry into the land at Penuel (Gen. 32:23–33 [Eng. 32:22–32]).

2. The narrative of the birth of Jacob's first eleven children (Gen. 29:31–30:24) is alien to its immediate context in the Jacob-Laban story. The context focuses primarily on Jacob's marriage to Laban's daughters and only mentions peripherally that Jacob had sons. In contrast, Gen. 29:31–30:24 carefully lists and names each son in anticipation of narratives following the Jacob-Laban story. Moreover, the section has been secondarily linked to its context by the addition of the maids in the text preceding the birth reports, Gen. 29:24, 29, and 30:33.[87]

3. God's protection of Jacob by appearing to Laban in a dream (Gen. 31:24), along with Laban's later mention of it (Gen. 31:29b) both appear to be additions to their contexts. The dream is secondarily linked to its context through resumptive repetition (31:25a, cf. 31:23b), and Laban's later mention of God's protection (31:29b) is not fully compatible with the menacing tone of the rest of his speech, one in which he argues

---

86. Blum, *Vätergeschichte*, 9–16.

87. Thus, for example, 29:24 interrupts the move from Jacob's unknowing marriage and sex with Leah (29:23), and his discovery of her identity (29:25). Moreover, the lack of specification that Jacob is the subject of the verb in 29:25 suggests that this verse originally attached not to 29:24, where Laban is the subject, but to 29:23 where Jacob is the specified subject. Eising, *Jakobserzählung*, 175; Blum, *Vätergeschichte*, 104n44. On the secondary character of this birth report, see most recently Van Seters, *Prologue to History*, 278.

that Jacob must cooperate because of Laban's power to hurt him (Gen. 31:26–29a).[88]

To be sure, such arguments are of differing weight, and they are often weaker than the combined arguments from seams and profile that have been used in previous chapters of this study. Nevertheless, even these often minor indicators of the secondary character of narrative cross-references in Genesis 25—31* disappear once we move to the texts concerning Jacob's return in Genesis 32—35*. Instead, this whole latter portion of the early Jacob narrative (Genesis 32—35*) appears to have been written from the perspective seen in the *secondary* cross-reference texts of Genesis 25—31* (Gen. 28:20–22; 29:31–30:24; 31:4–16, 24–25a, 29b, 41–42). To be sure, in isolated cases, like the Penuel encounter, the contours of an earlier tradition are noticeable. Nevertheless, the bulk of this narrative has been so thoroughly composed in light of what precedes that it is impossible to distinguish between secondary cross-reference texts, on the one hand, and their context, on the other.

Together, all these narrative cross-references display a conspicuous continuity of theme: travel and return, threat and protection by the god of the father(/fear of Isaac), fertility, divine providence, and overall anticipation in the life of Jacob of Israel's later national and cultic history—the emergence of a national group, "Israel"; Israel's dominance over Edom; the establishment of the Bethel temple and tithing there; and so forth. Such themes are by no means contradictory to those of the later, broader proto-Genesis framework that has now been built around them. Nevertheless, they are also distinct from it. Indeed, as observed before, certain cross-references, such as the reference in 31:13 to Jacob's oath at Bethel, do not display any signs that the author had knowledge of the later proto-Genesis promise texts. Moreover, this Jacob story network, like that seen in the primeval history composition, is remarkably self-contained. It requires nothing from the preceding Abraham and Isaac stories in order to be intelligible. Such indicators suggest that these cross-references in the Jacob story are part of a compositional layer predating the above-discussed, broader proto-Genesis compositional layer. They are part of a prepromise Jacob composition.

Background of the Early Jacob Composition

As Blum has argued, this Jacob composition has several clear linkages to the Northern Kingdom of Israel.

1. The above-discussed linkages focus on Northern Kingdom locales— Bethel, Gilead, Mizpah, Mahanaim, Penuel, Shechem, and the border between Benjamin and Judah.

---

88. Blum, *Vätergeschichte*, 125–26.

2. Bethel's particular prominence in the prepromise Jacob narrative corresponds strikingly with the importance of Bethel as a royal sanctuary in the Northern Kingdom. Blum notes that the focus on the Bethel sanctuary found in Gen. 28:10–22* presupposes an audience for whom this sanctuary was a living reality.[89] In particular, the prediction of tithing there indicates that this sanctuary was a reality for the audience of this text. In addition, the Jacob narrative incorporates not one but two legitimation traditions regarding Bethel (Gen. 28:10–22*; 35:6–8), and God is described in Jacob's speech to Rachel and Leah as introducing himself as the "God (El) who is in Bethel" (Gen. 35:7).[90] Such a designation of God then stands in contradiction to the Judean claim of "YHWH who dwells in Zion" (Isa. 8:18; Pss. 9:12 [Eng. 9:11]; 135:21) or "YHWH who is enthroned on the Cherubim" (1 Sam. 4:4; 2 Kings 19:15; Pss. 80:2; [Eng. 80:1] 99:1).[91]

3. Joseph, a frequent symbol of the North, is particularly prominent in these materials. The initial introduction of Jacob's first eleven sons culminates with Joseph's birth, and the double etiology for his name signals the special importance of his birth. The first etiology—"God has taken away my disgrace"—concludes the overall focus of the birth narrative on inter-wife dynamics and barrenness (cf. Gen. 29:31), while the second etiology—"YHWH will give me another son"—points to the end of the Jacob narrative with the birth of Benjamin.[92] In the following narrative Joseph is the only son of the eleven to be mentioned again by name (33:2, 7). Moreover, Bethel, and perhaps Mahanaim and Penuel as well, are located in territories associated with Joseph.[93] Such a focus on Joseph is particularly important in light of the fact that the Northern Kingdom was often characterized as the "house of Joseph," just as the Southern Kingdom was characterized as the "house of Judah."[94]

These connections to the North are further supported by evidence outside the book of Genesis that Jacob was a prominent figure in the preexilic Northern context. Not only is the audience frequently characterized as "Jacob/Israel" in Northern prophetic texts, but Hos. 12:4–5, 13 (Eng. 12:3–4, 12) appears to presuppose knowledge of the Jacob story in its Northern audience: Jacob's grabbing of Esau's foot at birth (Hos. 12:4a [Eng. 12:3a]; cf. Gen. 25:26); his flight to Aram and marriage there (Hos. 12:13; Eng. 12:12; cf. Gen. 27:43; 28:10–29:30); his wrestling with "God" at Penuel (Hos. 12:4b–5a [Eng. 12:3b–4]; cf. Gen. 32:23–33 [Eng. 32:22–32]); and Jacob's

---

89. Blum, *Vätergeschichte*, 93–96, 175–76.
90. Blum, *Vätergeschichte*, 186–90 (with survey and discussion of earlier literature).
91. Blum, *Vätergeschichte*, 180–81.
92. S. Lehming, "Zur Erzählung von der Geburt der Jakobsöhne," *VT* 13 (1963): 79; Gunkel, *Genesis*, 336; Blum, *Vätergeschichte*, 109–10.
93. See Blum, *Vätergeschichte*, 183n45, for discussion and literature.
94. Blum, *Vätergeschichte*, 183 and 490n71.

finding God at Bethel and speaking with God there (Hos. 12:5b [Eng. 12:4b]; cf. Gen. 28:10–22).[95] Evidence both internal and external to Genesis indicates a probable Northern origin for the pre-promise Jacob story.

Furthermore, the above-discussed features of the prepromise Jacob story suggest a date sometime during the Northern monarchy. The Northern monarchy would likely provide institutional infrastructure to support the authorship and preservation of an extensive narrative like the Jacob story. Moreover, the anticipation of Bethel as a living sanctuary suggests an original audience familiar with the temple and tithing there. This in turn suggests a date for the Jacob narrative sometime before the destruction of Bethel by Josiah. Blum argues on the basis of the prominence of Penuel in the Jacob narrative for a more exact placement of the narrative at the very beginning of the Northern Kingdom when Penuel was the temporary capital of Israel, just after the split from the South. This theory would not only explain the strategic placement of Jacob's renaming as "Israel" at Penuel, but it would also potentially provide background for certain anti-Judean aspects of the Jacob narrative, such as the implicitly counter-Jerusalem tone of formulations like "God who is at Bethel" (Gen. 31:13, versus the Judean "YHWH who dwells in Zion") and "El is the God of Israel" (Gen. 33:20).[96] To be sure, such an exact dating is risky in light of the paucity and multivalency of the data. Nevertheless, at the very least we can say the Jacob narrative shows multiple signs of origin in the Northern monarchy before its fall, making it an ancient pre-exilic composition.

Such a composition served to legitimate the Northern Kingdom and to present, in a sense, the national "character" of this kingdom through its depiction

---

95. Whitt, "The Jacob Traditions," 18–43 (see also Daniels, *Hosea and Salvation History*, 43–46, 51), argues against too quickly assuming that Hosea was familiar with the textual realization of the Jacob traditions now seen in the non-P Genesis material. In the process he has pointed out important divergences of Hosea 12 from the Genesis traditions, and rightly raised the possibility of Hosea's dependence on other Jacob traditions no longer attested in our narrative sources. Nevertheless, both (1) the breadth and (2) the closeness of the links between the prepromise Jacob narrative and Hosea 12 strongly suggest that Hosea was somehow familiar with the prepromise Jacob narrative. For example, Hos 12:4 (Eng. 12:3) asserts that Jacob "tricked" his brother in the womb, using the verb *'qb* that parallels the "heel" (*'aqēb*) of Esau that Jacob grabbed on his way out of the womb (Gen. 25:26). Hosea is representing the process differently from Genesis here. At the same time, however, the wordplay suggests a direct relationship between these textual formulations. So also, Israel "serves" (*šmr*) for a wife in Hos. 12:13 (Eng. 12:12), just as Jacob "guarded" (*šmr*) Laban's flocks (Gen. 30:31). Despite the different context, Hosea seems to be playing on the earlier tradition, even as he substantially redirects it. Especially when seen in the context of the broad number of parallels between Hosea 12 and the prepromise Jacob narrative, these verbal links suggest a special relationship between these two texts. Furthermore, since Hosea 12 appears to presuppose knowledge of these Jacob traditions in its audience—indeed the same breadth and type of traditions found in the prepromise Jacob narrative—the simplest and most elegant hypothesis is that the prepromise Jacob narrative was an important part of the block of traditions presupposed by Hosea.
96. Blum, *Vätergeschichte*, 184–86, notes other potential Northern associations of the Jacob narrative.

of Jacob. Already in the Egyptian Mernephtah stelae we have early attestation of association of the name "Israel" with the northern part of the country, and the name "Israel" seems to have retained this more specific reference to the north even after the Davidic monarchy laid claim to the term to characterize the broader territory covered by the Davidic chiefdom/kingdom. In the context of the split of the North from the South, the Jacob narrative locates Jacob's renaming as "Israel" in a Northern Kingdom capital. The use of the term *Israel* then serves a double function: while it has a special ancient association with the north, it verbalizes at the same time the broader territorial claims of the Northern Kingdom. Thus for example, the narrative of the birth of Jacob's sons includes the births of the purported progenitors of the Southern tribes. Yet at the same time the birth of Judah is subordinated to that of Joseph, and only Benjamin has a comparable place.[97] Other elements of the narrative, such as the description of Jacob's founding of the future Northern Kingdom's royal sanctuary in Bethel; the naming of God, "God who is in Bethel"; and the following reference to "El is the God of Israel" (Gen. 33:20) seem to articulate the emergent Northern Kingdom's right to exist.

Within this Northern context, the stories of Jacob's deception and counterdeception would have functioned to describe not just an individual but a culture hero who in a sense represents the character of the people he is said to have fathered. At Penuel, this individual-collective connection is even thematized on a textual level through the renaming of the individual, Jacob, by the national name, "Israel." Through this connection, the descriptions of Jacob's exploits do not just entertain but also claim for the *people* of "Israel" Jacob's craftiness, strength, virility, and riches. In addition, this connection works in other areas. Jacob's relations with Esau and Laban anticipate Israel's relations with the Edomites and Arameans. The claims of the narrative that God was "with" Jacob are, at the same time, claims that God is now "with" Northern Israel. And the narrative's consistent focus throughout on God's protection of Jacob implicitly asserts that God will likewise protect the people he fathered.

When making many of these links, the prepromise Jacob narrative drew on the resources of personal piety to articulate God's protection and sponsorship of the Northern Kingdom. Many of the traditional foci of personal piety were already present in the early traditions regarding Jacob. Just as personal piety often focuses on the everyday concerns of childbirth, fertility of flocks, and the dangers of journeys, so also these everyday concerns are found in the early traditions regarding Jacob's flight from his family and his acquisition of flocks and children in Haran.[98] The author of the prepromise Jacob story did

97. Blum, *Vätergeschichte*, 182–83.
98. Vorländer, *Mein Gott*, 69–90, 124–34, 146–48, 160–63; T. Jacobsen, *The Treasures of Darkness: A History of Mesopotamian Religion* (New Haven, Conn./London: Yale University Press, 1976), 155–64; Albertz, *Persönliche Frömmigkeit*, 58–70, 77–91, 101–39; idem, *Religionsgeschichte*, vol. 1, 53–62; (E.T., 29–36).

not introduce these elements. Nevertheless, as we look at the above-discussed secondary additions that bind together the prepromise Jacob story, these texts often build on the themes of personal piety, such as the allegiance of an ancestral deity to the clan patriarch, the claim that this deity is "with" him, and the promise of protection. Now, however, these themes are applied on a national level, so a link is built between the people Jacob fathered and his ancestral God, and in particular between that God's promise to be with him and that God's ongoing allegiance to Jacob's children.

In this way the prepromise Jacob narrative draws on the cultural resources of its audience to build a credible picture of God's protection of them and their fledgling kingdom. Moreover, it does so without needing to rely on the royal ideology of the Judean kingdom from which it is separating. The Jacob story shows how both the anti-authoritarian, trickster-Jacob, traditions and the personal piety of the highland clans could be important ideological resources for a Northern Kingdom splitting from the Southern monarchy and struggling for its own identity.

The Source Approach and the Question of Moving Further Backward

Certainly this Jacob narrative was not developed from whole cloth. As has long been recognized, it shows numerous signs of having been woven out of numerous traditions. Like the Old Babylonian Gilgamesh epic and the chronologically later Abraham section, the Jacob narrative under discussion appears to be rooted in earlier traditions. For example, it gathers a variety of ancient trickster traditions regarding Jacob. Moreover, several stories in it still preserve the faint outlines of what were once burial and sanctuary traditions of Israelite localities (Gen. 28:10–19*; 32:23–33* [Eng. 32:22–32]; 35:1–5*, 16–20*). The question to be considered at this point is, What model for the prehistory of the Jacob narrative is the most probable, if indeed we can even make any probable suggestions at all about its prehistory?

Past source analyses have argued that the non-P Jacob narrative is a conflation of parallel Yahwistic and Elohistic documents. Usually such analyses have been extensions of a conflation model initially developed for P and non-P materials in Genesis 1—11 and then reapplied to non-P material to posit parallel J and E sources in Genesis 12—25.[99] Once this model was established for the first half of Genesis, the source critics generally presupposed it for the Jacob story. Although the bulk of the Jacob narrative does not have the marks of conflation seen in a text block like Genesis 1—11, these scholars have dis-

---

99. Hupfeld, the original proponent of the three-source approach to Genesis that is being critiqued here, is an important exception. He began his arguments in the Jacob story (*Quellen der Genesis,* 38–47) before going on to identification of the Elohist in the Joseph (47–48) and Abraham (48–56) sections. With Wellhausen the movement is reversed, going from Abraham (*Composition,* 17–18) to Jacob (30–48) and Joseph (52–60).

sected certain key texts, such as Gen. 28:10–22 or 31:1–16, into separate sources and then worked outward from them to isolate the remnants of the purported Yahwistic and Elohistic sources connecting them. The results, however, have proven stubbornly variable because the texts do not offer evidence of the combination of parallel sources. Not only is a source approach to texts like Gen. 28:10–22 or 31:4–16 weak, but such an approach is completely contraindicated for many of the key texts surrounding them. For example, once critics have isolated the remnants of parallel "Yahwistic" and "Elohistic" Bethel stories in Gen. 28:10–22, many have tried to find parallel Yahwistic and Elohistic strands in the preceding non-P story of Jacob stealing his father's blessing (Gen. 27:1–45). Nevertheless, as Noth among others already noted, this chapter simply does not offer data to support any such reconstruction.[100] As a result, he and many other traditional source critics throw up their hands, positing that both sources "must" have had such a story, even though the text we have shows no evidence that they did.

The rest of the non-P Jacob story likewise lacks evidence of the combining of parallel Yahwistic and Elohistic sources. Both non-source and many source approaches have recognized the essential unity of the non-P material regarding Jacob's birth and marriages.[101] So also, the account of the birth of his sons, with the exception of the introduction of Dinah in 30:21, is unified. One can only reconstruct source strands here by dismantling the carefully composed whole and presupposing that largely complementary halves of J and E have been combined at this point.[102] Moving onward, the account of Jacob's acquisition of flocks, despite a few isolated interpolations,[103] is a unified whole. As Volz and others have pointed out, it moves logically through the following stages:[104]

1. Jacob's proposal to take as payment the black among the sheep and the spotted and speckled among the goats (Gen. 30:32–33)
2. Laban's acceptance of this proposal and separation of this "payment" from his herd and placement of it under the care of his sons (Gen. 30:34–35)

100. Noth, *Pentateuch*, 30n93; (E.T., 30); and Westermann, *Genesis 12—36*, 530–31; (E.T., 436). For critique of attempts to identify source strata here, see Volz, *Elohist*, 61–70; Blum, *Vätergeschichte*, 79–86; Boecker, *1. Moses 25.19–37.1*, 43–45.
101. See the overview in Westermann, *Genesis 12—36*, 565–66; (E.T., 464), and treatment in Blum, *Vätergeschichte*, 98–105. Those source approaches that have divided the chapter have usually divided it between 29:1, 15–30 (E) and 29:2–14 (J).
102. See in particular Blum's analysis on this point, *Vätergeschichte*, 105–10.
103. Good candidates for such glosses occur in 30:32 and 35. The phrase "every speckled and spotted sheep" (in Gen. 30:32) is missing in the Old Greek. "The male goats that were striped and spotted" standing at the outset of 30:35 is a third classification of animals that may have been added to this early section of the story so that it would better match the later description of Jacob's multiplication of "striped" animals in Gen. 30:39.
104. Eerdmans, *Studien*, 53–55; Jacob, *Genesis*, 603–9; Eising, *Jacobserzählung*, 193–202; Volz, *Elohist*, 90–92; Blum, *Vätergeschichte*, 112–16; Boecker, *1. Moses 25.19–37.1*, 78–80.

3. Jacob's use of magical means to cause Laban's flock to produce more speckled and spotted goats (Gen. 30:37–39) and black sheep (Gen. 30:40) for himself

4. Jacob's making sure the extra livestock he received were the strongest of Laban's flock (Gen. 30:41–42)

Finally, Jacob's preparations for his encounter with Esau in Genesis 32 can not be divided into a Yahwistic splitting of his flocks to protect them (Gen. 32:4–9, 14a [Eng. 32:3–8, 13a]) and Elohistic sending of his flocks as gifts (32:14b–22 [Eng. 32:13b–21]). Jacob's splitting his flocks in 32:4–9, 14a (Eng. 32:3–8, 13a) already looks forward in 32:6 (Eng. 32:5) to the sending of gifts in 32:14b–22 (Eng. 32:13b–21). Moreover, both halves of Genesis 32 are parallel to each other and form a continuous process (32:14a//22b [Eng. 32:13a//21b]);[105] both are united around wordplays involving the words "to camp" (ḥnh), "encampment" (maḥănēh), Mahanaim/"two encampments" (maḥănāyim), and "favor" (ḥēn;)[106] and both are presupposed in Genesis 33 (33:1; cf. 32:8–9 [Eng. 32:7–8]; 33:8–11 cf. 32:19–22 [Eng. 32:18–21]).[107]

To be sure there is evidence of transmission-historical complexity in various texts in the Jacob narrative. For example, one can trace the faint outlines of precursor traditions in texts such as the Gilead treaty on the one hand (Gen. 31:43–54) and various local traditions of the broader Jacob narrative on the other (Gen. 28:11–19*; 32:23–33 [Eng. 32:22–32]; 35:6–7). Nevertheless, these indicators are better explained by a theory of compositional incorporation and modification of earlier localized traditions than by any theory of parallel source strands.[108] The problem in many past analyses is not the assumption that the Jacob narrative may have undergone growth. Instead, many past analyses have been tripped up by the presupposition that the Jacob story underwent a particular kind of growth, an interweaving of parallel documentary sources analogous to that found in the P and non-P traditions. Once one stops assuming this and looks carefully at the non-P Jacob story as a whole, the careful composition of its various parts emerges into clearer focus and its prehistory is simplified.

That being said, it is extremely difficult to isolate the exact contours of any precursor traditions. Noting a system of integral cross-links between Gen. 25:21–34; 27:1–45; and 29:1–32:2a [Eng. 32:1a], along with the marked secondary character of broader narrative links in this section, Blum plausibly proposes that there may once have been a Jacob-Esau-Laban narrative that

---

105. Eising, *Jacobserzählung*, 143–46.
106. Gunkel, *Genesis*, 355–56; Blum *Vätergeschichte*, 142.
107. Kessler, "Querverweise," 132–33; Blum, *Vätergeschichte*, 142.
108. On the Gilead treaty, cf. Blum, *Vätergeschichte*, 132–38. Blum's argument that the border elements are part of an earlier tradition is persuasive, but whether one can reconstruct an unlocalized (!) border tradition here is questionable.

extended only up through Jacob and Laban's treaty (Genesis 25—31*). This narrative was later expanded by the author of the broader Jacob story, the same author who composed the early layer of Gen. 32:2b [Eng. 32:1b]–35:20 as a whole.[109] There is much to be said for this theory. Nevertheless, Blum also recognizes the relative unreconstructability of this precursor Jacob-Esau-Laban narrative.[110] Whatever the merit of his proposal, it lies on a qualitatively lower level of plausibility than exploring the shape and background of the above-discussed broader Jacob composition.[111]

Given this relative unreconstructability, the helpfulness of any hypothesis regarding the prehistory of the Jacob story lies less in its ability to outline the exact contours of a particular precursor tradition than in its capacity to help us distinguish the particular perspective of the Jacob-story author from the overall character of the traditions he used. That is how such observations have been used in this analysis. For example, I have distinguished in the preceding discussion between the trickster traditions leading up to Jacob's departure and the reconstrual of them by the author in Gen. 31:4–16 and related texts. Through such observations we can see how the bulk of the non-P Jacob narrative has been shaped by an author who was focused on depicting Jacob as a worthy precursor of the theological, moral, and political structures of the Northern Kingdom. To do so, he often radically reconstrued older Jacob materials at his disposal.

The Joseph Story

At this point we finally come to the heart of the Joseph story. In previous discussions I have isolated several levels of material in Genesis 37—50:

1. P and Priestly additions—Gen. 37:2; (41:46); 45:19–21; 46:5–7*, 8–27; [47:5–6a, 7–10]; 47:11, 27b–28; 49:1a, 29–33; 50:12–13, 22–3, 26a

2. A semi-Deuteronomistic transition to the Moses story—50:24–25

3. Secondary linkages of Joseph to the promise theme of the broad proto-Genesis composition—41:39–40; 39:2–3, 5–6aα, 21–23; 46:2–4*; 48:15–16, 21–22

4. Two additions focusing on Judah's destiny to rule—Genesis 38 and 49:1b–28

---

109. Blum, *Vätergeschichte*, 168–85, 200–3.
110. Blum, *Vätergeschichte*, 123–24, 174–75.
111. The same can be said for his positing an early Judean Jacob-Esau narrative that has been extended by the author of the Jacob-Esau-Laban narrative (Blum, *Vätergeschichte*, 67–88, 190–94). Although an early Judean background for Gen. 25:21–34; 27:1–41 makes good sense, there are few clear indications that it was decisively earlier than the Jacob-Laban traditions with which it is now combined. Instead, the Jacob-Esau-Laban materials appear to be composed out of a variety of precursor traditions, with some—such as 25:21–34; 27:1–41—having a particularly close relation to each other.

5. Two additions focusing on the Northern tribes of Ephraim and Manasseh—Gen. 41:50–52; 48:1–2, 8–14, 17–20

Each of these elements binds the Joseph story into a larger whole, whether a
proto-Pentateuchal composition or a smaller Jacob-Joseph complex. They
are placed in and around the contours of a broad narrative that begins with
Joseph's brothers selling him into slavery in Egypt (Gen. 37:3–36) and concludes with his final pronouncement that he will provide for them in Egypt
(Gen. 50:21).

As in the case of the Jacob story, this early Joseph narrative shows no clear
signs of having originally been connected to what precedes or follows it. The
beginning of the story in Gen. 37:3 is a standard narrative exposition and
would have been fully understandable to an ancient Israelite audience. The
following Joseph story, although sharing many common characters and
themes with the Jacob story, diverges in important respects from it as well.[112]

1. Although Joseph is presented in the Joseph story as Jacob's "son of old
   age" (Gen. 37:3), there is no clear reflection of this in the Jacob story
   (Gen. 30:23–24; 31:41).[113]
2. Although Rachel has already died in the Jacob narrative, she is presupposed as still living in Gen. 37:10.[114]
3. Although the Jacob story mentions only one daughter, and that only in
   a text probably belonging to a Judah-oriented compositional layer (Gen.
   30:21), the Joseph story speaks of many daughters (Gen. 37:35).[115]

---

112. Redford, *Joseph*, 247–48; Kessler, "Querverweise," 146–79, especially, 146, 178; Dietrich,
Die Josephserzählung, 45–46 (for his early Joseph novella). To be sure, some of their arguments
are based on later materials. For arguments for linkage of the Joseph narrative to a proto-Pentateuch, see especially G. Coats, *From Canaan to Egypt: Structural and Theological Context for
the Joseph Story* (CBQMS 4; Washington, D.C.: Catholic Biblical Association, 1976), 72–74 and
Dietrich, *Die Josephserzählung*, 46–52 (for his later Joseph narrative). Coats' main positive argument is based on the "Yahwistic" theme of blessing in Gen. 39:1–5, 21–23, an element that
has already been identified as part of a later proto-Genesis compositional layer. Dietrich likewise
bases many of his arguments for linkage between his expanded Joseph story and a broader proto-
Pentateuch on texts that have already been isolated as later, the semi-"Deuteronomistic" bridge
to Exodus in Gen. 50:26; Exod. 1:6, 8 (p. 47), links to the Jacob story in Gen. 41:50–52; 48*
(pp. 48–49), and the Judah-focused material in Genesis 49 (pp. 49–50). Other indicators named
by Dietrich, such as the use of "Israel" to designate Jacob and other terminological and cultural
practice linkages (48–49) do not establish that the Joseph narrative was originally embedded in
its present narrative context.
113. Kessler, "Querverweise," 146; Humphreys, *Joseph and His Family*, 195.
114. *b. Ber.* 55a,b; *Gen. Rab.* 72:11; Proksch, *Genesis*, 217, 249–50, 379; Kessler, "Querverweise," 146; Redford, *Joseph*, 248; Dietrich, *Josephserzählung*, 45; Humphreys, *Joseph and His
Family*, 195. Cf. Coats, *From Canaan to Egypt*, 73, who stretches when arguing that the inclusion of Rachel at this point is merely to provide an appropriate family parallel to the sun-moon imagery of Joseph's dream. Sarna, *Genesis*, 257, argues that this could not be an indicator of the independence of an early form of the Joseph story because "ten stars, not eleven, would be expected,
since Benjamin would not yet have been born." On the contrary, the argument is that this independent Joseph story begins as if all twelve sons were already born and Rachel were still alive.
115. Rudolph, *Elohist*, 181–82; Dietrich, *Josephserzählung*, 45; Schmidt, *Literarische Studien*,
149–51, 273–74.

Finally, the prepromise Joseph narrative reaches its full resolution in Joseph's final encounter with his brothers in 50:19–21. Although the story presupposes some kind of return of the brothers from Egypt, it requires no *textual* continuation in a story of an exodus.[116] Its themes and dynamics are already complete.

Initial Survey and Analysis of the Joseph Story

Scholars have long recognized the distinctive character of the Joseph story. Historical critics noted the unusual cohesiveness of the non-P Joseph materials. This among other indicators led them to posit that the Joseph "novella" derived from some sustained narrative effort, rather than the gradual accumulation of independent traditions. Recent literary studies such as those by Alter and Sternberg have brought into much sharper focus the subtlety of the narrative. Not only are various episodes fluidly linked through narrative forecasts and retrospectives, but the story uses irony and the interplay of perspective to involve the audience to an unusual extent. Through such means, the story achieves a particularly nuanced and complex characterization of Joseph, his brothers, and Jacob.[117]

For many modern readers familiar with modern narrative genres focused exclusively on the modern individual, the analysis does and can stop there. For the ancient Israelites, however, these characters were not just members of a family but were also representatives of specific political groups. Many ancient Near Eastern narratives worked this way. For example, the Babylonian edition of the Enuma Elish epic justified Babylonian domination by having the Babylonian national god, Marduk, defeat the god Anzu after the other gods had failed to do so. By the end of the epic, Marduk is king of the gods. When the epic, traveled to Assyria, the editors there replaced Marduk with their national god, Ashur, so that the narrative force of the epic now supported the political system in which they worked. In either case, the tradents were quite clear on the sociopolitical connections of the central character in the epic.[118] Now in the case of the prepromise Joseph story we are dealing with human, rather than divine, representatives of social groups.

---

116. Blum, *Vätergeschichte*, 238. Cf. Dietrich, *Die Josephserzählung*, 47–48, who argues that the mention of Goshen in 45:10; 46:28, 34; 47:1, 4, 6; 50:8, and then again in Exod. 9:26 indicates a narrative connection between his later Joseph narrative and the Exodus story. Exodus 9:26 falls out of the range of this analysis, but is in any case later than the Joseph material under discussion and most likely formed in relation to it.

117. E. D. McGuire, "The Joseph Story: A Tale of Son and Father," in *Images of Man and God: Short Stories in Literary Focus* (ed. B. O. Long; Sheffield: Almond, 1981), 9–26; Ackerman, "Joseph, Judah, and Jacob," 85–113; Alter, *The Art of Biblical Narrative*, 107–12, 137–40, 159–77; Sternberg, *Poetics of Biblical Narrative*, especially 285–308, 394–404; Humphreys, *Joseph and His Family*, 32–117.

118. For this and other examples, see B. Batto, "Creation Theology in Genesis," in *Creation in Biblical Traditions* (ed. R. J. Clifford and J. J. Collins; CBQMS 24; Washington, D.C.: Catholic Biblical Association of America, 1992), 25–26.

Nevertheless, the ancient Israelite audience of this story would not have failed to identify the characters of the Joseph story with social groups in their lives. Within ancient Israel, Joseph often stood for the Northern Kingdom, the "house of Joseph" (2 Sam. 19:21 [Eng. 2 Sam. 19:20]; 1 Kings 11:28; Amos 5:6; Obad. 18; Zech. 10:6; cf. Amos 5:15; 6:6), while Judah consistently represented the Southern people, "the house of Judah" (2 Sam. 2:4, 7, 10, 11; 1 Kings 12:21, 23; 2 Kings 19:30; Isa. 22:21; 37:31; Jer. 3:18; 5:11; 11:10, 17; 12:14; 13:11; 31:27, 31; 33:14; 36:3; Hos. 1:7; 5:12, 14).[119]

These political connections of the characters in the Joseph story are our first hint that the picture in the Joseph story of Joseph's divine destiny to rule almost certainly had political overtones to its early audience. It was not *just* a subtle characterization of human interactions. Rather it was *at the same time* a subtle argument for the North's destiny to rule both Northern and Southern Israelite groups. Let us turn to examine some other clues that suggest this early role for the story.

From the outset, the narrative repeatedly focuses the readers' attention on the theme of the power of Joseph over his brothers. Joseph receives from his father a garment associated with royalty and high officials (Gen. 37:3; cf. 2 Sam. 13:18–19; 15:32; Isa. 22:21), and his dreams seem to predict the brothers' performing an act of obeisance to Joseph, "lying prostrate" (37:5–7, 9). Indeed, the brothers are described as immediately drawing the political implications of this act when they unbelievingly exclaim, "Are you indeed to *reign* (*mlk*) over us? Are you indeed to *have dominion* (*mšl*) over us?" (37:8).[120]

The subsequent course of the narrative then thematizes the dreams and their dominance theme. This happens first when the brothers explicitly defy Joseph's dreams and plan to kill him (37:18–20), and then later when Joseph sees them bowing down to him in fulfillment of the first dream, despite all their efforts (42:6, 7). At precisely this latter point, the narrator intervenes to tell us that Joseph "remembered the dreams that he had dreamed about them" (42:9). As Blum points out, the reader could hardly hope for a clearer signal of interconnections in a narrative. In this case, the interconnections point the reader back to the initial anticipation of Joseph's "reign" and "dominion" over his brothers. At the same time, this conspicuous narrative comment begins the long, puzzling description of the process by which Joseph brings his brothers to experience some of what he did and to recognize their

---

119. Indeed, this future Northern "house of Joseph" is already anticipated by the appearance of the more mundane "house of Joseph" toward the end of the early Joseph narrative, a house that in each case is mentioned shortly before the brothers offer themselves as slaves to Joseph (Gen. 43:17, 18, 19, 24; cf. 44:16 and 50:8; cf. 50:18). Given the different meanings of the "house of Joseph" in these cases, it is difficult to know whether this link was intended at the level of the production of the text.
120. F. Crüsemann, *Der Widerstand gegen. das Königtum: Die antiköniglichen Texte des Alten Testaments und der Kampf um den frühen israelitischen Staat* (WMANT 49; Neukirchen-Vluyn: Neukirchener Verlag, 1978), 146–47.

responsibility toward Benjamin (Gen. 42:21–22, 28; 44:16, 18–34). The brothers later lie prostrate and fall down before Joseph at several strategic points (43:26, 28; 44:14; 50:18). In each of the last two times, they offer themselves as slaves (44:16; 50:18). Each time the offer is rejected by Joseph, who repeatedly asserts that God put him in his present position in order to provide for his family (45:5–8; 50:19–21).

Overall, the Joseph narrative is characterized by two movements: the divinely destined move of Joseph from the "pit" of prison in Egypt to being "lord of the entire land of Egypt," and Joseph's orchestration of his brothers' move from initial rebellion against the prediction of his rule to knowing self-subjugation to it. The former movement moves from Joseph's triple descent into the cistern (37:24), into Egypt (37:36; 39:1), and into prison (39:20; see 40:15). The latter movement likewise moves through several stages.

1. Joseph's initial elevation by Pharaoh (Gen. 41:41–45)
2. The narrative statement that he was "governor of the land" (Gen. 42:6)
3. The brothers' unknowingly addressing and describing him as "lord"/ "lord of the land" (Gen. 42:10, 30, 33; 44:8–9, 16, 18–20, 22, 24, 33), while characterizing themselves (42:10, 13; 44:18, 21, 23, 31) and even their father (43:28; 44:24, 27, 30, 31) as Joseph's "servants"
4. Joseph's assertion that he has become "a father to Pharaoh, head of his entire house, and ruler of the whole land of Egypt" (Gen. 45:8), and the brothers' communication of this to their father (45:26; cf. 45:9)

Within the context of this ongoing, irresistible rise of Joseph, the brothers' defiance of his dreams looks foolish (Gen. 37:8).[121]

Yet it is exactly this defiance that sets the narrative in motion (Gen. 37:18–20). Moreover, it is this defiance that defines the narrative's resolution. At first the brothers unknowingly fulfill the dreams by repeatedly lying prostrate and falling before Joseph. Then they are mute before Joseph when they realize who he is.[122] Only at the climactic end of the Joseph story do they express subservience to him again. This, then, is the first and only time they knowingly subject themselves to him and offer themselves as his slaves (Gen. 50:15–17a). Indeed, by designating themselves as servants of the God of their father (Gen. 50:17) and simultaneously servants of Joseph (Gen.

---

121. Notably, Joseph's second dream is never fulfilled (Gen. 37:9), and his father's doubt is never repudiated. Exactly what the presentation of this unfulfilled dream means is not clear. This is a fracture in the text that does not seem diachronically based. Nevertheless, the narrative never does repudiate Jacob's moderate doubt regarding this dream (Gen. 37:10–11). The distinction between the narrative's repudiation of the brothers' murderous defiance of the first dream and apparent validation of Jacob's moderate doubt heightens the focus of the narrative on the dream that is fulfilled and the wrongness of the brothers' attempt to work against it. Cf. Turner, *Announcements of Plot*, 147–69.
122. Crüsemann, *Widerstand*, 151–52.

50:18b) they implicitly equate Joseph with God.[123] Their resistance is over. They have moved full circle, from their initial denial of Joseph's dreams to their repeated subjugation to his mercy; from their resistance to divine destiny, to their cooperation with it. The end of the narrative has circled around to the beginning, and all implicitly focuses in some way on power, the divinely destined power of Joseph over his brothers and their final acceptance of it.

Joseph's reply to his brothers at this point is a crucial indicator of the type of authority being advocated here. He reassures them and explicitly distinguishes himself from God (Gen. 50:19). By reassuring them, he implicitly rejects their offer to be his slaves, thus distinguishing his authority over his brothers from that he exerted over the land of Egypt. The Egyptians came to Joseph in order to "live and not die," and he bought their livestock and land and enslaved them (Gen. 47:13–26). Joseph's family came for the same reason (Gen. 42:2; 43:8), but Joseph simply "provides for them" (45:11; 47:12; 50:21) because that is why God placed him in his position of authority (Gen. 45:5–8; 50:20). This contrast in types of rule is but one element in the narrative's overall emphasis on Joseph's mercy and the moderate character of his power over his brothers. Joseph could easily exact revenge on his brothers for what they did to him. Instead, he provides a privileged place for them once he sees their recognition of guilt (Gen. 44:16a) and their solidarity with Joseph's father and his full brother, Benjamin (44:16b, 18–34).

As Crüsemann points out, this constellation of themes addresses specific elements of the largely northern antimonarchal movement that resisted David's and Solomon's rule during the tenth century. In particular, this movement protested the forced labor and taxation policies of David and Solomon (1 Kings 12:3–4; 1 Sam. 8:11–17; cf. 2 Sam. 20:1–2),[124] charging, among other things, that the king will make his subjects his "slaves" (1 Sam. 8:17). In reply Joseph is described in the Joseph narrative as reserving enslavement and impoverishment for Egyptians, even as his brothers repeatedly offer themselves to him as his "slaves" (e.g., 43:18; 44:10, 17). In response to his brothers, Joseph maintains that he was placed by God over them in order to "provide" for them. In this way the narrative uses the extreme example of Joseph's oppression of the Egyptians as a foil against which Joseph's benevolent provision for his brothers looks good. This is a subtle argument in which objections to kingship are accounted for and displaced as an example of extreme subjugation of foreigners. In the process, the elements of royal ideology that stress the king's provision for his subjects are stressed, while other elements of royal ideology, such as the emphasis on domination and subjugation, are downplayed.[125]

---

123. Blum, *Vätergeschichte*, 241.
124. See Crüsemann, *Widerstand*, 19–127 for discussion of relevant texts.
125. For survey of both dimensions of royal ideology, see Albertz, *Religionsgeschichte*, vol. 1, 181–83; (E.T., 119–21); and (with special attention to iconography) Keel, *Bildsymbolik*, 259–85; (E.T., 280–306).

So also, the narrative represents a mediating position between the proroyal liturgy that stresses an extremely close link between the king and God (2 Sam. 7:8–16; 23:1–7; Pss. 2:6–9; 45:7 [Eng. 45:6]; 89:20–38 [Eng. 89:19–37]; 110:1–5; etc.) and antimonarchal material that consistently ignores such claims (1 Sam. 8:11–17; Judg. 9:8–15) or opposes them (1 Sam. 8:7; 12:12). Joseph denies his own brothers' implication that he stands in God's place (Gen. 50:17–19). Yet at the same time he repeatedly asserts, echoing royal ideology, that God alone was responsible for putting him in his present position (Gen. 45:5–8; 50:20).

Finally, the Joseph story brings a rhetoric of reconciliation to bear on the centrifugal antimonarchal forces calling for a return to more decentralized forms of rule. While people are calling "to your tents, O Israel" (2 Sam. 20:1; 1 Kings 12:16), the Joseph story calls for the "brothers" to pull together. Rather than arguing for a direct subjugation of the tribes to a monarch's authority, the narrative argues indirectly, using the narrative frame of a patriarchal story to argue for "brotherly solidarity."[126] Now aggression against Joseph and resistance to his destiny to rule is depicted as (1) resistance to divine authority and (2) lack of appropriate brotherly solidarity. To be sure, the narrative develops this picture through a sophisticated and realistic depiction of relationships between individuals. Nevertheless, the sophistication and realism of the narrative appears to be at least partly in the service of a broader aim related to a political problem: the legitimation of royal authority in a context where it is being questioned. Indeed, if it any more transparently reflected the situation it addresses, the narrative might well lose its persuasive power to address an audiance profoundly skeptical of monarchical structures.

The Historical Context of the Joseph Story

As we turn to look more closely at the possible historical context of such an argument, the answer is clear: the context is the North, and probably the North in the early stages of the formation of the Northern Kingdom.[127]

First, the characters of the story are not just any personalities but the purported ancestors of major political groups in later Israel. Given this, the North is the most likely context for the story's intricate case for "Joseph's" destiny

---

126. At the same time, the choice of this narrative frame, and setting it in Egypt in particular, imposed certain limits on the author of the story. Joseph could not be "king," and portrayal of him as "pharaoh" would not have enhanced the story's persuasive appeal to an Israelite audience. Nevertheless, particularly in its depiction of his authority in Genesis 45 and 47, the narrative comes as close to portraying Joseph as king as it can without actually making him pharaoh over Egypt. In any case—contra Crüsemann, *Widerstand*, 154—the picture of Joseph's absolute authority over Egypt would not have served as a good model for lower Northern officials in the Davidic monarchy.

127. For discussion of the reference to Hebron (37:14) and citations of other literature, see Blum, *Vätergeschichte*, 239n239, and Schmidt, *Literarische Studien*, 146n68. This is probably an addition that entered the text in the process of the adaptation of the Jacob-Joseph story by Judean tradents.

to rule his brothers and provide for them. Indeed, even the prominence of Judah in the material under discussion fits well into the hypothesis of an early Northern origin for the Joseph story. Both the above-discussed Northern Jacob narrative and the Joseph narrative share an apparent interest in Judah, yet he is a secondary character in both. In the Jacob narrative, the Judah figure is mentioned as one of Jacob's older sons, but he is never mentioned afterward. As a result, he plays a decisively minor role compared to Joseph.[128] In the Joseph narrative Judah repeatedly does obeisance before Joseph along with his brothers (Gen. 44:14 expressly; also 42:6; 50:18), and even his extended speech to Joseph recognizes Joseph's authority over them (Gen. 44:18–34). His prominence calls attention at the same time to his steadfast subservience to Joseph.[129] Moreover, as many have pointed out, much of his behavior is hardly exemplary.[130] Reuben's plan to free his brother Joseph (37:22, 29–30) and later to give up his own two sons if his brothers fail to return to Jacob with Benjamin (42:37) both compare favorably with their Judah counterparts (Gen. 37: 26–27; 43:9). Indeed, Judah's proposal to sell his brother into slavery is described elsewhere in Hebrew law as a death-penalty offence (Exod. 21:16; Deut 24:7).[131] At the same time, the prominence of Judah and eventual positive picture of him in the Joseph story (subjugating himself and his brothers to Joseph!) may help explain why later Judeans transmitted and adapted these Northern compositions, even though they are interlaced with a conspicuous promotion of Northern Kingdom causes. The Judah character was already there to be modified.[132]

Second, as Crüsemann has persuasively argued, the opposition to the monarchy against which the Joseph story appears to be arguing was centered particularly in the North, and the Northern Kingdom seems to have been founded partly in reaction to it. If Crüsemann's picture is accurate, there would have been many in the Northern Kingdom who questioned the establishment of a new monarchy in opposition to the old. They would have echoed Sheba's call "To your tents, O Israel" and criticized anyone wanting to set up one "brother" over others. In response, the Joseph story displaces the negative aspects of the Davidic and Solomonic reigns onto the Egyptians. Like Solomon, Joseph taxes and builds storage cities (Gen. 41:34–35, 48; cf. 1 Kings 4:7; 5:7 [Eng. 4:27]; 9:17–19). Nevertheless, it is the Egyptians

128. Blum, *Vätergeschichte,* 109–10, 169–70, 183.
129. Blum, *Vätergeschichte,* 235, 242.
130. Schmitt, *Josephsgeschichte,* 19–20; Coats, *From Canaan to Egypt,* 69; H. J. Boecker, "Überlegungen zur Josephsgeschichte," in *Alttestamentlicher Glaube und Biblische Theologie: Festschrift für Horst Dietrich Preuß* (ed. J. Hausmann and H.-J. Zobel; Stuttgart/Berlin/ Cologne: W. Kohlhammer, 1992), 43–44.
131. Kessler, "Querverweise," 153–54; Dietrich, *Die Josephserzählung,* 20; Levin, *Der Jahwist,* 271; cf. Seebass, *Geschichtliche Zeit,* 74.
132. This kind of upgrading of a narrative character has a number of analogies in the documented development of ancient Near Eastern literature. I will discuss one of these analogies in my treatment of the Southern Jacob-Joseph story in the conclusion of this book.

whom he taxes, and only them that he enslaves (47:19, 23; cf. 50:19 and 1 Sam 8:17), while he merely reassures and royally "provides" for his brothers (50:21a). The raw domination, impoverishment, and enslavement attributed to the Davidic monarchy are applied to Joseph's behavior toward foreigners while Joseph's behavior toward his brothers is presented as a model of a more moderate, benificent "brotherly rule."[133]

Third, as Dietrich has pointed out, the Egyptian connections of the Joseph story make good sense in an early Northern Kingdom setting. The early Joseph story is distinguished from other traditions not only by its overall Egyptian setting, but by its use of Egyptian tradition (Gen. 39:1–20) and infusion throughout with realia from Egyptian life.[134] Often, at least the "Yahwistic" elements of this picture have been attributed to an Egyptian-influenced Solomonic revival. Nevertheless, there is another more direct possibility, particularly if we are looking at a Northern origin for the story. Jeroboam I, the founder of the Northern Kingdom, is reported to have fled to Egypt for asylum under Pharaoh Shishak (1 Kings 11:26, 40) before he returned upon the death of Solomon. Indeed, he probably returned at least partially under the sponsorship of the Egyptian pharaoh, who may have sought through Jeroboam to reestablish a measure of Egyptian control over the region.[135] Dietrich even proposes that the positive picture of pharaoh in the Joseph story and his role in putting Joseph in power may be a reflection of Shishak's role in sponsoring the Northern dynasty.[136] Whether or not that is the case, the early Northern Kingdom under Jeroboam provides a plausible context not only for the Joseph-centered argument against antimonarchal forces, but also for the setting of such an argument in Egypt and for the detailed knowledge of Egypt evident in the narrative.

Fourth, the prominence of Benjamin in the Joseph story makes particular sense in the early stages of the Northern monarchy. Whereas Judah is an often-flawed leader, Benjamin is a passive figure and never speaks. He is Joseph's only full brother and the particular *object* of his father's and brothers' love. These various positions of the characters would have made narrative sense to an early Northern Kingdom audience perceiving these characters in relation to the groups they represent. Judah has just dominated the

---

133. Although Redford (*Joseph*, 103–4) in particular attacks Joseph's behavior as vindictive, the ancient audience would most likely have perceived it as remarkably merciful.
134. For a helpful overview of various details, see Dietrich, *Josephserzählung*, 60–61, 68–69. Dietrich, however, argues for a distinction between the similarly deep use of realia from a more positive picture of Egypt in an independent Joseph novella, and a more negative view in its later Judean redaction into a proto-Pentateuch. This distinction, however, is based more on his prior literary observations than on clear distinctions in the data itself. It ignores the unique level of knowledge of Egypt present in *both* sets of texts that Dietrich separates (cf. Dietrich, 69).
135. This picture would match the report that Shishak later attacked Jeroboam's opponent, Rehoboam, and plundered Jerusalem (1 Kings 14:25–26). Dietrich, *Josephserzählung*, 62–63.
136. Dietrich, *Josephserzählung*, 63.

North in the persons of David and Solomon, while Benjamin was a hotly disputed border area between North and South (1 Kings 15:16–22; cf. 1 Kings 12:21–24). Benjamin was the *object* of numerous ninth-century power struggles, associated with Judah in Judean traditions (1 Kings 12:21–24), yet also separate and occasionally occupied by the North (1 Kgs 15:16–22). Within this context, the Joseph story takes particular pains to describe the affinity between Joseph and Benjamin, and the importance of their being together.[137]

Fifth and finally, the affinities between the Joseph story and (Northern) Jacob story speak for their origin in a common Northern milieu. They share common characters (Jacob/Israel, Reuben, Simeon, Judah, Joseph, Benjamin, Rachel), a common emphasis on Joseph among Jacob's sons, and certain common information, such as Jacob's preference for Rachel. Moreover, the Jacob and Joseph stories share Northern political orientations. The Jacob narrative of Genesis 25—35 builds on trickster traditions regarding Jacob to associate him firmly with Northern sites and at the same time to legitimate Northern sanctuaries and cities through this association. The Joseph story responds to antimonarchal traditions through a picture of (Northern) Joseph's divinely-destined authority over his brothers versus their unbrotherly jealousy of him and defiance of his destiny. Finally, these two narratives share a striking number of themes.[138]

1. Prediction of the ascendancy of one brother over the other (Gen. 25:23; 37:5–11)
2. Exposition stating that the patriarch preferred one son over the other (Gen. 25:28; 37:3)[139]
3. Emergence of the younger son as the father's prospective successor (Gen. 25:29–34; 27:1–40; 37:4–14)
4. Will of the older son(s) to kill the younger son (Gen. 27:41; 37:18–20)
5. Departure of the younger son from his family for a stay abroad (Gen. 27:42–45; 28:10–29:1; 37:21–28, 36; 39:1)
6. The younger son's marrying and acquiring wealth (Gen. 29:1–30:43; 40:1–41:45)[140]
7. Reconciliation of the younger son with his brother(s) in an emotional scene (Gen. 33:4; 45:14–15; cf. also 46:29 for the father)

---

137. Dietrich, *Josephserzählung*, 63–64.
138. S. Niditch, *Underdogs and Tricksters: A Prelude to Biblical Folklore* (San Francisco: Harper & Row, 1987), 70–78.
139. Westermann, *Genesis 37—50*, 27; (E.T., 36–37).
140. Of course in this case, the present text of the prepromise Jacob and Joseph narratives are yet closer in that the heroes also have children in both sections (Gen. 29:31–30:24//41:50–52). Genesis 41:50–52, however, has already been isolated as a later addition to the Joseph story. This could be an argument that 41:50–52 was part of the early Joseph story. Alternatively, it is possible that the author of 41:50–52 did insert this material into the Joseph story, and indeed did it partly to fill a perceived gap in the presentation of Joseph as an archetypical hero figure.

Overall, as Niditch has persuasively argued, these similarities speak for the likelihood that the Jacob and Joseph stories are variants of a similar Israelite "hero myth."[141] More specifically, what is being advocated here is that these narratives are variants of a similar *Northern* Israelite hero myth, a myth tracing the life cycle of the Israelite protagonist with motifs particularly suited for and familiar to a Northern Kingdom audience.

Niditch points out that the Joseph story develops the above-mentioned "hero myth" in a decisively different way from the Jacob story. Whereas the Jacob story describes the rise of a trickster protagonist, the Joseph story describes the wise protagonist overcoming the tricks of his opponents. Whereas the Jacob story puts more focus on the hero's rise (Genesis 29—30; cf. 33:1–17), the Joseph story in its argument for "brotherly solidarity" puts great stress on Joseph's reconciliation with his brothers (Gen. 42:1–45:15; 50:15–21; cf. 40:1–41:45). Even the picture of God is different. Whereas God explodes into the narrative world of the Jacob story, the Joseph story has no such interventions in its earliest material. Instead, it is characterized by an abiding divine order to which all of its characters must conform. These and other elements indicate a distinctive emphasis on preserving order in the Joseph story, compared with the Jacob story's greater emphasis on craftily finding one's way in an unpredictable world.[142] Although the Joseph story is related to the Jacob story, it appears to be an originally independent variant of the hero myth presented in it.

Despite such differences, there are some subtle ways the Joseph story may allude to the Jacob story. Already, the outset of the Joseph story sets up certain resonances with the Jacob story. The brothers' use of a goat skin to fool Jacob

---

141. Niditch, *Underdogs and Tricksters,* 83–125. Note also R. Hendel's tracing of a common hero myth in the Jacob and Moses stories, *The Epic of the Patriarch: The Jacob Cycle and the Narrative Traditions of Canaan and Israel* (HSM 42; Atlanta: Scholars Press, 1987), 133–65.

Cf. Levin, *Der Jahwist,* 143, 161, who argues that the theme of strife and reconciliation is a specifically Yahwistic redactional theme spanning the whole of Genesis. First, Jacob's and Joseph's successes in overcoming brotherly strife are anticipated by Abraham's magnanimous overcoming of the "dispute" between his and his nephew Lot's shepherds (Gen. 13:7–12). Second, this stands in contrast to the Sodom story, where the primeval conditions already seen in the Cain and Abel story are continued. There the men of Sodom, whom Lot terms *brothers* (Gen. 19:7), fail to recognize the bond Lot claims (Gen. 19:9a) and do not respect the boundaries of Lot's home and hospitality (Gen. 19:9b). The former text, however, has no clear terminological links to the strife stories preceding and following it, and Lot's use of the term *brothers* in the Sodom story is not particularly emphasized and seems to stand as just a standard address. There are potential resonances with the theme to be picked up in a creative synchronic reading of these texts. Nevertheless, the compositional connection is too faint in this case to be reliable. The Cain and Abel, Jacob and Esau, and Joseph stories all develop the theme of brotherly conflict over preference, but there is little indication of a special compositional connection between them nor to any stories in the Abraham section on this topic.

142. Niditch, *Underdogs and Tricksters,* 99–125. In addition, Niditch observes in a previous chapter a more developed style in the Joseph story. Whereas the Jacob story moves from scene

into thinking Joseph was killed (Gen. 37:31–32) echoes Jacob's own use of a goat skin to fool his father into thinking he was Esau (Gen. 27:16, 21–23).[143] Later, the story of the successful search for Joseph's goblet in Benjamin's sack (Gen. 44:1–17) echoes the account of Laban's search for his household gods (Gen. 31:31–35). But whereas Rachel actually stole the household gods and escaped (Gen. 31:19, 34–35), Benjamin, her son, is "caught," despite his being innocent (Gen. 44:12).[144] This contrast with the Jacob story heightens the Joseph story's emphasis on the brothers' overall "guilt," despite their "innocence" at this point. Finally, the story's conclusion has Joseph respond to his brothers' demand for forgiveness with the same words Jacob used to respond to Rachel when she demanded children from him (Gen. 50:19b; cf. 30:2): "Am I in the place of God?"[145] In this way Joseph is associated with his recently deceased father, even as this final scene depicts a final brotherly reconciliation that Jacob never achieved with Esau (cf. Gen. 33:12–17).

To be sure, such verbal and thematic associations are often tenuous. It is difficult to know for sure how many of them were actually intended by the author or perceived by the audience. Nevertheless, the level of potential specific connections between the Joseph and Jacob stories is special. The Joseph story does not have the same range of potential allusions to other major sections of Genesis.[146] Insofar as these potential allusions are not coincidental,

---

to scene through implicit connections, the Joseph story is characterized by a sophisticated rhetoric of elaborative repetition (85–92).

143. *Gen. Rab.* 84.19; Sykes, "Patterns in Genesis," 73; Humphreys, *Joseph and His Family*, 197.

144. *Gen. Rab.* 92:8; Alter, *The Art of Biblical Narrative*, 172–73; Sternberg, *Poetics of Biblical Narrative*, 304–5; Steinmetz, *From Father to Son*, 124; G. Nichol, "Story Patterning in Genesis," in *Text as Pretext: Essays in Honour of Robert Davidson* (JSOTSup, 138; Sheffield: JSOT, 1992), 230–32.

145. This parallel has been used in transmission-historical analyses to assign Gen. 30:2 and 50:19 to the same source. See, for example, Gunkel, *Genesis*, 487. So also, Holzinger, *Einleitung*, 183, observes that just as Rachel's maid, Bilhah, "bears upon her knees" just after the parallel quote (Gen. 30:3), so also Joseph's grandsons are born "upon [Joseph's] knees" (Gen. 50:23). For Holzinger this is an indication of the common Elohistic origins of Gen. 30:2–3 and 50:19, 23. Nevertheless, although such verbal similarities are potential indicators of some kind of connection, they do not necessarily point to common authorship.

146. B. Dahlberg, "The Unity of Genesis," in *Literary Interpretations of Biblical Narratives*, vol. 2, 126–33, argues that some correspondences between the primeval history and the Joseph story indicate that Genesis is united by an inclusion between the two. In actuality, however, his correspondences are quite loose, and there are often closer correspondences between the elements of the Joseph story on which he comments and elements of the Jacob story. For example, he parallels Joseph's question, "Am I in the place of God?" (Gen. 50:19) with the snake's prediction that the humans will "be like God" (Gen. 3:4–5; p. 129). Nevertheless, the correspondence is much closer between Joseph's and Jacob's identical questions in 50:17 and 30:2. The other correspondences Dahlberg points out are quite weak: "administrative" (?) responsibilities of Adam and Eve for the garden//Joseph's authority over Egypt; expulsion from garden and from tree of life//Joseph's departure from Canaan to preserve life; lack of brotherly reconciliation between Cain and Abel//presence of reconciliation between Joseph and his brothers.

they point to yet another way the Joseph narrative builds on the Jacob narrative, even as it probably once stood separate from it. They are among many indications of an early intertextual relationship between the Jacob and Joseph narratives. They probably circulated in similar circles, despite the fact that they probably originally stood separate from one another.

The Source Approach and Moving Further Backward

It is likely the prepromise Joseph story has undergone some growth beyond that described above. The question is how much and when, and how much we can know about it. Although the earliest source critics refrained from dissecting the Joseph story and assigned it all to their E (e.g., Astruc, Hupfeld, and so forth), starting in the late nineteenth century many distinguished between a Yahwistic Israel-Judah source on the one hand and an Elohistic Jacob-Reuben source on the other (see Seebass, L. Schmidt).[147] More recently, many have followed Redford in positing an original Jacob-Reuben version of the Joseph story that has been redacted by an Israel-Judah editor (Redford, Dietrich, Van Seters; cf. Sandmel and Jepsen, as well).[148] Others have posited an early Yahwistic Israel-Judah layer that has been redacted by an author focusing on Reuben(-Jacob) (Schmitt, Boecker, Levin).[149] Still others have argued for an essentially unified Joseph story, apart from additions of the sort discussed above and a few minor additions (Mowinckel, Whybray, Coats, Crüsemann, Donner, Weimar, Kessler, Otto, Blum, Westermann, Willi-Plein, Humphreys).[150]

Although there is some continuity in the overall strata under discussion, the consistently fundamental variation in results indicates that the stratum of the Joseph story we have reached is difficult to analyze further. On the one hand, some of the identified difficulties can be ignored only by the most strenuously harmonistic reading. On the other hand, some difficulties appear to have been manufactured by source critics in search of a continuation of

---

147. Wellhausen, *Composition*, 52–60; Gunkel, *Genesis*, 401–88. For more recent advocates of this approach, see Seebass, *Geschichtliche Zeit*, and L. Schmidt, *Literarische Studien*.

148. Jepsen, "Vätergestalten," 265–68; S. Sandmel, "The Haggada within Scripture," *JBL* 80 (1961): 112; Redford, *Joseph*, 134–35, 139–76; Dietrich, *Josephserzählung*, 19–52; Van Seters, *Prologue to History*, 315, 317. Kebekus, *Joseferzählung*, follows this basic model, but has both a Reuben story and a Reuben expansion before his Judah layer.

149. Schmitt, *Josephsgeschichte;* Boecher, "Überlegungen," 37–45; Levin, *Der Jahwist*, 267, 271–72, 291.

150. Mowinckel, *Erwägungen zur Pentateuchquellenfrage,* 61–62; R. N. Whybray, "The Joseph Story and Pentateuchal Criticism," *VT* 18 (1968): 522–28; Coats, *From Canaan to Egypt,* 60–74; Crüsemann, *Widerstand,* 143–44; Donner, *Literarische Gestalt,* 27–47; Weimar, *Untersuchungen,* 24–25n6; Kessler, "Querverweise," 146–55; E. Otto, "Die 'synthetische Lebensauffassung' in der frühköniglichen Novellistik Israels—Ein Beitrag zur alttestamentlichen Anthropologie," *ZThK* 74 (1977): 377–78; Blum, *Vätergeschichte,* 231–34; Westermann, *Genesis 37—50;* Willi-Plein, "Josefsgeschichte," 305–22; Humphreys, *Joseph and His Family,* passim, particularly 198–99. Cf. also R. E. Longacre, *Joseph: A Story of Divine Providence—A Text Theoretical and Textlinguistic Analysis of Genesis 37 and 39—48* (Winona Lake, Ind.: Eisenbrauns, 1989).

parallel non-P Yahwistic and Elohistic sources identified in the Abraham and Jacob stories. Indeed, the Joseph story with its complex play of perspectives, irony, and backtracking has provided an unusually rich fund of material for those seeking parallel strands. Yet at the same time, the reconstructed source strands that emerge from such analyses consistently pale in comparison to the whole with which the critics start. So also the redaction approaches are not immune to difficulties. The reconstructed original source often lacks a beginning, middle, or end,[151] and the reasons for the redaction, such as the addition of a money motif[152] or Reuben,[153] for example, are often difficult to discern.

At this point it may be helpful to distinguish between clear indicators of growth and features of the narrative that only potentially can be read as problems. The following are among the clearer indicators of growth:

1. *The double speech introduction for Reuben's speech in Gen. 37:21 and 22.*
2. *Lack of clarity about who first sold Joseph.* In Gen. 37:25–28 the brothers decide to sell Joseph, but then the Midianites come along and pull him out to sell to the Ishmaelites before the brothers get their chance. Later, however, Joseph describes his brothers as themselves having sold him just as they had originally planned (Gen. 45:4–5).
3. *Reuben's unclear role with regard to Joseph's sale.* Genesis 37:27b simply states that "Judah's brothers" (cf. Gen. 37:26a), agreed to Judah's plan to sell Joseph, and later Joseph describes his brothers as a group selling him to Egypt (Gen. 45:4–5). Reuben is not described as objecting in any way to his brothers' plan, and he is even implicitly implicated in the brothers' deception of their father (Gen. 37:31–32). Yet the same narrative implies elsewhere that he was a nonparticipant in the sale. It describes him as coming to the pit and being surprised that Joseph is gone (Gen. 37:29) and later complaining to them as if he did not know or participate in the plan for sale (Gen. 42: 22).[154]
4. *Differing reports regarding who brought Joseph down to Egypt and sold him to Potiphar.* Genesis 37:36 states that the Midianites sold Joseph "to Egypt" and to Potiphar. Genesis 39:1 (see also 37:28) states that

---

151. E.g., Dietrich's Joseph novella lacks a beginning (he sees it as having been eliminated by P; *Josephsgeschichte*, 53n147), and Schmitt's original Judah narrative has a yawning gap between Genesis 37 and 43 (cf. Blum, *Vätergeschichte*, 234).

152. Schmitt, *Josephsgeschichte*, 44–45n173; Dietrich, *Josephserzählung*, 34–38; cf. Schmidt, *Literarische Studien*, 161.

153. Cf. Schmitt, *Josephsgeschichte*, 19–20; Boecher, "Überlegungen," 43–45; Levin, *Der Jahwist*, 271–72, 291.

154. The history of interpretation indicates there are a variety of ways to develop a subplot to explain Reuben's absence/presence here, but the variety also indicates the text itself is no help in this matter. It never explicitly states that he was not there, nor does it particularly thematize his participation/non-participation in the whole sale theme.

it was the Ishmaelites who brought him to Egypt and sold him to Potiphar.[155]

5. *Apparent later reconciliation of different accounts about where Joseph met the officials and how he got there.* Whereas Genesis 40 generally speaks of pharaoh placing his two officials "under guard in the house of the chief of the guard" (40:3; 41:10; cf. also "under guard" in 40:4, 7), two texts at the outset of the chapter conspicuously expand on their respective contexts to state that these officials were imprisoned in the same "prison" where Joseph was put (Gen. 40:3, 5bβ; cf. 39:20, especially 39:20aβγ). They appear to be minor additions aiming to clarify that Joseph's "prison" and their place of "custody" were the same place. Moreover, whereas Joseph's former master who imprisoned him is identified at the outset of Gen. 39:1 as the "chief of the guard," Gen. 40:4 describes this man as appointing Joseph over the officials without saying a word about this "chief's" roles as Joseph's former and later enraged boss.

6. *Double discovery of money in the sacks.* Both 42:26–27 and 42:35 describe the brothers' discovering the money Joseph had planted in their sacks and being surprised.

Many could and have argued that even these indicators are not decisive. Nevertheless, at the very least, the above indicators are clearer than many of the indicators often used in source and redaction analyses of the Joseph story.

1. *The outset of the narrative.* The escalating description of the enmity between Joseph's brothers and Joseph in Gen. 37:3–11 shows no clear signs of being combined from disparate materials. Instead it simply stresses the intensity of the rift that will eventually lead to their plans to kill him.[156]

2. *Purported doublets.* The doubled speech introduction at the outset of Genesis 42 (Gen. 42:1, 2) actually helps stress the silence of the brothers in response to Jacob's question. He asks a rhetorical question (42:1), they are silent, and he then makes a statement (42:2; cf. 45:3–4).[157]

---

155. Redford, *Joseph,* 145–46; Seebass, *Geschichtliche Zeit,* 73–75; cf. Longacre, *Joseph,* 30–31, 155, who resurrects an ancient strategy for handling this discrepancy, identifying the Ishmaelites with the Midianites. This approach may have been how the author of the final form of the text understood it, but does not adequately account for the switch to and away from Midianites before and after Gen. 37:28. See particularly Campbell and O'Brien (*Sources of the Pentateuch,* 227–35) on the importance of this indicator.

156. Redford, *Joseph,* 148; Donner, *Literarische Gestalt,* 36–37; Coats, *From Canaan to Egypt,* 61; Blum, *Vätergeschichte,* 233; Boecker, "Überlegungen," 38; cf. Schmidt, *Literarische Studien,* 144–45.

157. That in one case the silence is thematized (Gen. 45:3–4) and in the other it is not (42:1–2) is not decisive. A reader can make sense of both. Of course, if one is looking for parallel strands, this divergence becomes potentially significant. Nevertheless, this indicator of itself cannot establish the plausibility of such an assumption.

Other doublets, such as the doubled statement that Joseph recognized his brothers and they did not recognize him (Gen. 42:7, 8), or Joseph's later doubled introduction of himself to his brothers (Gen. 45:3, 4) likewise stress the surprise and importance of these events in the stretch of the narrative. They do not necessarily indicate the presence of different levels of material.[158]

3. *Divergences between Genesis 42 and 43—44.* None of the divergences between Genesis 42 and 43—44 are clear indicators of transmission history. Instead, the new elements in Genesis 43—44 point to the urgency of the new situation, on the one hand, and the modification of the brothers' story in the face of Jacob's criticism, on the other.[159]

In addition, many source and redaction analyses have used certain divergences in profile, such as naming Jacob "Israel" or "Jacob," as transmission-historical indicators as well. Nevertheless, the use of such variation as a transmission-historical indicator depends on the correlation of such variation with clear seams and breaks. If it is true that there are no clear indicators of seams in the two-stage description of the brothers' growing hatred for Joseph (Gen. 37:3–11) nor in the report of the brothers' two trips to Egypt (Genesis 42 and 43—44), then the variation in designations for Joseph's father, "Israel" (37:3–4; 43—44) and "Jacob" (42) in these narratives can not be used as a reliable indicator of transmission history. Whether one attempts to explain the usage of "Jacob" and "Israel" or just posits a random variation in the designations, there is no clear evidence that the variation in designations for Joseph's father matches clear indicators of seams in the Joseph story. To begin an argument for different levels in the Joseph story on the basis of such variation fails to insure that such a variation in designation for the father is

---

158. Redford, *Joseph,* 169; Blum, *Vätergeschichte,* 233. Indeed these two examples correspond exactly to each other: Joseph's two introductions of himself to his brothers correspond to the two statements that they did not first recognize him. Compare in particular the charge in 42:8–9 with Joseph's own interpretation of the reason for their trip in 45:4–8. Schmidt, *Literarische Studien,* 136–37, argues that Joseph could not have asked twice about his father's welfare in 43:27 and 45:3. Nevertheless, the second question in 45:3 takes on a wholly different cast now that it follows Joseph's self-introduction.

159. Blum, *Vätergeschichte,* 232. Note that Jacob's charge in 43:6 implicitly presupposes the brothers' earlier report in 42:29–32, not just the interaction in 43:3–5. Both source and redaction critics find this deviation difficult to explain because they see no point in the brothers' changing their story to (1) a father who has already heard a different, relatively unproblematic account and (2) Joseph, who was himself party to the interaction that is being falsely reported. Nevertheless, the brothers' altered story to their father in 43:7 does defend them better than the report in 42:29–32, and the shift offers a nuance to the depiction of the brothers as shifty and unreliable. So also Judah's continuation of this approach with Joseph helps emphasize the stress under which the brothers are suffering. In addition, the fact that the brothers keep shifting their story before characters like Joseph, who know better, helps depict them as fools. As such, they stand as the foil to Joseph's role as the ideal wise man. In both cases, this divergence is a prime

transmission-historically significant.[160] So also, the presence of Judah and Reuben in the story is not a priori an indicator of any kind of transmission history. Indeed, closer analysis indicates that they are carefully coordinated with each other, and the use of both corresponds to an overall tendency of the story to work with pairs.[161]

Thus, although there are some indicators of growth in the Joseph story, they diverge considerably in significance. Whereas some indicators, such as the divergence between Midianites and Ishmaelites in Gen. 37:36 and 39:1, are clear, other elements often used in transmission-historical analyses, such as the progressive description of the brothers' hatred of Joseph, are completely unproblematic. The transmission-historical question at this point then is, Are the more secure of the above-surveyed indicators merely indicators of isolated additions, or are they loose threads in the Joseph garment, threads that when pulled will help us "unravel" the whole?

Notably, we have manuscript evidence for the former model: minor, isolated additions. For example, the Old Greek provides textual evidence for the probable presence of an interpolation in 37:5b of the Hebrew text, one that anticipated the hate that would be mentioned later (Gen. 37:8b).[162] And this is not the only example of limited retouching, either in the Hebrew or the other textual traditions for the Joseph story. This complex text seems to have been particularly prone to being revised and connected with itself.[163]

Given this background, it is notable that most of the clearest indicators of growth can be easily accounted for as the result of just such minor revisions:

1. The double speech introduction in Gen. 37:21b–22 could have resulted from an insertion of an extra Reuben speech in 37:21b or 22.
2. The conflict regarding who first sold Joseph could have been caused by

---

example of the kind of use of repetition for characterization that is documented in Sternberg, *The Poetics of Biblical Narrative*, 365–440.

160. Rudolph, *Elohist*, 149–51; cf. Redford, *Joseph*, 131–32; and Schmidt, *Literarische Studien*, 133, who *begin* with such variation in profile. To be sure, both go on to argue that indicators of seams match this variation in usage. Yet I would maintain that the direction of argument should be the reverse. If one begins with the purported indicators of seams, they do not appear so decisive, and then the variation in designation of the father looks different as well.

161. Redford, *Joseph*, 74–76; Donner, *Literarische Gestalt*, 36–37.

162. On 37:5, see J. W. Wevers, *Notes on the Greek Text of Genesis* (SBLSCS 35; Atlanta: Scholars Press, 1993), 615–16; cf. D. Barthélemy, et al., *Preliminary and Interim Report on the Hebrew Old Testament Text Project*, vol. 1, *Pentateuch/Pentateuque* (Stuttgart: United Bible Society, 1976), 56; and especially B. Becking, "'They hated him even more': Literary Technique in Genesis 37.1–11," *BN* 60 (1991): 40–47. The last argues for the originality of Gen. 37:5b on the basis of the way the half-verse now can be read to function in its present context. His argument, however, depends on the idea that authors were artful and translators were not (cf. his 46). As we are learning from more recent literary studies of the ancient translations of the Bible, this is a highly problematic assumption.

163. For an overview of various candidates for such glosses, see Redford, *Joseph*, 28–32.

an insertion of the Midianites in 37:28, an insertion designed to take the blame off the brothers.[164]

3. The conflict regarding who brought Joseph down to Egypt and sold him to Potiphar could have been caused by the insertion of Gen. 37:36. This verse would have stood in anticipation of 39:1 (either simultaneous with the insertion in 37:28 or later) after the addition of Genesis 38.[165]

4. The double report of the brothers' discovery of the money may have resulted from the addition of a second account of discovering the money in the presence of their father (Gen. 42:35) so that he could refer to it later (43:12).[166]

In summary, several of the indicators that have been most important in the study of the early transmission history of the Joseph story are more likely clues to its latest transmission: the gradual retouching of the text after it has reached final form.

Other indicators are not so clear and are more amenable to other sorts of explanations.[167] Not only are the other indicators often used to posit such a redaction too weak; not only are the divergences in profile (e.g., Reuben-Judah; Jacob-Israel) often used to support such a theory unconfirmed as transmission-historically significant; but significant elements of the posited Judah-Israel layer, such as the sale motif, are important elements of the overall story. We can only isolate such materials as secondary by slashing through the heart of the story's fabric, a slashing that must be done without any clear indicators of seams to guide it.

To be sure, the author of the prepromise Joseph story probably did not create this broad narrative *ex nihilo*. Rather, as in the case of the Jacob and Abraham stories, he most likely adapted earlier traditions in the process of weaving his broader narrative. More specifically, the two stories of Joseph alone in Egypt, Genesis 39 and 40—41, appear to have existed in some form

---

164. Kessler, "Querverweise," 149–50; Blum, *Vätergeschichte*, 245; cf. Mowinckel, *Quellenfrage*, 62.

165. Schmitt, *Josephsgeschichte*, 23n75; Donner, *Literarische Gestalt*, 44–45; Rudolph, *Elohist*, 154–55; Otto, "Lebensauffassung," 388; Blum, *Vätergeschichte*, 245.

166. Redford, *Joseph*, 150–52; Seebass, *Geschichtliche Zeit*, 86n29; Donner, *Literarische Gestalt*, 46–47; Blum, *Vätergeschichte*, 231n8. This insertion would only have made explicit what the narrative already assumes in 43:12, that Jacob found out about the money. Genesis 42:27 is integrally bound to its context (Gen. 42:25–28) and is later explicitly referred to in the following narrative (Gen. 43:21). Note: although the latter reference refers to all of the brothers discovering their money, this does not at all conflict with the preceding report where one brother first discovers the money (Gen. 42:27) and then all discuss the meaning of it (Gen. 42:28).

167. For example, the lack of clarification of Reuben's role vis-à-vis the sale of Joseph is not easily explained as the result of a minor gloss. Perhaps the author of the Joseph story may not have shared our interest in this question. Certainly his focus was manifestly on Joseph and Judah, with Reuben playing a mere supporting role vis-à-vis these focal characters. In any case, this indicator is hardly a basis for positing a comprehensive Reuben-Israel version of the story that preceded a comprehensive Judah-Israel redaction of the story.

prior to their incorporation in their present context. Genesis 39:1–20 is distinct in style from the narrative that surrounds it and is markedly parallel to the Egyptian "tale of the two brothers."[168] In addition, Humphreys has argued persuasively for some kind of prehistory to the "court tale" of the rise of Joseph in Genesis 40—41.[169] These traditions appear to have developed in a common oral mileu, sharing certain fluid motifs, such as a focus on Joseph in Egypt and even a shared association of him with a "Potiphar" figure. In any case, both are distinguished from the broader Joseph story by their lack of specific attention to Joseph's family dynamics. In turn, the major themes of the broader Joseph story are confined to the family history in Genesis 37* and 42—50*. Given this thematic concentration, it is likely the author of the early Joseph story appropriated the traditions in Genesis 39 and 40—41 in some form, linked them, and built the bulk of his narrative around them. Furthermore, this hypothesis would account for the apparent late linkage of Genesis 39 with 40—41 (e.g., expansions in 40:3b and 5b). Indeed, it might also explain some of the doubling in the material toward the end of Genesis 41, where the author of the Joseph story may have added materials to make the transition from the Joseph traditions in Genesis 40—41 to the family history of Genesis 42ff.

In any case, the worth of any such hypothesis, as in the case of the Jacob story, lies more in the way it illuminates the broader (early) Joseph story than simply in isolation and investigation of its precursors. The traditions in Genesis 39 and 40—41 were probably transmitted in an unreconstructable, oral form before ever being used as the core for the broader Joseph story. Exact isolation of them is impossible. Nevertheless, identification of their general contours helps us recognize that the purest contribution of the author of the Joseph story is probably to be found in the family history surrounding the rise of Joseph (Genesis 37, 42—50*). It is exactly here that the above-discussed themes and allusions of the early Joseph story are concentrated.

168. Cf. Redford, *Joseph*, 93, for literature and some skepticism regarding a special link between these texts. Redford does establish the uniqueness of Genesis 39 vis-à-vis the rest of the Joseph story and argues that it is a later addition (*Joseph*, 147 [including n.2], 180–82). Likewise, I see a tradition-historical distinction between Genesis 39 and the rest of the prepromise Joseph story, but I see the story of Joseph and Potiphar's wife as one of the traditions used in the composition of the broader narrative.
169. Humphreys, *Joseph and His Family*, 136–75.

11

The Transmission History of the Non-P Materials

The Case for a Simpler Complexity

At this point we have moved far enough back in the transmission history of Genesis that the indicators become murkier and murkier. Nevertheless, already a basic shift in the compositional model from the source approach is possible. Rather than positing the combination of a Southern Yahwist with a Northern Elohist, I have followed Blum in arguing for the Southern adaptation of Northern Jacob-Joseph materials.[1] And there were yet earlier precursors to each major component of this model for the formation of the non-P materials. The fundamentals of the early part of this picture were already anticipated by Vater in 1798. He saw large Jacob and Joseph stories, as wholes, among the fragments standing at the outset of the composition of the Pentateuch.[2] Furthermore, neither this study nor Blum's were the first to suggest the Abraham materials are significantly later in date than the Jacob materials. Gunkel made the initial observations along these lines, and Noth followed this track in his classic study of the development of Pentateuchal traditions.[3] Finally, I am not the first to posit a layer of often semi-Deuteronomistic retouching of Genesis. This insight goes back to Colenso's work in 1879.[4] Put another way, using typical terms for the different models of Pentateuchal transmission history: I have advocated a "fragment" hypothesis for the precursors to the proto-Genesis composition (the primeval history, Jacob, and Joseph stories, and Jacob-Joseph composition), a combined "redaction"/"supplement" hypothesis for both the development of the Northern Jacob-Joseph story by Judean revisers and the later modification of the proto-Genesis composition, and a modified "source" hy-

---

1. My picture of the Joseph story largely agrees with his, with the minor exception that I assign certain texts to my proto-Genesis compositional layer, rather than to either the Joseph story (Gen. 39:2, 3, 5–6aα, 21–23; 41:39–40) or the semi-D layer (48:21–22). My overall picture diverges mainly in its argument that this proto-Genesis composition definitely included the primeval history and probably some form of the Moses story. For this model, cf. also Z. Weisman, "Diverse Historical and Social Reflections in the Shaping of Patriarchal History (Heb.)," *Zion* 50 (1985): 1–13; idem, "The Interrelationship between J and E in Jacob's Narrative," *ZAW* 104 (1992): 177–97 (with a comparison of his model with Blum's on 177).
2. Vater, *Genesis,* 256–57 (on Jacob) and 290–91 (on Joseph).
3. Gunkel, *Genesis,* 165; Noth, *Pentateuch,* 217; (E.T., 221).
4. Colenso, *Genesis,* 56–62, 73–74, 95–97, 117–18.

pothesis for the final combination of this non-P material with P by the Rp author/ redactor.

In the portion of this model devoted to non-P material, we see several crucial moves: (1) from a Northern core of prepromise compositions to the Southern Jacob-Joseph and proto-Genesis compositions; (2) from prepromise compositions written for life in the land to a broader proto-Genesis composition shifting the focus to assurances about the future; (3) from Northern compositions featuring delimited promises of protection to Jacob and dominance for Joseph to later editions of Genesis focusing on the promise of progeny/land/blessing to Israel; and finally (4) a movement from the (proto-)monarchal politics surrounding the formation of the Jacob-Joseph story to the proto-Genesis mixing of royal ideology with personal piety to sketch a new program for life in the midst of threat and possibly exile. Once these moves were accomplished, the resulting proto-Genesis composition was gradually modified in the late exilic and early postexilic periods. Yet by this point the shifts are less profound. The promise orientation, transfer of royal ideology to the people, and focus on Abraham among the ancestors is already in place. The author/revisors merely add new accents to the themes already established by the proto-Genesis author.

At each stage Israelite authors incorporated earlier traditions in this process of creating, combining, or expanding earlier compositions. Working within a predominantly oral culture, they constantly incorporated various fluid traditions, particularly those regarding the major Israelite characters: Jacob, Joseph, Abraham, and Isaac. Moreover, these authors, like many of their ancient Near Eastern counterparts, appear to have worked carefully around written precursors as well. The process began with the Northern combination of the Jacob and Joseph stories and continued with a subsequent Judean modification of this Northern Jacob-Joseph story that anticipates the Davidic dynasty. The latter move in particular appears to have drawn on earlier traditions, traditions regarding Jacob and his children (Genesis 34*), Tamar (Genesis 38*), and some kind of blessing tradition (Gen. 49:1b-28*). Later, an author composed new promise-centered sections regarding Abraham and Isaac based on Judean traditions concerning them, and adapted the primeval history and revised Jacob-Joseph story accordingly. This then formed the first composition extending from Creation through Joseph, "proto-Genesis." This composition, whether with or without a Moses story, then found its way into the broader, Deuteronomistically colored, stream of non-Priestly textual transmission. It was further revised in this context. Once again at this point we see the probable entry of independent traditions into the mix, traditions like the late story of Abraham's conquest of the Canaanite kings (Genesis 14) and the traditions standing behind the two halves of Genesis 15. Significantly, these are Judean traditions regarding Abraham. This then concludes the major formation of the non-P materials.

At first glance this several-stage transmission history of the non-P materials may seem overly complex. Nevertheless, the additions that have been isolated in any given text are relatively limited in number. The complexity only comes in the ordering of the additions across the entire book into separate levels: late retouching, proto-Genesis, and so forth. The four-source approach postulated only three or four major stages in the written transmission history of non-P Genesis (J, E, Rje, possibly a Rd). At the same time, the approach required reliance on insufficient data to hypothesize the intricate combination of largely non-extant Yahwistic and Elohistic sources. In contrast, I am arguing that the transmission-history of the non-P material is better explained as the result of a gradual and limited modification of certain core compositions. Where the documentary approach posited masses of fragments of J and E combined by Rje, mine posits a finite number of noticeable secondary additions.

This model not only fits the data in Genesis better than the traditional source approach. It also matches evidence outside Genesis.

First, we have at least two other examples of late Judean appropriation of preexilic Northern traditions. The Northern Deuteronomic law forms the core of the Southern Deuteronomistic history. So also the Northern prophecies of Hosea were highly influential in the Deuteronomistic movement, and the book of his sayings was revised in a Judean context and included at the head of the Judean collection of minor prophets. Both of these cases parallel the use of a Northern Jacob-Joseph story in Genesis as the core of a Judean Jacob-Joseph story and eventual proto-Genesis composition.

Second, references to Pentateuchal figures and events outside the Pentateuch match the development being sketched here. Texts outside the Pentateuch move from (1) preexilic Northern references to Jacob and Joseph, such as in Hos. 12:4–5, 13 (Eng. 12:3–4, 12) to (2) exilic and postexilic Southern references to Abraham and Isaac. This parallels the development postulated here from a preexilic Northern Jacob-Joseph story to an exilic story focusing ever more on the Southern figure of Abraham.

In summary, although there are areas of uncertainty, this overall model stays closer to the internal data in the text than the traditional source approach, *and* it matches patterns of biblical transmission history seen outside Genesis as well. The model does not require us to posit early Pentateuchal traditions hundreds of years before they are otherwise attested to in datable biblical texts. Moreover, it does not require us to postulate a multitude of divisions in the non-P materials where they are not to be found. There will always be debate about whether this or that feature in the text is an indicator of growth. Nevertheless, the approach being advocated here postulates a minimum of growth in any given portion of the text. In only a few cases have I identified more than one layer of secondary additions in a given pericope. The following are the most prominent examples (only secondary layers are named):

1. Gen. 41:37–57—Northern Jacob-Joseph and proto-Genesis layers;
2. Gen. 48:1–22—proto-Genesis, P, and post-P layers;
3. Gen. 50:22–26—retouching of non-P, P, and post-P layers. (This post-P text, located as it is at the end of the Genesis scroll, would have been particularly prone to later addition.)

Aside from these texts, the text units in Genesis appear basically unified, aside from the isolation of one layer of additions in a given context, additions that are usually marked as secondary by a combination of distinctive profile and indicators of seams.

Because my analysis does not generally posit layer upon layer of additions in any given text, my arguments are not as dependent on each other as an analysis of non-P material that posits a series of tightly connected additions to the same text. For example, even if one does not accept the hypothesis of a layer of revision of the non-P Genesis material, one could still consider my arguments for a distinctive proto-Genesis focusing on the Abraham story. The main difference would be that this proto-Genesis would now include texts like Genesis 14—15; 18:19; 22:15–18; and 26:3bβ–5. So also, one can consider my arguments for an early primeval history or prepromise form of the Jacob and Joseph stories without accepting my arguments that the Abraham section was a composition by the author of proto-Genesis. These levels of analysis are relatively independent of each other. In any case, my arguments for the isolation of various stages stand apart from my reflections on the dating and background of each layer.[5]

All this stresses a point made at the outset of this analysis: the purpose of this investigation is not to burrow back through the transmission history of Genesis in order to interpret its hypothetically earliest materials in relation to even more hypothetical historical contexts. The point is to reconstruct to the extent possible the different voices that have gone into the formation of Genesis so as to better understand its present complex, multivoiced, final form. Thus, this whole movement backward now turns forward for a final look at how elements of this transmission-historical analysis can inform analysis of the final form of Genesis. Let us turn to that task now.

---

5. To be sure, much does depend here on my isolation of an overall P strand. Nevertheless, my theories regarding the non-P materials do not rise or fall on the minutiae of this analysis of P. Whether or not Gen. 19:29; 37:2; or 46:5 was once part of P is not strategically important. Furthermore, the overall isolation of a distinctive block of P materials is comparatively secure for several reasons: (1) P's distinct profile and parallel character (as originally separate source) means it is marked off more clearly from the non-P materials than most other layers in Genesis; (2) most of P has been preserved in large contiguous blocks amidst the non-P material; and (3) the combination of P and non-P materials stands at the end of the transmission-historical process.

Part 4

Moving Forward

12
Reading
the Fractures

Much of this book has been devoted to showing: (1) that texts like Genesis are characterized by an intratextuality not so common in modern texts, and (2) that attention to this intratextuality could aid in sensing the fractured, multivoiced character of Genesis in its present form. Now we are finally able to look at some concrete ways in which this is true. To be sure, my reflections here will be limited, given the provisional nature of many of the conclusions presented in previous chapters.[1] Nevertheless, it is time to sketch some of the ways the diachronic analysis of the fractures of Genesis might illuminate its present form.

This chapter will move toward the final form of Genesis. I start with the earliest, most hypothetical pre-texts of Genesis and move later. Although this organization means that I start with the more insecure results, it also means that we can look at the relationship of each layer to earlier ones, their intratextuality, in the process of analyzing their impact on the final form of Genesis. This is important, because it is often the strong countertextual character of some of the changes that gives them the most impact on the final form. Layers that invert or radically swerve from earlier material are often the ones that have left the most fractures in the final form, fractures with which later interpreters struggle.

The Precursors to the First Genesis

Our trip back through the prehistory of Genesis starts with the prepromise compositions that stand at the beginning of the process: an independent primeval history, the Jacob and Joseph compositions, and then the successive Israelite and Judean editions of the Jacob-Joseph narrative. We can not exactly reconstruct the precursors to any of these compositions, particularly in the case of the primeval history. For that reason I will not discuss that block

---

1. When writing this chapter, I theoretically should place the adjectives "hypothetical" or "postulated" before every mention of a reconstructed text. Such insertions, however, would significantly disrupt the flow of the discussion, and my qualifications regarding these various layers are already clear from the preceding chapters. Let the reader understand the implicit intention of such adjectives despite their absence.

of material at this point. Nevertheless, there are some ways in which subtle, diachronically based fractures in the Jacob and Joseph stories affect interpretation of their final form.

The Jacob Story

The Jacob story is the composition with the clearest distinction between the authorial hand and his precursor traditions. In particular, it is possible in the earlier two-thirds of the story to distinguish between (1) apparent precursor traditions in Genesis 25, 27–31* and (2) later additions to these traditions from the perspective of the broader Jacob story extending to Genesis 35* (e.g., Gen. 28:20–22; 31:4–16, 24, 29). Many of the precursor materials are characterized by a celebration of trickster traditions associated with Jacob and his family, a celebration that would have had a likely home in Northern resistance movements to early Davidic-Solomonic power structures.[2] The later additions binding these trickster materials into a Jacob story introduced a number of important shifts—shifts that anticipate a new power structure centered in the North. Now God appears to Jacob at Bethel, and Jacob vows the establishment of a sanctuary and tithe there. Now highly theological birth notices for ancestors of Israelite subgroups are part of the account of Jacob's sojourn in Haran. Now Jacob's actions are justified vis-à-vis Laban's accusations by Jacob's speech and Laban's own daughters' acceptance of his speech. Then, in the new material of Genesis 32–35* the political connections continue. God appears to Jacob at Penuel and names him "Israel," thus explicitly linking him to a later ethnopolitical entity. Then Jacob goes on after his meeting with Esau to found cult places at Shechem, Bethel (again), and Rachel's burial place on the border with Benjamin.

The author of the Jacob story seems to have been focused on introducing a highly political form of theology into the new whole he created. This theology is closely linked with Jacob on the one hand, and with Northern cult sites on the other: the royal sanctuary at Bethel (twice), early capital at Penuel, Shechem, and so forth. Overall, we have moved from an emphasis on Jacob as national hero to Jacob as national ancestor, from vague localization of early Jacob traditions in Canaan and Haran, to intense localization of the Jacob narrative at Bethel, Mahanaim, Penuel, Sukkoth, Shechem, and the way to Ephratah.

As a result of these modifications, the Jacob narrative follows a concentric pattern: Jacob and Esau's interactions stand at either end, Bethel at the outset balances Penuel and Bethel at the end, and the Jacob-Laban sojourn stands at the middle. This narrative circle mirrors the tendency of this broader Jacob narrative to encompass the earlier traditions, to enclose them in a struc-

---

2. See Crüsemann, *Widerstand,* 19–127, for the best arguments for the existence of such a movement in ancient Israel.

ture more accommodating to an emergent political entity. This early Jacob narrative is a story that returns to its beginning. This same circular pattern then seems to have been influential in at least two other stages of the formation of the final form of Genesis. The same separation and reconciliation inclusio occurs in the early Joseph story, a story that likewise served a legitimating function for the early Northern monarchy. Then we see a concentric pattern in the proto-Genesis Abraham story, a story that appears to have been carefully formed to make Abraham parallel to Jacob. In the Abraham story, the concentric structure revolves around different issues, promise and heirship. Moreover, it functions not to legitimate an existing political structure but instead to support a structure of political hope. Nevertheless, by the point of the proto-Genesis composition, the correspondences of the broader Jacob story are rippling outward. In summary, starting with the pre-promise Jacob story, the ancestral traditions of Genesis are all narrative circles affirming social structure.

At the same time, the reader is faced with certain tensions that emerge out of these correspondences in the broader Jacob story. For example, some recent synchronic readings have rightly struggled with the contradiction between the promise that Jacob will dominate Esau in 25:23 and the picture of Jacob's (self-)subjugation to Esau in Genesis 33.[3] The former element is part of an early tradition appropriated by the author of the Jacob story, one justifying a broader Israelite domination of Edom during David's and Solomon's reigns.[4] The latter element, however, is part of the layer of material in Genesis 32—35* that appears to be more exclusively the product of the later Northern author of the Jacob story. With David's and Solomon's reign gone and their domination a bad memory in the North, this author writes a sequel to Jacob's and Esau's interaction, one that inverts their relationship. With this sequel in place, the final word is of Jacob's self-subjugation to the Edom he once overcame. Now readers of the whole must struggle with the result, and the variety of readings of this crosscurrent provides additional testimony to the existence of a fracture here.

So also, the reinterpretation of Jacob's trickery by this later compositional layer has not just produced problems exploited by source critics. For example, Calvin struggled with fractures produced by the formation of the Jacob story. He argued that Jacob's accusations against Laban in Gen. 31:7–8 and his assertions regarding God in Gen. 31:11–12 are merely descriptions of the same reality depicted in the earlier, quite different picture of Jacob's behavior in Gen. 30:37–43.[5] The adaptation of Jacob traditions into a narrative to

3. Turner, *Announcements of Plot in Genesis*, 119–24; Clines, "What Happens in Genesis," 59–60.
4. Blum, *Vätergeschichte*, 190–94.
5. J. Calvin, *Commentaries on the First Book of Moses Called Genesis* (trans. J. King; vol. 2; Grand Rapids: Eerdmans, 1948), 164–65.

legitimate the emergent Northern monarchy has not been seamless. The trickster has not been completely tamed. As a result, the reader is left with the task of making sense out of a subversive Jacob, on the one hand, and Jacob the divinely supported and morally justified ancestor of Israel, on the other.

The Joseph Story

Although there are some indicators of breaks in the Joseph story, we can not reconstruct its prehistory with any precision. The closest we can come to some kind of prehistory to the story is to postulate some kind of prehistory to the Joseph-in-Egypt traditions in Genesis 39 and 40—41. If these materials did preexist the Joseph story in some form, the Joseph story represents an interesting development of them. Rather than beginning with Joseph in Egypt, the broader Joseph story attributes his presence there to his brothers' jealousy and defiance of his destiny to rule them. Moreover, Joseph ends up ruling not just Egypt but his brothers as well. Thus, the overall story focuses not just on Joseph's rise, so Genesis 39 and 40—41, but on Joseph's rise *in order to rule and provide for his family* (Gen. 45:4–13). The broader Joseph story clothes a court story of Joseph's rise to power in the garments of family reconciliation, and this reconciliation is then integrally linked to Joseph's divine destiny to rule.

As we have seen, this story in turn is related in complex ways with its Jacob-story precursor. In particular, this postulated independent Joseph story represents an adaptation on a deeper level of the Israelite hero myth seen in the broader Jacob story. Joseph's dreams at the outset represent an interesting blend of Rebekah's oracle and Jacob's later dreams at Bethel (Gen. 28:10–22) and in the field (Gen. 31:11–13). Next, we see parallels in the father's preference, the brothers' intent to kill, the removal of the brother from his family, and the brothers' ultimate reconciliation. At the same time there are important contrasts between the Joseph story and its Jacob-story precursor. On the one hand, Joseph's descent from power is magnified in comparison with Jacob's because it is the result of his brothers' actual intent to kill (cf. Esau's waiting in Gen. 27:41). Moreover, Joseph is taken into slavery rather than fleeing like Jacob. On the other hand, Joseph's rise and ultimate power are stressed by his assuming many of the positions of power that characters in the Jacob story occupied. Joseph sees and dreams like Jacob, must be petitioned for forgiveness like Esau, and executes a search that surpasses Laban's. Just as Jacob could see, while his father was blind, so also Joseph recognizes his brothers, whereas they fail to recognize him. Whereas Jacob had to petition Esau for forgiveness, it is Joseph's brothers who must petition him for forgiveness. Finally, Laban failed in his search for the household gods, but Joseph successfully plants and searches for the household gods. Throughout, this concentration of narrative power in Joseph's hands is augmented by vanquishing the trickster theme of the Jacob story to the margins. All who cleverly try to frustrate Joseph's destiny to rule are defeated.

Overall, what we appear to have in the independent Joseph story is another step in the movement toward harnessing ancient Israelite traditions to support an existing political structure. Yet both the precursors and the new foci are different in the Joseph story. In contrast to the Jacob story, we are no longer looking at the elegant encompassing of subversive traditions. Instead, the Joseph story builds on court traditions (Joseph in Egypt, Genesis 39—41). Moreover, the new material plays a substantially bigger role in the Joseph story, setting up the narrative problem (Genesis 37*) and bringing it to an elaborate resolution (Genesis 42—50*). As we have seen, the new whole contrasts with the Jacob story in at least two respects: its marginalization of potentially subversive trickster themes and its concentration of narrative power positions in the hands of Joseph. Thus the institutionalization we saw in one form in the creation of the broader Jacob narrative out of the Jacob-Esau-Laban composition is present in a more intense form in the Joseph story. The Joseph story not only uses and alludes to the Jacob story. It also appears to be a further step along a similar textual-political trajectory.

Be that as it may, there are not many fractures here. We have only the faint outlines of some possible precursor traditions regarding Joseph's rise in Egypt (Genesis 39, 40—41). Nevertheless, these ripples in the text are quite minor. They relate more to emphasis than to conflicts in theme. In addition, the differences between the Jacob and Joseph stories do not significantly influence the final form of Genesis until the two are combined into a single composition. This then is the focus of the next section.

The Jacob-Joseph Compositions

The Northern Edition
of the Jacob-Joseph Composition

There really was no narrative alternative to putting the Joseph composition after the Jacob narrative. After all, Joseph is explicitly presented as Jacob's son in the Jacob story. Nevertheless, the ordering of these two compositions also represents yet another step in the above-discussed process of embedding Israelite traditions in monarchal power structures. The Joseph story was already characterized by marginalization of trickster antistructural characters and intensified polemic for benevolent monarchal power. Now standing after the Jacob story, it neutralizes many of the antistructural themes that appear earlier in the Jacob materials. Ordered differently, we would have had Jacob, the successful trickster, following Joseph, the one divinely destined to rule. As it is, however, we have Joseph providing the ultimate resolution to the process begun by Jacob.

Indeed, as we look at the first layer of material unique to this combined Jacob-Joseph composition (Gen. 41:50–52; 48:1–2, 8–14, 17–20), we see that it binds the whole into a narrative circle that gives a sense of the resolution. The Jacob-Joseph materials begin with a deathbed scene revolving around the blessing of a patriarch and his choice of one descendant over another (Genesis 27). Now, with the addition of Genesis 48*, they end with a similar deathbed scene. In this scene the one blessed in Genesis 27 is now doing the blessing, and the ones being blessed are not his sons but his grandsons through Joseph. Like his father, Isaac, Jacob of Genesis 48 is blind. Unlike his father, however, he is able to assert his preferences, despite the efforts of his son. Things have quieted down in the Genesis narrative world by now. Those in charge assert their/God's will, while those lower in the hierarchy must accommodate themselves to the will of those higher.

This combined Jacob-Joseph story originates in the early Northern Kingdom. The Genesis 27 story featured Jacob, along with a character representing a southern competitor (Esau/Edom). The origins of this tradition probably lie in the South as an articulation of David's right to dominate Edom. Now however, Genesis 48* focuses on Joseph as the father of two Northern groups, Ephraim and Manasseh. Whereas Genesis 27 establishes the dominance of an all-Israelite hero (Jacob) over a neighboring group (Edom), Genesis 48 focuses more exclusively on the precedence of one Northern group over the other, Ephraim over Manasseh. Thus the originally Southern model of Genesis 27 has been appropriated to articulate Northern intergroup power relationships. As in the case of the Jacob story itself (Genesis 25*; 27:1–45, and 32–33*), we have a diachronic inclusio in Genesis 27 and 48*. The earlier material (Genesis 27:1–45) anchors the beginning of a circle that is closed by later material (Genesis 48*). Genesis 48* appropriates elements from the earlier narrative (Genesis 27), but is strategically placed so that it resolves the narrative whole and has the last word.

Although this linkage of Jacob-Joseph materials played a crucial role in building toward the final form of Genesis, it does not seem to have introduced significant fractures into that form. This stage in the composition of Genesis involves no inversion or radical recontextualization of earlier materials. Instead, this move is more a collection of earlier traditions and an *extension* of their existing emphases. The Northern context remains constant. The increasing emphasis on order, particularly legitimizing a specific Northern Kingdom political order, remains constant. Even the overall interest in narrative circles is maintained. And the new materials added to this combined narrative are carefully linked into its existing narrative logic. Genesis 48:1–2 carefully reopens the earlier blessing scene to which Genesis 48* was added (Gen. 47:29–31 . . . 50:1ff.), and develops it in a way parallel to Genesis 27 and compatible with the Jacob-Joseph narrative as a whole. More significant fractures will emerge only when the traditions begin to be transmitted in a decisively different context.

The Southern Edition
of the Jacob-Joseph Composition

Just such a significant shift occurs with the transfer of the Northern Jacob-Joseph composition into a Southern monarchal context. To be sure, this Northern composition already included Judah as a major character in the Joseph story. Nevertheless, the trajectory of its development has led to an ever more resolute focus on the destiny of Northern groups to rule. We have already traced this development, from (1) the elegant modification of the Jacob, Esau, and Laban traditions to include Northern political and cultic sites, to (2) the argument for Joseph's destiny to rule his brothers in the early Joseph story, and finally to (3) the expanded Jacob-Joseph story focus on the destiny of Ephraim to have precedence among the Joseph tribes. Now, probably in the wake of the destruction of the Northern Kingdom in 722, this Jacob-Joseph composition appears to have found its way to Judah. Judean authors are faced with the task of making sense of such claims for Northern lordship in a southern context, indeed in a time where the North has been swept away.

Their answer was to (1) demote Joseph into just a ruler of Egypt and (2) promote an already prominent Judah character into the position of future ruler. Notably, there are many documented examples of such upgrading or downgrading of a character in the process of textual transmission. For example, Tigay discusses how the role of Shamash, the sun god, develops from helper of Gilgamesh on his journey to Cedar Mountain to instigator of this journey.[6] Notably, the presence of Shamash in the earlier materials seems to have been important. Neither Marduk nor Ashur, prominent national gods in the Middle and Late Babylonian periods, were included in the epic. Instead, the tradents of the Gilgamesh epic seem to have confined their efforts to enhancing the role of a god who was already there.[7] So also, the posited tradents of the Northern Jacob-Joseph story took the Judah character who was already in the Northern Jacob-Joseph story and used him as a pivot-point for a new reading of Israel's ancestral history.

The textual focus of most of their changes was the Joseph story, the section of the text with the most emphasis on interbrother relations. And the cultural principle used to articulate the dominance of Judah's and David's clan within Judah was the dynastic principle of preference for elder children. The Jacob-Joseph materials emphasized the role of the divine by focusing on the divine destiny of youngest children: Jacob, Rachel, Joseph, Benjamin, Ephraim. In contrast, the Judean revision of the Jacob-Joseph story under-

---

6. Tigay, *The Evolution of the Gilgamesh Epic*, 76–81. Tigay also notes how the Enkidu character shifts from being the servant of Gilgamesh in earlier material to being his friend in the Old Babylonian epic.
7. Tigay, *Evolution of the Gilgamesh Epic*, 244.

mines the earlier story's argument for Northern (Ephraimite) dominance by maintaining that Judah was the eldest legitimate successor of Jacob, and thus that it is he who is destined to rule.

As many have long recognized, there is a yet more specific model for this argument that Judah is the eldest legitimate heir: the narrative of David's succession (2 Sam. 13—20; 1 Kings 1—2). Just as David's eldest, Absalom, slept with his father's concubines on the way to his doom (2 Sam. 16:20–22), so also Reuben sleeps with his father's concubine (Gen. 35:22) and earns himself an unfavorable blessing (Gen. 49:3–4). David's next eldest, Ammon, sends himself to his doom by raping his sister (2 Samuel 13). So also, Jacob's next eldest sons, Simeon and Levi, earn themselves an unfavorable blessing by butchering the entire home town of the one who raped their sister (Genesis 34; 49:5–7). Finally, the succession narrative story of Ammon's rape of Tamar finds its last reflection in the quite different story of a different Tamar's heroic efforts to establish Judah's clan. It is at this point that Perez, the ancestor of David's clan, is born first from her womb (Gen. 38:27–30), thus anticipating David's future dominance over Israel (Gen. 49:8–12). Thus, not only does the eldest legitimate successor prevail at each stage, but the themes used to describe this process resonate at each point with the succession narrative.

In summary, the Judean authors of the Jacob-Joseph narrative strategically modified an earlier Northern composition. They did so by interlinking it with the different logic of their own Southern dynastic legitimating story, the succession narrative. The result was some conflicting currents in the final form of Genesis. On the one hand, God prefers the younger siblings in the cases of Jacob, Joseph, Rachel, and Ephraim. On the other hand, Judah emerges in the end as the proper future successor of Jacob *because of the disqualification of his elder siblings.* Such is the mixture of the ideology of divinely chosen power in the earlier, Northern Jacob-Joseph story and the ideology of dynastically legitimate power in the Southern succession narrative. The present narrative is characterized by an ongoing tension between the Reuben and Judah characters. This tension was strong enough that later Jewish interpreters attempted to explain Judah's eventual precedence over Reuben, despite the fact that both misbehave at points, as resulting from Judah's confession of his misdeed to Tamar (Gen. 38:26; *b. B.Qam.* 92a; *b.Mak* 116).

In addition, the shift toward a focus on Judah's future rule radically modified the significance of much of the Joseph narrative. Before, the dream prediction of Joseph's rule and his rise to that rule over his brothers was an allegory for the future domination of Joseph tribes over the others. Now, however, all these dynamics simply revolve around a narrative past. Joseph once ruled, but Judah rules now. As a result of this shift, the once politically laden interactions of Joseph and his brothers are now just the interpersonal relationships of Jacob's children. Thus, by (1) raising Judah and (2) relegating Joseph's rule to the past, the Judean author/redactors prepared the way to read the Joseph story as a more general lesson, a lesson regarding divine purpose, human relationships, and human response to and knowledge of the divine purpose. At the same time, these authors preserved the more explicitly Northern political elements of the Joseph story, such as Joseph's dreams, his arguments for God's endorsement of his rule, and the later depiction of Jacob's lifting Ephraim over Manasseh. Although such elements are not incompatible with a nonpolitical reading of the Joseph story, they are not fully accounted for by such a reading either. And indeed, the Joseph character has not been fully overcome by Judah in this Southern compositional revolution. As the major character of this section of Genesis, he is again the focus of the proto-Genesis composition, non-P retouchings of it, and P counterwriting.

The Proto-Genesis Composition

We take yet another significant step forward with the inclusion of the primeval history and (Southern edition of) the Jacob-Joseph story into a broader proto-Genesis composition. It is a step from exploration of established cosmicpolitical structures in the earlier narratives to a vision of hope for the *re*establishment, or at least reinforcement, of such structures. The cosmic narrative world of the primeval history is not enough. The political structures legitimated by the Judean version of the Jacob-Joseph story are either threatened or gone. In this context, the proto-Genesis composition extends these precursor texts and links them into a new whole.

Overall Shifts

This new whole transforms the earlier texts' anticipation of the audience's present circumstances into a secure prediction of the audience's future. The primeval history explored the shape and roots of the present human condition. The Jacob and Joseph stories anticipated various existing political structures, whether of the South (at beginning and end of the process) or North. In each case, the promises involved—preservation of seasons (Noah), protection (Jacob), and domination (Joseph)—are promises that have already been fulfilled in the audience's day. The narrative future in these precursor compositions is the audience's present. In the proto-Genesis composition, however, the narrative future *has become the audience's future*. Moreover, the earlier promises of the other narratives are encompassed in this reoriented perspective. God's promises to Jacob are now an extension of God's promises to Abraham, and so also with God's promises to Joseph and his sons. The proto-Genesis composition builds its vision for (re)establishment of Israel's power and prominence around promises that originally pointed to Israel's structures of the past.

One indicator of the shift toward the audience's future is the extent to which the proto-Genesis composition does not just predict the giving of nationhood, blessing, and so forth. Instead, it *strenuously argues* for the plausibility of such a promise against all odds. This is a strong promise, and the proto-Genesis author draws on all his cultural resources to depict its unshakability. For example, he builds on the theology of personal piety in order to describe the security of God's bond with Israel. Personal piety's faith in the loyalty of a god to an individual or family unit is a potent way to describe God's unshakable loyalty to Israel. In addition, the proto-Genesis author draws on Israel's royal ideological resources to describe the consequences of this divine loyalty.[8] This involves the addition of elements such as the promise that the patriarch will be a "great nation" or that he will be a paradigm of blessing. Both personal piety and royal ideology were present in precursor compositions. Personal piety was part of the Jacob story's narrative world, and royal ideology was the implicit subtext of the early Joseph narrative. The difference is that now both of these cultural resources are used to buttress the security of a promise that extends not into the audience's present but its future.

Most of all, the proto-Genesis author relentlessly anchors all such promises in God. The precursor compositions focused quite a bit on human blessing, such as Isaac's (Genesis 27) and Jacob's (Genesis 48). Divine communication generally took place in the form of *angelic* beings and/or dreams (Gen. 28:10–22*; 31:11–13; 32:2–3, 23–33 [Eng. 32:1–2, 22–32]; 37:5–9; 40—41). In contrast, the proto-Genesis composition emphasizes *divine* promise and blessing, and direct divine contact is now the norm. All human blessing and promise, such as Isaac's blessing Jacob, is now but an outgrowth of an earlier, constitutive promise of God in the proto-Genesis composition. The human will to believe in such promises may vary. Abraham does not immediately act as the protected one in Egypt (Gen. 12:10–20), Sarah and Abraham do not presuppose that God will provide (Gen. 16:1–14*), and later Sarah laughs at God's promise that she will have the promised child (Gen. 18:10–14). Nevertheless, the proto-Genesis composition insists on God's will to execute the promise, despite any such variables. This kind of marshalling of cultural resources—personal piety and royal ideology—and theological defense of the reliability of the promise is not required when the narrative future is the audience's present. Rather it occurs when the author must build a bridge from a given narrative to a future that does not yet exist for the narrative's audience.

This shift in the understanding of the narrative future means that the realia of the narrative world also function differently. The precursor compositions included etiological elements that reinterpreted aspects of the audience's present as testimonies to narrative events. Such people could look at Bethel and its tithes and see it as a reflection of Jacob's encounter and vow there. They could avoid eating the thigh muscle of the hip socket or hear the

---

8. Indeed, these two elements, personal piety and royal ideology, overlap more than is indicated in this discussion. Royal ideology is, to some extent, a form of personal/public piety for the king and his dynasty.

name "Penuel" and interpret both elements as outgrowths of the time Jacob was renamed after the nation he fathered. They could see the oak at Shechem and remember the burial of Laban's household gods there. They could look at the political prominence of Joseph/Ephraim and see it as a reflection of Joseph's early destiny to rule his brothers. Through such prepromise narratives, the audience's reality was textually transformed into a reflection of an earlier narrative world. This narrative world in turn legitimated the existing social structure as the way things ought to be.

In contrast, the proto-Genesis ancestral narratives point more *beyond* the audience's world. Their realia serve less to anticipate the audience's present *and more to bind various parts of the narrative together in order to point reliably to the future.* On the one hand, in narratives like the Sodom story, the proto-Genesis author builds on parallels to the primeval history in order to depict the world outside Israel in the somber colors of catastrophic crime and punishment. On the other hand, starting with the Abraham narrative, the proto-Genesis author constructs an Israelite genealogical line characterized substantially by the reliable transmission of the promise down the line. The somber colors of the primeval world are replaced by the steadfast loyalty of Abraham's, Isaac's, and Jacob's personal deity to each of them. By extending the genealogy backward from the Jacob-Joseph story, the proto-Genesis author does two things: (1) he focuses more on the Southern figures of Abraham and Isaac and (2) thus establishes an ongoing genealogical line of promise transmission of which the Judean audience can see themselves as a part.

Furthermore, the proto-Genesis author establishes certain repetitive patterns of promise, patterns that stress the reliable transmission of the promise down this single genealogical line. The readers are part of this genealogical line as descendants of Abraham, Isaac, and Jacob. The proto-Genesis composition's description of promise transmission from Abraham to Jacob and beyond helps establish that this audience can count on the continued transmission of the promise to them, despite all variables. Thus, the point is no longer so much the realia of the narrative world themselves. The point is that Abraham and Jacob are *both* part of a genealogical line that the readers share; they *both* travel a path to Canaan, Egypt, and back again that the readers can follow; they (along with Isaac) *both* receive an unbelievable set of promises that the readers can believe. This is not a matter of an isolated promise event or promise recipient. Proto-Genesis depicts for the Israelite reader a genealogically structured promise-community in which the audience members can see themselves as participants, and it stresses through its parallels between generations of that community an ongoing promise history in which that audience can believe.

Shaping and Fractures

Obviously this hypothesized step in the formation of Genesis was a crucial one in shaping the present book. The later retouchings of the non-P mater-

ial build around the proto-Genesis material already there, and the P document parallels and draws on the basic outline of the above-discussed proto-
Genesis composition. Finally, the similar outlines of the P and non-P materials allow them to be combined into a narrative that follows the basic lines
set down for the first time in the postulated proto-Genesis composition. At
each stage, the focus on the promise and genealogy intensifies, while emphasis on specific narrative subplots diminishes. The result is a genealogically
structured, promise-centered composition, one that leans ever more toward
the future and less toward explaining the present.

Thus the proto-Genesis composition represents a crucial loosening of the tie
of Israel's preland traditions to a specific sociocultural "present" of the readers.
This loosening, in turn, may be one factor that allowed these traditions to function in a wider range of sociocultural contexts. As long as the Genesis materials consisted of Jacob materials pointing toward Northern Kingdom sites, or a
Joseph narrative designed to convince Israelites of the value of monarchal rule,
they could not as easily speak to audiences for whom the Northern Kingdom
was but a distant reality. With the redirection of such materials to speak of a
promised future, more open elements were added to the text. These turned out
to be elements to which a wider variety of later readers, including Christians,
could relate. The readers only had to perceive themselves as somehow landless,
nameless, cursed, and vulnerable in order for the proto-Genesis composition
to speak to them. Although they might not exactly share the context in which
the narrative was written, such readers could gain hope from the future the narrative now stresses. And indeed, this interest in promise is borne out in the history of interpretation of Genesis. From early Jewish interpreters to Protestant
reformers and onward, later audiences of Genesis have found themselves particularly drawn to the promises of Genesis. They could find hope in the future
the proto-Genesis composition so painstakingly developed and secured.

At the same time, the proto-Genesis author did not create a future-ori-
ented composition from nothing. Instead he built around earlier compositions and traditions that had other interests. Usually, the interest of the
proto-Genesis author in establishing repetition and continuity meant that no
significant fractures were added to the text. For example, the proto-Genesis
author not only added a divine appearance and speech to an earlier, concen-
trically structured Bethel scene (Gen. 28:13–15), but he added a balancing
exclamation by Jacob as well (Gen. 28:16). In this way he preserved the circular pattern of the whole. So also, in the additions revolving around Joseph's
blessing, the proto-Genesis author only augmented existing stories of
Joseph's success with theological additions. Through such strategic insertions
of small bits of material, crucial parts of the Joseph story were given their present spin, one that attributes Joseph's success to divine blessing.

In other cases, however, the proto-Genesis author intervened more radically in earlier material, introducing themes that are sometimes alien to it. For

example, even as the proto-Genesis author so carefully worked around the circular pattern of the Bethel narrative, he introduced a set of promises that have little to do with the focus of the earlier materials on the holiness of Bethel. Here the broader future of the proto-Genesis narrative clashes to some extent with the narrower, sanctuary-centered future originally projected by the Bethel tradition. In a similar case, the proto-Genesis author binds Joseph to the promise by inserting a fatherly blessing on him in the midst of a scene that focuses on his grandsons (Gen. 48:15–16).

The main way the proto-Genesis author introduced fractures into the present form of Genesis was by expanding the essentially non-promise-centered Jacob and Joseph materials by adding to them the Abraham and Isaac materials. Although the new materials are carefully built around the older texts in order to redirect them, the two sets of ancestral materials have fundamentally different concerns. The more various unity-focused synchronic readings attempt to see these sections as parallel to one another, the more such readings run up against the resistance of the texts themselves. For example, in her book *From Father to Son,* Steinmetz reads the whole of the ancestral section in terms of family conflict and violence. This fits the Jacob-Esau and Joseph stories well, but this theme must be read into the Abraham story as an unconscious substructure to narratives that, to all appearances, do not have much to do with such themes.[9] In contrast, Steinberg, in her book *Kinship and Marriage in Genesis,* reads the whole of the ancestral section in terms of the struggle toward kinship continuity—the search for proper marriage and inheritance structures to transfer the promise. This fits the Abraham story very well and the Jacob story to a lesser extent. When Steinberg comes to the story of Joseph, however, she must awkwardly raise problems to prominence that the story treats as peripheral at best.[10] Overall, both Steinmetz's and Steinberg's studies have much to offer, and yet both must strain against the grain of significant portions of the ancestral material.

Once one correlates these different readings with the above-sketched diachronic analysis, it becomes clear that they resonate with different historical strata in Genesis. The interpretive base of Steinmetz's approach is primarily the stories of conflict in the earliest stratum of the Jacob and Joseph stories. In contrast, Steinberg's approach leans more on the materials stressing transferal of the promise, a theme characteristic of the proto-Genesis materials regarding Abraham and Jacob. Although the proto-Genesis materials have been elegantly built around the precursor materials regarding Jacob and Joseph, the major emphases of these two strata are not completely congruent. As a result, *any* synchronic reading of the ancestral

9. Genesis 22 is the main exception to this statement.
10. Cf. Steinberg, *Kinship and Marriage,* 120–34.

narratives must strain to a greater or lesser extent with the multivoiced character of Genesis at this point. The reader must choose, consciously or unconsciously, how to deal with the diachronically based, multivoiced character of the text.

The Revision of Proto-Genesis

Already with the late proto-Genesis materials we are moving to a modification of earlier texts (e.g., the Jacob-Joseph story) largely confined to inserting direct speech. This continues in the retouching of the proto-Genesis composition as it was transmitted in the exile and postexile by groups influenced by Deuteronomistic terminology and conceptuality. The additions in Gen. 9:18–27*; 10:16–18a; 15; 18:17–18, 19; and so forth do not all appear to have been made at the same time or by the same people. Nevertheless, most of these additions share a special relationship to the Deuteronomistic tradition, and they all tend to retouch earlier narratives, rather than adding entire new episodes. The main exception, of course, is Genesis 14—15. Nevertheless, even here we see later authors inserting and building around earlier traditions. Even here they appear to have confined the bulk of their own contributions to redactional transitions and direct speech.

As a result, these texts did not fundamentally change the final shape of Genesis. Instead, the additions strategically redirected or inverted existing structural units: an earlier curse by Noah on Ham, YHWH's reward to Abraham for passing the test in Genesis 22, YHWH's speech to Isaac before he departs for Gerar (Gen. 26:2–3bα), and so on.

Again, Genesis 15 (along with 14) is the main exception. This block is inserted into the heart of the proto-Genesis narrative circle once inhabited only by the Hagar-Ishmael story. As discussed previously, that Hagar-Ishmael story is remarkable for its description of Israelite oppression of a non-Israelite, a non-Israelite who then endures a forced "exodus" from Abraham's clan and receives a Sinai-like revelation in the wilderness. The antiforeign, semi-"Deuteronomistic" revisers of Genesis did not leave this alone at the heart of the Abraham account. Instead, they balanced it with elements expressing their perspective (Genesis [14—]15). As a result, most concentric diagrams of the present Abraham story done today now have Genesis 15 at or near the heart of their narrative circles.

Although these revisions of the proto-Genesis story are generally limited in scope and well integrated with the whole, they often introduce significant shifts into their narrative contexts. For example, Genesis Rabbah quotes rabbis as arguing that Canaan and not Ham is cursed because (1) the latter could not be cursed, since he had previously been blessed (Gen. 9:1), or (2) because Canaan was the one who informed his father, Ham, of Noah's nakedness, and/or (3) because Ham deprived his father of a young son by "exposing the nakedness" of his father and so was deprived of his own young son.[11] Luther reads the curse on Canaan as an example of the curse on the father falling on the son as well.[12] And these are but a few of many attempts to make sense of the story of Noah and his sons in its present form. All are struggling with the introduction of an anti-Canaanite swerve into a text that probably originally described a curse on Ham.[13]

In other cases, the gap between later additions and their contexts was not sensed until certain issues had emerged to the forefront of later religious debate. For example, the versions of the promise in Gen. 22:15–18 and 26:3bβ–5 both explicitly stress the importance of obedience to Deuteronomistic norms for the transmission of the promise to Isaac. Moreover, Gen. 18:19 stresses the importance of this principle for the ongoing genealogical line. This Deuteronomistic emphasis in turn contrasts with the lack of such a focus on such issues in the proto-Genesis material. That material begins with an unmotivated divine promise to Abraham (Gen. 12:1–3) and later describes the promise's (partial) fulfillment despite human lack of reliance on it. Later, rabbinic interpreters could base their halachic reading of Abraham's life partly on the semi-"Deuteronomistic" texts describing it, and Catholic opponents of the reformers later picked up on such an emphasis when they used texts like Gen. 22:15–18 and 26:3bβ–5 to counter the reformers' emphasis on unearned grace. In response, Luther points to the fact that the promise of Gen. 12:1–3 is not preceded by any act of obedience,[14] and he then spends an unusually large amount of time attempting to interpret 22:15–18; 26:2–5 in relationship to his theology of grace.[15] On the one hand, we have interpreters leaning toward the semi-"Deuteronomistic" retouching of the proto-Genesis composition. On the other hand, their opponents try to conform the semi-"Deuteronomistic" interventions to the text they built around. The reformers and counterreformers were working two sides of a diachronically based fracture in Genesis: the proto-Genesis promise, on the one hand, and the semi-"Deuteronomistic" revision of it, on the other.

---

11. *Gen. Rab.* 36:7; cf. also *b.Sanh.* 70a. The latter interpretation is augmented by the racist subnarrative that Canaan was the product of Ham's copulation with a dog in the ark. For a survey of attempts to fill this gap in the narrative, see W. Vogels, "Caham découvre les limites des son père Noé," *NRT* 109 (1987): 554–73.
12. M. Luther, *Lectures on Genesis* (trans. G. V. Schick; Luther's Works 2; St. Louis: Concordia, 1960), 174.
13. To be sure, even without this swerve, interpreters would need to struggle with the xenophobic thrust of the text, perhaps even more so. For without the fracture, the text would all the more univocally curse Ham. For survey and critique of the interpretive potential of this text, see C. H. Felder, *Troubling Biblical Waters: Race, 'Class and Family* (Studies in North American Black Religion 3; Maryknoll, N.Y.: Orbis, 1989), 40.
14. *Lectures on Genesis,* vol. 2, 245–46.
15. *Lectures on Genesis,* (vol. 4; 1960), 139–78.

The Priestly Document

With the priestly document, we come to a comprehensive counterpresentation of the Genesis story, indeed one designed to replace the account on which it is dependent. In the process of exploring the character of this material, I have already discussed its detailed intertextual relation to its non-P precursor. I will wait to discuss the impact of this material on the shape of Genesis until the next section, where we will look at the creation of Genesis out of a combination of P and non-P materials. The main task here is to discuss briefly ways the P material extended or subverted previous moves in the transmission history of the Genesis material.

As we saw in the last chapter, P is probably the second major priestly contribution to Genesis. The first was the early, independent primeval history that was used by the author of proto-Genesis. Nevertheless, despite their similar institutional origins, there are some important differences between the early "non-P" priestly primeval history and P. Within P, reference to human rebellion, so prominent in the early primeval history, is not only conspicuously, but even frequently contradicted, through devices such as the rhythmic assertions that creation was good or the assertion that God created humankind from the beginning to be in the material image and likeness of god. So also, elements of the early primeval history that focused on the problem of the divine-human boundary are not extended by the later P narrative. Instead, God is depicted as sovereignly setting the boundaries of the cosmos in Genesis 1 and then later providing through the tabernacle a means for divine-human communion across the divine-human boundary. In this way, the overall P primeval history replaces an earlier emphasis on the problematic character of the divine-human boundary with a confident assertion of God's ability to set up structures that can span that boundary. It inverts its precursor tradition.

In contrast, as we turn to the ancestral materials, the P document appears to have extended the emphases of the non-P material. Earlier, the retouching of the proto-Genesis material in Genesis 15 had transformed the Abrahamic promise into a covenant oath. So also the P document focuses in the ancestral section on El-Shaddai's covenant with Abraham, a covenant that is now made parallel to a new P story of God's postflood covenant with Noah. This focus on Abraham in P is a further development from the earlier emphasis on Abraham in both the proto-Genesis layer and the semi-D material.

Furthermore, the P material extends the interest of earlier layers in establishing the moral character and obedience of the ancestors. Where Abraham was portrayed in the revisions of the proto-Genesis composition as obeying God's commands, now in P, Abraham is described as circumcising himself and the males of his clan. Moreover, just as the broader Jacob narrative justified Jacob's trickery with the flocks and flight from Haran (Gen. 31:4–13), so also the P material deals with his trickery of Esau by replacing it with a story of Jacob's travel to Padan-Aram to find a proper wife. In this way, the P Jacob represents the final domestication of the trickster, a process already begun with the composition of the broader Jacob story, and continued with the composition of the Joseph story and the combination of the Jacob and Joseph stories.

Finally, just as the proto-Genesis composition and revisions of it deemphasized Joseph, so also the P material appears to have devoted a minimum of attention to him. To be sure, as has been observed above, we do not have crucial material from P on Joseph. Nevertheless, two indicators suggest that P did not have much in this portion of the story. First, the redactor responsible for combining P and non-P does appear to have preserved significant amounts of the less extensive P or non-P narratives in his work on the primeval history and Abraham sections. This would suggest that he would have included as much of the P Joseph narrative as possible. Second, if P had a minimal Joseph story, that would fit the broader trajectory of the relative lack of interest of Joseph we already saw in the proto-Genesis composition and revisions of it. By this point in the history of Israel, the future-focused, Judean Abraham figure appears to have captivated tradents far more than the Northern, kinglike Joseph figure.

As the ancestor of Israel, Jacob appears to have received a significant amount of attention in P as well. Much of this is difficult to gauge because some P material on Jacob appears to have been eliminated in favor of the more extended non-P Jacob account. Nevertheless, the portions of P that have been preserved are striking in the extent to which they subvert non-P materials in various ways. The P account of Jacob's departure has already been mentioned, but this subversion is also found in the P Bethel story. P retells the Bethel story so that it is clear Jacob established a pillar there only because God spoke to him there, not because of any special presence of angels or a gate of heaven at Bethel. The "angel ladder" and "gate of heaven" themes were part of a cultic theology standing behind the older Bethel story. They could compete with the distinctively different presence-theology standing at the heart of the P composition. Therefore, P in Gen. 35:9–15 explicitly contradicts the Bethel story with a new account that, as in the case of Gen. 27:46–28:9, depends for its original effect on a denial that things ever happened as described in the earlier, non-P story. It goes beyond earlier layers that merely built around the Bethel story, for example, proto-Genesis and revisions of it, to replace the story's precursor.

Overall, P represents the ultimate extension of several trends particularly characteristic of the proto-Genesis materials: linkage of ancestral and primeval history, establishment of genealogical links between major sections, coordination of the itineraries of the various patriarchs, and focus on the promise. Now the whole has become an extended genealogy, and this structure then spans both the primeval and ancestral periods. In contrast to the proto-

Genesis and later materials, the ancestral period is portrayed as an extension and intensification of covenantal dynamics already initiated after the Flood. The promise theme no longer serves to heighten the contrast between the primeval and ancestral periods. Instead the promise covenant makes the two periods parallel to one another. The parallel character of Abraham's and Jacob's travels in the non-P materials has been disrupted in P through its introduction of Terah's travel to Haran. Nevertheless, P continues the emphasis on itinerary through its focus on (1) the ancestors' travel to, sojourn in, and burial in the land and (2) the travel from the land by those of Abraham's children who do not inherit the promise. P hardly reflects all the details of the non-P narrative it was designed to replace. Nevertheless, it develops to a remarkable extent many of the overall emphases and tendencies of the later layers in the development of the non-P Genesis traditions.

The Combined P/Non-P Genesis Composition

The Nature of the Compositional Combination

At the end of the chapter on the P layer of Genesis, I already discussed some features of the redaction that combined the P and non-P materials. Now we are able to go beyond those initial observations and compare this stage of the composition of Genesis with earlier ones. It is, indeed, a decisively different stage. Whereas authors at earlier points often added substantial amounts of their own material, Rp appears to have composed only a minimum amount: the genealogical heading in Gen. 2:4a, several additions to the creation and flood accounts, genealogical material in Genesis 10, and some minor additions to the ancestral accounts of Genesis. Otherwise, the main work of Rp in Genesis lay in preserving and organizing the precursor texts before him.

Preservation: Indications of a New Step
Toward Proto-Scriptural Status of the Precursors

Rp appears to have attempted to preserve the maximum amount of material from both P and non-P without unproductive duplication. For example, Rp appears to have deemed unproductive duplication of P and non-P death reports. In this case, he preserved only the P accounts in the process of using the broader P genealogical structure. In the case of the theologically significant P and non-P flood accounts, however, Rp did preserve parallel death notices. At this point the duplication appears to have been judged theologically productive. Along similar lines, Rp seems to have only partially preserved P and non-P parallel birth accounts, but to have preserved more fully parallel P and non-P promise texts. This trend toward preservation of promise texts is Rp's extension of a more general trend seen from the proto-Genesis composition onward: to focus ever more on the future, particularly promises.

The difference is that Rp extends this focus on the future through selective preservation of earlier material, while earlier layers initiated this trend through creation of new material.

In most cases where the Rp author did eliminate parallel material, he seems to have eliminated the less extensive account.[16] Take the flood narrative as an example. Here, cases where parallel P and non-P accounts were both preserved suggest that the P flood account was more extensive than the non-P account. Furthermore, where material was eliminated, it seems to have been the less extensive non-P material. In contrast, in the Jacob and Joseph sections, Rp preserved large blocks of non-P material at the apparent expense of P accounts. From the proto-Genesis layer onward, we have seen decreasing interest in Jacob and Joseph coupled with increasing interest in the figure of Abraham. Indeed, the remnants of P in the Jacob-Joseph story indicate that this trend was probably continued in P as well. If this is so, Rp eliminated less extensive P materials regarding Jacob and Joseph and used the more extensive non-P narratives regarding these figures to fill out the broader genealogical structure. This selective elimination was itself an act of partial preservation. It allowed for (1) the implicit reflection of the substance of the less expansive account in the more expansive one, and (2) the preservation of the extras from the more expansive account as well.

At the same time, the case of the Jacob and Joseph materials indicates how much the impetus toward preservation has assumed a life of its own. Whereas earlier stages—proto-Genesis, revisions of it, and P—all deemphasized the Jacob and Joseph materials at the expense of the primeval and Abraham traditions, Rp appears to have preserved earlier, more expansive non-P Jacob and Joseph traditions at the expense of P's later, shorter accounts. Thus, the urge for maximum preservation resulted in much more emphasis on Jacob and Joseph than was reflected in all the more recent stages of the composition of Genesis.

Indeed, the kind of compositional preservation seen in Rp's work makes it an exception in a variety of ways: the minimal scope of Rp's own compositional contributions, the preservation of numerous parallel elements of P and non-P, and the preservation of the more expansive of parallel materials, even to the point of contradicting recent compositional trends and preserving older materials regarding older figures. In contrast, earlier compositional stages, as they have been reconstructed here, generally involved addition of new characters, scenes, and episodes; they extended earlier materials and/or elegantly redirected them without creating the number of doublets and breaks seen in Rp's work; and they often displayed clear trends—such as the emphasis seen across proto-Genesis, revisions, and P—that are contradicted in Rp's work by its interest in preservation. These earlier stages also involved

16. Noth, *Pentateuch*, 13–14; (E.T., 14); Levin, *Der Jahwist*, 439.

preservation of a kind, both in building onto earlier traditions seen in the non-P materials and in the use of non-P traditions by P. Nevertheless, with Rp such preservation has taken a new form, one where material is preserved as much for its own sake as because of its immediate relevance to broader compositional and theological aims.

Organization

That having been said, we would completely misunderstand Rp's work if we saw it as merely an exercise in maximum preservation. This is already clear in several elements: (1) Rp's orientation toward P's overall structural system, (2) Rp's use of Priestly terminology, and (3) Rp's complete preservation of some parallel materials and selective preservation of others. Although Rp appears to have authored only a minimal amount of the current text of Genesis, his authorial contribution to the text's final shape was fundamental. Many of the aspects of the present structure of Genesis derive from him: (1) the use of the P genealogical structure to organize the whole (Gen. 2:4a; 5:1; 6:9, etc.), (2) the placement of Gen. 1:1–2:3 at the head of the structure as its programmatic introduction, (3) the use of the non-P creation account (Gen. 2:4b–25) as a reprise of the sixth day of the P creation account (Gen. 1:26–31), (4) the balancing of both P and non-P creation accounts with the non-P story of crime and punishment (Gen. 3:1–24), (5) and the placement of the Priestly covenant with Abraham (Genesis 17) parallel to the semi-Deuteronomistic covenant (Genesis 15) at the center of the Abraham story.

Rp's influence also extends to the microstructure of the ancestral sections. In the Abraham story, Rp was responsible for the broader genealogical structure, and he used the P framework to divide the Abraham material into accounts of Terah's and Abraham's lives. In the Jacob story, Rp not only combined the P and non-P accounts of Jacob's departure, but he balanced the non-P story of the Bethel promise (Gen. 28:10–22) with the P version of the Bethel epiphany (Gen. 35:9–15). Now the P version stands last and has the final word. Finally, in the Joseph story, where Rp appears to have had the least P material to work with, Rp once again appears to have used the P genealogical system to frame non-P material. Moreover, he created a combined P and non-P deathbed scene. Now the P adoption of Ephraim and Manasseh serves as a rationale for the non-P version of Jacob's promises to them, and the non-P blessings by Jacob on his twelve sons occur in the midst of the P version of Jacob's final instructions to them.

In most cases, even though the P material is allowed to sound a decisive first or final note and non-P material is often conformed to it, the non-P material adds an important dimension. For example, the P material appears to have emphasized divine sovereignty at the expense of description of human rebellion. In the process it minimized and/or eliminated accounts of human rebellion in the creation, ancestral, and even flood sections of Genesis. P reserved narratives focusing on sin for the post-Sinai period. Now, however, the new combined composition frames non-P narratives regarding human striving and/or rebellion with P narratives describing the establishment of the divine order. Now the Garden of Eden crime and punishment story occurs in the context of God's orderly creation in Gen. 1:1–2:3. Now the problem of borders raised in Gen. 6:1–4 and especially in 11:1–9 is partially resolved through the establishment of the tabernacle in the midst of the cultic community of Israel. In these and other ways, Rp allows the non-P material to depict a more chaotic narrative world than that found in P, and yet has P envelope that world in order. The result is a more multifaceted whole than that presented by either of Rp's precursors, one that better allows its audience to interpret the balance of chaos and order in their own worlds.

A Fractured Whole: Crosscurrents Introduced by the Combination of P and Non-P

At no point in the composition of Genesis were more crosscurrents introduced into its final form than in the combination of the P account with the non-P account it was designed to replace. There is not space here to explore all of the places where this combination has affected the final form of Genesis. Instead, in the following I explore just a few key examples.

Creation and Crime

The best initial example stands at the outset of the book, Genesis 1—3. Here we have a good example of account, counteraccount, and combination of accounts. We start with the non-P creation and crime story (Gen. 2:4b–3:24). Its picture of the original human crime, resulting bodily shame, and divine curse is then countered by P's picture of original goodness, creation in the bodily image of God, and blessing. Then, one of Rp's most decisive moves was his placement of this P creation account before the non-P account it was designed to replace. In some ways this works well, since the P material was almost certainly composed in relation to these non-P materials. Both feature a primary focus on humans' role vis-à-vis their context. Moreover, both move from plants, to animals, to the creation of a fully gendered humanity, and finally to a celebration of the creation by God (Gen. 1:31) or humanity (Gen. 2:23). Thus, in many ways Genesis 2 serves well as a specification of Genesis 1, particularly its sixth day. God decides to make humanity as a living statue of the divinity in Genesis 1, and then Genesis 2 uses pottery and building imagery to describe *how* God did this.

Nevertheless, already in Genesis 2 the crosscurrents begin. Whereas God was in sovereign control in Genesis 1, God seems to have lost some of that control in Genesis 2. Instead, God fumbles when creating a partner for the first human and makes animals instead. As the story continues, God seems to have second thoughts about having made humans godlike. The humans gain godlike knowledge by eating of the tree of knowledge, and God ends up expelling them lest they gain godlike immortality. Here human striving toward God does not issue in blessing but in curse. Rather than bearing in their body a stamp of their godlike authority over creation, the human body becomes in Genesis 3 an object of shame to be covered by clothing. Blessed with a call to be fruitful and multiply at the start, their multiplication keeps ending up in a violation of divine-human boundaries, whether from the divine side, as in Gen. 6:1–4, or from the human side, as in Gen 11:1–9.

The audience of Genesis 1—3 is faced with a creation that has suddenly and inexplicably gone wrong. On the one hand, there is the intensely orderly P world. This world was created as an answer to the chaos of life in exile, created out of orderly priestly categories in order to assert God's potential to order the audience's world and send them home. On the other hand, there is the much more contingent "non-P" world of Gen. 2:4bff. Here earlier (Priestly) authors appear to have attempted to explain present contingencies of human existence as God's punishment for an original human crime, the search for wisdom. Both narrative worlds are built on a presupposition that disorder and contingency are bad, but they differ profoundly on how they conceive such disorder and contingency emerging. Whereas the non-P material looks at the emergence of human rebellion in the primeval period, P is focused on God's firm and uncontested establishment of order from Creation on. Standing at the end of a long period of exile, the audience of P was already faced with a potentially chaotic social world, and the P material offered them an orderly narrative world to help them structure their experience. Now, in the present combined P/non-P text, these two narrative worlds are juxtaposed without being resolved into each other. The non-P creation crime follows quickly on the P account of God's sovereign creation of order.

Much subsequent interpretation of Genesis 1—3 has focused on developing a subtext to make the transition from one account to the other, from the more orderly narrative world of P to the more fractured world of its precursor. The text itself does not decisively guide us in constructing continuity here. As Eco, among others, has argued, this readerly process of constructing a narrative world involves a number of what he terms "inferential walks." That means that when a reader takes the text and tries to make sense out its characters and plot, she or he tests various plausible hypotheses about what is happening in the narrative and correlates them with how she or he views the world.[17] In this sense, building a narrative world out of a complex text like Genesis 1—3 and following is already a theological task.

For example, we start in Genesis 1 with a picture of God creating humanity in God's own image to rule the earth, but already by the end of the Eden story God appears to be having second thoughts, and we see similar divine

17. Eco, *The Role of the Reader*, 31–37.

reflections on the need for divine-human boundaries in the sons of God and Tower of Babel stories. It is almost as if God has set a process in motion in Genesis 1 that has gotten out of hand. Yet this development does not square with the sovereign deity of Genesis 1. Perhaps we can follow early Jewish and Christian interpreters who dealt with this narrative break by elevating the snake character to a semidivine demonic power, well capable of introducing evil into God's orderly world.[18] By doing so, they were able to enrich the text with certain dualistic categories in order to make sense of the power of evil in their world. Alternatively, we might attribute the development here to a divine mistake: God just did too good a job of making godlike humans, and they got out of hand. Or, there is always the possibility that God changes either God's attitude toward the divine-human boundary, or God's control of the situation in general.[19]

In any case, the text leaves these questions open. How coherence is established here will depend on a critical interaction between the reader's own world view and the complex data in the text. The text's fractures are an invitation to readers to interpret the fractures of their own world, challenging them to account for both the sovereign divine order of the Priestly account and the more contingent, cyclical narrative world of the non-Priestly account.

The Tension Between Genealogy and Narrative

As synchronic studies have shown, the present form of Genesis is now organized by genealogical headings starting in Gen. 2:4a and extending to Gen. 37:2. The whole begins with the programmatic creation narrative in Gen. 1:1–2:3, and then continues with carefully labeled genealogical sections culminating in the sons of Jacob, the progenitors of the people who will be featured in the Moses story. It is Rp who has so organized this material between Creation and Moses through use of the P genealogical structure.

As we look more closely at this narrative, a similar balance of order and contingency dominates the whole of the book that was found in Genesis 1—3. Robinson's observations are particularly helpful at this point and worth quoting at some length:

> For their own part, the narratives of Genesis are inherently messy, an apt counterpoise to the order of the genealogies. Before they reach a relative closure and approximate moral balance, the narratives must

---

18. This connection was already made by R. Rendtorff, "Hermeneutische Probleme der biblischen Urgeschichte" in *Festschrift für Friedrich Smend zum 70. Geburtstag* (Berlin: Merseburger (1963); 28–29; reprinted in *Gesammelte Studien zum Alten Testament* [Munich: Kaiser, 1975]), 207–8. Compare also Genesis Rabbah 21:1, 2, 4 for solutions linking God's majestic destiny for humans in Gen. 1:26–27 with the eschaton, while 3:22 is related to the human present.
19. Note the failure already in creating the animals in Gen. 2:19–20 and the more general problem with life in general, not just human life, in Gen. 6:10–13.

take account of much that is problematic and contingent, all the vagaries of actual life. If the genealogies seem almost stolidly linear and do not bend easily or broaden, the narratives are skittish and mercurial, pursuing a far less predictable course of surprises and unanticipated events. The basic orderliness of the genealogies often stands, therefore, in a profound and productive tension with the untidy economy of the narrative. Much of the density and depth of Genesis comes from this tension between what may be called at great risk, order and contingency.[20]

When Robinson is talking about the tension between genealogy and narrative, he is essentially describing Rp's mix between P's genealogical structure and non-P's narrative material. To be sure, P has narratives, and the non-P material has genealogies. Nevertheless, the "stolidly linear" genealogies that Robinson is discussing belong to the P genealogical framework, and the narratives with "surprises" and "unexpected events" are non-Priestly. Thus Robinson's resolutely synchronic study has uncovered a diachronically based tension in the text of Genesis. The tension lies between the orderly world of P's carefully structured genealogies and the often unpredictable narrative world of the non-P narratives. This combination of two narrative worlds results in a tensive whole that is far deeper and more multifaceted than either body of material alone would have been.

Robinson carefully avoids any attempt to resolve the tension between these worlds. Nevertheless, the drive of any reading toward coherent meaning could easily move one toward tilting the balance toward one side of this narrative continuum or the other. For example, Fokkelman accents the genealogies in his reading of Genesis, with the narratives sounding the discordant counterthemes to the relentless expansion of human fertility.[21] On the other hand, working out of different interpretive interests, we could also choose to read some of the non-P narratives as subversions of the order the genealogies attempt to maintain.

Either approach is possible, and there are yet other options. The point is that the tension Robinson observes here is diachronically based, and it is irresolvable on a purely textual level. The tension results from a mix of different textual voices not fully accommodated to each other. When reading the text, the reader must make certain choices about the extent to which she or he construes unity here and how such unity is achieved. A diachronic analysis merely helps us to hold on to the tensions between the P and non-P voices at this point, and to recognize the options presented to the reader here.

20. R. B. Robinson, "The Literary Function of the Genealogies of Genesis," *CBQ* 48 (1986): 598.
21. J. P. Fokkelman, "Genesis," in *The Literary Guide to the Bible* (ed. R. Alter and F. Kermode; Cambridge, Mass.: Belknap, 1987), 40–44.

Jacob's Departure

The above-discussed tension between order and contingency is present in microcosm in the account of Jacob's departure (Gen. 26:34–28:9). This text has been elegantly composed out of two elements: (1) the non-P account of Jacob's deception of Esau (Gen. 27:1–41) and (2) a P account of Esau's marriages to bad wives (Gen. 26:34–35) and Jacob's departure to marry better wives (Gen. 27:46–28:9). This latter P account appears to have been designed to absolve Jacob of any charge of wrongdoing. It explains his departure as a planned trip to marry properly, rather than a hurried departure to escape the consequences of having deceived his father and cheated his brother. Thus, P attempts to *replace* the antinomian non-P trickster story with a narrative that better fits into an orderly moral world. Moreover, to fully achieve this effect, the P account needed to stand apart from and in place of the non-P account it was designed to contradict. Now, however, the two accounts stand side by side. The non-P material is sandwiched between the P account of Esau' marriages (Gen. 26:34–35) and Jacob's reception of blessing and departure (Gen. 27:46–28:9). Now, the more ordered world of P surrounds the comparatively unruly non-P narrative world.

P surrounds non-P but does not completely subdue it. Instead, the two now form a fractured whole, and there are various ways to make sense of it. On the one hand, some synchronic readings, such as those by Sternberg and Alter, have tended to read the Jacob story from the perspective of the P material. They argue that the Jacob story slowly builds a case against Esau, up to and including his improper marriages. Read this way, Jacob's stealing the blessing is but a means to transfer the blessing to one who would marry better.[22] Notably, this reading of the Esau character is remarkably congruent with an older Jewish interpretive tradition that Esau had already given up his right to Isaac's blessing by marrying the wrong women.[23] Both older and newer synchronic readings tend to frame the story of deception within the broader context of the issue of proper marriages. On the other hand, the final form of the text does not fully cooperate with this approach. As we saw previously, the present text juxtaposes Rebekah's actual instructions to Jacob (Gen. 27:42–45) with her divergent rationale to Isaac for Jacob's trip (Gen. 27:46). Especially given Rebekah's earlier manipulation of Isaac for Jacob's sake, it appears that her expression of concern about marriage to Isaac is merely a ruse to get Isaac involved in saving Jacob from Esau. In other words, saving Jacob from the results of her plan for him is Rebekah's main concern; marriage is not. If we read the whole through Rebekah's eyes, it revolves around Jacob's deceit and flight, the themes of the non-P material.

22. Alter, *The Art of Biblical Narrative*, 42–45; Sternberg, *The Poetics of Biblical Narrative*, 494–95.
23. See, for example, *Gen. Rab.* 76:4; also 65:1–4. I owe initial recognition of this issue in Jewish interpretation to a personal communication from E. Blum.

To be sure, we need not read the narrative through Rebekah's eyes. There are others who potentially can focalize the text—Jacob, Isaac, even Esau. Nevertheless, Gen. 26:34–28:9 is itself ambiguous. On the one hand, there is enough emphasis in it on the improper character of Esau's marriages that later Jewish interpreters, many of whose communities probably struggled with intermarriage themselves, saw the issue of proper marriage as primary. Reading the story through their eyes, Jacob's deception functions only to get the blessing to the proper heir. On the other hand, the text's later portrayal of Rebekah's actions suggests the issue of proper marriage in the end is just a means to help Jacob escape the consequences of his deception of Esau. Later readers are left with different options as they mix their own interpretive interests with the interpretive potential of the mixed P and non-P text before them.

The Blessing by/of the Clans of the Earth in Gen. 12:3

Finally, at certain points, Rp's juxtaposition of P and non-P material has widened existing fractures in the interpretive potential of non-P texts. For example, the multivalent character of the blessing on the nations has already been discussed above. Proto-Genesis texts like Gen. 12:3 and 28:14 develop the idea that other "clans of the earth," having recognized the Israelites' blessing from God, will bless themselves by Abraham and his descendants. This proto-Genesis theme of blessing *by* the clans of the earth is a way of stressing the specialness of Abraham's and his descendants' blessing.

Next, the first layer of revision of this proto-Genesis story, Gen. 18:17–18, 22b-33, refers to this promise and describes a situation where the "nations" might benefit from Abraham without any action on their part. God decides to share with Abraham God's plans for Sodom and Gomorrah because "Abraham will definitely become a great and mighty nation and all nations of the world will bless themselves by him/be blessed through him" (Gen. 18:17–18). Right after this reference to the blessing by/of the nations, Abraham then manages to talk God into agreeing to spare "the city" if God can find ten righteous ones in it (Gen. 18:22b–33). Read in conjunction with the reference to Abraham's blessing, this dialogue is easily taken as an example of the blessing *of* the nations through Abraham. Indeed, Wolff, in his influential study of the theology of the Yahwist, interpreted the dialogue in exactly this way.[24] When doing so, he was exploiting the multivalence of the verb form for "bless" used in Gen. 12:3 and 18:18. We have already seen how this verb form, *nibrĕkû*, can mean either "bless oneself by" or "be blessed through" someone. What is important for our purposes is the recognition that the addition of Gen. 18:17–18 and 22b–33 added, whether intentionally or not,

24. Wolff, "Kerygma," 88–99 (*Gesammelte Studien*, 362–63; [E.T., *Int*, 147–48; *Vitality*, 55–56]).

ammunition for interpreting this verb form as passive ("be blessed through") by juxtaposing God's reference to this blessing with Abraham's pleas on Sodom's behalf.

The story does not stop here. Instead, still later revisers of the non-P material appear to have attempted to close off this interpretation of Abraham's blessing by reformulating the blessing promise with an explicitly reflexive verb, so that now the "nations" unequivocally "bless themselves" by Abraham and his heirs (Gen. 22:18; 26:4b). The nations are not blessed through them. When doing so, these revisers were introducing an antiforeign focus typical of much later Israelite literature and found in late revisions of Genesis as well.

Finally, the P authors completely revised this picture of blessing. In P the "clans" and "nations" are blessed directly by God, but Abraham and his heirs receive a special, more intensified form of the same blessing. Thus, P puts the Abrahamic blessing in the context of a preexisting blessing of the creator on the creation as a whole. In P no one is blessed through Abraham, nor do any people bless themselves by him. All are blessed by God, with Israel blessed most of all.

With the combination of P and non-P materials, all these perspectives on blessing are placed in juxtaposition with each other. As a result, we do not just have the multifaceted interpretive potential of the proto-Genesis materials and revisions of it. In addition, all the non-P materials are now placed in the context of the P creation blessing. This move does not solve the interpretive problem but, rather, heightens it.

On the one hand, we can read the Abrahamic promise in Gen. 12:3 through the lens of what precedes it. In the P material of Genesis 1—11 God has blessed humanity from the outset and then again after the Flood, even as humanity has rebelled and frustrated God's will for the world. Within this context, Gen. 12:3 is easily interpreted as God's answer to this cosmic problem. It sets up Abraham as a conduit of blessing to the "clans" of the earth surveyed in Genesis 10.

On the other hand, the problem with such a reading is that the promise is not actually fulfilled in the text following Gen. 12:3. On the contrary, if we read Gen. 12:3 in light of what follows, the blessing-as-paradigm approach becomes more plausible: Abimelek and Laban recognize Abraham's blessing; Abimelek recognizes Isaac's blessing; Laban recognizes Jacob's blessing; and Potiphar and the jailer recognize Joseph's blessing. For each of them, Abraham's descendants are paradigms of blessing. Nevertheless, this reading does not link as tightly with the primeval history as the reading of the blessing of the clans of the earth as a blessing *to* them.

Once again this element of multivalency in Genesis is diachronically based. More specifically, it results from the combination of multiple voices in the non-P material with each other *and* with the P material as well. The result is an irresolvably multivalent whole. The reader must make certain choices about how to make sense out of the final product. In this case, Jews have been more inclined than Christians to exploit the potential of the text toward an interpretation of Abraham's blessing as paradigmatic. Christians have tended more univocally to read the text as implying a blessing through Abraham to non-Israelites. The text itself offers both readings as part of its range of interpretive possibilities. It is the interpretive interests and aims of the readers that then play an important role in determining which of these interpretive possibilities is actualized.

Further Fractures and Reflections

These are but a few of the examples of fractures and crosscurrents resulting from the combination of the P account with the account it was designed to counter. Many of the other fractures have been briefly examined from another perspective in the diachronic portion of the study: the problems in the age notices for Sarah, Ishmael, and Joseph; disagreement about when Ishmael separated from Abraham and Esau from Isaac; competing versions of God's promise of a son to Abraham; parallel and yet divergent accounts of Jacob at Bethel; and so forth. Some of these fractures have had a tangible effect on the later history of interpretation, while others have not. By now, however, the pattern of argumentation is clear. The combination of P and non-P materials introduced fractures into the narrative substance of Genesis, both its whole and its parts. This then ties back to the earlier discussion of the strong move toward preservation on the part of Rp. It was not just that Rp combined the P counteraccount with the non-P account it was designed to counter. In addition, Rp thoroughly attempted to preserve the substance of both. It is this combination of factors that produced much of the remarkable depth and range of interpretive potential that characterizes the present form of Genesis.

The Sociohistorical Context of the Combination of P and Non-P

Looking back on the previous discussion, the distinctive character of Rp's work has repeatedly risen to the forefront. At the end of the section on Rp's preservation of earlier material, I already commented on the exceptional character of Rp's work: his minimal writing of his own material, his preservation of numerous doublets and chronological and geographical contradictions, and his contradiction of earlier trends in the composition of Genesis out of interest in preserving the more expansive account. This exceptional character has emerged yet more clearly in the survey of fractures in Genesis that resulted from Rp's work. More than at any other stage in Genesis, Rp juxtaposed opposing narrative worlds with each other. As a result, more fractures and crosscurrents appear to have resulted from his work than from the earlier stages combined.

Internal Judean Dynamics

So far all of my reflections have focused on the unusual internal dynamics of the combined P/non-P composition. I have not yet discussed what kind of sociohistorical context might have encouraged this unusual compositional move. After all, the subsequent history of the formation of the Torah indicates that its earliest interpreters tended to bridge the gaps between P and non-P material, not create new ones.[25] Any theory attempting a diachronic explanation of the sometimes major fractures between P and non-P material in Genesis must account for the reasons the Jewish community might have brought these often disparate blocks of material together into one document, even attempting to preserve such large portions of each.

My starting point for consideration of this question is Rp's precursors. In the previous chapters, the P composition was dated in the early postexilic period and the non-P composition shortly before that. If this is correct, then Rp must be working some time in the postexilic period.

Indeed, Rp's precursors correspond strikingly to divisions in the major leadership groups present in the postexilic period. As Albertz in particular has highlighted, leadership in Judah was basically tripartite. At the top of the political structure stood the Persian governmental apparatus, including the governor (whether Persian or Jewish), his family, retinue, and various officials. Then there were two main components of the specifically Judean political structure, the college of priests and the council of lay elders. Often we hear of these groups separately, but occasionally we see all three together, as in letter AP 30 from Elephantine:[26]

> [the Persian governor] We sent a letter to your lordship

> [the priests] and to Johanan the high priest and his colleagues the priests who are in Jerusalem,

> [the lay council of elders] and to Ostanes the brother of 'Anani, and the nobles of Judah."

We know little of the exact relations of these groups to one another, and they must have shifted over time. For example, as a lay Jewish governor of Judah, Nehemiah appears to worked intensively to influence and correct the "elders of Judah," while his relations with the priests appear to have been more distant and his clashes with them unresolved. This was probably different from the situation under Ezra, also functioning as part of the Persian governmental structure, but a priest.

---

25. Otto, "Kritik der Pentateuchkomposition," 169–70.
26. AP 30, lines 18–19, from Cowley, *Aramaic Papyri,* 112 (trans. on 114).

What is important for our purposes is the fact that the two main in-
digenous leadership groups in postexilic Judah, the councils of priests and
of elders, were the probable sponsors of the two main streams incorporated
by Rp into the present combined P/non-P work. As discussed previously,
the non-P tradition appears to have been transmitted and adapted by lay
leaders like the council of elders and Nehemiah. The college of priests is
the most likely context for the transmission and extension of the Priestly
counterrepresentation of Israel's preland history. In other words, the P
and non-P precursors to Rp's work stood as competing founding myths
that were transmitted and nurtured by the two main leadership groups in
Judah.

In summary, when Rp combined P and non-P, he was probably combining documents that were important to distinct priestly and non-priestly
leadership groups in postexilic Judah. This could explain Rp's attention to
preserving the substance of both precursors. In so far as he was successful in
maintaining what was essential to both documents, the resulting text could
be accepted by both groups.

And indeed, Genesis along with the rest of the Torah did achieve remarkably wide acceptance in postexilic Judah. Whereas the prophetic and liturgi-
cal books were not always recognized as authoritative by some Jewish groups,
the Torah appears to have been almost universally recognized from early on
in the postexilic period.[27] Even Second Temple Jews, who did work with a
Torah and Prophets canon, appear to have treated the latter collection as a
less clearly organized and less closed entity than the Torah.[28] Surveying the
data on perceptions of authority of texts in Second Temple Judaism, contrasts
outlined in Chart 12-1 emerge.

Chart 12–1: Contrasts Between Torah and Prophets

Torah	Non-Torah Authoritative Books (Prophets)
Accepted by all Jewish groups	Accepted by most Jewish groups
Clearly circumscribed and ordered	Variously defined and ordered
Translated into Greek by the second century B.C.E.	Translated into Greek at various times and contexts through the first century C.E.

27. For an excellent, brief survey of what diversity did exist in recognition of the Torah, see
O. H. Steck, "Der Kanon des hebräischen Alten Testaments: Historische Materialien für eine
ökumenische Perspektive," in *Vernunft des Glaubens: Wissenschaftliche Theologie und kirchliche
Lehre, Festschrift zum 60. Geburtstag von Wolfhart Pannenberg* (ed. J. Rohls and G. Wenz; Göttingen: Vandenhoeck & Ruprecht, 1988), 236–37.
28. T. Swanson, "The Closing of Holy Scripture: A Study in the History of the Canonization of the Old Testament," (Ph.D. diss., Vanderbilt, 1970), 198; J. Barr, *Holy Scripture: Canon,*

Part of what may have created this divergence in perception and acceptance of Torah and non-Torah books was that the Torah was the combination of foundational documents of priestly and non-priestly leadership groups in Judah, a combination that almost all were able to accept.

The Possible Role of the Persians in Supporting the Rp Synthesis

There is yet an additional factor, however, that could help explain (1) why divergent leadership groups of Judah may have been compelled to accept a hybrid document in place of their own and (2) why the result was so widely accepted: the probable support by the Persian government of the collection, "publication," and enforcement of the Torah as the local law of Judah. Ever since P. Frei's study of Persian *Reichsautorization* ("governmental authorization"), a number of scholars have more seriously considered the possibility that Persian sponsorship may have played a role in the collection of various streams of tradition into the Torah, and publication of the Torah as the standard Jewish law.[29] Overall, the Persians appear to have supported their claim to legitimacy to rule local provinces by executing the responsibility of ancient monarchs to maintain the cults of the area's local gods.[30] They appear to have played a role in rebuilding the temple of Jerusalem. Moreover, they even seem to have participated in the regulation of local cults. A letter found at Elephantine, dated to the fifth year of Darius (419/8), discusses what appears to be a ruling issued under the sponsorship of Darius to his local satrap regarding the Jewish Passover.[31] So also, a second-century Greek inscription found in Sardes contains a copy of an earlier ruling by a Persian governor regarding the erection of an image of Zeus and the staffing of the cult dedicated to the image.[32]

Most important for our purposes, however, are two extrabiblical examples of Persian involvement in the authorization of local laws:

1. Demotic papyrus 215 from the Paris National Library: This papyrus is dated by Spiegelberg to the beginning of the Ptolemaic period, and con-

---

Authority, Criticism (Philadelphia: Westminster, 1983), 54–56; J. Barton, " 'The Law and the Prophets': Who Are the Prophets?," *OTS* 23 (1984): 1–18; idem, *Oracles of God*, 35–55.

29. P. Frei, "Zentralgewalt und Lokalautonomie im Achämenidenreich," in P. Frei and K. Koch, *Reichsidee und Reichsorganisation im Perserreich* (OBO 55; Freiburg/Göttingen: Vandenhoeck & Ruprecht, 1984), 10–26; Blum, *Studien*, 345–60; Crüsemann, *Die Tora*, 387–93.

30. J. M. Miller and J. H. Hayes, *A History of Ancient Israel and Judah* (Philadelphia: Westminster, 1986), 450–56, 462–65.

31. AP 21, Cowley, *Aramaic Papyri*, 63. See Frei, "Zentral Gewalt," 15–16, and Blum, *Studien*, 349–50, for discussion of the crucial gap in this text and refutation of earlier proposals that the Persian decree and Passover ruling were separate concerns.

32. M. L. Robert, "Une nouvelle inscription grecque de Sardes: Règlement de l'autorité perse relatif à un culte de Zeus," *Comptes rendus des séances de l'année—Académie des inscriptions et belles-lettres* (Paris: Editions Klincksieck, 1976), 306–31; see also Frei, "Zentralgewalt," 21.

tains a number of different sorts of texts on its backside, including a report of how Darius commissioned the gathering and copying of Egyptian law up through the forty-fourth year of Pharaoh Amasis. This corresponds with Diodor's (I, 94–95) report that Darius was the sixth and last lawgiver of Egypt, following Amasis, the fifth lawgiver.[33]

On lines 8–12 of column C the text reports the following decree by Darius to his satraps: "let the wise [and those] among the warriors, the priests, the scribes of Egypt, who come out of it, may they write down the early law of Egypt until the year forty-four of Pharaoh Amasis for me, may the . . . law of Pharaoh, the temple and the people be brought here." Lines 12–16 describe the execution of this decree, emphasizing that the laws were written "in the manner of Egyptian law," with a copy made in the official language of the Persian empire, Aramaic. The writing concludes by emphasizing that everything was "written" and nothing left out. This is the sixth time "writing" is mentioned in this short sixteen-line text.

2. The Letoon inscription from Xanthos: This inscription is dated by its editors to 358 or 337, depending on which Artaxerses is meant in its initial dating notice. The stele contains three more or less parallel texts in Greek, Lycian, and Aramaic, and concerns the establishment of a cult for two gods. The Lycian and Greek texts are full descriptions of an initiative by the citizens of Xanthos to set up a cult for Karian gods. The Aramaic version represents the Persian satrap's publication of their stipulations as official law. Interestingly this publication is not identical with the citizens' own Greek and Lycien texts. Instead, it abbreviates and occasionally sharpens the formulations in its parallels, and, most important, stresses the Persian governor's central function to "write" and thus establish the law proposed by the citizens.[34] Just before the curses protecting the inscription itself, the Aramaic portion concludes with the assertion that "this law [*dat*], he [the Persian satrap] had written" (line 19).[35]

Both texts emphasize the Persian authority's role in authorizing local cultic regulations through publishing them, having them "written." In both cases this publication starts with a body of material originating in the local citizenry, whether the laws accumulated through Amasis in Egypt or the initiative of the citizens of Xanthos. And in both cases the process concludes with the Persian authority's publication of this local law in the imperial language,

33. W. Spiegelberg, *Die sogenannte demotische Chronik: Des Pap. 215 der Bibliothèque Nationale zu Paris nebst auf der Rückseite des Papyrus stehenden Texten* (Demotische Studien 7; Leipzig: J. C. Hinrichs'sche Buchhandlung, 1914), 30–31.
34. A. Dupont-Sommer in H. Metzger, et al., *Fouilles de Xanthos*, vol. 6, *La stäle trilingue du Létôon* (Paris: Librairie C. Klincksiek, 1979), 143, 151–53, 161–62.
35. Dupont-Sommer, *La stèle trilingue du Létôon*, 136–37. Cf. 143 for commentary on how this concept of law in the Aramaic portion differs from that found in its Lycian and Greek parallels.

Aramaic. As Frei points out, the issue of publication in writing should not be underestimated. The story of Esther features two occasions where the Persian king issues laws in writing so that they may not be changed (Esth. 1:21–22; cf. 1:19 and 8:10–14; cf. 8:8), and it ends with Queen Esther, now herself part of the Persian structure, confirming the Jewish festal regulations for Purim by having Mordecai's proposal likewise "written down" and sent throughout the Persian empire (Esth. 9:20–32). This is not an issue of the historicity of the events in the narrative world. Rather, the story of Esther suggests that its early Jewish audience would have found this picture credible, a picture where Persian decrees once written were irreversible.[36]

This is the most important data suggesting that the Persian rulers may have played a supportive role in the collection and publication of the combined P/non-P Torah composition as official, irreversible, local Persian cultic law. To be sure, all we have in the Hebrew Torah is a local law, and there is absolutely no indication that the Persians published a parallel Aramaic version that specially stressed their role in authorizing it.[37] The closest we come to documentation of direct Persian involvement in local Jewish law is the above-mentioned Elephantine letter discussing a Persian decree regarding Passover. Nevertheless, Persian sponsorship of the broader Torah process would help explain some of the internal features of the combined P/non-P composition that have been discussed previously. In particular, Persian involvement might have been some kind of external impetus for the remarkable combination and preservation of two such different narratives (P and non-P), narratives probably sponsored by very distinct groups in Judah. We see a similar sort of collection of local law and interest in the preservation of earlier traditions in the above-discussed Demotic papyrus. Furthermore, the particular priestly and cultic focus of the combined P/non-P composition would correspond with the predominantly cultic regulations with which the Persians are associated elsewhere. Finally, insofar as there was an idea in the Persian empire that official written materials were irreversible, this would help explain why the component parts of the combined P/non-P composition were so well preserved, even in the many places where both laws and narratives in them

---

36. Frei, "Zentralgewalt," 23–25; Crüsemann, *Die Tora*, 404–7.

37. H. C. Schmitt, "Die Suche nach der Identität des Jahweglaubens im nachexilischen Israel: Bemerkungen zur theologischen Intention des Pentateuch," in *Pluralismus und Identität* (ed. J. Mehlhausen; Munich: Chr. Kaiser, 1995), 264–65, emphasizes this point. He sets certain very strict criteria for what might be Persian-sponsored on the basis of a very small sample of examples of this phenomenon. His protests are a helpful reminder of the hypothetical nature of any proposal about the background of the composition of the Pentateuch. Nevertheless, they are not decisive in establishing that the Persians could not have been behind the combination of the P and non-P materials. There may have been special reasons for Israelites to avoid such an attribution, such as the antiforeign tendencies of the Deuteronomistic tradition and the tendency of Israelite tradition to attribute law exclusively to God. What is crucial here is the correspondence of internal data in the formation of the Pentateuch with external testimony to the role of Persians in the collection, publication, and enforcement of local cultic laws.

clashed with one another.[38] To be sure, in this case the crucial precursor materials to be gathered into an authoritative law, P and non-P, included an unusually large amount of narrative material. Nevertheless, given the parallels to Persian sponsorship of collection and publication of local law elsewhere, and given the highly unusual character of the final redaction of Pentateuchal books like Genesis, it is likely that some kind of Persian collection and publication practice played a role in sponsoring and/or confirming the tensive P/non-P composition that we now have before us.

It is in light of this kind of reflection that the famous Aramaic letter to Ezra in Ezra 7:12–26 should be read. This letter describes how Ezra was commissioned by Artaxerses to enforce a law that is at the same time the law of the God of heaven and of the king. Once again, this letter appears to be written out of the conception that the Persians played a role in the certification, enforcement, and publication of particular legal texts in local populations. What has made the letter particularly interesting is that it claims Persian involvement in the enforcement of an undefined "law," one that has been identified with a variety of existing and imagined legal corpora. Be that as it may, the importance of the letter should certainly not be limited to its possible use as testimony to what Artaxerses actually did. The authenticity of some parts of it are in dispute, and we can not know for sure what kind of "law" is meant, even if those sections were authentic.[39] Nevertheless, the letter is good testimony to an ancient Jewish perception of the plausibility of Persian involvement in the publication and enforcement of local Jewish law.[40] Thus, even if Ezra 7:12–26 were completely inauthentic, it would still stand as a sort of ancient Jewish "governmental authorization" hypothesis. It was not inconceivable to ancient Jews much closer to the period that Artaxerses might sponsor their local law as the law of the king. Their entertainment of that possibility stands alongside the other examples of Persian governmental authorization as additional evidence for some kind of Persian involvement in the final formation of the Torah.

Now, it would be a mistake to portray Rp's work as entirely an outgrowth of Persian *Realpolitik*.[41] We can not know exactly how or how much the Per-

---

38. Crüsemann, *Die Tora*, 405–7.
39. See the nuanced discussion by Crüsemann, *Die Tora*, 388–93.
40. Frei, "Zentralgewalt," 17.
41. Schmitt, "Die Suche nach der Identität des Jahweglaubens," 266–67. Let it be clear, however, that no one in the current discussion is advocating such an exclusive explanation of this compositional move. E. Otto (citing a comment by J. Ska in *Bib* 72 [1991]: 261) objects that the Persians would never have sponsored a legal document with military and nationalistic elements such as are found in the present Pentateuch ("Kritik der Pentateuchkomposition," *ThRu* 60 [1995]: 169). Such an argument, however, is difficult to verify. Moreover, it is difficult to find any national story in the ancient Near East that did not have nationalistic and militaristic elements. The Persians would have probably balked at supporting an openly anti-Persian document or a clear prophetic call for rebellion, but there is nothing in the Pentateuch that would necessarily have been problematic. Indeed, as Crüsemann has observed, the Pentateuch is conspicuously lacking in some of the prophetic elements that might have been most problematic (*Die Tora*, 400–3).

sians were involved, and the examples of Persian governmental authorization suggest a broad range of different relationships between local initiative and Persian sponsorship and support. Furthermore, as we have seen, Rp's own compositional contribution to the whole was not inconsiderable. Looking back on the disappointments and strife in the postexilic period, he created a document that tempered P's emphasis on the sovereign power of the creator God with the non-P emphasis on the primeval power of human rebellion. The result was not only a document that appears to have achieved political acceptance by a wide range of Second Temple Jewish groups, but also a narrative with a much deeper and broader potential to offer hope in the midst of chaos to countless later readers in other times and cultures.

If this reconstruction is correct, then we are looking not just at a step in the transmission history of Genesis. This is a step in the process leading to the recognition of Genesis as scripture within early Jewish communities. At the outset of Rp's work, we see two precursors that are regarded as somehow specially authoritative by the respective groups transmitting them. We might term these precursors "proto-scriptural." To be sure, P and non-P are not preserved in their totality, nor were they copied with the vigilance of later scriptures. Nevertheless, Rp works with P and non-P as if their substance is understood to be somehow sacrosanct. He organizes and connects where earlier authors tended to supplement and redirect. Moreover, he preserves the distinctive elements of P and non-P even to the point of creating repeated doublets and breaks—between the creation accounts, flood materials, ancestral promises, and so forth. This impetus toward preservation reflects a different view of precursor texts than was evident in earlier stages of the formation of Genesis, a new level of consideration of their content as worthy of preservation and further transmission regardless of their immediate relevance. Although it would be misleading to speak of canonization here, we can say that Rp's view of P and non-P reflects a step toward the scriptural end of the canonical continuum.[42]

Once Rp combines these proto-scriptural precursors, once his result is accepted by various Judean leadership groups, and once it is supported by the Persian government as Judean law, the combined result then assumes a yet new level of authority. This result is regarded as authoritative not only within certain subgroups of Judah but across almost the entire spectrum of Second Temple Judaism. Moreover, Rp's work of preservation of older documents and emphases suggests an important shift toward transmission of text without primary regard for its immediate relevance. Both this acceptance across groups and orientation across time are crucial steps in the creation of a scripture that can become the authorizing locus of meaning for a community, rather than itself being modified in relation to other loci of meaning within a community's leadership elites.

42. On this term, see Sanders, *Canon and Community*, 28.

Furthermore, the more widely this new combined Genesis was published and accepted, the more difficult it would have become to modify it. Indeed, Rp's own work suggests that much depended on the minimization of individual additions to the combined P/non-P product by one group or another. Rp, at least, seems to have confined his additions to a minimum. Then, insofar as Rp's work did achieve broad acceptance across various groups of Second Temple Judaism, it would have been progressively more difficult to modify the whole and still maintain the transgroup authority that made the common text worth modifying. To be sure, the textual history of Genesis indicates that one could still modify individual manuscripts of Genesis, and we do have evidence for more restricted and expansionist harmonistic texts. Nevertheless, this same history also shows that such modifications did not tend to find their way into the broader transmission of the Torah by other groups.

These reflections suggest that Rp's work stands toward the very end of the transmission history of Genesis. Not only was his work probably done under Persian sponsorship and supported by Palestine's governing authorities, but it was designed to gain for Genesis the kind of written publication, distribution, and transgroup acceptance that would preclude further major shifts in its content.[43] To be sure, many have argued that texts in the Moses story were added after Rp's work. Such arguments lie outside the scope of this study.[44] Nevertheless, at least in Genesis, there is little material clearly identifiable as postdating Rp's work. With Rp, we are truly dealing with the final redaction of Genesis, albeit a highly fractured and multifaceted final redaction.

This hardly means that communities stopped radically adapting Genesis to speak to new conditions and problems. The locus of interpretive play has merely shifted. Before interpretive communities could redirect (proto-Genesis, semi-D, and earlier levels) and/or replace (P) precursor documents. Now they had to actualize the interpretive potential of such texts in free-standing interpretations. At the same time, the nature of Rp's work may have supported this process. For in the very process of combining opposing representations of Israel's prehistory, Rp introduced a depth into the final result and a tensive multivalency that contributed to the usability of the text by a variety of later communities in a variety of times. The combined result spoke not just to the postexilic communities that originally accepted the Torah, but also to later Jews in the Diaspora and in Palestine grappling with

---

43. This preclusion of shifts excludes minor clarifying and harmonizing additions such as are found in expansionist editions of the Torah.
44. It is possible that the Moses story is an exception to the above observations. Certainly, Moses was important in the postexilic period, his importance far surpassing that of interpretive focal points of Genesis such as the primeval history or Abraham. Moreover, there was an apparent tendency of postexilic groups to add legislation to the Moses story that anticipated present structures and/or envisioned improvements to them. Nevertheless, any such theory must then state whether such changes were made to a common Torah, and if so, how the changes were then held in common.

the destruction of the Second Temple; Jews in the ghetto looking toward the promise of nationhood, blessing, and land; Gentiles through the ages rereading the primeval history and promise in relation to themselves; and now contemporary interpreters exploring the interpretive potential of Genesis outside a specific confessional framework.

Insofar as this is true, the canonical and/or classical status of Genesis lies in its fractures as well as its shape. Modern defenders of the Bible, Genesis in particular, have often stressed its unitary character. Indeed, this kind of emphasis on unity has even found its way into some—though not all!—modern canonical interpretations of biblical texts. Yet, as we have seen, the complexity of the textual data resists this struggle toward coherence. Indeed, there are simpler texts than the Torah. Eco terms them "closed" texts and describes how they lead the reader down a predetermined path by repeating certain patterns and playing on the reader's ideology. The Torah on the other hand more closely resembles what Eco terms an "open" text. Such a text challenges the reader to construct the textual world for themselves.[45] Yet in contrast to Eco's examples of open texts, the openness of the Torah is not the product of a single author's conscious attempt to build a multivalent text that the readers must then construct for themselves. Instead, the openness of the Torah is more the product of its inclusion of multiple perspectives on life, perspectives that now capture contrasting aspects of reality without being conclusively resolved into each other.

In summary, the interpretive potential of Genesis, and indeed part of the draw it exerts on later interpreters, is to be found not just in an overarching shape of the final form, but also in the diachronically based fractures that make it difficult to find any such comprehensive overarching shape. Such fractures are part of what make Genesis and other biblical books so remarkably open for interpretation, and diachronic analysis can be one way of sharpening our focus on the magnificent openness of biblical texts to ever new readings.

Concluding Reflections

More could be done, but by now the above examples should indicate ways a diachronic approach might sharpen attention to the fractures of a text like Genesis. Genesis bears in itself fractures and crosscurrents left from a complex transmission history. Some of these fractures and crosscurrents have even been reflected in divergences in the river of interpretation history. Others still lie submerged, waiting for interpreters with the right constellation of interpretive interests to exploit the text's potential to be read in a new way.

Reading for such fractures, whether using a diachronic or other method, holds the text open for such new readings. Such an approach loosens the interpreter's hold on the text. Many of the more unity-focused synchronic

---

45. Eco, *The Role of the Reader,* passim, especially 7–10, 33–34, 47–66.

approaches tend to try to gather all parts of the text into themselves. They attempt to translate fully the unruly discourse of the text into a new form of discourse more understandable and/or meaningful to its audience. There is nothing inherently wrong with this. A diachronic approach, however, can help put any such effort into perspective. Not only can a study of a book's formation call attention to specific crosscurrents and fractures in the book, but it can also highlight ways the text as a whole can never be fully tamed by a given synchronic reading. Done in the context of such a diachronic approach, a unity-focused synchronic approach appears more clearly as a specific attempt to produce meaning out of interaction with a complex text. This attempt is governed by specific rules and resonates with the problems and interests of specific interpretive contexts. Even when we do not know for sure just when or where a given verse was composed, an overall consciousness of a text's fractured quality helps highlight the particularity of any synchronic approach: the tentative quality of such an approach vis-à-vis the reality of a text, and the linkage of any such approach to specific interpretive rules and interests.

To be sure, there are synchronic ways to focus on textual fractures. Barthes, Miscall, Fewell, and Gunn are among the scholars who have read for the fractures in Genesis without relating these to possible diachronic crosscurrents in the text.[46] Such synchronic reading for gaps and crosscurrents also makes sense. There are many fractures in Genesis that are not diachronically based, just as in any text that tries to bridge the fractures of a world with narrative.

The virtue of a diachronic approach is that the picture it produces of the text's fractured quality is potentially rooted not only in a specific interpreter's sense of the text's gaps and crosscurrents, but also in a historical analysis of how certain fractures might be more likely in a text like Genesis than others. For example, I have followed others in identifying a certain set of texts in Genesis, the P texts, as a strong counterreading of non-P texts. This counterreading bears the marks of having been executed in the specific institutional locus of the Israelite priesthood, a locus to whose worldview and norms we have indirect access through other sources. So also, I have shown how an otherwise attested shift in non-priestly, exilic Israel toward Deuteronomistic norms is reflected in the retouching of Genesis from the perspective of some of these norms. There are other fractures in Genesis. Nevertheless, we have particular access to diachronically based fractures such as these by way of correlation of them with (1) historical data on the institutions and history of Israel and (2) our knowledge of how texts like Genesis sometimes developed over time.

The more a diachronic or other approach highlights the way any synchronic reading is a choice, the more clearly the limited character of biblical

46. Barthes, "La lutte," 27–39; (E.T., 125–41); Miscall, *The Workings of Old Testament Narrative;* idem, "Garden of Eden," 1–9; Fewell and Gunn, *Gender, Power and Promise,* 22–91; cf. also Pardes, *Countertraditions.*

scholarship comes into focus. As is becoming more and more clear, biblical scholarship, whether diachronic or synchronic, is ill equipped to decisively narrow the reading of a given biblical text, let alone to determine any single normative meaning. Studies can offer new options for making meaning out of a text like Genesis through attention to the language and historical context in which it was written. They can sharpen our sense of the competing voices in a text and thus highlight the choice and responsibility involved in any attempt to produce meaning out of it. In the end, however, offering a "reading" of a text is an ideological/theological task. Such a reading must not only interact with crucial aspects of the text, but it must also answer to the other norms of critical reflection. For example, it must be self-consciously contextual and ideologically self-critical, among other things. No such reading is a simple extension of the Bible's conceptuality, final form, or transmission-historical process. It stands or falls on more general theological criteria. In this case, my hope is that my pre-"reading" of the fractures of Genesis may contribute to leveling the interpretive playing field, highlighting the extent to which no method can claim to offer a final account of Genesis, and the extent to which any reading of the book is a specific resolution of the irresolvably divergent voices embedded in it.

Abbreviations

AnBib	Analecta biblica
AOAT	Alter Orient und Altes Testament
AP	Aramaic Papyri
ASTI	*Annual of the Swedish Theological Institute*
ATANT	Abhandlungen zur Theologie des Alten und Neuen Testaments
ATDSup	Das Alte Testament Deutsch, Supplements
BA	*Biblical Archaeologist*
BBB	Bonner biblische Beiträge
b.Ber.	*Tractate Berakot of the Babylonian Talmud*
b.B.Meṣ.	*Tractate Baba Meṣia of the Babylonian Talmud*
b.B.Qam.	*Tractate Baba Qamma of the Babylonian Talmud*
BETL	Bibliotheca ephemeridum theologicarum Lovaniensium
Bib	*Biblica*
BKAT	Biblischer Kommentar: Altes Testament
b.Mak.	*Tractate Makkot of the Babylonia Talmud*
BN	*Biblische Notizen*
b.Sanh.	*Tractate Sanhedrin of the Babylonian Talmud*
b.Sota.	*Tractate Soṭa of the Babylonian Talmud*
BThSt	Biblical and Theological Studies
BWANT	Beiträge zur Wissenschaft vom Alten und Neuen Testament
BZ	*Biblische Zeitschrift*
BZAW	Beihefte zur Zeitschrift für die alttestamentliche Wissenschaft
CARB	Cahiers de la Revue biblique
CBOTS	Coniectanea biblica, Old Testament
CBQ	*Catholic Biblical Quarterly*
CBQMS	Catholic Biblical Quarterly Monograph Series
CTM	*Concordia Theological Monthly*
DBAT	*Dielheimer Blätter zur Alten Testament*
D-stem	piel stem
EB	Echter Bibel
EstBib	*Estudios biblicos*
EvT	*Evangelische Theologie*

FAT	Forschungen zum Alten Testament
FOTL	The Forms of the Old Testament Literature
FRLANT	Forschungen zur Religion und Literatur des Alten und Neuen Testaments
Gen.Rab.	*Genesis Rabbah*
G-stem	paal stem
HSM	Harvard Semitic Monographs
H-stem	hiphil stem
Htd-stem	hithpael stem
HUCA	*Hebrew Union College Annual*
IBS	*Irish Biblical Studies*
ICC	International Critical Commentary
Int	*Interpretation*
JAAR	*Journal of the American Academy of Religion*
JBL	*Journal of Biblical Literature*
JDT	*Jahrbücher für deutsche Theologie*
JETS	*Journal of the Evangelical Theological Society*
JJS	*Journal of Jewish Studies*
JRelS	*Journal of Religious Studies*
JSOT	*Journal for the Study of the Old Testament*
JSOTSup	Journal for the Study of the Old Testament Supplement Series
JTS	*Journal of Theological Studies*
KB	L. Koehler and W. Baumgartner, *Lexicon in Veteris Testamenti libros*
KEHAT	Kurzgefasstes exegetisches Handbuch zum Alten Testament
KHC	Kurzer Hand-Commentar zum Alten Testament
McCQ	*McCormick Quarterly*
NRT	*La nouvelle revue theologique*
N-stem	niphal stem
Num.Rab.	*Numbers Rabbah*
OBO	Orbis biblicus et orientalis
Or	*Orientalia*
OTL	Old Testament Library
OTS	*Oudtestamentische studien*
RB	*Revue biblique*
SBB	Stuttgarter biblische Beiträge
SBLDS	SBL Dissertation Series
SBLMS	SBL Monograph Series
SBLSCS	SBL Septuagint and Cognate Studies
SBS	Stuttgarter Bibelstudien
SSN	Studia semitica Neerlandica
TB	Theologische Bücherei
TQ	*Theologische Quartalschrift*

TynBul	*Tyndale Bulletin*
TZ	*Theologische Zeitschrift*
USQR	*Union Seminary Quarterly Review*
VT	*Vetus Testamentum*
VTSup	Vetus Testamentum, Supplements
WBC	Word Biblical Commentary
WMANT	Wissenschaftliche Monographien zum Alten und Neuen Testament
ZAW	*Zeitschrift für die alttestamentliche Wissenschaft*
ZAWSup	*Zeitschrift für die alttestamentliche Wissenschaft Supplement*
ZBK	Zürcher Bibelkommentar
Zion	*Zion*
ZThK	*Zeitschrift für Theologie und Kirche*

Appendix:
A Model of Transmission History

The following is a summary of the previously argued reconstruction of the transmission history of Genesis. The chart on this page depicts Genesis 1:1–25:18; the chart on p. 340 shows Genesis 25:19–35:20. Grades of relative probability are not noted here.

Primeval History	Proto-Genesis	Revisions of Non-P	Toledot Book (in P)	P Source	Rp and Later
2:4b–4:26a	4:26b			1:1–2:3	2:4a
					2:19*, 20*
5:28*–29			5:1a, 3–28*	5:1–28*, 30–32	
6:1–7aα			5:30–2		
6:7b–8					6:7aβ
7:1–2				6:9–22	
7:3b–5,					7:3a
7:7				7:6	7:8–9
7:10, 12,				7:11, 13–	
7:[16b]–17				16a, 18–21,	
7:22–23aαb*				23aβ, 24	7:23aα*
8:2b–3a				8:1–2a,	
8:6–12, 13b				8:3b–5	8:13
8:20–22				8:14–19	
				9:1–17	
9:18a, 19		9:18b			
9:20–27*		9:22a*, 25–27*			10:1a, 2–7
10:1b, 8–15					10:20
10:18b–19		10:16–18a			10:22–23
10:21					10:31–32
10:24–30					
11:1–9					
	11:28–30*			11:10–27	
				11:31–32	
	12:1–4a			12:4b–5	
	12:6–13:18*			13:6	
				13:11b–12abα	
				19:29bβγ	
				[19:29abα]	
	16:1–2, 4–14	14:1–15:21		16:3	
				16:15–16	
				17:1–24	
	18:1–19:28*	18:17–18,			
		22b–33			
	19:30–22:14	18:19		21:3–5 +	
	22:19–24	22:15–18			23:1–20
	24:1–67a				24:67b
	25:1–6			25:7–17	25:18
				[21:21]	

339

Jacob Story*	Northern Jacob-Joseph Story	Judean Jacob-Joseph Story	Proto-Genesis	Revisions of Non-P	P Source	Late P, Rp, and Later
25:21-34			26:1-3bα 26:6-33	26:3bβ-5	25:19-20 26:34-35	
27:1-45			28:13-15aα		27:46-28:9	
28:10-12, 13-22*			28:16aβγb	28:15*? 28:21b		
29:1-30:20		30:21				
30:22-43						
31:1-2, 4-16			31:3			
31:19-54					31:17-18	
32:1-9, 13-33				32:10-13		
33:1-20*						33:18aβ
35:1-8		34:1-31				35:9*
35:16-20		35:21-22a		35:2*, 4*??	35:9-15 35:22b-29 36:1-43*	
Joseph Story*						37:2*
37:3-35		37:14*? 37:36-38:30			37:2	
39:1, 4, 6aβ-20			39:2-3, 5-6aα 39:21-23			
40:1-41:38						
41:41-45, 47-49	41:50-52		41:39-40		41:46	46:8-27
41:53-57		46:1?	46:2-4			
42:1-45:28					45:19-21	
47:1-4, 6b					46:5-7*	
47:12-27a					47:5-6a	
47:29-31	48:1-2				47:7-11	
	48:8-14		48:15-16		47:27b-28	
	48:17-20		48:21-22		48:3-6	48:7
		49:1b-28			49:1a, 29-33	
50:1-11					50:12-13	
50:14-21					50:22-23	
				50:24-25	50:26a	50:26b

Texts isolated as specific to the Jacob story compositional layer include: 28:20-22 (incorporating the Bethel tradition of 28:10-12, 17-19 into the Jacob story); 29:31-30:24 (excepting 30:21); 31:4-16, 24-25a, 29b, 41-42, and the Jacob story material following 31:54. Texts isolated as specific to the Joseph story compositional layer are 37:3-35 and the Joseph story material following 42:1.

Bibliography

Ackerman, J. "Joseph, Judah, and Jacob." In *Literary Interpretations of Biblical Narratives*. Vol. 2. Ed. K. R. R. Gros Louis with James S. Ackerman, 85–113. Nashville: Abingdon, 1982.

Albertz, R. "Die Kulturarbeit im Atramḫasī Epos im Vergleich zur biblischen Urgeschichte." In *Werden und Wirkung des Alten Testaments: Festschrift für C. Westermann*. Eds. R. Albertz, et al., 38–57. Göttingen: Vandenhoeck & Ruprecht and Neukirchen-Vluyn: Neukirchener-Verlag, 1980.

———. *Persönliche Frömmigkeit und offizielle Religion. Religionsinterner Pluralismus in Israel und Babylon*. CTM A9. Stuttgart: Calwer Verlag, 1978.

———. *Religionsgeschichte Israels*. Vol. 1. *Von den Anfängen bis zum Ende der Königszeit*. ATDSup 8/1. Göttingen: Vandenhoeck & Ruprecht, 1992. (E.T., *A History of Israelite Religion in the Old Testament Period*. Vol. 1. *From the Beginnings to the End of the Monarchy*. OTL. Louisville, Ky.: Westminster John Knox Press, 1994.)

———. *Religionsgeschichte Israels in alttestamentlicher Zeit*. Vol. 2. *Vom Exil bis zu den Makkabäern*. ATDSup, 8/2. Göttingen: Vandenhoeck & Ruprecht, 1992. (E.T., *A History of Israelite Religion in the Old Testament Period*. Vol. 2. *From the Exile to the Maccabees*. Trans. J. Bowden. OTL. London: SCM, 1994.)

Alter, R. *The Art of Biblical Narrative*. New York: Basic Books, 1981.

———. "Sodom as Nexus: The Web of Design in Biblical Narrative." In *The Book and the Text: The Bible and Literary Theory*. Ed. R. M. Schwartz, 146–60. Oxford: Basil Blackwell, 1990.

———. *The World of Biblical Literature*. New York: Basic Books, 1992.

Anbar, M. "Genesis 15: A Conflation of Two Deuteronomic Narratives." *JBL* 101 (1982): 39–55.

———. "La 'reprise.' " *VT* 38 (1988): 385–98.

Astour, M. C. "Political and cosmic symbolism in Genesis 14 and in its Babylonian sources." In *Biblical Motifs: Origins and Transformations*. Ed. A. Altmann, 65–112. Cambridge, Mass.: Harvard University Press, 1966.

Astruc, J. J. *Conjectures sur les mémoires originaux dont il paroît que Moyse s'est servi pour composer le livre de la Genèse*. Paris: Chez Fricx, 1753.

Auerbach, E. "Die babylonische Datierung im Pentateuch." *VT* 2 (1952): 334–41.

Bakhtin, M. M., and P. N. Medvedev, *The Formal Method in Literary Scholarship: A Critical Introduction to Sociological Poetics*. Trans. A. J. Wehrle. Baltimore/London: Johns Hopkins University Press, 1978.

Bal, M. *Lethal Love: Feminist Literary Readings of Biblical Love Stories*. Bloomington, Ind.: Indiana University Press, 1987.

Baltzer, K. *Die Biographie der Propheten*. Neukirchen-Vluyn: Neukirchener Verlag, 1975.

Barr, J. *Holy Scripture: Canon, Authority, Criticism*. Philadelphia: Westminster Press, 1983.

Barthélemy, D. et al. *The Story of David and Goliath. Textual and Literary Criticism. Papers of a Joint Research Venture*. OBO 73. Fribourg: Editions Universitaires, 1986.

———. *Preliminary and Interim Report on the Hebrew Old Testament Text Project*. Vol. 1. *Pentateuch/Pentateuque*. Stuttgart: United Bible Society, 1976.

Barthes, R. "La lutte avec l'ange: analyse textuelle de Genèse 32.23–33." In *Analyse structurale et Exégèse Biblique; Essais d'interprétation*, 27–39. Bibliothèqe théologique. Neuchâtel: Delachaux et Niestlé, 1971. (E.T., "The Struggle with the Angel." In *Image, Music, Text*. Trans. Stephen Heath, 125–41. London: Fontana Collins, 1977.)

Barton, J. " 'The Law and the Prophets': Who Are the Prophets?" *OTS* 23 (1984): 1–18.

———. *Oracles of God: Perceptions of Ancient Prophecy in Israel After the Exile*. London: Darton, Longman and Todd, 1986.

———. *Reading the Old Testament: Method in Biblical Study*. London: Darton, Longman & Todd, 1984.

Batto, B. F. "Creation Theology in Genesis." In *Creation in Biblical Traditions*. Eds. R. J. Clifford and J. J. Collins, 16–38. CBQMS 24. Washington, D.C.: Catholic Biblical Association of America, 1992.

———. *Slaying the Dragon: Mythmaking in the Biblical Tradition*. Louisville, Ky.: Westminster John Knox Press, 1992.

———. "The Sleeping God: An Ancient Near Eastern Motif of Divine Sovereignty." *Bib* 68 (1987): 153–76.

Beal, T. "Glossary." In *Reading Between Texts: Intertextuality and the Hebrew Bible*. Ed. D. Nolan Fewell, 21–24. Louisville, Ky.: Westminster John Knox Press, 1992.

Becking, B. " 'They hated him even more': Literary Technique in Genesis 37.1–11." *BN* 60 (1991): 40–47.

Begrich, J. "Die priesterliche Torah." *Werden und Wesen des Alten Testaments*. Eds. P. Volz, F. Stummer, and J. Hempel, 63–88. BZAW 66. Berlin: W. de Gruyter, 1936.

Bendavid, A. *Parallels in the Bible*. Jerusalem: Carta, 1972.

Bentzen, A. *Introduction to the Old Testament*. 4th ed. Copenhagen: Gad, 1958.

Berge, K. *Die Zeit des Jahwisten. Ein Beitrag zur Datierung jahwistischer Vätertexte*. BZAW 186. Berlin/New York: W. de Gruyter, 1990.

Bleek, F. *Insunt de libri Geneseos origine atque indole historica observationes quaedam contra Bohlenium*. Bonn: Typis Caroli Georgii, 1836.

Blenkinsopp, J. *The Pentateuch: An Introduction to the First Five Books of the Bible*. AB Reference Library. New York: Doubleday, 1992.

———. "The Structure of P." *CBQ* 38 (1976): 275–92.

Bloom, H. *The Anxiety of Influence*. New York: Oxford University Press, 1973.

———. *A Map of Misreading*. New York: Oxford University Press, 1975.

Blum, E. "Gibt es die Endgestalt des Pentateuch?" In *The Congress Volume Leuven, 1989*. Ed. J. Emerton, 46–57. VTSup 43. Leiden: Brill, 1991.

————. *Die Komposition der Vätergeschichte.* WMANT 57. Neukirchen-Vluyn: Neukirchener Verlag, 1984.

————. *Studien zur Komposition des Pentateuch.* BZAW 189. Berlin: W. de Gruyter, 1990.

Boecker, H.-J. *1 Moses 25.19–37.1.* ZBK 1,3. Zurich: Theologischer Verlag, 1992.

————. "Überlegungen zur Josephsgeschichte." In *Alttestamentlicher Glaube und Biblische Theologie: Festschrift für Horst Dietrich Preuß.* Eds. J. Hausmann and H.-J. Zobel, 35–45. Stuttgart/Berlin/Cologne: W. Kohlhammer, 1992.

Boorer, S. "The Importance of a Diachronic Approach: The Case of Genesis-Kings." *CBQ* 51 (1989): 195–208.

————. *The Promise of the Land as Oath: A Key to the Formation of the Pentateuch.* BZAW 205. Berlin/New York: W. de Gruyter, 1992.

Brett, M. *Biblical Criticism in Crisis?: The Impact of the Canonical Approach on Old Testament Studies.* Cambridge: Cambridge University Press, 1991.

Breukelman, F. "Das Buch Genesis als das Buch der תולדות Adams, des Menschen— eine Analyse der Komposition des Buches." In *Störenfriedels Zeddelkasten: Geschenkpapiere zum 60. Geburtstag von Friedrich-Wilhelm Marquardt.* Eds. Ute Gniewoss, et al., 72–97. Berlin: Alektor, 1991.

Brisman, L. *The Voice of Jacob: On the Composition of Genesis.* Indiana Studies in Biblical Literature. Bloomington/Indianapolis, Ind.: Indiana University Press, 1990.

Buber, M. "Der Mensch von heute und die jüdische Bibel." In *Die Schrift und ihre Verdeutschung.* Eds. M. Buber and F. Rosenzweig, 13–45. Berlin: Schocken, 1936.

Budde, K. *Die biblische Urgeschichte (Gen 1–12,5).* Giessen: J. Ricker, 1883.

Calvin, J. *Commentaries on the First Book of Moses Called Genesis.* Trans. J. King. Vol. 2. Grand Rapids: Eerdmans, 1948.

Campbell, A. F. "The Priestly Text: Redaction or Source?" In *Biblische Theologie und gesellschaftlicher Wandel: Für Norbert Lohfink SJ.* Eds. G. Braulik, W. Gross, S. McEvenue, 32–47. Freiburg/Basel/Vienna: Herder, 1993.

Campbell, A. F., and O'Brien, M. A. *Sources of the Pentateuch: Texts, Introductions, Annotations.* Minneapolis: Fortress Press, 1993.

Cancik, H. *Mythische und historische Wahrheit.* SBS 48. Stuttgart: Verlag Katholisches Bibelwerk, 1970.

Caquot, A. "L'alliance avec Abraham (Genèse 15)." *Semitica* 12 (1962): 51–66.

Carpenter, J. E. *The Composition of the Hexateuch.* London/New York/Bombay: Longmans, Green & Co., 1902.

Carr, D. M. *From D to Q: A Study of Early Jewish Interpretations of Solomon's Dream at Gibeon.* SBLMS 44. Atlanta: Scholars Press, 1991.

————. "The Politics of Textual Subversion: A Diachronic Perspective on the Garden of Eden Story." *JBL* 112 (1993): 577–95.

Cassuto, U. *A Commentary on the Book of Genesis.* Vol. 2. *From Noah to Abraham. Genesis VI 9–XI 32 with an Appendix: A Fragment of Part III.* Trans. I. Abrahams. Jerusalem: Magnes, 1964.

————. *La questione della Genesi.* Firenze: Le Monnier, 1934.

Childs, B. *Biblical Theology of the Old and New Testaments: Theological Reflection on the Christian Bible.* London: SCM, 1992.

————. *Exodus.* OTL. London: SCM, 1974.

————. *Introduction to the Old Testament as Scripture.* Philadelphia: Fortress, 1979.

Clark, W. M. "The Flood and the Structure of the Pre-patriarchal History." *ZAW* 83 (1971): 184–211.

Clements, R. E. *Abraham and David.* SBT 2/5. London: SCM, 1967.

Clines, D. J. A. *The Theme of the Pentateuch.* JSOTSup 10. Sheffield: JSOT Press, 1982.

———. *What Does Eve Do to Help?* JSOTSup 94. Sheffield: JSOT Press, 1990.

Coats, G. W. *From Canaan to Egypt: Structural and Theological Context for the Joseph Story.* CBQMS 4. Washington, D. C.: Catholic Biblical Association, 1976.

———. *Genesis with an Introduction to Narrative Literature.* FOTL 1. Grand Rapids: Eerdmans, 1983.

———. "Redactional Unity in Genesis 37—50." *JBL* 93 (1974): 15–21.

Cohn, R. L. "Narrative Structure and Canonical Perspective in Genesis." *JSOT* 25 (1983): 3–16.

Colenso, J. W. *Critical Analysis of the Pentateuch and the Book of Joshua.* Part V. *Critical Analysis of Genesis.* London: Longmans, Green & Co., 1865.

Coote, R. B., and D. R. Ord. *The Bible's First History.* Philadelphia: Fortress Press, 1989.

Cowley, A. *Aramaic Papyri of the Fifth Century B.C.* Oxford: Clarendon, 1923.

Cross, F. M. *Canaanite Myth and Hebrew Epic.* Cambridge: Harvard University Press, 1973.

Crüsemann, F. "Die Eigenständigkeit der Urgeschichte: Ein Beitrag zur Diskussion um den 'Jahwisten.'" In *Die Botschaft und die Boten: Festschrift für H. W. Wolff.* Eds. J. Jeremias and L. Perlitt, 9–29. Neukirchen-Vluyn: Neukirchener Verlag, 1981.

———. "Israel in der Perserzeit: Eine Skizze in Auseinandersetzung mit Max Weber." In W. Schluchter, ed. *Max Webers Sicht des antiken Christentums: Interpretation und Kritik,* 205–32. Frankfurt am Main: Suhrkamp, 1985.

———. *Die Tora. Theologie und Sozialgeschichte des alttestamentlichen Gesetzes.* Munich: Kaiser, 1992.

———. *Der Widerstand gegen das Königtum: Die antiköniglichen Texte des Alten Testaments und der Kampf um den frühen israelitischen Staat.* WMANT 49. Neukirchen-Vluyn: Neukirchener Verlag, 1978.

Culley, R. C. *Studies in the Structure of Hebrew Narrative.* Philadelphia: Fortress Press; Missoula, Mont.: Scholars Press, 1976.

Dahlberg, B. "The Unity of Genesis." In *Literary Interpretations of Biblical Narratives.* Vol. 2. Ed. K. R. R. Gros Louis with James S. Ackerman, 126–34. Nashville: Abingdon, 1982.

Damrosch, D. *The Narrative Covenant.* San Francisco: Harper & Row, 1987.

Daniels, D. *Hosea and Salvation History: The Early Traditions of Israel in the Prophecy of Hosea.* BZAW 191. Berlin/New York: W. de Gruyter, 1990.

Davies, P. *In Search of 'Ancient Israel.'* JSOTSup 148. Sheffield: JSOT Press, 1992.

———. "Sons of Cain." In *A Word in Season: Essays in Honour of William McKane,* 35–56. JSOTSup 42. Sheffield: JSOT Press, 1986.

Diebner, B. "'Isaak' und 'Abraham' in der alttestamentlichen Literatur außerhalb Gen 12—50. Eine Sammlung literaturgeschichtlicher Beobachtungen nebst einigen überlieferungsgeschichtlichen Spekulationen." *DBAT* 7 (1974): 38–50.

Dietrich, W. *Die Josephserzählung als Novelle und Geschichtsschreibung. Zugleich ein*

Beitrag zur Pentateuchfrage. BThSt, 14. Neukirchen-Vluyn: Neukirchener Verlag, 1989.

Dillmann, A. *Die Genesis.* 3d ed. KEHAT 11. Leipzig: S. Hirzel, 1886. (E.T., *Genesis Critically and Exegetically Expounded.* Trans. W. B. Stevenson. Edinburgh: T. & T. Clark, 1897.)

————. *Die Bücher Numeri, Deuteronomium und Josua.* 2d ed. Leipzig: S. Hirzel, 1886.

Doane, A. N. "Oral Texts, Intertexts, and Intratexts: Editing Old English." In *Influence and Intertextuality in Literary History.* Eds. J. Clayton and E. Rothstein, 75–113. Madison, Wis.: University of Wisconsin Press, 1991.

Dohmen, C. *Schöpfung und Tod: Die Entfaltung theologischer und anthropologischer Konzeptionen in Gen 2/3.* SBS 17. Stuttgart: Verlag Katholisches Bibelwerk, 1988.

Donner, H. *Die literarische Gestalt der alttestamentlichen Josephsgeschichte.* Heidelberg: Carl Winter Universitätsverlag, 1976.

————. "Der Redaktor: Überlegungen zum vorkritischen Umgang mit der Heiligen Schrift." *Henoch* 2 (1980): 1–30.

Doukhan, J. B. *The Genesis Creation Story: Its Literary Structure.* Berrien Springs, Mich.: Andrews Univ. Press, 1982.

Eco, U. *The Role of the Reader: Explorations in the Semiotics of Texts.* Bloomington, Ind.: Indiana University Press, 1979.

Edgerton, W. D. *The Passion of Interpretation.* Literary Currents in Biblical Interpretation. Louisville, Ky.: Westminster John Knox, 1992.

Eerdmans, B. D. *Alttestamentliche Studien.* Vol. 1. *Die Komposition der Genesis.* Giessen: Töpelmann, 1908.

Eichhorn, J. E. *Einleitung ins Alte Testament.* Vol. 2. Leipzig: Ben Weidmanns, Erben & Reich, 1781.

Eichrodt, W. *Die Quellen der Genesis von neuem untersucht.* BZAW 31. Giessen: Töpelmann, 1916.

Eising, H. *Formgeschichtliche Untersuchung zur Jakobserzählung der Genesis.* Emsdetten, 1940.

Eissfeldt, O. "Biblos Geneseōs." In *Kleine Schriften.* Vol. 3. Eds. R. Sellheim and F. Maass, 458–70. Tübingen: J. C. B. Mohr, 1966.

————. *Einleitung in das Alte Testament.* 3d ed. Tübingen: J. C. B. Mohr, 1964. (E.T., *The Old Testament: An Introduction.* Trans. P. Ackroyd. New York/London: Harper and Row, 1965.)

————. *Die Genesis der Genesis: Vom Werdegang des ersten Buches der Bibel.* 2d ed. Tübingen: J. C. B. Mohr, 1981.

————. *Hexateuch-Synopse.* Darmstadt: Wissenschaftliche Buchgesellschaft, 1962.

Eitz, A. "Studien zum Verhältnis von Priesterschrift und Deuterojesaja." Ph.D. diss., Heidelberg, 1970.

Elliger, K. "Sinn und Ursprung der priesterlichen Geschichtserzählung." *ZThK* 49 (1952): 121–43.

Ellis, P. *The Yahwist: The Bible's First Theologian.* London/Dublin/Melbourne: G. Chapman, 1969.

Emerton, J. A. "An Examination of Some Attempts to Defend the Unity of the Flood Narrative in Genesis: Part One." *VT* 37 (1987): 401–20.

————. "An Examination of Some Attempts to Defend the Unity of the Flood Narrative in Genesis: Part Two." *VT* 38 (1988): 1–21.

————. "The Origin of the Promises to the Patriarchs in the Older Sources of the Book of Genesis." *VT* 32 (1982): 14–32.

————. "The Priestly Writer in Genesis." *JTS* 39 (1988): 381–400.

————. "The Riddle of Genesis XIV." *VT* 21 (1971): 403–39.

————. "Some False Clues in the Study of Genesis XIV." *VT* 21 (1971): 24–47.

————. "Some problems in Genesis xiv." In *Studies in the Pentateuch.* VTSup 41. Ed. J. A. Emerton, 73–102. Leiden/New York: Brill, 1990.

————. "The Source Analysis of Genesis XI 27–32." *VT* 42 (1992): 37–46.

Ewald, H. G. A. "(Review of J. J. Stähelin, *Kritische Untersuchungen über die Genesis*)." *Theologische Studien und Kritiken* 4 (1831): 595–606.

Farmer, W. R. "Basic Affirmation with Some Demurrals: A Response to Roland Mushat Frye." In *The Relationships Among the Gospels: An Interdisciplinary Dialogue.* Ed. W. O. Walker, 303–22. San Antonio, Tex: Trinity University Press, 1978.

Felder, C. H. *Troubling Biblical Waters: Race, Class and Family.* Studies in North American Black Religion, 3. Maryknoll, N.Y.: Orbis, 1989.

Fewell, D. Nolan and Gunn, D. M. *Gender, Power and Promise: The Subject of the Bible's First Story.* Nashville: Abingdon Press, 1993.

Fish, S. *Is There a Text in This Class?: The Authority of Interpretive Communities.* Cambridge, Mass./London: Harvard University Press, 1980.

Fishbane, M. *Biblical Interpretation in Ancient Israel.* Oxford: Clarendon Press, 1985.

————. "Composition and Structure in the Jacob Cycles (Gen. 25:19–35:22)." *JJS* 26 (1975): 15–38.

————. *Text and Texture: Close Readings of Selected Biblical Texts.* New York: Schocken Books, 1979.

Flanagan, J. W. *David's Social Drama: A Hologram of Israel's Early Iron Age.* The Social World of Biblical Antiquity Series 7. Sheffield: Almond, 1988.

Fleischer, G. "Jakob träumt. Eine Auseinandersetzung mit Erhard Blums methodischem Ansatz am Beispiel von Gen 28,10–22." *BN* 76 (1995): 82–102.

Fohrer, G. *Einleitung in das Alte Testament.* 10th ed. Heidelberg: Quelle & Meyer, 1965. (E.T., *Introduction to the Old Testament.* Trans. D. Green. Nashville: Abingdon Press, 1968.)

Fokkelman, J. P. "Genesis." In *The Literary Guide to the Bible.* Eds. R. Alter and F. Kermode, 36–55. Cambridge, Mass.: Belknap, 1987.

————. *Narrative Art in Genesis. Specimens of Stylistic and Structural Analysis.* SSN 17. Assen: Gorcum, 1975.

Foster, B. R. *Before the Muses: An Anthology of Akkadian Literature.* Bethesda, Md: CDL Press, 1993.

Fox, M. V. *The Redaction of the Books of Esther: On Reading Composite Texts.* SBLMS 40. Atlanta: Scholars Press, 1991.

Frei, P. "Zentralgewalt und Lokalautonomie im Achämenidenreich." In *Reichsidee und Reichsorganisation im Perserreich.* P. Frei and K. Koch, 9–43. OBO 55. Freiburg/Göttingen: Vandenhoeck & Ruprecht, 1984.

Friedman, R. *The Exile and Biblical Narrative: The Formation of the Deuteronomistic and Priestly Works.* HSM 22. Chico, Calif.: Scholars Press, 1981.

————. "The Hiding of the Face: An Essay on the Literary Unity of Biblical Narrative." In *Judaic Perspectives on Ancient Israel.* Eds. J. Neusner, et al., 207–22. Philadelphia: Fortress Press, 1987.

Frye, N. *Spiritus Mundi: Essays on Literature, Myth, and Society.* Bloomington: Indiana University Press, 1976.

Frye, R. M. "The Synoptic Problems and Analogies in Other Literatures." In *The Relationships Among the Gospels: An Interdisciplinary Dialogue.* Ed. W. O. Walker, 261–302. San Antonio, Tex.: Trinity University Press, 1978.

Frymer-Kensky, T. "The Atrahasis Epic and Its Significance for Our Understanding of Genesis 1—9." *BA* 40 (1977): 147–55.

Gammie, J. "Theological Interpretation by Way of Literary and Tradition Analysis: Genesis 25—36." In *Encounter with the Text: Form and History in the Hebrew Bible.* Ed. M. J. Buss, 117–37. Philadelphia: Fortress; Missoula, Mont.: Scholars, 1979.

Geddes, A. *Critical Remarks on the Holy Scriptures, corresponding with a new translation of the Bible.* Vol. 1, *Containing Remarks on the Pentateuch.* London: Davis, Wilks and Taylor, 1800.

Gese, H. "Der bewachte Lebensbaum und die Heroen: zwei mythologische Ergänzungen zur Urgeschichte der Quelle J." In *Wort und Geschichte: Festschrift für Karl Elliger zum 70. Geburtstag.* Eds. H. Gese, H. P. Rüger, 77–85. AOAT 18. Neukirchen-Vluyn: Neukirchener Verlag, 1973. Reprinted in *Vom Sinai zum Zion: Alttestamentliche Beiträge zur biblischen Theologie,* 99–112. Beiträge zur evangelischen Theologie, 64. Munich: Kaiser, 1974.

Goldman, Y. *Prophétie et royauté au retour de l'exil: Les origines littéraires de la forme massorétique du livre de Jérémie.* OBO 118. Göttingen: Vandenhoeck & Ruprecht, 1992.

Görg, M., " 'Wo Lag das Paradies?' Einige Beobachtungen zu einer alten Frage." *BN* 2 (1977): 30–32.

Gosse, B. "La tradition yahviste en Gn 6,5–9,17." *Henoch* 15 (1993): 139–53.

Gottwald, N. *The Hebrew Bible: A Socio-Literary Introduction.* Philadelphia: Fortress Press, 1985.

Greenberg, M. "The Redaction of the Plague Narrative in Exodus." In *Near Eastern Studies in Honor of William Foxwell Albright.* Ed. H. Goedicke, 243–52. Baltimore/London: Johns Hopkins University Press, 1971.

Greenspahn, F. *When Brothers Dwell Together: The Preeminence of Younger Siblings in the Hebrew Bible.* New York/Oxford: Oxford University Press, 1994.

Greenstein, E. "An Equivocal Reading of the Sale of Joseph." In *Literary Interpretations of Biblical Narratives.* Vol. 2. Ed. K. R. R. Gros Louis with James S. Ackerman, 114–25. Nashville: Abingdon, 1982.

Grintz, Y. " 'Do not eat the Blood': Reconsiderations upon Setting and Date of the Priestly Code" (Heb.). In *Studies in Early Biblical Ethnology and History,* 201–21. Tel Aviv: Hakibbutz Hameuchad Publishing House, 1969.

Gros Louis, K. R. R. "Genesis 3–11." In *Literary Interpretations of Biblical Narratives.* Vol. 2. Ed. K. R. R. Gros Louis with James S. Ackerman, 37–53. Nashville: Abingdon Press, 1982.

Gross, W. "Die Gottebenbildlichkeit des Menschen im Kontext der Priesterschrift." *TQ* 161 (1981): 244–64.

———. "Die Gottebenbildlichkeit des Menschen nach Gen 1,26.27 in der Diskussion des letzten Jahrzehnts." In *Lebendige Überlieferung - Prozesse der Annäherung und*

Auslegung: Festschrift für Hermann-Josef Vogt zum 60. Geburtstag. Eds. N. el-Khoury, H. Crouzel, R. Reinhardt, 118–35. Beirut: Friedrich-Rückert Verlag; Ostfildern: Schwaben-Verlag, 1992.

———. "Jakob, der Mann des Segens." *Bib* 49 (1968): 321–44.

———. "Syntaktische Erscheinungen am Anfang althebräischer Erzählungen: Hintergrund und Vordergrund." In *The Congress Volume: Vienna 1980.* VTSup 32. Leiden: Brill, 1981.

Gunkel, H. *Genesis.* 3d ed. Göttingen: Vandenhoeck & Ruprecht, 1910.

Gunn, D. "Narrative Criticism." In *To Each Its Own Meaning: An Introduction to Biblical Criticisms and Their Application.* Eds. S. Haynes and S. McKenzie, 171–95. Louisville Ky.: Westminster John Knox, 1993.

Gutiérrez, M. "'L'homme créé à l'image de Dieu' dans l'ensemble littéraire et canonique Genèse, chapitres 1—11." Ph.D. diss., University of Strasbourg, 1993.

Ha, J. *Genesis 15: A Theological Compendium of Pentateuchal History.* BZAW 181. Berlin/New York: W. de Gruyter, 1989.

Halevy, J. *Recherches Bibliques.* Vol. 1. *L'histoire des origines d'après la Genèse.* Paris: E. Leroux, 1895.

Haran, M. "Behind the Scenes of History: Determining the Date of the Priestly Source." *JBL* 100 (1981): 321–33.

———. *Temples and Temple Service in Ancient Israel.* Oxford: Clarendon Press, 1978.

———. "The Law Code of Ezekiel XL–XLVIII and its Relation to the Priestly School." *HUCA* 50 (1979): 45–71.

Hardmeier, C. *Prophetie im Streit vor dem Untergang Judas: Erzählkommunkative Studien zur Entstehungssituation der Jesaja- und Jeremiaerzählungen in II Reg 18—20 und Jer 37—40.* BZAW 187. Berlin/New York: W. de Gruyter, 1990.

Hart, K. "The Poetics of the Negative." In *Reading the Text: Biblical Criticism and Literary Theory.* Ed. Stephen Prickett, 280–340. Cambridge, Mass.: Basil Blackwell, 1991.

Hartman, G. H. "The Struggle for the Text." In *Midrash and Literature.* Eds. G. H. Hartman and S. Budick, 3–18. New Haven, Conn./London: Yale University Press, 1986.

Hauser, A. J. "Linguistic and Thematic Links between Genesis 4:1–16 and Genesis 2—3." *JETS* 23 (1980): 297–305.

Hazra, R. C. *Studies in the Purāṇic Records on Hindu Rites and Customs.* Calcutta: University of Dacca, 1940.

Hendel, R. *The Epic of the Patriarch: The Jacob Cycle and the Narrative Traditions of Canaan and Israel.* HSM 42. Atlanta: Scholars Press, 1987.

Henry, M. L. *Jahwist und Priesterschrift: Zwei Glaubenszeugnisse des Alten Testaments.* Arbeiten zur Theologie 3. Stuttgart: Calwer Verlag, 1960.

Hess, R. S. "Genesis 1—2 in its Literary Context." *TynBul* 41 (1990): 143–53.

Hoffman, Y. "The Lexicography of the P Document and the Problem Concerning its Dating" (Heb.). In *Studies in Judaica,* 13–22. Te'uda 4. Tel-Aviv: Tel-Aviv University, 1986.

Holloway, S. W. "What Ship Goes There: The Flood Narratives in the Gilgamesh Epic and Genesis Considered in Light of Ancient Near Eastern Temple Ideology." *ZAW* 103 (1991): 328–55.

Holzinger, H. *Einleitung in den Hexateuch.* Freiburg: J.C.B. Mohr, 1893.

———. *Genesis.* KHC. Freiburg: J.C.B. Mohr, 1898.

Hopkins, T. J. *The Hindu Religious Tradition*. Encino and Belmont, Calif.: Dickenson Pub. Co., 1971.

Hoskisson, P. Y. "Emar as an Empirical Model of the Transmission of Canon." In *The Biblical Canon in Comparative Perspective: Scripture in Context IV*. Ancient Near Eastern Texts and Studies 11. Eds. K. Lawson Younger, Jr., et al., 21–32. Lewiston, N.Y.: Mellen Press, 1991.

Houtman, C. *Der Pentateuch: Die Geschichte seiner Erforschung neben einer Auswertung*. Contributions to Biblical Exegesis and Theology 9. Kampen: Kok Pharos, 1994.

Humbert, P. *Études sur le récit du pardis et de la chute dans la Genèse*. Memoires de l'Université de Neuchâtel 14. Neuchâtel: Secretariat de l'Université, 1940.

Humphreys, W. L. *Joseph and His Family: A Literary Study*. Studies on Personalities of the Old Testament. Columbia, S.C.: Univ. of South Carolina Press, 1988.

Hupfeld, H. *Die Quellen der Genesis und die Art ihrer Zusammensetzung von neuem untersucht*. Berlin: Verlag von Wiegandt und Grieben, 1853.

Hurvitz, H. "The Evidence of Language in Dating the Priestly Code." *RB* 81 (1974): 24–56.

———. *A Linguistic Study of the Relationship between the Priestly Source and the Book of Ezekiel*. CARB 20. Paris: J. Gabalda et Cie, 1982.

Ilgen, K. D. *Die Urkunden des Jerusalemischen Tempelarchivs in ihrer Urgestalt . . . : Theil I: Die Urkunden des ersten Buchs von Moses*. Halle: Hemmerde und Schwetschke, 1798.

Jacob, B. *Das erste Buch der Tora. Genesis*. Berlin: Schocken, 1934.

Jacobsen, T. *The Treasures of Darkness: A History of Mesopotamian Religion*. New Haven, Conn./London: Yale University Press, 1976.

Jamieson-Drake, D. W. *Scribes and Schools in Monarchic Judah: A Socio-Archeological Approach*. JSOTSup 109. Social World of Biblical Antiquity Series 9. Sheffield: Almond, 1991.

Janowski, B. "Herrschaft über die Tiere: Gen 1,26–28 und die Semantik von רדה." In *Biblische Theologie und gesellschaftlicher Wandel: Für Norbert Lohfink, S.J.* Eds. G. Braulik, W. Groβ, S. McEvenue, 183–98. Freiburg/Basel/Vienna: Herder, 1993.

———. "Tempel und Schöpfung: Schöpfungstheologische Aspekte der priesterschriftlichen Heiligtumskonzeption." *Jahrbuch für Biblische Theologie* 5 (1990): 37–69. Reprinted in *Gottes Gegenwart in Israel: Beiträge zur Theologie des Alten Testaments*, 214–46. Neukirchen-Vluyn: Neukirchener Verlag, 1993.

Japhet, S. "The Laws of Manumission of Slaves and the Question of the Relationship Between the Collection of Laws in the Pentateuch." In *Studies in Bible and the Ancient Near East: Presented to S. E. Loewenstamm on his Seventieth Birthday*, 231–49. Jerusalem: E. Rubenstein's Publishing House, 1978.

Jeansonne, S. *The Women of Genesis: From Sarah to Potiphar's Wife*. Minneapolis: Fortress Press, 1990.

Jenkins, A. K. "A Great Name: Genesis 12:2 and the Editing of the Pentateuch." *JSOT* 10 (1978): 41–57.

Jensen, H. J. L. "Über den Ursprung der Kultur und der Völker: Eine transformationskritische Analyse von Komplementarität und Verlauf in der jahwistischen Urgeschichte." *SJOT* 2 (1987): 28–48.

Jepsen, A. "Zur Überlieferungsgeschichte der Vätergestalten." *Wissenschaftliche*

Zeitschrift der Karl-Marx-Universität Leipzig, gesellschafts- und sprachwissenschaftliche Reihe 3 (1953/4): 265–81.

Jeremias, J. *Jerusalem zur Zeit Jesu: Eine kulturgeschichtliche Untersuchung zur neutestamentlichen Zeitgeschichte.* 3d. ed. Göttingen: Vandenhoeck & Ruprecht, 1962.

Johnstone, W. "Reactivating the Chronicles Analogy in Pentateuchal Studies, with Special Reference to the Sinai Pericope in Exodus." *ZAW* 99 (1987): 16–37.

Kaiser, O. *Grundriss der Einleitung in die kanonischen und deuteronkanonischen Schriften des Alten Testaments.* Gütersloh: Gerd Mohn, 1992.

———. "Traditionsgeschichtliche Untersuchung von Genesis 15." *ZAW* 70 (1958): 107–26.

Kapelrud, A. S. "The Date of the Priestly Code (P)." *ASTI* 3 (1964): 158–64.

Kaufman, S. "The Temple Scroll and Higher Criticism." *HUCA* 53 (1982): 29–43.

———. "Deuteronomy 15 and Recent Research on the Dating of P." In *Das Deuteronomium: Entstehung, Gestalt, und Botschaft.* Ed. N. Lohfink, 273–6. Leuven: University Press, 1985.

Kaufmann, Y. "Der Kalender und das Alter des Priesterkodex." *VT* 4 (1954): 307–13.

———. *The Religion of Israel: From Its Beginning to the Babylonian Exile* (Heb.). 7th ed.; Jerusalem: Bialik Institute and Dvir, 1967. Trans. and abridged by M. Greenberg. New York: Schocken Books, 1960.

Kebekus, N. *Die Joseferzählung: Literarkritische und redaktionsgeschichtliche Untersuchungen zu Genesis 37—50.* Internationale Hochschulschriften. Münster/New York: Waxmann, 1989.

Keel, O., and Uehlinger, C. *Göttinen, Götter und Gottessymbole: neue Erkenntnisse zur Religionsgeschichte Kanaans und Israels aufgrund bislang unerschlossener ikonographischer Quellen.* 2d ed. Questionones Disputatae 134. Freiburg/Basel/Vienna: Herder, 1993.

Keel, O. *Die Welt der altorientalischen Bildsymbolik und das Alte Testament am Beispiel der Psalmen.* Darmstadt: Wissenschaftliche Buchgesellschaft, 1972. (E.T., *The Symbolism of the Biblical World: Ancient Near Eastern Iconography and the Book of Psalms.* Trans. T. J. Hallett. New York: Seabury, 1978.)

Kermode, F. *The Genesis of Secrecy: On the Interpretation of Narrative.* Cambridge, Mass.: Harvard University Press, 1979.

Kessler, R. "Die Querverweise im Pentateuch. Überlieferungsgeschichtliche Untersuchung der expliziten Querverbindungen innerhalb des vorpriesterlichen Pentateuchs." Ph.D. diss., Heidelberg, 1972.

Kikiwada, I. M., and Quinn, A. *Before Abraham Was.* Nashville: Abingdon Press, 1985.

Kilian, R. *Die vorpriesterlichen Abrahamsüberlieferungen: Literarisch und traditionsgeschichtlich untersucht.* BBB 24. Bonn: Peter Hanstein Verlag, 1966.

———. "Die Hoffnung auf Heimkehr in der Priesterschrift." *Bibel und Leben* 7 (1966): 39–51.

Kilmer, A. D. "The Mesopotamian Concept of Overpopulation and Its Solution as Reflected in Mythology." *Or* 41 (1972): 160–75.

Kippenberg, H. G. *Religion und Klassenbildung im antiken Judäa: Eine religionssoziologische Studie zum Verhältnis von Tradition und gesellschaftlicher Entwicklung.* Göttingen: Vandenhoeck & Ruprecht, 1978.

Klein, R. W. *Israel in Exile.* Philadelphia: Fortress Press, 1979.

Klostermann, A. *Der Pentateuch: Beiträge zu seinem Verständnis und seiner Entstehungsgeschichte.* Leipzig: A. Dreicherische Verlagsbuchhandlung, 1907.

Knierim, R. "The Composition of the Pentateuch." *Society of Biblical Literature 1985 Seminar Papers.* Ed. K. H. Richards, 393–405. Atlanta: Scholars Press, 1985.

———. "Criticism of Literary Features, Form, Tradition and Redaction." In *The Hebrew Bible and Its Modern Interpreters.* Eds. G. Tucker and D. Knight, 123–65. Philadelphia: Fortress Press; Chico, Calif.: Scholars Press, 1985.

Knohl, I. *The Sanctuary of Silence: The Priestly Torah and the Holiness School.* Minneapolis: Fortress Press, 1995.

Koch, K. "P–kein Redaktor! Erinnerung an zwei Eckdaten der Quellenscheidung." *VT* 37 (1987): 446–67.

Köckert, M. *Vätergott und Väterverheißungen: Eine Auseinandersetzung mit Albrecht Alt und seinen Erben.* FRLANT 142. Göttingen: Vandenhoeck & Ruprecht, 1988.

Kohata, F. *Jahwist und Priesterschrift in Exodus 3—14.* BZAW 166. Berlin/New York: W. de Gruyter, 1986.

Kraus, H. J. *Geschichte der historisch-kritischen Erforschung des Alten Testaments.* 3d ed. Neukirchen-Vluyn: Neukirchener Verlag, 1982.

Kristeva, J. *Desire in Language: A Semiotic Approach to Literature and Art.* Ed. L. S. Roudiez. Trans. T. Gora, et al. New York: Columbia University Press, 1980.

Kugel, J. "On the Bible and Literary Criticism." *Prooftexts* 1 (1981): 217–36.

Kuhl, C. "Die 'Wiederaufnahme'—ein literarisches Prinzip?" *ZAW* 64 (1952): 1–11.

Lamotte, E. "La critique d'authenticité dans le bouddhisme." In *India Antiqua,* 213–22. Leyden: Brill, 1947.

———. "La critique d'interprétation dans le bouddhisme." *Annuaire de l'Institut de philologie et d'histoire orientales et slaves* 9 (1949): 341–61.

———. "Sur la formation du Mahayana." In *Asiatica: Festschrift Friedrich Weller,* 377–96. Leipzig: O. Harrassowitz, 1954.

———. *Histoire du bouddhisme indien: des origines à l'ère śaka.* Louvain: Institut Orientaliste, 1958.

Lanser, S. "Feminist Criticism in the Garden: Inferring Genesis 2—3." *Semeia* 41 (1988): 67–84.

Lehming, S. "Zur Erzählung von der Geburt der Jakobsöhne." *VT* 13 (1963): 74–81.

Lemche, N. P. "The Chronology in the Story of the Flood." *JSOT* 18 (1980): 52–62.

Levin, C. *Der Jahwist.* FRLANT 157. Göttingen: Vandenhoeck & Ruprecht, 1993.

Levine, B. A. "Late Language in the Priestly Source: Some Literary and Historical Observations" (Heb.). In *Proceedings of the Eighth World Congress of Jewish Studies,* Vol. 5, 69–94. Jerusalem: World Union of Jewish Studies, 1983.

———. "Research in the Priestly Source: The Linguistic Factor." (Heb.) *Eretz Israel* 16 (1982): 124–31.

Levinson, B. "The human voice in divine revelation: The problem of authority in Biblical law." In *Innovation in Religious Traditions: Essays in the Interpretation of Religious Change,* 35–61. Berlin/New York: Mouton de Gruyter, 1992.

———. "The Right Chorale: From the Poetics to the Hermeneutics of the Hebrew Bible." In *"Not in Heaven": Coherence and Complexity in Biblical Narrative.* Eds. Jason P. Rosenblatt and Joseph C. Sitterson, Jr., 131–53. Indiana Studies in Biblical Literature. Bloomington/Indianapolis, Ind.: Indiana University Press, 1991.

Licht, J. *Storytelling in the Bible.* Jerusalem: Magnes, 1978.

Lindbeck, G. A. *The Nature of Doctrine: Religion and Theology in a Postliberal Age.* Philadelphia: Westminster Press, 1984.

Lods, A. "Un précurseur allemand de Jean Astruc: Henning Bernhard Witter." *ZAW* 43 (1925): 134–5.

Lohfink, N. "Gab es eine deuteronomistische Bewegung?" In *Jeremia und die "deuteronomistische Bewegung,"* ed. W. Gross, 313–82. BBB 98. Weinheim: Beltz Athenäum Verlag, 1995.

———. *Die Landverheißung als Eid.* SBS 28. Stuttgart: Verlag Katholisches Bibelwerk, 1967.

———. "Die Priesterschrift und die Geschichte." *The Congress Volume: Göttingen, 1977,* 189–225. VTSup 29. Leiden: Brill, 1978.

———. "Die Ursünden in der priesterlichen Geschichtserzählung." In *Die Zeit Jesu: Festschrift für Heinrich Schlier.* Eds. G. Bornkamm and K. Rahner, 38–57. Freiburg/Basel/Vienna: Herder, 1970. Reprinted in idem, *Studien zum Pentateuch,* 169–89. SBAB 4. Stuttgart: Verlag Katholisches Bibelwerk, 1988.

———. *Die Väter Israels im Deuteronomium mit einer Stellungnahme von Thomas Römer.* OBO 111. Göttingen: Vandenhoeck & Ruprecht, 1991.

Longacre, R. "The Discourse Structure of the Flood Narrative." *JAAR* 47 (1979; supplement B): 89–133.

———. *Joseph: A Story of Divine Providence—A Text Theoretical and Textlinguistic Analysis of Genesis 37 and 39—48.* Winona Lake, Ind.: Eisenbrauns, 1989.

Longstaff, T.R.W. *Evidence of Conflation in Mark? A Study in the Synoptic Problem.* SBLDS 28. Missoula, Mont. Scholars Press, 1977.

Luther, M. *Lectures on Genesis.* Trans. G. V. Schick. Luther's Works, 1–6. St. Louis: Concordia, 1960.

Machholz, C. "Israel und das Land. Vorarbeiten zu einem Vergleich zwischen Priesterschrift und deuteronomistischem Geschichtswerk." Habil., Heidelberg Universität, 1969.

McEvenue, S. *The Narrative Style of the Priestly Writer.* AnBib 50. Rome: Biblical Institute Press, 1971.

McGuire, E. D. "The Joseph Story: A Tale of Son and Father." In *Images of Man and God: Short Stories in Literary Focus.* Ed. B. O. Long, 9–26. Sheffield: Almond, 1981.

Mack, B. "Under the Shadow of Moses: Authorship and Authority in Hellenistic Judaism." *SBLSP* 21 (1982): 299–318.

McKenzie, S. *The Chronicler's Use of the Deuteronomistic History.* HSM 33. Atlanta: Scholars Press, 1984.

Magonet, J. "Die Söhne Abrahams." *Bibel und Leben* 14 (1973): 204–10.

Mann, T. *The Book of the Torah: The Narrative Integrity of the Pentateuch.* Atlanta: John Knox Press, 1988.

Metzger, H., et al. *Fouilles de Xanthos.* Vol. 6. *La stèle trilingue du Létôon.* Paris: Librairie C. Klincksiek, 1979.

Meyer, E. *Die Entstehung des Judentums: Eine historische Untersuchung.* Halle: Max Niemeyer, 1896.

Milgrom, J. *Leviticus 1—16.* AB. New York: Doubleday, 1991.

———. "Profane Slaughter and a Formulaic Key to the Composition of Deuteronomy." *HUCA* 47 (1976): 1–17.

Milik, J. T. *The Books of Enoch: Aramaic Fragments of Qumran Cave 4.* Oxford: Clarendon Press, 1976.

Millard, A. R. "A New Babylonian 'Genesis' Story." *TynB* 18 (1967): 3–18. Reprinted in *I Studied Inscriptions from before the Flood: Ancient Near Eastern, Literary, and Linguistic Approaches to Genesis 1—11.* Eds. R. S. Hess and D. T. Tsumura, 114–28. Winona Lake, Ind.: Eisenbrauns, 1994.

Miller, J. M., and J. H. Hayes, *A History of Ancient Israel and Judah.* Philadelphia: Westminster Press, 1986.

Miller, P. D. *Genesis 1–11: Studies in Structure and Theme.* JSOTSup 8. Sheffield: JSOT Press, 1978.

Miscall, P. "Jacques Derrida in the Garden of Eden." *USQR* 44 (1990): 1–9.

———. *The Workings of Old Testament Narrative.* Semeia Studies. Philadelphia: Fortress; Chico, Calif.: Scholars, 1983.

Moore, G. F. "Tatian's *Diatessaron* and the Analysis of the Pentateuch." *JBL* 9 (1890): 201–15. Reprinted in *Empirical Models for Biblical Criticism,* 243–56. Philadelphia: University of Pennsylvania Press, 1985.

Moore, S. D. *Poststructuralism and the New Testament: Derrida and Foucault at the Foot of the Cross.* Minneapolis: Fortress, 1994.

Moran, W. L. "Atrahasis: The Babylonian Story of the Flood." *Bib* 52 (1971): 51–61.

———. "The Literary Connection between Lv. 11,13–19 and Dt. 14,12–18." *CBQ* 28 (1966): 271–77.

Morgan, R., with Barton, J. *Biblical Interpretation.* Oxford Bible Series. New York/Oxford: Oxford University Press, 1988.

Mowinckel, S. *Erwägungen zur Pentateuch Quellenfrage.* Oslo: Universitetsforlaget, 1964.

———. *The Two Sources of the Pre-Deuteronomistic Primeval History in Genesis 1—11.* Oslo: J. Dybwad, 1937.

Müller, H. P. *Ursprünge und Strukturen alttestamentlicher Eschatologie.* BZAW 109. Berlin: Töpelmann, 1967.

Nelson, R. D. *The Double Redaction of the Deuteronomistic History.* JSOTSup 18. Sheffield: Univ. of Sheffield, 1981.

Nichol, G. "Story Patterning in Genesis." In *Text as Pretext: Essays in Honour of Robert Davidson,* 215–33. JSOTSup 138. Sheffield: JSOT, 1992.

Nicholson, E. W. "P as an Originally Independent Source in the Pentateuch." *IBS* 10 (1988): 192–206.

———. "The Pentateuch in Recent Research: A Time for Caution." In *The Congress Volume: Leuven, 1989,* 10–21. VTSup 43. Leiden: E. J. Brill, 1991.

Niditch, S. *Chaos to Cosmos: Studies in Biblical Patterns of Creation.* Scholars Press Studies in the Humanities 6. Chico, Calif.: Scholars Press, 1985.

———. *Underdogs and Tricksters: A Prelude to Biblical Folklore.* San Francisco: Harper & Row, 1987.

Noble, P. "Synchronic and Diachronic Approaches to Biblical Interpretation." *Literature and Theology* 7 (1993): 130–48.

Nöldeke, T. *Untersuchungen zur Kritik des Alten Testaments.* Kiel: Schivers, 1869.

Noth, M. *Überlieferungsgeschichte des Pentateuch.* 2d ed. Darmstadt/Stuttgart: Kohlhammer, 1948. (E.T., *A History of Pentateuchal Traditions.* Trans. B. W.

Anderson. Englewood Cliffs, N.J.: Prentice-Hall, 1972. Reprint, Chico, Calif.: Scholars Press, 1981.)

Oden, Jr., R. *The Bible without Theology: The Theological Tradition and Alternatives to It.* San Francisco: Harper & Row, 1987.

———. "Divine Aspirations in Atrahasis and in Genesis 1—11." *ZAW* 93 (1981): 197–216.

Otto, E. "Jakob in Bethel." *ZAW* 88 (1976): 165–90.

———. "Kritik der Pentateuchkomposition." *ThRu* 60 (1995): 163–91.

———. "Die 'synthetische Lebensauffassung' in der frühköniglichen Novellistik Israels - Ein Beitrag zur alttestamentlichen Anthropologie." *ZThK* 74 (1977): 371–400.

Pardes, I. *Countertraditions in the Bible: A Feminist Approach.* Cambridge, Mass.: Harvard University Press, 1992.

Perlitt, L. "Priesterschrift im Deuteronomium?" *ZAWSup* 100 (1988): 65–88. Reprint in *Deuteronomium-Studien,* 123–43. FAT 8. Tübingen: J.C.B. Mohr, 1994.

Pettinato, G. "Die Bestrafung des Menschengeschlechts durch die Sintflut." *Or* 37 (1968): 165–200.

Pfeiffer, R. H. *Introduction to the Old Testament.* 2d ed. New York/London: A. and C. Black, 1948.

———. "A Non-Israelite Source of the Book of Genesis." *ZAW* 48 (1930): 66–73.

Pola, T. *Die ursprüngliche Priesterschrift.* WMANT 70. Neukirchen-Vluyn: Neukirchener Verlag, 1995.

Polzin, R. *Late Biblical Hebrew: Toward an Historical Typology of Biblical Hebrew Prose.* HSM 12. Missoula, Mont.: Scholars Press, 1976.

Powell, M. A. *The Bible and Modern Literary Criticism: A Critical Assessment and Annotated Bibliography.* Bibliographies and Indexes in Religious Studies 22. New York: Greenwood, 1992.

Procksch, O. *Die Genesis.* 3d ed. Leipzig: A. Dreicherische Verlagsbuchhandlung, 1924.

de Pury, A. *Promesse divine et légende cultuelle dans le cycle de Jacob: Genèse 28 et les traditions patriarcales.* EB. Paris: J. Gabalda et Cie, 1975.

Rad, G. von. *Das erste Buch Mose: Genesis.* ATD 2/4. Göttingen: Vandenhoeck & Ruprecht, 1961. (E.T.: *Genesis: A Commentary.* Rev. ed. OTL. Philadelphia: Westminster, 1972.)

———. "Das formgeschichtliche Problem des Hexateuch." In *Gesammelte Studien zum Alten Testament,* 9–86. TB 8. Munich: Kaiser, 1961. (E.T., "The Form-Critical Problem of the Hexateuch." In *The Problem of the Hexateuch and Other Essays,* 1–78. Trans. T. Dicken. New York: McGraw Hill, 1966.)

———. *Die Priesterschrift im Hexateuch. Literarisch untersucht und theologisch gewertet.* BWANT 65. Stuttgart/Berlin: W. Kohlhammer, 1934.

———. *Theologie des Alten Testaments.* Vol. 1. *Die Theologie der geschichtlichen Überlieferungen Israels.* 4th ed. Munich: Kaiser, 1962. (E.T., *Old Testament Theology.* Vol. 1, *The Theology of Israel's Historical Traditions.* Trans. D. M. G. Stalker. New York: Harper & Row, 1962.)

Redford, D. B. *A Study of the Biblical Story of Joseph (Genesis 37—50).* VTSup 20. Leiden: Brill, 1970.

Renaud, B. "Les genealogies et la structure de l'histoire sacerdotale dans le livre de la Genèse." *RB* 97 (1990): 5–30.

Rendsburg, G. A. *The Redaction of Genesis.* Winona Lake, Ind.: Eisenbrauns, 1986.

Rendtorff, R. "Between Historical Criticism and Holistic Interpretation: New Trends in Old Testament Exegesis." In *The Congress Volume: Jerusalem, 1986,* 298–303. VTSup 40. Leiden: Brill, 1988. Republished in *Canon and Theology,* 25–30. OBT. Minneapolis: Fortress, 1993.

———. "Hermeneutische Probleme der biblischen Urgeschichte." In *Festschrift für Friedrich Smend zum 70. Geburtstag,* 19–29. Berlin: Merseburger, 1963. Reprinted in *Gesammelte Studien zum Alten Testament,* 198–208. Munich: Kaiser, 1975.

———. "L'histoire biblique des origines (Gen 1—11) dans le contexte de la rédaction 'sacerdotale' du Pentateuque." In *Le Pentateuque en question.* 2d ed. Ed. A. de Pury, 83–94. Le monde de la Bible 19. Geneva: Labor et Fides, 1989.

———. "Martin Noth and Tradition Criticism." *The History of Israel's Traditions: The Heritage of Martin Noth,* ed. S. L. McKenzie and M. P. Graham, 91–100. JSOTSup 182. Sheffield: Sheffield Academic Press, 1994.

———. "The Paradigm is Changing: Hopes and Fears." *Biblical Interpretation* 1 (1993): 34–53.

———. *Das überlieferungsgeschichtliche Problem des Pentateuch.* BZAW 147. Berlin/ New York: W. de Gruyter, 1976. (E.T.: *The Problem of the Process of Transmission in the Pentateuch.* Trans. J. J. Scullion. JSOTSup 89. Sheffield: JSOT Press, 1990.)

Renou, L. *Indian Literature.* Trans. P. Evans. New York: Walker and Co., 1964.

———. *Vedic India.* Trans. P. Spratt. Classical India 3. Calcutta: Susil Gupta, 1957.

Richter, W. *Die Bearbeitungen des 'Retterbuches' in der deuteronomistichen Epoche.* BBB 21. Bonn: P. Hanstein, 1964.

Robert, M. L. "Une nouvelle inscription grecque de Sardes: Règlement de l'autorité perse relatif à un culte de Zeus." In *Comptes rendus des séances de l'année— Académie des inscriptions et belles-lettres,* 306–31. Paris: Editions Klincksieck, 1976.

Robertson-Smith, W. *The Old Testament in the Jewish Church.* London: Adam and Charles Black, 1908.

Robinson, R. B. "The Literary Function of the Genealogies of Genesis." *CBQ* 48 (1986): 595–608.

Römer, T. "Genesis 15 und Genesis 17: Beobachtungen und Anfragen zu einem Dogma der 'neueren' und 'neuesten' Pentateuchkritik." *DBAT* 26 (1989/90): 32–47.

———. *Israels Väter: Untersuchungen zur Väterthematik im Deuteronomium und in der deuteronomistischen Tradition.* OBO 99. Freiburg and Göttingen: Vandenhoeck & Ruprecht, 1990.

Rosenberg, J. *King and Kin: Political Allegory in the Hebrew Bible.* Indiana Studies in Biblical Literature. Bloomington, Ind.: Indiana University Press, 1986.

Rudin O'Brasky, T. *The Patriarchs in Hebron and Sodom (Gen 18—19): A Study of the Structure and Composition of a Biblical Story* (Heb.). Jerusalem: Simor, 1982.

Rudolph, W., and Volz, P. *Der Elohist als Erzähler. Ein Irrweg der Pentateuchkritik?* BZAW 63. Giessen: Töpelmann, 1933.

Ruppert, L. *Die Josephserzählung der Genesis: Ein Beitrag zur Theologie der Penta-teuchquellen.* Studien zum Alten und Neuen Testament 11. Munich: Kösel Verlag, 1965.

————. "'Machen wir uns einen Namen . . . ' (Gen 11,4). Zur Anthropologie der vorpriesterschriftlichen Urgeschichte." In *Der Weg zum Menschen: Zur philosophischen und theologischen Anthropologie: Für Alfons Deissler.* Eds. R. Mosis and L. Ruppert, 28–45. Freiburg/Basel/Vienna: Herder, 1989.

Sanders, J. A. *Canon and Community: A Guide to Canonical Criticism.* Philadelphia: Fortress Press, 1984.

————. "Cave 11 Surprises and the Question of Canon." *McCQ* 21 (1968): 284–98. Republished in *The Canon and Masorah of the Hebrew Bible: An Introductory Reader.* Ed. Sid Leiman, 37–51. Library of Biblical Studies. New York: KTAV, 1974.

————. *From Sacred Story to Sacred Text: Canon as Paradigm.* Philadelphia: Fortress Press, 1987.

————. "The Integrity of Biblical Pluralism." In *"Not in Heaven": Coherence and Complexity in Biblical Narrative.* Eds. Jason P. Rosenblatt and Joseph C. Sitterson, Jr., 154–69. Indiana Studies in Biblical Literature. Bloomington/Indianapolis, Ind.: Indiana University Press, 1991.

————. *Torah and Canon.* Philadelphia: Fortress Press, 1972.

Sandmel, S. "The Haggada within Scripture." *JBL* 80 (1961): 105–22.

Sarna, N. M. *Genesis.* JPS Torah Commentary. Philadelphia/New York/Jerusalem: Jewish Publication Society, 1989.

Sasson, J. M. "The 'Tower of Babel' as a Clue to the Redactional Structuring of the Primeval History (Gen. 1–11:9)." In *The Bible World: Essays in Honor of Cyrus H. Gordon.* Ed. G. Rendsburg, 211–219. New York: KTAV and the Institute of Hebrew Culture and Education of New York University, 1980.

Sawyer, J. F. A. "The image of God, the wisdom of serpents, and the knowledge of good and evil." In *A Walk in the Garden.* Eds. P. Morris and D. Sawyer, 64–73. JSOTSup 136. Sheffield: JSOT, 1992.

Scharbert, J. "Der Sinn der Toledoth-Formel in der Priesterschrift." In *Wort-Gebot-Glaube: Beiträge zur Theologie des Alten Testaments: W. Eichrodt zum 80. Geburtstag.* Eds. J. J. Stamm, et al., 45–56. ATANT 59. Zurich: Zwingli Verlag, 1970.

Schart, A. *Mose und Israel im Konflikt: Eine redaktionsgeschichtliche Studie zu den Wüstenerzählungen.* OBO 98. Göttingen: Vandenhoeck & Ruprecht, 1990.

Schatz, W. *Genesis 14: Eine Untersuchung.* Bern: H. Lang; Frankfurt am Main: P. Lang, 1972.

Schmid, H. H. *Der sogenannte Jahwist: Beobachtungen und Fragen zur Pentateuch-forschung.* Zurich: Theologischer Verlag, 1976.

Schmidt, L. *'De Deo,' Studien zur Literarkritik und Theologie des Buches Jona, des Gesprächs zwischen Abraham und Jahwe in Gen 18,22ff. und von Hi 1.* BZAW 143. Berlin/New York: W. de Gruyter, 1976.

————. "Israel ein Segen für die Völker?" *Theologia viatorum* 12 (1975): 135–51.

————. *Literarische Studien zur Josephsgeschichte.* BZAW 167. New York/Berlin: W. de Gruyter, 1986.

————. *Studien zur Priesterschrift.* BZAW 214. Berlin/New York: W. de Gruyter, 1993.

————. "Überlegungen zum Jahwisten." *EvTh* 37 (1977): 230–47.

————. "Väterverheißungen und Pentateuchfrage." *ZAW* 104 (1992): 2–27.

Schmidt, W. H. "Elementare Erwägungen zur Quellenscheidung im Pentateuch." In *The Congress Volume Leuven, 1989*, 22–45. VTSup 43. Leiden: Brill, 1991.

————. *Exodus*. BKAT 2. Neukirchen-Vluyn: Neukirchener Verlag, 1974.

————. *Die Schöpfungsgeschichte der Priesterschrift*. 3d ed. WMANT 17. Neukirchen-Vluyn: Neukirchener Verlag, 1973.

————. "Ein Theologe in solomonischer Zeit? Plädoyer für den Jahwisten." *BZ* 25 (1981): 82–102. (E.T., "A Theologian of the Solomonic Era? A Plea for the Yahwist." In *Studies in the Period of David and Solomon and Other Essays*. Ed. T. Ishida, 55–73. Tokyo: Yamakawa-Shuppansha, 1982.)

Schmitt, H. C. *Die nichtpriesterliche Josephsgeschichte: Ein Beitrag zur neuesten Pentateuchkritik*. BZAW 154. Berlin/New York: W. de Gruyter, 1980.

————. "Die Suche nach der Identität des Jahweglaubens im nachexilischen Israel: Bemerkungen zur theologischen Intention des Pentateuch." In *Pluralismus und Identität*. Ed. J. Mehlhausen, 259–78. Munich: Chr. Kaiser, 1995.

Schottroff, W. *Der altisraelitische Fluchspruch*. WMANT 30. Neukirchen-Vluyn: Neukirchener Verlag, 1969.

Schrader, E. *Studien zur Kritik und Erklärung der biblischen Urgeschichte*. Zurich: Meyer & Zeller, 1863.

Seebass, H. "Zur geistigen Welt des sog. Jahwisten." *BN* 4 (1977): 39–47.

————. *Geschichtliche Zeit und theonome Tradition in der Joseph-Erzählung*. Gütersloh: Gütersloher Verlagshaus Gerd Mohn, 1978.

————. "Que reste-t-il du yahwiste et de l'élohiste?" in *Le Pentateuque en question*. 2d ed. Ed. A. de Pury, 199–214. Le monde de la Bible 19. Geneva: Labor et Fides, 1989.

Seeligmann, I. L. "Loans, Security, and Interest in Biblical Law and in Its World-View." In *Studies in the Bible and the Ancient Near East: Presented to S. E. Loewenstamm on his Seventieth Birthday*, 183–205. Jerusalem: E. Rubenstein's Publishing House, 1978.

Shea, W. "The Unity of the Creation Account." *Origins* 5 (1978): 9–38.

Simpson, C. A. *The Early Traditions of Israel: A Critical Analysis of the Predeuteronomic Narrative of the Hexateuch*. Oxford: Basil Blackwell, 1948.

Ska, J. L. "El relato del Diluvio: un relato sacerotal y algunos fragmentos redaccionales posteriores." *EstBib* 52 (1994): 37–62.

————. "La place d'Ex 6,2–8 dans la narration de l'exode." *ZAW* 94 (1982): 530–48.

————. "Quelques remarques sur Pg et la dernière rédaction du Pentateuque." In *Le Pentateuque en question*. 2d ed. Ed. A. de Pury, 95–125. Le monde de la Bible 19. Geneva: Labor et Fides, 1989.

Skinner, J. *A Critical and Exegetical Commentary on Genesis*. 2d ed. ICC. Edinburgh: T. & T. Clark, 1930.

Smend, R. *Die Erzählung des Hexateuch auf ihre Quellen untersucht*. Berlin: G. Reimer, 1912.

————. *Die Entstehung des Alten Testaments*. 4th ed. Stuttgart: W. Kohlhammer, 1989.

Smith, D. *Religion of the Landless: The Social Context of the Babylonian Exile*. Bloomington, Ind.: Meyer-Stone Books, 1989.

Smith, J. Z. "Wisdom and Apocalyptic." In *Map Is Not Territory: Studies in the History of Religions,* 67–87. Studies in Judaism in Late Antiquity. Leiden: Brill, 1978.

Smith, W. C. "The Study of Religion and the Study of the Bible." In *Rethinking Scripture.* Ed. M. Levering, 18–28. Albany, N.Y.: State University of New York Press, 1989.

———. *What is Scripture?: A Comparative Approach.* Minneapolis: Fortress Press, 1993.

Specht, H. "Von Gott enttäuscht—Die priesterschriftliche Abrahamgeschichte." *EvTh* 47 (1987): 395–411.

Spieckermann, H. *Juda unter Assur in der Sargonidenzeit.* FRLANT 129. Göttingen: Vandenhoeck & Ruprecht, 1982.

Spiegelberg, W. *Die sogenannte demotische Chronik: Des Pap. 215 der Bibliothèque Nationale zu Paris nebst auf der Rückseite des Papyrus stehenden Texten.* Demotische Studien 7. Leipzig: J. C. Hinrichs'sche Buchhandlung, 1914.

Steck, O. H. "Genesis 12,1–3 und die Urgeschichte des Jahwisten." In *Probleme biblischer Theologie: Festschrift für G. von Rad.* Ed. H. W. Wolff, 525–54. Munich: Kaiser, 1971.

———. *Israel und das gewaltsame Geschick der Propheten: Untersuchungen zur Überlieferung des deuteronomistischen Geschichtsbildes im Alten Testament, Spätjudentum und Urchristentum.* WMANT 23. Neukirchen-Vluyn: Neukirchener Verlag, 1967.

———. "Der Kanon des hebräischen Alten Testaments: Historische Materialien für eine ökumenische Perspektive." In *Vernunft des Glaubens: Wissenschaftliche Theologie und kirchliche Lehre, Festschrift zum 60. Geburtstag von Wolfhart Pannenberg.* Ed. J. Rohls and G. Wenz, 231–52. Göttingen: Vandenhoeck & Ruprecht, 1988.

———. "Strömungen theologischer Tradition im Alten Israel." In *Zu Tradition und Theologie im Alten Testament.* Ed. O. H. Steck, 27–56. Biblische-Theologische Studien 2. Neukirchen-Vluyn: Neukirchener Verlag, 1978.

Stegemann, H. "Die Bedeutung der Qumranfunde für die Erforschung der Apokalyptik." In *Apocalypticism in the Mediterranean World and the Near East: Proceedings of the International Colloquium on Apocalypticism, Uppsala, August 12–17, 1979.* Ed. D. Hellholm, 495–530. Tübingen: J.C.B. Mohr, 1983.

Steinberg, N. "Alliance or Descent? The Function of Marriage in Genesis." *JSOT* 51 (1991): 45–55.

———. *Kinship and Marriage in Genesis: A Household Economics Perspective.* Minneapolis: Fortress Press, 1993.

Steinmetz, D. *From Father to Son: Kinship, Conflict and Continuity in Genesis.* Literary Currents in Biblical Interpretation. Louisville, Ky.: Westminster John Knox Press, 1991.

———. "Vineyard, Farm and Garden: The Drunkenness of Noah in the Context of Primeval History." *JBL* 113 (1994): 193–207.

Sternberg, M. *The Poetics of Biblical Narrative: Ideological Literature and the Drama of Reading.* Indiana Studies in Biblical Literature. Bloomington, Ind.: Indiana University Press, 1985.

Stoellger, P. "Deuteronomium 34 ohne Priesterschrift." *ZAW* 105 (1993): 26–51.

Stordalen, T. "Genesis 2,4—Restudying a *locus classicus.*" *ZAW* 104 (1992): 163–67.

Swanson, T. "The Closing of Holy Scripture: A Study in the History of the Canonization of the Old Testament." Ph.D. diss., Vanderbilt University, 1970.

Sykes, D. K. "Patterns in Genesis." Ph.D. diss., Yeshiva University, 1985.

Talmon, S. "The Textual Study of the Bible—A New Outlook." In *Qumran and the History of the Biblical Text*. Eds. F. M. Cross and S. Talmon, 328–332. Cambridge, Mass./London: Harvard University Press, 1976.

Talshir, Z. *The Alternative Story: 3 Kingdoms 12:24a–z*. Jerusalem Biblical Studies 6. Jerusalem: Simor, 1993.

———. "The Contribution of Diverging Traditions Preserved in the Septuagint to the Methodology of Biblical Criticism." Paper to be published in the Proceedings of the International Organization for Septuagint and Cognate Studies.

Talstra, E. *Solomon's Prayer. Synchrony and Diachrony in the Composition of 1 Kings 8,14–61*. Contributions to Biblical Exegesis and Theology 3. Kampen: Kok Pharos, 1993.

Tengström, S. *Die Toledotformel und die literarische Struktur der priesterlichen Erweiterungsschicht im Pentateuch*. CBOTS, 17. Lund: Gleerup, 1981.

Tertel, H. J. *Text and Transmission: An Empirical Model for the Literary Development of Old Testament Narratives*. BZAW 221. Berlin/New York: W. de Gruyter, 1994.

Thiel, W. *Die deuteronomistische Redaktion von Jeremia 1—25*. WMANT 41. Neukirchen-Vluyn: Neukirchener Verlag, 1973.

Tigay, J. "Conflation as a Redactional Technique." In *Empirical Models for Biblical Criticism*, 61–83. Philadelphia: University of Pennsylvania Press, 1985.

———. *The Evolution of the Gilgamesh Epic*. Philadelphia: University of Pennsylvania Press, 1982.

———. "The Evolution of the Pentateuchal Narratives in the Light of the Evolution of the Gilgamesh Epic." In *Empirical Models for Biblical Criticism*, 21–52. Philadelphia: University of Pennsylvania Press, 1985.

———. "The Stylistic Criterion of Source Criticism in the Light of Ancient Near Eastern and Postbiblical Literature." In *Empirical Models for Biblical Criticism*, 149–73. Philadelphia: University of Pennsylvania Press, 1985.

Tov, E. "The Composition of 1 Samuel 16—18 in the Light of the Septuagint Version." In *Empirical Models for Biblical Criticism*, 98–130. Philadelphia: University of Pennsylvania Press, 1985.

———. "Glosses, Interpolations and Other Types of Scribal Additions in the Text of the Hebrew Bible." In *Language, Theology, and the Bible: Essays in Honour of James Barr*, ed. S. Balentine and J. Barton, 40–66. Oxford: Clarendon Press, 1994.

———. "The Literary History of the Book of Jeremiah." In *Empirical Models for Biblical Criticism*, 212–37. Philadelphia: University of Pennsylvania Press, 1985.

———. *Textual Criticism of the Hebrew Bible*. Minneapolis: Fortress Press, 1992.

———. "The Textual Status of 4Q364-7 (4QPP)." In *The Madrid Qumran Congress: Proceedings of the International Congress on the Dead Sea Scrolls, Madrid, 18-21 March 1991*. Ed. J. Trebolle Barrera and L. Vegas Montaner, 43-82. Studies on the Texts of the Desert of Judah 11; Madrid: Universidad Complutense; Leiden: Brill, 1992.

Tov, E., and S. White. "364-67. 4QReworked Pentateuch*b-e* and 365a. 4QTemple?" In *Qumran Cave 4*, vol. 8, *Parabiblical Texts, Part I*. DJD 13; Oxford, Clarendon Press, 1994.

Trible, P. "Genesis 22: The Sacrifice of Sarah." In *"Not in Heaven": Coherence and Complexity in Biblical Narrative*. Eds. Jason P. Rosenblatt and Joseph C. Sitterson, Jr., 170–91. Indiana Studies in Biblical Literature. Bloomington/Indianapolis, Ind.: Indiana University Press, 1991.

———. *God and the Rhetoric of Sexuality*. OBT. Philadelphia: Fortress, 1978.

———. *Texts of Terror: Literary-Feminist Readings of Biblical Narratives*. OBT. Philadelphia: Fortress Press, 1984.

Tuch, J. C. F. *Kommentar über die Genesis*. Halle: Buchhandlung des Waisenhauses, 1838.

Turner, L. *Announcements of Plot in Genesis*. JSOTSup 96. Sheffield: JSOT Press, 1990.

Uehlinger, C. *Weltreich und 'eine Rede': Eine neue Deutung der sogenannten Turmbauerzählung (Gen 11,1–9)*. OBO 101. Göttingen: Vandenhoeck & Ruprecht, 1990.

Utzschneider, H. "Das hermeneutische Problem der Uneindeutigkeit biblischer Texte: dargestellt an Text und Rezeption der Erzählung von Jakob am Jabbok." *EvT* 48 (1988): 182–198.

Van Dijk-Hemmes, F. "Tamar and the Limits of Patriarchy: Between Rape and Seduction." In *Anti-Covenant: Counter-Reading Women's Lives in the Hebrew Bible*. Ed. M. Bal, 135–56. JSOTSup 81. Sheffield: Almond, 1989.

Van Seters, J. *Abraham in History and Tradition*. New Haven, Conn.: Yale University Press, 1975.

———. "Confessional Reformulation in the Exilic Period." *VT* 22 (1972): 448–59.

———. *The Life of Moses*. Louisville, Ky.: Westminster/John Knox Press 1994.

———. *Prologue to History: The Yahwist as Historian in Genesis*. Louisville, Ky.: Westminster John Knox Press, 1992.

Vater, J. S. *Commentar über den Pentateuch*. Vol. 1. Halle: Waisenhaus Buchhandlung, 1802.

de Vaux, R. *Histoire ancienne d'Israël: Des origines à l'installation en Canaan*. EB. Paris: J. Gabalda et Cie, 1971. (E.T., *The Early History of Israel*. Trans. D. Smith. Philadelphia: Westminster Press, 1978.)

———. "A propos du second centenaire d'Astruc: Réflexions sur l'état actuel de la critique du Pentateuque." In *The Congress Volume: Copenhagen, 1953*, 182–98. VTSup 1. Leiden: Brill, 1953.

Vervenne, M. "The 'P' Tradition in the Pentateuch: Document and/or Redaction?— The 'Sea Narrative' (Ex 13:17–14:31) as a Test Case." In *Pentateuchal and Deuteronomistic Studies*. Eds. C. Brekelmans and J. Lust, 67–90. BETL 94. Leuven: University Press, 1990.

Vogels, W. "Caham découvre les limites des son père Noé." *NRT* 109 (1987): 554–73.

von Soden, W. "Der Mensch bescheidet sich nicht: Überlegungen zu Schöpfungserzählungen in Babylonien und Israel." In *Symbolae Biblicae et Mesopotamicae: Francisco Mario Theodoro de Liagre Böhl Dedicatae*. Eds. M. Beek, et al., 349–58. Leiden: Brill, 1973.

Vorländer, H. *Die Entstehungszeit des jehowistischen Geschichtswerkes*. Europäische Hochschulschriften, Theology Series 109. Frankfurt am Main/Bern/Las Vegas: Peter Lang, 1978.

———. *Mein Gott. Die Vorstellungen vom persönlichen Gott im Alten Orient und im Alten Testament.* AOAT 23. Kevelaer: Butzon & Bercker; Neukirchen-Vluyn: Neukirchener Verlag, 1975.

Vriezen, T. "Bemerkungen zu Genesis 12:1–7." In *Symbolae Biblicae et Mesopotamicae: Francisco Mario Theodoro de Liagre Böhl Dedicatae.* Eds. M. Beek, et al., 380–92. Leiden: Brill, 1973.

Wagner, N. E. "Abraham and David?" In *Studies on the Ancient Palestinian World Presented to F. V. Winnett.* Eds. J. W. Wevers and D. B. Redford, 117–40. Toronto Semitic Texts and Studies 2. Toronto/Buffalo: University of Toronto Press, 1972.

Wallace, H. N. "The Toledot of Adam." In *Studies in the Pentateuch.* Ed. J. A. Emerton, 17–33. VTSup 41. Leiden: E. J. Brill, 1990.

Weimar, P., "Sinai und Schöpfung. Komposition und Theologie der priesterschriftlichen Sinaigeschichte." *RB* 95 (1988): 337–85.

———. "Struktur und Komposition der priesterschiftlichen Geschichtsdarstellung." *BN* 23 (1984): 81–134 and 24 (1985): 138–62.

———. "Die Toledot Formel in der priesterschriftlichen Geschichtsdarstellung." *BZ* 18 (1974): 65–93.

———. *Untersuchungen zur Redaktionsgeschichte des Pentateuch.* BZAW 146. Berlin/New York: W. de Gruyter, 1977.

Weinfeld, M. *Deuteronomy and the Deuteronomic School.* Oxford: Clarendon Press, 1972.

———. "God the Creator in Gen. I and in the Prophecy of Second Isaiah" (Heb.). *Tarbiz* 37 (1967–8): 105–32.

———. "Social and Cultic Institutions in the Priestly Source Against Their Ancient Near Eastern Background." In *Proceedings of the Eighth World Congress of Jewish Studies, Jerusalem, August 16–21, 1981,* 95–138. Jerusalem: World Union of Jewish Studies, 1983.

———. "Towards the Concept of Law in Israel and Elsewhere." *Beit Miqra* 8 (1964): 58–63.

Weisman, Z. "Diverse Historical and Social Reflections in the Shaping of Patriarchal History" (Heb.). *Zion* 50 (1985): 1–13.

———. "The Interrelationship between J and E in Jacob's Narrative." *ZAW* 104 (1992): 177–97.

Wellhausen, J. "Die Composition des Hexateuchs und der historischen Bücher des Alten Testaments." *JDT* 21 (1876): 392–450. Reprinted as *Die Composition des Hexateuchs und der historischen Bücher des Alten Testaments.* 4th ed. Berlin: W. de Gruyter, 1963.

———. *Geschichte Israels: Erster Band - Prolegomena zur Geschichte Israels.* Berlin: G. Reimer, 1883. (E.T., *Prolegomena to the History of Ancient Israel.* Trans. J. S. Black and A. Menzies. Cleveland and New York: World Publishing, 1957.)

Wenham, G. J. "The Coherence of the Flood Narrative." *VT* 28 (1978): 336–48.

———. *Genesis 16—50.* WBC 2. Dallas: Word Books, 1994.

———. "Method in Pentateuchal Source Criticism." *VT* 41 (1991): 84–109.

———. "Sanctuary Symbolism in the Garden of Eden Story." In *Proceedings of the Ninth World Congress of Jewish Studies, Jerusalem, August 4–12, 1985.* Vol. 1, 19–25. Jerusalem: World Union of Jewish Studies, 1986. Reprinted in "I

Studied Inscriptions from before the Flood": Ancient Near Eastern, Literary, and Linguistic Approaches to Genesis 1—11. Eds. R. S. Hess and D. T. Tsumura, 399–404. Winona Lake, Ind.: Eisenbrauns, 1994.

Westermann, C. *Genesis 1—11.* BKAT I/1. Neukirchen-Vluyn: Neukirchener Verlag, 1974. (E.T., *Genesis 1—11.* Trans. J. J. Scullion. Minneapolis: Augsburg Press, 1984.)

———. *Genesis 12—36.* BKAT I/2. Neukirchen-Vluyn: Neukirchener Verlag, 1977. (E.T.,: *Genesis 12—36.* Trans. J. J. Scullion. Minneapolis: Augsburg Press, 1985.)

———. *Genesis 37—50.* BKAT I/3. Neukirchen-Vluyn: Neukirchener Verlag, 1982. (E.T., *Genesis 37—50.* Trans. J. J. Scullion. Minneapolis: Augsburg Press, 1986.)

de Wette, W. M. L. *Lehrbuch der historisch-kritischen Einleitung in die kanonischen und apokryphischen Bücher des Alten Testaments.* 6th ed. Berlin: G. Reimer, 1845.

Wevers, J. W. *Notes on the Greek Text of Genesis.* SBLSCS 35. Atlanta, Ga.: Scholars Press, 1993.

Whitt, W. "The Jacob Traditions and Their Relation to Genesis." *ZAW* 103 (1991): 18–43.

Whybray, R. N. "The Joseph Story and Pentateuchal Criticism." *VT* 18 (1968): 522–28.

———. *The Making of the Pentateuch: A Methodological Study.* JSOTSup 53. Sheffield: JSOT Press, 1987.

Williams, J. G. "Symphony No. 1: The Genesis—An Analysis of the First two Movements." *JRelS* 9 (1982): 24–33.

Willi-Plein, I. "Historiographische Aspekte der Josefsgeschichte." *Hennoch* 1 (1979): 305–31.

Wolff, H. W. "Das Kerygma des Jahwisten." *EvT* 24 (1964): 73–98. Reprinted in *Gesammelte Studien zum Alten Testament,* 345–73. TB 22. Munich: Kaiser, 1964. (E.T., W. Benware, trans. "The Kerygma of the Yahwist," *Int* 20: 131–58. Republished in *The Vitality of Old Testament Traditions.* Eds. W. Brueggemann and H. W. Wolff, 41–66. Atlanta: John Knox, 1975.)

Wood, W. "The Congregation of Yahweh: A Study of the Theology and Purpose of the Priestly Document." Ph.D. diss., Princeton University, 1974.

Wurster, P. "Zur Charakteristik und Geschichte des Priestercodex und Heiligkeitsgesetzes." *ZAW* 4 (1884): 112–33.

Zakowitch, Y. *'For Three and for Four'* (Heb.). Jerusalem: Makor, 1979.

Zenger, E. "Beobachtungen zu Komposition und Theologie der jahwistischen Urgeschichte." In *Dynamik im Wort: Lehre von der Bibel, Leben aus der Bibel.* Eds. E. Zenger and J. Gnilka, 35–54. Stuttgart: Verlag Katholisches Bibelwerk, 1983.

———. *Gottes Bogen in den Wolken: Untersuchungen zu Komposition und Theologie der priesterschriftlichen Urgeschichte.* SBS 112. Stuttgart: Katholisches Bibelwerk, 1983.

Zevit, Z. "Converging Lines of Evidence Bearing on the Date of P." *ZAW* 94 (1982): 481–511.

Zimmerli, W. *1. Moses 12—25: Abraham.* ZB. Zurich: Theologischer Verlag, 1976.

———. "Sinaibund und Abrahambund: Ein Beitrag zum Verständnis der Priesterschrift." *TZ* 16 (1960): 268–80.

Zwickel, W. "Der Altarbau Abrahams zwischen Bethel und Ai (Gen 12f)." *BZ* 36 (1992): 207–19.

Index of Scripture and Other Ancient Sources

Boldface indicates the most significant discussion of Genesis passages analyzed in this book. English equivalents are given in brackets where they differ from the Hebrew Bible. Scripture books are listed in the order of the Hebrew Bible.

Index of Authors

Index of Subjects

Adapa, 245
antimonarchal movement, 276–80, 298
Ashurbanipal inscriptions, 18

canon
    See scripture
Chronicles (books of), 17
conflation, 19–20, 65, 67, 114–17,
    143–47, 150–51, 268–69,
    283, 290–93, 314–17

Daniel (book of), 166 n.37
Davidic-Solomonic kingdom, 143,
    220–21, 223, 224, 226, 267,
    276, 277 n.126, 278–80,
    298–99, 302
descendant labels
    See toledot
Deuteronomistic History, 17, 114, 136,
    150, 156, 157–159, 169–72,
    173–75, 218 n.84, 219,
    221–22, 226, 227–28, 292
Diatessaron, 19–20, 24–25, 26, 32, 36,
    37–38, 45, 117 n.5
direction of dependence (P/non-P),
    65–67, 84, 84 n.12, 87–88,
    89
divine designation, 46, 51–53, 70, 70
    n.42, 73, 76, 80–81, 114,
    118, 143–46, 168, 168 n.42,
    197 n.40, 200–202
divine name
    See divine designation
documented transmission history, 3,
    16–20, 24–39, 65, 114–15,
    117 n.5, 119–20, 148, 150,
    152, 173, 218–19, 268, 278
    n.132, 303
Diodor I, 94–95, 328

E
    See Elohist
elders (of Judah), 175–76, 325–26
Elohist, 144–48, 150–51, 165–66 n.35,
    177, 196–202, 207–8, 208
    n.60, 226 n.109, 255 nn.67,
    68; 259 n.76; 261–62,
    268–70, 282 n.145, 283–88,
    290, 292
empirical studies
    See documented transmission his-
    tory
Enuma Elish, 273
etiology, 90 n.26, 136–37, 140, 172,
    205, 240, 241, 252, 256, 259
    n.76, 265, 306–7
exile, 133–40, 143, 149, 170, 171,
    173–76, 221 n.94, 227–32,
    246–47, 293, 310, 318, 334
expanionist edition of the Pentateuch,
    18, 18 n.60, 30–32, 152, 332
    n.43

Gilgamesh (epic), 16–17, 26–27, 30
    (flood), 33, 34, 44, 148, 150,
    218–19, 234, 245, 268, 303

final redaction, 6–9, 47, 314–17, 332

Hammurabi legal proclamations, 18
history of interpretation and transmis-
    sion history, 11, 12–15, 22,
    299–300, 304, 308, 309–10,
    310–11, 318–19, 320,
    321–22, 324, 332–33

interpretive interests, 7–8, 320, 322,
    324
intratextuality, 12–16, 297